AF892499

Sebastian Michael Lehrig

Efficiently Conducting Quality-of-Service Analyses by Templating Architectural Knowledge

The Karlsruhe Series on Software Design and Quality
Volume 25

Chair Software Design and Quality
Faculty of Computer Science
Karlsruhe Institute of Technology

and

Software Engineering Division
Research Center for Information Technology (FZI), Karlsruhe

Editor: Prof. Dr. Ralf Reussner

Efficiently Conducting Quality-of-Service Analyses by Templating Architectural Knowledge

by
Sebastian Michael Lehrig

KIT Scientific Publishing

Dissertation, Universität Stuttgart
Fakultät 5: Informatik, Elektrotechnik und Informationstechnik

Tag der mündlichen Prüfung: 24. November 2017
Referenten: Prof. Dr.-Ing. Steffen Becker, Prof. Dr. Ralf H. Reussner

Impressum

KIT Scientific Publishing

Karlsruher Institut für Technologie (KIT)
KIT Scientific Publishing
Straße am Forum 2
D-76131 Karlsruhe

KIT Scientific Publishing is a registered trademark
of Karlsruhe Institute of Technology.
Reprint using the book cover is not allowed.

www.ksp.kit.edu

This document – excluding the cover, pictures and graphs – is licensed under a Creative Commons Attribution-Share Alike 4.0 International License (CC BY-SA 4.0): https://creativecommons.org/licenses/by-sa/4.0/deed.en

The cover page is licensed under a Creative Commons Attribution-No Derivatives 4.0 International License (CC BY-ND 4.0): https://creativecommons.org/licenses/by-nd/4.0/deed.en

Print on Demand 2018 – Gedruckt auf FSC-zertifiziertem Papier

ISSN 1867-0067
ISBN 978-3-7315-0756-7
DOI: 10.5445/KSP/1000079766

Efficiently Conducting Quality-of-Service Analyses by Templating Architectural Knowledge

Von der Fakultät Informatik, Elektrotechnik
und Informationstechnik der Universität Stuttgart
zur Erlangung der Würde eines
Doktors der Naturwissenschaften (Dr. rer. nat.)
genehmigte Abhandlung

Vorgelegt von

Sebastian Michael Lehrig M. Sc.

aus Lennestadt, Deutschland

Hauptberichter:	Prof. Dr.-Ing. Steffen Becker
Mitberichter:	Prof. Dr. Ralf H. Reussner
Tag der mündlichen Prüfung:	24. November 2017

Institut für Softwaretechnologie (ISTE) der Universität Stuttgart

2017

Abstract

Software architects engineer software systems, i.e., they design, document, implement, test, operate, and maintain such systems in a systematic, disciplined, and quantifiable manner. Here, software architects make design decisions that define the system-wide boundaries of achievable software quality. Because of this far-reaching impact and potentially high realization efforts, taken decisions are expensive to revise. To reduce the risk of such revisions, software architects can apply architectural analyses. Such architectural analyses quantify a system's quality properties based on architectural models that (semi-)formally capture taken decisions, e.g., the structure of the planned software. Subsequently, software architects can compare quantifications against pre-specified software quality requirements. If requirements are violated, software architects only have to iteratively revise their architectural models and not the whole software to be realized. As soon as requirements are feasible, software architects can initiate the realization of the planned software.

However, the creation of suitable architectural models can cause high initial efforts for software architects. During creation, software architects formerly had to manually apply architectural knowledge, e.g., by looking up architectural styles and architectural patterns. Existing architectural analysis approaches like Palladio [BKR09] lack support for directly reusing architectural knowledge. This lack makes the design-space for software architects unnecessarily large; architects potentially consider designs that violate prescribed constraints. Moreover, this lack makes an automatic processing of architectural knowledge impossible; architects have to manually model architectural styles and patterns over and over again, even in recurring situations. These issues point to an unused potential to make the work of software architects more efficient.

To use this potential, I propose the *Architectural Template* (AT) method, a software engineering method that makes architectural analyses of quality-of-service (QoS) properties more effective and efficient. In the AT method, software architects quantify QoS properties based on so-called Architectural Templates (ATs), i.e., reusable design and analysis templates that capture recurring architectural knowledge. Software architects only have to customize such templates with the parts specific to their software application. ATs therefore reduce effort and lead to a more effective and efficient engineering method.

For evaluating the AT method, I have extended the architectural analysis approach Palladio [BKR09] with the AT method and have followed the AT method in three case studies and a preliminary controlled experiment. The case studies focus on the domains of distributed computing, cloud computing, and big data and associated QoS properties performance, scalability, elasticity, and cost-efficiency. Concrete cases are CloudStore, a distributed online book shop that is migrated to a cloud computing environment, WordCount, a statistical analysis in big data to be operated in Apache's Hadoop, and Znn.com, a distributed news service to be analyzed by an external software architect. The case studies show that the AT method is applicable to the investigated domains and associated QoS properties. Moreover, evaluation results indicate that AT application is a matter of minutes while saving more than 90 % of recurring modeling efforts. The preliminary controlled experiment has confirmed these results in an experiment with 7 involved software architects. A main limitation is the high effort for specifying ATs; AT specification can take several person months of effort. However, these efforts pay off when ATs are reused often.

Abstract (in German)

Softwarearchitekten gehen ingenieurmäßig bei der Entwicklung von Softwaresystemen vor, d.h., sie entwerfen, dokumentieren, implementieren, testen, betreiben und warten diese Systeme auf systematische, disziplinierte und quantifizierbare Art und Weise. Hierbei treffen Softwarearchitekten Entwurfsentscheidungen, die die systemweiten Grenzen der erreichbaren Softwarequalität bestimmen. Aufgrund dieser weitreichenden Auswirkungen und potenziell hoher Entwicklungskosten sind einmal getroffener Entwurfsentscheidungen nur unter hohem Aufwand zu revidieren. Um das Risiko solcher Revisionen zu reduzieren, können Softwarearchitekten sogenannte Architekturanalysen verwenden. Diese Architekturanalysen ermöglichen es Softwarearchitekten, die Qualitätseigenschaften eines Systems zu quantifizieren. Eine solche Quantifizierung basiert auf Architekturmodellen, die die getroffenen Entwurfsentscheidungen (semi-)formal erfassen, z.B. die Struktur der geplanten Software. Nachfolgend können Softwarearchitekten erhaltene Quantifizierungen mit vorgegebenen Anforderungen an die benötigte Softwarequalität vergleichen. Sind diese Anforderungen verletzt, so müssen Softwarearchitekten lediglich ihre Architekturmodelle iterativ revidieren und nicht das gesamte zu realisierende Softwaresystem. Sobald die Anforderungen erfüllbar sind, können Softwarearchitekten die Realisierung des geplanten Systems einleiten.

Allerdings kann die Erstellung geeigneter Architekturmodelle einen hohen Initialaufwand für Softwarearchitekten bedeuten. Während einer solchen Erstellung mussten Softwarearchitekten zuvor Architekturwissen manuell anwenden, z.B. durch das Nachschlagen von Architekturstilen und Architekturmustern. Existierenden Ansätzen zur Architekturanalyse, wie z.B. Palladio [BKR09], mangelt es an Unterstützung, solches Architekturwissen direkt wiederzuverwenden. Dieser Mangel macht den Entwurfsraum für Softwarearchitekten unnötig groß; Softwarearchitekten erwägen potentiell sogar Entwürfe, die vorgeschriebene Designeinschränkungen verletzen.

Ferner macht dieser Mangel eine automatische Verarbeitung von Architekturwissen unmöglich; Softwarearchitekten müssen Architekturstile und Architekturmuster immer und immer wieder modellieren, sogar in wiederkehrenden Situationen. Diese Probleme zeigen ein ungenutztes Potential auf, um die Arbeit von Softwarearchitekten effizienter zu gestalten.

Um dieses Potential zu nutzen, schlage ich die *Architectural Template* (AT)-Methode vor; eine Softwareengineeringmethode, welche Architekturanalysen für QoS-Eigenschaften[1] effektiver und effizienter macht. Mit der AT-Methode quantifizieren Softwarearchitekten QoS-Eigenschaften auf Basis von sogenannten Architectural Templates (ATs), d.h., wiederverwendbaren Entwurfs- und Analysevorlagen, die wiederkehrendes Architekturwissen erfassen. Softwarearchitekten müssen diese Vorlagen lediglich an Stellen anpassen, die spezifisch für ihre Softwareapplikation sind. ATs reduzieren daher Aufwand und führen zu einem effektiveren und effizienteren ingenieurmäßigen Vorgehen.

Zur Evaluation der AT-Methode habe ich den Architekturanalyseansatz Palladio [BKR09] mit der AT-Methode erweitert und in drei Fallstudien sowie einem vorläufigen kontrollierten Experiment angewendet. Die Fallstudien konzentrieren sich auf die Cloud Computing, verteilte Systeme und Big Data Domänen und den assoziierten QoS-Eigenschaften Performance, Skalierbarkeit, Elastizität und Kosteneffizienz. Bei den konkreten Fällen handelt es sich um CloudStore, einem verteilten Onlinebuchhandel, der in eine Cloud Computing Umgebung migriert werden soll, WordCount, einer statistischen Big Data Analyse, die in Apache's Hadoop betrieben werden soll, und Znn.com, einem verteilten Nachrichtendienst, der durch einen externen Softwarearchitekten analysiert werden soll. Die Fallstudien zeigen, dass die AT-Methode in den untersuchten Domänen und für die assoziierten QoS-Eigenschaften anwendbar ist. Zudem zeigen die Evaluationsergebnisse, dass ATs innerhalb von wenigen Minuten angewendet werden können und gleichzeitig über 90 % wiederkehrender Modellierungsaufwände einsparen. Das vorläufige kontrollierte Experiment hat diese Ergebnisse in einem Experiment mit 7 Softwarearchitekten bestätigt. Eine Haupteinschränkung ist der hohe Aufwand für die Spezifikation von ATs; eine AT-Spezifikation kann mehrere Personenmonate an Aufwand verursachen. Allerdings zahlen sich diese Aufwände aus, wenn ATs oft wiederverwendet werden.

[1] QoS (Quality of Service): Dienstgüte.

Acknowledgements

When I was little, I have adored my father for being such a versatile and skilled programmer: among the first computer games I have ever played in good ol' DOS times was a maze game, home-brewed by my father, that even allowed me to design my own mazes. He was (and still is!) a great role model for me; so great that, already at the age of eight, I have decided that I would learn programming and study computer science as soon as I grew older. I have never changed my mind about that decision, nor have I regretted it.

Now, several years later, you, the interested reader (well, at least of this acknowledgement), have one of my proudest achievements in your hands—a scientific treatise, my PhD thesis, that is settled in the context of my favorite topic in computer science: software architecture (but more about that later...). Since my decision to study computer science, a lot of people have helped me to reach this achievement, especially during the years I was writing up this thesis. Without these people, I would certainly have never succeeded, so it's time for a big thanks to all of these people that became so important to me.

First of all, I want to thank my family for the incessant unconditional support: thank you Papa, thank you Mama, I love you both! I also want to thank my beloved wife, Maxi, for her perseverance in times that turned out to be much harder than expected. You have always stood by me and given me the stability I have needed. Thank you, Maxi, I truly love you! Christel and Edith, thank you for the genuine warmth with which you have welcomed me in your family. Hans and Christoph, you're the coolest brothers-in-law I could have imagined—cheers!

Writing up a thesis is not only hard for the author but also for his whole environment—I therefore have to thank all my friends that kept on going with me—you guys never left my heart! Patrick, thanks for being one of the best friends I have ever had. Christina, I have loved growing up with you—you were the best sister I have never had. Jens and Moritz, you rock! It feels like Artsem has ever existed and I cannot imagine a world without it anymore, so cheers to our next sessions, let them be legendary! Oli and Anka. I was actually not sure whether I should rather put you to "family". Thanks for all the good time we had together (and for the shelter). You'll always get shelter (and a coffee) wherever future brings Maxi and me. Tobi, you were one of the best things that happened to me during my Chemnitz time: thanks for being there! Sergej and Gosia, thanks for all the warm-hearted help—you managed what I was unable to manage! I'll be there whenever you need me!

Next, I want to thank all my direct colleagues I have worked with. You did a great job, not only content-wise, but also at an interpersonal level; most of you I can certainly call my friends! I especially want to thank Steffen, my supervisor, for being the best "Doktorvater" one can have. Your feedback was always constructive and has helped me to improve myself. In this context, I also thank Steffi, Balzac, and Felix for their enduring psychological support. A special thanks goes to all of my "Doktorgeschwister" Matthias, Christian S., Anas, Marie, Stefan, Markus F., Marcus, Christian H., Claudia, Jörg, Uwe, Christopher, and Markus v. D. Our mutual assistance was extraordinary—thank you and keep on going! Matthias and Marcus, thank you again for your extensive reviewing; that has helped me so much! Wilhelm, I also wish you all the best, thanks for the good time at the Zukunftsmeile! Jutta, Kristin, and Sammy—without you, literally nothing would have worked—thanks for everything!

Having worked in well-financed projects, I was so lucky to get my own group of minions, my faithful student workers. All of you guys did exceptional work, thank you so much, I'm deeply indebted to you! Daria, you were the very first and most loyal one—I wish you all the best! Hendrik, you got what it takes to become a great researcher! Max, you made it all work—thanks! Christian, that was an impressive work, thanks! Marcel and Edith, I also want to thank you for your very good work!

Also the students that I have supervised during their Bachelor's and Master's theses did extraordinary jobs. Daria, Alex, and Hendrik, you did an amazing job in bringing the AT method to a whole new level—thank you! Daniel, you have extremely helped me with OpenStack, thanks! Mohammed, Vinay, Christoph, and Manoveg—thanks for your good contributions!

A big thanks goes to all members of the CloudScale project. Guys (and Ivana), you were the best! Thanks for the good time and the success we had!

Another big thanks goes to our friends at the KIT and all other members of the Palladio community. Ralf, you're the best "Doktoropa" I could wish for! It feels good to know that I'm always received with open arms in Karlsruhe—thank you and again thanks to the whole team for what we achieved together!

I'm also thankful for the good time I had during my research stay in L'Aquila. Thanks Vittorio for being an exceptional host and thanks Catia and Davide for all the fun we had.

Finally, I want to thank all the researchers I have met on countless conferences for their valuable ideas and feedback. A special thanks goes to Clemens Szyperski (remember the burger from Montréal?), Raffaela Mirandola (remember presentation bingo Palladio Days 2011?), Murray Woodside, Dorina Petriu, Jan Bosch, and Philippe Kruchten.

It appears that getting a PhD means not only writing up a thesis. If I look at this acknowledgement, a pathbreaking decision, an extensive process, adventure, and a large chunk of luck were involved. Most prominently, I had great luck with you folks and a great time! Thank you!

Dublin, 1st of December 2017 *Sebastian Michael Lehrig*

Contents

List of Figures

List of Tables

"Each problem that I solved became a rule, which served afterwards to solve other problems."

— *René Descartes 1596 – 1650*

1. Introduction

A system's software architecture is its fundamental organization of software components, their relations, and their environment [ISO07]. Additionally, software architecture describes the set of design decisions that have led to such an organization [TMD09, p. 58]. Once taken, these design decisions define the system-wide boundaries of achievable software quality [HAZ07, BCK98, Chap. 1]. Because of this far-reaching impact and potentially high realization efforts of the system, design decisions are expensive to revise [BCK98, Chap. 2] and should consequently be evaluated as early as possible [CKK02, BT03, Gar14].

The main task of software architects is to make design decisions such that a system's quality requirements are finally met and optimal trade-offs have been achieved [TMD09, Sec. 17.1]. For effectively fulfilling this task without risking revisions, software architects can *engineer* software architectures. In engineering, software architects approach the design, documentation, implementation, testing, operation, and maintenance of software architectures in a systematic, disciplined, and quantifiable manner [IEE10]. Such an engineering approach helps software architects in making informed design decisions, that is, decisions with predictable, intended (i.e., requirement-satisfying) outcomes.

This thesis focuses on a concrete category of such engineering approaches: architectural analyses. Architectural analyses allow software architects to quantify quality-of-service (QoS) properties based on architectural models of their system. These quantifications enable early evaluations and, thus, inexpensive revisions of disadvantageous design decisions. However, the creation of suitable architectural models for architectural analyses formerly required a high modeling effort [SW02, p. 458]—even in recurring modeling situations [Leh13].

To approach this problem, this thesis contributes the Architectural Template (AT) method as an extension to architectural analyses. The AT method provides software architects with templates that formally capture reusable architectural knowledge (such as architectural styles and architectural patterns) for recurring modeling situations. By applying such templates to architectural models, software architects become more effective and efficient because captured design decisions can automatically be integrated into architectural models, checked for consistency, and be analyzed.

This introductory chapter refines this motivation and idea behind the AT method and gives an overview of this thesis. Section 1.1 details how architectural analyses allow to quantify QoS properties while Section 1.2 outlines the benefits of exploiting reusable architectural knowledge for the creation of architectural models. Subsequently, Section 1.3 derives requirements to profit from these benefits in architectural analyses and Section 1.4 inspects concrete architectural analysis methods to illustrate their lack of support for these requirements. Section 1.5 explains how the AT method copes with this lack and Section 1.6 lists concrete, scientific contributions of this thesis. Finally, Section 1.7 explains the structure of this thesis.

1.1. Analyzing Quality-of-Service

A concrete category of engineering approaches are architectural analyses [TMD09, p. 291]. Architectural analyses quantify a system's quality-of-service (QoS) properties based on architectural models that (semi-)formally capture taken decisions, e.g., the structure of the planned software. Subsequently, software architects can compare quantifications against prespecified QoS requirements. If requirements are violated, software architects only have to iteratively revise their architectural models and not the whole software to be realized. As soon as requirements are feasible, software architects can initiate the realization of the planned software.

Figure 1.1 illustrates the data flow of such architectural analyses as introduced by Koziolek [Koz08, p. 3]. Involved artifacts are denoted with a representative symbol and data flow via thick arrows.

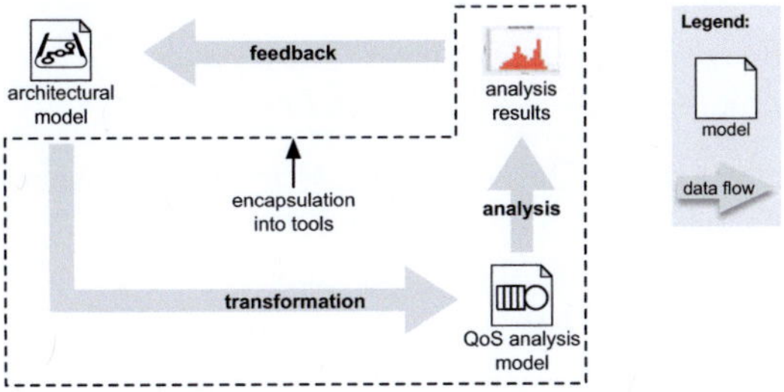

Figure 1.1.: Architectural analyses of QoS properties (based on [Koz08, p. 3]).

As shown in Figure 1.1 (left), the data flow starts with an architectural model that is transformed to a QoS analysis model (e.g., Markov chains [Tri82], queuing networks [LZGS84], stochastic Petri nets [BK98], or stochastic process algebras [HHK02]). Figure 1.1 (right) shows that such analysis models can be analyzed. The resulting analysis results provide quantifications of the QoS properties of interest. These analysis results serve software architects as feedback for revising the architectural model.

The dashed border in Figure 1.1 shows that appropriate tools encapsulate the steps from architectural model to analysis results. Underlying QoS analysis models are therefore transparent to software architects and cause no creation efforts. However, the creation of suitable architectural models can cause high initial efforts for software architects [SW02, p. 458]. As described in the next section, such efforts can be lowered by exploiting design decisions that can be reused over multiple architectural models.

1.2. Exploiting Reusable Architectural Knowledge

Software architects commonly commit "theft" [Kru95] to efficiently create architectural models. That is, software architects reuse ("steal" [Kru95]) design decisions that have been proven to solve previous but similar design problems [Ale77, p. x]. If given a name, such proven design decisions form reusable architectural knowledge [KLvV06]. Concrete examples of reusable architectural knowledge are architectural styles, architectural patterns, and reference architectures [TMD09].

The application of reusable architectural knowledge to architectural models can have several benefits for software architects:

Generic documentation. Design decisions included in reusable architectural knowledge can be documented generically [HAZ07], e.g., as pattern descriptions in architectural handbooks [BCK98, TMD09, BMR+96, SSRB00, KJ04, KJ04, BHS07a, BHS07b]. This generality saves documentation efforts; only the design decision to apply such knowledge requires documentation.

Conformance checks. Reusable architectural knowledge can include design decisions about constraints on the architectural model [KLvV06]. Software architects can check whether these decisions conform to their architectural models. These conformance checks ensure that knowledge is consistently applied, thus, particularly ensuring an effective application of reusable architectural knowledge.

Knowledge integration. Reusable architectural knowledge can include design decisions about the existence of elements and their interaction [KLvV06]. Software architects can reuse these existential decisions for integrating associated elements into their architectural models efficiently.

Figure 1.2 extends Figure 1.1 to illustrate these benefits. Figure 1.2 (left) illustrates that sources of reusable architectural knowledge provide software architects with generic information that they can use for effectively and efficiently creating architectural models.

Figure 1.2 particularly annotates the benefits outside of the dashed border, which indicates that software architects may manually apply reusable architectural knowledge. To relieve software architects from such manual efforts as much as possible, the next section describes requirements for an appropriate tool support.

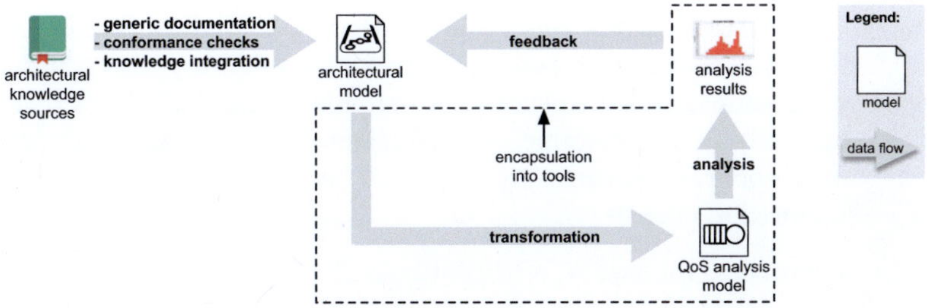

Figure 1.2.: Exploiting reusable architectural knowledge for creating architectural models.

1.3. Requirements for Supporting Reusable Architectural Knowledge

The benefits previously described in Section 1.2 enable software architects to become more effective and efficient in their engineering task. However, to fully profit from these benefits within architectural analyses, the following requirements must be satisfied:

R_{formal}: **Capture knowledge in a formal way.** Reusable architectural knowledge shall be captured formally. Only formally captured knowledge allows to automate both conformance checks and knowledge integrations.

$R_{architecture}$: **Give architecture-level feedback.** Software architects shall be able to check conformance to reusable architectural knowledge automatically and already during the creation of architectural models. This early feedback allows software architects to maintain conformance to knowledge throughout model creation, thus, avoiding revision risks due to inconsistently made design decisions at the architectural level.

$R_{semantics}$: **Define semantics for architectural analyses.** Once it has been integrated, knowledge shall be interpretable by architectural analyses. That is, integrated elements must have well-defined semantics that are understood by the employed architectural analysis.

$R_{additions}$: Allow to formalize additional knowledge. It shall be possible to formalize additional reusable architectural knowledge. This possibility acknowledges the plethora of reusable architectural knowledge available as, e.g., described in architectural handbooks. For an optimal support for formalizing additional knowledge, it is particularly required to provide:

- a process for such a formalization and
- quality assurance steps to ensure that said formalizations capture reusable architectural knowledge correctly.

1.4. Problem Statement

Unfortunately, no existing architectural analysis approach satisfies all the requirements described in Section 1.3 [Leh13]. Some existing approaches on architectural analyses satisfy $\mathbf{R_{formal}}$ and $\mathbf{R_{semantics}}$ while approaches from the software architecture domain exemplify the realization of $\mathbf{R_{formal}}$, $\mathbf{R_{architecture}}$, and $\mathbf{R_{additions}}$ but lack analysis capabilities:

Architectural analysis approaches. Koziolek surveys [Koz10] architectural analysis approaches, e.g., SPE [SW02], that lack formalisms for capturing reusable architectural knowledge, thus, violating all requirements of Section 1.3. Some architectural analysis approaches [PW00, CG02, MPW15, WPS02, VDGD05, Bec08, Hap09, Hap11, MGMS11, Rat13] support an integration of formally captured knowledge with well-defined semantics ($\mathbf{R_{formal}}$ and $\mathbf{R_{semantics}}$). However, neither of these approaches supports the exploitation of conformance checks at the architectural level ($\mathbf{R_{architecture}}$) while allowing to formalize additional reusable architectural knowledge ($\mathbf{R_{additions}}$).

Software architecture domain. Some approaches from the software architecture domain [GMW00, GAO94, LKA+95, MR97, All97, MHG01, KFGS03, TTSOF16] support automated conformance checks while allowing to formalize additional reusable architectural knowledge ($\mathbf{R_{formal}}$, $\mathbf{R_{architecture}}$, and $\mathbf{R_{additions}}$). However, these approaches lack support for integrating knowledge into architectural models suited for architectural analyses of QoS properties ($\mathbf{R_{semantics}}$).

Therefore, software architects are currently required to conduct all or some knowledge application steps manually when constructing architectural models suited for architectural analyses. For example, when preparing architectural models for architectural analyses, software architects have to manually check whether design decisions are consistently applied. In consequence, software architects can have high efforts in creating such architectural models, even in recurring situations.

These issues underline the unused potential to fully profit from the benefits of Section 1.2. That is, there is potential to make the work of software architects more effective and efficient, e.g., by introducing concepts from the software architecture domain into architectural analyses.

1.5. Solution Overview

To benefit from the unused potential described in Section 1.4, I propose the *Architectural Template* (AT) method, a software engineering method that makes architectural analyses of QoS properties more effective and efficient. In the AT method, software architects quantify QoS properties based on so-called Architectural Templates (ATs), i.e., reusable design and analysis templates that capture reusable architectural knowledge. Software architects only have to customize such templates with the parts specific to their software application. ATs therefore reduce effort and lead to a more effective and efficient engineering method.

Figure 1.3 illustrates the creation of architectural models and the conduction of architectural analyses with AT support. As shown in Figure 1.3 (top-left), software architects can apply ATs from a pre-specified AT catalog when creating architectural models. Figure 1.3 (center) shows that such applications are formally applied to architectural models.

Formalized applications allow to profit from the three benefits described in Section 1.2. First, as shown in Figure 1.3 (top-left), each AT comes with a generic documentation of the captured reusable architectural knowledge; an AT's application allows software architects to inspect this documentation. Second, as shown in Figure 1.3 (bottom-left), ATs formally capture constraints of reusable architectural knowledge, thus, enabling an automated conformance checking. Detected constraint violations serve software architects as feedback for revising their architectural models. Third, as shown in Figure 1.3 (bottom-right), ATs formally capture decisions about the existence of elements, thus, enabling an automated knowledge integration. Knowledge is integrated prior to the transformation to QoS analysis models.

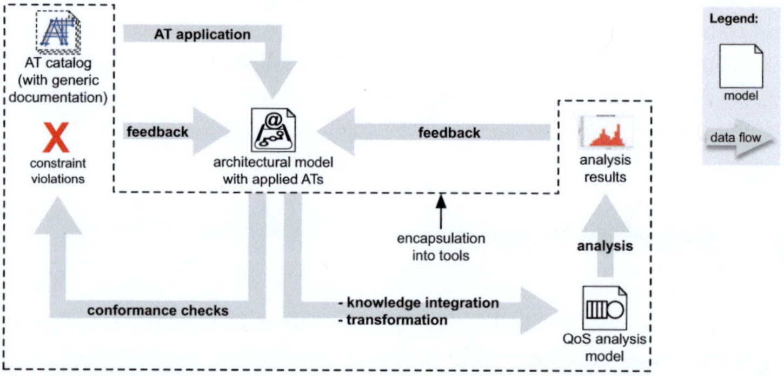

Figure 1.3.: Creating and analyzing architectural models with ATs.

Figure 1.2 is similar to Figure 1.3 but shows that the benefits from Section 1.2 are now encapsulated into tools. The encapsulation particularly satisfied the first three requirements from Section 1.3: ATs formally capture knowledge ($\mathbf{R_{formal}}$), give architecture-level feedback ($\mathbf{R_{architecture}}$), and define semantics for architectural analyses ($\mathbf{R_{semantics}}$).

The fourth and final requirement ($\mathbf{R_{additions}}$) demands that further reusable architectural knowledge can be formalized. The AT method satisfied this requirement by introducing a domain-specific language—the AT language—for the specification (and application) of ATs. Moreover, the AT method provides processes and quality assurance steps explaining how so-called AT engineers can formalize custom ATs using the AT language.

The AT method accordingly satisfies all requirements defined in Section 1.3 and provides a solution to the problem stated in Section 1.4.

1.6. Scientific Contributions

The main contributions of this PhD thesis are the following[1]:

(1) AT method. The AT method is introduced as a software engineering method that uses ATs to make approaches for architectural analyses of QoS properties more effective and efficient. The AT method consists of:

AT processes: AT processes describe in natural language how software architects apply ATs and how AT engineers specify ATs.

AT language: The AT language provides formalizations to document and specify ATs.

AT tooling: AT tooling supports AT processes and serves as a reference implementation.

(2) Evaluation of the AT method. For evaluating the AT method, we (i.e., my colleagues and I) have conducted three case studies and a preliminary controlled experiment. We have used and extended the architectural analysis approach Palladio [BKR09] for these evaluations.

The three case studies focus on the domains of distributed computing, cloud computing, and big data. These domains are suited because they come with interesting quality properties, and a large amount of architectural constraints to foster these properties. First, we migrate CloudStore [LB16], a distributed online book shop, from a classical distributed bare metal setup to a virtualized cloud computing environment. We guide our migration along appropriate architectural knowledge captured via ATs. Second, we model and analyze the statistical analysis WordCount [Whi09] when it is operated in Apache Hadoop, a processing pipeline commonly used in big data. We create and apply an AT that captures Apache Hadoop as a reference architecture. Third, an external software architect models and analyzes Znn.com [CGS09], a distributed news service. The software architect successfully reuses an AT previously created during the CloudStore case study.

[1] A summary of these results has been published in a scientific journal [LHB17].

The case studies show that the AT method is applicable to the investigated domains and suited for the associated QoS properties performance, scalability, elasticity, and cost-efficiency. Moreover, our results indicate that AT application is a matter of minutes while saving more than 90 % of recurring modeling efforts. The preliminary controlled experiment has confirmed these results in an experiment with 7 involved software architects.

A detailed threads to validity discussion highlights remaining limitations. A main limitation is the high effort for AT engineers; AT specification can take several person months of effort. Another limitation is that further evaluation is needed for generalizing gained results, e.g., to other domains and QoS properties. Otherwise, mainly technical issues in AT tooling remain.

(3) Extensions of the AT method. I illustrate two optional extensions to the AT method:

Reuse mechanism: For making AT engineers more efficient, we have extended the AT method with a reuse mechanism that allows to derive new ATs from existing ones. The evaluation of this mechanism indicates that AT engineers become over 200 % more productive in reuse scenarios.

Optimization: We have integrated the optimization framework PerOpteryx [KKR11] into the AT method to automatically determine optimal configurations for AT applications using genetic algorithms. This addition makes software architects even more efficient because they save effort to manually determine such configurations. We have conducted a proof-of-concept evaluation of the optimization mechanism on a small example, which shows that such optimizations are possible.

(4) Classification. I provide a novel classification schema for combining reusable architectural knowledge with architectural analyses of QoS properties. Moreover, I use this schema to systematically classify related works of the AT method and to highlight several opportunities for future works.

1.7. Thesis Structure

The remainder of this thesis is structured into the following chapters:

Chapter 2 describes the foundations relevant for the AT method. Foundations include the evaluation and research methods employed by this thesis as well as fundamentals on software architecture, model-driven software engineering, templates, and architectural analyses of QoS properties.

Chapter 3 introduces an online book shop as a simple example system to illustrate the AT method. In a fictional scenario, a software architect follows the AT method to engineer this book shop. The software architect starts with engineering requirements, continues with an AT-based specification of an architectural model, and eventually conducts an architectural analysis with the architectural model. This illustration of the AT method subsequently allows to discuss some first lessons learned that confirm the promised benefits of the AT method.

Because of its simplicity, the book shop example is used throughout this thesis for illustrative purposes. Particularly the evaluation in Chapter 5 extends the book shop example to a full case study—the CloudStore case study.

Chapter 4 introduces the AT method. Each of the AT method's constituents (AT processes, AT language, and AT tooling) is described in full detail. Moreover, the two extensions of the AT method (reuse mechanism and optimization mechanism) are described. A discussion of assumptions and limitations of the AT method complements this chapter.

Chapter 5 describes the evaluation of the AT method. After discussing related studies and introducing the general evaluation design, each of the conducted case studies—CloudStore, WordCount, and Znn.com—are described in detail. Afterwards, the conduction of further (but smaller) case studies is outlined, the controlled experiment is described, and the evaluation of AT method extensions is described. A summary of lessons learned closes the evaluation chapter.

Chapter 6 surveys related works on the AT method by investigating four different domains: architectural knowledge management, architectural description languages, the pattern community, and architectural analyses of QoS properties. The chapter compiles a model of common features from this investigation; particularly allowing the chapter to systematically classify both the investigated related works and the AT method. Based on this classification, related works are discussed and related to the AT method.

Chapter 7 concludes this thesis with a summary of lessons learned, a discussion of assumptions and limitations, and with prospects on future works.

"Invention, strictly speaking, is little more than a new combination of those images which have been previously gathered and deposited in the memory; nothing can come of nothing."

— Joshua Reynolds 1723 – 1792

2. Foundations

This section describes the fundamentals of the AT method. These fundamentals provide and explain the vocabulary to describe how the AT method helps software architects to analyze quality-of-service (QoS) properties (see Definition 2.1). For example, performance is a QoS property that analyses can quantify, e.g., in terms of response times and throughput.

Definition 2.1 (Quality-of-Service)

- *"[Quality-of-service] denote[s] all non-functional aspects of a service which may be used by clients to judge service quality." [DLS05]*
- *"The quality of service (QoS) offered by a distributed system reflects the system's ability to deliver its services dependably and with a response time and throughput that is acceptable to its users." [Som10, p. 484]*

The input to such analyses are architectural models that manifest the design decisions that software architects have made. Based on quantified analysis results, software architects can judge whether made design decisions foster a system's QoS properties and optimal trade-offs have been achieved. Therefore, QoS analyses enable software architects to make informed design decisions. The AT method enables software architects to reuse recurring and well-proven design decisions effectively and efficiently, i.e., reusable architectural knowledge like architectural styles and architectural patterns.

This chapter introduces the fundamentals for the AT method as follows. Section 2.1 describes empirical evaluation and research methods for quantifying QoS properties that the AT method utilizes. Moreover, Section 2.2 overviews fundamentals on software architecture and reusable architectural knowledge. The AT method formally captures this knowledge based on techniques from model-driven software engineering that are described in Section 2.3 and based on templates that are described in Section 2.4. Finally, Section 2.5 provides fundamentals on architectural analyses of QoS properties. The AT method allows software architects to integrate previously captured reusable architectural knowledge into architectural models for such analyses.

2.1. Evaluation and Research Methods

Prechelt [Pre01, p. 30] describes software engineering as an engineering discipline. Consequently, methods in the area of software engineering have to be evaluated with respect to their quality properties (see Definition 2.2). This claim particularly holds for QoS properties, which are a special kind of quality property covering non-functional aspects (cf. Definition 2.1). Typically, evaluations of quality properties are conducted empirically, based on experience, and with a concrete goal in mind.

Definition 2.2 (Quality Property) *"[The] inherent property or characteristic of an entity that can be distinguished quantitatively or qualitatively by human or automated means." [ISO14]*

One of the main goal-oriented approaches to measure properties of software systems is the Goal/Question/Metric (GQM) method [vSB99, pp. 21-25]. The GQM method is based on defining goals, deriving questions related to these goals, and specifying metrics (see Definition 2.3) that shall help to answer these questions.

Definition 2.3 (Metric) *"[A metric is a] precisely defined method which is used to associate an element of an (ordered) set V to a system S." [BF08]*

In the AT method, the GQM method is used to systematically derive metrics of quality properties to be analyzed. This section therefore continues with detailing the GQM method in Section 2.1.1. Afterwards, Section 2.1.2 describes quality models, which specify possible quality properties of software products. To quantify such quality properties, Section 2.1.3 describes data collection procedures. Finally, Section 2.1.4 defines the term method and describes how to systematically construct methods like the AT method.

2.1.1. Goal/Question/Metric (GQM) Method

The Goal/Question/Metric (GQM) method is a goal-oriented approach to establish a software measurement program. The approach was developed by Basili and Weiss [BW84] and later expanded by Basili et al. [BCR02]. Furthermore, Solingen and Berghout [vSB99] contribute to the original work by providing further analyses and examples as well as by adding techniques like a cost/benefit analysis. They particularly describe the GQM method in the form of a practical guide. Because of its practical nature, this thesis refers to this guide of Solingen and Berghout [vSB99] regarding the GQM method.

The GQM method, as illustrated in Figure 2.1, consists of four phases: the planning, definition, data collection, and interpretation phase [vSB99, pp. 21-22]. Figure 2.1 visualizes each of the four phases as a grey-shaded box; white boxes denote involved deliverables.

Planning Phase. The planning phase is the first phase and constitutes the framework of the measurement program. It includes the selection, specification and characterization, and the planning of a project the measurement is applied on. The main deliverable of this phase is a *project plan*.

Definition Phase. The second phase is the definition phase. It compiles a GQM plan that specifies the measurement program. The definition phase consists of three main parts which are developed top-down [vSB99, p. 23].

The GQM plan includes a set of explicit measurement *goals* and refines these goals to *questions* making the goal attainment operational: by analyzing the answers to the questions, engineers can decide whether the goals are attained. Moreover, the GQM plan identifies *metrics* that, when measured, provide the data to answer the questions. Additionally specified *hypotheses* state the expected answers to the questions. Specifying hypotheses is important to increase the learning effect from the measurement by eventually comparing measurement-based answers with expected answers (cf. [vSB99, pp. 55-56]).

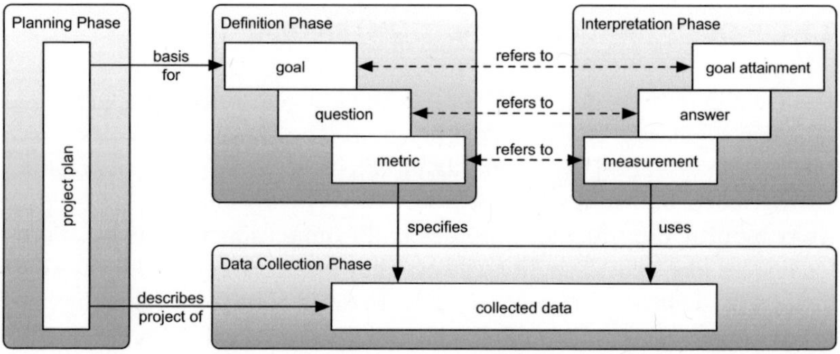

Figure 2.1.: Phases and deliverables of the GQM method: planning phase, definition phase, data collection phase, and interpretation phase (derived from [vSB99, p. 22]).

Data Collection Phase. The data collection phase is the third phase. It executes the measurements of the project and collects the data as specified by the metrics of the GQM plan.

For collection, engineers use so-called *data collection procedures*, which are further described in Section 2.1.2. The phase includes the implementation of the data collection procedure as well as the data collection and storage itself.

Interpretation Phase. The interpretation phase is the fourth and final phase. Its purpose is to use, interpret, and evaluate the collected data to draw conclusions regarding the measurement program. Like the definition phase, it consists of three main parts but interprets the parts bottom-up instead of top-down [vSB99, p. 23].

The *measurement* results are the first part. A measurement result refers to a concrete metric and uses the collected data to provide the result. Secondly, the measurement results allow to *answer* the respective questions of the GQM plan. Thirdly, the answers are used to evaluate the *goal attainment.*

Besides these three parts, the interpretation phase compares the hypotheses of the GQM plan to the measurement-based answers. In the case that a hypothesis and a measurement-based answer differ, an engineer has to find the reason for this difference. The engineer can, for instance, further inspect and analyze the collected data or take additional measurements.

The AT method employs the GQM method to elaborate new definitions and metrics for QoS properties (cf. Section 4.1.3.2). Moreover, the evaluation of the AT method in Chapter 5 is designed and executed based on the GQM method.

2.1.2. Software Quality Models

Software quality is a software product's capability to satisfy the different needs by its users, developers, and other stakeholders [ISO14]. These needs are captured by various quality properties. For software systems, software quality models provide a categorization of these quality properties (see Definition 2.4). Thus, they allow to refine the general term "quality" into concrete properties that can be handled individually. In the context of the GQM method, quality models are useful to derive concrete questions ("What is the product's quality property X?") whenever a goal is related to quality. Furthermore, the GQM method can profit from the existing literature that addresses metrics related to the quality properties.

Definition 2.4 (Software Quality Model) *"[A] defined set of characteristics, and of relationships between them, which provides a framework for specifying quality requirements and evaluating quality." [ISO14]*

In the past, several quality models were developed as, for instance, by Boehm [Boe78] or McCall et al. [MRW77]. Based on these first developments, the ISO/IEC defined the ISO/IEC 9126-1 [ISO01] standard that presents ISO/IEC's quality model. The successor of this standard is the ISO/IEC 25010 [ISO11] standard. As the latter is the newest standard currently available, this thesis concentrates on the ISO/IEC 25010 quality model only and does not evaluate other quality models.

The feature diagram[1] in Figure 2.2 shows the eight main quality properties of the ISO/IEC 25010 product quality model: functional suitability, performance efficiency, compatibility, usability, reliability, security, maintainability, and portability. ISO/IEC 25010 composes each of these main properties to subproperties. For instance, performance efficiency includes time behavior, resource utilization, and compliance. For concrete descriptions of each (sub)property, this thesis refers to the ISO/IEC 25010 [ISO11] standard as the (sub)properties should be well-known by software engineers. Nonetheless, this thesis gives a detailed description of a used property at the relevant place.

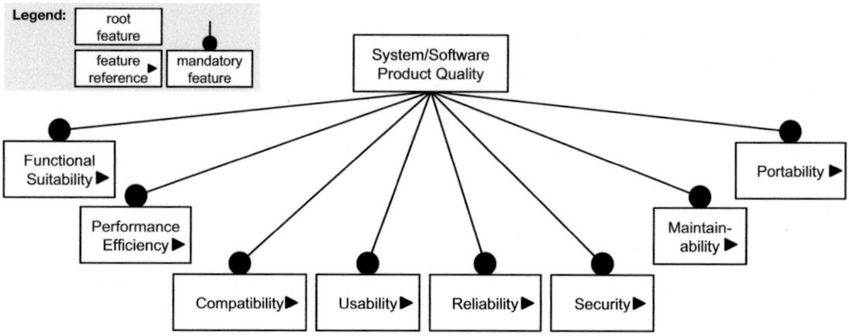

Figure 2.2.: ISO/IEC's Product Quality Model (derived from [ISO11]).

In addition to the quality model, the ISO/IEC describes suitable metrics for each quality property. The ISO/IEC 25023 [ISO16b] (formerly ISO/IEC 9126-3 [ISO03b]) standard describes these metrics for each quality property of the product quality model. Whenever this thesis refers to one of ISO/IEC's metrics, the thesis describes the metric at the relevant place.

[1] See Appendix A for a detailed description of syntax and semantics of feature diagrams.

2.1.3. Data Collection Procedures

Data collection procedures execute data collection tasks, e.g., the measurements as specified by a GQM plan [vSB99, p. 66]. According to Solingen and Berghout, data collection procedures can utilize manual forms, electronic forms, and automated data collection tools [vSB99, pp. 67-68]. Manual and electronic forms provide the means for collecting data from human participants of the measurement. Automated data collection tools use predefined algorithms for calculating metrics on the respective artifact.

Prechelt [Pre01, pp. 35-48] provides a wider scope concerning data collection procedures. He distinguishes between six empirical methods:

Questionnaires cumulate subjective data from its participants by collecting answers to a set of specified questions. For this collection, questionnaires can utilize manual and electronic forms as well as conduct structured interviews. For example, a questionnaire can ask a participant for advantages and disadvantages observed during the usage of a tool.

Case studies collect data of methods by means of application examples in a realistic application domain. For example, a realistic application domain can be a public cloud computing environment. A case study may then inspect methods to migrate a simple application into such an environment.

Case studies allow to compare methods without keeping every influencing factor constant, thus, also limiting the expressiveness of the comparison. For instance, in the example above, different engineers may use the methods, there may be no time restrictions, it may be allowed to discuss the migration with colleagues and to use web resource, etc.

Benchmarks are precisely specified use cases for tools or methods. Furthermore, benchmarks specify algorithms for calculating quantitative properties of the tool or method. Thus, they are like automated data collection tools and are a special case of case studies.

For example, TPC-W [Tra02] is a standardized benchmark for an e-commerce application. The TPC-W specification [Tra02] describes browsing and shopping use cases and states how to calculate whether these use cases achieved their QoS requirements.

Field studies are also like case studies but observe real software projects instead of artificial ones. Their advantage is that they provide more realistic results. Their disadvantage is that their results are hard to interpret and reproduce.

The example for case studies above describes a simple application to be migrated. Instead of a simple application, a field study may inspect the migration of a real industrial-size application.

Controlled experiments compare tools or methods like case studies but keep the number of variable properties low. Their advantage is that the low number of variable properties makes the interpretation of the data easy and statistically significant as varying comparison results can be explained by the variable properties. Their disadvantage is that they are costly. For instance, whenever artifacts created by an engineer are compared, individual traits need to be removed. Hence, many other engineers need to create these artifacts, too.

Meta studies cumulate their data from studies related to a common topic. Typically, meta studies are inexpensive but require several studies on the same subject.

A concrete meta study method is a systematic literature review (SLR) [KC07]. In an SLR, a set of sources (e.g., journals, conference papers, and books) on a common topic is investigated based on predefined criteria (e.g., definitions and metrics for quality properties). The result is a set of synthesized data with key insights on the common topic (e.g., a concrete definition and typical metrics for a quality property).

Because several factors influence the AT method (e.g., the software architect applying it, the kind of architectural knowledge applied, the actual system to be engineered, etc.), evaluating the whole AT method within a controlled experiment is hard. This thesis therefore uses case studies for evaluating the AT method as a whole (see Section 5.3). In addition, a pre-study to a controlled experiment with particular focus on the effort for software architects when following the AT method is conducted (see Section 5.4).

The AT method itself incorporates data collection procedures for finding and deriving suitable definitions and metrics of the quality properties of interest. For finding metrics and definitions, the AT method employs systematic literature reviews as a concrete meta study method. For deriving metrics, the AT method employs the GQM method (cf. Section 2.1.1).

2.1.4. Systematically Engineering Methods

A core contribution of this thesis is the AT method. This section therefore defines what constitutes a method (Section 2.1.4.1) and describes how to systematically construct methods via method engineering (Section 2.1.4.2).

2.1.4.1. Methods

Given that the AT method is applied for engineering information system, only methods specialized for this purpose are of interest. Definition 2.5 acknowledges this purpose by defining a method[2] as a set of means for engineering such systems.

Definition 2.5 (Method) *"A method for information systems engineering is an integrated collection of documentation and specification techniques, processes, and tools, for effective, efficient, and consistent support of the information system engineering process." (based on [Har97, p. 25])*

As stated in Definition 2.5, the means of a method include documentation and specification techniques, processes, and tools. These means need particularly to be *integrated* into the whole engineering process. The purpose of a method is to provide support for engineering processes effectively, efficiently, and consistently.

The AT method is an example of such a method. As outlined in Figure 2.3, the AT method provides a set of different means: the AT language for documentation and specification of ATs, AT processes to be followed, and an AT tooling that supports these processes. These means are intended to

[2] For brevity, this thesis treats "method" and "information systems engineering method" as synonyms.

make the work of engineers more effective and efficient while ensuring a consistent application of ATs. Chapter 4 describes each of these means in detail.

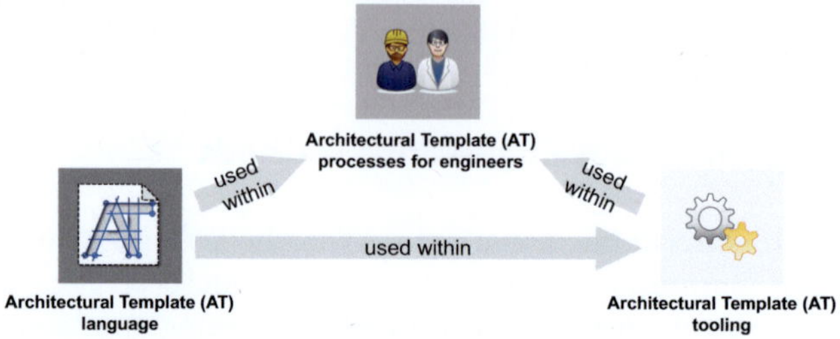

Figure 2.3.: The Architectural Template (AT) method is an example for a method and consists of a set of different means—AT language, AT processes, and AT tooling.

2.1.4.2. Method Engineering

Method engineering is an engineering discipline for constructing methods:

Definition 2.6 (Method Engineering) *"Method engineering is an engineering discipline to adopt, tailor, and develop methods for the engineering of information systems." (based on [Bri96])*

Optimally, method engineers construct methods from existing methods [MCF$^+$95, p. 8]. As stated in Definition 2.6, method engineers can either directly *adopt* existing methods (complete reuse) or *tailor* existing methods to the concrete situation at hand (application of minor modifications). If reuse is impossible, method engineers must *develop* a method from scratch.

Figure 2.4 illustrates the according process for constructing methods. The rounded rectangles represent actions that need to be conducted during the process. Thick arrows between actions denote allowed traversals from an action to another action. Actions can be traversed both forwards and backwards, thus allowing for an iterative refinement of methods.

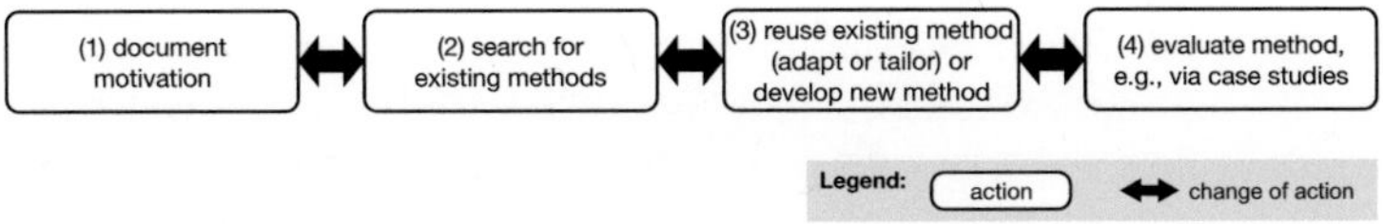

Figure 2.4.: Overview of the method engineering process (based on [MCF+95, p. 7]).

As shown in Figure 2.4, the method engineering process consists of four actions:

(1) document motivation. In the first action, method engineers document the motivation to construct a method. The motivation includes several aspects of the method (cf. [MCF+95, p. 7]): a first attunement of basic intuitions and concepts, potential users, and advantages and disadvantages in state-of-the-art methods. Method engineers document these aspects in cooperation with experts of the domain in which the method will be used.

In this thesis, Chapter 1 documents the motivation for the AT method.

(2) search for existing methods. The previously documented motivation helps method engineers in searching for existing methods [MCF+95, p. 8]. For domains with a plethora of existing methods, systematic literature reviews (see Section 2.1.3) help method engineers in conducting systematic searches. The result of the search is a set of existing methods that are related to the documented motivation.

In this thesis, Chapter 6 describes methods related to the AT method. Moreover, Section 2.3.3 describes a method for testing and Section 2.5 a method for architectural analyses. Both of these methods are related to the AT method as described in the next action.

(3) reuse existing methods (adapt or tailor) or develop new method. In action (3), method engineers construct the method. The previously documented motivation and the identified set of existing methods allows method engineers to decide whether to reuse an existing method or to develop a new method [MCF+95, p. 8].

Chapter 4 describes the AT method as a new method. However, the AT method extends the existing method for architectural analyses described in Section 2.5. Moreover, for quality assurance of ATs, the AT method includes the testing method described in Section 2.3.3. The methods described in Chapter 6 are unsuited for being reused in the construction of the AT method because these methods have different pragmatisms, however, individual features were integrated into the AT method where relevant.

(4) evaluate method, e.g., via case studies. Once constructed, method engineers evaluate the method [MCF+95, p. 8]. The means of the method (techniques, processes, tools) can be evaluated using data collection procedures like case studies and controlled experiments (see Section 2.1.3). Lessons learned from such evaluations serve method engineers as input to an iterative refinement of the method [MCF+95, p. 8].

In this thesis, Section 5.3 evaluates the AT method based on case studies. Furthermore, Section 5.4 describes a pre-study to a controlled experiment for the AT method. The lessons learned from these evaluations have partly been considered for iterative refinements of the AT method. Chapter 4 describes the AT method after these refinements have been integrated.

2.2. Software Architecture

Software architecture is the fundamental organization of a software system in terms of software components, their relations, and their environment (first part of Definition 2.7). For example, an online book shop may be organized via software components that deliver web pages, which request data from a database. The book shop may be operated in a local on-premise environment or a public cloud computing environment.

Software architecture particularly describes the set of design decisions that have led to such an organization (second part of Definition 2.7). The main task of software architects is to make these decisions such that the system's service level objectives are finally met and optimal trade-offs have been achieved [TMD09, Sec. 17.1].

Definition 2.7 (Software Architecture)

- *"The fundamental organization of a system embodied in its components, their relationships to each other, and to the environment, and the principles guiding its design and evolution." [ISO07]*
- *"A software system's architecture is the set of principal design decisions made about the system." [TMD09, p. 58]*

This section details the aspects of software architecture important for the AT method. Being first-class citizens in software architecture, the concept of software components and their types are detailed in Section 2.2.1. Afterwards, Section 2.2.2 describes service level objectives as a means for software architects to formulate requirements for their software architecture. To fulfill such requirements, software architects make design decisions, which are described in Section 2.2.3. Software architects' decision making can be governed by reusable architectural knowledge, e.g., in the form of architectural styles and architectural patterns, which is overviewed in Section 2.2.4. The AT method allows to formalize this knowledge. This formalization enables software architects to be governed consistently and automatically, which makes them more efficient in ensuring the fulfillment of service level objectives.

2.2.1. Software Components and their Types

According to Szyperski[3], software components are units of composition for software entities:

Definition 2.8 (Software Component) *"A software component is a unit of composition with contractually specified interfaces and explicit context dependencies only. A software component can be deployed independently and is subject to composition by third parties." [Szy02, p. 41]*

[3] Szyperski's definition is well-accepted in component-based software engineering because of its focus on composability (cf. [GTWJ03, p. 7]).

Compositions are based on exposed and contractually specified interfaces because interfaces are the only way components[4] interact with their environment (cf. Meyer's design-by-contract principle [Mey97, Chap. 11]). Accordingly, a component that requires a certain interface can only be composed with a component that provides this interface. The contract between these two components states that if the preconditions specified in the interface hold, the providing component can guarantee specified postconditions. The scope of such guarantees can cover both functional properties (e.g., operation signatures and protocols) and non-functional properties (e.g., QoS characteristics) [BJPW99].

Szyperski emphasizes that software components have explicit context dependencies only. That is, components expose every dependency to their environment that they need to fulfill their guarantees. Required interfaces are the typical concept to express such dependencies to other components, e.g., the UML follows this approach [Obj11, Sec. 7.3.24]. Besides required interfaces, explicit context dependencies also relate to the environment into which components are deployed [Szy02, Sec. 4.1.7].

The second sentence of Definition 2.8 illustrates implications of the interface-based component definition. The encapsulation of features behind interfaces makes components well-separated from their context. This separation allows components to be deployed independently. Components particularly become units of deployment, i.e., they cannot be deployed partially.

A further implication is that components can be composed by third parties, i.e., other stakeholders than the creators of components. Third parties compose only based on the exposed interfaces of components; without knowing the components' internals (black-box principle [Dry07, Sec. 3.1.2]). For example, in the component-based development process by Cheesman and Daniels [CD00], software architects act as third parties and let component developers provision components.

Such a process allows for an iterative development as illustrated in the left-hand action (3) of Figure 2.13 (see Section 2.5.1.1 for a detailed description of Figure 2.13). Initially, software architects request components from component developers by specifying the interfaces these components need to provide, i.e., they specify component types as defined in Definition 2.9.

[4] For brevity, this thesis treats "component" and "software component" as synonyms.

This way, software architects can already plan an initial software architecture without having component internals available. Meanwhile, component developers can implement the components that conform to the requested component types. Once implemented, software architects can finally refine their initial software architecture by substituting component types with conforming components.

Definition 2.9 (Software Component Type) *"The specification of a set of interfaces that conforming components need to expose." (based on [CD00, p. 8][5])*

2.2.2. Service Level Objectives

Service level objectives (SLOs) are the quality-of-service targets of a software system (see Definition 2.10). To specify an SLO, requirements engineers need to determine a suitable metric and a threshold for this metric. The metric is "a defined measurement method and measurement scale" [Clo14] and the threshold the lower limit for which a metric measurement violates the SLO.

Definition 2.10 (Service Level Objective) *"The quality-of-service target to be achieved—for each service activity, function, and process." (based on [Gar03])*

An example SLO is the performance metric *maximum response time* combined with a concrete threshold of 1 second. A guarantee of 1 second response time in 100 % of the time can be unrealistic depending on the context of the system. Therefore, a refined threshold of 1 second *for* 90 % *of all requests within one month* can be a viable alternative. The resulting performance SLO accordingly states that "the system shall respond with a maximum response time of 1 second for 90 % of all request within one month".

[5] Cheesman and Daniels [CD00, p. 8] refer to "component specifications" instead of "software component types". This thesis uses the latter to be consistent with the vocabulary used in Palladio (cf. Section 2.5.3).

Violations of SLOs potentially lead to contractually specified penalties, e.g., system users may get discounts for system usage. As described in the next section, software architects thus need to make design decisions that fulfill SLOs as best as possible.

2.2.3. Design Decisions

Design decisions describe why and how software architects have applied changes to a software architecture (see Definition 2.11). These decisions therefore characterize the system-wide boundaries of achievable software quality and, thus, fulfillable SLOs.

Definition 2.11 (Design Decision) *"A description of the set of architectural additions, subtractions and modifications to the software architecture, the rationale, and the design rules, design constraints and additional requirements that (partially) realize one or more requirements on a given architecture." [JB05]*

The "why" is covered by a rationale that gives the reasons for applied changes. For example, the rationale may state that a design decision ensures the fulfillment of a performance requirement. An example for a performance requirement is the SLO defined in Section 2.2.2 ("the system shall respond with a maximum response time of 1 second for 90 % of all request within one month").

The "how" is covered by a description of restrictions for future elements (design constraints) and of actual changes to elements (additions, subtractions, and modifications) according to documented design rules.

Making design decisions potentially results in new requirements that have to be addressed by future design decisions (last part of Definition 2.11).

2.2.4. Reusable Architectural Knowledge

Based on Definition 2.12, architectural knowledge is the combination of design decisions with the resulting (changes in the) software architecture when these decisions are made.

Definition 2.12 (Architectural Knowledge)
"Architectural Knowledge = Design Decisions + Design" [KLvV06]

Software architects repeatedly create and extend architectural knowledge when designing software architectures. Hereby, architects become more efficient if they reuse previously created knowledge. Such a reuse is possible for recurring design problems that allow for the same changes in software architecture to be applied.

Examples of reusable architectural knowledge are architectural styles, architectural patterns, and reference architectures [TMD09]. These kinds of reusable knowledge use the concept of roles, as defined in Definition 2.13, to assign responsibilities to architectural elements [BHS07b, p. 309], e.g., to components, connectors, and resource containers.

Definition 2.13 (Role) *"The responsibility of a design element within a context of related elements." [BHS07b, p. 395]*

A role's responsibilities can be specified as a set of design decisions [BHS07b, p. 309]. The assignment of roles then leads to the application of these design decisions [BHS07b, Sec. 11.2]. For reusable architectural knowledge, roles may include well-proven design decisions to solve a given recurring problem [Ale77, p. x]. These design decisions are well-proven because they provided solutions for previous but similar problems.

A key goal for software architects is to apply reusable architectural knowledge consistently [BCK98, Sec. 12.2]. That is, software architects should avoid both partial applications of architectural knowledge (e.g., by missing role assignments) and violations of a role's responsibilities (e.g., by introducing state to a component that acts in a stateless role). This consistency between software architecture and applied architectural knowledge is captured in the quality property *conceptual integrity* (see Definition 2.14).

Definition 2.14 (Conceptual Integrity) *"Conceptual integrity refers to consistency in the design of the architecture, and it contributes to the understandability of the architecture and leads to fewer errors of confusion." [BCK98, Sec. 12.2]*

To exemplify reusable architectural knowledge and the role concept, the remainder of this section describes architectural styles, architectural patterns, and reference architectures. Figure 2.5 illustrates the main differences between these kinds of reusable architectural knowledge.

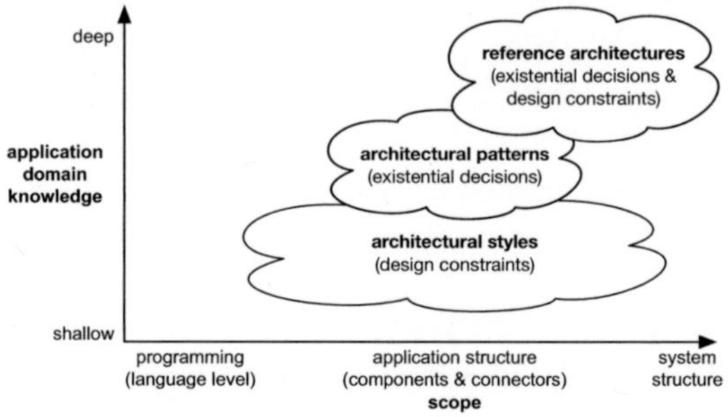

Figure 2.5.: Reusable architectural knowledge (cloud symbols) differs in scope (X-axis), application domain knowledge (Y-axis), and kinds of design decisions (parentheses within cloud symbols). The figure is based on [TMD09, p. 92].

The X-axis and Y-axis of Figure 2.5 show Taylor et al.'s [TMD09, p. 92] classification of reusable architectural knowledge into scope (X-axis) and application domain knowledge (Y-axis). The scope dimension gives the targeted level of abstraction of reusable architectural knowledge; ranging from a programming level over the application level to the system level. The application domain knowledge dimension gives the amount of domain-specific knowledge inherent to reusable architectural knowledge; ranging from shallow domain dependence (i.e., the knowledge is general) to a deep domain dependence (i.e., the knowledge is domain-specific).

In Figure 2.5, cloud symbols denote different kinds of reusable architectural knowledge—architectural styles, architectural patterns, and reference architectures. The position of these symbols provides the classification based on scope and application domain knowledge. For example, architectural styles and architectural patterns mainly target the application structure scope but architectural styles provide more shallow knowledge than architectural patterns. As in Taylor et al.'s [TMD09, p. 92] classification, cloud symbols are used because this classification serves only as a rough guide. This fuzziness acknowledges that the difference, e.g., between architectural patterns and architectural styles, is often subject to discussion [BMR+96, p. 394ff.].

In contrast to Taylor et al.'s [TMD09, p. 92] classification, a cloud symbol's text in parentheses additionally denotes the kinds of design decisions defining the associated reusable architectural knowledge. While architectural styles only contain design decisions about design constraints, architectural patterns contain existential decisions, i.e., decisions about the existence of elements. Reference architectures define a set of domain-specific architectural styles and architectural patterns, thus, including both kinds of design decisions.

The advantage of this additional classification dimension is that design decisions provide a more distinct differentiation criterion. The AT method particularly allows to formalize the different kinds of design decisions. Based on this formalization, the AT method allows to capture the illustrated kinds of reusable architectural knowledge as a whole. Because these kinds of reusable architectural knowledge are in the focus of the AT method, the following sections describe and exemplify these kinds in detail.

2.2.4.1. Architectural Styles

An architectural style introduces a set of roles that constrain a system, i.e., include only design decision about design constraints. When an architectural style is applied, these constraints foster particular quality properties. Definition 2.15 covers these aspects by paraphrasing roles as a "named collection of architectural design decisions".

Definition 2.15 (Architectural Style) *"An architectural style is a named collection of architectural design decisions that (1) are applicable in a given development context, (2) constrain architectural design decisions that are specific to a particular system within that context, and (3) elicit beneficial qualities in each resulting system." [TMD09, p. 73]*

Moreover, Definition 2.15 points out that architectural styles are applicable in specific contexts. For example, in the context of information systems, the *three-layer* architectural style is often applied [BMR+96, p. 47]. The three-layer architectural style introduces roles to structure a system into three different logical layers: a presentation layer, an application layer, and a data access layer. The roles' constraints dictate that each of these layers can only access the respective lower-level layer. Because of this restriction, a three-layer system becomes loosely coupled and therefore more maintainable.

2.2.4.2. Architectural Patterns

An architectural pattern introduces a set of roles that refine a system (see first item of Definition 2.16). For this refinement, roles include design decisions about the existence of additional elements. These additional elements are intended to solve a recurring design problem.

Roles can be parametrized to introduce variation points to select different design decisions (see second item of Definition 2.16). Variation points are configured based on the context of the system, e.g., the expected workload.

Definition 2.16 (Architectural Pattern)

- *"[An architectural] pattern provides a scheme for refining elements of a software system or the relationships between them. It describes a commonly-recurring structure of interacting roles that solves a general design problem within a particular context." [BHS07b, p. 392]*
- *"An architectural pattern is a named collection of architectural design decisions that are applicable to a recurring design problem, parametrized to account for different software development contexts in which that problem appears." [TMD09, p. 73]*

For example, the *loadbalancing* architectural pattern [BHS07a] requires the existence of a component acting as a loadbalancer. Figure 2.6 (left) shows such a loadbalancer component as deployed on a dedicated loadbalancer server. As loadbalancer, the component distributes workload (i.e., incoming requests) over replicas of a given architectural element. In Figure 2.6 (right), the architectural element is a resource container that is replicated *n* times

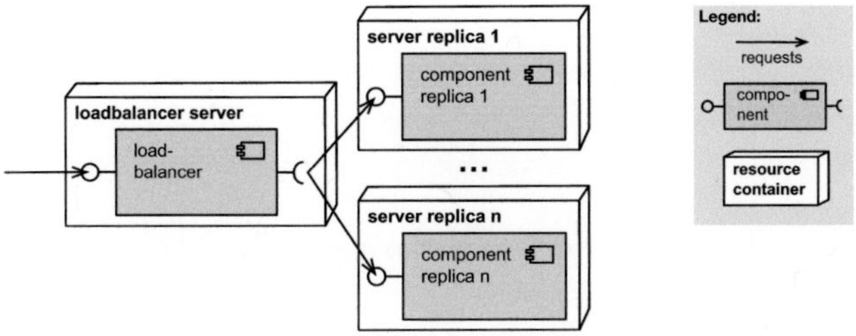

Figure 2.6.: The loadbalancing architectural pattern introduces a loadbalancer component to distribute workload.

(server replica 1 to server replica n), including allocated components (component replica 1 to component replica n).

Workload distribution is a common way to improve a system's performance. Typical variation points are the concrete architectural element (e.g., a resource container with all deployed components or only a single component), the number of replicas, and the loadbalancing strategy (e.g., round-robin).

2.2.4.3. Reference Architectures

A reference architecture defines a domain-specific architectural style and a set of domain-specific architectural patterns to be applied in that style (see Definition 2.17). These patterns provide the variation points to account for different domains and contexts.

Definition 2.17 (Reference Architecture) *"A reference architecture is the set of principal design decisions that are simultaneously applicable to multiple related systems, typically within a single application domain, with explicitly defined points of variation." [TMD09, p. 58]*

For example, AUTOSAR [Wie13] (AUTomotive Open System ARchitecture) defines a reference architecture for software in automobiles—independent of concrete vendors and cars. AUTOSAR prescribes a *three-layered* architectural style with a basic software layer, a runtime environment layer, and an application layer [Wie13]. Architectural patterns are prescribed for these layers, e.g., describing which component interfaces are required on the basic software layer.

2.3. Model-Driven Software Engineering

In model-driven software engineering (MDSE), models describe a domain's problem in an *abstract* and *(semi-)formal* way. Abstraction allows, e.g., software architects during architectural modeling, to concentrate on the essential parts of the problem by omitting irrelevant details and, thus, keeping the model compact. Because models are (semi-)formal[6], models can be transformed into other models and textual artifacts. This way, models can both become part of the software and serve for documentation [VSC06, p. 366]. To specify models, *Domain-Specific Languages* (DSLs) are used, i.e., (semi-)formal languages designed and implemented for a specific domain.

This section describes MDSE topics relevant for this thesis: the AT method introduces a DSL—the AT language—for the specification and application of ATs. Once specified, software architects can apply ATs to their architectural models and map these models to analysis models for QoS analyses. Therefore, Section 2.3.1 gives clear definitions for models and metamodels (that allow to specify DSLs like the AT language). Afterwards, Section 2.3.2 describes model transformations (as used for the mapping of architectural to analysis models). Section 2.3.3 describes how test engineers can ensure the quality of model transformations via testing (to ensure that AT mappings are correct). To extend DSLs, Section 2.3.4 describes profiles and stereotypes (which are used by ATs to extend architectural models with AT applications). The semantics for these extensions can be defined as described in Section 2.3.5.

2.3.1. Metamodeling

Metamodeling is concerned with engineering models and metamodels—the central artifacts of MDSE. Therefore, this section gives clear definitions for

[6] Models are semi-formal if "their notations have a formal syntax, but no formal semantics" [APS07].

these artifacts (Section 2.3.1.1 and Section 2.3.1.2). Moreover, this section details how to specify these artifacts formally and systematically (Section 2.3.1.3).

2.3.1.1. Models

Models have the most important role in MDSE. Nonetheless, there are several different definitions for this term. Baier et al. [BBJ+08, p. 94] give a definition of a model that fits the needs of this thesis.

Definition 2.18 (Model) *"A model describes a (real) system in a simplified (abstract) manner in pursuance of a concrete goal." [BBJ+08, p. 94] (translated by the author)*

Based on a fundamental book of Stachowiak [Sta73, p. 207], Baier et al. [BBJ+08, p. 94] emphasize that a model has three characteristics: abstraction, pragmatics, and homomorphism[7]. *Abstraction* describes the property that the model removes details which are unnecessary to serve a specific purpose. The purpose reflects the goal of creating the model (*pragmatics*). Thus, the pragmatics dictate the attributes of interest when abstracting. Additionally, statements of the model should also relate to the modeled entity (with respect to the pragmatics), i.e., there must be a *homomorphism* between model and represented entity.

2.3.1.2. Metamodels

Metamodels specify syntax and semantics of models. Baier et al. [BBJ+08, p. 94] define metamodels as follows.

Definition 2.19 (Metamodel) *"A metamodel is a precise definition of constructs and rules for the creation of models. It includes an abstract syntax, at least one concrete syntax as well as static and dynamic semantics." [BBJ+08, p. 94] (translated by the author)*

[7] Stachowiak [Sta73, p. 207] uses the German words "Verkürzungsmerkmal", "Pragmatisches Merkmal", and "Abbildungsmerkmal". Abstraction, pragmatics, and homomorphism are no literal translations of these words but precisely reflect their meaning (cf. [Bec08, p. 31]).

With these characteristics, metamodels can be used to define DSLs [Küh06]: a metamodel describes a set of models that conform to it, i.e., each model uses the constructs and obeys the rules dictated by the metamodel. Metamodel constructs—the elements of a metamodel—are called metaclasses.

A model conforming to a metamodel is called an *instance* of the metamodel. The shorter forms *model instance* and just *model* are also common. Furthermore, a metamodel can have its own metamodel, the so-called *meta metamodel*, and so forth.

Definition 2.19 is based on the concepts introduced by Völter et al. [VSC06, pp. 56-58]. Accordingly, the *abstract syntax* specifies the set of syntactically correct model instances independent of its concrete representation. A concrete representation is specified by a *concrete syntax* that complies with the abstract syntax. There can be several concrete syntaxes, e.g., a textual and a graphical syntax.

The *static semantics* put further constraints (criteria for well-formedness) on the set of syntactically valid model instances. These semantics can be checked without knowing the meaning of the model. In contrast, the *dynamic semantics* specify its meaning, which allows to interpret the model in a given context.

2.3.1.3. Formally and Systematically Defining DSLs

The AT method introduces with the AT language a DSL (as detailed in Section 4.2). To make this introduction as precise and systematic as possible, this thesis applies the metamodeling concepts introduced by Kühne [Küh06]. Therefore, this section briefly outlines Kühne's main concepts for formally and systematically defining DSLs.

According to Kühne, a language $\mathcal{L}$ can equivalently be defined by the metamodel $\mathcal{MM}$ or by the intension ι of the language, i.e., $\mathcal{MM}(\mathcal{L}) \sim \iota(\mathcal{L})$ [Küh06]. The intension of a language is the sum of its attributes [Car88], e.g., an AT "represents an architectural style" $\wedge$ "has a name" $\wedge \ldots$. Therefore, there are two options to approach the definition of a language $\mathcal{L}$: (a) collect all required attributes of $\mathcal{L}$, i.e., derive $\iota(\mathcal{L})$, or (b) specify the metamodel of $\mathcal{L}$, i.e., define $\mathcal{MM}(\mathcal{L})$ directly.

In any case, users of a DSL eventually need $\mathcal{MM}(\mathcal{L})$ to apply $\mathcal{L}$ in a model-driven way. For example, model transformations and graphical editors require the specification of metamodels. To derive such a metamodel systematically, software engineers can proceed using a combination of options (a) and (b) [Leh14a].

Software engineers begin with option (a) by deriving required attributes, e.g., based on pragmatism and example usage scenarios of the DSL. After collecting the attributes of $\mathcal{L}$, software engineers have a first version of $\iota(\mathcal{L})$. The intension for the AT language is derived like this in Section 4.2.3.

Based on this intension, software engineers can subsequently derive a first version of $\mathcal{MM}(\mathcal{L})$. The crux of the matter is that software engineers can, by this approach, assure that the metamodel is correct by construction, i.e., that $\mathcal{MM}(\mathcal{L}) \sim \iota(\mathcal{L})$ holds. Following this principle, the AT metamodel is derived in Section 4.2.5.

Once a first version of $\mathcal{MM}(\mathcal{L})$ exists, software engineers can iteratively refine this metamodel based on feedback by its users. Such iterations have indeed occurred for the AT metamodel: after an initial version of the results was published [Leh14a], the role concept of the AT metamodel has been refined, e.g., by further constraints (cf. Section 4.2.5).

2.3.2. Model Transformations

In MDSE, models play the most important role and become "at least as import as source code" [VSC06, p. 4]. Consequently, software engineers need mechanisms to convert one model into another model in order to apply a refinement, a refactoring, etc. to the former one. For this purpose, MDSE uses model transformations as a key technology (see Definition 2.20).

Definition 2.20 (Model Transformation) *"A model transformation is a computable function that maps model instances of a set of source metamodels onto model instances of a set of target metamodels." [BBJ+08, p. 97] (translated by the author)*

The attribute *computable* is essential for an automated processing of transformations[8]. Computability allows to reuse transformations, which particularly decreases development costs and increases development speed and software quality [VSC06, p. 13].

Figure 2.7 illustrates a transformation. Figure 2.7 (left) depicts a source model instantiated from a source metamodel. Figure 2.7 (right) depicts a target model instantiated from a target metamodel. The transformation depicted between the two models computes the target model based on the source model. Typically, the metamodels of source and target model are different. Still, they can have the same metamodels, e.g., for refactorings. Such transformations are so-called in-place transformations [CH06].

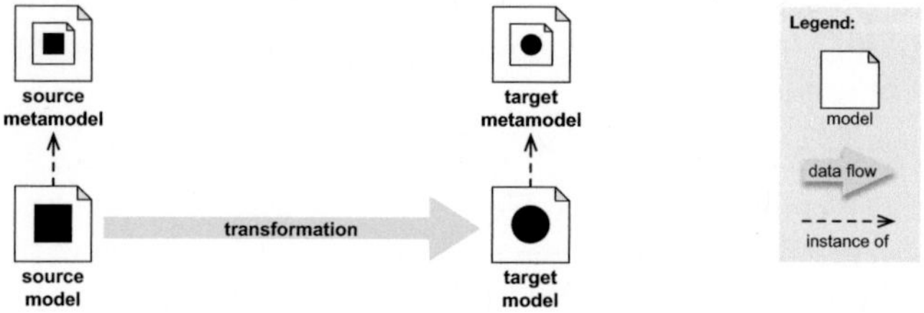

Figure 2.7.: Transformations map a source model to a target model.

Another common classification of transformations is to distinguish between model-to-model (M2M) transformations and model-to-text (M2T) transformations [BBJ+08, p. 97]. While an M2M transformation generally follows the above scheme, an M2T transformation generates texts like source code, configuration files, XML, etc. from a source model. Consequently, M2T transformations are a special case of M2M transformations where the target metamodel is an arbitrary or structured text file [CH06].

In this thesis, M2M transformations are used to map architectural models to QoS analysis models. For the specification of these transformations, the QVT Operational Mapping (QVT-O) [Obj16] language is used, i.e., an imperative approach. In unidirectional scenarios like the mapping from architectural models to QoS analysis models, QVT-O has the advantages that it is more maintainable and easier to learn than common alternatives [Leh12].

[8] For brevity, this thesis treats "transformation" and "model transformation" as synonyms.

2.3.3. Quality Assurance of Model Transformations via Testing

Model transformations are manually specified by software engineers and, thus, prone to implementation errors. For example, a software engineer can easily forget to specify how to map seldomly instantiated metaclasses from a source to a target model. Still, a correct mapping may require a mapping for *each* metaclass of a source metamodel. Because of this error-proneness, quality assurance of transformations is required.

This section describes transformation testing as a concrete quality assurance approach. The AT method employs transformation testing for assuring the conceptual integrity (cf. Definition 2.14) of applied architectural knowledge.

According to Definition 2.21, transformation testing is a process in which test engineers execute a transformation on a set of source models. Subsequently, they validate the transformation by comparing the resulting target models with the expected output.

Definition 2.21 (Transformation Testing) *"Transformation testing executes a transformation on input models and validates that the actual output matches the expected output [...]." [SCD12]*

Testing is more lightweight when compared to formal approaches like mathematical proofs, model checking, theorem proving, and static analysis [CS13]. Although testing is unable to *verify* conceptual integrity (like formal approaches), testing can be automated, easily uncover faults, and involves low computational effort.

Section 2.3.3.1 details how software engineers can specify expectations to transformations via contracts and Section 2.3.3.2 how they proceed when testing transformations.

2.3.3.1. Contracts of Transformations

Following Meyer's design-by-contract principle [Mey97, Chap. 11], transformation contracts declare *what* a transformations computes (but not *how*) [CMSD04]. Definition 2.22 states that such declarations are realized as three sets of constraints.

Definition 2.22 (Transformation contract) *"A transformation contract is a tuple of three sets of constraints:*

- *pre-conditions—a set of constraints to be matched for a model to be candidate as a source model of the transformation,*
- *post-conditions—a set of constraints to be matched for a model to be considered as a valid target model produced by the transformation, and*
- *source-target-conditions—a set of constraints on the relationships and evolution of elements from the source to the target model." (based on [CMSD04])*

Figure 2.8 illustrates transformation contracts based on these constraint sets. Figure 2.8 illustrates a transformation like Figure 2.7. In addition, black boxes represent constraint sets that are matched for source and target models. Pre-conditions match for the source model, post-conditions for the target model, and source-target-conditions match for both. The conformance of source and target models to source and target metamodels are implicit pre- and post-conditions, respectively.

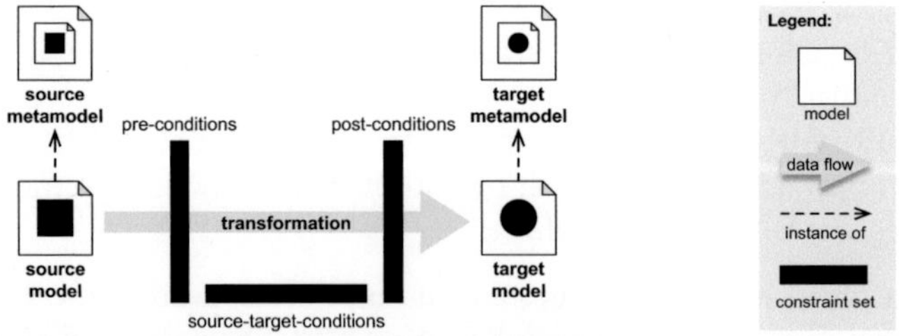

Figure 2.8.: Transformation contracts consist of three sets of constraints: pre-conditions, post-conditions, and source-target-conditions.

Transformation contracts are commonly specified via OCL [SCD12]. OCL is suited because it is a constraint expression language, well-supported by tools, and well-known by software engineers [CBBD09]. In these aspects, OCL outperforms alternatives like B and the Java Modeling Language (cf. [CMSD04]).

The benefit of transformation contracts is that software engineers can characterize transformations as application conditions (pre-conditions) and expected results (post-conditions and source-target-conditions) [CMSD04]. Therefore, transformation contracts can particularly be used as oracle functions for testing models, which is described in the next section.

2.3.3.2. Process for Transformation Testing

Figure 2.9 illustrates Selim et al.'s [SCD12] process for transformation testing. Rounded rectangles in Figure 2.9 represent actions that need to be conducted during the process. While rectangles of high-level actions are white, rectangles for sub-actions are grey-shaded. The roles that conduct high-level actions are annotated as well. The thick arrows between actions denote allowed traversals from an action to another action. Actions can be traversed both forwards and backwards, thus allowing for an iterative and incremental approach. The thin arrows represent flow of artifacts during development. Each concrete artifact is denoted with an according name and a representative icon.

According to Figure 2.9, software engineers develop a model transformation to be tested. Once developed, software engineers hand this model transformations over to test engineers. These engineers test the model transformation and provide feedback to the software engineers in terms of a fault report.

Test engineers execute the following sub-actions to test the model transformation:

(1) specify test goals and adequacy criteria. First, test engineers must specify their test goals [FH86], e.g., to test functional correctness. Moreover, test engineers specify for each test goal a set of adequacy criteria [SCD12]. For example, when transforming class diagrams, an adequacy criterion may state that for each class attribute, each representative value must be instantiated in at least one test source model.

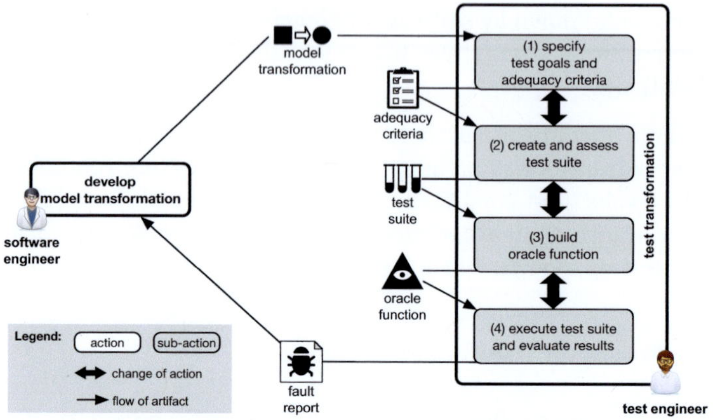

Figure 2.9.: Test engineers systematically test model transformations provided by software engineers.

Adequacy criteria differ depending on whether a black-box or a white-box testing approach is used [SCD12]. In black-box testing, test engineers can only access transformation contracts—transformation implementations are unavailable. In white-box testing, test engineers have in contrast full access to transformation implementations.

The adequacy criterion for the coverage of class attributes as exemplified above can be applied in black-box testing. However, a criterion that checks for the coverage of transformation implementation code requires white-box testing. Also testing single units of the transformation implementation requires white-box testing. For these reasons, white-box testing is typically applied by the developers of the transformation whereas black-box testing is applied by dedicated test engineers for quality assurance [Moh12].

(2) create and assess test suite. In the second action, test engineers create a test suite that includes a set of source models to be tested with a transformation. Test engineers derive this test suite based on the previously specified adequacy criteria [SCD12]: the goal is to cover as many criteria as possible. Based on assessing this coverage, transformation engineers can determine whether a test suite is likely to uncover faults within a transformation.

For example, the adequacy criterion for the coverage of class attributes implies that each representative value of each class attribute needs to be covered. To derive a test suite, test engineers accordingly must iterate over each class attribute and each representative value while specifying appropriate test source models. After these iterations, the adequacy criterion for the coverage of class attributes is covered and the likelihood to uncover faults with the test suite is increased.

(3) build oracle function. In this action, test engineers build an oracle function. The oracle function checks whether a transformation produces the correct target models [SCD12].

For conducting such checks, the oracle function compares produced target models with expected outcomes. Test engineers can specify expected outcomes via concrete models and via transformation contracts [SCD12]. If specified via concrete models, the oracle function checks whether these models equal the corresponding target models (model differencing [KPP06]). If specified as transformation contracts, the oracle function validates the contract's constraints on source and target models.

(4) execute test suite and evaluate results. In the fourth and final action, test engineers execute the test suite and subsequently use the oracle function to evaluate transformation results [SCD12]. Each failed check of the oracle function points to a potential fault within the transformation.

Test engineers create a report of these faults and hand this report over to the developers of the transformation. Afterwards, the developers can resolve reported faults or ask test engineers to revise their oracle function in case expectations about outcome were wrong.

2.3.4. Profiles and Stereotypes

Profiles are extensions of metamodels with a specific purpose (see Definition 2.23). For example, ATs use profiles to extend metamodels of architectural models with facilities to apply reusable architectural knowledge (see Section 2.2.4 for a description of reusable architectural knowledge). These facilities allow to bind elements of architectural models to roles of previously captured reusable architectural knowledge. Without a profile-based extension, the creation of bindings would be unsupported by the architectural model.

Definition 2.23 (Profile) *"A profile defines limited extensions to a reference metamodel with the purpose of adapting the metamodel to a specific platform or domain." [Obj11, p. 670]*

Profiles specify extensions as a set of *stereotypes*, which define how the elements of a metamodel are extended (see Definition 2.24). Stereotypes mark the extended elements and optionally enrich these elements with further attributes—so-called tagged values. For example, profiles used by ATs include stereotypes for each role of the formalized architectural knowledge. Tagged values allow to model the parameters of such roles.

Definition 2.24 (Stereotype) *"A stereotype defines how an existing metaclass may be extended, and enables the use of platform or domain specific terminology or notation in place of, or in addition to, the ones used for the extended metaclass." [Obj11, p. 679]*

Profiles and their stereotypes are on the same level of abstraction as the extended metamodel. In contrast, *profile applications* (see Definition 2.25) specify which profiles are applied to a model, i.e., they are on the metamodel instance level. Profile applications particularly specify where and which stereotypes are applied, including an assignment of actual parameters to their tagged values. For example, the application of an AT and its roles to an architectural model is realized as profile application (cf. Chapter 4).

Definition 2.25 (Profile Application) *"A profile application is used to show which profiles have been applied to a package." [Obj11, p. 677]*

Because profiles do not change a metamodel itself (which would be a heavyweight extension), profiles are referred to as lightweight extensions [Obj11, p. 659]. The benefit of such lightweight extensions is that tools depending on a given metamodel do not break due to metamodel changes and can even provide a generic support for stereotype extensions. For example, an editor for models of a metamodel can show which stereotypes have been applied to a model element and provide editing support for assigning actual parameters to tagged values. For these reasons, ATs use profiles for applying architectural knowledge to architectural models.

2.3.5. Ways to Describe Semantics of Metamodels

As mentioned in Section 2.3.1, the semantics of a metamodel specify its meaning, allowing to interpret metamodel instances in a given context. There are two metamodel-related aspects in the AT method: (1) the AT method defines with the AT language a metamodel on its own and (2) the AT language itself allows to extend metamodels (of architectural models) by additional semantics. The semantics of both aspects must be described.

While descriptions in natural language are possible, their ambiguity gives reason for more formal ways. According to Kleppe [Kle08, p. 135], more formal ways to describe semantics are denotational, pragmatic, translational, and operational. A brief overview of these ways allows to argue why the AT method follows the pragmatic way for aspect (1) and the translational way for aspect (2):

Denotational semantic descriptions are based on mathematical constructs—so-called denotations. Denotations represent metamodel elements and can be collected in sets. Such sets formalize the state of the modeled entity. The semantics of operations, e.g., to insert an element into a model, can then be formalized as partial functions that alter this state accordingly.

Pragmatic semantic descriptions provide an executable tool that takes metamodel instances as input—a so-called reference implementation. The execution of this reference implementation with a concrete model allows to observe the model's intension.

Translational semantic descriptions specify a translation from a source metamodel to a target metamodel with well-described semantics. This combination of translation and existing semantics indirectly defines the semantics for the source metamodel. To specify a translation, model transformations (cf. Section 2.3.2) can be used.

Operational semantic descriptions specify how an abstract machine, e.g., a state transition system, executes instances of a metamodel. Similar to translational semantics, source model instances therefore have to be translated, e.g., into state representations. In addition, the execution behavior of the abstract machine needs to be specified, e.g., via state transitions.

For aspect (1), i.e., the AT metamodel, the pragmatic way is chosen for its simplicity [Kle08, p. 135]. The so-called AT tooling (see Section 4.3) provides a reference implementation interpreting instances of the AT metamodel, thus, realizing the pragmatic way. To complement this formal semantics definition, Section 4.2.5 informally describes the AT metamodel in natural language. This informal description allows to grasp the semantics of the AT metamodel more intuitively and to check AT tooling for conformance.

For aspect (2), i.e., extensions of architectural models, the AT method uses the translational way because it is expected to be the "best" and quickest formal way if a suitable target metamodel exists [Kle08, p. 138]. In the AT method, target metamodels are well-described languages for architectural models. With ATs, recurring elements in instances of these languages (i.e., reusable architectural knowledge) can be formalized. Because this architectural knowledge can be expressed in the target architectural model language (by definition), such languages are also suitable targets for translational semantic descriptions. Section 4.2.5.6 describes the AT method's use of transformations to implement the translational way.

2.3.6. Standards and Technologies

Several standards and technologies have emerged to help software engineers in effectively and efficiently applying MDSD. This section overviews the standards and technologies relevant for the AT method.

The Meta Object Facility (MOF) [Obj15] provides a standard for specifying metamodels. For metamodel specification, MOF specifies the *MOF model* as a standardized metamodel for metamodels.

The Eclipse Modeling Project—an MDSD project of the Eclipse Foundation [Gro09, p. 8]—is related to the MOF. The core of the project is the Eclipse Modeling Framework (EMF) that includes a MOF implementation, the so-called Ecore metamodel [SBPM09]. The Ecore metamodel, thus, allows to specify metamodels technically.

Several projects exist that use EMF to provide MDSD capabilities, e.g., for abstract and concrete syntax development and for working with model transformations. Particularly, the transformation language QVT-O (cf. Section 2.3.2) is part of the Eclipse Modeling Project and makes use of EMF.

Another standard and technology is the Object Constraint Language (OCL) [Obj14]. OCL is a declarative language that initially was specified for describing constraints on UML models. In fact, the OCL is nowadays able to specify queries and constraints on any MOF-based modeling language [VSC06, p. 96]. For MDSD, OCL is especially important because OCL can enrich metamodels with constraints, thus, allowing to formalize static semantics, and because transformations can use OCL to operate on models.

2.4. Templates

Template is a common English term characterizing some kind of blueprint [Oxf16b, Ame11]. Templates are used in a variety of domains and contexts, amongst others in model-driven software engineering. In this particular domain, several examples for templates can be found [BG07b, TA05b, HJS+09, Cza98, CA05, Obj11, VCC15]; however, no common definition for the term exists. This section therefore derives a definition for templates that best fits the understanding within the model-driven context of this thesis, thus, providing a clear and consistent view on templates:

Definition 2.26 (Template) *"In model-driven software engineering, a **template** is a reusable model blueprint from which (parts of) concrete models can be instantiated. As such, their purpose is to make knowledge for recurring* *modeling situations reusable. For a controlled reuse, templates come with static parts that cannot be customized and dynamic parts that are intended to be customized within prescribed constraints." (author's definition)*

In the AT method (see Chapter 4), such templates—Architectural Templates (ATs)—are used as proposed by Riehle [Rie03]. Riehle argues to use templates to formalize reusable architectural knowledge like illustrated in Figure 2.10.

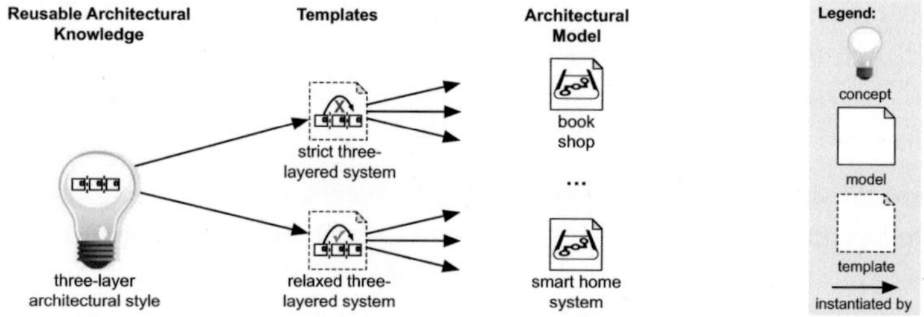

Figure 2.10.: Capturing variants of reusable architectural knowledge via templates that can be instantiated by architectural models (based on [Rie03]).

Figure 2.10 (left) shows that reusable architectural knowledge is on a conceptual level. For example, a description of the three-layer architectural style may be documented in natural language and mainly serve communication purposes, e.g., providing software architects a representative name and a rough understanding of the knowledge.

Because such an informal documentation deliberately leaves room for interpretation, different realization variants of the knowledge exist. As shown in Figure 2.10 (middle), Riehle proposes to use templates for capturing different variants. For example, a strict three-layered system captures the three-layer architectural style described in Section 2.2.4.1 where the presentation layer can only access the application layer but not the data access layer. In contrast, a relaxed three-layered system [BMR+96, pp. 45/46] allows direct accesses from presentation to data access layer. In terms of QoS properties, the relaxed variant comes with an improved performance (due to the allowed shortcut) but sacrifices maintainability (due to a tighter coupling of layers).

Figure 2.10 (right) shows that templates finally allow software architects to apply the captured knowledge to architectural models. For example, an online book shop may apply the strict three-layered system template whereas a smart home system may apply the relaxed three-layer system template. For realizing such an application of templates, software architects use appropriate modeling tools. In particular, these tools can check whether architectural models maintain the conformance to prescribed constraints as formally captured within the applied templates (cf. last sentence of Definition 2.26).

Because templates are the central concept of the AT method, the remainder of this section thoroughly derives and explains the template definition given in Definition 2.26 and describes typical template characteristics. Definition 2.26 is derived from common terms associated to templates described in Section 2.4.1 and template examples described in Section 2.4.2. The set of examples allows Section 2.4.3 to generalize to common template categories and Section 2.4.4 to derive common template characteristics. Such categories and characteristics become important for precisely classifying ATs.

2.4.1. Template Terms

Common English dictionaries define a template as a "model for others to copy" [Oxf16b], "preset format" [Oxf16b, Ame11], "pattern" [Oxf16b, Ame11], "gauge" [Ame11], and "blueprint" [Oxf16a]. In the IT domain, common terms characterizing templates are "document" [MWR14, Kri98], "pattern" [VJ02], "parametrized element" [Obj11], and "model schema" [VCC15].

While all of these terms cover valid template characteristics, Definition 2.26 uses the term blueprint because it best fits to the context in which the templates of this thesis are applied: ATs serve as blueprints for software architecture models, similar to blueprints in civil engineering. Additionally, the term blueprint allows to clearly separate ATs from patterns and styles in software architecture (cf. Section 2.2.4).

2.4.2. Template Examples

In the IT domain, templates are applied for the creation of IT-related artifacts. Examples include:

- document templates, e.g., for creating initial documents in office tools like Microsoft Word where actually "every [...] document is based on a template" [MWR14, p. 498],
- preset forms, e.g., used as starting point to document architectural knowledge like architectural styles and patterns [BG07b, BMR+96, TA05b],
- templates in metaprogramming, e.g., in the C++ programming language where a template is "a pattern from which actual classes or functions can be generated" [VJ02, p. 514],
- web templates, e.g., for web documents like HTML pages that serve as a "prototypical document or part thereof" [Kri98], and
- various templates in model-driven software engineering that provide "built-in support for variability" [HJS+09] such as:
  - templates in generative programming and software product lines that are combined with a data model to generated textual artifacts [Cza98, CA05],
  - UML templates where a template is a "parameterized element that can be used to generate other model elements" [Obj11, p. 632], and
  - so-called aspectual templates that "inject new functionalities" [VCC15] into a model via model weaving [MKBJ08].

2.4.3. Template Categories

The examples from Section 2.4.2 differ in their data flow characteristics. These differences allow to induce three categories for templates: (a) initiator templates, (b) generator templates, and (c) bound templates. Sections 2.4.3.1 to 2.4.3.3 detail these categories based on Figure 2.11 (which visualizes these three template categories in terms of their data flow). Afterwards,

Section 2.4.3.4 describes hybrid approaches as a combination of the former three template categories.

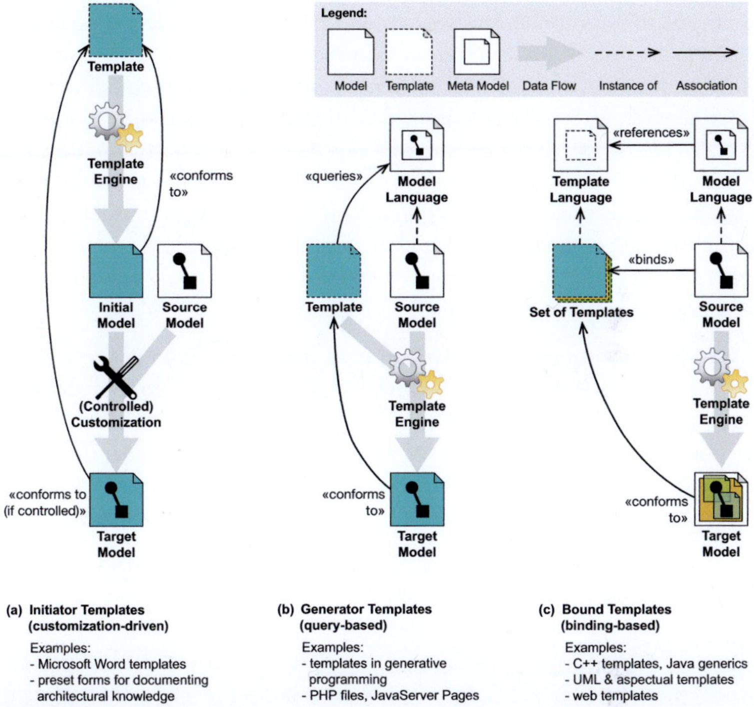

Figure 2.11.: Data flow of different template categories. (a) For initiator templates, a template engine creates an initial model that conforms to a given template. To maintain conformance, a subsequent customization with source model elements might be controlled by an appropriate tool. (b) For generator templates, a template engine evaluates queries from a template to a source model and subsequently embeds query results within the template instance. (c) For bound templates, source models link (bind) a set of templates. A template engine can subsequently weave bound templates into the source models.

2.4.3.1. Initiator Templates

Figure 2.11 (a) illustrates the case of initiator templates. A template is the input to a template engine, which instantiates the input template to produce an initial model. The initial model conforms to the template by construction, i.e., it adheres all template constraints. After construction, the initial model needs to be customized with elements of a source model. Such a source model can either be a mental or a (semi-)formal model with custom information. During customization, source model elements are integrated into the initial model to form a target model. The target model conforms to the original template as long as it satisfies all template constraints. To ensure conformance, an appropriate customization tool can be employed for a controlled customization.

Due to their customization-driven nature, initiator templates serve as starting points for specifying more concrete target models, guided along template constraints. Examples from Section 2.4.2 that fit into this category are classical document templates in office tools and preset forms (where template instantiation and conformance checks to constraints are typical manual tasks).

2.4.3.2. Generator Templates

Figure 2.11 (b) illustrates the case of generator templates. A template and a source model with custom information are the input to a template engine, which produces a final target model out of these inputs. For the integration of source model elements into the template, the template includes queries formulated against the model language of the source model. This dependency on the model language decouples the template from the concrete instance of the model language, i.e., the concrete source model. The template engine executes the template's queries against the concrete source model to determine the elements to be integrated within the template. After these elements are determined, the template engine instantiates the target model by copying the template into the target model and by substituting each query with the respective query result. Once instantiated, the target model therefore conforms to the template by construction.

Generator templates advocate customization only within the source model; generated target models typically remain untouched and are "ready to use". Examples from Section 2.4.2 that fit into this category are templates used in generative programming. Particularly PHP files and JavaServer Pages fit into this category.

2.4.3.3. Bound Templates

Figure 2.11 (c) illustrates the case of bound templates. A source model that binds a set of templates is the input to a template engine, which transforms the source model to a target model by including bound template constructs. Each binding (1) associates the source model to a respective template and (2) specifies which template parameters shall be substituted with which source model elements. For enabling such bindings, the model language of the source model accordingly needs appropriate means to reference the template language. Such references can be realized either within the model language directly (i.e., the model language includes direct associations to the template language) or indirectly via extension mechanisms of the model language (e.g., the model language supports profiles similar to UML's profiles; cf. Section 2.3.4). In any case, the template engine can derive how to include templates from such bindings: (1) it copies each associated template into the source model while (2) substituting template parameters with bound model elements. After such an instantiation, the affected parts of the resulting target model conform to the previously bound templates.

Bound templates suggest customization either for the original model itself or for the binding (for example, by updating existing bindings and by adding bindings to further templates; cf. [OVDPB01a]). As for generator templates, generated models typically remain untouched and are "ready to use". Examples from Section 2.4.2 that fit into this category are templates from template metaprogramming (e.g., C++ templates and Java generics), UML templates, and aspectual templates.

2.4.3.4. Hybrid Templates

Besides the pure categories illustrated in Figure 2.11, hybrid template approaches combine these categories. For example, a hybrid template approach may combine initiator templates (to generate an initial model and to get support for controlled customization) with bound templates (to add further aspects to the model).

The templates introduced in this thesis (Architectural Templates; ATs) indeed realize such a combination for specifying architectural models (cf. Chapter 4). Firstly, ATs can generate an initial architectural model, e.g., satisfying the constraints of a particular architectural style. Secondly, further ATs can be added to the initial architectural model, e.g., to apply various architectural patterns.

2.4.4. Template Characteristics

This section describes common template characteristics derived from the template examples and categories of the previous sections. These characteristics were the basis for the template definition (Definition 2.26): templates allow (1) to instantiate (parts of) concrete models, (2) are reusable for recurring modeling situations, and (3) come with static and dynamic parts.

Templates can instantiate (parts of) concrete models. Templates classify the artifacts created from such templates, i.e., each concrete artifact conforms to the respective template [CA05]. Because of this classification aspect, templates can be seen as type models and conforming artifacts as instance models (cf. [Küh06]). This observation particularly implies that templates have to be instantiated (i.e., an instance of the type model has to be created) when being applied.

Such an instantiation either directly or indirectly results in a concrete model. In the direct case (initiator templates and generator templates), template instances manifest directly in a concrete model (an initial model for initiator templates and a target model for generator templates). In the indirect case (bound templates), template instances modify parts of an existing source model that, after integration of such instances, serves as the concrete target model.

In Figure 2.11, the template engine executes the instantiation task. Here, instantiation can either be fully automated by a tool (e.g., Microsoft Word) or manually be conducted by a user of the template (e.g., when manually copying a preset form as a preparation for documenting architectural patterns).

Templates are reusable for recurring modeling situations. The classification characteristic of templates (see previous paragraph) induces the main benefit of templates: their reusability [Rie03]. However, not every template is reusable. Reusability of a template generally increases with the number of artifacts classified by the template. (Because templates can be seen as type models, they classify a set of concrete instance models/artifacts.)

In the case that a template only classifies one element, a template is too specific and loses its classification characteristic. In this case, the template becomes useless because the concrete artifact could directly be used in place of the template.

However, if the number of classified elements increases too much, a template can become too abstract. A template becomes too abstract as soon as it abstracts from the knowledge it intends to make reusable for recurring modeling situations. For example, a document template for a letter will include knowledge about addresses. If this letter template would abstract from addresses, it would classify more documents, however, loose letter-specific knowledge and thus its pragmatics. When writing letters, such a template makes too few knowledge reusable and consequently causes more manual modeling effort. Therefore, template engineers must determine a good trade-off between specialization and abstraction when designing templates, e.g., by getting feedback from template users.

Templates come with static and dynamic parts. Concrete models resulting from template applications are customized towards the concrete modeling situation at hand [OVDPB01b, Kri98, Par04, Obj11]. Such a customization initializes the situation-specific information that differentiates the template instance from the template.

To maintain conformance to the template during customization, templates internally consist of two parts: a static part that cannot be customized and a dynamic part that can only be customized within prescribed constraints [Kri98]. Static parts cover the knowledge that will be reused in every recurring modeling situation. For example, a template for a letter would always prescribe an address field. Dynamic parts cover variable information that are situation-specific. For example, the letter template would allow to customize the contents of the address field. Templates constrain customizations of dynamic parts based on the knowledge of the recurring modeling situation. For example, the letter template would prescribe different address-related constraints, e.g., that the zip code is required within an address field and that it must consist of numbers only.

It depends on the template category how static and dynamic parts are technically handled. Initiator templates allow customization after the creation of the initial model. In case such a customization is controlled by a suitable tool, only dynamic parts can be customized as exemplified with the letter example. In other cases, customization is unconstrained, for example, Microsoft Word allows arbitrary changes to the initial model and preset forms for documentation can be used manually, i.e., without tool support.

Generator templates include queries against a model language; these queries represent their dynamic parts. Customization can only occur within the concrete source model that is queried. Query results are finally embedded within the static parts of the template.

Bound templates include formal template parameters within their static parts that have to be bound; these parameters represent their dynamic parts. Customization is only possible by binding conforming actual parameters to these formal parameters.

2.5. Architectural Analyses of Quality-of-Service Properties

With architectural analyses, software architects can quantify a system's QoS properties based on architectural models of the system (see Definition 2.27). These quantifications allow architects to assess SLOs (see Section 2.2.2). For example, an SLO for performance may require 90 % of response times to stay below 1 second. With an architectural analysis for performance, architects can analyze whether this SLO is fulfilled for their current system design.

Definition 2.27 (Architectural Analysis) *"Architectural analysis is the activity of discovering important system properties using the system's architectural models." [TMD09, p. 291]*

Koziolek surveys several architectural analysis approaches [Koz10]. The principal idea of these approaches is to map architectural models annotated with QoS-relevant attributes to suitable formal analysis models like Markov chains [Tri82], queuing networks [LZGS84], stochastic Petri nets [BK98], and stochastic process algebras [HHK02]. After this mapping, existing solvers and simulations of these analysis models can quantify the QoS metrics of interest while reporting their results to software architects.

The AT method extends such architectural analyses by a build-in support for reusing and processing architectural knowledge [Leh14b, LHB17]. This section therefore describes the fundamentals for such extensions: the development process with architectural analyses (Section 2.5.1) and architectural models annotated with QoS-relevant attributes (Section 2.5.2). Additionally, this section describes Palladio [BKR09] as an example of an architectural analysis approach (Section 2.5.3). Palladio is particularly used for the evaluation of the AT method.

2.5.1. Integration of Architectural Analyses in Development Processes

Koziolek and Happe [KH06] introduce a process that integrates architectural analyses in the component-based development process of Cheesman and Daniels [CD00]. This section summarizes the process of Koziolek and Happe based on Figure 2.12.

In Figure 2.12, rounded rectangles represent actions that need to be conducted during development. The thick arrows between these actions denote allowed traversals from an action to another action. Actions can be traversed both forwards and backwards, thus allowing for iterative and incremental developments (in contrast to the classical waterfall model). The thin arrows represent flow of artifacts during development. Each concrete artifact is denoted with an according name and a representative icon.

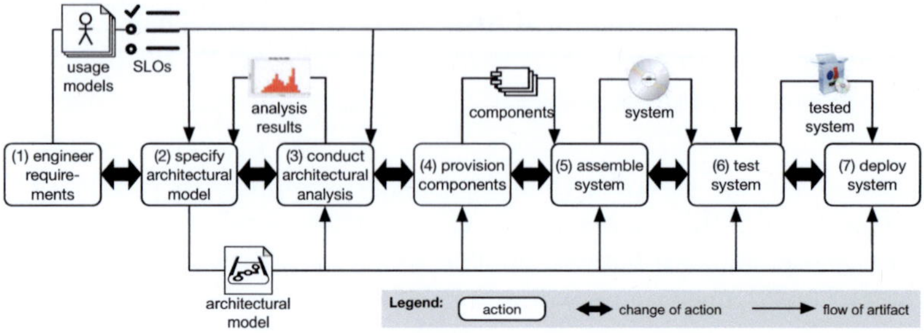

Figure 2.12.: Development process with integrated architectural analysis (based on [KH06]).

The development process starts with action (1) and progresses until action (7). The AT method extends actions (2) and (3), i.e., the specification of architectural models and the conduction of architectural analyses. After briefly overviewing all actions (to understand the context of the AT method), dedicated subsections describe these two actions in detail (to focus on the actions extended by the AT method):

(1) engineer requirements. Requirements engineers elicit, identify, analyze, and specify requirements of a system. For these tasks, requirements engineers collaborate (e.g., via meetings and interviews) with stakeholders of the system (e.g., with system users and domain experts).

The outcome are usage models and SLOs for the system to be developed. Usage models specify functional requirements and how users interact with the system. SLOs characterize the quality-of-service targets for such interactions (cf. Definition 2.10).

(2) specify architectural model. In this action, software architects create architectural models based on usage models, SLOs, and previously collected analysis results (if architectural analyses have already been conducted in an earlier iteration).

The resulting architectural model includes the design decisions that the software architects have made, e.g., existential decisions[9] about

[9] Existential decisions are decisions about the existence of elements (cf. Section 2.2.4).

software components and their allocation to specific processing resources. For making these decisions, software architects collaborate with component developers and system deployers.

(3) conduct architectural analysis. Software architects run an architectural analysis based on usage models and the architectural model of the system. The analysis results serve as feedback for revising the architectural model if results indicate that SLOs are violated.

Architectural analyses require that SLO-relevant information are provided within the input models. For example, usage models need to cover the probabilities with which users request system operations. Another example is that the architectural model needs to cover the envisioned characterization of processing resources, e.g., CPU processing rates. Software architects need to ensure that such information are present in the input models. If not present, software architects collaborate with domain experts, requirements engineers, component developers, and system deployers, respectively, to gather the required information and to enrich the models accordingly.

(4) provision components. Software architects and project managers decide which software components are bought, reused from existing component repositories, or newly implemented. Here, software components need to conform to their specification as given by the architectural model. Afterwards, software components are provisioned based on the made decisions.

(5) assemble system. Software architects manage the creation of the software system by assembling the given components according to the architectural model. During assembly, software components are configured, e.g., regarding specific frameworks and component containers. Moreover, legacy components potentially require adapters that provide the interfaces specified in the architectural model by delegating to these legacy components. The final output of this action is a completely assembled software system, including all its code artifacts.

(6) test system. Test engineers assess, in a test environment and according to the usage models, whether the system's functional requirements and SLOs can be fulfilled. Testing is important because of several risks: the architectural analysis may have missed SLO-relevant factors, provisioned components and the assembled system may include bugs, and the system may not conform to the architectural model. If issues are revealed, test engineers trigger software architects to resolve the issues by iterating through previous actions. Once test results are satisfying, the software system is tested and ready for deployment.

(7) deploy system. System deployers install the tested system in the target environment where system users can request system operations. The architectural model serves again as input because it specifies on which resources the components of the system need to be allocated. After successful execution of this action, the system is in operation.

2.5.1.1. Specify Architectural Model

Software architects specify architectural models based on usage models, SLOs, and—if already available—results from previously conducted analyses (action (2) in Figure 2.12). During this process, software architects make design decisions about components, their assembly into a system, and the allocation of these components on processing resources. Their decision-making is particularly governed by architectural knowledge. This section details this specification of architectural models based on Figure 2.13.

Figure 2.13 generally uses the same syntax as Figure 2.12. Additionally, rounded rectangles of high-level actions include grey-shaded rounded rectangles that represent the sub-actions that are conducted within these high-level actions. The roles that conduct these actions are annotated as well. In Figure 2.13, the role of the software architect conducts the high-level action *specify architectural model* while cooperating with component developers that *newly implement components* and with system deployers that *specify deployment* information. The cooperation with component developers is facilitated with a repository—represented as cylinder—that allows to store and interchange assets like interfaces, component types, and components. In the following, each of these high-level actions is described in detail.

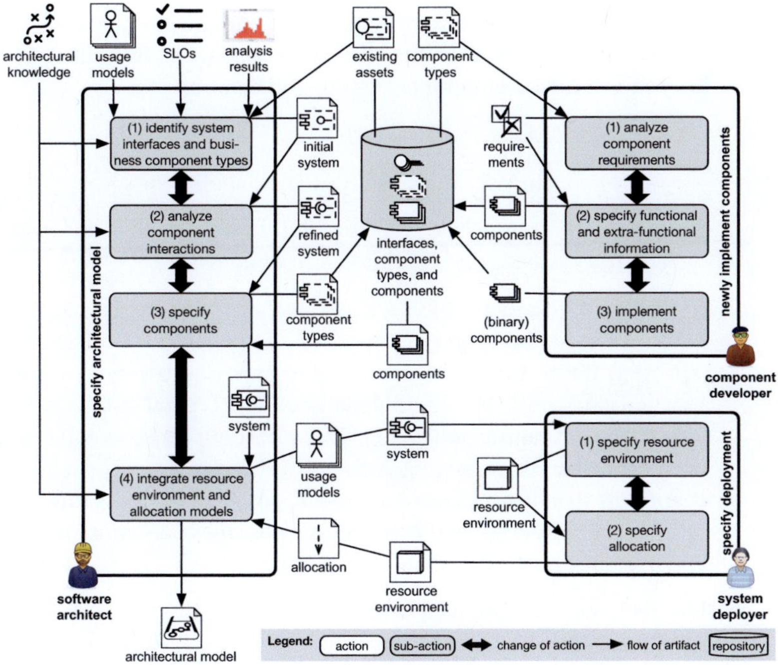

Figure 2.13.: Software architects specify an architectural model; component developers may provision components by implementing them anew; system deployers specify the allocation of the system to resources (based on [KH06]).

Software Architect: Specify Architectural Model To specify an architectural model, Figure 2.13 (left) shows that software architects proceed from (1) the identification of system interfaces and business components types over (2) the analysis of component interactions and (3) the specification of components to (4) the integration of models describing how components are allocated to a resource environment:

(1) identify system interfaces and business component types. At first, software architects create an initial system model. Here, the tasks for software architects are to identify the interfaces of the system, to identify business interfaces and business component types that provide these business interfaces, and to apply architectural knowledge where feasible. If possible, they reuse existing assets from the repository of interfaces, component types, and components.

For system interfaces, software architects require one interface for each use case of the given usage models [CD00, p. 86]. The system interactions needed for fulfilling these use cases define the operations of the respective interface [CD00, p. 86]. In the model of the initial system, the system provides these system interfaces.

For business interfaces, software architects require one interface for each core business type [CD00, p. 92]. These core business types represent the primary business information that the system manages [CD00, p. 92]. For example, a book is a typical core business type within an online book shop. The according business interfaces are responsible for managing such business types, e.g., by providing operations to add, alter, and buy books. For each business interface, software architects specify a dedicated business component type that provides this interface [CD00, p. 99].

The relevant architectural knowledge during the first action are architectural styles and reference architectures [BBB+16, p. 223].

Software architects apply architectural styles (cf. Definition 2.15) to prescribe the role of business components inside the system. For example, when applying the three-layer architectural style (cf. Section 2.2.4.1) to a system, business components play the role of data access layer components while further components will be needed for the roles of presentation layer and application layer.

Similarly, architects can apply reference architectures (cf. Definition 2.17) if available for the system's domain. For example, in the automotive domain, the AUTOSAR reference architecture (cf. Section 2.2.4.3) prescribes a three-layer architectural style where business components reside on the basic software layer. Additionally, AUTOSAR prescribes which automotive-specific component interfaces and component types are required on each layer.

(2) analyze component interactions. In this action, software architects refine the model of the initial system with operations of business interfaces, further component types, connectors, and by applying architectural patterns. For this refinement, software architects need to analyze component interactions as follows.

First, architects discover business operations for the business interfaces as identified in action (1). For this discovery, they inspect each operation of each system interface and decide how the system should interact with business components to provide these operations [CD00, p. 104]. From these interactions, software architects can derive the operation signatures that the business interfaces of business component types need to cover. For example, getting details about a book in an online book shop requires an interaction with the business component that manages books. A suitable operation signature for the components' business interface is `Book : getDetails(String : bookID)` where the operation `getDetails` returns a data transfer object of type `Book` with detailed book information as identified by a unique book identifier `bookID` of type `String`.

Second, software architects model the interactions between system operations and business component types [CD00, p. 104]. Depending on the previously selected architectural styles and reference architectures, these interactions are either direct or indirect.

In the direct case, business component types provide the same interfaces as the system. Therefore, software architects can simply create delegation connectors from provided interfaces of the system to provided interfaces of business component types. For example, when following the microservice architectural style [New15], business component types can be designed to provide presentation, application, and data access logic altogether and, thus, directly provide all operations of a system interface.

In the indirect case, intermediate component types intervene interactions between operations of the system and business component types. Software architects therefore need to create these component types and connect them appropriately. For example, when following the three-layer architectural style, business component types acting as data access layer components are preceded by component types on presentation layer and application layer. Here, software architects need to specify suitable component types and assemble them via assembly connectors with the business component types on the data access layer. Software architects further create delegation connectors from provided system interfaces to component types on the presentation layer.

Finally, software architects apply architectural knowledge in the form of architectural patterns (cf. Definition 2.16) to refine the system [BBB+16, p. 223]. Such a refinement is necessary if a particular design problem needs to be solved. For example, already available analysis results can indicate that performance SLOs are violated because of a bottleneck component at the application layer. A software architect can therefore apply performance architectural patterns to solve this problem, e.g., the loadbalancing architectural pattern (cf. Section 2.2.4.2).

(3) specify components. In this action, software architects complete the model of the system by substituting component types with concrete components. In contrast to component types, these concrete components contain both functional and extra-functional behavior specifications for each provided operation.

Software architects request concrete components from component developers. For executing such requests, software architects put their specifications of component types into the shared repository (cf. Figure 2.13). Afterwards, software architects trigger component developers to specify concrete components that realize these component types. Once component developers have specified these components, they share them again via the repository and trigger software architects. Software architects finally use the shared components to substitute the corresponding component types in their system model. As soon as every component type is substituted with a concrete component specification, the system model is completed.

(4) integrate resource environment and allocation models. Next, software architects create an architectural model that refines the previously created system model with information of the systems' deployment context. The deployment context describes how system components are allocated to resource environments with processing resources.

Software architects request a specification for such deployment contexts from system deployers. For executing such requests, software architects hand usage models and the system model over to these system deployers. Subsequently, the system deployers can specify resource environment and allocation models suitable for the planned system and its usage.

Once specified, system deployers pass resource environment and allocation models back to software architects. In turn, software architects then integrate these models into the system model. Software architects particularly check the interoperability of these models and whether no constraints of the previously applied architectural knowledge are violated. For example, in action (1), software architects can have decided for an architectural style in which each logical layer needs to be allocated to a dedicated tier. Now, in action (4), software architects can check whether system deployers obeyed this architectural style and trigger another specification iteration if constraints were violated. The integration of system, resource environment, and allocation models finally results in a completely specified architectural model.

Component Developer: Newly Implement Components Letting component developers implement components anew is a sub-action of the *provision components* action of the overall development process, i.e., of action (4) in Figure 2.12. In this sub-action, component developers specify and implement components that realize a given set of component type specifications as requested by software architects.

For each component to be specified and implemented, Figure 2.13 (upper right) shows that component developers proceed from (1) an analysis of the component's requirements over (2) the specification of the component's (extra-)functional information within a model to (3) the implementation of the specified component as a binary artifact:

(1) analyze component requirements. In this action, component developers determine the specification and implementation requirements of the components [KH06]. If information from a component's type specification are insufficient for this determination, component developers interact with software architects for clarification.

For example, component developers may need to clarify which dependencies a component responsible for ordering books can have. Payments for ordered books, for instance, can either be realized by depending on an external payment service or by including payment functionality directly within the component. Software architects may assess both options and clarify, based on the assessment result, which option component developers should implement.

(2) specify functional and extra-functional information. Component developers specify appropriate, i.e., requirements-fulfilling, functional and extra-functional information of the components [KH06]. These information can be utilized by architectural analyses and guide component developers in implementing these components.

The specification of functional information covers provided and required interfaces as well as the internal dependencies between provided and required operations of these interfaces. State machines can, for instance, be used for specifying these dependencies [KH06].

The specification of extra-functional information covers resource demands, reliability values, data flow, and transition probabilities for these dependencies [KH06]. These information cover factors that have an impact on the QoS of the component's operations. Therefore, the specification of these information is especially important for architectural analyses.

After the specification of (extra-)functional information, component developers share their specifications with software architects via the repository (cf. Figure 2.13). Therefore, software architects can subsequently refine component types within their system model with the corresponding component specifications. Component developers continue by implementing the just specified components.

(3) implement components. In this action, component developers implement the components according to their specification. For this implementation, software developers use a target technology such as Enterprise Java Beans (EJBs) [CD00, p.147ff]. The final results are binary implementations of the specified components. Component developers store the implemented components in the repository. Software architects can later assemble the system out of these components (action (5) of the overall development process in Figure 2.12).

System Deployer: Specify Deployment For specifying an architectural model, software architects need to integrate deployment information of the modeled system. System deployers provide these information by modeling the system's allocation to the target environment of processing resources.

For a given set of usage models and a system model, Figure 2.13 (lower right) shows that system deployers proceed from (1) the specification of an environment model of processing resources to (2) the specification of an allocation of system components to these resources:

(1) specify resource environment. In this action, system deployers create a model of the environment of processing resources where the system will operate. Because this environment needs to be aligned to the system and its usage, the system model and the usage models are input to this action.

These inputs allow system deployers to derive the required physical and virtual processing resources, e.g., in terms of interconnected servers with various CPU and hard disk drive characterizations. As additional source of information, system deployers can also take existing processing resources into account.

(2) specify allocation. In this action, system deployers specify how system components are allocated to the previously specified resource environment. Every component of the system needs an allocation to an available processing resource. The resulting allocation model and the resource environment model are finally passed to software architects for an integration into the architectural model.

2.5.1.2. Conduct Architectural Analysis

Software architects conduct architectural analyses (action (3) in Figure 2.12) based on usage models, SLOs, and the previously specified architectural model. During this process, software architects specify which QoS properties they want to analyze and conduct the analysis by transforming all inputs to a suitable analysis model. This section details such a conduction of architectural analyses based on Figure 2.14.

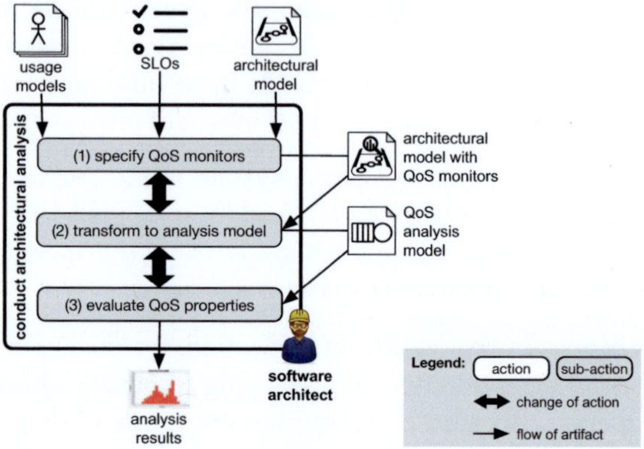

Figure 2.14.: Software architects conduct architectural analyses based on information from usage models, SLOs, and architectural models (based on [KH06]).

Figure 2.14 uses the same syntax as the figures of the previously describe processes (Figure 2.12 and Figure 2.13). In the following, the three sub-actions of architectural analyses as conducted by software architects are discussed in detail.

(1) specify QoS monitors. Software architects configure which metrics will be measured—via so-called QoS monitors [BBL17, Sec. 6.3.1]. A QoS monitor points to (1) an architectural element for which measurements need to be taken and (2) a set of concrete metrics that have to be measured for that element. In setting up these monitors, architectural analyses are configured to measure the configured metrics.

(2) transform to analysis model. In this action, software architects transform the architectural model (with annotated QoS monitors) to a QoS analysis model [KH06]. Depending on the metrics of interest and the analysis approach used, different kinds of QoS analysis models are created. For example, simulation and layered queuing network models can be used to analyze performance metrics (cf. Section 2.5.3.1). In case the architectural model can directly be analyzed (e.g., by a simulation that directly interprets the architectural model), no transformation is needed.

(3) evaluate QoS properties. In this action, software architects evaluate the monitored QoS properties by running a suitable analysis tool and interpreting its analysis results. Such tools take the previously created QoS analysis models as input. For example, simulation tools can be used for simulation models and analytical solvers for layered queuing network models (cf. Section 2.5.3.1).

For the interpretation of analysis results, software architects compare the results to the predefined SLOs. If SLOs are violated, software architects either modify the architectural model or renegotiate SLOs; afterwards they reevaluate the monitored QoS properties. Software architects iteratively proceed like this until all SLOs are fulfilled.

2.5.2. Architectural Models with Quality-of-Service Attributes

Architectural analyses as described in Section 2.5.1.2 are based on QoS analysis models. Clearly, these models must cover the attributes required to analyze the QoS properties of interest. This observation induces that also the transformations that create these models need to have access to such QoS-specific attributes; otherwise they would be unable to create them. However, most languages for specifying architectural models—the input to such transformations—cannot express QoS-specific attributes. For example, the UML [Obj11] lacks several attributes that would be required for performance analyses (e.g., resource demands, workload specifications, characterizations of input data, etc.).

The options to resolve this issue are either to use languages for architectural models that cover the required QoS-specific attributes directly or to annotate architectural models with such attributes. Either way, the relevant QoS attributes to be included in architectural models have to be derived. The GQM method as introduced in Section 2.1.1 can be used to make such a derivation goal-driven (Section 2.5.2.1). Moreover, if annotated to architectural models, QoS attributes have to be integrated during the transformation to QoS analysis models. So-called completions can realize such an integration (Section 2.5.2.2).

2.5.2.1. Goal-Driven Derivation of Quality-of-Service Attributes

Pragmatic architectural models for QoS analyses are tailored to answer QoS-related questions [BBB+16, p. 103], e.g., "how many servers are needed to serve a particular workload with acceptable performance?". To answer such questions, architectural models should optimally only include the minimally required QoS attributes (i.e., the model needs an appropriate abstraction level; cf. Section 2.3.1). For example, if only performance is of interest, architectural models should only cover performance-relevant attributes like component behavior, dependencies to other components, usage characteristics, and deployment information (cf. [BGMO06]).

Software architects can use the GQM method (cf. Section 2.1.1) to derive the QoS attributes to be included in architectural models [BBB+16, p. 104]. In this context, goals correspond to QoS requirements formulated as SLOs (cf. Section 2.2.2). For example, a performance goal can be formulated as the SLO "the system shall respond with a maximum response time of 1 *second* for 90% of monthly requests". Such goals allow to formulate questions like "how many servers are needed to fulfill the performance goal?". An exemplary metric to answer this question is the "response time of the system for monthly peak workloads and 3 *servers*". Given the metric to be analyzed, only those factors that impact its measurement need to become attributes of the architectural model. For the previous example metric, the number of servers needs to be covered, for instance.

2.5.2.2. Integration of Quality-of-Service Attributes via Completions

Architectural models are kept on a high level of abstraction such that software architects can focus on key design decisions. However, for architectural analyses to be accurate, QoS-relevant details (identified as described in Section 2.5.2.1) need to be present in the QoS analysis model generated from the architectural model. So-called completions [WPS02] provide a means to integrate such details into architectural models (see Definition 2.28).

Definition 2.28 (Completion) *"A completion is a general means to capture QoS attributes, modify architectural models, and describe all of the expected elements." (based on [WPS02])*

For this integration, completions modify architectural models with relevant QoS attributes and expected elements. Completions technically realize their modification via in-place model transformations (see Section 2.3.2). Happe et al. [HFBR08] detail such a realization as illustrated in Figure 2.15.

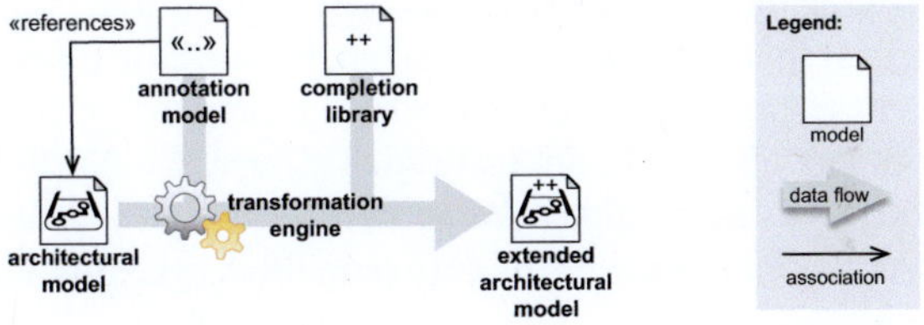

Figure 2.15.: Realization of completions (based on [HFBR08]).

On the left side of Figure 2.15, an annotation model references elements of an architectural model, e.g., components and connectors. The annotation model can be realized as a profile application if the language of the architectural model supports extensions via profiles (cf. Section 2.3.4).

Annotations mark the elements that need to be refined with QoS-relevant details. On the bottom of Figure 2.15, a transformation engine executes this refinement in the form of a M2M transformation (cf. Section 2.3.2). The inputs to this transformation are the annotated architectural model and a completion library. The completion library provides the transformation specifications (completions) that include the logics for refining annotated elements with QoS-relevant details. Accordingly, the output of the transformation is an extended architectural model that includes these details (right side of Figure 2.15).

2.5.3. Palladio

Palladio [BKR09] is a concrete example of an architectural analysis method and serves as evaluation and application example of the AT method. Palladio supports several QoS properties, for example, performance [BKR09], scalability [LB14a], elasticity [LB14a], cost-efficiency [LE15], reliability [BKBR12], energy-efficiency [OGW+14], as well as security [HFL16]. Moreover, Palladio has the advantage that its architectural language, the Palladio Component Model (PCM), is UML-like and therefore expected to have a high acceptance by software architects [BKR09]. Initial empirical results indeed confirm this expectation [Mar07, p. 99], despite pointing out some improvement opportunities in usability, e.g., regarding high initial and overall modeling efforts. To alleviate such efforts, the AT method extends Palladio with a build-in support for applying reusable architectural knowledge. The AT method's extensions are exemplified in Chapter 3 and detailed in Chapter 4.

Being the targeted architectural analysis of the AT method, the remainder of this section details concepts of Palladio. Section 2.5.3.1 describes the basic paradigms for architectural modeling with the PCM. Afterwards, Section 2.5.3.2 details Palladio's extensions for elastic environments, which are needed for the evaluation of the AT method within the cloud computing domain in Chapter 5.

2.5.3.1. The Palladio Component Model

The Palladio Component Model (PCM) [BKR09] is an architecture description language that particularly supports QoS-relevant attributes, e.g., for performance and reliability. Instances of the PCM can therefore be analyzed with respect to QoS metrics like response times, utilization, throughput, and mean time to failure. In the following, this section details the idea behind the PCM based on Figure 2.16.

Figure 2.16 (left) illustrates that PCM models are constituted of partial models. Each of these partial models is inspired by the UML and covers QoS-relevant attributes of the system to be modeled:

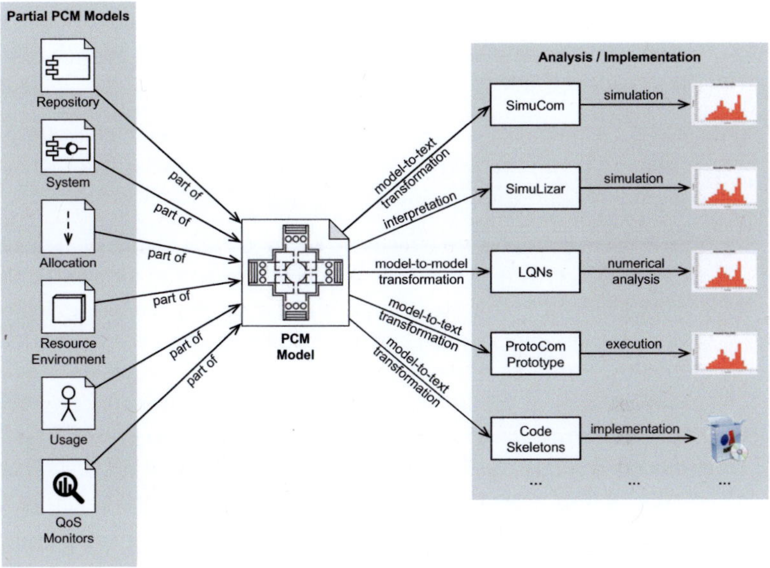

Figure 2.16.: The PCM includes partial, UML-like models for specifying QoS-relevant attributes of software systems (left). PCM models can then be analyzed and implemented in various tools (right).

Repository Model. Models a repository of components and component types, thus allowing for an iterative development (cf. Section 2.2.1). Components and component types provide and optionally require a set of interfaces.

Components conform to a component type if they (1) at least provide the provided interfaces of the type and (2) at most require the required interfaces of the type. Components can substitute conforming component types whenever such types are used. This substitutability particularly allows to reuse components whenever their provided interfaces are required.

In contrast to component types, components include behavior specifications for each operation of a provided interface. For example, software architects can model requests to operations of required interfaces and demands to resources like CPUs and hard disk drives. In Palladio, these behavior specifications are called *Service Effect Specifications* (SEFFs).

System Model. Models a system that instantiates and assembles components and component types from repository models. Instances of components and component types are called *assembly contexts.*

The system provides interfaces on its own such that its users can externally access it. For implementing its provided interfaces, the system delegates requests to appropriate assembly contexts. If these assembly contexts require further interfaces, the system includes assembly connectors that delegate requests to appropriate providing interfaces of further assembly contexts. Moreover, a system can require interfaces if assembly contexts depend on services of external systems. In this case, the system delegates requests from corresponding assembly contexts to its required interfaces.

Allocation Model. Models the allocation from assembly contexts (system) to containers (resource environment). Therefore, the allocation specifies from which container assembly contexts demand resources.

Resource Environment Model. Models the resource environment (e.g., in terms of hardware) on which the system is allocated. The environment consists of containers connected via networks. Containers can, for instance, represent bare-metal or virtualized servers. Containers particularly include a set of active resources like CPUs and hard disk drives. Each of these resources comes with different processing rates and scheduling strategies.

Usage Model. Models the workload to a system in terms of its users. The usage model consists of different usage scenarios, each either being a closed workload (fixed number of users) or an open workload (users enter based on inter-arrival rates). In each usage scenario, users can access operations provided by the system. Users access such operations with a certain probability and with specific work parameters, e.g., characterizing the size of input data.

QoS Monitors. Models which metrics are measured during analysis [BBL17, Sec. 6.3.1]. A QoS monitor points to (1) a PCM element for which measurements need to be taken and (2) a set of concrete metrics that have to be measured for that element. For example, a QoS monitor can be configured to measure response times of an operation of a system interface.

In sum, these partial models form a complete PCM model. PCM models can then serve as input to various analysis tools as illustrated in Figure 2.16 (right):

SimuCom. SimuCom is a simulation of the modeled system. Simulation logic is generated by a M2T transformation according to the input PCM model. During simulation, SimuCom can take measurements for QoS metrics like response times.

SimuLizar. SimuLizar is a simulation of the modeled system. The simulation interprets the input PCM model to provide measurements for QoS metrics like response times.

Because SimuLizar interprets PCM models, it can also acknowledge changes of these instances during simulation-time. This feature therefore allows to model self-adaptive systems. SimuLizar was extended with support for dedicated models for these self-adaptive systems (see Section 2.5.3.2).

LQNs. Layered Queuing Networks (LQNs) extend queuing networks with layered structures and related elements, e.g., to fork/join different layers. Based on input PCM models, M2M transformations can create LQN models. These models can then be solved with numerical mean-value approximation methods, e.g., to provide mean response times as output. In contrast to simulations, these methods require less time for analyses; however, provide only information about mean values.

ProtoCom Prototype. ProtoCom transforms PCM models into runnable QoS prototypes. Such QoS prototypes can execute in different target environments and mimic demands to different types of processing resources. Their execution therefore allows to take QoS measurements for an early assessment of the modeled software system within a real environment.

Code Skeletons. Based on a PCM model, a M2T transformation generates appropriate code skeletons. These skeletons serve developers as starting point for implementing the modeled system. Code skeletons are therefore especially important in greenfield and forward engineering.

2.5.3.2. Extensions for Elastic Environments

Palladio was initially designed for static environments, i.e., for resource environments that do not change the amount of their computing resource over time. However, the usage of information systems shifted from a static to a highly dynamic behavior that challenged such static environments. For example, online shops often observe workload increases before Christmas. In such scenarios, static environments demand that resources are aligned to the maximum workload to be expected (over-provisioning). Otherwise, customers will remain unserved, which eventually leads to business losses. The disadvantage of this solution is that over-provisioning is expensive during non-peak times.

Elastic environments—like found in the cloud computing domain [MG11]—revise the assumption that resource environments are static: to minimize expenses for resources, their amount is now elastically adapted to changing workloads. Because the AT method is evaluated in the cloud computing domain, this section reports on Palladio extensions for modeling and analyzing these elastic resource environments as shown in Figure 2.17.

Figure 2.17 (bottom) shows that Palladio's modeling extensions cover workloads that change over time (so-called Usage Evolutions) and self-adaptation rules that react on these changes by adapting the amount of resources:

Usage Evolution Model. Usage Evolution models specify how workload parameters, as characterized in PCM usage models, change over time [Gop14, BSL16, KHK$^+$17]. For example, steadily increasing and periodically varying arrivals of users can be modeled.

Self-Adaptation Rules. Self-adaptation rules react on changes to measurements of QoS monitors. For example, when a certain response time threshold is exceeded, a self-adaptation rule could trigger a scaling-out of bottleneck resources. These rules therefore consist of two parts, a trigger and an action that can be activated by the trigger.

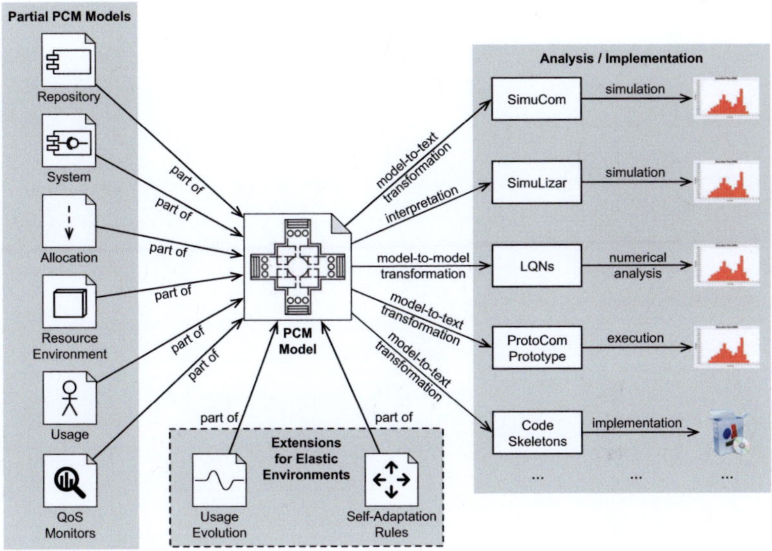

Figure 2.17.: PCM extensions enrich the PCM with models for elastic environments, i.e., with Usage Evolutions and Self-Adaptation Rules.

> The trigger relates measurements to pre-specified thresholds to determine whether to activate the action. The action describes the change in the system to be applied.

As of the time of writing this thesis, only SimuLizar supports analyzing PCM models with these extensions. At simulation-time, SimuLizar updates workload parameters according to an input Usage Evolution model. For these updates, SimuLizar samples the Usage Evolution model once per simulated time unit to receive the concrete workload parameter for the current simulation time.

Moreover, SimuLizar supports actions (of self-adaptation rules) formulated in the M2M transformation languages QVT-O (described in Section 2.3.2), Story Diagrams [vDHP+12], and Henshin [ABJ+10]. The execution of an action therefore involves the transformation of the currently simulated PCM instance into an adapted version. SimuLizar subsequently continues by simulating the adapted version.

"Few things are harder to put up with than the annoyance of a good example."

— Mark Twain 1835 – 1910

3. Example System: An Online Book Shop

This chapter illustrates the fundamentals introduced in Chapter 2 along an online book shop example system. The book shop is based on an architectural model suited for architectural analyses that we previously specified [LB16]. Our model particularly reflects the QoS properties of an implemented and deployed book shop version [LB16].

The book shop example is intentionally described on a high level of abstraction. The example is therefore suited for illustrative purposes throughout this thesis. Moreover, Chapter 5 refines the book shop example to a full case study—the CloudStore case study—to evaluate the AT method.

This chapter takes the perspective of the book shop's requirements engineer and software architect. These roles execute the first three actions of the development process with architectural analyses (see Section 2.5.1). Firstly, the requirements engineer collects requirements in the form of usage models and SLOs (Section 3.1). Secondly, the software architect specifies the book shop's architectural model (Section 3.2). Thirdly and finally, the software architect conducts an architectural analysis with the architectural model to check whether the book shop's SLOs can be fulfilled for the given usage model (Section 3.3). The chapter closes with a discussion of the book shop example (Section 3.4).

3.1. Engineer Requirements of the Book Shop

In the first step of the development process with architectural analyses (cf. Section 2.5.1), the requirements engineer captures the book shop's requirements via a usage model (Section 3.1.1) and SLOs (Section 3.1.2).

3.1.1. The Book Shop's Usage Model

After collaborating with the book shop's stakeholders, the requirements engineer identifies the two main use cases of the shop: customers shall be able to *browse books* and to *order books*. The requirements engineer further expects that 100 concurrent customers steadily use the book shop, i.e., a closed workload of 100 customers. These customers browse books in 95 % of the cases and order books in 5 % of the cases.

Figure 3.1 illustrates how the requirements engineer documents these use cases and workloads in a usage model. A customer (UML actor symbol) can request (UML association symbol) the use cases (UML use case symbols) browse books and order books within the Book Shop system (UML system symbol).

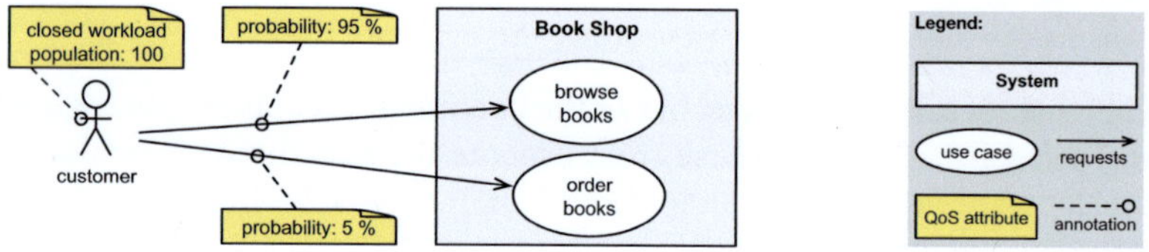

Figure 3.1.: Illustration of the book shop's usage model.

Besides these functional specifications, the requirements engineer annotates (dashed line with a circle) QoS-relevant attributes (UML note symbol). In Figure 3.1, customer and customer's requests are annotated. The customer workload is a closed workload of population 100 and the requests follow a probabilistic distribution where 95 % of requests browse books and 5 % of requests order books. These attributes are QoS-relevant because several QoS properties depend on the workload of the system. For example, performance can vary depending on the number of requests per time interval. Also security properties are impacted by workload, e.g., evident from denial-of-service attacks.

3.1.2. The Book Shop's Service Level Objectives

During the collaboration with the book shop's stakeholders, the requirements engineer identifies that a response time of 1 second is satisfactory for potential customers if met in at least 90 % of the cases. Moreover, the requirements engineer notes that the number of initial customers (100 customers) is expected to increase to 500 customers in 1 year.

These observations induce a performance and a capacity requirement. To capture these requirements, the requirements engineer specifies the following SLOs:

$SLO_{\textbf{Performance}}$**:** 90 % of the book shop's responses for browsing and ordering books shall have a maximum response time of 1 second.

$SLO_{\textbf{Capacity}}$**:** The book shop shall handle up to 500 concurrent customers without violating $SLO_{\textbf{Performance}}$.

3.2. Specify Architectural Model of the Book Shop

Given the book shop's requirements, its software architect can create an appropriate architectural model (step two of the development process; cf. Section 2.5.1). The software architect first specifies component types and lets component developers realize implementing components (Section 3.2.1). Second, the software architect assembles these components into a system (Section 3.2.2). Third, the software architect collaborates with system deployers to compile an architectural model of the shop (Section 3.2.3). Fourth, the software architect applies architectural knowledge in the form of ATs to this model (Section 3.2.4). This application of ATs exemplifies how templates can be bound to models.

3.2.1. The Book Shop's Repository Model

By following the process for specifying architectural models (as described in Section 2.5.1.1), the software architect derives which component types are needed for the book shop. Figure 3.2 illustrates the resulting repository of component types and their interfaces.

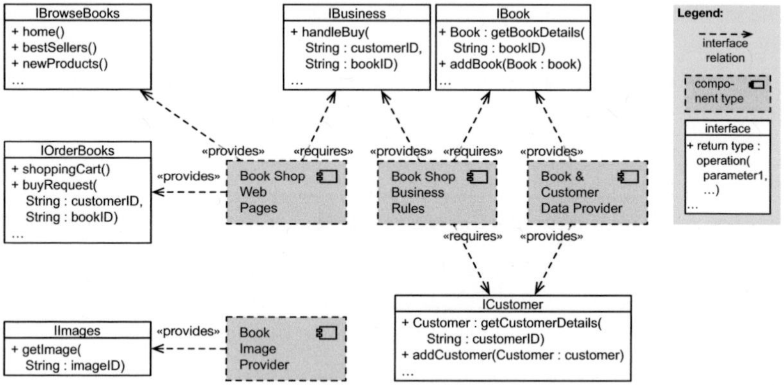

Figure 3.2.: Illustration of the book shop's repository model.

In Figure 3.2, component types (UML component symbols with dashed border) provide and require various interfaces (UML class symbols). Each interface defines various operations (second compartment of interface symbols). An operation (starting with a +-symbol followed by the operation name) can optionally have return types (prepended to the operation name) and multiple parameters (appended to the operation name in parentheses).

As shown in Figure 3.2 (top), each previously specified use case (*browse books* and *order books*) requires a dedicated interface (IBrowseBooks and IOrderBooks) and a component type (Book Shop Web Pages) that provides these interfaces. Also each core business type (*books* and *customers*) requires a dedicated interface (IBook and ICustomer) and a providing component type (Book & Customer Data Provider). The software architect has further decided to use a dedicated component type (Book Shop Business Rules) to determine how data about books and customers is created, changed, and received. Book Shop Business Rules exposes the IBusiness interface to provide this functionality.

As shown in Figure 3.2 (bottom), the software architect specifies a dedicated component type for retrieving images of books (Book Image Provider). With this component, the software architect wants to support the typical behavior of web browsers—receiving an HTML page and subsequently its image references [JW04].

After specifying these component types, the software architect collaborates with component developers that implement corresponding components. The component developers particularly provide models of implemented components to the software architect (cf. Section 2.5.1.1). Using these models of the components, the software architect assembles a model of the book shop's system as describe in the next section.

3.2.2. The Book Shop's System Model

By assembling the previously specified components, the software architect creates a system model for the book shop. Figure 3.3 illustrates this model.

Figure 3.3.: Illustration of the book shop's system model.

In this model, the software architect specifies which business components (UML component symbols) are part of the book shop system (UML system symbol). Components expose their provided interfaces via providing roles (UML symbol for implementing interfaces) and their required interfaces via requiring roles (UML symbol for using interfaces). Possible requests are illustrated via UML connectors from requiring to providing roles. Interfaces of providing roles outside of the system's border are accessible by customers.

In Figure 3.3, the Book Shop Web Pages component provides such interfaces to browse and order books. To provide its functionality, Book Shop Web Pages requests information from the Book Shop Business Rules component, which in turn can request data about books and customers from the Book & Customer Data Provider component. If a web page returned by Book Shop Web Pages references images, these references can be fetched via the Book Image Provider component.

3.2.3. The Book Shop's Architectural Model

The software architect refines the previously specified system model with deployment information, which results in an architectural model for the book shop (cf. Section 2.5.1.1). For this refinement, the software architect collaborates with a system deployer to integrate information about the book shop's allocation into a resource environment. Figure 3.4 gives a high-level overview of the resulting architectural model.

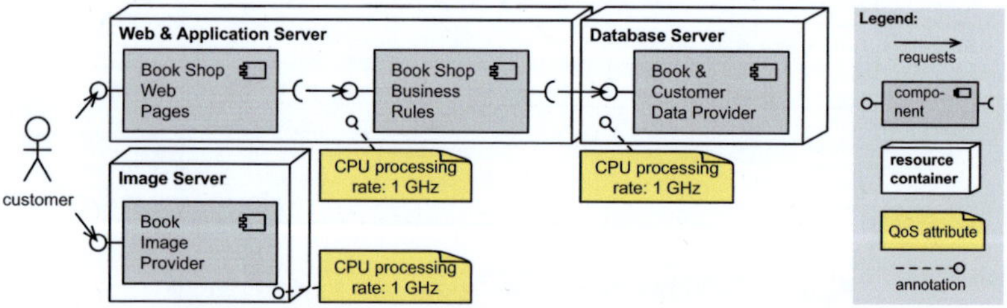

Figure 3.4.: Overview of the book shop's architectural model.

With this overview, software architects can easily follow the requests (UML connector symbols) from customers through the book shop's business components (UML component symbols) allocated on various resource containers (UML node symbols).

Like Figure 3.3, Figure 3.4 shows that customers access the book shop via the Book Shop Web Pages component to browse and order books. If a web page returned by Book Shop Web Pages references images, a customer's browser subsequently fetches these reference via the Book Image Provider component.

Additionally, Figure 3.4 shows that Book Shop Web Pages and Book Shop Business Rules are allocated on a Web & Application Server, Book & Customer Data Provider on a Database Server, and Book Image Provider on a dedicated Image Server. The software architect has received these information from the system deployer.

The system deployer particularly annotated QoS attributes to the resource containers. In the current setup, each resource container contains a CPU with a processing rate of 1 GHz. This attribute is QoS-relevant because the processing rate impacts how long it takes to serve CPU demands as caused by executing a component's operations. In consequence, performance metrics like response times and throughput are directly impacted.

3.2.4. The Book Shop's Applications of Architectural Templates

The software architect is interested in applying architectural knowledge to make the book shop maintainable and to ensure that the shop fulfills its SLOs. For maintainability, the software architect wants to apply the *three-layer* architectural style (cf. Section 2.2.4.1). For fulfilling the book shop's SLOs, the software architect investigates the option to use the *loadbalancing* architectural pattern (cf. Section 2.2.4.2). To apply such knowledge in a formalized way, the software architect uses ATs.

Figure 3.5 illustrates the book shop's architectural model after the application of corresponding ATs (bold italic text in dashed boxes). Following the idea of bound templates (see Section 2.4), the software architect has bound the roles of the formalized knowledge (italic text prepended with an @-sign) to appropriate architectural elements, including a set of actual parameters (appended to a role in parentheses). Architectural modeling tools and architectural analyses can utilize ATs as exemplified in the following.

The *three-layer* AT introduces roles to structure the book shop into a *presentation layer* (bound to Book Shop Web Pages), an *application layer* (bound to

Book Shop Business Rules), and a *data access layer* (bound to Book & Customer Data Provider). These roles constrain the bound components to only access the respective lower-level layer (in Figure 3.5 shown from left to right). Because ATs formalize such constraints, an architecture tool with AT support can ensure their fulfillment, e.g., by forbidding direct connections from Book Shop Web Pages to Book & Customer Data Provider. Such an assurance becomes especially useful in maintenance scenarios that potentially violate taken design decisions.

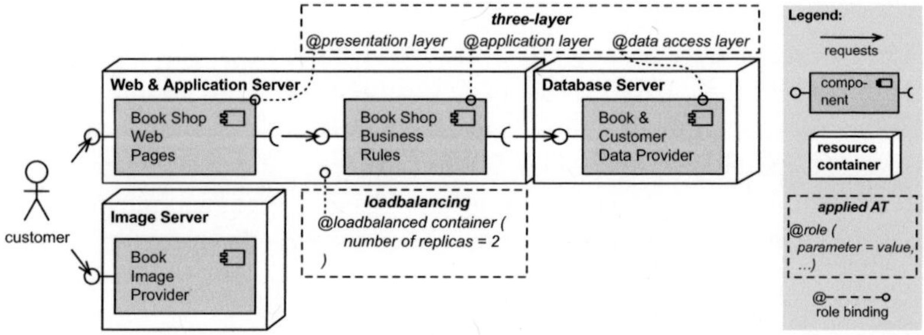

Figure 3.5.: Applying Architectural Templates to the book shop's architectural model.

The *loadbalancing* AT (bottom middle of Figure 3.5) introduces a *loadbalanced container* role bound to the Web & Application Server. In a preprocessing step of an architectural analysis, a template engine will reflect the performance impact of this binding by creating a loadbalancer in front of the container that distributes workload. According to the parameter given in Figure 3.5, the loadbalancer will distribute workload over 2 replicas of the Web & Application Server container.

3.2.5. The Book Shop's Validation of Architectural Template Constraints

The architectural modeling tool of the software architect automatically validates the constraints of applied ATs. This validation reveals that the software architect did not bind a logical layer to the Book Image Provider. This is an issue because the *three-layer* AT requires an assignment for every component.

The Book Image Provider presents images directly to customers. Therefore, to resolve the issue, the software architect decides to additionally bind the *presentation layer* role to the Book Image Provider. At this point, the *three-layer* AT has helped the software architect to maintain a model conforming to the three-layer architectural style, i.e., it improved maintainability of the modeled system.

3.3. Conduct Architectural Analysis of the Book Shop

The applied *loadbalancing* AT allows the software architect to analyze the book shop's SLOs by varying the parameter *number of replicas* of the *loadbalanced container* role. First, the software architect configures an architectural analysis for *number of replicas = 1* to calculate $SLO_{\mathbf{Capacity}}$. The architectural analysis yields 400 concurrent customers as a result, which implies that $SLO_{\mathbf{Capacity}}$ is violated.

The architectural analysis particularly reports how response times are distributed. Figure 3.6 illustrates these response times as a cumulative distribution function. For 400 customers, Figure 3.6 shows that indeed 90 % (Y-axis) of the response times are under the 1 second mark (X-axis).

To resolve the SLO violation, the software architect repeats this analysis for *number of replicas = 2*. Interestingly, this analysis results in a capacity of only 180 concurrent customers, thus, pointing to an even more severe violation of $SLO_{\mathbf{Capacity}}$. Figure 3.6 illustrates the corresponding response time distribution for 180 customers.

To explain this capacity degradation, the software architect investigates the number of jobs waiting at the Database Server: for 400 customers and *number of replicas = 1*, approximately 50 jobs wait at the Database Server; for 180 customers and *number of replicas = 2*, the number of waiting jobs increases to 90. This observation points to the Database Server as a reason for the capacity degradation. Because of the replicated Web & Application Server,

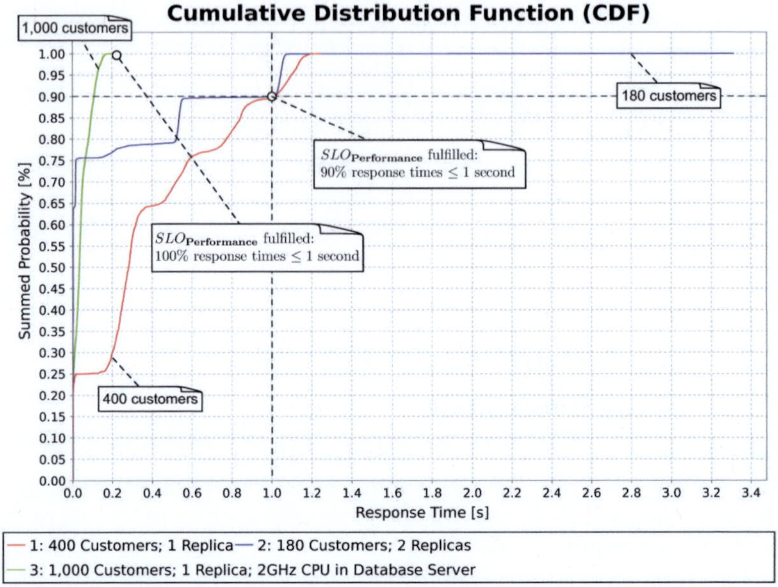

Figure 3.6.: Cumulative distribution function of response times for different workloads and configurations.

an increased number of concurrent jobs arrives at the Database Server. The increased workload at the Database Server makes this server the book shop's bottleneck.

After identifying this bottleneck, the software architect wants to analyze whether increasing the processing rate of the Database Server's CPU helps to increase capacity. Therefore, the software architect changes the corresponding processing rate from 1 GHz to 2 GHz. Additionally, the software architect sets *number of replicas = 1* again to save costs for the additional server that did not help to increase the book shop's capacity.

After having the architectural model modified, the software architect runs another architectural analysis. In the modified version, the book shop's capacity increases to over 1, 000 concurrent customers (the maximum number the software architect considered for the analysis). Because the CPU of the Database Server now processes with 2 GHz, it services jobs twice as fast, which evidently removes the capacity degradation: even for 1,000 concurrent customers, response times are below the 0.2 seconds mark as highlighted in Figure 3.6.

Being confident that the book shop will fulfill all specified SLOs, the software architect can continue now to implement, deploy, and operate the shop according to its architectural model.

3.4. Discussion of the Book Shop Example

The book shop example illustrates how software architects make use of reusable architectural knowledge during the development process with architectural analyses. While state-of-the-art approaches let software architects informally apply reusable architectural knowledge, the AT method represents a formal approach for such applications. This combination of formalized architectural knowledge and architectural analyses offers advantages for software architects. In detail, the book shop example illustrates the following advantages:

Automated detection of constraint violations of architectural styles.
Violations of constraints of architectural styles (cf. Definition 2.15) can automatically be detected. For example, the software architect automatically discovers a missing binding of the presentation layer role in Section 3.2.5. These discoveries help software architects to maintain the conceptual integrity between architectural models and applied architectural styles.

Automated generation of additional elements of architectural patterns.
Architectural patterns refine systems with additional elements (cf. Definition 2.16). If architectural patterns are formalized, these additional elements can automatically be generated. For example, the application of the loadbalancing AT has ensured that a loadbalancer and replicas of the annotated resource container were automatically generated for the architectural analysis in Section 3.3.

Context-aware application of architectural knowledge.
In Section 3.3, the software architect is surprised that an increased

number of load-balanced server replicas can degrade capacity. This degradation is in contrast to what the loadbalancing pattern promises. However, the architectural analysis reveals that the book shop's database server—a context factor for the loadbalancing pattern—actually becomes overloaded when too many replicas exist. For such situations, the combination of reusable architectural knowledge with architectural analyses is beneficial.

Declarative application of reusable architectural knowledge.
Section 3.2.4 illustrates how the concept of bound template (cf. Section 2.4.3.3) can be applied to architectural models. Bindings are specified declaratively. Based on this declaration, a template engine takes care of weaving relevant elements into the architectural model. Therefore, this kind of specification relieves software architects from potentially complex, manual adaptations of architectural models.

Overall, these advantages show that ATs can make software architects more effective and efficient in their modeling tasks. The challenge is, however, to provide software architects with a suitable set of such ATs. The AT method therefore includes an appropriate process for engineering ATs. The next chapter introduces the AT method in detail.

"We are what we repeatedly do. Excellence, then, is not an act, but a habit."

— Aristotle 384 B.C. – 322 B.C.

4. The Architectural Template Method

The *Architectural Template* method is a software engineering method with which software architects can reuse architectural knowledge from pre-specified templates—Architectural Templates (ATs; see Definition 4.1)—for architectural modeling and architectural analyses. ATs are specified by AT engineers, i.e., implemented, quality-assured, and provided within catalogs. In applying ATs from such catalogs, software architects reuse knowledge and become more effective and efficient in their architectural analysis tasks (see Definition 4.2).

Definition 4.1 (Architectural Template) *"An Architectural Template (AT) is a template for reusable architectural knowledge that software architects can apply for architectural modeling and architectural analyses." (author's definition)*

Definition 4.2 (Architectural Template method) *"The Architectural Template method (AT method) is a software engineering method that uses ATs to make approaches for architectural analyses of QoS properties more effective and efficient." (author's definition)*

This chapter describes the AT method by covering the processes of the AT method in Section 4.1, the AT language for specifying and applying ATs in Section 4.2, and an accompanying AT tooling in Section 4.3. Additionally, Section 4.4 describes extensions to these core aspects: a reuse mechanism for AT specification and an optimization mechanism for configuring AT applications. Section 4.5 closes this chapter with a discussion of assumptions and limitations of the AT method.

4.1. Architectural Template Processes

The AT method extends existing processes for architectural analyses. During the *specify architectural model* process (cf. Section 2.5.1.1), software architects can additionally apply architectural knowledge via ATs, which allows to automatically check for constraint violations of applied architectural knowledge. Moreover, during the *conduct architectural analysis* process (cf. Section 2.5.1.2), a template engine automatically integrates elements induced by applied architectural knowledge into architectural models. AT engineers specify ATs with such capabilities and provide them within catalogs.

Section 4.1.1 describes these extensions for architectural modeling and Section 4.1.2 for architectural analysis. Section 4.1.3 details the process of AT engineers to specify ATs.

4.1.1. Architectural Template Application

When following the AT method, software architects use their modeling tools to apply ATs to architectural models. For example, Section 3.2.4 illustrates how a software architect applies ATs to the architectural model of the book shop example. This section details this process for AT applications.

During modeling, software architects can *select and apply suitable ATs* to their architectural model. Figure 4.1 illustrates this addition as an extended version of Figure 2.13. In Figure 4.1, unfilled thick arrows denote where the AT method extends existing actions. There are two of these extensions: one for the *identify system interfaces and business component types* action and one for the *analyze component interactions* action.

While these actions originally prescribed to apply architectural knowledge informally (cf. Section 2.5.1.1), their extensions allow to apply architectural knowledge formally via ATs. For applying ATs, software architects create appropriate role bindings and set actual parameters like illustrated for the

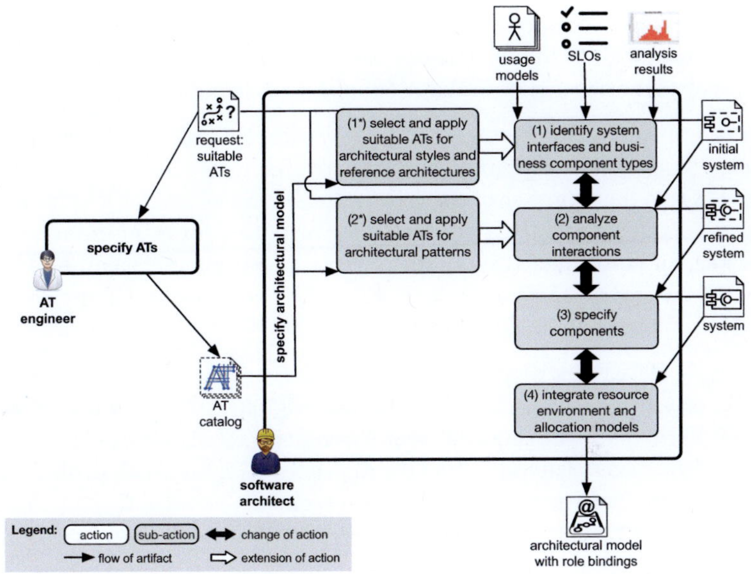

Figure 4.1.: Software architects apply ATs from a catalog of ATs specified by AT engineers.

book shop example in Figure 3.5. The final result of the *specify architectural model* process is therefore an architectural model with role bindings (bottom right in Figure 4.1).

Like the original process in Figure 2.13, the extending actions distinguish the kind of architectural knowledge to be applied. While the first action (action (1*) in Figure 4.1) targets architectural styles and reference architectures, the second action (action (2*) in Figure 4.1) targets architectural patterns. This distinction acknowledges the higher level of abstraction of architectural styles and reference architectures compared to architectural patterns (cf. Section 2.2.4).

Software architects can particularly use ATs of architectural styles and reference architectures to instantiate their architectural model. For example, a software architect may instantiate an architectural model according to the AUTOSAR reference architecture (cf. Section 2.2.4.3) and refine this initial model with additional business component types. Conceptually, ATs thus realize the concept of initiator templates (cf. Section 2.4.3.1).

Before software architects apply ATs, they select suitable ATs from an AT catalog (bottom left in Figure 4.1). Software architects select by matching their SLOs to the promises of the architectural knowledge that was formalized as ATs. ATs provide an informal documentation for this purpose. For example, for performance SLOs, software architects may select an AT that promises to improve response times, e.g., the *loadbalancing* AT applied to the book shop example in Figure 3.5.

If existing AT catalogs lack such suitable ATs, software architects either continue without ATs (thus, following the original architectural analysis process) or request suitable ATs from AT engineers (left side of Figure 4.1). Once AT engineers have specified the requested ATs, they include them in an AT catalog. Software architects can subsequently select and apply these ATs. Section 4.1.3 details the specification process for AT engineers.

Once ATs have been applied, architecture modeling tools can prevent software architects from violations of constraints captured in the applied ATs. For example, modeling tools can avoid the creation of invalid connections and point to missing elements or existing but invalid elements. This way, software architects can easily maintain the conceptual integrity between architectural models and applied architectural knowledge. Software architects are particularly relieved from manual integrity checks as was originally required during the *integrate resource environment and allocation models* action (cf. Section 2.5.1.1).

Figure 4.2 exemplifies an AT-based constraint validation for the book shop example. The X-symbol marks constraint violations of the applied *three-layer* AT. There are two of such constraint violations; each annotated with a brief description. First, the Book Image Provider lacks a role binding. This is a constraint violation because the *three-layer* AT requires every component to have such a binding (Section 3.2.5 describes this situation in detail). Second, a direct connection from a component of the presentation layer to a component of the data access layer exists. This is a constraint violation because the *three-layer* AT prescribes that presentation layer components can only request data from presentation and application layer components.

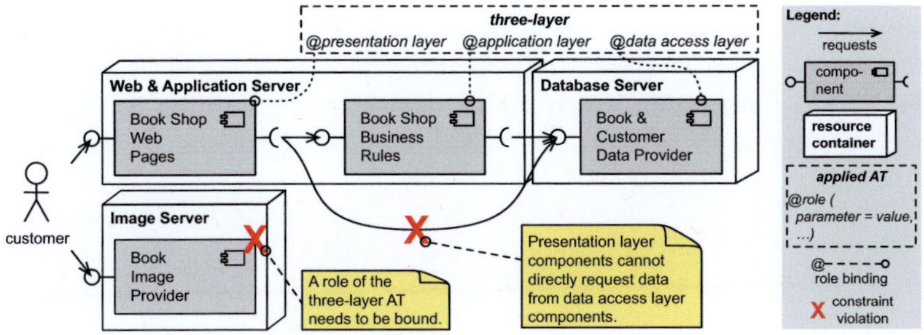

Figure 4.2.: An architectural model of the book shop with two constraint violations.

4.1.2. Architectural Template Analysis Integration

In the AT method, software architects apply ATs by binding roles to their architectural models. These roles formally reflect the semantics of their associated architectural knowledge. For roles that constrain architectural models, e.g., for roles of architectural styles, semantics are reflected by automatic constraint checks as described in the previous section. For roles that refine an architectural model by additional elements, e.g., for roles of architectural patterns (cf. Section 2.2.4.2), semantics are reflected by an automated integration of these additional elements into the architectural model. This section describes the required process extensions for this integration.

Figure 4.3 illustrates these process extensions as an extended version of Figure 2.14. As before, software architects transform their architectural model to a QoS analysis model for conducting architectural analyses. Additionally, if roles of ATs are bound to the architectural model, this transformation additionally needs to integrate role-induced elements. Figure 4.3 denotes this addition by extending the *transform to analysis model* action with an action to *integrate AT-induced elements.*

Conceptually, this integration of ATs conforms to bound templates (cf. Section 2.4.3.3). That is, a template engine automatically weaves elements induced by AT roles into the annotated architectural model. Technically, this integration is realized as a completion (cf. Section 2.5.2.2): bound roles annotate the architectural model and a completion instructs a transformation engine (representing the template engine) how to weave elements into the architectural model. Such a realization causes no additional effort for software architects because the execution of the completion is completely automatic.

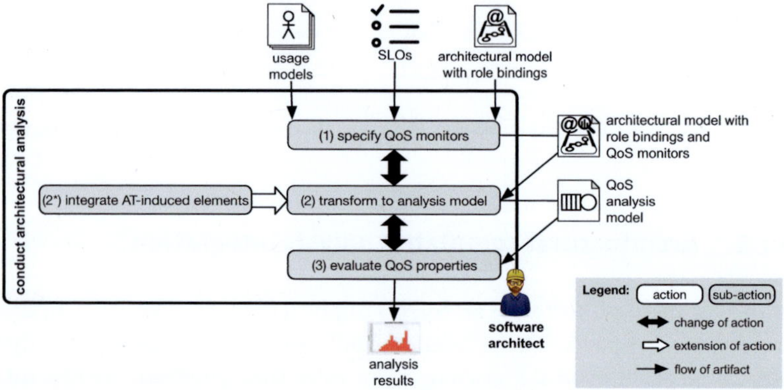

Figure 4.3.: AT-induced elements are automatically integrated during the transformation of an architectural model to a QoS analysis model.

By using a completion to map bound roles to elements of an architectural model, the semantics of these roles are defined via translational semantics (cf. Section 2.3.5). Here, it is important that only elements already supported by the underlying language for architectural models are created because translational semantics require a translation to a language with well-described semantics.

Figure 4.4 illustrates such a translation using the book shop example from Section 3.2.4. Figure 4.4 (top) shows that the *loadbalanced container* role of the *loadbalancing* AT is bound to the book shop. A completion can map this architectural model with a role binding to a semantically equivalent architectural model without a role binding.

As shown in Figure 4.4 (bottom), an appropriate completion may create a loadbalancer component allocated on a dedicated Loadbalancer Server. According to the *number of replicas* parameter, the loadbalancer component is

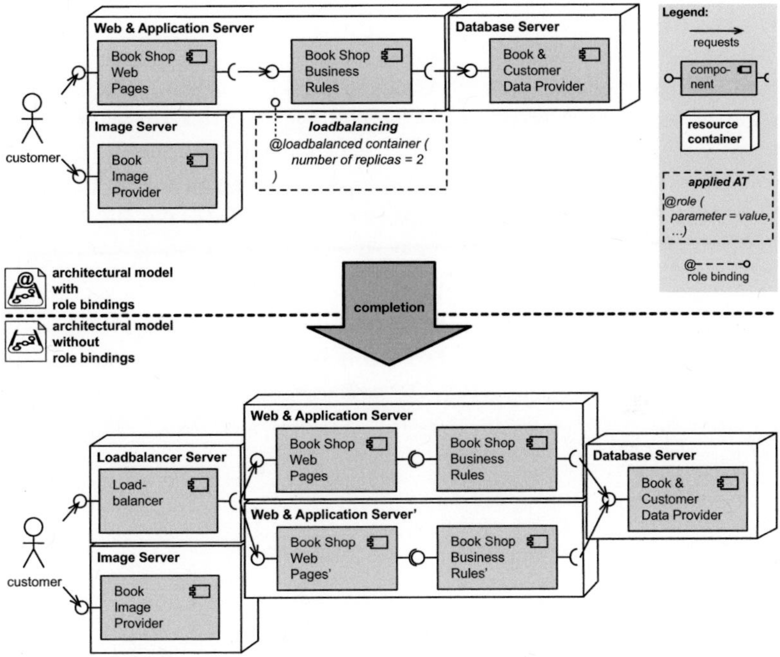

Figure 4.4.: A completion integrates elements induced by the loadbalancing AT into the book shop's architectural model, which defines the semantics of the bound role.

connected with two replicas of the *loadbalanced container*, i.e., of the Web & Application Server. These constructs (component, connector, and resource container) are completely supported by architectural modeling languages like the PCM and therefore precisely define the semantics of the *loadbalanced container* role of the *loadbalancing* AT.

Once completions have integrated all AT-induced elements, the transformation to the QoS analysis model can be executed exactly like in the original process. The next section describes how AT engineers specify ATs and include completions with such capabilities.

4.1.3. Architectural Template Specification

So-called AT engineers specify ATs to be used by software architects. AT engineers are triggered by a request for ATs, e.g., when a software architects needs a concrete architectural style formalized as AT. During the specification of ATs, AT engineers cooperate with AT testers who assure the quality of ATs via testing. Once quality-assured, AT engineers put the specified ATs into an AT catalog that can be used by software architects.

In Figure 4.5, the AT specification process is illustrated as a refinement of the *specify ATs* action from Figure 4.1. Figure 4.5 (left) illustrates the *specify ATs* action for AT engineers while Figure 4.5 (right) illustrates the *assure quality of ATs* action for AT testers. After describing the possible contents of requests for ATs, each of these high-level actions is described in the following.

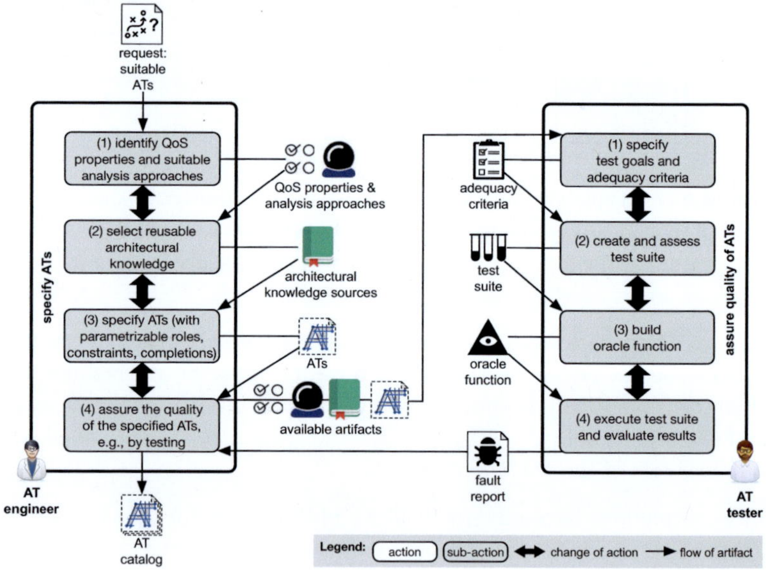

Figure 4.5.: AT engineers specify ATs in cooperation with AT testers to assure a high quality.

4.1.3.1. Contents of Requests for ATs

Requests for suitable ATs trigger the specification process of AT engineers. This section classifies possible contents of such requests.

A classification of requests is important because the contents of requests impact the actions that AT engineers have to perform. If the contents of requests only broadly characterize the ATs to be formalized, AT engineers have to gather the missing information. For instance, if a request only contains the QoS properties that are of interest, AT engineers first have to select appropriate reusable architectural knowledge for fostering such properties. In contrast, AT engineers can save the effort to perform such a selection if a request directly contains the concrete reusable architectural knowledge to be formalized.

Generally, AT engineers need to identify the reusable architectural knowledge to be formalized and the architectural analysis approaches to be supported. Both aspects are described and discussed in the following.

Reusable Architectural Knowledge. To select the reusable architectural knowledge to be formalized, requests for ATs may contain the following information; ordered from the most specific to the broadest information:

Direct request. Often, software architects need particular reusable architectural knowledge to be formalized. In this case, AT engineers have a precise and focused formalization task.

For example, if a software architect wants to apply the loadbalancing architectural pattern, the software architect may request a formalization of this concrete pattern from an AT engineer.[1]

QoS properties. Reusable architectural knowledge can indirectly be requested based on the QoS properties of interest. In this case, AT engineers are required to search and select appropriate architectural knowledge that fosters these QoS properties.

[1] In personal communication with members of the Palladio (cf. Section 2.5.3) community on established conferences and workshops, I was in fact asked for the formalization of the loadbalancing architectural pattern.

For example, the CloudScale project [BSL⁺13] has requested ATs for the QoS properties scalability, elasticity, and cost-efficiency. This request has driven the selection of typical reusable architectural knowledge for these properties and the formalization of this knowledge via ATs (see Section 5.3.1).

Application domains. Requestors may be interested in reusable architectural knowledge for a whole application domain. In this case, requests are even broader formulated than requests for QoS properties because AT engineers first have to identify which QoS properties are relevant in the requested application domain. Once identified, AT engineers can continue as for requests for QoS properties.

For example, the CloudScale project [BSL⁺13] started with a general interest in the cloud computing domain. Only after scalability, elasticity, and cost-efficiency had been identified as relevant QoS properties in this domain [LEB15], the specification of suitable ATs was able to continue.

Architectural Analysis Approaches. To identify the architectural analysis approaches for which ATs have to be formalized, requests for ATs may contain the following information; ordered from the most specific to the broadest information:

Direct request. Software architects usually have a preferred architectural analysis approach. Therefore, software architects may directly request such an approach. In this case, AT engineers precisely know for which architectural analysis they have to formalize ATs.

For example, a software architect may request Palladio (Section 2.5.3) as the target architectural analysis approach. Given that the tooling of the AT method is fully compliant with Palladio (cf. Section 4.3), this request has the benefit that the AT method can be used out-of-the-box.

QoS properties. A requestor may be interested in analyzing particular QoS properties and not in the concrete architectural analysis approach used for such analyses. Moreover, architectural analysis approaches differ in supported QoS properties. Therefore, AT engineers have to identify architectural analysis approaches that support the QoS properties of interest. If no suitable approach is available, AT engineers have to integrate support for the requested QoS properties into an existing or a new approach.

For example, the CloudScale project [BSL$^+$13] requested to analyze the QoS properties scalability, elasticity, and cost-efficiency. However, no existing architectural analysis approach had support for all of these properties. CloudScale's request has consequently driven the integration of metrics for scalability, elasticity, and cost-efficiency into Palladio [LB14a].

Different Request Scenarios. Requests for ATs may vary in the provided information about both reusable architectural knowledge and approaches on architectural analyses. These variations stem from different scenarios that requestors (e.g., software architects, researchers, and companies) want to realize.

Software architects typically request concrete architectural knowledge for a concrete architectural analysis approach. In contrast, researchers and companies are often interested in several ATs. For example, because ATs create value for software architects, companies can be interested in selling AT catalogs for a specific application domain. Vendors of architectural modeling tools can also be interested in the integration of ATs to increase the value of such tools.

4.1.3.2. AT Engineer: Specify ATs

Figure 4.5 (left) illustrates the actions for AT engineers to specify ATs. AT engineers proceed from (1) the identification of QoS properties and suitable analysis approaches over (2) the selection of reusable architectural knowledge and (3) the specification of ATs to (4) the assurance of the ATs' quality:

(1) identify QoS properties and suitable analysis approaches. The first action of AT engineers is the identification of QoS properties and suitable architectural analysis approaches. That is, for the QoS properties of interest (e.g., performance), AT engineers select or derive definitions and metrics (e.g., response times) and identify, extend, or implement a suitable analysis approach for these metrics (e.g., Palladio). New definitions and metrics can systematically be selected with systematic literature reviews (cf. Section 2.1.3) and derived by elaborating GQM plans (cf. Section 2.1.1). As shown in Figure 4.5, the outputs of this action are the QoS properties of interest along with the selected analysis approaches.

The input to this action determines the required effort, i.e., the contents of a request for ATs (cf. Section 4.1.3.1). The more specific the contents, the less effort AT engineers require gathering the required information. In the extreme case, the request contains the QoS properties of interest (e.g., performance) along with a suitable architectural analysis approach (e.g., Palladio supports performance metrics like response times, utilization, and throughput). In this case, AT engineers have no effort in this action. The other extreme is a broad request for ATs for a whole application domain; especially if QoS properties and metrics for this domain have to be identified and a suitable architectural analysis approach is lacking. In this case, AT engineers have to conduct a systematic literature review, elaborate a GQM plan, and implement or extend an architectural analysis appropriately.

(2) select reusable architectural knowledge. In the second action, AT engineers select reusable architectural knowledge to be formalized. If not directly provided in the request for ATs, AT engineers select this knowledge from sources that fit to the previously identified QoS properties, e.g., from books on appropriate styles, patterns, and reference architectures. As shown in Figure 4.5, the selected sources are particularly the output of this action.

A generally good source are books on software architecture, e.g., [BCK98, TMD09, BMR+96, SSRB00, KJ04, KJ04, BHS07a, BHS07b]. These books document architectural knowledge in the form of architectural styles and patterns for general and distributed software.

For more specific domains, specialized software architecture books document appropriate architectural knowledge. For example, for the domain of cloud computing, several of such books exist [RH11, Wil12, EPM13, FLR+14].

Besides such books, specialized architectural knowledge is often directly documented by providers of services and frameworks. For example, Amazon Web Services (AWS) provides architectural knowledge for their cloud computing services in the “AWS Architecture Center” [AWS16].

(3) specify ATs (with parametrizable roles, constraints, completions). In the third action, AT engineers formalize the previously selected knowledge via ATs. The roles of ATs provide the means to capture this knowledge, e.g., in terms of decisions about constraints (i.e., roles contain constraints) and about the existence of elements (i.e., roles contain a completion to create such elements). Roles can include parameters to account for variation points, e.g., to configure the number of replicas for a loadbalancer. AT engineers create roles, constraints, and completions step-wise and iteratively, analogously to existing processes for pattern creation (cf. Section 6.3.5).

Roles are particularly tied to the architectural elements of the analysis approach’s language: roles can only be bound to such elements and completions can only create such elements. For example, if Palladio (cf. Section 2.5.3) is selected as analysis approach, the PCM—Palladio’s architectural description language—defines the set of suitable elements.

(4) assure the quality of the specified ATs, e.g., by testing. Before AT engineers add specified ATs to an AT catalog, AT engineers have to assure the quality of these ATs. ATs need quality assurance because ATs interpret the architectural knowledge to be formalized. Still, this interpretation has to consistently maintain the architectural decisions of the formalized knowledge, i.e., the interpretation must have a high conceptual integrity (cf. Definition 2.14). For ATs, conceptual integrity relates to decisions about constraints (in the form of role constraints) and the existence of elements (as created by role completions).

The AT method suggests testing as a quality assurance technique because testing is lightweight (cf. Section 2.3.3). Testing allows to assure the conceptual integrity of ATs, e.g., by checking whether a completion’s output includes the expected elements.

As shown in Figure 4.5, AT engineers closely collaborate with AT testers that execute the concrete testing actions. For triggering these actions, AT engineers hand the previously gathered artifacts over to AT testers. These inputs serve AT testers for a rigorous planning and execution of AT testing. Once finished with testing, AT testers provide AT engineers with a report of faults detected during testing.

AT engineers use the fault report to resolve problems of specified ATs. These problems can be either due to faulty AT specifications or due to misinterpretations of formalized architectural knowledge by AT testers. In the former case, AT engineers return to action (3) and add missing elements or correct existing elements of ATs. In the latter case, AT engineers inform AT testers and together collaborate on resolving misinterpretations.

Flexibility of Collaboration. The collaboration between AT engineers and AT testers is flexible. In action (3), AT engineers may specify a preliminary version of ATs that only contains role and parameter specifications (i.e., the signature of ATs). Afterwards, AT engineers can directly hand the available artifacts over to AT testers in action (4). AT testers can then prepare testing while AT engineers, in parallel, continue to specify constraints and completions of the ATs back in action (3). Once both tasks are finished, AT testers execute all testing tasks on the completely specified ATs to finalize action (4).

The advantage of this approach is that AT specification and AT testing are parallelized. Therefore, the overall duration for the specification of ATs is lowered.

4.1.3.3. AT Tester: Assure Quality of ATs

Conceptually, quality assurance of model transformations and ATs is similar for two reasons. First, ATs include completions that are implemented as transformations. Second, ATs include constraints that particularly define the pre-conditions for these completions. For these reasons, the process for quality assurance of ATs refines the testing process for transformations described in Section 2.3.3.2.

Figure 4.5 (right) illustrates the refined process for quality assurance of ATs along the actions for so-called AT testers. AT testers proceed from (1) the specification of test goals and adequacy criteria over (2) the creation and assessment of a test suite and (3) the building of an oracle function to (4) the execution of the test suite and the evaluation of execution results; with the following specifics for AT testing:

(1) specify test goals and adequacy criteria. The main goal of AT testers is to test ATs' conceptual integrity (cf. Definition 2.14). For specifying adequacy criteria for this goal, AT testers need to be aware of typical root causes for AT faults. Giacinto identified the following typical root causes in her Master's thesis [Gia16, Sec. 6.3]:

- **Missing applications of AT roles:** Software architects may forget to assign required AT roles to their architectural models. In this case, the validation of the architectural model should fail. If the validation is nonetheless successful, the AT is faulty.

  Therefore, an appropriate adequacy criterion is the coverage of missing applications of AT roles. Full coverage is achieved if each possible combination of role applications is missing in at least one test case of a test suite. For n roles of an AT, there are 2^n of these combinations (also counting the special case where the set of missing applications is empty; i.e., the positive test case).

- **Faulty actual parameters of AT roles:** Software architects may specify invalid actual parameters for AT roles. For example, a software architect may specify -1 *number of replicas* for the *loadbalanced container* role of the *loadbalancing* AT (see Figure 4.4). An actual parameter of -1 is obviously invalid because a negative number of replicas cannot occur. In this case, the validation of the architectural model should fail. If the validation is nonetheless successful, the AT is faulty.

  The parameters of AT roles induce different groups of possible actual parameters: normal, boundary, and faulty actual parameters. Normal actual parameters are typical valid values for an AT parameter, e.g., 2 *number of replicas*. Boundary actual parameters are extreme but valid values for an AT parameter, e.g., the special cases 1 and *MAXIMUM_INTEGER number of replicas.* Faulty actual parameters are invalid values for an AT parameter, e.g., −1 and 0 *number of replicas.*

According to the partition testing strategy [Som10, Chap. 8.1.2], each of these groups should be covered by at least one test case. Therefore, an appropriate adequacy criterion is the coverage of normal, boundary, and faulty actual parameters for applications of AT roles.

The number of required test cases for full coverage depends on the type of an AT's formal parameter and its usage. For example, the only faulty values of a formal parameter of type *String* may be a null pointer and an empty string. Covering these two cases in the test suite thus leads to a full coverage of faulty actual parameters.

- **Missing constraints of AT roles:** An architectural model with an applied AT may violate constraints of the architectural knowledge formalized by the AT. For example, when the *three-layer* AT is applied, a component of the presentation layer may directly request data from a data layer component like illustrated in Figure 4.2. In this case, the validation of the architectural model should fail. If the validation is nonetheless successful, the AT is faulty.

  The reason for such faults is that AT engineers have missed to formalize constraints of the corresponding architectural knowledge. During the specification of ATs (step (3) of the AT specification process in Figure 4.5), AT engineers interpret the architectural knowledge to be formalized. Because such interpretations are conducted manually, AT engineers may simply forget the formalization of certain constraints. Also wrongly formalized constraints are possible, e.g., when AT engineers misunderstand the corresponding architectural knowledge.

  Fortunately, the likelihood is low that both AT engineers and AT testers forget or misunderstand the same constraints. The only precondition is that they interpret the architectural knowledge independently from each other.

  Consequently, an appropriate adequacy criterion is the coverage of constraints of AT roles. For full coverage, AT testers have to specify at least a positive and a negative test case for each constraint of the formalized architectural knowledge. For identifying constraints, AT testers manually interpret the architectural knowledge to be formalized. This identification is redundant to and independent from the interpretation AT engineers, which increases the likelihood to discover missing constraints.

- **Uncovered metamodel elements in completions:** Software architects may use arbitrary elements of the metamodel of an architectural model to which an AT is applied; as long as no metamodel or AT constraints are violated. For example, the book shop model in Figure 4.4 (top) will remain valid if the Web & Application Server would additionally include a model element for a virtual machine (if supported by the metamodel). In this case, the output of the completion should not only be valid but also acknowledge the additional metamodel element correctly. In above example, the completion result in Figure 4.4 (bottom) should include a virtual machine in both replicas of the Web & Application Server. If this is not the case, the AT is faulty.

  The reason for such faults is that AT engineers missed to cover the metamodel element in question within an AT's completion. For example, the completion illustrated in Figure 4.4 may lack the logic to copy the element for virtual machines. Faults like this typically occur for rarely-used and newer metamodel elements because it is less likely that AT engineers think of these situations (cf. [Gia16, Sec. 7.1.1]).

  Therefore, an appropriate adequacy criterion is the coverage of metamodel elements. For full coverage, AT testers have to provide at least one test case per metamodel element. If full coverage is unrealistic, especially rarely-used and newer metamodel elements should be tested.

- **Coding errors:** Faulty ATs may contain coding errors within their completions. In this case, the pre-conditions of a completion are fulfilled but its post- and source-target-conditions are violated (cf. Section 2.3.3.1). The typical causes for such a situation range from simple faults (e.g., assigning a wrong value) to complex and conceptual faults (e.g., allocating a replicated component on the wrong server).

Coding errors are the most generic type of root cause, which makes the suggestion of concrete adequacy criteria hard. Still, because a completion is a refinement transformation that enriches architectural models with additional expected elements (cf. Definition 2.28), AT testers should explicitly test whether a completion creates such elements correctly.

Therefore, an appropriate adequacy criterion is the coverage of AT-induced elements (cf. Section 4.1.2). Full coverage is achieved if each element to be created is tested with at least one test case.

(2) create and assess test suite. AT testers create and assess a test suite exactly like described for the testing of transformations in Section 2.3.3.2. In summary, AT testers derive the test suite directly from the specified adequacy criteria and use the coverage of these criteria to assess the test suite.

(3) build oracle function. As described in Section 2.3.3.2, testers can specify oracle functions either via concrete models for model differencing or via transformation contracts. Both approaches have been applied for testing ATs by Giacinto [Gia16]. Her results support the following statements.

In case of faults in completions, model differencing is well-suited for identifying the cause for these faults [Gia16, Sec. 6.3]. The differences between target and expected model typically point to the concrete issues at hand. For example, a missing connector directly points to the completion logic where connectors are created. Similarly, a wrong value of an attribute directly points to the completion logic where the value is set. The downside, however, is that model differencing is computationally expensive [SCD12] and requires one expected model per test case, thus, causing high specification efforts [Gia16, Sec. 7.2]. Giacinto has therefore only applied model differencing to identify fault causes that were otherwise hard to find.

In contrast, transformation contracts are more lightweight because they check only particular constraints instead of comparing whole models. Moreover, transformation contracts are reusable over various test cases because the contract's constraints have to hold independently of specific models.

Instead of OCL, Giacinto uses QVT-O (cf. Section 2.3.2) for specifying transformation contracts [Gia16, Sec. 5.3.4]. The use of QVT-O allows to overcome OCL's limitation of only working within the context of one metamodel [CMSD04]. In contrast, QVT-O transformations can use two models as input, i.e., both the source and the target model of a completion. QVT-O transformations can therefore check a contract's source-target-conditions and output whether these conditions are fulfilled. QVT-O particularly includes an extended OCL version [Obj16, Chap. 8.2.2], thus, allowing AT testers to benefit from OCL as well.

(4) execute test suite and evaluate results. AT testers execute the test suite and evaluate execution results using the oracle function as described for transformations testing in Section 2.3.3.2. Based on evaluation results, AT testers create a fault report that helps AT engineers to resolve any problems (cf. action (4) in Section 4.1.3.2)

4.2. Architectural Template Language

The AT language allows AT engineers to specify ATs and software architects to apply ATs (see Definition 4.3). Given this pragmatism, the AT language becomes an integral part of the AT method because it impacts both AT processes and AT tooling.

Definition 4.3 (Architectural Template language) *"The Architectural Template (AT) language is the language to specify and apply ATs." (author's definition)*

This section details the theoretical foundations and the formalization of the AT language. The AT language's formalization is realized as a metamodel—the AT metamodel.

ATs are classified as hybrid templates that combine initiator and bound templates (Section 4.2.1). A core characteristic of such templates is the differentiation between types and instances, which motivates the formalization of AT types and AT instances (Section 4.2.2). After clarifying these theoretic foundations, the intension of the AT language is derived as a basis for metamodel specification (Section 4.2.3) and the technical realization of types and instances is described (Section 4.2.4). Finally, the AT metamodel is described that follows this technical realization while adhering to the AT language's intension (Section 4.2.5). The overall process therefore follows the formal and systematic definition process for DSLs described in Section 2.3.1.3.

4.2.1. Classification of Architectural Templates

In the AT application process (Section 4.1), software architects can both instantiate architectural models with ATs and bind further ATs to their architectural model. According to the template categories from Section 2.4.3, ATs can thus be classified as hybrid templates that combine initiator and bound templates. Figure 4.6 illustrates this combination from the viewpoint of software architects.

The data flow for ATs starts at the left side of Figure 4.6 where an AT of an AT catalog serves as initiator template. The AT initiator (part of AT tooling) acts as template engine to create an initial architectural model from this AT. A subsequent customization is controlled via the editors of the AT tooling, i.e., AT tooling prevents software architects from violating AT constraints when they specify the architectural model (see the AT application process in Section 4.1.1). Within AT constraints, AT editors allow customization with application-specific elements (from an application-specific model) and bindings to additional ATs (from an AT catalog). Because of these bindings, ATs not only act as initiator but also as bound templates. The result after customization is, therefore, only an intermediate architectural model into which bound ATs have to be integrated in a subsequent task. To execute this integration task, the AT engine (part of AT tooling) acts as a second template engine. The final result is an architectural model that conforms to all previously bound ATs, i.e., the model satisfies all constraints of each AT within the set of ATs.

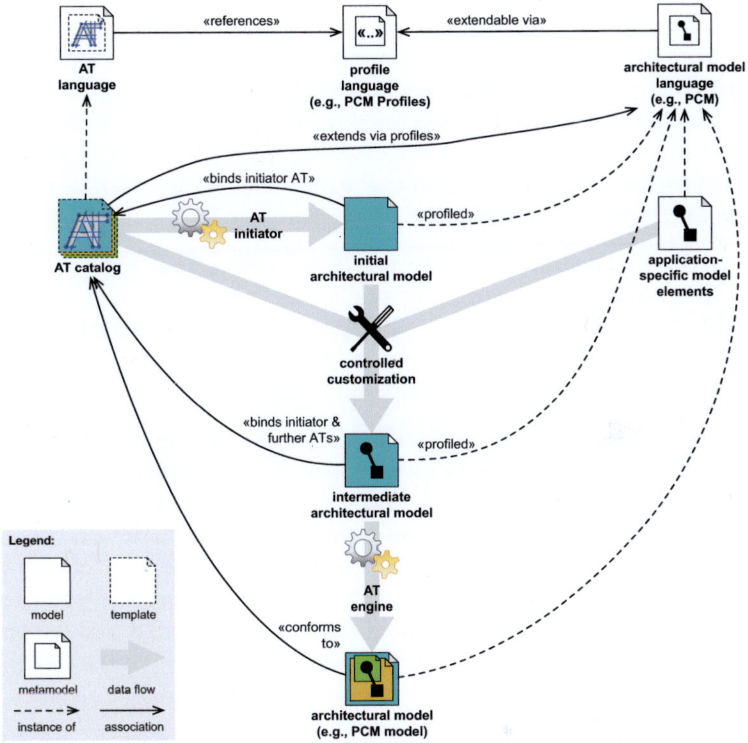

Figure 4.6.: Data flow of Architectural Templates (ATs). ATs are hybrid templates that combine initiator templates (for the creation of initial models and a controlled customization) and bound templates (for embedding further templates).

The models illustrated in Figure 4.6 are instances of different metamodels: while ATs are instances of the AT language, all architectural models are instances of an architectural model language such as the PCM. However, a strict separation between these two metamodels would make binding templates within architectural models impossible. Bound templates therefore require that there is an according mean to reference from architectural model language to template language (cf. Section 2.4.3).

To realize such a reference, the AT language depends on a profile language (cf. Section 2.3.4). This dependency allows the AT language to externally extend architectural model languages in a lightweight manner. The prerequisite for such an extension is that the architectural model language supports such a profile language. For example, the PCM supports PCM profiles [KDH+12] for external extensions, an integration of EMF profiles [LWWC12] within the PCM tooling.[2]

Given this prerequisite, a concrete AT can provide a profile for a particular architectural model language. The profile extends this language by the capability to bind the AT. The initial architectural model and the intermediate architectural model in Figure 4.6 can realize such bindings because they are instances of the profiled architectural model language.

A metamodel extension by profiles also requires a precise semantics definition of the extension. In the AT method, extension semantics are defined via translational semantics as described in Section 4.1.2: The AT engine eventually embeds bound templates into an unprofiled instance of the architectural model language. This embedding particularly specifies the semantics of the AT application because the target architectural model language is assumed to have well-defined semantics. Here, the main condition is that template constructs can be expressed (and thus finally embedded) in the target architectural model language. Technically, each AT therefore includes an appropriate completion.

4.2.2. Formalization of Types and Instances

ATs are templates that fulfill the template characteristics described in Section 2.4.4. Accordingly, the AT metamodel needs to distinguish between AT types (or short ATs) and AT instances. The notion of types and instances is indeed suitable because ATs *classify* the AT instances that can be created based on them (classification is needed for instance-of relationships; cf. [Küh06]). For example, the software architect of the book shop (Section 3.2.4) may use a different set of components to engineer an online shop for flowers and the resulting architecture would still conform to the bound

[2] EMF profiles can similarly be integrated into other EMF-based architectural model languages [LWWC12].

three-layer AT. This section formalizes these core concepts—ATs and AT instances—of the AT metamodel.

Following the terminology of Kühne [Küh06], ATs are type models for AT instances, i.e., $AT_{instance} \lhd_t AT$, and AT instances are prescriptive token models of the planned software, i.e., $software \lhd_i AT_{instance}$. The instance-of relation between ATs and AT instances describes an ontological instantiation because both reside on the same linguistic level, i.e., $AT_{instance} \lhd_t^o AT$.

A change to a higher linguistic level is needed to *specify* such ATs and AT instances. This specification is enabled by the AT language $\mathcal{L}_{\mathcal{AT}}$. Accordingly, a specified AT is a linguistic instance of the AT metaclass of the AT language, i.e., $AT \lhd_t^l \mathcal{L}_{\mathcal{AT}}(AT)$. Analogously, a specified AT instance is a linguistic instance of the AT instance metaclass of the AT language, i.e., $AT_{instance} \lhd_t^l \mathcal{L}_{\mathcal{AT}}(AT\ instance)$. The latter two metaclasses of the AT language require an association describing the ontological instance-of relation, i.e., $\mathcal{L}_{\mathcal{AT}}(AT\ instance)$ is instance of $\mathcal{L}_{\mathcal{AT}}(AT)$ and $\mathcal{L}_{\mathcal{AT}}(AT)$ is type of $\mathcal{L}_{\mathcal{AT}}(AT\ instance)$.

Figure 4.7 illustrates the discussed instance-of relationships based on the *three-layer* AT. The upper-right of the figure shows these relationships along the two linguistic levels L_0 and L_1 and the two ontological levels O_0 and O_1.

Furthermore, Figure 4.7 uses Kühne's notion of a meaning μ that "assigns meaning to a model (element)" [Küh06]. The AT language defines the meaning for elements of linguistic level L_1 using $\iota(\mathcal{L}_{\mathcal{AT}})$ (see Section 2.3.1.3 for the definition of the intention ι). The meaning of the *three-layer* AT (O_1 on L_0) is based on the referred architectural knowledge concept using ι(*three-layer*). This concept defines the meaning of the book shop model (O_0 on L_0) via its extension ϵ(*three-layer*), i.e., all elements falling under the three-layer concept [Küh06]. Also the AT language spans an extension $\epsilon(\mathcal{L}_{\mathcal{AT}})$, defining all valid models that the language can specify, e.g., a three-layer book shop model.

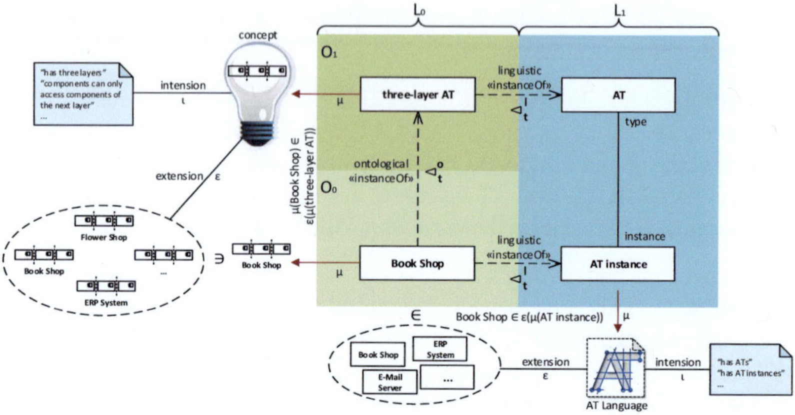

Figure 4.7.: Instance-of relationships of the book shop example (based on [Küh06]).

4.2.3. Intension of the Architectural Template Language

This section provides the intension—and thus the required attributes—of the AT language. The AT languages' intension particularly serves as basis for defining the AT language via a metamodel in subsequent sections.

As described in Section 2.3.1.3, a language's typical usage scenarios allow to derive a language's intension. The typical usage scenarios of the AT language $\mathcal{L}_{\mathcal{AT}}$ are reflected in the AT processes from Section 4.1. Therefore, the intension of the AT language $\iota(\mathcal{L}_{\mathcal{AT}})$ can be derived by analyzing the minimally required attributes to enable these AT processes.

Table 4.1 summarizes the results of this analysis.[3] The first column of Table 4.1 provides the core elements of the AT language, i.e., AT catalogs, ATs, AT roles, AT constraints, AT completions, and AT instances. The second column of Table 4.1 lists the attributes associated to these elements. These attributes can be derived from the AT processes in Section 4.1 as follows.

[3] An initial version of these results was published in [Leh14a].

Table 4.1.: Intension of the AT language ($\iota(\mathcal{L}_{\mathcal{AT}})$)

Element	Attributes
AT catalog	"has ID", "has name", "collects ATs"
AT	"has ID", "has name", "represents and documents architectural knowledge", "supports architectural analyses", "has default AT instance", "has roles"
AT role	"has ID", "has name", "has AT constraints", "has formal parameters", "has AT completion"
AT constraint	"has ID", "has name"
AT completion	"references model transformation"
AT instance	"classified by ATs", "has bindings between architectural elements and AT roles", "bindings have actual parameters"

The selection of ATs (first task of actions (1*) and (2*) of AT application in Figure 4.1) induces the need of a uniquely identifiable, named catalog of ATs to select from ("AT catalog has ID", "AT catalog has name", and "AT catalog collects ATs"). A selection particularly requires ATs to have unique identifiers ("AT has ID") and convenient names ("AT has name"). The selection criteria are based on the architectural knowledge represented and documented by the AT ("AT represents and documents architectural knowledge") and supported architectural analyses ("AT supports architectural analyses"). For example, a software architect who wants to improve the maintainability of a Palladio model may select the *three-layer* AT: the AT represents the three-layer architectural style (along with its promise to improve maintainability) and is supported by Palladio. As discussed in the previous section, the selection also induces the need of AT types and instances ("AT language has ATs", "AT language has AT instances", and "AT instances are classified by ATs").

Given these fundamental formalisms of the AT language, the application of ATs (second task of actions (1*) and (2*) of AT application in Figure 4.1) can be inspected next. As described in Section 4.1.1, software architects apply an AT either by instantiating a new architectural model from the AT ("AT has default AT instance") or by binding the AT's uniquely identifiable, named roles to an existing architectural model ("AT has roles", "AT role has ID", and "AT role has name"). Furthermore, AT roles define constraints and are parametrizable ("AT role has AT constraints" and "AT role has formal parameters"; cf. action (3) of AT specification in Figure 4.5). Constraints are uniquely identifiable and named, which allows software architects to quickly recognize the meaning of a constraint in natural language ("AT constraint has ID" and "AT constraint has name").

For the assignment of roles to architectural elements, AT instances have to maintain an appropriate binding ("AT instance has bindings between architectural elements and AT roles"). These bindings can particularly have actual parameters for each formal parameter of an AT role ("AT instance bindings have actual parameters").

The quality property analysis (described in Section 4.1.2) requires that AT roles specify a completion ("AT role has AT completion"). Technically, such a completion is realized by a suitable model transformation that integrates AT-induced elements (cf. Section 4.1.2). Therefore, a completion needs to reference an implementing transformation ("AT completion references model transformation"). Figure 4.4 illustrates a completion for the *loadbalanced container* role of the *loadbalancing* AT.

4.2.4. Technical Realization of Types and Instances

AT types and AT instances are the core concepts of the AT language. Therefore, this section describes how these concepts are technically realized in the AT metamodel. After selecting a suitable realization option (Section 4.2.4.1), the induced structural dependencies for the AT metamodel are described (Section 4.2.4.2).

4.2.4.1. Selection of Realization Option

The intension of the AT language (Section 4.2.3) requires that AT instances bind AT roles to architectural elements and assign actual parameters to formal parameters of bound AT roles. These requirements may be realized by extending the targeted architectural model:

(a) externally via an annotation model, e.g., by defining a metamodel for bindings that reference a PCM element and an AT role while assigning actual parameters to each formal parameter of an AT role,

(b) heavyweight, e.g., by extending the architectural elements of the PCM to specify role bindings and parameter assignments, or

(c) lightweight, e.g., by reusing EMF profiles [LWWC12] to bind roles and to assign actual parameters.

Options (a) and (b) both have the disadvantage that existing tools have to be extended or newly be developed, e.g., to provide editing support for role bindings and parameter assignments. As described in Section 2.3.4, profiles instead have the advantage that existing tools may already provide tool support for profile-based extensions. For example, Palladio has an integrated support for EMF profiles [KDH$^+$12] that enables software architects to use the normal PCM editors to apply profiles, including stereotype applications and assignments of actual parameters to tagged values. For this reason, the AT metamodel employs option (c) for realizing role bindings and parameter assignments.

4.2.4.2. Structural Dependencies of Selected Realization Option

This section explains the structural dependencies for the AT metamodel that are induced from the metatmodel's realization via profiles (i.e., the realization option selected in Section 4.2.4.1).[4]

In terms of structure, the realization via profiles requires that a dedicated profile is associated to an AT. For each AT role, the dedicated profile provides a stereotype that represents the role and specifies the role's formal parameters as tagged values. Once such a profile is available, a corresponding profile application allows to bind the profile's stereotypes to architectural elements and to assign actual values to tagged values. Therefore, such profile applications realize the concept of AT instances, including the attributes required by the AT language's intension (cf. Table 4.1).

Figure 4.8 illustrates the described structural dependencies and the resulting instantiation relationships between involved (meta)models. Linguistic instantiation levels are depicted via white rectangles. Figure 4.8 orders these instantiation levels from the highest linguistic level (top) to the lowest linguistic level (bottom):

[4] Section 4.2.1 describes this realization from a data flow perspective.

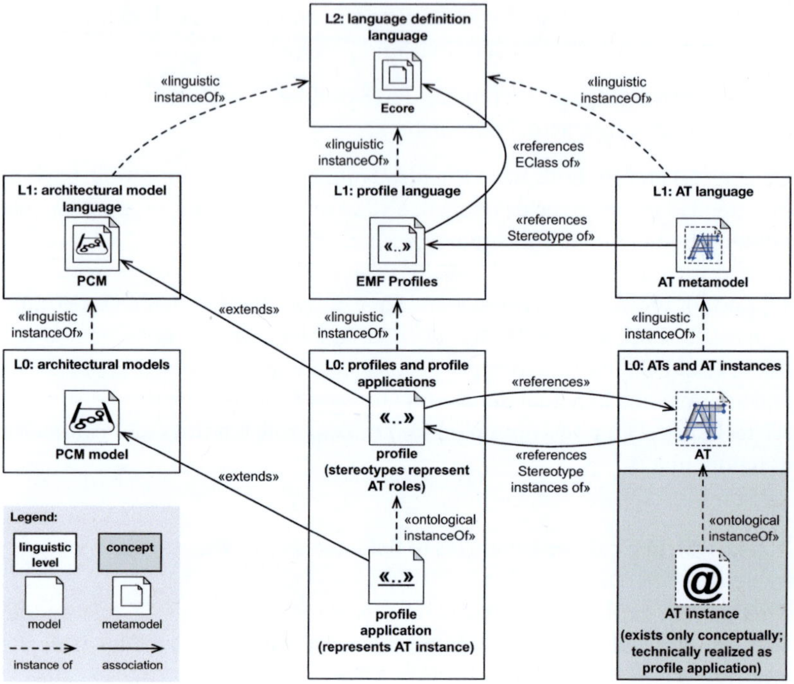

Figure 4.8.: Instance-of relationships of architectural models, profiles, and ATs.

L2: The highest linguistic level (top of Figure 4.8) describes the level for languages to define languages (i.e., meta metamodels). EMF's Ecore metamodel is an example for such a language (cf. Section 2.3.6).

L1: The languages of the next lower level (middle of Figure 4.8) are specified with the language from **L2**, thus, linguistic instances of the **L2** language. Figure 4.8 shows that the architectural modeling language (e.g., the PCM), the profile language (e.g., EMF Profiles), and the AT language (i.e., the AT metamodel) are specified at this linguistic level. In particular, the PCM, EMF profiles, and the AT metamodel are all linguistic instances of Ecore.

L0: Analogously, the languages of the lowest level (bottom of Figure 4.8) are specified with the corresponding languages from **L1**, thus, linguistic instances of these **L1** languages. Figure 4.8 shows that architectural models (e.g., PCM models), profiles and profile applications, and ATs and AT instances are specified at this linguistic level.

Besides linguistic instance-of relationships, Figure 4.8 illustrates two ontological instance-of relationships at **L0**: profile applications are ontological instances of profiles and AT instances are ontological instances of ATs. Section 4.2.2 describes the rationale for ontological instantiation of ATs and AT instances; the argumentation is analogous for profiles and profile applications.

Figure 4.8 illustrates that AT instances are only defined conceptually and are technically realized via profile applications. For this reason, a profile holds a reference to an AT and an AT's roles reference corresponding stereotypes of a profile. These references enable the navigation from profiles and profile applications to ATs and vice-versa. Particularly, the stereotype that represents an AT role (and vice-versa) can be identified.

As shown in Figure 4.8, these references are enabled at **L1**. ATs can reference profiles because the AT metamodel references EMF Profiles' Stereotype metaclass. Profiles can reference ATs because the EMF Profiles metamodel references ECore's EClass metaclass, which allows profiles to reference arbitrary elements of Ecore-based models. Because the AT metamodel is specified via Ecore, profiles can thus reference ATs.

For the same reason, profiles and profile applications can particularly reference elements of the PCM and of PCM models. That is, a profile can specify which PCM elements are extended by a profile's stereotypes and a profile application can specify to which concrete PCM model elements such stereotypes are applied.

4.2.5. The Architectural Template Metamodel

This section describes the AT metamodel as specified via EMF's Ecore (cf. Section 2.3.6). The AT metamodel realizes ATs and AT instances as described in Section 4.2.4. The remaining elements of the AT metamodel are derived from the AT language's intension described in Section 4.2.3.

For each language element of the intension, a representing metaclass is created. Each metaclass is then enriched with the corresponding intension attributes as defined in Table 4.1. Therefore, the AT metamodel adheres to the AT language's intension by construction.

In this section, the semantics of the AT metamodel are informally described in natural language. AT tooling (Section 4.3) serves as a reference implementation for these semantics. Therefore, AT tooling formally defines semantics in a pragmatic way (cf. pragmatic semantics in Section 2.3.5).

The remainder of this section is structured as follows. First, an overview of the metamodel and its main elements is given (Section 4.2.5.1). Second, abstract syntax, semantics, and concrete syntax are detailed for each metaclass. The AT metamodel includes metaclasses for catalogs (Section 4.2.5.2), ATs (Section 4.2.5.3), roles (Section 4.2.5.4), constraints (Section 4.2.5.5), completions (Section 4.2.5.6), stereotypes (Section 4.2.5.7), and AT instances (Section 4.2.5.8).

4.2.5.1. Overview of the Metamodel

This section describes the main elements of the AT language. Main elements are highlighted in **bold**.

Software architects *apply* an AT by creating an AT instance. **AT instances** formalize the set of **bindings** with **actual parameters** from architectural elements to AT roles (cf. bound templates in Section 2.4.3.3). The bound roles in Figure 3.5 exemplify such bindings and their graphical syntax.

AT engineers *specify* the ATs (i.e., AT types) to be bound. Each **AT** consists of:

(1) A set of **roles** to refine and restrict elements of architectural models—AT instances bind such roles similar to models that bind stereotypes of UML profiles (cf. Section 2.3.4). Each role may include:

- **formal parameters** to acknowledge for variation points (cf. action (3) in Section 4.1.3.2)—formal parameters are realized by assigning each role a stereotype (cf. Section 2.3.4) that defines these parameters,

- **constraints** to express restrictions as, e.g., shown in Figure 4.2, and
- a **completion** that can map bound roles to a semantically equivalent architectural model construct—this mapping defines the semantics of the role via translational semantics (cf. Section 2.3.5). For instance, the *loadbalanced container* role in Figure 4.4 refines the bound resource container with a loadbalancer—its completion expresses this refinement formally.

(2) A **documentation** that describes the architectural knowledge that is modeled, e.g., to point to the QoS properties potentially impacted by this knowledge.

(3) An optional **default AT instance** to be used as initiator template (cf. Section 2.4.3.1).

These constituents allow to formalize architectural knowledge, e.g., coming in the form of architectural styles (i.e., roles with constrains) and architectural patterns (i.e., roles that refine elements via completions). Such ATs are finally collected in **AT catalogs**.

4.2.5.2. Metamodel: Catalog

An AT catalog is a collection of ATs within a common repository. Software architects can select ATs from and AT engineers can put ATs into such catalogs. According to the AT language's intension (cf. Table 4.1), AT catalogs further have a unique identifier and a name.

Abstract Syntax Figure 4.9 illustrates the metaclass Catalog that realizes the concept of AT catalogs.

Catalog inherits from Entity, which provides Catalog with attributes for a unique identifier (id; inherited from Identifier) and a name (entityName; inherited from NamedElement). In Figure 4.9, the metaclasses Entity, Identifier, and NamedElement are abstract and reused from the PCM (cf. Section 2.5.3.1) but may be analogously defined without PCM dependency.

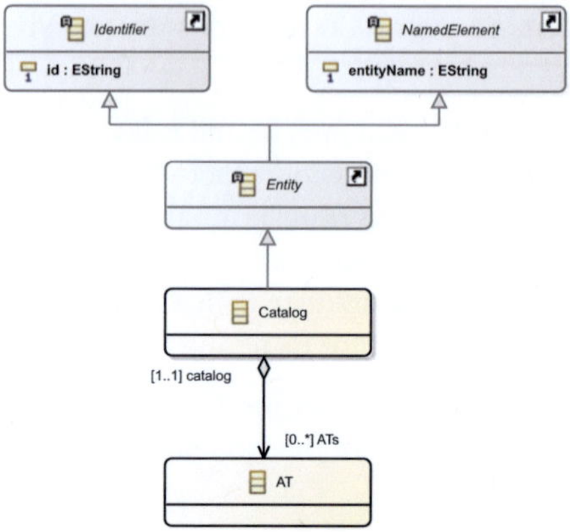

Figure 4.9.: The metaclass Catalog inherits from Entity and contains a set of ATs.

Moreover, Catalog has a containment reference to the AT metaclass. As shown in Figure 4.9, a Catalog includes an arbitrary number of ATs and each AT is contained in exactly one catalog.

Semantics AT engineers put an AT into an AT catalog by adding an instance of the AT metaclass to the containment reference of an instance of the Catalog metaclass. Software architects can subsequently select and use the added AT from this catalog. AT tooling (Section 4.3) supports these use cases.

Concrete Syntax Table 4.2 illustrates the concrete syntax of AT catalogs. There are two alternative notions to depict AT catalogs: a compact and an expanded notion.

The first row in Table 4.2 shows the compact notion of Catalog instances. A catalog is depicted as a stacked AT logo with the catalog name (e.g., "Catalog Name") underneath. This notion is useful to illustrate data flow of ATs as, e.g., used in Figure 4.1, without explicitly stating contained ATs.

Table 4.2.: Catalog notations

Metaclass	Notation	Description
Catalog	 Catalog Name	Compact notion of an AT catalog with the name "Catalog Name", e.g., used in Figure 4.1.
Catalog	Catalog Catalog Name AT An AT Name AT Another AT Name	Expanded notion of an AT catalog with the name "Catalog Name". Subentries illustrate two contained ATs named "An AT Name" and "Another AT Name".

The second row in Table 4.2 shows the expanded notion of Catalog instances. A catalog is depicted as an expanded list where the list head contains an entry for the catalog name (e.g., "Catalog Name") prepended with a stacked template symbol and the string "Catalog". Each list entry represents a contained AT. An AT entry provides the AT's name prepended with a template symbol and the string "AT". The example in Table 4.2 shows two ATs named "An AT Name" and "Another AT Name". This notion is useful to illustrate the ATs contained in a catalog.

4.2.5.3. Metamodel: AT

As stated in Definition 4.1, an AT is a template representing and documenting reusable architectural knowledge. Software architects can apply ATs for both architectural modeling and architectural analyses while AT engineers specify ATs. An optional default AT instance provides software architects with an initial architectural model corresponding to the represented architectural knowledge, e.g., a reference architecture.

ATs formalize reusable architectural knowledge in terms of the architectural knowledge's roles (cf. Section 2.2.4). Furthermore, ATs have a unique identifier and a name for selection purposes (cf. the AT language's intension in Table 4.1).

Abstract Syntax Figure 4.10 illustrates the metaclass AT that realizes the concept of ATs.

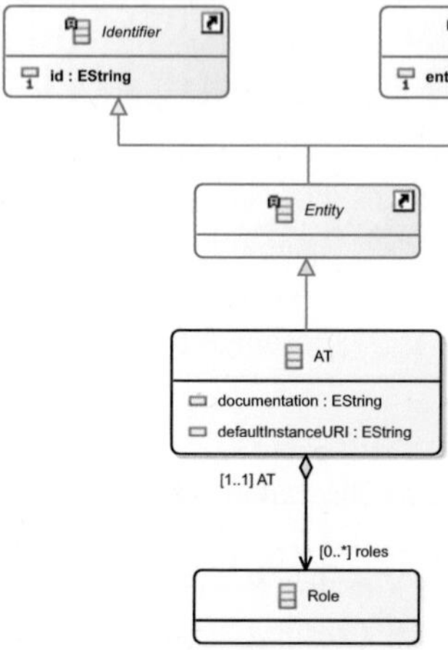

Figure 4.10.: The metaclass AT inherits from Entity and contains a set of roles.

AT inherits from Entity, which provides AT with attributes for a unique identifier and a name (as detailed for the Catalog metaclass in Section 4.2.5.2). AT engineers use the documentation attribute to point to the modeled architectural knowledge, e.g., via a natural language description or a hyperlink to such a description. Moreover, the defaultInstanceURI references the location of the AT's default instance as a uniform resource identifier (URI).

AT has a containment reference to the Role metaclass. As shown in Figure 4.10, an AT includes an arbitrary number of roles and each Role is contained in exactly one AT.

Semantics AT semantics are mainly determined by an AT's roles, which constrain and refine architectural elements. In addition, the semantics of the attributes of the AT metaclass are as follows.

The id attribute is a unique identifier of an AT, thus, suited as identifier for ATs within tools. In contrast, the entityName attribute represents a human readable (but not necessarily unique) version of this identifier. The entityName of an AT is, thus, a convenient mean for AT engineers and software architects to identify an AT.

The documentation attribute is an informal mean to describe the represented architectural knowledge. A tool with AT support must be able to show the documentation attribute to involved stakeholders. For example, the documentation helps software architects in determining the suitability of an AT and AT testers in developing their interpretation of the described architectural knowledge.

The defaultInstanceURI attribute must be a unique identifier of the location of a default AT instance. Software architects must be able to use this default AT instance as initiator template for a new architectural model (initiator templates are described in Section 2.4.3.1). A tool with AT support must provide an according wizard.

AT tooling (Section 4.3) serves as a reference implementation for above use cases.

Concrete Syntax Table 4.3 illustrates the concrete syntax of ATs. There are two alternative notions to depict ATs: a compact and an expanded notion.

Table 4.3.: AT notations

Metaclass	Notation	Description
AT		Compact notion of an AT with the name "AT Name", e.g., used in Figure 4.5.
AT		Expanded notion of an AT with the name "AT Name". Inner dashed boxes depict two contained AT roles named "A Role" and "Another Role" (cf. Section 4.2.5.4).

The first row in Table 4.3 shows the compact notion of instances of the AT metaclass. An AT is depicted as an AT logo with the AT name (e.g., "AT Name") underneath. This notion is useful to illustrate data flow of ATs as, e.g., used in Figure 4.5, without explicitly stating contained roles.

The second row in Table 4.3 shows the expanded notion of instances of the AT metaclass. An AT is depicted as dashed box where the top left of the box contains the AT name (e.g., “AT Name”) prepended with an @-symbol. Contained dashed boxes represent AT roles as described in Section 4.2.5.4. The example in Table 4.3 shows two roles named “A Role” and “Another Role”. This notion is useful to illustrate the roles contained in an AT.

4.2.5.4. Metamodel: Role

In correspondence to the general role definition (Definition 2.13), a role of an AT specifies the responsibility of an architectural element within a context of related elements. When software architects assign AT roles to architectural elements, AT roles thus restrict and refine assigned elements. AT engineers specify how AT roles realize such restrictions (via constraints) and refinements (via completions). Furthermore, AT roles have a unique identifier and a name for clarity when being illustrated (cf. the AT language’s intension in Table 4.1).

An AT role references exactly one stereotype of a profile associated to the AT (cf. Section 2.3.4). As described in Section 4.2.1, the referenced profile allows to externally extend architectural model languages in a lightweight manner. In the case of AT roles, profiles provide AT role with formal parameters (tagged values of a stereotype) to acknowledge for variation points (cf. action (3) in Section 4.1.3.2). Moreover, profiles allow software architects to create AT instances by creating profile applications (cf. Definition 2.25). Profile applications bind the associated roles to architectural elements and support the specification of actual parameters via tagged values.

Abstract Syntax Figure 4.11 illustrates the metaclass Role that realizes the concept of AT roles.

Role inherits from Entity, which provides Role with attributes for a unique identifier and a name. Entity and its superclasses are detailed for the Catalog metaclass in Section 4.2.5.2.

Role has a containment reference to the Constraint metaclass. As shown in Figure 4.11, a Role includes an arbitrary number of constraints and each Constraint is contained in exactly one role. Constraint is abstract to acknowledge

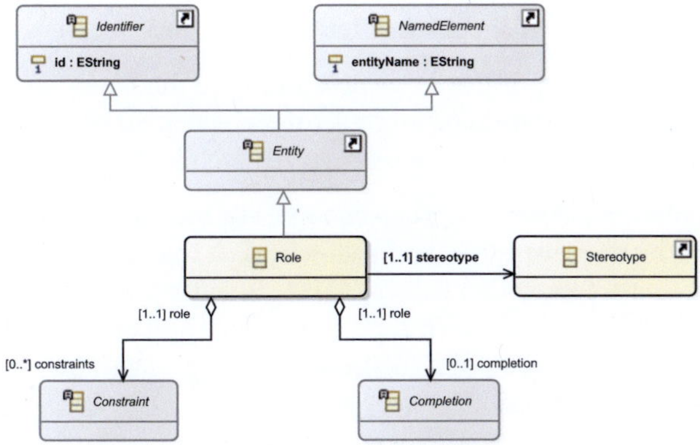

Figure 4.11.: The metaclass Role inherits from Entity, contains a set of constraints and an optional completion, and references a stereotype.

for different kinds of constraints, e.g., constraints formulated via the OCL (cf. Section 2.3.6). Section 4.2.5.5 details the Constraint metaclass.

Role further has a containment reference to the Completion metaclass. As shown in Figure 4.11, a Role contains either no or exactly one completion and each Completion is contained in exactly one role. Completion is abstract to acknowledge for different kinds of completions, e.g., a completion implemented via QVT-O (cf. Section 2.3.2). Section 4.2.5.6 details the Completion metaclass.

Furthermore, Role has a reference to exactly one Stereotype. Stereotype indirectly provides Role with formal parameters (via tagged values) and allows to bind roles to architectural elements (via profile applications). Section 4.2.5.7 details the Stereotype metaclass.

Semantics AT roles formalize the roles of the represented architectural knowledge. As such, AT roles restrict and refine bound architectural elements. An AT role is bound by applying the referenced stereotype.

If an AT role is bound to an architectural element, the following conditions must be met before an architectural analysis can be started:

- all constraints of the AT role have to hold and
- the completion of the AT is able to refine the bound architectural element with additional architectural elements if such elements are needed to conform to the represented architectural knowledge.

If no completion is specified, the semantics of an applied role are solely determined by its constraints (and vice-versa). A role that contains neither constraints nor a completion is invalid. For usability purposes, architecture modeling tools of software architects can prevent software architects from constraint violations and point to already existing constraint violations as exemplified in Figure 4.2.

Moreover, the semantics of the attributes of the Role metaclass are as follows. The id attribute is a unique identifier of a role, thus, suited as identifier for roles within tools. The entityName attribute represents a human readable (but not necessarily unique) version of this identifier. The entityName of a role is, thus, a convenient mean for AT engineers and software architects to identify a role.

AT tooling (Section 4.3) serves as a reference implementation for integrating constraint checks, executing completions, and for applying roles via stereotypes.

Concrete Syntax Table 4.4 illustrates the concrete syntax of AT roles. Different notions can be used depending on whether a role contains constraints, formal parameters, and a completion.

The first row in Table 4.4 shows a role without constraints and parameters. A role is depicted as dashed box where the top left of the box contains the role name (e.g., "Role") prepended with an @-symbol.

The second row in Table 4.4 shows a role with constraints. In addition to the notion in the first row, a role's box contains a straight horizontal line with its constraints displayed underneath. Each constraint starts with a bold text "inv" (an abbreviation for "invariant" in the style of OCL expressions) followed by the constraint's name and a colon. In the next line, a representative expression for the constraint follows. This expression can, for instance, be an OCL expression (cf. Section 2.3.6). The example in Table 4.4

Table 4.4.: Role notations

Metaclass	Notation	Description
Role	**@Role**	A role with the name “Role”.
Role	**@Role** **inv** constraint 1: expression 1 **inv** constraint 2: expression 2 ...	A role with constraints. The name of each constraint (“constraint 1”, “constraint 2”, etc.) is depicted after a bold “inv” (invariant) text. Each concrete constraint is visualized via a textual expression (“expression 1”, “expression 2”, etc.). For example, an OCL expression can be used as expression.
Role	**@Role (** parameter 1 : type 1, parameter 2 : type 2, ... **)**	A role with formal parameters “parameter 1” of type “type 1”, “parameter 2” of type “type 2”, etc. Technically, formal parameters are realized as tagged values of stereotypes; accordingly the names and types of tagged values are illustrated.
Role	**@Role** ⇨ completion.qvto	A role with a completion referencing a QVT-O transformation located at “completion.qvto”.

shows two constraints named “constraint 1” and “constraint 2” and with the expressions “expression 1” respectively “expression 2”.

The third row in Table 4.4 shows a role with formal parameters. In addition to the notion in the first row, a role’s name is appended with an opening and a closing parenthesis. Between these parentheses, formal role parameters are denoted as a comma-separated list. For each formal parameter, its name and its type separated by a colon are given. Technically, parameters (including names and types) are derived from the tagged values of a role’s referenced stereotype. The example in Table 4.4 shows two parameters named “parameter 1” and “parameter 2” and with the type “type 1” respectively “type 2”.

The fourth row in Table 4.4 shows a role with a completion. In addition to the notion in the first row, a role's box contains a straight horizontal line with its completion displayed underneath. A completion starts with a bold arrow-symbol followed by the location of the completion's transformation file. The example in Table 4.4 shows a completion that references the QVT-O transformation “completion.qvto”.

A role can contain constraints, formal parameters, and a completion altogether. The corresponding notions can therefore be combined.

4.2.5.5. Metamodel: Constraint

AT constraints specify what software architects are forbidden to change in a software architecture (cf. [JB05]). Such restrictions prescribe software architects possible design decisions, which can ensure that architectural design remains sound. AT constraints can, thus, formalize reusable architectural knowledge applied to an architectural model. These constraints can then ensure the conformance to the architectural knowledge by prohibiting design decisions that would violate conformance.

Technically, constraints can be formulated via different constraint languages, e.g., via the OCL (Section 2.3.6), Alloy [Jac12], B [Abr96], VDM [Jon90], and Z [Spi92]. The AT language and AT tooling (cf. Section 4.3) are exemplified with constraints formulated in OCL. In contrast to the other constraint languages, OCL has the advantage that it is integrated with UML and, thus, the best-known language to software architects [Abr96, p. 303]. Moreover, the applicability and suitability of OCL for formalizing architectural constraints has been shown by Tibermacine et al. [TFS10a].

In the AT language, the extensibility for different constraint languages is acknowledged by defining an abstract metaclass for constraints. A dedicated subclass is used for adding support for OCL constraints; alternatives like Alloy may be realized analogously. Furthermore, constraints have a unique identifier and a name for selection purposes (cf. the AT language's intension in Table 4.1).

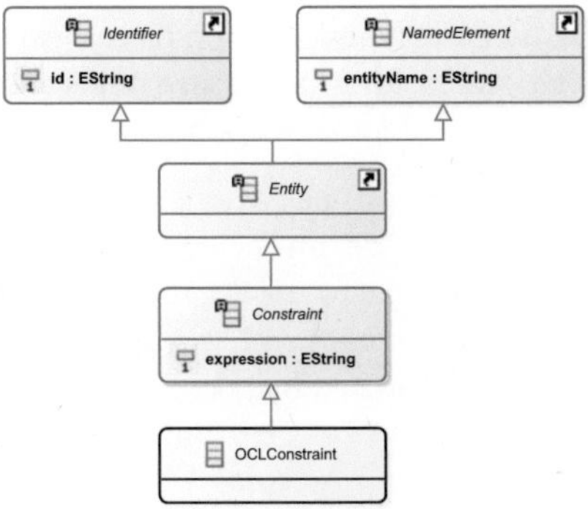

Figure 4.12.: The abstract metaclass Constraint inherits from Entity. The metaclass OCLConstraint realizes a concrete Constraint.

Abstract Syntax Figure 4.12 illustrates the metaclass Constraint that realizes the concept of AT constraints.

The metaclass Constraint is abstract to acknowledge for different kinds of constraints, e.g., OCL constraints. The attribute expression holds a corresponding string representation of an OCL constraint. Moreover, Constraint inherits from Entity, which provides Constraint with attributes for a unique identifier and a name. Entity and its superclasses are detailed for the Catalog metaclass in Section 4.2.5.2.

The metaclass OCLConstraint inherits from Constraint, thus, realizing a concrete constraint kind. OCLConstraint represents constraints formulated via OCL (cf. Section 2.3.6). The attribute expression of an OCLConstraint holds a corresponding string representation of an OCL constraint. Accordingly, OCL syntax and semantics [Obj14] hold for this expression.

Semantics A constraint specifies a restriction for elements of an architectural model. Software architects can evaluate whether such a constraint holds for a given architectural model.

The evaluation context of a constraint is the AT role that contains the constraint. Starting from this context, AT engineers specify restrictions on the role itself, on the bound element, and on directly and indirectly related elements and roles. A constraint's expression holds an evaluation rule for such restrictions.

For instance, an OCL constraint—i.e., a concrete variant of a constraint—must hold an OCL expression within the expression attribute. An example constraint can easily be formulated for the number of replicas of the load-balancer in Figure 4.4. The number of replicas should be strictly greater than zero because a loadbalancer always needs at least one component attached. In OCL, this constraint can be formulated as self.numberOfReplicas > 0 in the context of the associated AT role.

In case the evaluation of a constraint indicates a violation of the restriction, software architects are informed about this violation. For convenience, software architects are provided with the constraint's name. If software architects need more details, they can inspect the concrete expression of a constraint.

AT tooling (Section 4.3) exemplifies constraint evaluations for OCL constraints. AT tooling also serves as a reference implementation for such evaluations.

Concrete Syntax Table 4.5 shows the concrete syntax of AT constraints.

Table 4.5.: Constraint notation

Metaclass	Notation	Description
Constraint	**inv** constraint name: expression	A constraint named "constraint name" is depicted after a bold "inv" (invariant) text. After a colon, the constraint's textual expression is denoted underneath, e.g., formulated in OCL.

Table 4.5 shows that a constraint is denoted with a textual syntax similar to OCL. A constraint starts with a bold text "inv" (an abbreviation for "invariant" in the style of OCL expressions) followed by the constraint's name and a colon. In the next line, the constraint's expression is given. This expression can, for instance, be an OCL expression as exemplified in the previous paragraph about constraint semantics.

4.2.5.6. Metamodel: Completion

In the AT method, completions (cf. Section 2.5.2.2) integrate QoS-relevant elements and attributes into architectural models to which AT roles have been bound. The QoS-relevant elements and attributes are inherent to the architectural knowledge captured by the associated AT role. For instance, the *loadbalanced container* role in Figure 4.4 refines the bound resource container with a loadbalancer—its completion expresses this refinement formally.

Like constraints that can be formulated in various constraint languages, completions can be realized with various M2M transformation languages, e.g., QVT-O (Section 2.3.2) and ATL [JABK08]. The AT language and AT tooling (cf. Section 4.3) are exemplified with completions formulated in QVT-O for the reasons given in Section 2.3.2. Still, the AT language acknowledges for extensions with different transformation languages by defining the metaclass for completions as abstract. A dedicated subclass is used for adding support for QVT-O completions; alternatives like ATL may be realized analogously.

Abstract Syntax Figure 4.13 illustrates the metaclass Completion that realizes the concept of completions of AT roles.

Completion is abstract to acknowledge for different kinds of M2M languages. The attribute completionFileURI of a Completion references the location of the corresponding transformation file via a uniform resource identifier (URI). QVTOCompletion inherits from Completion, thus, realizing a concrete completion kind for completions formulated via QVT-O (cf. Section 2.3.2).

Moreover, a Completion has one or more parameters that describe which models a completion uses. The metaclass CompletionParameter is abstract to acknowledge for different types of concrete parameters. Concrete parameters differ in their kind of use (input or output), supported metamodels (e.g., the PCM), and how parameters are received (for input parameters) respectively stored (for output parameters). Given these characteristics, parameters become part of a completion's transformation contract (cf. Section 2.3.3.1).

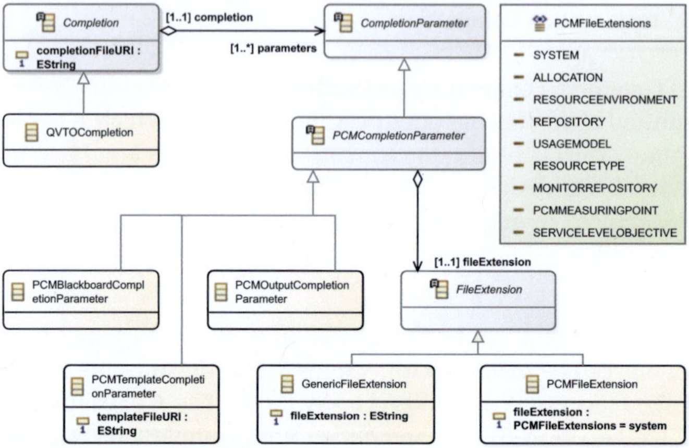

Figure 4.13.: The abstract metaclass Completion contains one or more parameters, which can be of different kinds. The metaclass QVTOCompletion realizes a concrete Completion.

The subclasses of CompletionParameter shown in Figure 4.13 are all specific to Palladio. During Palladio-based analyses, models are stored in and received from a blackboard. A model from the blackboard is identified by the file extension of the model (conceptually, this corresponds to the identification via a metamodel). Therefore, the subclass PCMCompletionParameter contains a fileExtension. Common PCM file extensions like "system" for PCM system models are captured in the PCMFileExtensions enumeration, which is used as fileExtension type for the PCMFileExtension metaclass. Other file extensions are generically covered by typing fileExtension as a string for the GenericFileExtension metaclass.

PCMCompletionParameter is abstract because it lacks information about how models are received and stored. Its subclasses introduce this information:

- PCMBlackboxCompletionParameter receives a model from the blackboard of Palladio. Changes to the model of the completion are stored on the blackboard.

- PCMTemplateCompletionParameter loads a template model to Palladio's blackboard and then proceeds like PCMBlackboxCompletionParameter. The templateFileURI attribute references the location of the corresponding template model via a URI.
- PCMOutputCompletionParameter is created as completion output and then stored on Palladio's blackboard.

Semantics Completions specify further semantics of AT roles (i.e., in addition to constraints). While constraint semantics rely on the applied constraint language, completion semantics rely on the applied M2M transformation language for specifying completions, the execution of the completion, and the requirements of the AT method to a completion's in- and output models.

Semantics of the applied M2M language are defined by the transformation language itself. For example, the QVT specification [Obj16] describes the semantics of QVT-O.

Moreover, if an AT role with a completion is bound to an architectural model, the completion is executed prior to the architectural model's transformation to a QoS analysis model (as described in Section 4.1.2). If several roles with completions are bound to an architectural model, all of these completions are executed in their binding order (however, software architects may change this order by using editors for AT application).

Furthermore, the AT method requires that:

- the input model of a completion is an architectural model to which the completion's role has been bound,
- the output model of a completion is an architectural model extended by a role's induced QoS-relevant elements and attributes,
- the output model of a completion, i.e., the extended architectural model, has well-defined semantics in the architectural modeling language regarding the completion's extensions.

The last requirement assures that tools for architectural analyses can process the extended architectural model. Because completions map to models with well-defined semantics, completions define semantics of AT roles in a translational way (cf. Section 2.3.5). That is, the completion maps the bounded role—for which semantics have to be defined—to a semantically equivalent architectural model. This model expresses the induced elements and attributes in terms of a well-defined architectural modeling language. For this reason, the extended architectural model can be analyzed with QoS analysis tools.

Concrete Syntax Table 4.6 illustrates the concrete syntax of AT completions.

Table 4.6.: Completion notations

Metaclass	Notation	Description
Completion	⇨ completion.qvto	A completion is depicted as a bold arrow-symbol followed by its file URI, e.g., referencing a QVT-O transformation "completion.qvto".

Table 4.6 shows that a completion is denoted with a bold arrow-symbol because arrows are common for visualizing model transformations. After the arrow-symbol, the URI of the transformation file's location is denoted. The example in Table 4.6 shows a completion for which a QVT-O transformation file is located at "completion.qvto".

The concrete syntax of the referenced transformation depends on the concrete transformation language. For example, the QVT specification [Obj16] describes a textual concrete syntax for QVT-O.

4.2.5.7. Metamodel: Stereotype (Formal Parameters and Role Bindings)

Each AT role references a stereotype (cf. Section 4.2.4.2) that:

- provides roles with formal parameters via tagged values and
- allows to bind roles to architectural elements via profile applications.

Regarding the AT language's intension (cf. Table 4.1), a referenced stereotype thus realizes an AT role's attribute "has formal parameters". Stereotypes are particularly a prerequisite for software architect to apply corresponding profiles to their architectural models. In a profile application, an AT instance's attributes "has bindings between architectural elements and AT roles" and "bindings have actual parameters" are realized because profile applications specify where and which stereotypes are applied, including an assignment of actual parameters to their tagged values (cf. Section 2.3.4). Section 4.2.5.8 details profile applications.

As described in Section 4.2.4.2, AT roles reference stereotypes of the EMF profile metamodel [LWWC12] that provides an adaptation of UML profiles [Obj11, Chap. 18] for metamodels specified via EMF's Ecore metamodel, e.g., the PCM and the AT metamodel. The PCM particularly has full support for EMF profiles [KDH+12], which allows for lightweight extensions of the PCM with ATs.

The following paragraphs describe the abstract syntax, semantics, and concrete syntax of profiles and stereotypes of the EMF profile metamodel. Additionally, the relation to ATs and AT roles is detailed.

Abstract Syntax Figure 4.14 illustrates the metaclasses Profile and Stereotype that realizes the concept of EMF Profile's profiles and stereotypes.

The metaclasses of the EMF Profile metamodel (Figure 4.14 bottom) extend metaclasses of ECore, i.e., EMF's metamodel (Figure 4.14 top). Extended metaclasses provide the basic mechanisms for profiles to contain stereotypes and for stereotypes to extend metaclasses and to contain tagged values.

As described in the note in Figure 4.14, a Profile instance needs to reference an AT. Given a profile (respectively its application), this reference allows to identify the represented AT (respectively its AT instance). Furthermore, the metaclass Profile inherits from EPackage, which allows a Profile to contain a set of EClassifier instances. Because Stereotype (indirectly) inherits from EClassifier, a Profile can particularly contain a set of Stereotype instances. The operation getStereotypes of Profile returns these instances as a result. Likewise, a Stereotype provides the operation getProfile to return its containing Profile.

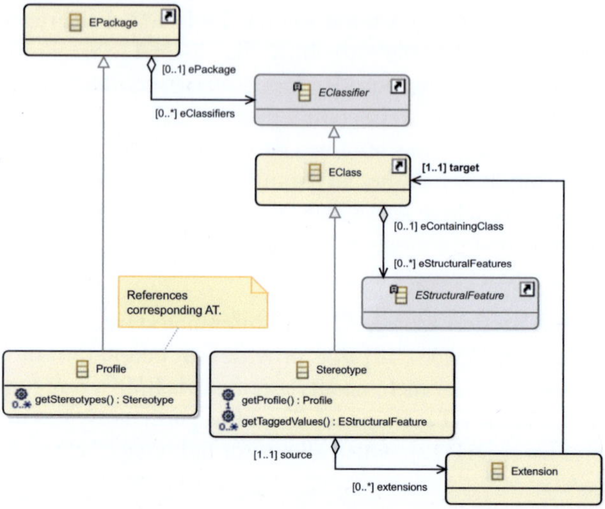

Figure 4.14.: The metamodel of EMF Profiles extends metaclasses of the metamodel of EMF. This extension enables a Profile to reference its corresponding AT and to contain Stereotypes. A Stereotype contains tagged values (realized as EStructuralFeatures) and extends metaclasses (EClasses) that are referenced via contained Extensions.

Stereotype directly inherits from EClass and can, thus, contain a set of EStructuralFeature instances. An EStructuralFeature allows to specify a typed attribute, e.g., a parameter of a method or a member variable of a class [SBPM09, Sec. 5.3]. In the EMF Profile metamodel, Stereotype uses instances of EStructuralFeature to specify tagged values. The operation getTaggedValues of Stereotype provides these instances as a result. In the context of the AT language, these tagged values correspond to formal parameters of AT roles.

Moreover, a Stereotype contains extensions that specify which metaclasses the Stereotype extends. The target of an Extension references the extended metaclass (in ECore typed as EClass).

Semantics The EMF metamodel defines profiles as extensions of EMF-based metamodels. A profile's stereotypes define how and which metaclasses can be extended by applications of these stereotypes. As stated in Definition 2.24, a stereotype's extension can extend metaclasses by platform or domain specific terminology, e.g., by role names of reusable architectural knowledge as in the AT method. A stereotype's tagged values further enrich extended metaclasses by additional attributes, e.g., used to specify formal parameters of AT roles. A profile particularly references the concrete AT that the profile and its stereotypes represent.

Further details on the semantics of EMF profiles are provided by Langer et al. [LWWC12]. Langer et al. detail the semantics both in natural language and in a pragmatic way via a reference implementation.

Concrete Syntax AT engineers can specify profiles and stereotypes in a dedicated view, thus, demanding a concrete syntax of profiles and stereotypes. Once specified and referenced by an AT role, a stereotype and its tagged values can, however, be denoted as part of the AT role (as described in Section 4.2.5.4).

EMF profiles' concrete syntax for profiles and stereotypes [LWWC12] follows UML's notion for profiles and stereotypes [Obj11, Chap. 18]. Table 4.7 illustrates this concrete syntax.

The first row in Table 4.7 shows that a profile is denoted via UML's package symbol. The top rectangle of the package symbol includes the name of the profile prepended with the "profile" string in guillemets (« and »). The stereotypes contained by a profile are denoted—according to their own concrete syntax—inside the bottom rectangle of the package symbol. The example in Table 4.7 shows a profile named "Profile Name" that contains the stereotypes "Stereotype 1" and "Stereotype 2".

The second row in Table 4.7 shows a stereotype without tagged values. Such a stereotype is depicted as a rectangle that contains the stereotype's name in bold; located underneath the "stereotype" string in guillemets. The example in Table 4.7 shows a stereotype named "Stereotype Name".

The third row in Table 4.7 shows a stereotype with tagged values. In addition to the notion in the second row, a stereotype's rectangle contains a straight horizontal line with its tagged values displayed underneath. For each tagged value, its name and its type separated by a colon are given.

Table 4.7.: Profile, stereotype, and extension notations

Metaclass	Notation	Description
Profile (for ATs)	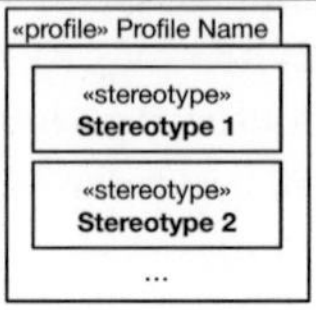	A profile is depicted as a UML package symbol. In the top rectangle of the package symbol, the string "profile" in guillemets followed by the profile's name "Profile Name" is included. Inner rectangles depict the contained stereotypes named "Stereotype 1", "Stereotype 2", etc.
Stereotype (for AT roles)		A stereotype is depicted using a rectangle that includes the string "stereotype" in guillemets and gives the stereotype's name "Stereotype Name" underneath in bold.
Stereotype (for AT roles)	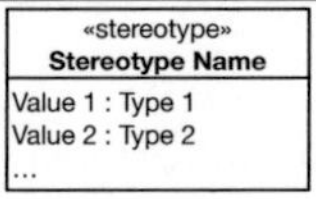	A stereotype with tagged values "Value 1" of type "Type 1", "Value 2" of type "Type 2", etc. for each EStructuralFeature contained by the stereotype.
Extension		An extension is denoted as an arrow with a black-filled head. The arrow starts at an extension's source Stereotype and ends an extension's target EClass.

The example in Table 4.7 shows two tagged values named "Value 1" and "Value 2" and with the type "Type 1" respectively "Type 2".

The fourth row in Table 4.7 shows the notion of an extension. An extension is illustrated as an arrow with a black-filled arrow head. The source role of the Extension metaclass references the Stereotype at which the arrow starts. The target role of the Extension metaclass references the EClass at which the arrow ends.

4.2.5.8. Metamodel: Profile Application (AT Instances)

An AT instance is the application of an AT to an architectural model. Because there can be several AT applications for a single AT, the AT classifies these AT instances (attribute "AT instance classified by ATs" of the AT language's intension in Table 4.1). Software architects realize AT applications by specifying a binding between an AT's roles and the architectural elements of the architectural model where the roles are applied on (attribute "AT instance has bindings between architectural elements and AT roles" in Table 4.1). Such bindings particularly specify the actual parameters for the formal parameters of AT roles (attribute "AT instance bindings have actual parameters" in Table 4.1).

While AT instances are a conceptual part of the AT language, the AT metamodel does not have a dedicated AT instance metaclass for their technical realization. Instead, Section 4.2.4 argues that AT instances are technically realized as profile applications.

The principle idea behind this realization is that profile applications describe where and which stereotypes are applied to a model, including an assignment of actual parameters to their tagged values. Because each AT role references exactly one stereotype, a corresponding profile application to an architectural model (indirectly) binds the AT role to an architectural element. In particular, because an AT role's formal parameters are realized as tagged values of the referenced stereotype (cf. Section 4.2.5.7), a corresponding profile application assigns actual parameters to the formal parameters of the AT role.

Similar to the use of stereotypes of the EMF profile metamodel by AT roles (cf. Section 4.2.5.7), the realization of AT instances is based on profile applications of the EMF profile metamodel. The following paragraphs describe the abstract syntax and semantics of these profile applications, including the relation to AT instances. For the concrete syntax, a dedicated notion for AT instances is introduced.

Abstract Syntax Figure 4.15 illustrates the metaclasses ProfileApplication and StereotypeApplication that realize the concept of EMF Profile's profile applications.

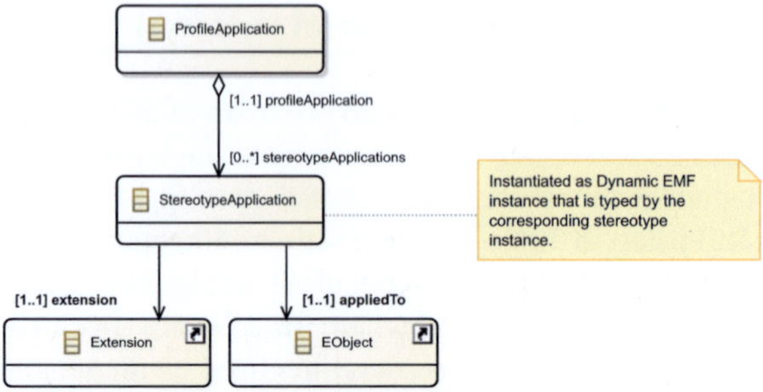

Figure 4.15.: A ProfileApplication contains stereotypeApplications. A StereotypeApplication applies a Stereotype (referenced via its Extension) to an EObject. Moreover, a StereotypeApplication is dynamically instantiated from a corresponding Stereotype instance, which allows StereotypeApplication to assign actual parameters to tagged values.

The metaclass ProfileApplication conceptually corresponds to the application of an AT (i.e., ProfileApplication realizes the concept of AT instances). Furthermore, a ProfileApplication contains an arbitrary number of stereotypeApplications.

A StereotypeApplication conceptually corresponds to the application of an AT role to an architectural element. The StereotypeApplication references the Extension of a stereotype that represents the AT role (cf. the metamodel for stereotypes in Section 4.2.5.7). The concrete AT role can, thus, be derived by navigating from the Stereotype associated to the Extension over the containing Profile and the referenced AT to the AT's Role that references the Stereotype.

A StereotypeApplication's appliedTo reference identifies the architectural element to which the AT role is applied. The appliedTo reference points to exactly one EObject. Because each EMF-based metaclass inherits from EObject, a StereotypeApplication can thus reference arbitrary elements of architectural models specified in an EMF-based language. The PCM is realized based on EMF and therefore fulfills this prerequisite.

Moreover, a StereotypeApplication needs to assign actual parameters to the tagged values defined in a Stereotype instance. As described in the note in Figure 4.15, EMF profiles realize such assignments using the Dynamic

EMF instantiation mechanism [SBPM09, Sec. 14.3]. Because AT engineers specify the tagged values of stereotypes at run time, also the concrete data model—that includes the concrete tagged values—for a stereotype instance is only known at run time. In such situations, Dynamic EMF allows to create a run time object that is typed by the stereotype instance. This dynamically created object then provides the means to assign actual parameters to the tagged values of its type (i.e., the stereotype instance). To create a StereotypeApplication instance, first such a dynamic object needs to be created and then the remaining attributes that make up a StereotypeApplication (i.e., the referenced Extension and EObject) can be initialized.

Semantics A profile application specifies which elements of a model are extended according to the stereotypes of a profile. Extended elements are marked with the stereotype, which provides additional type information. Moreover, extended elements can assign actual parameters to the tagged values defined in the stereotype.

In the AT language, a profile application represents the concept of an AT instance. Because each stereotype has a corresponding AT role, the application of such a stereotype represents the binding of an AT role. Similarly, the assignment of actual parameters to a stereotype's tagged values corresponds to the assignment of actual parameters to an AT role's formal parameters.

Further details on the semantics of EMF profile applications are provided by Langer et al. [LWWC12]. Langer et al. detail the semantics both in natural language and in a pragmatic way via a reference implementation.

Concrete Syntax Software architects specify AT instances (via profile applications) directly in their editors for architectural models. Accordingly, AT instances need a concrete syntax for their representation in such editors.

Because AT instances are realized via profile applications, UML's notion for profile applications [Obj11, Sec. 18.3.9] can easily be adapted for illustrating AT instances. The UML describes three alternative notion options:

the external notion annotates a model element outside of the element's graphic node,

the internal/joined notion annotates a model element inside of the element's graphic node joined above the element's name, and

the internal/separated notion annotates a model element inside of the element's graphic node via a separated compartment.

Table 4.8 describes all of these notion options for AT instances.

Table 4.8.: Profile Application notations for AT instances

Metaclass	Notation	Description
ProfileApplication (for AT instances)	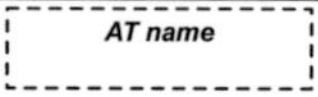	An AT instance (which is represented using a profile application) is depicted as a dashed rectangle. The rectangle includes the name "AT name" of the referenced AT at the middle top and in a bold and italic font.
StereotypeApplication (for AT role bindings)	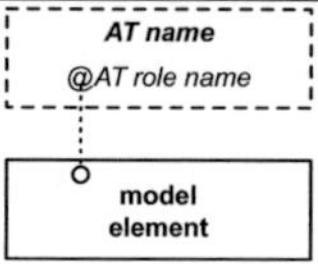	The external notion of an AT role binding (as represented by a stereotype application). The name of the AT role "AT role name" is denoted as part of the containing AT instance "AT name" (represented by a profile application) and in an italic font. The name is prepended with the @-symbol and linked to the target model element named "model element" with a dashed line that ends with a circle.

StereotypeApplication (for AT role bindings)	*@AT role name* **model element**	Internal/joined notion of an AT role binding (represented by a stereotype application). The role name “AT role name” is given above the name of the target model element named “model element”. The name is prepended with the @-symbol.
StereotypeApplication (for AT role bindings)	*@AT role name* **model element**	Internal/separated notion of an AT role binding (represented by a stereotype application). The name of the AT role “AT role name” is given within a separate compartment (visualized as rectangle) of the target model element named “model element”. The AT role name is prepended with the @-symbol.
StereotypeApplication (for actual parameters)	*@AT role name (* *parameter 1 = value 1,* *parameter 2 = value 2,* *...* *)*	A binding of an AT role named “AT role name” with actual parameters for the external and internal/joined notions. The binding assigns “value 1” to “parameter 1”, “value 2” to “parameter 2”, etc. for each EStructuralFeature contained by the Stereotype representing the AT role.

StereotypeApplication (for actual parameters)	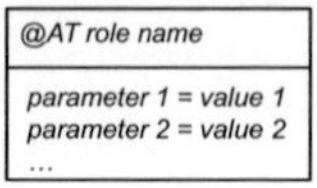	A binding of an AT role named "AT role name" with actual parameters for the internal/separated notion. The binding assigns "value 1" to "parameter 1", "value 2" to "parameter 2", etc. for each EStructuralFeature contained by the Stereotype representing the AT role.

The first row in Table 4.8 shows that an AT instance (realized as profile application) is denoted as a dashed rectangle; similar to UML's symbol for template class parameters [Obj11, Sec. 17.4.7]. The rectangle contains the name of the AT that belongs to the AT instance (a profile application references its corresponding profile, which in turn references the AT). The name is denoted in a bold and italic font. The example in Table 4.8 shows an AT application of an AT named "AT name". In the book shop example in Section 3.2.4, the ATs named "three-layer" and "loadbalancing" are applied.

The second row in Table 4.8 shows an AT role binding (realized as stereotype application) in the external notion. Accordingly, the bound role is annotated outside of the graphic node of the bound model element. While the UML suggests an annotation within a dedicated comment symbol (cf. [Obj11, Sec. 18.3.9]), bindings of AT roles are annotated in the rectangle of the corresponding AT instance. The annotation is realized using the name of the bound AT role prepended with an @-symbol. Embedding bound roles in the AT instance's rectangle has the advantage that bound roles can easily be associated to their corresponding ATs. The reference to the targeted model element is then visualized using a dashed line that ends with a circle. The example in Table 4.8 shows an AT role binding of an AT role named "AT role name" of an AT named "AT name" that is bound to a model element named "model element". The book shop example in Section 3.2.4 uses the external notion for illustrating role bindings of the ATs named "three-layer" and "loadbalancing".

The third row in Table 4.8 shows an AT role binding (realized as stereotype application) in the internal/joined notion. Accordingly, the bound role is annotated inside of the graphic node of the bound model element. In accordance to the UML (cf. [Obj11, Sec. 18.3.9]), the name (prepended with an @-symbol) of the bound AT role is directly attached above the name of the targeted model element. The example in Table 4.8 shows an AT role binding of an AT role named "AT role name" that is bound to a model element named "model element".

The fourth row in Table 4.8 shows an AT role binding (realized as stereotype application) in the internal/separated notion. The notion is similar to the internal/joined notion. The only difference is that the annotation is located in a separate compartment (i.e., a surrounding rectangle).

The fifth row in Table 4.8 shows an AT role binding with actual parameters; such a notion is suited in conjunction with the external notion and the internal/joined notion. For each formal parameter of the bound AT, the parameter name and a value conforming to the parameter type are given (separated by a colon). The example in Table 4.8 shows two actual parameters that assign "value 1" to "parameter 1" and "value 2" to "parameter 2".

The sixth row in Table 4.8 shows an AT role binding with actual parameters; such a notion is suited in conjunction with the external notion and the internal/joined notion. The notion is similar to the previously described alternative notion but contains a dedicated inner compartment for visualizing the assignment of actual parameters.

4.3. Architectural Template Tooling

A typical mean of a method are tools (cf. Section 2.1.4.1). Tools help engineers to follow the processes of a method effectively, efficiently, and consistently, e.g., by automating process actions and by technically realizing method artifacts. Another benefit of tools is that they can define the semantics of method artifacts in a pragmatic way, i.e., in the form of a reference implementation (cf. Section 2.3.5).

Therefore, the AT method provides an accompanying set of tools—the AT tooling [ATt]. AT tooling extends Palladio (cf. Section 2.5.3) by a wizard for AT-based instantiation of architectural models, an engine that executes AT mappings specified as in-place QVT Operational (QVT-O) model transformations (cf. Section 2.3.2), and editors for AT specification and application, including constraint checks via OCL (cf. Section 2.3.6). Palladio has the advantage that it is suited for software architects and supports several QoS metrics (cf. Section 2.5.3). Palladio therefore serves for illustrating and evaluating the AT method for a particular architectural analysis approach. Moreover, AT tooling provides a reference implementation for the AT metamodel (Section 4.2.5), thus defining the metamodel's semantics (in the preceding section informally described in natural language) in a pragmatic way. Appendix B provides details on AT tooling.

4.4. Extensions of the Architectural Template Method

The preceding sections describe the AT method's core. This section describes extensions to this core that make AT engineers and software architects even more efficient.

For making AT engineers more efficient, Openkowski [Ope17] introduces a reuse mechanism for ATs. This mechanism allows to derive new ATs from existing ones.

For making software architects more efficient, I have integrated the optimization framework PerOpteryx [KKR11] into the AT method. The integration allows software architects to automatically determine optimal configurations for AT parameters using evolutionary algorithms, thus, saving effort to determine such parameters manually.

Openkowski's reuse mechanism is described in Section 4.4.1. Afterwards, Section 4.4.2 details the integration of the optimization framework. An evaluation—indicating the effectiveness of both extensions—is provided in Section 5.5.

4.4.1. Reuse Mechanism for AT Specification

In his Master's thesis [Ope17], Openkowski introduces a reuse mechanism for the specification of ATs. The mechanism allows AT engineers to specify child AT roles that inherit properties from one or more parent AT roles, i.e., realizing multiple inheritance on the level of AT roles. Inherited properties are parameters, constraints, and completions of parent AT roles.

For example, an AT engineer may specify an AT that enriches the *load-balancing* AT with a cache in front of the loadbalancer (cf. the caching architectural pattern [BHS07a, Sec. 7.10]). In this case, a new role *cached and loadbalanced container* can, for instance, inherit from the *loadbalanced container* role while providing an additional completion to attach a cache in front of the loadbalancer.

In detail, Openkowski has extended each means of the AT method (AT processes, AT language, and AT tooling) as follows:

Extension of AT processes: For specifying ATs based on reuse mechanisms, only the AT specification process from Section 4.1.3 requires an extension. More precisely, only action (3), i.e., the specification of ATs (with parametrizable roles, constraints, completions), requires an extension: AT engineers are additionally required to identify reuse opportunities and, in case such opportunities exist, to specify appropriate role inheritance relationships to existing AT roles (cf. [Ope17, Sec. 7.2] for details).

Extension of AT language: Openkowski has extended the metamodel of AT roles from Section 4.2.5.4 as illustrated in Figure 4.16.

The Role metaclass includes a new association superRoles to itself, thus, allowing to specify parent roles for roles. A role can have an arbitrary number of parent roles, thus, particularly allowing to specify multiple-inheritance relationships. The association roleIncludingInherited is a derived attribute—an ordered set of all roles directly and indirectly accessible from a role via superRoles united with the role itself. The C3 linearization algorithm [BCH+96] is used for obtaining the order. The algorithm assures that the linearization does not reorder the linearizations of its parent roles and avoids the diamond problem (cf. [Ope17, Sec. 7.4]).

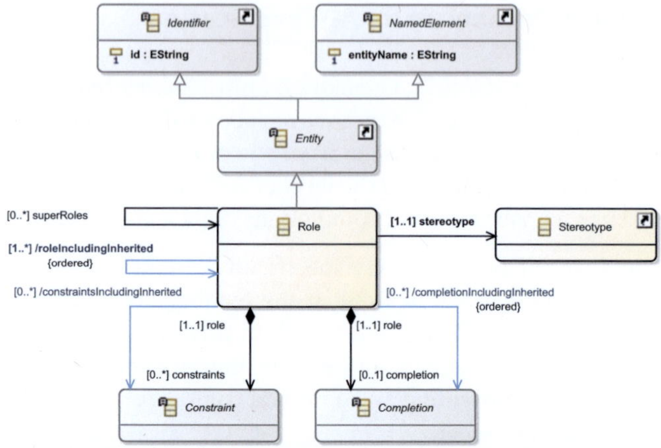

Figure 4.16.: The metaclass Role is extended by a new self-association superRoles that allows to specify inheritance relationships. Based on this relationship, the associations roleIncludingInherited, constraintsIncludingInherited, and completionIncludingInherited can be derived.

Semantically, when a role inherits from one or more other roles, their sets of parameters and constraints are united. While parameter union is modeled via stereotypes inheriting from other stereotypes (cf. [Ope17, Sec. 8.3.4]), constraint union is modeled by the derived attribute constraintsIncludingInherited as shown in Figure 4.16.

Completions, in contrast, are orchestrated to be executed one after the other [Ope17, Sec. 7.4]. The set of inherited completions must therefore be ordered. For this ordering, the C3 linearization order as described above is used. The derived attribute completionIncludingInherited includes the resulting ordered set of completions.

More detailed semantics and a concrete syntax are provided by Openkowski [Ope17, Sec. 7.4–Sec. 8.2].

Extension of AT tooling: Openkowski and I have fully integrated the reuse mechanism for AT specification in AT tooling. Our integration covers the extended metamodel, the implementation of the C3 linearization algorithm to determine derived attributes, modified conformance checks to check against inherited constraints, and an extended AT integration support to orchestrate the execution of completions. Openkowski provides details on this integration in his Master's thesis [Ope17, Sec. 8.3].

4.4.2. Optimization of Actual AT Parameters

This section overviews an extension of the AT method that allows to optimize AT-based architectural models. The optimization is realized based on an integration of the PerOpteryx optimization framework [KKR11] into the AT method. The integration allows software architects to automatically determine optimal configurations of AT parameters. This automation makes software architects more efficient as parameters have not to be determined manually.

Koziolek et al. [KKR11] introduce PerOpteryx as an approach and framework for optimizing architectural models. PerOpteryx optimizes by automatically varying design decisions and assessing the impact on quality properties via architectural analyses. Variations are determined by evolutionary algorithms; given their suitability for multi-objective optimization [DK01].

Technically, the variations executed by PerOpteryx are formalized via so-called degrees of freedom [Koz11a, Sec. 6.3.2.2]. A degree of freedom specifies how to vary design decisions of a specific type. For example, design decisions of type "allocation" specify that allocation decisions can be varied over a given set of target resource containers.

For the integration of PerOpteryx in the AT method, I have introduced a new type of degree of freedom: a type for actual AT parameters. Actual AT parameters can be varied depending on their data types. For example, for the *loadbalancing* AT, actual parameters for the *number of replicas* may be automatically varied between 1 and 10. The rationale behind this new degree of freedom is that AT parameters, as part of captured reusable architectural knowledge, cover high-level architectural decisions with huge impact on QoS properties.

In detail, I have extended each means of the AT method (AT processes, AT language, and AT tooling) for the integration of PerOpteryx as follows:

Extension of AT processes: For enabling software architects to optimize AT parameters, the specification and analysis of architectural models (cf. Section 4.1.3) additionally requires an identification of concrete degrees of freedom and the configuration and execution of the optimization itself. Koziolek details these process extensions in her PhD thesis [Koz11a, Sec. 5.2].

Extension of AT language: For the integration of PerOpteryx, the AT language has required no extensions.

Extension of AT tooling: For the integration of AT tooling with PerOpteryx, PerOpteryx must be able to run Experiment Automation workflows (cf. Appendix B.2) and to use actual AT parameters as degree of freedom. I have implemented an appropriate PerOpteryx plug-in that lets PerOpteryx use Experiment Automation [Perb]. Moreover, I directly included the degree of freedom for actual AT parameters in the PerOpteryx framework [Pera].

4.5. Assumptions and Limitations of the Architectural Template Method

The AT method currently has several assumptions and limitations. The following list describes the most important ones.

Embedding AT-induced elements via completions. AT engineers specify completions to embed AT-induced elements into architectural models (action (3) in Section 4.1.3.2). Here, the AT method assumes that such elements can be expressed in the targeted architectural modeling language. Given this assumption, AT engineers can legitimately use completions to define AT semantics in a translational way (cf. Section 2.3.5).

However, AT engineers may want to specify ATs that induce elements that are inexpressible within the targeted architectural modeling language. For example, self-adaptive systems require elements to characterize self-adaptation rules; however, such elements do not exist, e.g., in Palladio. For this example, AT engineers cannot directly specify a legit completion that accurately covers the semantics of architectural knowledge for self-adaptation rules.

The lacking support for a special kind of architectural elements can motivate an extension of the targeted architectural modeling language. For example, the lack of elements to characterize self-adaptations in Palladio has motivated Palladio's extension of such elements (cf. Section 2.5.3.2). Once extended, the described expressibility assumption holds and AT engineers can legitimately specify semantic-preserving completions.

If the extension of the targeted architectural modeling language is no option, AT engineers may specify ATs that do not integrate AT-induced elements via completions. In this case, architectural analyses will not reflect any QoS-impacts of such elements. Still, such ATs can be useful for documenting decisions to apply a specific kind of reusable architectural knowledge. This way, at least subsequent development actions (as described in Section 2.5.1) can consider the applied architectural knowledge. For example, when deploying a system, system deployers may configure self-adaptations as specified by a software architect within an AT application.

Focus on QVT-O for completions. Completions can generally be implemented in various model transformation languages (Section 2.5.2.2). For example, the related work investigated in Section 6.4.2 uses completions implemented as graph transformations (Woodside et al. [WPS02]), QVT-R (L. Happe [Hap11]), QVT-O (J. Happe [Hap09] and Rathfelder [Rat13]), and completion components (a dedicated completion language introduced by Becker [Bec08]).

The AT language and AT tooling (cf. Section 4.3) are exemplified with completions formulated in QVT-O for the reasons given in Section 2.3.2. Still, the AT language acknowledges for extensions with different transformation languages by defining the metaclass for completions as abstract. A dedicated subclass is used for adding support for QVT-O completions; alternatives like Becker's completion components may be realized analogously.

Focus on Palladio for architectural analyses. The AT method is introduced as a method to extend architectural analyses (cf. Definition 4.2). However, the AT method currently focuses on Palladio as a concrete architectural analysis approach. While AT processes (Section 4.1) are described independently of Palladio, the AT language and AT tooling partly depend on Palladio:

- In the AT language, the metamodel for completions (described in Section 4.2.5.6) provides dedicated PCM parameters. Other approaches are required to provide their own parameters by extending the abstract CompletionParameter metaclass appropriately.
- In the AT tooling, the support for the application (Appendix B.1) and integration (Appendix B.2) of ATs is tailored to Palladio. Other approaches may add application support analogously.

Because there are only these direct dependencies to Palladio, the AT method is likely to suit other approaches as well. An indication for this suitability is given by the integration of the AT method not only with the Palladio approach but also with the CloudScale method [LB15b, BBL17]. However, a detailed evaluation of this kind of generalizability is left as a future work.

ATs are cross-cutting. ATs are cross-cutting architectural models both horizontally and vertically. Horizontally, ATs can impact elements of one level of abstraction, e.g., by constraining relationships between components of an architectural model's system. Vertically, ATs can impact elements between different levels of abstraction, e.g., by introducing a new component in an architectural model's system while allocating this component to a new resource container in an architectural model's resource environment.

The application of ATs to the online book shop in Section 4.1.2 exemplifies such cross-cuts. In the book shop, the constraints of the *three-layer* AT are checked against multiple components of the system model, i.e., horizontally. Moreover, the completion of the *loadbalancing* AT induces elements for both system and resource environments models, i.e., vertically. AT roles are particularly bound to elements of the system model and the resource environment model, thus, impacting multiple views on the architectural model.

Still, the cross-cutting characteristic of an AT captures a single concern: the formalization of a particular reusable architectural knowledge. In that sense, ATs conform to Dijkstra's "separation of concerns" [Dij82] principle. To integrate this concern, ATs weave knowledge-induced elements into architectural models (via completions) and allow to check constraints of the architectural model as a whole.

ATs are therefore similar to aspect-oriented [CB05] and view-based [ASB10, Bur14] modeling approaches[5]; and to aspectual templates (cf. Section 2.4.2) in particular. In contrast to some of these approaches, the AT method is however limited in visualizing AT-specific views, i.e., a single view that illustrate how the concern covered by an AT is applied to the targeted architectural model. For example, the related work COMLAN provides such a feature (see Section 6.3.4). Providing and analyzing specific views of AT applications is left as a future work.

AT tooling only covers systems and resource environments. The application support of AT tooling for ATs (Appendix B.1) is currently limited to PCM's system and resource environment editors. Software architects therefore have no integrated tool support to bind AT roles to other PCM models, e.g., PCM's allocation model.

The ATs evaluated in this thesis (Chapter 5) only had to be applied to system and resource environment models; the existing tool support was sufficient here. If ATs formalize architectural knowledge that impacts other PCM models, software architects may apply such ATs using Palladio's generic profiling mechanisms. In such a case, however, future works should optimally provide an integrated AT application support for such models like for system and resource environment editors due to an improved usability for software architects.

AT tooling lacks integrated support for AT specification. AT tooling's specification support for ATs (Appendix B.3) is currently restricted to generic tree-based editors and externally specified profiles, completions, and tests. An integrated specification environment for these

[5] Wimmer et al. [WSK+11] provide a survey of such approaches.

specifications potentially makes AT engineers more effective and efficient when specifying ATs. Such an environment should particularly support the concrete graphical syntax for ATs as described in Section 4.2.5.

Because the focus of this thesis is on the effectiveness and efficiency of software architects, I saved the effort to develop such an integrated environment. This development is therefore left as a future work.

"When you can measure what you are speaking about, and express it in numbers, you know something about it; but when you cannot express it in numbers, your knowledge is of a meagre and unsatisfactory kind."

— Lord Kelvin 1824 – 1907

5. Evaluation

In this chapter, I evaluate the AT method to derive lessons learned regarding its effectivity and efficiency. The main target groups of the evaluation are software architects and AT engineers because of their predominant role in the AT method. For deriving representative lessons learned, I focus on realistic software systems, e.g., a more detailed and realistic version of the book shop example from Chapter 3. Using the Goal-Question-Metric (GQM) template [BCR02], typically used to describe goals of empirical studies, the evaluation goal therefore is to:

Analyze: the AT method

For the purpose of: conducting architectural analyses

With respect to: effectivity and efficiency

From the viewpoint of: software architects and AT engineers

In the context of: realistic software systems.

In order to achieve this evaluation goal, I employ the empirical data collection procedures described in Section 2.1.3. Because the evaluation goal is set in the context of realistic software systems, I focus on case studies as a concrete data collection procedure. Additionally, I outline how a controlled experiment on the efficiency of software architects can be designed and describe a preliminary execution of this experiment.

The case studies are set in the domains of distributed computing, cloud computing, and big data. These domains cover the quality properties maintainability, performance, scalability, elasticity, and cost-efficiency. This coverage illustrates the generalizability of the AT method to various domains and quality properties.

For software architects, the evaluation results of the case studies indicate that the AT method can effectively and efficiently be applied: AT application is a matter of minutes while saving more than 90 % of recurring modeling efforts. This result is particularly confirmed by the preliminary controlled experiment. The evaluation of the optimization mechanism (i.e., the AT method extension described in Section 4.4.2) shows that AT parameters can automatically be optimized, thus, reducing efforts of software architects even more. However, in situations where software architects suspect bugs in ATs or AT tooling, software architects mistrust analysis results. This mistrust leads to effort-intensive analysis iterations to pin-point the causes of suspected bugs. The case studies reveal that mistrust is often (but not always) inappropriate because applied ATs reflect the corresponding reusable architectural knowledge correctly. In the evaluation of the AT method, an observed cause of mistrust was that the promised QoS improvements of applied knowledge were missed (judging based on analysis results). This miss has led software architects to suspecting bugs in ATs and AT tooling instead of context factors that rendered the applied knowledge inappropriate. For example, a software architect in one case study replicated a non-bottleneck resource and was expecting performance gains. After missing performance improvements, the software architect blamed the applied AT instead of inspecting further analysis results that would have revealed the bottleneck resource. The main derived lessons are that (1) AT tooling should be further improved to strengthen trust in its implementation (and to resolve actual bugs) and (2) software architects need further training in resolving unsuspected analysis results. Resolving these lessons is left as future work.

For AT engineers, the evaluation results of the case studies indicate that AT engineers can effectively create ATs but often need high efforts: evaluation results show that AT specification can take several person months. The benefits for software architects typically outweigh these efforts, especially if ATs are reused often. Observed causes for high efforts were difficulties in debugging ATs, lack of an integrated specification environment, and a missing support of reusing previously specified (elements of) ATs. The main derived lessons are that (1) AT tooling should be enriched with an integrated specification environment with debugging support and (2) reuse mechanisms for ATs need to be supported. The integrated environment (lesson (1)) is left as future work. However, after the conduction of the case studies, lesson (2) has led to the AT method extension of the reuse mechanisms for the specification of ATs described in Section 4.4.1. As the evaluation of this mechanism shows, the mechanism can increase productivity of AT engineers by over 200 %.

The remainder of this chapter is structured as follows. To establish a sound evaluation basis, Section 5.1 inspects previously conducted empirical studies. These studies show that software architects can apply architectural analyses effectively; however, inspections of involved efforts are often missing. Afterwards, Section 5.2 elaborates a generic GQM plan for evaluating the AT method. This plan is used for evaluating both the case studies and the controlled experiment. The case studies are described and discussed in Section 5.3. Subsequently, Section 5.4 outlines the controlled experiment and its preliminary conduction. Section 5.5 describes the evaluations of the extensions of the AT method (introduced in Section 4.4). Section 5.6 finally summarizes the lessons learned from all of these empirical investigations.

5.1. Related Studies

Following empirical evaluations reporting guidelines [JP05, JCP08, RH09], this section overviews earlier empirical studies related to architectural analyses. Such an overview of related studies clarifies the context and provides a sound evaluation basis [JCP08]. More general related work—without focus on empirical evidence—is described in Chapter 6.

Potential empirical evaluation approaches vary in their amount of qualitative vs. quantitative investigation [Bas07]. In the context of more qualitative studies, Section 5.1.1 describes related case studies. In the context of more quantitative studies, Section 5.1.2 describes related controlled experiments.

5.1.1. Related Case Studies

Several existing case studies on architectural analyses report their effectivity over various domains (e.g., business information systems) and technologies (e.g., virtualization). Section 5.1.1.1 describes such case studies with a focus on performance; the QoS property most closely related to the investigations in this chapter.[1] Despite its relevance, only few of the described case studies inspect the effort for architectural analyses as well. Section 5.1.1.2 summarizes the results of these inspections and concludes that currently no existing study inspects the impact on effort when exploiting reusable architectural knowledge.

5.1.1.1. Effectivity of Architectural Analyses

In their pioneering work on Software Performance Engineering (SPE) [SW02], Smith and Williams report the first successfully executed case studies on architectural analyses of performance. Their case studies cover the domains of business information systems for web applications and the financial sector, computer-aided design, distributed systems, and embedded real-time systems. They therefore show that architectural analyses are generally applicable to a variety of domains.

Smith and Williams particularly describe reusable architectural knowledge in the form of patterns [SW02, Chap. 10] and anti-patterns [SW02, Chap. 11]. Their case studies confirm the effectivity of exploiting such knowledge. However, opposed to the AT method, they require software architects to apply reusable architectural knowledge manually.

More closely related to this thesis, we have previously conducted a case study with Palladio (see Section 2.5.3) and within our virtualized on-premise infrastructure [LZ11]. For the four cases we consider, our architectural analysis provides accurate results (e.g., our prediction error regarding throughput was below 14 % on average), indicating that architectural analyses are applicable to virtualized environments. However, we have not investigated the application of reusable architectural knowledge during modeling.

[1] The described case studies have been systematically selected as described in [LB16].

Rathfelder et al. [RBKR12] also conduct a case study with Palladio but within a more realistic, industrial context: the e-mail system of the 1&1 Internet AG, which is Germany's largest e-mail provider. Their case study shows that Palladio is applicable in this realistic context while maintaining high accuracy (their prediction error regarding resource utilization was "mostly less than 10 %" [RBKR12]). Unfortunately, this case study does not inspect the exploitation of reusable architectural knowledge.

Huber et al. [HBR$^+$10b] provide further evidence for Palladio's applicability in industry within their case study on the IBM System z9 mainframe for storage virtualization. Their results indicate that Palladio accurately analyzes such virtualized environments because their prediction error regarding throughput is ~20 %. Again, no exploitation of reusable architectural knowledge is considered in this study.

De Gooijer et al. [dGJKK12] use Palladio to analyze an industrial distributed system from ABB with several million lines of code that is deployed in a virtualized environment. They provide further evidence that architectural analyses are applicable to such environments because their predictions regarding resource utilization deviate at most by 30 %. As the studies mentioned before, they do not describe the application of reusable architectural knowledge for creating their models.

5.1.1.2. Effort of Architectural Analyses

Both Rathfelder et al. [RBKR12] and Huber et al. [HBR$^+$10b] argue that software architects have to trade-off between analysis accuracy and modeling effort. While all authors from Section 5.1.1.1 describe means to lower such effort, quantifications of effort are only provided by Huber et al. [HBR$^+$10b], Smith and Williams [SW02], and Koziolek et al. [KSBH12] (who extend the work of de Gooijer et al. on the ABB case study [dGJKK12]):

Huber et al. [HBR$^+$10b] estimate that non-Palladio experts can create accurate performance models for similar systems like IBM System z9 with an effort of 4 person months.

Smith and Williams [SW02, p. 458] estimate that architectural analysis efforts may cause up to 10 % of total project costs. In a later work [WS03], they confirm this estimate by conducting a case study with an artificial business case where they estimate that one full-time performance engineer is needed in addition to a team of 15 developers.

Koziolek et al. [KSBH12] provide several effort estimates for the case study on ABB's system, i.e., for an existing system with several million lines of code. Their estimates include post-mortem estimates of the actual effort (126 person hours) and optimistic (24 person hours), realistic (65 person hours), and pessimistic (162 person hours) estimates of expected efforts for similar projects. The estimates of these expected efforts assume that some issues, e.g., immaturity of tool support, are resolved (cf. [KSBH12]).

Such estimates can serve as good base lines for effort estimations, e.g., of new projects. However, these estimates are unsuited if software architects heavily exploit reusable architectural knowledge like in the AT method. Additional studies are required to quantify the expected lower effort due to reuse.

5.1.2. Related Controlled Experiments

The case studies previously described in Section 5.1.1 indicate that architectural analyses are applicable to the domain of web applications (where also the AT method is evaluated). This insight, however, should be considered with care because case study results are not necessarily generalizable [SDAH08]; they are more exploratory. For more generalizable theories, controlled experiments are favorable [SDAH08].

According to our recent survey [LB15c], only Martens et al. [MKPR11] conducted such experiments on the accuracy and effort of architectural analyses. For reuse scenarios of architectural models, their results indicate that component-based architectural analysis approaches like Palladio save effort without sacrificing accuracy—compared to monolithic performance modeling approaches like SPE [SW02], UML Performance Simulator [Mar04], and Capacity Planning [MDA04] for which no component reuse is intended.

The results of Martens et al. [MKPR11] show that reuse of (parts of) architectural models in the context of architectural analyses is possible. This possibility particularly holds for Palladio. However, Martens et al. restrict their reuse to components and lack an investigation of higher-level reusable architectural knowledge.

5.2. Evaluation Design

This section describes a generic design for evaluating the AT method. Concrete data collection procedures (cf. Section 2.1.3) can reuse and refine this generic design. The case studies in Section 5.3.1 to Section 5.3.4 and the controlled experiment in Section 5.4 exemplify such a reuse and refinement.

The section is organized according to the reporting guidelines for experimental designs by Runeson and Höst [RH09] and based on the GQM method (cf. Section 2.1.1) to derive the design. At first, Section 5.2.1 derives research questions from the overall evaluation goal of the AT method. For answering these research questions, Section 5.2.2 derives metrics for the collection of empirical data. Section 5.2.3 specifies how this data is analyzed to answer the research questions and defines hypotheses stating which answers are expected. A description of validity procedures concludes the evaluation design in Section 5.2.4.

Table 5.1 overviews all research questions, along with associated metrics and hypotheses. The following subsections describe this table in detail.

Table 5.1.: Overview of research questions and associated metrics and hypotheses

$Q_{\text{application effort}}$	**How much effort do software architects require to apply ATs?**
$M_{\text{time for AT selection}}$	Exclusive time for executing the AT selection action of the AT application process (cf. Section 4.1.1), i.e., time from start to finish of the action minus time not spend on the action during this interval.
$M_{\text{time for AT application}}$	Exclusive time for executing the AT application action of the AT application process (cf. Section 4.1.1), i.e., time from start to finish of the action minus time not spend on the action during this interval.
$M_{\text{\#ATs}}$	Number of ATs within the employed AT catalog.
$M_{\text{\#AT roles}}$	Number of AT roles of the applied AT.
$M_{\text{\#AT parameters}}$	Number of parameters as sum over all AT roles of the applied AT.
$H_{\text{time-size correlation}}$	The time metric $M_{\text{time for AT selection}}$ positively correlates with the size metric $M_{\text{\#ATs}}$ and the time metric $M_{\text{time for AT application}}$ positively correlates with the size metrics $M_{\text{\#AT roles}}$ and $M_{\text{\#AT parameters}}$. *Rejection:* The correlation is not positive, i.e., the correlation coefficient is *not* greater than 0.0.

$H_{\textbf{effort is low}}$	Compared to the overall efforts for specifying architectural models suited for architectural analyses, AT selection and AT application effort is low. *Rejection:* The sum of $M_{\textbf{time for AT selection}}$ and $M_{\textbf{time for AT application}}$ is higher than 40 person minutes.

$Q_{\textbf{effort saving}}$	**How much creation effort can software architects save when applying ATs?**
$M_{\Delta\textbf{time}}$	Difference between the time for manually creating AT-induced elements and the time for selecting and applying an AT. (Note: requires a redundant manual creation by a control group.)
$M_{\Delta\textbf{components}}$	Difference between the number of components (i.e., types of components) after and before the execution of AT completions.
$M_{\Delta\textbf{assembly ctx.}}$	Difference between the number of assembly contexts (i.e., instances of components) after and before the execution of AT completions.
$M_{\Delta\textbf{operations}}$	Difference between the number of operations as sum over all interfaces (provided by components) after and before the execution of AT completions.
$M_{\Delta\textbf{self-adapt.}}$	Difference between the number of lines of self-adaptation rules after and before the execution of AT completions.
$H_{\Delta\textbf{time-}\Delta\textbf{size correlation}}$	The time metric $M_{\Delta\textbf{time}}$ positively correlates with all of the four size metrics $M_{\Delta\textbf{components}}$, $M_{\Delta\textbf{assembly ctx.}}$, $M_{\Delta\textbf{operations}}$, and $M_{\Delta\textbf{self-adapt.}}$. *Rejection:* The correlation is not positive, i.e., the correlation coefficient is *not* greater than 0.0.
$H_{\textbf{effort is lowered}}$	Applying the AT method lowers effort compared to manually creating architectural models directly in the targeted architectural analysis approach. *Rejection:* Any of above metrics ($M_{\Delta\textbf{time}}$, $M_{\Delta\textbf{components}}$, $M_{\Delta\textbf{assembly ctx.}}$, $M_{\Delta\textbf{operations}}$, $M_{\Delta\textbf{self-adapt.}}$) is negative.

$Q_{\textbf{conformance}}$	**Do software architects effectively benefit from checking whether their architectural models violate conformance to applied ATs?**
$M_{\textbf{\#detected violations}}$	Total number of actually detected conformance violations.
$M_{\textbf{\#resolved violations}}$	Total number of resolved violations after they have been detected.
$H_{\textbf{violations are detected}}$	Violations are detected, which indicates that conformance checks are possible and helpful. *Rejection:* $M_{\textbf{\#detected violations}}$ equals 0.
$H_{\textbf{violations are resolved}}$	All detected violations are resolved, which indicates an increased benefit of conformance checks. *Rejection:* $M_{\textbf{\#resolved violations}} < M_{\textbf{\#detected violations}}$.

$Q_{\textbf{benefits}}$	**What are effective benefits of the AT method?**
$M_{\textbf{benefits}}$	Any benefits of the AT method observed during its empirical investigation.
$H_{\textbf{benefits exist}}$	Benefits are observed and subjectively reported. *Rejection:* $M_{\textbf{benefits}}$ is empty.

$Q_{\textbf{limitations}}$	**What are effective limitations of the AT method?**

$M_{\textbf{limitations}}$	Whenever a limitation is observed, it is collected, e.g., an AT has to be adapted for its application or a potential AT application is not performed due to any kind of problem.
$H_{\textbf{limitations exist}}$	Some limitations will be discovered, thus helping to identify future work directions. No critical limitations are excepted, i.e., limitations that render the AT method generally unsuitable. *Rejection:* $M_{\textbf{limitations}}$ is empty.
$Q_{\textbf{specification effort}}$	**How much effort do AT engineers require for specifying ATs?**
$M_{\textbf{time for AT specification}}$	Exclusive time for executing each of the AT specification actions of the AT specification process (cf. Section 4.1.3), i.e., time from start to finish of an action minus time not spend on an action during this interval.
$M_{\textbf{\#AT roles}}$	Number of roles of an AT.
$M_{\textbf{\#AT constraints}}$	Number of constraints of an AT.
$M_{\textbf{\#completion LOC}}$	Number of lines of completions of an AT.
$H_{\textbf{time-size correlation}}$	The time metric $M_{\textbf{time for AT specification}}$ positively correlates with the size metrics $M_{\textbf{\#AT roles}}$, $M_{\textbf{\#AT constraints}}$, and $M_{\textbf{\#completion LOC}}$. *Rejection:* The correlation is not positive, i.e., the correlation coefficient is *not* greater than 0.0.
$H_{\textbf{effort is high}}$	Compared to the overall efforts for specifying architectural models suited for architectural analyses, AT specification effort is high. *Rejection:* $M_{\textbf{time for AT specification}}$ is lower than 6.5 person hours.
$Q_{\textbf{quality assurance}}$	**Does quality assurance help AT engineers to improve the conceptual integrity of specified ATs effectively?**
$M_{\textbf{\#detected errors}}$	Total number of actually detected errors by following the AT method's test-based quality assurance process.
$M_{\textbf{\#resolved errors}}$	Total number of resolved errors after they have been detected.
$H_{\textbf{errors are detected}}$	Errors are detected, which indicates that quality assurance is possible and helpful. *Rejection:* $M_{\textbf{\#detected errors}}$ equals 0.
$H_{\textbf{errors are resolved}}$	All detected errors are resolved, which indicates an increased benefit of the AT method's quality assurance steps. *Rejection:* $M_{\textbf{\#resolved errors}} < M_{\textbf{\#detected errors}}$.

5.2.1. Research Questions

As stated in the introduction of Chapter 5, the overall evaluation goal of the AT method is to analyze the effectivity and efficiency of the AT method for conducting architectural analyses. From these properties—effectivity and efficiency—and involved roles—software architects and AT engineers—research questions for evaluating the AT method can be derived.

The following list provides these research questions along with their rationale (the list starts with questions related to software architects and ends with questions related to AT engineers):

$Q_{\text{application effort}}$: **How much effort do software architects require to apply ATs?**
A criterion for efficiency is the needed effort to achieve a task [LB15c]. This question addresses this criterion from the viewpoint of software architects.

$Q_{\text{effort saving}}$: **How much creation effort can software architects save when applying ATs?**
Similar to the previous question (and for the same motivation), this question addresses effort. However, the focus of this question in on how much effort can be *saved*, thus, more directly targeting the AT method's main promise of making architectural analyses more efficient.

$Q_{\text{conformance}}$: **Do software architects effectively benefit from checking whether their architectural models violate conformance to applied ATs?**
Section 1.2 describes conformance checks as a main benefit for software architects when exploiting reusable architectural knowledge. Therefore, this question asks whether the AT method indeed provides this benefit.

Q_{benefits}: **What are effective benefits of the AT method?**
During the conduction of an evaluation, other benefits than the AT method's main benefits may be observed. Therefore, this question openly asks for such benefits; such open questions typically accompany empirical evaluations [RH09].

$Q_{\text{limitations}}$: **What are effective limitations of the AT method?**
Analogously to the previous question, limitations of the AT method may be observed. Therefore, this question openly asks for such limitations.

$Q_{\text{specification effort}}$: **How much effort do AT engineers require for specifying ATs?**
As the first question, this question inspects the effort criterion. However, the focus is on the viewpoint of AT engineers.

$Q_{\text{quality assurance}}$: **Does quality assurance help AT engineers improve the conceptual integrity of specified ATs effectively?**
As a major part of the AT method, the effectiveness of its testing-based quality assurance approach needs to be inspected. Therefore, this question calls for such an inspection.

Table 5.1 is structured along these research questions. In addition, the table provides associated metrics and hypotheses as described next.

5.2.2. Data Collection Procedure(s)

Data collection procedures specify how the empirical data for answering research questions is gained [RH09]. Fitting to the GQM method (cf. Section 2.1.1), I specify these procedures via metrics aligned to the research questions from Section 5.2.1.

In the following, for each question, a dedicated subsection describes its associated metrics. Table 5.1 provides a summary of these metrics.

5.2.2.1. Metrics: How much effort do software architects require to apply ATs?

Question $Q_{\text{application effort}}$ ("How much effort do software architects require to apply ATs?") can be quantified based upon the following metrics:

Time-based metrics quantify effort by measuring the time software architects require for executing the actions of the AT application process (cf. Section 4.1.1); a commonly applied type of metric for quantifying effort [LB15c]. The AT application process for software architects comes with two main actions (AT selection and AT application) that motivate the following two metrics:

$M_{\text{time for AT selection}}$ measures the exclusive time for executing the AT selection action of the AT application process (cf. Section 4.1.1), i.e., the time from the start to the finish of the action minus time not spend on the action during this interval. For example, a software architect may require 30 *minutes* to study an AT catalog and to select a suitable AT for a given context.

$M_{\text{time for AT application}}$ measures the exclusive time for executing the AT application action of the AT application process (cf. Section 4.1.1), i.e., the time from start to finish of the action minus time not spend on the action during this interval. For example, a software architect may require 20 *minutes* to bind an AT's roles and to set actual parameters.

Size-based metrics quantify effort by measuring the number of elements that software architects have to investigate and create during the actions of the AT application process (cf. Section 4.1.1). Martens et al. [MKPR11] have showcased the utility of size-based metrics in the context of architectural analyses. For the selection of an AT, the number of ATs within AT catalogs is relevant; for the application of an AT, the number of the AT's roles and parameters are relevant:

$M_{\#\text{ATs}}$ measures the number of ATs within the employed AT catalog. For example, a software architect may require more effort to select a suitable AT if an AT catalog contains 100 ATs instead of 10 ATs.

$M_{\#\text{AT roles}}$ measures the number of AT roles of the applied AT. For example, a software architect may require more effort to apply an AT with 10 roles instead of 1 role.

$M_{\#\text{AT parameters}}$ measures the number of parameters as sum over all AT roles of the applied AT. For example, a software architect may require more effort to apply an AT with 10 parameters instead of 1 parameter.

5.2.2.2. Metrics: How much creation effort can software architects save when applying ATs?

Question $Q_{\text{effort saving}}$ ("How much creation effort can software architects save when applying ATs?") can be quantified based upon similar metrics than described for the previous question ($Q_{\text{application effort}}$). However, quantifications compare the application of ATs against manual knowledge application approaches:

Time-based metrics quantify effort saving by measuring the time difference between AT-based and manual applications of reusable architectural knowledge. Such time-based metrics are typically applied by controlled experiments to measure the efficiency of methods [LB15c]. The following metric is the most relevant and most direct time-based metric in the AT method's context:

$M_{\Delta\text{time}}$ measures the difference between the time for manually creating AT-induced elements and the time for selecting and applying an AT. For example, a manual knowledge application may take 100 *minutes* while an AT-based application may take 50 *minutes*, thus, resulting in a measurement of $100\ minutes - 50\ minutes = 50\ minutes$.

To measure this metric, software architects are required to create two redundant versions of an architectural model—a version where knowledge is integrated via ATs and a version where knowledge is integrated manually. Typically, the AT-based architectural model is created by a treatment group of software architects while the other architectural model is created by a control group of different software architects [LB15c]. For computing a value for the metric for multiple time measurements, statistical aggregation functions, e.g., for median and mean values, can be employed [LB15c].

Size-based metrics quantify effort saving by measuring the difference in the number of architectural model elements after and before the execution of AT completions. The rationale behind this difference is that AT-induced elements would have to be created manually without completions, i.e., by manually modifying the targeted architectural model. In such modification scenarios, our previously conducted case study [LB16] indicates that measuring differences reflects involved efforts appropriately.

According to Martens et al. [MKPR11], relevant elements of architectural models are components, assembly contexts, and interface operations (cf. Section 2.5.3.1); additionally, in the context of elastic environments (cf. Section 2.5.3.2), self-adaptations are relevant:

$M_{\Delta\text{components}}$ measures the difference between the number of components (i.e., types of components) after and before the execution of AT completions. For example, a completion may integrate 10 additional components into an architectural model.

$M_{\Delta \textbf{assembly ctx.}}$ measures the difference between the number of assembly contexts (i.e., instances of components) after and before the execution of AT completions. For example, a completion may integrate 10 additional assembly contexts into an architectural model.

$M_{\Delta \textbf{operations}}$ measures the difference between the number of operations as sum over all interfaces (provided by components) after and before the execution of AT completions. For example, a completion may integrate 10 additional operations into an architectural model.

$M_{\Delta \textbf{self-adapt.}}$ measures the difference between the number of lines of self-adaptation rules after and before the execution of AT completions. For example, a completion may integrate 100 additional lines of self-adaptation rules into an architectural model.

5.2.2.3. Metrics: Do software architects effectively benefit from checking whether their architectural models violate conformance to applied ATs?

Question $Q_{\textbf{conformance}}$ ("Do software architects effectively benefit from checking whether their architectural models violate conformance to applied ATs?") can be quantified based upon the metrics derived by Giacinto [Gia16, Chap. 7]:

$M_{\textbf{\#detected violations}}$ measures the total number of actually detected conformance violations, thus, directly measuring the effectivity of conformance checks. For example, during the AT-based creation of an architectural model, software architects may detect 10 *violations* to constraints of an applied AT.

$M_{\textbf{\#resolved violations}}$ measures the total number of resolved violations after they have been detected. For example, after detecting 10 *violations* to constraints of an applied AT, software architects may only resolve 9 *violations*. The rationale behind this metric is that it gives an indication whether software architects successfully exploit detected violations as feedback for revising their architectural model.

5.2.2.4. Metrics: What are effective benefits of the AT method?

Question $Q_{\textbf{benefits}}$ ("What are effective benefits of the AT method?") is an open question for benefits. Open questions suggest a broad range of answers formulated in natural language [RH09] and are directly asked to participants of empirical investigations [RH09]. The participant's answers often provide additional and unexpected insights. Accordingly, the following metric simply collects the answers to $Q_{\textbf{benefits}}$:

$M_{\textbf{benefits}}$ collects any benefits of the AT method observed during its empirical investigation in natural language. For example, a software architect may state: "The AT method's formalization of an architectural pattern helped me to better understand the pattern itself."

5.2.2.5. Metrics: What are effective limitations of the AT method?

Question $Q_{\textbf{limitations}}$ ("What are effective limitations of the AT method?") is an open question for limitations. Therefore, $Q_{\textbf{limitations}}$ forms the counterpart of $Q_{\textbf{benefits}}$ and can analogously be answered:

$M_{\textbf{limitations}}$ collects any limitations of the AT method observed during the empirical investigation, e.g., an AT has to be adapted for its application or a potential AT application is not performed due to any kind of problem. For example, a software architect may state: "I was unsure whether this AT was the right one, so I ignored it."

5.2.2.6. Metrics: How much effort do AT engineers require for specifying ATs?

Question $Q_{\textbf{specification effort}}$ ("How much effort do AT engineers require for specifying ATs?") can be quantified based upon the following metrics:

Time-based metrics quantify effort by measuring the time AT engineers require for executing the actions of the AT specification process (cf. Section 4.1.3); analogously to the time-based metrics of $Q_{\textbf{application effort}}$:

$M_{\textbf{time for AT specification}}$ measures the exclusive time for executing each of the AT specification actions of the AT specification process (identification, selection, specification, and quality assurance; cf. Section 4.1.3), i.e., the time from start to the finish of the action minus time not spend on the action during this interval. For example, an AT engineer may require 8 *hours* to specify a requested AT in a controlled environment.

Size-based metrics quantify effort by measuring the number of elements that AT engineers have to investigate and create during the actions of the AT specification process (cf. Section 4.1.3); analogously to the size-based metrics of $Q_{\textbf{application effort}}$. Major elements when creating ATs are AT roles, AT constraints, and AT completions:

$M_{\textbf{\#AT roles}}$ measures the number of roles of an AT. For example, an AT engineer may require more effort to specify an AT with 10 *roles* instead of 1 role.

$M_{\textbf{\#AT constraints}}$ measures the number of constraints of an AT. For example, an AT engineer may require more effort to specify an AT with 50 *constraints* instead of 10 *constraints*.

$M_{\textbf{\#completion LOC}}$ measures the number of lines of completions of an AT. For example, an AT engineer may require more effort to specify an AT with $1,000$ *LOCs* instead of 100 *LOCs*.

5.2.2.7. Metrics: Does quality assurance help AT engineers to improve the conceptual integrity of specified ATs effectively?

Question $Q_{\textbf{quality assurance}}$ ("Does quality assurance help AT engineers to improve the conceptual integrity of specified ATs effectively?") is similar to $Q_{\textbf{conformance}}$ but with a focus on AT engineers and their quality assurance process:

$M_{\textbf{\#detected errors}}$ measures the total number of actually detected errors by following the AT method's test-based quality assurance process, thus, directly measuring the effectivity of quality assurance. For example, during quality assurance, AT engineers may detect 10 *errors* in an AT completion.

$M_{\#\text{resolved errors}}$ measures the total number of resolved errors after they have been detected. For example, after detecting 10 *errors* in an AT completion, AT engineers may only resolved 9 *errors*. The rationale behind this metric is that it gives an indication whether AT engineers successfully exploit detected errors as feedback for revising ATs.

5.2.3. Analysis Procedure(s)

Analysis procedures precisely specify how to interpret empirical data gained from measuring metrics [RH09]. To specify these procedures, I follow again the GQM method: for each question, I formulate expected answers as hypotheses. Along with hypotheses, I state appropriate rejection criteria.

In the following, for each question, a dedicated subsection describes its associated hypotheses and rejection criteria. Table 5.1 provides a summary of these hypotheses and rejection criteria.

5.2.3.1. Hypotheses: How much effort do software architects require to apply ATs?

The following hypotheses characterize the expected answers to question $Q_{\text{application effort}}$ ("How much effort do software architects require to apply ATs?"):

$H_{\text{time-size correlation}}$ states that there are positive correlations between the time metric $M_{\text{time for AT selection}}$ and the size metric $M_{\#\text{ATs}}$ as well as between the time metric $M_{\text{time for AT application}}$ and the size metrics $M_{\#\text{AT roles}}$ and $M_{\#\text{AT parameters}}$.

Martens et al. [MKPR11] provide evidence that time- and size-based effort metrics positively correlate. A correlation would confirm that results regarding effort can be triangulated over such metrics. Moreover, a correlation would allow future studies to estimate effort based on size, i.e., without depending on human interactions like time-based metrics require.

Rejection: The correlation is not positive, i.e., the correlation coefficient is *not* greater than 0.0. Because all considered metrics are ratio scaled, the Pearson correlation coefficient [WRH+00, Sec. 10.1] is employed.

$H_{\textbf{effort is low}}$ states that AT selection and AT application effort is low, compared to the overall efforts for specifying architectural models suited for architectural analyses.

For the comparison to overall efforts, Koziolek's realistic estimates of 65 person hours are used as a reference point (cf. Section 5.1.1.2). I assume that "low" means that AT efforts cause at most 1 % of the overall efforts, i.e., at most 40 person minutes (1 % · 65 person hours ≈ 40 person minutes).

Rejection: The sum of $M_{\textbf{time for AT selection}}$ and $M_{\textbf{time for AT application}}$ is higher than 40 person minutes.

5.2.3.2. Hypotheses: How much creation effort can software architects save when applying ATs?

The following hypotheses characterize the expected answers to question $Q_{\textbf{effort saving}}$ ("How much creation effort can software architects save when applying ATs?"):

$H_{\boldsymbol{\Delta}\textbf{time-}\boldsymbol{\Delta}\textbf{size correlation}}$ states that the time metric $M_{\boldsymbol{\Delta}\textbf{time}}$ positively correlates with the size metrics $M_{\boldsymbol{\Delta}\textbf{components}}$, $M_{\boldsymbol{\Delta}\textbf{assembly ctx.}}$, $M_{\boldsymbol{\Delta}\textbf{operations}}$, and $M_{\boldsymbol{\Delta}\textbf{self-adapt.}}$.

As for $H_{\textbf{time-size correlation}}$, the motivation behind this hypothesis is the expected positive correlation of time- and size-based effort metrics [MKPR11].

Rejection: The correlation is not positive, i.e., the correlation coefficient is *not* greater than 0.0. Because all considered metrics are ratio scaled, the Pearson correlation coefficient [WRH+00, Sec. 10.1] is employed.

$H_{\textbf{effort is lowered}}$ states that applying the AT method lowers effort compared to manually creating architectural models directly in the targeted architectural analysis approach.

This hypothesis describes and follows directly from the main promise of the AT method (cf. Chapter 4), i.e., that the AT method makes architectural analyses more efficient. The subsequent rejection criterion employs the previously introduced difference metrics to quantify the saved effort—only if effort is actually saved, this hypothesis is accepted.

Rejection: Any of the difference metrics from Section 5.2.2.2 ($M_{\Delta\textbf{time}}$, $M_{\Delta\textbf{components}}$, $M_{\Delta\textbf{assembly ctx.}}$, $M_{\Delta\textbf{operations}}$, $M_{\Delta\textbf{self-adapt.}}$) is negative.

5.2.3.3. Hypotheses: Do software architects effectively benefit from checking whether their architectural models violate conformance to applied ATs?

The following hypotheses characterize the expected answers to question $Q_{\textbf{conformance}}$ ("Do software architects effectively benefit from checking whether their architectural models violate conformance to applied ATs?"):

$H_{\textbf{violations are detected}}$ states that violations are detected.

Accepting this hypothesis indicates that conformance checks are possible and helpful, thus, directly targeting the effectivity of such checks. Its acceptance particularly shows that software architects became aware of violations, thus, indicating that AT tooling provides a sufficient reporting mechanism of violations.

Rejection: $M_{\textbf{\#detected violations}}$ equals 0.

$H_{\textbf{violations are resolved}}$ states that all detected violations are resolved.

Accepting this hypothesis indicates that software architects successfully use detected violations as feedback for revising their architectural models. Therefore, conformance checks are beneficial both for "diagnosis" and "therapy" of conformance violations.

Rejection: $M_{\textbf{\#resolved violations}} < M_{\textbf{\#detected violations}}$.

5.2.3.4. Hypotheses: What are effective benefits of the AT method?

The following hypothesis characterizes the expected answer to question $Q_{\textbf{benefits}}$ ("What are effective benefits of the AT method?"):

$H_{\textbf{benefits exist}}$ states that benefits are observed and subjectively reported.

The rationale behind this hypothesis is that it is unlikely that each positive aspect in the usage of the AT method can be foreseen. Foreseeing is especially hard because of human-based activities [WRH+00, Chap. 9].

Rejection: $M_{\textbf{benefits}}$ is empty.

5.2.3.5. Hypotheses: What are effective limitations of the AT method?

The following hypothesis characterizes the expected answer to question $Q_{\textbf{limitations}}$ ("What are effective limitations of the AT method?"):

$H_{\textbf{limitations exist}}$ states that some limitations will be discovered.

The rationale behind this hypothesis is analogous to hypothesis $H_{\textbf{benefits exist}}$: foreseeing limitations is hard because of human involvement [WRH+00, Chap. 9]. I expect no critical limitations, i.e., limitations that render the AT method generally unsuitable. Detected limitations therefore help to identify future work directions, e.g., in the form of additional features, correctable bugs in AT tooling, and improvements in usability.

Rejection: $M_{\textbf{limitations}}$ is empty.

5.2.3.6. Hypotheses: How much effort do AT engineers require for specifying ATs?

The following hypotheses characterize the expected answers to question $Q_{\textbf{specification effort}}$ ("How much effort do AT engineers require for specifying ATs?"):

$H_{\textsf{time-size correlation}}$ states that the time metric $M_{\textbf{time for AT specification}}$ positively correlates with the size metrics $M_{\textbf{\#AT roles}}$, $M_{\textbf{\#AT constraints}}$, and $M_{\textbf{\#completion LOC}}$.

Similar to $H_{\textbf{time-size correlation}}$ for software architects (associated to $Q_{\textbf{application effort}}$), the motivation behind this hypothesis is the the expected positive correlation of time- and size-based effort metrics [MKPR11].

Rejection: The correlation is not positive, i.e., the correlation coefficient is *not* greater than 0.0. Because all considered metrics are ratio scaled, the Pearson correlation coefficient [WRH⁺00, Sec. 10.1] is employed.

$H_{\textsf{effort is high}}$ states that AT specification effort is high, compared to the overall efforts for specifying architectural models suited for architectural analyses.

For the comparison to overall efforts, Koziolek's realistic estimates of 65 person hours are used as a reference point (cf. Section 5.1.1.2). I assume that "high" means that AT efforts cause at least 10 % of the overall efforts, i.e., at least 6.5 person hours ($10\% \cdot 65$ person hours $= 6.5$ person hours).

Rejection: $M_{\textbf{time for AT specification}}$ is lower than 6.5 person hours.

5.2.3.7. Hypotheses: Does quality assurance help AT engineers to improve the conceptual integrity of specified ATs effectively?

The following hypotheses characterize the expected answers to question $Q_{\textbf{quality assurance}}$ ("Does quality assurance help AT engineers to improve the conceptual integrity of specified ATs effectively?"):

$H_{\textsf{errors are detected}}$ states that errors are detected.

Accepting this hypothesis indicates that quality assurance is possible and helpful, thus, directly targeting the effectivity of quality assurance. The hypothesis' acceptance particularly shows that AT engineers became aware of errors, thus, indicating that the AT method's quality assurance steps are sufficiently described.

Rejection: $M_{\#\textbf{detected errors}}$ equals 0.

$H_{\textbf{errors are resolved}}$ states that all detected errors are resolved.

Accepting this hypothesis indicates that AT engineers successfully use detected errors as feedback for revising ATs. Therefore, the AT method's quality assurance is beneficial both for "diagnosis" and "therapy" of errors in ATs.

Rejection: $M_{\#\textbf{resolved errors}} < M_{\#\textbf{detected errors}}$.

5.2.4. Validity Procedure(s)

Especially measuring effort comes with high validity threats because effort is often measured based on human interactions [WRH+00, Chap. 9]. Human-based measurements can, for instance, result in poor reproducibility of case studies. To cope with such threats, the evaluation design describes hypotheses (e.g., $H_{\textbf{time-size correlation}}$) that triangulate [Sea99] results from human-based measurements (i.e., measurements of time-based metrics) and size-based measurements.

Another aspect is the quality of the evaluation design itself. I try to maximize its quality by following case study reporting guidelines [RH09] and by letting colleagues review the evaluation design two times regarding reproducibility. Moreover, parts of the evaluation plan have been published [LB15c, LB16], i.e., these parts were externally reviewed and accepted. This external acceptance is an indication for a high quality of the evaluation design.

5.3. Case Studies

We have used the evaluation design from Section 5.2 in several case studies to evaluate the AT method. This section provides brief summaries of these case studies: Section 5.3.1 summarizes the CloudStore case study, Section 5.3.2 the WordCount case study, Section 5.3.3 the Znn.com case study, and Section 5.3.4 further (but smaller) case studies. Detailed reports of the first three case studies are provided in Appendix C.

5.3.1. Case Study: CloudStore

This section summarizes the case study on CloudStore, an online book shop similar to the book shop example from Chapter 3. A detailed case study report is provided in Appendix C.1.

5.3.1.1. CloudStore: Description

CloudStore [LSB+17] represents a distributed, CPU-bound online book shop where customers can search and order books, similar to (but more complex than) the book shop example from Chapter 3. CloudStore's implementation is based on a legacy implementation of the TPC-W benchmark [Tra02]. In our previous efforts [LB16, LSB+17], we have conducted a case study to migrate this legacy version to a version that operates in a cloud computing environment. We have applied the AT method for planning this migration, e.g., to analyze whether CloudStore would benefit from the loadbalancing architectural pattern inside the cloud computing environment. Accordingly, CloudStore has two main advantages: (1) it refers to the well-specified TPC-W benchmark [Tra02] that is popular both in academia and industry and (2) it represents a typical distributed legacy system for which a migration needs to be planned, thus, fitting to a typical purpose of architectural analyses.

5.3.1.2. CloudStore: Goal

The CloudStore case study refines the overall evaluation goal by focusing on planning a migration within the distributed and cloud computing domains. Therefore, the AT method's effectivity and efficiency is evaluated in these domains and their typical QoS properties (performance, scalability, elasticity, and cost-efficiency). By including this refinement into the GQM template for the overall evaluation goal, the particular goal of the CloudStore case study is to:

Analyze: the AT method

For the purpose of: conducting architectural analyses *for planning migrations*

With respect to: effectivity and efficiency

From the viewpoint of: software architects and AT engineers

In the context of: realistic *distributed and cloud computing* systems.

5.3.1.3. CloudStore: Case Description

To achieve the goal of the CloudStore case study, CloudStore's software architect requests a set of suitable ATs from an AT engineer. In this request scenario, the software architect's request is of the broadest kind (cf. Section 4.1.3.1): the software architect requests ATs for a whole application domain (cloud computing) and is interested in several QoS properties (performance, scalability, elasticity, and cost-efficiency). Therefore, the AT engineer is required to extensively work on each action of the AT specification process (cf. Section 4.1.3).

5.3.1.4. CloudStore: Summary of Lessons Learned

This section briefly summarizes the main lessons learned within the CloudStore case study; a detailed analysis and interpretation is provided in Appendix C.1. The summary is aligned along the questions of the evaluation design (cf. Section 5.2).

$Q_{\text{application effort}}$: **How much effort do software architects require to apply ATs?** Software architects have only low effort for applying ATs (compared to the overall efforts for specifying architectural models). Indeed, on average, we have required only about 5 *minutes* to apply ATs. This result is in line with the AT method's goal to make software architects more efficient because only low effort is introduced for benefiting from the exploitation of reusable architectural knowledge (cf. Section 1.2). However, the result is biased because we are experts on the AT method and already knew which ATs we required, thus, minimizing selection times of appropriate ATs from the AT catalog.

Effort for software architects varies depending on the number of ATs in the employed AT catalog and the number of roles and parameters of the applied

AT. We additionally noted that effort is caused by the number of *applied* roles, e.g., the *three-layer* AT includes only 4 roles but we have bound these roles to a total of 8 architectural elements of CloudStore. Therefore, a metric for the number of applied roles should be applied for future empirical investigations.

Predicting the time for selecting and applying ATs solely based on the identified correlation will result in inaccurate estimates. Future work may investigate whether metrics with strong correlations with selection and application time can be defined, e.g., similar to the complexity metrics by Martens et al. [MKPR11].

$Q_{\textbf{effort saving}}$: **How much creation effort can software architects save when applying ATs?** Effort can effectively be lowered by applying ATs. Investigated ATs have saved creation efforts for assembly contexts and for specifying self-adaptive behavior by providing generic self-adaptation rules.

We were unable to provide estimates of the saved time when applying ATs because we lacked a control group *not* following the AT method (as is required by the employed metrics). Future empirical investigations may tackle this lack; the controlled experiment outlined in Section 5.4 exemplifies such an investigation.

$Q_{\textbf{conformance}}$: **Do software architects have effective benefits from checking whether their architectural models violate conformance to applied ATs?** Software architects can effectively benefit from the AT method's conformance checks. Our results particularly indicate that conformance checks help to apply ATs correctly.

However, during the CloudStore case study, we only detected one conformance violation. Therefore, no conclusive insights have been gained—especially regarding the long-term benefits of conformance checks (e.g., regarding maintainability) and regarding software architects that have not participated in creating the applied ATs. Future investigations may focus on these aspects.

Q$_{\textbf{benefits}}$**: What are effective benefits of the AT method?** We have collected 3 benefits of the AT method during the CloudStore case study. These benefits both confirm expected and reveal unexpected benefits.

The first benefit ("detected constraint violations helped to correctly apply the *three-layer* AT") shows that conformance checks not only maintain and ensure conformance but also help software architects to apply ATs. We expect that such a help will be most beneficial for software architects not involved in AT specification and, especially, novice software architects.

The second benefit ("as an expert, AT application is a matter of a few minutes") confirms that AT application can come with low efforts. It would, however, be interesting to inspect whether such benefits are observed by non-experts of the AT method as well.

The third benefit ("the architectural analysis showed that the application of the loadbalancing AT was not beneficial in the given context; without analysis, this issue would have been hard to show") empirically confirms that architectural analyses help in making context-aware informed decisions. During the case study, we were actually surprised that an increased number of loadbalanced replicas can degrade capacity. This degradation is in contrast to what the loadbalancing architectural pattern promises. However, the architectural analysis has revealed that CloudStore's Database Server—a context factor for the loadbalancer—actually becomes overloaded when too many replica exist. Here, the combination of reusable architectural knowledge with architectural analyses was beneficial.

Q$_{\textbf{limitations}}$**: What are effective limitations of the AT method?** We have collected 5 limitations of the AT method during the CloudStore case study. The limitations point to technical issues in AT tooling (first 4 limitations) and an issue in selecting suitable ATs (last limitation).

AT tooling issues relate to EMF profiles and debugging mechanisms (first limitation), missing reuse mechanisms for ATs (second limitation), lack of in-editor syntax checks when specifying OCL constraints (third limitation), and customizability of self-adaptations (fourth limitation). Fortunately, all of these issues are of technical nature and do not render the AT method infeasible. However, for making the AT method more practically relevant, these issues should be resolved. Openkowski has—meanwhile—already resolved the second limitation by introducing reuse mechanisms for the specification of ATs (cf. Section 4.4.1). Resolving the remaining limitations remains as a future work.

The fifth and last limitation ("conceptually, the *three-layer* AT does not completely fit to CloudStore") is not of technical nature but relates to a conceptual mismatch between the selected AT and the targeted system. In CloudStore, assembly contexts for web pages, e.g., Home Page, communicate over a dedicated Database Access assembly context to CloudStore's Database. Because this structure defines three logical layer, we have applied the *three-layer* AT to CloudStore as illustrated in Figure C.7. While all constraints of the captured knowledge are fulfilled, the role names of the *three-layer* AT do not perfectly fit to CloudStore: the *application layer* role is applied to CloudStore's Database Access assembly context and the *data access layer* role is applied to CloudStore's Database assembly context. We may argue that Database Access also includes application layer logic and that Database models the access to CloudStore's database. However, the alternative (and common) role names "presentation layer", "middle layer", and "data layer" of the *three-layer* architectural style may be more intuitive in the context of CloudStore. A next step in the CloudStore case would therefore be to let software architects and AT engineers re-agree on this terminology. We conclude that, in general, software architects and AT engineers must steadily cooperate to avoid confusion due to unsuitable role names.

$Q_{\text{specification effort}}$: **How much effort do AT engineers require for specifying ATs?** AT engineers have high efforts for specifying ATs (compared to the overall efforts for specifying architectural models). The identification of suitable QoS properties and their integration into Palladio has caused the most effort, i.e., approximately 2.5 *person months*. We had high efforts in this step because neither established metrics for scalability, elasticity, and cost-efficiency nor a suitable architectural analysis have existed when we started with the case study. However, we expect that only little effort is required in domains with well-established metrics and analysis approaches.

Once we had finished with our integration into Palladio, on average, we have required about 8 *hours* to select, specify, and quality-assure a single AT. Given the potential effort that software architects save when applying the AT method, we believe that 8 *hours* are affordable. Moreover, resolving some limitations in AT tooling promises to lower AT specification efforts (see previous lesson learned).

Not all suspected effort-causing factors indeed cause effort. For example, we identified a negative correlation between specification time and the number of AT roles and constraints. This correlation even suggests that "the more roles and constraints an AT needs to capture, the less time is required for its specification". Because such a statement makes no causal sense, we suggest a more controlled inspection of these factors. Furthermore, we identified a positive correlation of 0.83 between specification time and completion lines of code, indicating that the size of completions indeed influences the effort for specifying ATs. According to Evans' classification [Eva96], this correlation is even "very strong"; thus, making completions a primary factor for specification efforts.

$Q_{\text{quality assurance}}$: **Does quality assurance help AT engineers to improve the conceptual integrity of specified ATs effectively?** The AT method's quality assurance helps in effectively improving conceptual integrity of specified ATs: testing has revealed faults in the specification of several ATs. This testing is a lightweight quality assurance technique because it requires little effort compared to a full-blown formal verification. The typical root causes for AT faults (cf. Section 4.1.3.3) particularly have helped to efficiently detect the actual faults. Once detected, we have shown that faults can be removed, thus, leading to an improved conceptual integrity. We therefore suggest to always include the proposed quality assurance steps in any AT specification efforts.

Given its importance, future work should target a more extensive support for quality assurance. For example, an automated generation of test models that cover the typical root causes for AT faults is a promising future work direction.

5.3.2. Case Study: WordCount

This section summarizes a case study that we have conducted in the big data domain; a domain concerned with processing large data sets [Whi09]. The concrete case is the WordCount application [Whi09], which is a commonly used example application in the big data domain. A detailed case study report is provided in Appendix C.2.

5.3.2.1. WordCount: Description

The WordCount application [Whi09] counts the number of occurrences of each word over a set of input texts. For example, the texts "software architects apply an AT" and "AT engineers create an AT" may be processed. WordCount then outputs a count of 3 for the word "AT", a count of 2 for the word "an", and a count of 1 for the remaining words.

5.3.2.2. WordCount: Goal

In our case study, we have created and analyzed an architectural model for WordCount. We have created this model based on an AT that captures a typical reference architecture for big data applications. The reference architecture is based on Apache's Hadoop framework [Whi09] that implements the MapReduce architectural style [DG08]. Compared to the ATs specified during the CloudStore case study, the unique feature of the *Hadoop MapReduce* AT is that it provides a default AT instance (cf. Section 4.2.5.3), i.e., can be used as initiator template.

Accordingly, the goal of the WordCount case study was to:

Analyze: the AT method

For the purpose of: conducting architectural analyses *based on initiator templates*

With respect to: effectivity and efficiency

From the viewpoint of: software architects and AT engineers

In the context of: realistic *big data* systems.

5.3.2.3. WordCount: Case Description

We have achieved the goal of the WordCount case study in three consecutive steps. First, in the context of his Master's thesis [Sax15], Manoveg Saxena has acted as software architect to create a reference model for Hadoop applications—with full support for Palladio-based analyses. Second, I have acted as AT engineer to extract the *Hadoop MapReduce* AT from this reference model. Third, I have acted as software architect to showcase the application of this AT to the WordCount case. The third and last step has required only minor effort (less than 1 *hour*) compared to setting up, running, and analyzing the WordCount application on an actual computing cluster. Therefore, our results point to an improved efficiency when using ATs as initiator templates.

5.3.2.4. WordCount: Summary of Lessons Learned

This section briefly summarizes the main lessons learned within the WordCount case study; a detailed analysis and interpretation is provided in Appendix C.2. The summary is aligned along the questions of the evaluation design (cf. Section 5.2).

$Q_{\text{application effort}}$: **How much effort do software architects require to apply ATs?** The application of the *Hadoop MapReduce* AT involves minor effort for software architects: the AT-based initialization of WordCount's architectural model took us less than 2 *minutes*. We expect that this result can be generalized to other AT-based initializations because the initialization wizard requires no complicated configuration and automates most creation tasks; the selection of an AT with default AT instance is enough.

$Q_{\text{effort saving}}$: **How much creation effort can software architects save when applying ATs?** Effort can effectively be lowered by applying ATs. An interesting observation is that, compared to the size-based metric measurements in the CloudStore case study, the measurements of size-based metrics are significantly higher for the *Hadoop MapReduce* AT. Furthermore, the *Hadoop MapReduce* AT is the first inspected AT for which additional operations were created by completions.

We account both of these observations to the fact that we captured a reference architecture within the AT; opposed to the architectural styles and architectural patterns captured during the CloudStore case study. As described in Section 2.2.4.3, reference architectures can provide additional component interfaces with additional operations, define an architectural style, and group sets of architectural patterns. Based on this definition, the higher values for the taken metric measurements can be explained.

We conclude that ATs that capture reference architectures can save software architects more effort than ATs that capture different kinds of architectural knowledge. However, we note that reference architectures have the downside of being domain-specific (cf. Section 2.2.4.3), thus, being not as universally applicable as architectural styles and architectural patterns.

$Q_{\textbf{conformance}}$: **Do software architects have effective benefits from checking whether their architectural models violate conformance to applied ATs?** At least for WordCount and the *Hadoop MapReduce* AT, no benefits were gained from automated conformance checks. However, that such benefits generally exist has been shown during the CloudStore case study.

Moreover, two factors about the *Hadoop MapReduce* AT make it hard to cause conformance violations at all. First, the AT contains only two constraints; each checking that roles are bound to the correct architectural element (i.e., to assembly contexts). However, AT tooling allows only to bind roles to the correct elements; the tool does not allow binding roles to wrong target elements. Second, the AT-based initialization also prevents software architects from violating conformance compared to a completely manually created architectural model.

In such situations, software architects do not necessarily require conformance checks. Fortunately, software architects then face situations where conformance violations are unlikely—grounded in the capabilities of applied ATs and AT tooling.

$Q_{\textbf{benefits}}$: **What are effective benefits of the AT method?** We have collected 2 benefits of the AT method during the WordCount case study. These benefits confirm the lessons learned about application effort: we were clearly impressed by the little effort we have spent to model a complex Hadoop-based system.

The first benefit ("we had very little effort with the AT-based instantiation of the architectural model") covers the effort aspect. As our measurements show, we only required 2 *minutes* for the instantiation of the model, which confirms our impression.

The second benefit ("the bound AT heavily reduces the complexity of the underlying Hadoop infrastructure") covers the complexity aspect. Indeed, we had minor analyzing effort using our architectural model; compared to setting up, running, and analyzing the Apache Hadoop application on actual hardware.

We conclude that we were able to confirm the main promise of the AT method, i.e., to make software architects more efficient.

$Q_{\text{limitations}}$**: What are effective limitations of the AT method?** We have collected 3 limitations during the WordCount case study. These limitations point to current drawbacks of the *Hadoop MapReduce* AT and in SimuLizar.

The first limitation ("the AT is currently inflexible and misses parameters, e.g., for configuring the number of map and reduce replicas") shows that the AT is only a first proof-of-concept for an AT-based initialization. Future work is needed to make the AT more flexible, however, the proof-of-concept of an AT-based initialization was successful.

The second limitation ("the AT-annotated architectural model appears incomplete because map and reduce assembly context are unconnected") points to a potential visualization issue of AT-based architectural models. Due to the fact that missing elements are created by AT completions, AT-based architectural models potentially appear incomplete as, e.g., shown in Figure C.17. A possible solution to this issue is to provide software architects with a view on the architectural model that previews the elements to be generated, e.g., by depicting missing elements in a greyed-out form along with the remaining elements. Future work may inspect this issue further.

The third limitation ("the applied analysis tool (SimuLizar) lacks support for asynchronous map and reduce tasks, which can generally lead to inaccurate analysis results") relates to a tooling issue in SimuLizar; i.e., a tool on which AT tooling depends. Saxena [Sax15, Sec. 7] has identified this issue in his Master's thesis and reports on it in detail. Because the issue influences prediction accuracy, Saxena suggests improving SimuLizar with support for asynchronous communication. Rathfelder [Rat13] provides a good starting point for such an improvement because he describes such an improvement for other Palladio analysis tools, e.g., for SimuCom.

$Q_{\textbf{specification effort}}$: **How much effort do AT engineers require for specifying ATs?** The case study again confirms that AT engineers have high efforts for specifying ATs (compared to the overall efforts for specifying architectural models). In contrast to the CloudStore case study, the specification of the AT itself has caused the most effort, i.e., approximately $2.5\,person\,months$.

We had high efforts in this step because Saxena's reference model has required extensive investigations of and experimentation with Hadoop's processing pipeline. We suspect that such an amount of effort can even be generalized to most reference architectures, given their typically high amount of (domain-specific) design decisions. However, we expect that such efforts pay-off when captured in ATs that are reused often.

It remains open how time- and size-based metrics correlate, thus, more experiments that provide the required data are needed. In the CloudStore case study, we have established first results in this direction, however, not with focus on an AT-based initialization of architectural models. Future work may continue with investigations in this direction.

$Q_{\textbf{quality assurance}}$: **Does quality assurance help AT engineers to improve the conceptual integrity of specified ATs effectively?** The AT method's quality assurance helps in effectively improving conceptual integrity of specified ATs. The discussion of this result is analogous to the CloudStore case study.

5.3.3. Case Study: Znn.com

This section summarizes a case study where a student, Igor Rogic [Rog16], has applied ATs to analyzing the elastic news service Znn.com [CGS09].

The Znn.com case study serves as an external validation of AT application; I only interacted with the student via mail in case of concrete questions. A detailed case study report is provided in Appendix C.3.

5.3.3.1. Znn.com: Description

Znn.com [CGS09] represents a typical news service. The main requirement is to provide news content to customers within reasonable response time.

Moreover, due to the nature of news, Znn.com is expected to face varying workloads (cf. [CGS09]), e.g., peak workloads in the event of breaking news. Znn.com therefore requires the implementation of suitable elasticity mechanisms.

5.3.3.2. Znn.com: Goal

The context of Znn.com is the same as in the CloudStore case study (realistic distributed and cloud computing systems; cf. Section 5.3.1). Therefore, the goal was to analyze whether ATs for elasticity that we have specified during the CloudStore case study can be reused and configured for Znn.com:

Analyze: the AT method

For the purpose of: conducting architectural analyses *for determining suitable parameters for elasticity mechanisms*

With respect to: effectivity and efficiency

From the viewpoint of: *external software architects*

In the context of: realistic *distributed and cloud computing* systems.

5.3.3.3. Znn.com: Case Description

To cope with varying workloads cost-efficiently, the provider of Znn.com requires that the Znn.com service shall employ elasticity mechanisms. These elasticity mechanisms shall be able to dynamically adapt both the number of load-balanced server replicas and the content mode (multimedia vs. textual) of Znn.com.

Therefore, in the Znn.com case, a software architect has to determine suitable parameters for Znn.com's elasticity mechanisms. Parameters to be determined can relate to the dynamic load-balancing strategy (e.g., the determination of a threshold when a scale-out should be triggered) and the selection strategy of the content mode (e.g., determining a peak workload when content mode should optimally be switched to textual).

5.3.3.4. Znn.com: Summary of Lessons Learned

This section briefly summarizes the main lessons learned within the case study on Znn.com; a detailed analysis and interpretation is provided in Appendix C.3. The summary is aligned along the questions of the evaluation design (cf. Section 5.2). Only questions relevant for AT application are considered because the Znn.com case study does not involve the specification of new ATs.

$Q_{\text{application effort}}$: **How much effort do software architects require to apply ATs?** The data provided by Rogic unfortunately does not allow to precisely analyze AT application efforts, especially since Rogic has only measured the total time for creating and analyzing Znn.com's architectural model and not the exclusive time for AT-related actions. However, Rogic's total time of 46 *hours* can be compared to the total time of 214 *hours* for the creation of the CloudStore model (cf. Section C.1.1): we required approximately 4.5 times more time to create the CloudStore model. Therefore, CloudStore can be considered significantly more complex than Znn.com.

A lowered complexity of Znn.com (compared to CloudStore) implies different expectations for its evaluation. For example, it is less likely that conformance to applied reusable architectural knowledge is violated and less benefits and limitations may be observed during the conduction of the case study. When answering the subsequent questions, the lowered complexity of Znn.com is therefore taken into account.

$Q_{\text{effort saving}}$: **How much creation effort can software architects save when applying ATs?** Effort can effectively be lowered by applying ATs. The interpretation of this result is analogous to the CloudStore case study because the *horizontal scaling* AT was applied there as well.

$Q_{\text{conformance}}$: **Do software architects have effective benefits from checking whether their architectural models violate conformance to applied ATs?** At least for Znn.com and the *horizontal scaling* AT, no benefits were gained from automated conformance checks. That such benefits generally exist has been shown during the CloudStore case study, however, even in the CloudStore case study, only other ATs than the *horizontal scaling* AT have triggered conformance violations.

A possible explanation for these observations is that software architects apply the *horizontal scaling* AT correctly because it involves no complex constraints. Indeed, the constraints of this AT mainly check that actual parameters are set correctly, e.g., that the *number of initial replicas* is positive. Software architects potentially do not violate such constraints as parameter names often suggest valid values intuitively. Future investigations may provide more conclusive answers for this question.

Q_{benefits}: **What are effective benefits of the AT method?** We have collected 2 benefits during the Znn.com case study. These benefits indicate that even novice software architects can reuse pre-specified ATs and correctly apply these ATs to architectural models.

The first benefit ("the *horizontal scaling* AT—specified in the context of the CloudStore case study—has been reused during the Znn.com case study") covers the reuse aspect. Because Rogic was able to reuse the previously specified *horizontal scaling* AT within another case study, reuse of ATs is possible. This result holds at least for intra-domain reuse: both CloudStore and Znn.com are located in the context of distributed and cloud computing systems. The *horizontal scaling* AT particularly captures a typical cloud computing architectural pattern [EPM13, FLR+14]. More general ATs like the *three-layer* AT potentially allow for an inter-domain reuse; however, this expectation requires confirmation in future empirical studies.

The second benefit ("a novice software architect was able to correctly apply an AT and to conduct an AT-based architectural analysis") points to a main benefit of the AT method—an increased efficiency of software architects. As the benefit shows, an increased efficiency (due to the time-efficient application of reusable architectural knowledge) is not only achieved for expert software architects. An increase efficiency is particularly achieved for novice software architects without deep architectural knowledge—because the required architectural knowledge is correctly captured within ATs.

$Q_{\text{limitations}}$**: What are effective limitations of the AT method?** We have collected 2 limitations during the Znn.com case study. These limitations show that software architects may distrust ATs and that the tooling extended by the AT method requires improvement.

The first limitation ("the software architect has suspected the AT to be faulty based on unsatisfying analysis results; however, the unsatisfying results were caused by a performance bottleneck unrelated to the applied AT") covers the distrust aspect. An inspection of Znn.com's Database Server after re-analyzing the Znn.com model shows that this server is over-utilized and cannot cope with the number of requests. Therefore, Znn.com is unable to scale by adding additional Application Servers—a similar results as we have observed during the CloudStore case study. To resolve this issue Rogic could have, for example, increased the processing rate of the Database Server's CPU. The interesting observation, however, is that Rogic did not resolve the issue at all but suspected a faulty AT.

A solution to lower such distrust in ATs is to train software architects more in interpreting analysis results and inspecting the causes of quality issues such as performance bottlenecks. Software architects can also be supported by an automated detection of quality anti-patterns (cf. [BBL17, Chap. 7]) and hotspot detections (cf. [Str13, Sec. 4.3]). Again, further empirical investigations are needed to analyze the impact of these solutions on the trust in ATs of (novice) software architects.

The second limitation ("mail support was required pointing to the Experimentation Automation Framework for conducting AT-based analyses") relates to a tooling issue in the Experimentation Automation Framework as extended by AT tooling (cf. Appendix B.2). In its current form, the Experimentation Automation Framework provides the required functionality to extend architectural analyses with AT support. However, the Experiment Automation Framework lacks an intuitive user interface for configuring architectural analyses. Due to this lack, Rogic has particularly ran into problems to create a correct configuration and, consequently, has requested my support via mail. Upon having received this request, I have pointed Rogic to an example configuration. Based on this example, Rogic finally managed to create a correct configuration to run architectural analyses with the Experimentation Automation Framework.

Given the observed issue, future work should target improving the usability of the Experiment Automation Framework. A promising direction for such an improvement is provided by the CloudScale Environment [Cloa]: the CloudScale Environment also extends the Experiment Automation Framework but enriches it with a dedicated and intuitive user interface. An integration of this user interface into the Experiment Automation Framework itself is, however, missing at the moment.

5.3.4. Further Case Studies

Because only the WordCount case study (cf. Section 5.3.2) involves an AT with initiator template capabilities, I have conducted further (but smaller) case studies with a special focus on ATs used as initiator templates. This section briefly points to these case studies: a migration of previously existing initiator templates of Palladio projects (Section 5.3.4.1) and the creation of initiator templates for the book shop example and CloudStore (Section 5.3.4.2).

5.3.4.1. Migration of Templates from the Palladio Template Wizard

The wizard coming with AT tooling (cf. Section B.1.1) was inspired by the original Palladio project wizard [Palb]. The original wizard comes with four initiator templates ("Minimum Example Template", "Minimum Event Template", "PCM Standard Components and Interfaces Repository", "Techreport Component Type Example"). These templates are normal Palladio projects that are simply copied by the wizard into a new Palladio project during a wizard-based initialization.

With AT tooling, such a behavior can be similarly realized by an AT that contains just a default AT instance pointing to a templated Palladio project; no AT roles are needed. I have accordingly created an AT for migrating each of the four templates from the original wizard. Moreover, the AT catalog containing these templates is shipped along with AT tooling (see [ATt]). AT tooling therefore provides full support for initializing the Palladio projects available in the old Palladio wizard.

Given that I only had to link the originally used templates from the new ATs, AT creation required only minor effort. On average, I required approximately 2 *minutes* for creating such ATs.

I conclude that such simple initiator templates—without AT roles and planned variation points—can be created with less effort than reference architectures as, e.g., investigated in the WordCount case study (cf. Section 5.3.2). The fact that I was able to migrate pre-existing templates (that have existed independently of the AT method) particularly indicates that this result has a high external validity.

5.3.4.2. Creation of ATs for the Book Shop Example and CloudStore

Similarly to the initiator templates described in the preceding section, I have created ATs to initialize the book shop example from Chapter 3 and for the CloudStore model from Section 5.3.1. Again, the AT catalog containing these templates is shipped along with AT tooling (see [ATt]) and provides an efficient means to instantiate these models. Confirming the results from the preceding section, I have only required approximately 2 *minutes* for creating these ATs.

5.4. Controlled Experiment

Motivated by threats to validity for the conducted case studies (cf. Appendix C), controlled experiments should be conducted to analyze the AT method further. Such controlled experiments promise more reproducible and statistically solid results.

To ease planning such controlled experiments in future works, this section outlines a design for such experiments and summarizes an already conducted pre-study based on this design. The design follows the lessons learned for conducting controlled experiments in the context of architectural analyses that we have derived within a survey [LB15c]. Moreover, the pre-study was conducted by Nützel in the context of his Bachelor's thesis [Nï15]. While this section only provides a summary, Appendix E provides a detailed report of the execution, analysis, and interpretation of the pre-study.

5.4.1. Controlled Experiment Design

The goal of a controlled experiment for the AT method will typically be a refinement of the goal given in the introduction of this chapter. The case studies on Section 5.3.1, Section 5.3.2, and Section 5.3.3 each exemplify such a refinement. Also Nützel's goal corresponds to the goal stated in this chapter's introduction [Nï15, Sec. 1.2].

Analogously to case studies, controlled experiments are reported according to a typical structure like described by Jedlitschka et al. [JCP08]. The subsequent sections follow this structure to describe the design of controlled experiments for the AT method. Section 5.4.1.1 describes potential research questions and empirical procedures. Afterwards, Section 5.4.1.2 outlines a plan for a controlled experiment (required experiment material, tasks, and scenarios). Subjects involved in controlled experiments are characterized in Section 5.4.1.3.

5.4.1.1. Controlled Experiment: Research Questions and Procedures

The evaluation design described in Section 5.2 provides a good resource for research questions and procedures for data collection, analysis, and validity. The evaluation design has proven to be applicable in the previously described case studies. Moreover, also Nützel's controlled experiment uses research questions [Nï5, Sec. 3.5] and procedures [Nï5, Sec. 3.8] from this evaluation design.

Additionally, our survey [LB15c] reveals that experiments often assess the quality with which subjects achieve their tasks, e.g., in terms of correctness and analysis accuracy. For architectural analyses, our survey particularly reveals that achieved prediction accuracy can be assessed, e.g., against a reference solution. Nützel follows this idea as described in his experiment design [Nï5, Sec. 3.5].

5.4.1.2. Controlled Experiment: Experiment Planning

During experiment planning, a protocol for the experiment is created that reproducibly describes how to conduct the experiment [JCP08]. This section outlines relevant aspects of experiment planning for the AT method: the general experiment design, scenarios used within the experiment, required material for experimentation, and concrete tasks to be conducted by subjects during the experiment.

Design Nützel [Nï5, Sec. 3.2] suggests a between-subject design for the controlled experiment, i.e., an experiment involving a treatment and a control group.

In the treatment group, software architects first have to attend a one-day workshop on Palladio, SimuLizar, and the AT method. Afterwards, the software architects follow the AT method to solve a common task—the modification and analysis of a given architectural model.

The control group consists of software architects that have to use Palladio and SimuLizar natively to solve the common task. In contrast to the treatment group, experts on SimuLizar are selected as subjects, thus, no preceding training is required.

Nützel's hypothesis [Nï5, Sec. 3.5] is that, after the workshop, even novice software architects out-perform (regarding prediction accuracy and required effort) the SimuLizar experts in modifying and analyzing a given architectural model when following the AT method. The questions and procedures from Section 5.4.1.1 are used to test this hypothesis.

Scenarios During the controlled experiment, subjects have to solve tasks for one or more architectural analysis scenarios. For receiving reproducible and comparable results, these scenarios must be characterized in detail. Moreover, selected scenarios must find a balance between complexity and simplicity; given that subjects will have a limited amount of time to solve the task. Goal and research questions generally allow to set a focus, determining the required level of complexity.

In the controlled experiment planned by Nützel [Nï5, Sec. 3.3], a simple variant of CloudStore (cf. Section 5.3.1) is used as scenario. The scenario starts with a given CloudStore model that violates pre-specified SLOs. The task of subjects is to resolve these violations by applying reusable architectural knowledge (the vertical scaling and the horizontal scaling architectural patterns).

In the following, CloudStore is used to exemplify other aspects of experiment planning.

Experiment Material Experiment materials are objects used during controlled experiments [JCP08]. For the AT method, Nützel [Nï5, Sec. 3.3] provides the following experiment materials:

Installation guides (Appendix D.1 and Appendix D.2): A set of documents explaining the setup of the tooling environment (Palladio, SimuLizar, and AT tooling). The documents include installation guidelines for the Eclipse IDE and required plug-ins. Moreover, they describe how an example project can be imported.

Workshop document (Appendix D.3): A document describing who to train software architects in using Palladio, SimuLizar, and AT tooling. The document comes in the form of a hands-on workshop with tasks to be executed.

CloudStore description (Appendix D.4): A description of CloudStore; similar to the description given in Appendix C.1.1. CloudStore is used as a scenario during the experiment.

CloudStore models (*evaluation* project available at [ATt]): A set of Palladio projects (for treatment and control group, respectively) containing the CloudStore model.

Task descriptions (Appendix D.5 and Appendix D.6): Descriptions of tasks to be executed by the human subjects of the controlled experiment. For each of the two groups, i.e., the treatment and the control group, a dedicated task description document is provided.

Tasks Nützel [Nï15, Sec. 3.4] structures the experiment in tasks to be executed by involved human subjects. The previously described experiment materials contain detailed descriptions of these tasks (see Appendix D.5 and Appendix D.6). In summary, treatment and control group have to proceed as follows:

(1) answer background questions to collect information about characteristics and context of the human subject. For example, subjects are asked to rate their knowledge of Eclipse, ATs, SimuLizar, and model transformations. These factors potentially help to interpret experimentation results once collected.

(2) understand architectural analysis scenario to become familiar to the given case that is investigated. In Nützel's experiment [Nï15, Sec. 3.3], CloudStore without self-adaptation capabilities and with a performance bottleneck is given as a scenario.

Subjects first have to read a description of CloudStore as given in Appendix D.4. Because each subject is given the same description, it is expected that each subject gains the same level knowledge about CloudStore.

Afterwards, subjects have to answer control questions about CloudStore, e.g., asking for the rationale of CloudStore's worker pools. These questions are expected to help subjects understanding the scenario. Moreover, the answers to these questions allow to assess whether subjects have indeed understood the given description of CloudStore or whether there are deviations among subjects.

Finally, subjects have to import a given CloudStore model (*evaluation* project at [ATt]) into their workspace and analyze this model to detect the performance issue. These tasks are expected to help subjects deepen their understanding of CloudStore further. As before, control questions allow to assess whether subjects have executed the tasks correctly or whether there are deviations among subjects.

(3) resolve QoS issues either with support for ATs (treatment group) or without such support (control group).

Similar to the case descriptions of this chapter's case studies, Nützel's task description first states the targeted SLOs for performance, elasticity, and cost-efficiency. From the analysis of the previous task, it is evident that the current CloudStore version violates these SLOs and, thus, a QoS issue needs to be resolved.

Subjects are therefore asked to analyze whether the application of reusable architectural knowledge would help to fulfill these SLOs. First, subjects have to investigate the application of the vertical scaling architectural pattern (cf. Appendix C.1.4.3). Second, subjects have to investigate the application of the horizontal scaling architectural pattern for resource containers (cf. Appendix C.1.4.3).

For both of these knowledge applications, subjects get a brief description of the respective architectural pattern. Moreover, subjects get configuration parameters, e.g., stating when a self-adaptation shall be triggered. As before, control questions check whether subjects were successful, e.g., in knowledge application, architectural analysis, and in resolving the QoS issue.

The treatment group is pointed to the documentation of the AT catalog to be used [Clob]. Subjects have to select and apply the *vertical scaling* and *horizontal scaling* ATs based on the descriptions of this catalog. No subject has applied these ATs before because, during the workshop, only other ATs are used for training.

The control group, in contrast, is forbidden to apply ATs. However, subjects are explicitly allowed to reuse any existing reconfigurations

("You may copy transformation code from existing reconfigurations or completely reuse an existing transformation, if you know any."). For example, subjects may reuse the default examples for vertical scaling coming with SimuLizar or they may copy reconfigurations included within corresponding ATs. Given that we have selected subjects from a group of SimuLizar experts that partly even know the AT method, the expectation was that subjects indeed make use of this possibility (which, however, turned out to be not the case).

(4) finalize experiment by handing-over the filled-out task description and any other produced results (e.g., screenshots from architectural analyses) to the experimenter.

5.4.1.3. Controlled Experiment: Subjects

The design of the controlled experiment requires the selection of human subjects that are divided into a treatment and a control group. While subjects of the treatment group are assumed to be software architects with no experience with the AT method, subjects of the control group are assumed to be experts on Palladio and SimuLizar. Therefore, the treatment group undergoes a training prior to executing experiment tasks; the control group directly executes experiment tasks.

In Nützel's pre-study [N15, Sec. 4.2], 5 subjects participated in the treatment group and 3 subjects in the control group. These subjects have the following characteristics.

The 5 subjects from the treatment group were selected from employees of the Software Engineering Chair of the TU Chemnitz. Out of these subjects, 3 subjects were student workers with a Bachelor's degree in computer science, i.e., with a basic understanding of software engineering. The other 2 subjects were PhD students with a Master's degree in computer science, i.e., potentially with a more solid understanding of software engineering. Moreover, the experiment was accounted for their normal work as employees.

The 3 subjects in the control group were selected from the Software Engineering Group and Heinz Nixdorf Institute of the Paderborn University and volunteered to participate in the experiment. All subjects had at least a

Bachelor's degree in computer science and extensively worked on both Palladio and SimuLizar (at least one year active development and usage). These subjects can therefore be seen as experts on Palladio and SimuLizar. Moreover, 2 subjects (Daria Giacinto and Matthias Becker; cf. Appendix C.1.3.3) had experience with the AT method; however, being in the control group, were forbidden to follow the AT method.

5.4.2. Summary of Preliminary Lessons Learned

This section briefly summarizes the main lessons learned within Nützel's preliminary controlled experiment [Nï15, Chap. 4–6]; a detailed analysis and interpretation is provided in Appendix E. The summary is aligned along the questions of the evaluation design (cf. Section 5.2). Only questions relevant for AT application are considered because the controlled experiment does not involve the specification of new ATs.

$Q_{\text{application effort}}$: **How much effort do software architects require to apply ATs?** Software architects have low effort in using ATs for architectural analyses (compared to the overall efforts for specifying architectural models). Indeed, with an average of 9.4 *minutes* for the *horizontal scaling* AT, subjects of the controlled experiment were close to our efforts of 6 *minutes* to apply this AT during the CloudStore case study (cf. Section 5.3.1). Given that inexperienced software architects were selected as subjects, our results from Section 5.3.3.4 are therefore confirmed: the AT method indeed achieves an increase efficiency for novice software architects.

$Q_{\text{effort saving}}$: **How much creation effort can software architects save when applying ATs?** Saved efforts increase with the amount of self-adaptations included in ATs. Indeed, we can confirm that we had significant efforts for specifying the self-adaptation rules of the investigated ATs (cf. Appendix C.1.4.4) and, thus, reusing these rules saves a significant amount of effort. The two investigated ATs indicate that the faced time can range from half an hour to more than two hours. Compared to the typical time for applying ATs (3 *minutes* on average; cf. the CloudStore case study), the saved time of 36.7 *minutes* (*vertical scaling* AT) and 110.6 *minutes* (*horizontal scaling* AT) is significant because these values range from approximately 92 % to approximately 97 % saved time.

Moreover, the data for these adaptation-intensive ATs shows that reuse of adaptation rules can render other effort-saving factors less significant. For example, our data shows that the number of captured components is a bad indicator for saved effort of the investigated ATs. The data therefore indicates that combining various metrics (e.g., via a linear combination) potentially yields a better predictor for effort saving than considering each metric in separation.

Moreover, the data indicates that effort can effectively be lowered by applying ATs. The interpretation of this result is analogous to the CloudStore case study because both the *vertical scaling* AT and the *horizontal scaling* AT were applied there as well.

$Q_{\text{conformance}}$: **Do software architects have effective benefits from checking whether their architectural models violate conformance to applied ATs?** At least for this setup of the controlled experiment where the *vertical scaling* AT and *horizontal scaling* AT are applied to CloudStore, no benefits were gained from automated conformance checks. Appendix C.3.3.3 discusses this observation in detail.

Q_{benefits}: **What are effective benefits of the AT method?** We have collected 2 benefits during the experiment. These benefits indicate that experiment tasks were clear and that AT application is manageable in the context of controlled experiments.

The first benefit ("the instructions for the experiment were good") covers the clarity of experiment tasks. A subject of the control group explicitly wrote this statement in a free text field of the task description. The fact that the subject did so without being asked explicitly about the quality of the instructions is an indication that the task description is indeed comprehensible. Another indication for comprehensibility is that we received no clarification questions regarding the task description. We conclude that experiments in future work can reuse our task description or create similar ones.

The second benefit ("based on an AT's documentation, AT application is straight-forward") points to the suitability of AT applications within controlled experiments and a good usability of ATs in general. However, for the *vertical scaling* AT, we observed confusion about how to apply the AT. Only after we have again pointed to the Wiki with the AT's documentation [Clob], participants were able to correctly apply the AT. Afterwards, for the *horizontal scaling* AT, participants had no problems to apply the AT. We conclude that AT documentation is essential. While the Wiki [Clob] has the advantage that it is easily accessible, its disadvantage is that it is not tightly integrated into AT tooling—software architects currently have to manually access the Wiki. Future versions of AT tooling should therefore strive for a tight integration of AT documentation in addition to the Wiki, e.g., by offering a context help during AT application.

$Q_{\text{limitations}}$**: What are effective limitations of the AT method?** We have collected 3 limitations during the experiment. The limitations mainly point to technical issues in AT tooling and in tools extended by AT tooling.

The first limitation ("the main issue is with compilation errors produced when something is wrong with the QVT-O file and with debugging support") was reported by a subject of the control group and relates to difficulties when specifying reconfiguration rules for SimuLizar. The subject notes that debugging is difficult when using QVT-O in conjunction with SimuLizar. SimuLizar indeed lacks support for a debugging mode in which breakpoints in the QVT-O file are considered; debugging is purely based on logging. Furthermore, we have experienced the same issue when we acted as AT engineers to specify ATs that include reusable self-adaptation rules. While this is only a technical issue and no conceptual one, future work on SimuLizar on improving debugging support can increase SimuLizar's practical relevance.

The second limitation ("the reconfiguration engine does not work correctly") describes an issue observed by a subject of the control group. Instead of using *QVT-O*, the subject tried to use Story Diagrams [vDHP+12] as an alternative M2M transformation language to specify reconfiguration rules (cf. Section 2.5.3.2). Unfortunately, SimuLizar's engine for executing reconfiguration rules for Story Diagrams suffers from bugs causing a wrong reconfiguration behavior. Because of this technical issue, the subject was unable to provide correct analysis result. This issue should be fixed in future works, despite not affecting the utility of ATs as long as QVT-O reconfiguration rules are used.

The third limitation ("tooling problems still exist") is an observation we made during the controlled experiment with the treatment group. As described in Appendix E.1, we had to intervene because of problems in AT tooling. However, at the time of writing, the reported problem has been already resolved in AT tooling.

This example shows that Nützel's pre-study has helped in improving the AT method. Moreover, despite conceptually unimportant, tooling issues bias subjects in empirical evaluations. These biases can lead to questionable conclusions that, most notably, may not reflect the properties of the concepts under investigation. We therefore conclude that future empirical investigations should optimally first resolve currently known tooling issues or explicitly explain subjects how to handle such issues.

5.5. Evaluation of AT Method Extensions

The evaluation of the extensions of the AT method (described in Section 4.4) indicates the effectiveness of these extensions. Section 5.5.1 briefly outlines Openkowski's evaluation of the reuse mechanism for AT specification that indicates an increase in productivity of AT engineers. Afterwards, Section 5.5.2 summarizes a successful proof-of-concept evaluation of the optimization approach for actual AT parameters.

5.5.1. Evaluation of the Reuse Mechanism for AT Specification

Openkowski has evaluated the reuse mechanism for AT specification (cf. Section 4.4.1) in his Master's thesis [Ope17, Chap. 9]. His results indicate an increased productivity of AT engineers when reuse is possible.

Openkowski started the evaluation by selecting reuse scenarios, e.g., the combination of the *loadbalancing* AT with an AT capturing the caching architectural pattern [BHS07a, Sec. 7.10]. Afterwards, he has realized each scenario in two variants: a variant based on the novel reuse mechanism and a variant based on copying specification elements from two existing ATs into a new AT that combines the two ATs. Finally, he has compared both variants for each reuse scenario regarding specification effort and quality of the resulting AT. While quality has remained constant, his results indicate a significantly lower effort; resulting in an average productivity increase of 210 % over all investigated reuse scenarios.

Openkowski's Master's thesis [Ope17, Chap. 9] provides a detailed description of this evaluation, including a threads to validity discussion.

5.5.2. Evaluation of the Optimization of Actual AT Parameters

We have successfully conducted a small proof-of-concept evaluation for the optimization of actual AT parameters (cf. Section 4.4.2). For this evaluation, we have created a minimal example architectural model where the *loadbalancing* AT is applied [Loa]. Afterwards, we configured PerOpteryx with a degree of freedom that varies the value of the *number of replicas* parameter. Running PerOpteryx with this configuration takes about 2 *minutes* total execution time and points to an optimal value of 2 replicas. We have concluded that the optimization of such parameters is possible, however, further investigations are needed for more generalizable results.

5.6. Lessons Learned

This section summarizes the evaluation of the AT method. Section 5.6.1 lists and discusses the main lessons learned from the conducted empirical studies. These lessons show that the goal to analyze the AT method (cf. introduction of this chapter) is attained to a great extent. Moreover, further experiments are required to strengthen the validity and the extend of gained insights as summarized in Section 5.6.2. The generalizability of gained insights is finally discussed in Section 5.6.3.

5.6.1. Summary of Answers to Research Questions

Overall, learned lessons point to a gained effectivity and efficiency for software architects. The work of AT engineers is effectively supported by the proposed quality assurance techniques while their effort is high compared to the overall specification effort for a single architectural model. However, these efforts pay-off when ATs are reused for specifying and analyzing further models.

In detail, we have learned the following lessons; formulated as answers to (and ordered by) the questions posed in the evaluation design in Section 5.2:

(1) **AT application is a matter of minutes; the required effort increases slightly with the number of ATs to select from, an AT's roles and parameters, and the number of AT roles to be bound.**

Experienced software architects with existing knowledge of the AT method manage to select and apply ATs to architectural models in up to 7 minutes (cf. the CloudStore case study). Using ATs as initiator templates involves less effort, i.e., approximately 2 minutes for experienced software architects (cf. the WordCount case study). The pre-study of the controlled experiment particularly shows that even inexperience software architects manage AT applications within 7 minutes after having completed a one-day training.

Furthermore, the measurements of size-based metrics point to factors impacting the required efforts of software architects. The effort for selecting ATs is impacted by the size of employed AT catalogs. The effort for binding a selected AT is impacted by the number of AT roles, parameters, and actually bound AT roles. As discussed for the CloudStore case study (Appendix C.1.4.5), a single factor alone is a bad predictor for estimating the time that software architects will require applying a given AT. However, a metric that combines these factors via a weighted function promises to be a good predictor; similar to the complexity metrics discussed by Martens et al. [MKPR11]. Future work on determining these weights and assessing the resulting metric is still needed, though.

The evaluation of the optimization mechanism (Section 5.5.2) has shown that the determination of suitable AT parameters can be automated. This automation promises to make software architects even more efficient, however, further evaluations of this optimization are required.

(2) **Depending on the kind of knowledge, software architects can save hours (i.e., more than 90 %) of recurring modeling efforts by applying ATs; the saved efforts increase with the number of AT-induced elements (components, assembly contexts, operations, self-adaptation rules, etc.).**

ATs can be seen as an automation of recurring modeling tasks. In this sense, it is quite obvious that software architects save effort when applying ATs. Indeed, we, acting as software architects, have required only a maximum of 7 minutes (cf. the CloudStore case study) to select and apply a single AT while we have measured time savings beyond 2 hours (i.e., more than 90 % of modeling time; cf. the pre-study to the controlled experiment). Interestingly, we have observed differences in the amount of saved effort depending on the kind of captured architectural knowledge (architectural styles, architectural patterns, and reference architectures).

At the lower end of the scale, captured architectural styles appear to save the least effort: the size-based effort metrics for the *three-layer* AT in the CloudStore case study indicate that no effort is saved at all. However, given that architectural styles only provide design decisions that constrain systems (cf. Section 2.2.4.1), effort saving cannot be measured in terms of size-based metrics, which quantify existential decisions only. Better measures for architectural styles are, for instance, metrics that quantify saved maintainability efforts due to automated conformance checks. An investigation of such measures for maintainability scenarios and saved maintainability efforts is left as future work.

Higher on the scale, ATs that capture architectural patterns achieve the effort savings over 90 % as described above. Opposed to architectural styles, size-based metrics are suitable indicators for these effort savings. The reason is that architectural patterns provide existential decisions (cf. Section 2.2.4.2) and size-based metrics quantify the impact of captured existential decisions. The CloudStore case study shows that ATs that capture architectural patterns can save effort for the creation of components, assembly contexts, and self-adaptation rules. However, analogously to the metrics that quantify effort of software architects (discussed in the preceding lesson), sticking only to a single size-based metric leads to bad predictions for saved efforts. Again, combining and weighting these metrics within a composed metric promises a more universal predictor; its derivation and assessment is left as future work.

At the upper end of the scale, the WordCount case study indicates that captured reference architectures save the most creation effort: size-based metrics for the *Hadoop MapReduce* AT have higher values than the ATs investigated in the other studies. As reasoned in Section 5.3.2.4, the increased effort saving can be explained by the property of reference architectures to provide an architectural style and a set of architectural patterns (cf. Section 2.2.4.3). Moreover, reference architectures can even define additional operations; as measured via $M_{\Delta\mathbf{operations}}$. A downside of reference architectures is, however, their restriction to specific domains and, thus, their more limited reusability.

(3) **Conformance checks can help maintaining conformance to captured architectural knowledge while AT tooling often ensures conformance by construction; however, additional long-term investigations regarding maintainability are missing.**

In the CloudStore case study, we, acting as software architects, have successfully detected and resolved a conformance violation to the applied *three-layer* AT. Therefore, we concluded that ATs can help maintaining the conformance to architectural styles imposed on architectural models.

For other kinds of architectural knowledge, we have observed that AT tooling often ensures conformance by construction, i.e., no explicit detection of conformance violation is necessary. As discussed in the WordCount case study, AT tooling ensures that AT roles can only be bound to architectural elements, thus, making wrong bindings impossible. Moreover, the AT-based initialization of captured reference architectures creates conforming models automatically, which again avoids conformance violations.

In the Znn.com case study and the controlled experiment, we have observed that ATs of architectural patterns often involve no complex constraints because they only focus on correctly set AT parameters. For example, a constraint of the *horizontal scaling* AT checks that only positive values are assigned to the *number of initial replicas* parameter. Because no subject violated such constraints, we have concluded that names of AT parameters suggest valid values intuitively; making conformance violations unlikely.

However, our evaluation only covers short-term investigations for conformance checks. As we discuss in the context of the CloudStore case study, long-term benefits of conformance checks regarding maintainability are expected, especially if further software architects get involved in modifications. Therefore, an interesting future work is an investigation of such long-term benefits.

(4) **Several effective benefits (beyond saved efforts and consistency checks) have been observed during the evaluation; highlights are the possibility of making context-aware informed decisions, complexity hiding, reusability of ATs, an increased effectivity and efficiency of novice software architects, and the learnability of the AT method based on the available documentation.**

The preceding lessons point to the main promises of the AT method: an increased effectivity and efficiency for software architects, e.g., due to an automated consistency checking. In addition to these benefits, we have observed further benefits during our evaluation. The most interesting of these benefits are the following:

context-aware informed decisions: during the CloudStore case study, we were surprised that an increased number of load-balanced replica can degrade capacity. This degradation is in contrast to what the loadbalancing architectural pattern promises. However, the architectural analysis has revealed that CloudStore's Database Server—a context factor for the loadbalancer—actually becomes overloaded when too many replica exist. In general, recurring architectural knowledge therefore does not help per se; it depends on the context.

Fortunately, combining recurring architectural knowledge with architectural analyses has enabled us to detect this issue and to make appropriate design decisions as countermeasures. Results from architectural analyses have particularly allowed us to make these decisions in an informed manner.

complexity hiding: in the WordCount case study, we have observed that the *Hadoop MapReduce* AT hides complexity of the captured architectural knowledge. Complexity is caused by the size of Apache's MapReduce framework that would, without AT support, require software architects to understand how to setup, operate, and analyze Apache Hadoop applications. In capturing these information via an AT, software architects can directly analyze such applications without deep knowledge of Apache's MapReduce framework.

This example suggests that complexity hiding is especially high for captured reference architectures, due to the higher amount of captured design decisions. Future work may inspect this benefit further, e.g., for other kinds of architectural knowledge.

reusability of ATs: in both, the Znn.com case study and the controlled experiment, software architects have reused ATs specified during the CloudStore case study. While we have therefore observed successful intra-domain reuse, future empirical studies may inspect inter-domain reuse as well (cf. Section 5.3.3.4).

increased effectivity and efficiency of novice architects: during both the case study on Znn.com and the controlled experiment, novice software architects have successfully applied ATs. We have therefore concluded that the AT method leverages deep architectural knowledge to an abstraction level at which even novice software architects can apply this knowledge. This benefit is therefore a consequence of complexity hiding (see above).

learnability of the AT method via the available documentation: after the pre-study on the controlled experiment, subjects have stated that AT application is straight-forward based on an AT's documentation. These statements indicate that the documentation of the AT method and concrete ATs is easy to learn, given that novice software architects successfully applied previously unknown ATs.

Moreover, documentation of ATs appears to be essential and, thus, needs to be easily accessible by software architects. While our current approach of documenting ATs in a Wiki [Clob] provides a platform-independent and ubiquitous way of documentation, a tighter integration with AT tooling potentially eases documentation access further. Such a tight integration is therefore planned as a future work.

(5) **Several effective limitations have been observed during the evaluation; main limitations are technical issues in AT tooling and external tools, immature ATs, visualization issues, and distrust in ATs.**

We have observed several limitations of the AT method during our evaluation. The main limitations fit into the following categories:

technical issues in AT tooling: AT tooling currently has some limitations of technical nature that should be fixed in the future. While these limitations are conceptually unimportant, such fixes will improve the practical relevance of the AT method and lower potential threats to the validity of future empirical investigations.

In detail, we have identified the following issues in AT tooling:

- the editor for specifying constraints via OCL lacks a static syntax analysis and syntax highlighting (cf. Section 5.3.1.4),
- the EMF profiles framework is error-prone and hard to debug in case of errors (cf. Section 5.3.1.4), and
- altering self-adaptation rules contained in an AT requires the adaptation of the whole AT (cf. Section 5.3.1.4).

For resolving these issues, we suggest an integrated AT specification environment that hides the EMF profiles framework in the background, provides debugging support, and supports static syntax checks and syntax highlighting of constraints formulated in OCL.

technical issues in external tools: we have observed some technical issues in external tools that are extended by AT tooling. Similarly to the preceding issues, these issues are conceptually unimportant but should be fixed for an increased practical relevance and fewer threats in future empirical investigations.

In detail, we have identified the following issues in external tools:

- SimuLizar lacks support for asynchronous communication, which should be added (cf. Section 5.3.2.4),
- SimuLizar lacks support for debugging QVT-O reconfiguration rules, which should also be added (cf. Section 5.4.2),
- SimuLizar suffers from bugs in its execution engine for Story Diagrams that should be fixed (cf. Section 5.4.2), and
- the Experiment Automation Framework lacks an intuitive user interface; future work should provide such an interface based on the interface provided in the CloudScale Environment (cf. Section 5.3.3.4).

immature ATs: the *Hadoop MapReduce* AT is only a proof-of-concept realization and requires further improvement; the maturity of other ATs needs to be assessed in further reuse scenarios (cf. Section 5.3.2.4).

visualization issues: the *Hadoop MapReduce* ATs has shown that AT-based architectural models can appear incomplete, due to missing elements that will be created by AT completions. We have therefore suggested to enrich views on AT-based architectural models with previews of AT-induced elements (cf. Section 5.3.2.4).

distrust in ATs: software architects may doubt whether ATs function correctly even if these ATs are correct. We have observed such a distrust in ATs in the Znn.com case study where a novice software architect has blamed the AT for causing unexpected analysis results, despite context factors were the actual cause. We have therefore suggested to train software architects for such situations and to support them via automated quality anti-pattern and hotspot detections (cf. Section 5.3.3.4).

(6) **AT specification efforts can take several person months for (1) identifying suitable QoS properties and analysis approaches in domains lacking established metrics and analyses and (2) specifying complex and exhaustive architectural knowledge, for instance, large reference architectures. Otherwise, the specification and quality assurance of a single AT is a matter of hours; depending on the number of captured constraints for architectural styles, the size of an AT's completion for architectural patterns, and the complexity of the knowledge to be captured for reference architectures. Initiator ATs without variation points can be created within minutes.**

In domains where novel QoS properties and metrics have to be identified and integrated into architectural analyses (as part of AT specification), efforts for these tasks can take several person months. For example, we, acting as AT engineers, have spent 2.5 *person months* for these tasks in the CloudStore case study due to the novelty of scalability, elasticity, and cost-efficiency in the cloud computing domain. Fortunately, such efforts have only to be investigated once per novel QoS property and can be reused for further AT specifications.

Moreover, similarly high specification efforts can arise if the captured knowledge is complex and exhaustive. For example, we have spent 2.5 *person months* for creating the reference architectural model of Apache's MapReduce framework (Hadoop) in the WordCount case study. We suspect that such high efforts only occur for reference architectures because we have not observed such high efforts for capturing other kinds of reusable architectural knowledge (cf. Section 5.3.1.4).

For other kinds of knowledge, we have observed that AT engineers require approximately 8 *hours* for creating a single AT in the CloudStore case study. Of these 8 *hours*, AT engineers have typically spend 1 *hour* on selecting the architectural knowledge to be specified, 4 *hours* on the specification itself, and 3 *hours* on quality assurance.

Furthermore, the measurements of size-based metrics point to factors impacting the required efforts of AT engineers. While we have not revealed relevant factors over each kind of architectural knowledge (cf. Section 5.3.1.4), we have identified potential factors for each kind in separation. The effort for capturing architectural styles is impacted by the number of captured constraints. Based on the *three-layer* AT (cf. Section 5.3.1.4), we estimate that AT specification requires approximately 10 *minutes* per captured constraint. The effort for capturing architectural patterns is reflected in the size of an AT's completions. Based on the architectural patterns specified in the CloudStore case study, we estimate that AT specification requires approximately 1 *hour* per 100 to 150 *lines of code* of an AT's completion. As argued above, the efforts for reference architectures mainly depend on the complexity of the captured architectural knowledge. Finally, we have found no indication that the number of AT roles plays a significant role for specification efforts.

The specification of the ATs used as initiator templates in Section 5.3.4 has shown that such simple initiator ATs require only minor effort, i.e., approximately only 2 *minutes* per AT. These ATs are simple because they only link pre-existing architectural models via default AT instances; without defining AT roles and variation points. An interesting future work is therefore to inspect how such simple ATs can systematically be enriched with variation points, e.g., in a step-wise process. The outcome of such a process can, for instance, be a more complex reference architecture. Moreover, insights in the evolution of ATs can be gained when analyzing such a process.

The evaluation of the reuse mechanism for AT specification in Section 5.5.1 indicates that specification efforts can significantly be decreased in scenarios where reuse is possible. An external evaluation and further experimentation with further reuse scenarios is still needed, though.

In summary, this lesson provides a good first base line for estimating AT specification efforts. However, these estimates suffer from some validity threats, e.g., resulting from the fact that I (as an expert) have been involved in specifying most ATs. Further experimentation is therefore required to provide more solid estimates.

(7) **Quality assurance of ATs is effective because it enabled us to successfully detect and resolve faults.** AT testing has revealed faults in the specification of several ATs (cf. Section 5.3.1.4 and Section 5.3.3.4). Given that testing is a light-weight quality assurance technique, we have required little effort for quality assurance compared to a full-blown formal verification. The typical root causes for AT faults (cf. Section 4.1.3.3) have particularly helped to efficiently detect the actual faults. Once detected, we have shown that faults can be removed, thus, leading to an improved conceptual integrity. We therefore suggest to always include the proposed quality assurance steps in any AT specification efforts.

Given its importance, future work should target a more extensive tool support for quality assurance. For example, an automated generation of test models that cover the typical root causes for AT faults is a promising future work direction.

5.6.2. Summary of Threats to Validity

For the CloudStore case study, threats to validity are discussed in detail (Appendix C.1.4.6). Threats regarding WordCount, Znn.com, and the pre-study to the controlled experiment are briefly highlighted and related to the threats from the CloudStore case study in Appendix C.2.3.4, Appendix C.3.3.4, and Appendix E.4, respectively.

Being typical for empirical studies, a main threat to internal validity remains "low statistical power" (cf. Appendix C.1.4.6) because only few subjects—often only myself—were involved in executing actions of the AT method. The pre-study to the controlled experiment alleviates this threat for software architects (as multiple software architects have executed the same actions), however, for AT engineers, such an experiment is still left as future work.

Regarding external validity, some threats remain that affect the generalizability of the learned lessons. Generalizability is therefore discussed in the next section.

5.6.3. Discussion of Generalizability

Within the assumptions and limitations discussed in Section 4.5, our evaluation indicates that the AT method can be generalized to various computing paradigms and QoS properties. This section briefly discusses such generalization aspects.

We specified and applied ATs in the domains of distributed computing, cloud computing, and big data to conduct architectural analyses regarding performance, scalability, elasticity, and cost-efficiency. Our success shows that the AT method is applicable to these domains and QoS properties, and can potentially be generalized to further domains and QoS properties.

However, further empirical studies are needed for more conclusive results. The investigation of other domains (e.g., automotive) and QoS properties (e.g., reliability) is needed. A more detailed investigation of maintainability (an internal quality and not a QoS property) would especially be interesting as the *three-layer* AT already indicates that such quality properties can be covered as well.

"Inventing is a combination of brains and materials. The more brains you use, the less material you need."

— Charles Kettering 1876 – 1958

6. Related Work

The AT method is related to approaches that capture reusable architectural knowledge, especially in the context of architectural analyses. This chapter surveys such related works by analyzing appropriate research domains. The chapter inspects the following domains[1] (a typical key feature of the domain is given in parentheses and bold text at the end of the domain description):

Architectural knowledge management. In architectural knowledge management, design decisions are documented systematically. An example for such a design decision is the decision to apply reusable architectural knowledge, e.g., an architectural pattern. For documenting this kind of decision, approaches in architectural knowledge management typically link to informally captured knowledge (**informal documentation**).

Architectural description languages. The domain of architectural description languages (ADLs) focuses on the (semi-)formal specification of architectural models. Several approaches in this domain formally capture architectural styles and provide mechanisms to check whether architectural models conform to these styles (**conformance checks to architectural styles**).

Pattern community. The pattern community focuses on capturing patterns, e.g., design patterns and architectural patterns. Some approaches

[1] Related works on templates are described in Section 2.4 and on empirical studies in Section 5.1.

in this domain allow to formally capture such patterns and provide mechanisms to check whether architectural models conform to these patterns (**conformance checks to (architectural) patterns**).

Architectural analyses. The domain of architectural analyses provides approaches that quantify QoS properties based on analysis models that have been generated from architectural models. For the generation of analysis models, several of these approaches exploit formally captured knowledge (**QoS analysis**).

Figure 6.1 illustrates these domains, their key features, and associated approaches as investigated in this chapter. Each circle denotes a feature and includes the approaches that provide this feature. Analogously, each dashed rectangle denotes a domain and the approaches that belong to this domain. Approaches are denoted by a representative name in square brackets. For example, this chapter investigates the ADDSS approach (in Section 6.1.1), which belongs to the domain of architectural knowledge management and provides the informal documentation feature.

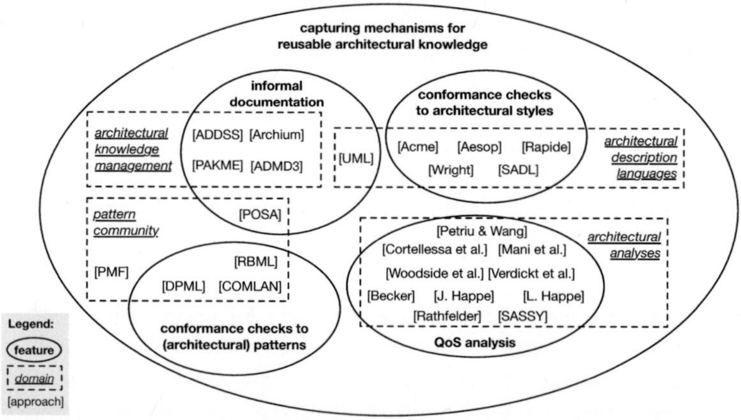

Figure 6.1.: Features and domains of approaches that can capture architectural knowledge.

As can be seen in Figure 6.1, all approaches provide capturing mechanisms for reusable architectural knowledge. Besides PMF, each approach additionally provides exactly one of the above-described key features (informal documentation, conformance checks to architectural patterns, conformance checks to architectural styles, or QoS analysis). In particular, the additional feature is typical for exactly one domain; only PMF, UML, and POSA deviate from this scheme.

Figure 6.1 shows that no approach provides a combination of these additional features. The AT method provides this combination, i.e., it uniquely combines:

capturing mechanisms for reusable architectural knowledge to enable architects to effectively and efficiently apply reusable architectural knowledge to architectural models,

informal documentation to ease software architects the selection of captured architectural knowledge,

conformance checks to ensure that captured knowledge is consistently applied, and

QoS analysis to provide software architects with quantitative data, allowing them to make more informed decisions about the suitability of applied knowledge.

In the remainder of this chapter, I detail this classification of related works and the AT method itself. I start with a detailed description and discussion of the domains and associated approaches, i.e., the architectural knowledge management domain (Section 6.1), the architectural description language (ADL) domain (Section 6.2), the pattern community domain (Section 6.3), and the architectural analysis domain (Section 6.4). Based on my per-domain discussions, I compile a feature model for methods that exploit reusable knowledge in architectural analyses (Section 6.5). This feature model allows me to classify each investigated approach and the AT method in detail (Section 6.6). Finally, I discuss this detailed classification, which confirms that the AT method provides a unique combination of existing features (Section 6.7). In the discussion, I particularly highlight which features would complement the AT method, thus, providing opportunities for future works.

6.1. Architectural Knowledge Management

Tyree and Akerman [TA05b] argue for documenting design decisions[2] to communicate the rationale of a software architecture among involved stakeholders. Moreover, for documenting design decisions, they propose an initiator template[3] [TA05b]. This initiator template is similar to initiator templates for documenting reusable architectural knowledge [HAZ07]. Given this similarity, the application of reusable architectural knowledge itself documents relevant design decisions in a reusable manner [HAZ07].

This thesis complies to these ideas by viewing reusable architectural knowledge as a set of proven design decisions (cf. Section 2.2.4). The application of ATs particularly documents the design decision to apply concrete reusable architectural knowledge. Therefore, the AT method is related to management tools for architectural knowledge. This section describes such tools and discusses their relation to the AT method.

Tang et al. [TAJ+10] compare tools to manage architectural knowledge. From these tools, only three support the application of reusable architectural knowledge as described above [TAJ+10]: ADDSS (Section 6.1.1), Archium (Section 6.1.2), and PAKME (Section 6.1.3). Moreover, in the Palladio community, a similar tool has been introduced—ADMD3 (Section 6.1.4).

Given their support for reusable architectural knowledge, all of these tools are closely related to the AT method. However, in contrast to the AT method, these tools lack support for automatically quantifying QoS properties with architectural analyses. To detail these issues, each of the four tools is described and related to the AT method in the following.

6.1.1. Architecture Design Decision Support System (ADDSS)

The Architecture Design Decision Support System (ADDSS) [CNPDn06] is a web-based tool for managing architectural knowledge in the form of architectural styles and architectural patterns. Using this tool, software architects can link requirements over design decisions to architectural models. Moreover, ADDSS captures the evolution of architectural knowledge, which

[2] Design decisions are described in Section 2.2.3.

[3] Initiator templates are described in Section 2.4.3.1.

allows software architects to inspect different versions, e.g., of architectural models as illustrated in Figure 6.2 and linked design decisions.

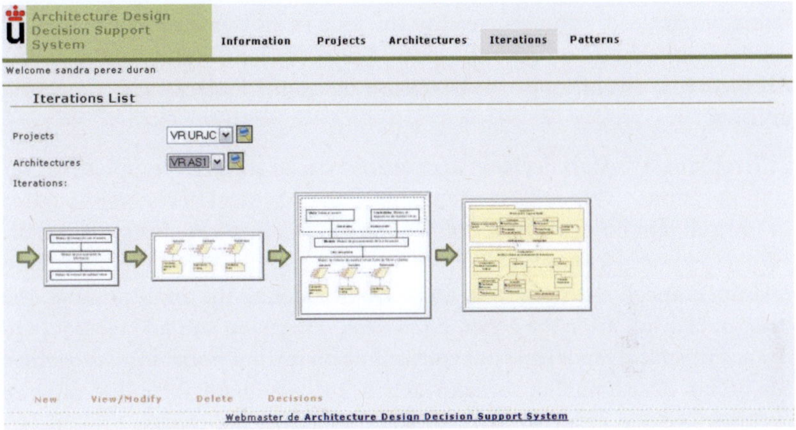

Figure 6.2.: Different model versions depicted as images (from [CNPDn06]).

Like the AT method, ADDSS allows software architects to document the application of reusable architectural knowledge with a focus on architectural styles and architectural patterns. ADDSS informally captures this reusable architectural knowledge with a unique name, a description in natural language, and a representative image.

However, ADDSS is limited regarding its integration into architectural analyses. For example, architectural models can only be captured as image files and ADDSS' reusable architectural knowledge covers only informal data such as a description in natural language. Therefore, ADDSS is suited for documentation tasks only. In contrast, the AT method both documents the application of reusable architectural knowledge and utilizes information from the reused knowledge within architectural analyses.

6.1.2. Archium

Jansen and Bosch introduce Archium [JB05] as an architectural knowledge management tool centered around the idea of software architecture as a set of design decisions (see the second part of Definition 2.7 at page 25). Accordingly, Archium provides design decisions as first-class modeling entities.

In Archium, a design decision is captured via an initiator template for design decisions. This initiator template covers typical decision attributes in natural language, for example, a general description, design rules, design constraints, consequences, advantages, and disadvantages. Software architects specify architectural models by modeling the application of one design decision after the other. Each design decision can add elements to the architectural model and put constraints on further decisions. Altogether, the design decisions that software architects have made form the software architecture and induce a corresponding architectural model.

Archium allows to formalize reusable architectural knowledge via a specialization of so-called design fragments. Design fragments capture a set of design decisions as modeled in Archium. Such a design fragment formalizes reusable architectural knowledge if exactly the knowledge's design decisions are captured by the fragment. Once specified, software architects can make the design decision to apply a design fragment—similar to applying an AT in the AT method.

Archium defines design decisions over a targeted architectural description language with common concepts like components and connectors. Therefore, Archium can better be integrated into architectural analyses as ADDSS (Section 6.1.1) that only captures architectural models via image files.

The implementation of Archium integrates the targeted architectural description language with the programming language Java [JvdVAH07]. In consequence, Archium's implementation only supports architectural decisions made within source code. The advantage of this close integration with a system's realization is that architectural knowledge is less likely to vaporize—the knowledge can explicitly be linked from source code to architectural model. The disadvantage of this close integration is that software architects have to work on a low level of abstraction. However, as described in Section 2.2, software architects often make design decisions before the actual source code is available. Furthermore, some design decisions cannot directly be linked to source code elements, e.g., decisions about the non-existence of elements and decisions motivated by the business environment (cf. [KLvV06]). For example, the design decision to develop a system in Java barely makes sense to be annotated in Java source code.

In the AT method, software architects can apply reusable architectural knowledge directly at the level of architectural models. In contrast to Archium, software architects can therefore make high level design decisions. Moreover, the AT method supports architectural analyses to quantify the impact of design decisions on a system's quality properties. Such analyses are not supported by Archium. For lower level decisions, the tight integration of Archium with source code is, however, a promising extension for actions that follow after the architectural analysis action in the development process (cf. Section 2.5.1). Langhammer and Krogmann [LK15] inspect such an extension in the context of architectural analyses; their extension is complementary to the AT method.

6.1.3. Process-Centric Architecture Knowledge Management Environment (PAKME)

A further web-based management tool for architectural knowledge is the Process-centric Architecture Knowledge Management Environment (PAKME) [ABGJ05]. PAKME follows a collaborative software architecture process that allows multiple stakeholders to manage architectural knowledge [BGK06]. PAKME's implementation [BG07a] uses initiator templates to capture such knowledge uniformly. Once captured, software architects can refer to this knowledge to reason about design decisions.

Compared to ADDSS (Section 6.1.1), the initiator templates of PAKME for reusable architectural knowledge are more fine-grained. For example, the template for architectural patterns in PAKME includes attributes for a pattern's application context, targeted problem, proposed solution, and affected QoS properties. ADDSS only provides a general description attribute for capturing such issues.

As for ADDSS, PAKME suffers from the fact that attributes are only captured in natural language, thus, making PAKME mainly suitable for documentation tasks. In contrast, the AT method both documents the application of reusable architectural knowledge and utilizes information from the reused knowledge within architectural analyses.

Moreover, PAKME lacks an explicit representation of architectural models; despite captured design decisions can imply such models [JvdVAH07]. Therefore, knowledge management and architectural models are decoupled in PAKME. This decoupling can foster the vaporization of architectural knowledge because software architects have to manually synchronize design decisions and architectural models. In the AT method, the application of reusable architectural knowledge is closely coupled with the targeted architectural model, thus, avoiding this potential for vaporization of knowledge.

6.1.4. Architectural Design and Modelling with Design Decision Documentation (ADMD3)

The Architectural Design and Modelling with Design Decision Documentation (ADMD3) approach [DR12, Dur16] introduces a method for architectural knowledge management. ADMD3's process, language, and tool combine a systematic requirement elicitation with architectural pattern selection and application to architectural models for documentation.

Whenever software architects want to select an architectural pattern from ADMD3's pattern catalog, they have to answer validation questions that are associated to this pattern. For example, a validation question associated to the loadbalancing architectural pattern may ask whether the targeted system is performance-critical. If software architects answer with "yes", the selected pattern is validated and software architects can apply the pattern. If software architects answer with "no", the selected pattern is invalidated and software architects have to continue with other architectural decisions than applying the pattern. If software architects cannot answer the associated questions, they have to elicit further requirements that allow them to eventually answer the questions. Analogously, if a selected and validated architectural pattern includes variants (e.g., a loadbalancer can be variable in its loadbalancing strategy), additional questions associated to the pattern determine a concrete variant. These additional questions either result in the selection of a variant, a variant's rejection, or in the elicitation of further requirements.

Finally, software architects can apply the selected and validated pattern variant to an architectural model. ADMD3 formalizes such applications based on roles, similar to the AT method. ADMD3's formalization approach reuses a dedicated framework for this purpose; the PMF as described in Section 6.3.5. Another commonality is that ADMD3's targeted architectural description language is the PCM (cf. Section 2.5.3.1).

Besides associated questions, ADMD3 formalizes architectural patterns using typical attributes of initiator templates for architectural patterns (Section 6.3.1 details a typical template) such as goal, keywords, advantages, drawbacks, QoS properties, and relations to other patterns. As for ADDSS (Section 6.1.1) and PAKME (Section 6.1.3), these attributes are captured in natural language, thus, only serving documentation and design decision tracing.

For documenting pattern advantages and drawbacks, ADMD3 assumes that a pattern's impact on QoS properties cannot accurately be evaluated [DR12]. Therefore, ADMD3 does not quantify such impacts but only documents whether the impact is generally positive or negative. The AT method rejects this assumption by providing means to evaluate QoS properties based on formalized reusable architectural knowledge—the main difference between ADMD3 and the AT method. Still, ADMD3 is interesting as an orthogonal extension of the AT method for earlier actions in the development process, i.e., requirement elicitation and systematic selection and validation of reusable architectural knowledge.

6.1.5. Discussion of Architectural Knowledge Management

The described tools for managing architectural knowledge all provide means to document reusable architectural knowledge and its application to architectural models. This documentation allows a system's stakeholders to comprehend taken design decisions. Applications of ATs are similar in this respect. Differences in the following concepts can be observed among the investigated tools.

Selection mechanism Most tools provide no systematic approach for selecting reusable architectural knowledge. Only ADMD3 provides an approach for this purpose; based on a systematic questioning technique.

The AT method currently lets software architects select ATs from AT catalogs, without further guidance. It would therefore be interesting to extend the AT method with an approach similar to ADMD3. Such an extension potentially makes the selection of ATs more systematic and efficient.

Capturing mechanism The tools vary in attributes to capture reusable architectural knowledge in natural language. While ADDSS provides a generic "description" attribute, PAKME and ADMD3 employ typical attributes of initiator templates for architectural knowledge. Archium uses an initiator template for design decisions; reusable architectural knowledge is captured as a composite design decision (a design fragment) that groups a set of sub-decisions.

The AT language formally captures reusable architectural knowledge via AT roles. AT roles capture decisions about constraints (via OCL) and the existence of elements (via completions). In addition, ATs provide a generic and informal "documentation" attribute in natural language; similar to ADDSS. Informal documentation is not the focus of the AT method—its focus is a formal combination of reusable architectural knowledge with architectural analyses. Future work may inspect the benefits (e.g., in terms of understandability) for software architects when using a more structured approach like Archium, PAKME, and ADMD3 for informal documentation.

Architectural models The described tools also vary in their dependency to architectural models. ADDSS only links to an image representing a system's software architecture and PAKME does not explicitly reference an architectural model at all. In contrast, Archium integrates the targeted architectural description language directly in source code, which requires existing source code but reduces knowledge vaporization.

Both ADMD3 and the AT method follow a role-based approach to bind reusable architectural knowledge to architectural models. The advantage of this approach is that design decisions are precisely and explicitly linked to architectural models (in contrast to ADDSS and PAKME) and that high-level decisions can be expressed (in contrast to Archium). Still, Archium's approach is an interesting extension for the AT method for actions that follow the architectural analysis action in a system's development process.

Support for architectural analyses The main difference between the AT method and the described tools is that none of these tools supports quantitative architectural analyses. These analyses allow software architects to quantify the impact of applied reusable architectural knowledge on QoS properties. Given such quantifications, software architects can make more informed decisions for the selection and application of reusable architectural knowledge. Particularly, software architects can reason on quantitative data when documenting the design decision to apply reusable architectural knowledge—here, the AT method provides a valuable extension to the domain of architectural knowledge management.

6.2. Architectural Knowledge in Architectural Description Languages

Formalizations of architectural styles originate from the architectural description language (ADL) community [Gie08, p. 51]. Therefore, several related works can be found in the ADL community, given that ATs can also formalize architectural styles as a concrete kind of reusable architectural knowledge. This section describes these related works and relates them to the AT method.

Medvidovic and Taylor [MT00] survey ten ADLs. From these ADLs, the following ones are related to the AT method because they allow for specifying architectural styles: Acme (Section 6.2.1), Aesop (Section 6.2.2), Rapide

(Section 6.2.3), SADL (Section 6.2.4), and Wright (Section 6.2.5).[4] The UML is relevant as well because the UML can be counted as an ADL, provides similar constructs as the AT method, and is of high practical relevance (Section 6.2.6). As the discussion of these ADLs shows (Section 6.2.7), the formalization of architectural knowledge in these ADLs is often similar to ATs, however, all of these ADLs lack support for architectural analyses of QoS properties.

6.2.1. Acme

Acme [GMW00] is an ADL with support for architectural constraints and architectural styles, including a reuse mechanism for these architectural styles and an accompanying specification process [Kom98].

Architectural constraints are formulated via an OCL-like, custom-build constraint language that is based on first-order predicate logic. Software architects can associate constraints to any architectural element of architectural models specified with Acme. Moreover, Acme distinguishes two types of constraints: invariant and heuristic constraints. Violations of invariant constraints make architectural models invalid whereas violations of heuristic constraints only produce a warning for software architects.

Architectural styles are formulated as (1) a set of element types, (2) additional constraints and parameters, and (3) a default instance of the architectural style.[5] Software architects can use a style's types to instantiate concrete architectural elements. These elements then provide the type's parameters as attributes and conform to the type's constraints. A style's additional constraints and parameters hold for the whole system to which the style is applied. A style's default instance prescribes the minimal set of architectural elements that must be part of such a system.

The reuse mechanism of Acme for architectural styles is based on subtyping via inheritance [Mon99, Sec. 4.4.6]. When a child architectural style

[4] In his Master's thesis [Ope17, Chap. 6], Openkowski relates the AT method to a subset of these ADLs (Acme, SADL, Wright) and provides detailed examples. His work has served as a starting point for this section.

[5] Acme refers to architectural styles as *families*, to element types as *structural types*, to parameters as *properties*, and to a default instance as *default structure*.

extends a parent architectural style, the child style inherits all element types, constraints, parameters, and the default instance of the parent style. Subsequently, the child style may add further or extend existing element types, constraints, and parameters. A child style is however forbidden to redefine elements of the parent architectural style. This restriction ensures that any architectural model that conforms to the child style also conforms to the parent style.

Some works [KG10, TFS10a] provide extensions to Acme that are related to the AT method. Kim and Garlan [KG10] show how to use the SAT solver Alloy [Jac12] to analyze properties of architectural styles, e.g., to analyze whether a style's constraints are contradictory to each other. They conclude that such analyses are applicable to realistic systems. Instead of using Alloy, Tibermacine et al. [TFS10a] suggest an approach based on OCL for specifying and checking constraints of architectural styles. They argue that modeling with the OCL is easier to learn and, thus, more efficient. To the best of my knowledge, they do not provide empirical evidence for this hypothesis.

The AT method follows the suggestion of Tibermacine et al. [TFS10a] by allowing AT engineers to specify and check constraints via the OCL. Constraint violations are shown to software architects as warnings as long as no architectural analysis is started (similar to Acme's heuristic constraints). However, an architectural analysis first triggers a constraint check and returns an error when any constraints are violated (similar to Acme's invariant constraints). This more restrictive approach ensures that AT completions have strong guarantees that their preconditions hold, however, comes at the cost of a less flexible constraint violation handling. Investigating the impact of this lowered flexibility on usability remains as a future work.

Regarding the formalization of architectural styles, Acme and the AT method differ in the general approach: Acme follows a type-based approach while the AT method follows a role-based approach. The type-based approach lets software architects directly instantiate architectural elements conforming to a particular architectural style. In contrast, the AT method's role-based approach lets software architects first instantiate general architectural elements (e.g., a component) and subsequently bind roles to these elements. While the role-based approach requires this additional binding step, it is more flexible when multiple roles need to be applied and when changes to styles or the architectural model are required.

Apart from that, Acme and the AT method have several commonalities. Acme's additional constraints and parameters associated to an architectural style can analogously be represented via an AT that contains a role for a system with according constraints and parameters. Acme's default instance is similar to an AT's default instance, however, prescribes a minimal set of architectural elements. The default instance of an AT does not prescribe that its elements are required. An AT's default instance instead provides an initiator template to software architects, i.e., it serves as an (optional) starting point for architectural modeling. Also the reuse mechanisms of Acme and AT method are similar; the only difference is that the AT method defines additional semantics for reusing completions (which do not exist in Acme).

The main difference between Acme and the AT method is that Acme lacks support for architectural analyses of QoS properties. Here, the AT method provides software architects with a more extensive decision support for applying architectural styles.

6.2.2. Aesop

Aesop [GAO94] is a framework for developing architectural modeling tools that are specific to an architectural style. Aesop comes with a generic component-based ADL that definitions of architectural styles can refine. Out of such style definitions, Aesop can generate a corresponding modeling tool.

In Aesop, architectural styles are defined by subtyping C++ classes via inheritance. Engineers can subtype either Aesop's basic ADL classes for components, connectors, etc. or classes of other architectural styles.

Constraints of architectural styles are hardcoded within the methods of the associated classes. As already the original authors note [GAO94], the downside of this approach is that constraints are obscured within imperative code. This approach particularly makes it hard to analyze constraints, e.g., to check whether two constraints are conflicting.

In the AT method, constraints are represented in a dedicated modeling construct, thus, not suffering from these disadvantages. The reuse mechanisms of Aeosp and AT method are similar in the sense that both are based on subtyping by inheritance. In contrast to Aesop, the AT method supports architectural analyses of QoS properties.

6.2.3. Rapide

Rapide [LKA+95] is a component-based ADL specialized to event-based and distributed systems. The ADL supports the specification of communication patterns to constrain inter-component interaction, thus, characterizing communication aspects of the employed architectural style. For example, a communication pattern may express that a set of outgoing connectors of a component has to follow a multicast communication. An accompanying simulation tool allows software architects to check whether an architectural model conforms to these communication patterns.

In contrast to Rapide, the OCL-based constraints of the AT method check only structural constraints. Therefore, Rapide's constraints for restricting the communication between components are an interesting extension for the AT method. Additions to Palladio's simulations are particularly required to dynamically check for violations of communication constraints; analogously to Rapide's simulation.

Rapide lacks support for capturing other architectural knowledge, e.g., architectural patterns and structural constraints of architectural styles. Here, the AT method outperforms Rapide. Moreover, Rapide's simulation is restricted to analyses of the correct communication behavior. Analyses of QoS properties, e.g., related to performance, are not provided.

6.2.4. Structural Architecture Description Language (SADL)

The Structural Architecture Description Language (SADL) [MR97] is a component-based ADL to formally specify architectural models via a first-order predicate logic. SADL supports completion-like refinement mappings from abstract to more concrete architectural models. Moreover, SADL supports the formalization of architectural styles via element types. These types can include formal constraints to restrict inter-type relationships and refinement mappings.

SADL provides a reuse mechanism that allows architectural styles to subtype other architectural styles via inheritance. Architectural styles inherit types including associated constraints from parent styles. Similar to Acme's reuse mechanism (cf. Section 6.2.1), SADL allows to extend inherited element types with further constraints but forbids to override existing constraints; adding further element types is also possible. In contrast to Acme, SADL additionally provides constructs for exporting and importing element types of architectural styles. These constructs enable engineers to explicitly mark element types that are suited for reuse and to selectively import only the element types required within an inheriting architectural style.

SADL's refinement mappings relate elements of an abstract source model to corresponding elements of a concrete target model. Being a refinement mapping, each source element is associated to at least one target element. These associations are formally specified via a first-order predicate logic that allows to check whether a concrete model correctly implements an abstract model. If correctly implemented, the concrete model satisfies the abstract model's constraints exactly as the abstract model itself. Checking this kind of correctness is a means to formally ensure the conceptual integrity (cf. Definition 2.14) of the refined architectural model.

SADL's completions (implemented as refinement mappings) are more formal than the AT method's completions (implemented as QVT-O transformations). In that sense, SADL takes its place alongside related formal specification approaches like the Z language [Spi92] and the UML+Z framework [APS07].

The benefit of such formal approaches is that they are amenable to formal analyses and to consistency checking [APS07]. For example, SADL's first-order predicate logic allows for mathematically proving conformance of the refined model to the original model, thus formally ensuring conceptual integrity.

The downside of formal approaches is that they are more complex and, consequently, unintuitive and impractical for engineers [APS07]. The reason for this complexity is that refinements in formal approaches require mathematical proofs. At best, the correctness of refinements can be generically proven for reusable refinement patterns as particularly suggested by SADL and the UML+Z framework [APS07]. However, even such generic proofs come at high costs for engineers: conducting such proofs in the first place is still time consuming, expensive, and requires training; changes in refinement patterns (e.g., for introducing a new variation point) require engineers to prove correctness anew; and mathematical notions are hard to communicate among (non-technical) stakeholders.

For these reasons, the AT method follows a more practical approach by using a less formal transformation language (QVT-O) for specifying completions. Quality is assured via testing, which is more lightweight than formal approaches. Although testing is unable to verify correctness as described above, testing can be automated, easily uncover faults, and involves low computational effort.

The AT method is inspired by SADL's import/export mechanism to select/-expose reusable element types. In the AT method, each AT role is allowed for being reused, i.e., the AT method is less restrictive than SADL. A reusing AT can however select only the AT roles from other ATs that are relevant. Moreover, in contrast to SADL, the AT method supports architectural analyses of QoS properties.

6.2.5. Wright

Wright [All97] is another component-based ADL with support for architectural styles. Similar to ADLs like Acme (Section 6.2.1) and SADL (Section 6.2.4), Wright formalizes architectural styles based on element types with constraints. Element types can be used to instantiate conforming architectural elements. As a reuse mechanism for defining architectural styles, Wright allows that architectural styles inherit all element types of a parent style; engineers may add further element types and constraints (analogously to Acme's reuse mechanism; cf. Section 6.2.1).

Wright's structural constraints are formulated in a first-order predicate logic. Behavioral constraints can be formulated via additional predicates that reference communicating sequential process (CSP) [Hoa78] models.

These CSP models formally describe allowed and forbidden communication patterns, similar to the patterns used in Rapide (cf. Section 6.2.3).

Like the AT method, Wright combines several features of other ADLs (e.g., reuse mechanism and constraints in first-order predicate logic). In contrast to the AT method, Wright has a focus on behavioral constraints of architectural styles. For behavior-intensive architectural styles, Wright's approach of using CSP models for specifying communication patterns is therefore a promising extension to the AT method's constraints that currently only support structural OCL expressions. The AT method goes beyond Wright's capabilities by additionally supporting completions and architectural analyses.

6.2.6. Unified Modeling Language (UML)

The Unified Modeling Language (UML) [Obj11] is a general-purpose modeling language for software systems. Despite there has been some discussion on whether the UML can be counted as an ADL [Pan10], the UML certainly includes several aspects of ADLs, e.g., modeling constructs for components and connectors [HNS99], and has explicitly been related to ADLs, e.g., to SADL [KCSS02]. Moreover, the UML has a high practical relevance because software architects indeed use the UML for documenting software architectures in industrial organizations [LCM06].

This section therefore describes the UML constructs closely related to the AT method: collaborations (Section 6.2.6.1), templates (Section 6.2.6.2), and profiles (Section 6.2.6.3).

6.2.6.1. UML Collaborations

The UML proposes collaborations [Obj11, Sec. 9.3.3] as a means to capture and describe design patterns, e.g., the observer pattern. A UML collaboration defines a set of roles and their connections to each other, e.g., subject and observer of the observer pattern. Via so-called *collaboration uses*, collaboration roles can be bound to concrete entities, e.g., to components. Bound entities have to provide the attributes and operations required by the role they play. The collaboration can then be used to describe how bound entities achieve a joint task. For example, a collaboration for the observer pattern can be used to describe how observers are registered at a subject. The collaboration can particularly describe constraints for the communication behavior among its roles.

Additionally, the UML describes a reuse mechanism for collaborations. Child collaborations may inherit and extend roles of parent collaborations. Analogously to Acme (cf. Section 6.2.1), child roles cannot override constraints from their parents and have to comply to these constraints.

Concrete syntaxes for collaborations are a dashed ellipse icon or, alternatively, a rectangle icon (like in UML composite structure diagrams). These icons contain the name of the collaboration and a compartment with its roles and connectors. Figure 6.3 illustrates this syntax for the observer pattern, including a constraint on the size of the observed queue.

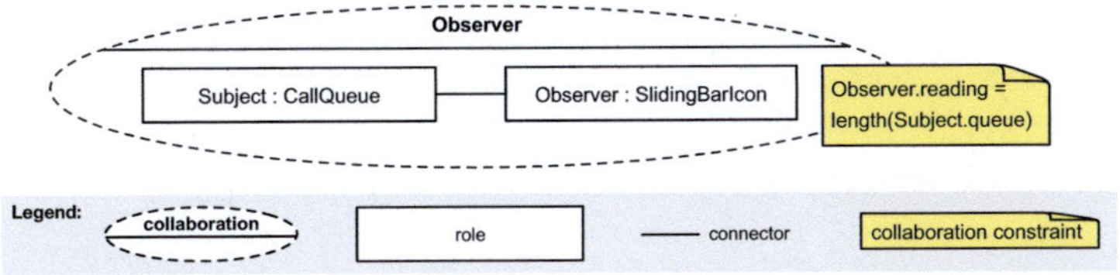

Figure 6.3.: A UML collaboration for the observer pattern (based on [Obj11, Sec. 9.3.3]).

Collaborations are only of descriptive nature, i.e., collaborations provide no semantics for integrating structures or behavior into bound entities. Rather, collaborations require that bound entities already comply to the structure and behavior described by the collaboration. In contrast, ATs provide integration semantics in the form of completions that ensure that applied architectural knowledge is integrated in the targeted architectural model. This approach to integration particularly enables architectural analyses with the targeted architectural model.

Otherwise, there are several similarities between collaborations and ATs. Both follow a role-based approach to bind architectural knowledge. The concrete syntax of ATs is also similar to the one of collaborations. Furthermore, collaborations and ATs both use an inheritance-based reuse mechanism.

6.2.6.2. UML Templates

In Section 2.4, UML templates [Obj11, Sec. 17.4] are classified as bound templates. As such, UML templates provide a facility to let models (e.g., an architectural model) bind model elements to template parameters. Once bound, a template engine can appropriately weave template constructs into the binding model. Other related works have particularly used UML's templates to weave design patterns [VCC15] and resource environments [BTN+14] into architectural models.

ATs are a similar means to weave recurring architectural knowledge into architectural models. Instead of a pure substitution mechanism to include parameters in templates (cf. Section 2.4.3.3), ATs use completions for such an inclusion. Completions provide a higher flexibility for weaving parameters into templates, e.g., enabling the processing of the number of replicas parameter of the Loadbalancing AT (cf. Section 3.2.4). However, completions are more complex to specify than simple substitutions. For this reason, the AT method includes a dedicated quality assurance step (cf. Section 4.1.3.3). In addition to this difference, UML templates have—in contrast to the AT method—not been applied in the context of architectural analyses.

6.2.6.3. UML Profiles

UML profiles [Obj11, Chap. 18] are described in Section 2.3.4. The AT method employs such profiles to extend languages for specifying architectural models in a lightweight manner. In the AT method, these extensions allow software architects to bind ATs to architectural models; including the specification of actual parameters for the formal parameters of ATs.

6.2.7. Discussion of Architectural Description Languages

ADLs focus on one particular kind of reusable architectural knowledge—the formalization of architectural styles (as defined in Section 2.2.4.1). All described ADLs therefore provide means to capture constraints on architectural models. UML collaborations additionally provide means to capture design patterns. The investigated ADLs differ in the following concepts and features.

Types vs. roles To formalize architectural knowledge, the investigated ADLs mainly follow a type-based approach (Acme, Aesop, Rapide, SADL, Wright). UML follows a role-based approach.

In type-based approaches, architectural elements are created as instances of a type that is specific to an architectural style. For example, in the three-layer architectural style, software architects are only allowed to create "presentation layer components", "middle layer components", and "data access layer components". Type-based approaches have in common that targeted architectural elements are of exactly one type. The advantage of this limitation is that software architects can create appropriate elements in a single instantiation step; simply by selecting the type to be instantiated. For example, style-specific architectural modeling tools generated with Aesop provide software architects with a palette of style-specific types of components and connectors for instantiation. However, in scenarios where software architects want to modify styles (e.g., to combine a three-layer architectural style with additional company-specific constraints), completely new types have to be created; and based on these new types the architectural model has to be modified. Therefore, type-based approaches can slow-down software architects in maintenance and evolution scenarios.

In role-based approaches, architectural elements are created in their general form and subsequently bound to roles of architectural styles (or of design patterns like for UML's collaborations). For example, in the three-layer architectural style, software architects may first create an architectural model with several components and then assign each component either the "presentation layer component role", the "middle layer component role", or the "data access layer component role". In contrast to type-based approaches, software architects accordingly require two steps to create elements with an applied architectural style: (1) instantiate the element and (2) bind a role. While the additional role-binding step may cause a higher effort initially, binding roles is more flexible than a type-based instantiation: bound roles can naturally be unapplied or modified and multiple roles can be bound to architectural elements. For example, in addition to roles of the three-layer style, roles with company-specific constraints can be bound to components. This flexibility provides a clean separation of different concerns (e.g., of the three-layer style and a company-specific style) and a natural means to support maintenance and evolution scenarios. For this reason, the AT method employs such a role-based approach.

Invariant vs. heuristic constraints Acme is the only approach that distinguishes between invariant and heuristic constraints, i.e., the severity of constraint violations. In case of constraint violations, this difference allows modeling tools to show software architects errors (invariant constraints) or just warnings (heuristic constraints).

In the AT method, constraint violations are similarly distinguished. During modeling, software architects get warnings when violating constraints, e.g., to point to missing but required architectural elements. When starting an architectural analysis, however, such violations are shown as errors to software architects, thus, forcing them to create architectural models that conform to applied architectural knowledge.

Structural vs. behavioral constraints Most ADLs (Acme, Aesop, SADL, Wright, UML) support structural constraints, e.g., to forbid direct connections from presentation to data access layer components. Aesop embeds these constraints in imperative code, which obscures constraints. All other ADLs formulate constraints via some kind of first-order predicate logic. The first-order predicate logic is either custom-build (Acme, SADL, Wright) or based on existing languages like Alloy (Kim and Garlan's Acme extension [KG10]) and OCL (Tibermacine et al.'s Acme extension [TFS10a], UML).

Rapide, Wright, and the UML support behavioral constraints; specified as allowed or forbidden communication patterns between components. Rapide and Wright formulate communication patterns via some kind of process algebra—a custom-build algebra in Rapide and CSPs in Wright. Communication patterns can then be checked against a simulation of the modeled software. The UML only provides informally documented behavioral constraints, which makes conformance checks infeasible.

ATs currently support structural constraints formulated via OCL. Future work may investigate extending ATs with support for behavioral constraints, e.g., based on CSPs like in Wright. The metaclass `Constraint` of the AT language is defined as an abstract class (cf. Section 4.2.5.5), thus, only an appropriate subclass for CSPs and support for checking constraints needs to be added, e.g., in Palladio-based simulations.

Consistency checks Besides checking the conformance to structural and behavioral constraints, some ADLs provide additional analysis mechanisms for constraints. These mechanisms include inter-constraint consistency checks (Kim and Garlan's Acme extension [KG10]) and formal consistency checks of refinements (SADL).

Consistency checks complement the conformance checks of the AT method and, consequently, may be included in future works. Besides constraint checks, the AT method supports architectural analyses of QoS properties. None of the investigated ADLs has support for such analyses.

Refinement semantics From the investigated ADLs, only SADL describes semantics for refining abstract architectural models to more concrete architectural models. Conceptually, such refinements define completions for abstract architectural models as particularly employed by the AT method.

In contrast to the AT method, SADL follows a formal refinement approach, similar to Z [Spi92] and UML+Z [APS07]. While this formal approach allows for verifying conceptual integrity, the AT method's approach of testing is more practical for ensuring conceptual integrity. Analyzing the suitability of a more formal approach than QVT-O completions is still a promising prospect for future work.

Concrete syntaxes Most of the investigated ADLs (Acme, Aesop, Rapide, SADL, Wright) provide a concrete syntax for specifying and applying architectural styles that is *textual*. For the specification of architectural styles, only the UML provides a concrete *graphical* syntax. For the application of architectural styles, Acme, Aesop, and the UML provide a concrete *graphical* syntax. The type-based approach of Acme and Aesop enables them to define an icon for each type to be applied, e.g., different icons for components of presentation, middle, and data access layer. UML's role-based approach suggests annotating existing icons for architectural elements, e.g., by prepending element names with the names of bound roles in guillemets [Obj11, Chap. 18].

Because the AT method follows a role-based approach, its graphical syntax for specifying and applying ATs is inspired by the UML. For example, AT instances (Section 4.2.5.8) also prepend role names to element names while using an @-symbol instead of guillemets (to distinguish from UML stereotype applications).

The AT method particularly uses a graphical concrete syntax (instead of a textual one) for specifying AT applications because the targeted ADL (the PCM) also provides a graphical syntax. This way, AT applications can be internally specified in PCM editors. A textual concrete syntax of AT applications would require either an external specification or a concrete textual syntax for the PCM (into which AT applications can be internally embedded). An investigation of such realizations is left as potential future work because it is out of this thesis' scope.

Reuse mechanisms Except for Rapide, all investigated ADLs provide a reuse mechanism for specifying new architectural styles based on existing ones. For all of these ADLs, the reuse mechanism is based on inheritance to subtype architectural styles.

Inheritance semantics are similar over all ADLs. Depending on the approach, child architectural styles inherit all element types (respectively roles) of parent styles; including their constraints. Only SADL allows element types to selectively inherit parent element types. Additional constraints and element types (respectively roles) can be specified on child styles. However, existing constraints cannot be changed.

The reuse mechanism of ATs follows SADL's approach of selective inheritance, i.e., AT engineers can specify (select) the parent AT roles from which child AT roles inherit. Additionally, the reuse mechanism defines semantics for reusing completions: when reusing multiple roles, the C3 linearization algorithm defines a total order in which completions have to be executed (cf. Section 4.4.1).

6.3. Architectural Knowledge in the Pattern Community

The pattern community originates in Christopher Alexander's work on patterns for buildings and towns [Ale77]. In the introduction of his book,

Alexander notes: "Each pattern describes a problem which occurs over and over again in our environment, and then describes the core of the solution to that problem, in such a way that you can use this solution a million times over, without ever doing it the same way twice" [Ale77, p. x]. Beck and Cunningham [BC87] have first applied this idea of patterns to the software engineering discipline. Afterwards, patterns in software engineering became especially popular with the "Gang of Four"[6] book [GHJV95], which includes 23—nowadays well-known—design patterns for object-oriented software. In their book series on "Pattern-Oriented Software Architecture" (POSA) [BMR+96, SSRB00, KJ04, BHS07a, BHS07b], Buschmann et al. have lifted the idea of these design patterns to the architectural level, i.e., to architectural patterns as described in Section 2.2.4.2.

As a concrete kind of architectural knowledge, architectural patterns are related to the AT method. Especially the formalization of such patterns in the context of model-driven engineering is relevant. This section therefore describes related works in this area.

The POSA book series provides a good starting point (Section 6.3.1). In addition, Taibi's book [Tai07] describes 16 pattern formalization approaches. Of these approaches, the most related ones are DPML (Section 6.3.2) and RBML (Section 6.3.3) because they are model-based (as the AT method) and not purely mathematical (as the other approaches described by Taibi [Tai07]; cf. [Ope17, Chap. 6]). Furthermore, a Google Scholar[7] search with the term "architectural pattern" "formalization" "model-based" OR "model-driven" yields the work of That et al. on COMLAN as another relevant work (Section 6.3.4). PMF (Section 6.3.5) is also relevant because PMF is used by ADMD3 (described in Section 6.1.4) as formalization mechanism. As the discussion of these approaches shows (Section 6.3.6), the formalization of architectural patterns is typically role-based like ATs, however, all approaches lack support for architectural analyses of QoS properties.

6 The "Gang of Four" are the four authors of the book [GHJV95]—Erich Gamma, Richard Helm, Ralph Johnson, and John Vlissides.

7 Google Scholar (`https://scholar.google.de`) is a search engine for scientific publications.

6.3.1. Pattern-Oriented Software Architecture (POSA)

The Pattern-Oriented Software Architecture (POSA) book series [BMR+96, SSRB00, KJ04, BHS07a, BHS07b] follows a role-based approach to architectural patterns. This thesis has adapted this approach as described in Section 2.2.4.2.

Furthermore, POSA introduces an initiator template for documenting architectural patterns (Section 6.3.1.1) and so-called pattern compounds to document combinations of architectural patterns (Section 6.3.1.2).

6.3.1.1. POSA's Initiator Template

POSA's initiator template [BMR+96, Sec. 1.5] covers the following information regarding an architectural pattern: name and aliases, example usages, typical application contexts, descriptions of the addressed problem and the general solution idea, detailed descriptions about structural and dynamic aspects, guidelines for implementation, descriptions of variants, known uses in existing systems, positive and negative consequences on system quality, and relations to other patterns. These information help software architects in selecting a suitable pattern and in applying the pattern. For this reason, architectural knowledge management tools, e.g., ADMD3 (Section 6.1.4), typically use POSA's or a similar initiator template for pattern documentation.

In contrast to POSA's structured initiator template for documentation, ATs only include a generic documentation attribute of type String (see Section 4.2.5.3). Therefore, ATs are more flexible but guide AT engineers less in structuring their documentation of architectural knowledge. In the AT catalog created for this thesis, ATs refer with their documentation attribute to a Wiki [Clob] if they formalize an architectural pattern. By convention, the Wiki itself documents the architectural pattern according to POSA's template. The advantage of this approach is that an AT's documentation can be accessed independently of AT tooling. In future works, an empirical evaluation may investigate benefits for AT engineers and software architects when using more structured documentation attributes within the AT metaclass.

6.3.1.2. POSA's Pattern Compounds

POSA's pattern compounds [BHS07b, Chap. 6] document a composition-based combination of other patterns. Pattern compounds are therefore closely related to reuse mechanisms for architectural knowledge.[8] To document a pattern compound in graphical syntax, POSA suggests using Vlissides' [Vli98] *pattern:role* notation, i.e., to prepend names of reused roles with the name of the reused architectural pattern (separated by a colon). This way, multiple applied roles from different patterns can easily be distinguished from each other, even when their names are equal.

In the AT method, the *pattern:role* notation may be used to visualize a role's inherited roles and roles bound to architectural elements. The graphical syntax of bound AT roles is described in Section 4.2.5.8: in its current form, only role names are given. Given that ATs often have long names and that no role name occurred twice in the evaluation (Chapter 5), this notion was sufficient so far. As a potential extension, however, the *pattern:role* notation may be integrated as an optional alternative notion to visualize reused and applied roles.

6.3.2. Design Pattern Modeling Language (DPML)

The Design Pattern Modeling Language (DPML) [MHG01, MHG02, Tai07, Chap. 2] is a dimension-based language to formalize design patterns. DPML defines a dimension as a set of elements that act in a certain role. For example, a "replica" dimension for the loadbalancing architectural pattern may contain the set of elements acting in roles that require replication when being load-balanced. DPML then allows to associate such dimensions to a pattern's roles. For example, as shown in Figure 6.4, the "replica" dimension may be assigned to the the "load-balanced container" role and the corresponding "assembly connectors" roles that have to be replicated. DPML's semantics demand that each so-assigned role refers to the same number of elements as defined in the dimension. In the previous example, each assigned role therefore refers to the same number of replicas, thus, requiring a load-balanced container, an incoming assembly connector, and an outgoing assembly connector for each replica. A dimension therefore

8 For concrete examples, the interested reader is referred to [BHS07b, Chap. 6].

represents a dedicated construct to ensure that cardinalities of assigned roles are consistent.

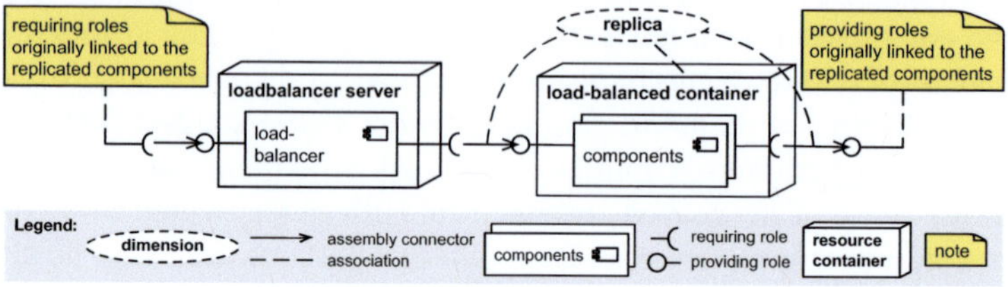

Figure 6.4.: The replica dimension ensures that replicated elements have the same cardinality.

In contrast, other role-based approaches either include dedicated cardinality constraints (e.g., RBML as described in Section 6.3.3) or require formulating appropriate constraints in a constraint language such as in OCL. The AT method follows an OCL-based approach because the OCL is well-known [LCM06] and, thus, more practical for software architects. Moreover, the evaluation of DPML [Tai07, Chap. 2]—conducted by DPML's original authors—has shown that software architects have difficulties in understanding the dimension concept. On the architectural level, the dimension-based approach further seems to divide roles into too fine-granular elements, e.g., the loadbalancing architectural pattern formalized as AT only requires binding a loadbalancing role to the entity to be loadbalanced. The dimension-based formalization as exemplified above requires more bindings, thus, appearing more complicated in practice.

6.3.3. Role-Based Metamodeling Language (RBML)

The Role-Based Metamodeling Language (RBML) [KFGS03, Tai07, Chap. 9] is a role-based language to formalize design patterns. Despite not explicitly focused on architectural patterns, RDML introduces a role concept for models [KFGS03] that is similar to the role concept employed by ATs.

According to RDML's role concept [KFGS03], roles (1) have structural and behavioral properties that can be inherited from parent roles, (2) define conformance constraints, and (3) are context-sensitive. AT roles share these characteristics. First, parameters and completions of ATs provide bound elements with additional structural and behavioral properties. AT roles particularly support inheritance for these properties. Second, ATs contain constraints for conformance checks (which are also inherited). Third, context-sensitivity is reflected in the fact that AT roles can only be bound to specific architectural elements. For example, if an AT role is applied in the context of a system model, attributes associated to the AT role are hidden in the context of a resource environment model (and vice-versa).

RBML extends the UML with its role concept, e.g., allowing to capture structural aspects of design patterns via UML classes. Here, RBML's roles restrict UML base metaclasses, e.g., a UML class. RBML specifies its restrictions via the OCL. These restrictions define a subset of the UML that only allows to create instances that conform to the formalized pattern. For example, a restriction for a class may demand that the class is abstract; a suitable restriction when, e.g., implementing the abstract factory pattern (cf. [GHJV95, p. 87ff.]).

Interestingly, RDML's approach to capture design patterns by restricting UML's design space has more in common with this thesis' definition of architectural styles (Section 2.2.4.1) than it has with the one of architectural patterns (Section 2.2.4.2). Similar to RDML's patterns, architectural styles are collections of constraints to restrict systems. Architectural patterns, instead, are typically associated with design decisions about the existence of elements (cf. Section 2.2.4.2). This distinction becomes unfortunately fuzzy when restricting the design space to such an extent that only few existential design decisions remain (like RDML does). For this reason, the difference between architectural patterns and architectural styles is often subject to discussion (e.g., in [BMR+96, p. 394ff.]). Here, RDML lies somewhere in between; and ATs provide facilities to capture both kinds of architectural knowledge, thus, leaving the resolution of such discussions to AT engineers.

6.3.4. Composition-Centered Architectural Pattern Description Language (COMLAN)

That et al. [TSO12, TSOB15, TTSOF16] define the Composition-Centered Architectural Pattern Description Language (COMLAN) as a role-based language to capture architectural patterns. COMLAN's roles can extend existing component-based languages [TTSOF16], e.g., Acme (cf. Section 6.2.1). Role characteristics are captured via constraints formulated in the OCL.

Software architects can apply COMLAN's patterns to architectural models via a dedicated mapping model. The mapping model specifies bindings of pattern roles to architectural elements. Once applied, COMLAN allows to create views that visualize only those elements that are related to an applied pattern. COMLAN uses completion-like transformations to create dedicated models for these views.

Another key concept in COMLAN is its reuse mechanism to compose architectural patterns, motivated by the observation that software architects often combine preexisting patterns into new ones [TSOB15]. COMLAN provides dedicated combining operations for its reuse mechanism [TTSOF16]: the stringing and overlapping operators. The stringing operator creates a connector between two components of two distinct patterns. The overlapping operator merges two components of two distinct patterns into a new component. Using these operators, complex patterns can be composed out of more simple patterns.

In contrast to most other approaches, COMLAN's reuse mechanism is based on composition instead of subtyping by inheritance. In the AT method, AT roles may inherit from other roles. Here, the C3 algorithm determines a total order in which inherited completions are executed. This ordering can be seen as a dedicated composition operator for completions, similar to the operators in COMLAN. However, a fundamental difference between these operators is that COMLAN's operators are only used to combine patterns whereas the AT method's total ordering specifies a whole completion. COMLAN's views are only capable of weaving single architectural patterns into an architectural model; the AT method's completions instead weave *each* applied AT into an architectural model. In that sense, COMLAN's mechanism is more fine-grained than the one of the AT method and has a focus on creating pattern-specific views. The creation of such pattern-specific views is a potential extension to the AT method.

The role-based binding of COMLAN and AT method is similar. However, COMLAN requires defining a dedicated adapter metamodel for each target architectural description language. The AT method employs a lightweight metamodel extension based on profiles instead. A particular advantage of this approach is that software architects can create role-bindings internally in the architectural description language. In contrast, COMLAN requires an external creation of a mapping model.

6.3.5. Pattern Modeling Framework (PMF)

The Pattern Modeling Framework (PMF) [EBL06] is a method providing a process, tool support, and a language (EPattern) to specify patterns for Ecore (see Section 2.3.6) metamodels. Patterns are used for detection purposes and not for application, thus, PMF provides no instantiation- or binding-based application mechanism. Still, the EPattern language uses the concept of roles to characterize targeted model elements, e.g., components in architectural models. Like related approaches, a pattern's roles characterize targeted elements with constraints; PMF's tooling supports the OCL for constraint specification.

EPattern supports a combination of inheritance and composition as reuse mechanism for patterns. A child pattern may inherit from a parent pattern. Analogously to approaches in the ADL domain (cf. Section 6.2.7), child patterns inherit roles including their constraints and may add additional roles and constraints. Additionally, pattern roles can relate to roles of other patterns over explicitly exposed ports for roles. Using these relations, additional constraints can be formulated.

In contrast to most other approaches, PMF provides a pattern creation process for engineers. Engineers start by understanding a pattern's structure, continue with a step-wise specification of model elements for pattern, roles, ports, and constraints, and finish with an optimization step to simplify the pattern model. The whole process is of iterative nature.

PMF's creation processes has served as a basis for the AT specification process (described in Section 4.1.3.2). Both processes describe the required steps to capture the architectural knowledge to be formalized. In contrast to patterns specified via the EPattern language, ATs additionally require engineers to specify completions. These completions provide additional semantics for weaving AT-induced elements into the targeted architectural model.

Another fundamental difference is that software architects can apply ATs to architectural models. PMF only provides the possibility to detect pattern occurrences in (architectural) models. Accordingly, PMF also lacks support for improving architectural analyses by utilizing information from applied patterns.

6.3.6. Discussion of Approaches in the Pattern Community

While related work on ADLs focuses on architectural styles (cf. Section 6.2.7), the pattern community (not surprisingly) has a strong focus on patterns—ranging from design patterns (DPML, RBML) over architectural patterns (POSA, COMLAN) to general model patterns (PMF). Other differences of the investigated approaches rely in the following concepts.

Roles vs. dimensions The predominant approach to capture patterns is based on roles (POSA, RBML, COMLAN, PMF). Only DPML provides with dimensions an addition to this concept.

Even though a dimension-based approach is an interesting alternative, pure role-based approaches have proven to be more intuitive to software architects (cf. Section 6.3.2). For this reason, the AT method is role-based but does not employ the dimension concept.

Informal vs. formal From the investigated approaches, only the POSA series captures patterns in an informal way. POSA proposes an initiator template for documentation purposes—stating which information should be given for documenting a pattern. Other related works suggest using this (or similar) templates for documentation as well, e.g., ADMD3 (Section 6.1.4) and the AT method itself.

The rationale behind more formal approaches is that formalized patterns can provide additional analysis capabilities, going beyond documentation only. Such analyses are discussed next.

Analyses Approaches on pattern formalization focus on conformance checks of constraints to improve conceptual integrity (DPML, RBML, COMLAN). All of these approaches have in common that they check only structural constraints and not behavioral aspects.

COMLAN explicitly documents applications of patterns as annotations to the targeted architectural model. Even if all elements playing roles in a pattern are removed, COMLAN can therefore point to constraint violations (e.g., missing required elements). The other approaches lack this kind of constraint check, however, the AT method follows a similar approach as AT applications are also annotated on the architectural model.

PMF can detect its formalized patterns in targeted models. This detection allows software architects to check whether models conform to a required pattern or whether an anti-pattern occurs that should be removed. Such an automatic detection is still a current research topic (cf. [vL13, Gie08, p. 53]) and an extension opportunity for the AT method.

In contrast to the AT method, no investigated approach provides support for architectural analyses of QoS properties.

Constraints The investigated approaches either informally document constraints (POSA) or suggest to additionally use a dedicated constraint language such as the OCL (DPML, RBML, COMLAN, PMF). The AT method is in line with these suggestions: AT constraints may be documented in natural language but each role requires also constraints formulated in a constraint language. AT tooling currently supports constraints formulated in the OCL.

Refinement semantics No investigated approach provides refinement semantics (like completions) to weave patterns into the targeted model. Instead, the approaches require that elements acting in a pattern's role already exist in the targeted model. Patterns can then manually (DPML, RBML,

COMLAN) or automatically (PMF) be linked to the target model, giving the benefit of conformance checks as described above.

In the AT method, architectural knowledge is instead imposed on the targeted architectural model, i.e., AT-induced elements are woven into the architectural model. ATs include completions for this purpose, which particularly ensure that architectural analyses can be conducted that accurately reflect the formalized architectural knowledge.

Reuse mechanisms As reuse mechanisms, the investigated approaches support subtyping by inheritance on a per-role basis (RBML, PMF) and compositions of patterns (POSA's pattern compounds, COMLAN, PMF). DPML provides no reuse mechanism for patterns.

ATs analogously support inheritance for AT roles. Additionally, the completion execution order is specified when reusing completions. An integration of further reuse semantics is left as future work, e.g., via similar composition approaches as above. In his Master's thesis, Openkowski [Ope17, Sec. 7.1] provides details about the possible integration options.

6.4. Architectural Knowledge in Architectural Analyses

Architectural analyses—as investigated in this thesis—are methods to quantify a system's QoS properties based on architectural models (see Section 2.5 for a detailed description). The focus of the AT method is on such quantitative methods instead of qualitative methods like SAAM [KBWA94] and ATAM [KBK+99].[9] Qualitative methods may complement quantitative methods, e.g., by identifying the most relevant QoS properties to be quantified. However, due to a different focus of the AT method, this section only discusses quantitative methods.

Quantitative methods have been surveyed by Koziolek [Koz10]. Koziolek investigates component-based methods, which fits to the AT method's focus on software architecture (cf. Section 2.2). Component-based methods

[9] See [DN02, BZJ04, KBK+05, SS12] for surveys of qualitative methods.

originate in the pioneering work of Smith on the Software Performance Engineering (SPE) [SW02] method. SPE allows to quantify performance properties on the level of UML-like architectural models. The methods surveyed by Koziolek extend SPE by models of software components that software engineers can reuse within further analyses, along with tool support for model editing and model-driven transformations to underlying analysis models. For example, CB-SPE [BM04] and Palladio (cf. Section 2.5.3) provide such extensions.

These methods are related to the AT method because their components capture reusable architectural knowledge within reusable components. SPE and Palladio particularly provide the basis for the AT method: SPE processes and Palladio's tooling are extended by the AT method. However, the methods that Koziolek [Koz10] has investigated lack support for reusing higher-level architectural knowledge (cf. [HBR+10a]), e.g., guiding software architects in composing components. The AT method extends these methods as a complementary method for capturing and applying reusable architectural knowledge like architectural styles, architectural patterns, and reference architectures. Regarding such reusable architectural knowledge, Koziolek only mentions Smith's informal descriptions of performance patterns and anti-patterns [SW02] and Happe's use of completions for integrating messaging patterns of a message-oriented middleware in PCM models (discussed in Section 6.4.2.4).

In the following, this section therefore supplements Koziolek's survey with architectural analysis methods with support for high-level reusable architectural knowledge.[10] For such existing analysis methods, there are two major categories: methods that transform architectural models to analysis models utilizing knowledge-specific information (Section 6.4.1) and methods that capture knowledge via completions (Section 6.4.2). In these major categories, software architects apply reusable architectural knowledge manually. Instead, the SASSY method employs an optimization algorithm for such applications (Section 6.4.3). The discussion of these methods (Section 6.4.4) shows that methods either have too strong dependencies to analysis models or do not exploit reusable architectural knowledge already for the design of architectural models.

[10] In her Master's thesis [Gia16, Chap. 3], Giacinto systematically identifies several of the investigated methods and briefly relates these to the AT method. Her work has served as a starting point for this section.

6.4.1. Knowledge-Specific Generation of Analysis Models

Some architectural analysis approaches [PW00, CG02, MPW15] provide techniques to generate analysis models that are knowledge-specific. These approaches have in common that generation techniques directly target the level of analysis models, thus, are directly depending on concrete analysis models.

In contrast, the AT method is independent of concrete analysis models because AT completions weave knowledge-induced elements directly in the targeted architectural model. After these elements have been woven into the architectural model, transformations to various analysis models can be chained. For example, Palladio's transformations to analysis models can be applied after AT-induced elements have been woven into a PCM model. This independence therefore allows to reuse existing transformations to various analysis models instead of requiring engineers to specify such transformations anew.

The following subsections relate the AT method to each approach in detail.

6.4.1.1. Petriu and Wang [PW00]

Petriu and Wang [PW00] use style-specific UML collaborations (cf. Section 6.2.6.1) to type UML models with style-specific roles. For each UML collaboration, a dedicated model transformation is specified. These transformations allow to generate analysis models (LQN models as described in Section 2.5.3.1) from UML models with bound collaborations. The authors exemplify their approach with the client-server [BCK98, p. 217ff], pipes and filters [BMR+96, p. 53ff], and blackboard [BMR+96, p. 71ff] architectural styles.

For example, Figure 6.5 (left) illustrates a collaboration for the "client-server with forwarding broker" style bound to a UML model. Figure 6.5 (right) illustrates the result of a corresponding transformation of this model to an LQN model. Following the idea of the captured style, the client and the server are now intervened by a broker that forwards requests.

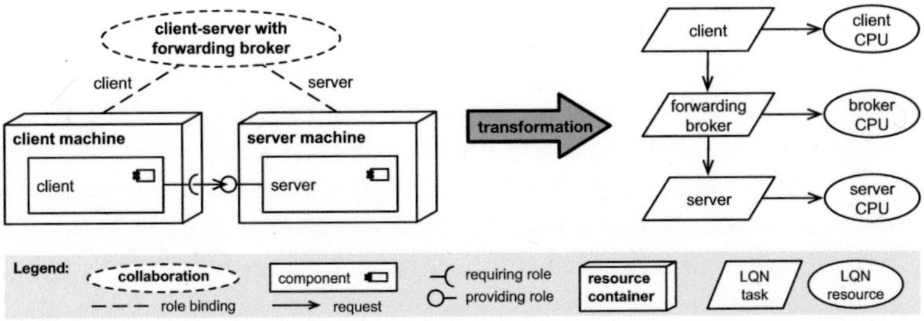

Figure 6.5.: A transformation from a UML model with a bound collaboration to a corresponding LQN model (based on [PW00]).

Given that Petriu and Wang formalize architectural knowledge for an ADL and utilize this formalization in transformations to analysis models, their approach is closely related to the AT method. While their approach allows to type architectural elements only with one role, the role-based approach of the AT method provides support for binding multiple roles. Software architects therefore have a higher flexibility in the AT method (see Section 6.2.7 for a detailed discussion). Additionally, the AT method comes with support for constraint checks and a general process for extending architectural analyses with ATs, e.g., describing quality assurance steps for the conceptual integrity of the formalized knowledge. Another difference is that the AT method employs completions (that weave AT-induced elements directly in the architectural model) instead of transforming to analysis models.

6.4.1.2. Cortellessa et al. [CG02]

Cortellessa and Grassi [CG02] specify component and connector types of an architectural style for mobile code. These types can be used in ADLs like Acme (cf. Section 6.2.1) to create architectural models. For so-created architectural models, the authors specify a transformation to an analysis model (a Markov decision process model; cf. [Bel57]). This analysis model can be used to analyze performance-related QoS properties.

Cortellessa and Grassi show how a particular architectural style can be formalized for ADLs while utilizing this formalization for generating analysis models. Therefore, the work of Cortellessa and Grassi is closely related to the AT method, similar to Petriu and Wang's approach. However, their work suffers from the same issues as Petriu and Wang's approach: the type-based approach is inflexible and transformations directly to the analysis model have to be specified. Moreover, Cortellessa and Grassi focus only on one architectural style (code mobility) and provide no guidelines to formalize further architectural knowledge.

6.4.1.3. Mani et al. [MPW15]

Mani et al. [MPW15] introduce a method to synchronize applications of architectural patterns within an architectural model with a previously created analysis model. In a first step, a transformation creates the analysis model (an LQN model as described in Section 2.5.3.1) from an initial architectural model. In a second step, software architects can bind roles of architectural patterns to their architectural model. These patterns are formalized via RBML (described in Section 6.3.3), i.e., via a role-based approach. In a third step, software architects specify and execute a transformation that weaves pattern-induced elements into the architectural model. In a fourth and final step, a corresponding transformation for the previously created analysis model is automatically derived and executed, thus, keeping the analysis model in sync with the architectural model. The automatic derivation of this transformation in based on information of the original mapping from architectural model to analysis model (first step) and the transformation that modified the architectural model (third step).

The method of Mani et al. is similar to the AT method because it follows a role-based formalization approach and applies transformations to integrate pattern-induced elements into architectural models. Both methods also provide processes for software architects and an accompanying tool support. Mani et al.'s method is especially interesting because pattern applications do not require a complete regeneration of the corresponding analysis model; the existing analysis model is instead directly modified via generated transformations. A downside of this approach is that the generated transformations are LQN-specific. If additional analysis models have to be supported, additional transformation generators have to be engineered. The AT method saves this effort because existing transformations to analysis models can completely be reused. Mani et al. particularly require software architects to specify transformations for modifying architectural models; the AT method instead lets AT engineers specify transformations in a reusable fashion. Besides these main differences, ATs additionally include a reuse mechanism and support constraint checks of the formalized knowledge on the architectural level. Moreover, the AT method provides a quality assurance process for the formalized knowledge.

6.4.2. Knowledge Captured via Completions

Several architectural analysis approaches [WPS02, VDGD05, Bec08, Hap09, Hap11, Rat13] use completions (as described in Section 2.5.2.2) to integrate QoS-relevant details into architectural models that subsequently serve as input to architectural analyses. For example, Verdickt et al. [VDGD05] integrate details about the Common Object Request Broker Architecture (CORBA) [Obj12] middleware. A subsequent architectural analysis can then accurately reflect the impact of choosing CORBA as middleware.

The focus of these approaches is the integration of lower-level, technology-specific factors that impact QoS properties. These approaches therefore do not utilize reusable architectural knowledge directly on the level of architectural models, e.g., to check whether an architectural pattern has been consistently applied. In contrast, the AT method combines the idea of completions (for integrating AT-induced elements) with concepts from the ADL and pattern domains (for providing feedback to software architects when applying ATs). This combination allows, for example, to check for a consistent application of an architectural pattern while integrating pattern-induced elements for architectural analyses.

The following subsections relate the AT method to each approach in detail.

6.4.2.1. Woodside et al. [WPS02]

Woodside et al. [WPS02] have introduced the idea of completions as a general means to refine and extend architectural models with QoS-relevant elements. Being QoS-relevant, the inclusion of these elements improves the accuracy of subsequent architectural analyses. For example, elements may be included that model the CORBA middleware, execution delays of web browsers, and assumptions about internet delays. To indicate where a completion is applied, architectural models are annotated, e.g., based on UML profiles (cf. Section 2.3.4).

The AT method builds up on Woodside et al.'s idea of completions to weave elements induced by AT roles into architectural models. However, the AT language is specialized in capturing reusable architectural knowledge while Woodside et al. describe a more general approach. This generality prohibits Woodside et al.'s completions to exploit specific constraints of reusable architectural knowledge, e.g., to check for a consistent annotation of multiple architectural elements. In contrast, AT roles additionally contain constraints that allow for consistency checks. This way, the semantics of reusable architectural knowledge can better be reflected. Besides this main difference, the AT method comes with an engineering process for ATs, which particularly includes quality assurance for completions.

6.4.2.2. Verdickt et al. [VDGD05]

Verdickt et al. [VDGD05] use completions for integrating details about the CORBA middleware into UML models for performance analyses. For example, their completions enrich a client-server communication captured via UML collaborations (cf. Section 6.2.6.1) by CORBA-specific communication elements like object request brokers. Their completions transform the whole UML model, without depending on dedicated annotations like Woodside et al. [WPS02] suggest.

Verdickt et al. [VDGD05] focus on a concrete kind of completions—on completions that integrate middleware details. This concreteness allows them to focus on the elements of UML models that are impacted by middleware decisions (UML activities, UML deployments, UML collaborations). However, their focus is different than the focus of the AT method, which focuses on capturing architectural knowledge at the application layer. Software architects can apply AT roles (and, thus, completions) selectively to architectural elements and check for consistency via AT constraints. Verdickt et al., in contrast, always transform the whole architectural model, e.g., integrating CORBA details into each possible inter-component communication, and lack a constraint mechanism.

6.4.2.3. Becker [Bec08]

Becker [Bec08] uses completions to include details about middleware and runtime container services into PCM models. For example, he describes completions for the protocols SOAP and RMI and for processing overheads due to encryption, compression, and authorization [Bec08, p. 182]. Becker uses feature models (cf. Appendix A) as annotatable roles to configure which completions will be executed [Bec08, Sec. 4.5.2]. Moreover, he introduces so-called *completion components* as a special kind of components that include the QoS-impact of infrastructure layers as configured via the feature models [Bec08, Sec. 4.5.3]. When a quality analysis is started, Becker's completions can replace connectors (*connector completions*) or wrap components (*container completions*).

Becker's completions are complementary to ATs as they focus on a different kind of knowledge (knowledge about lower application layers). Feature models for configuring completions are a viable alternative to the AT method's use of profiles. Becker rejected profiles as option because profiles were unavailable for EMF-based metamodels when he wrote his thesis [Bec08, p. 158]. However, EMF profiles (cf. Section 4.2.4.1) have resolved this problem. Profiles have the advantage that their extensions can easily be integrated in existing editors, thus, providing software architects with an internal DSL for applying architectural knowledge. Feature models instead annotate architectural models externally, which is better suited for configuring lower application layers (like Becker does) but less suited for coping with application-layer concerns (like the AT method does).

Several ATs (e.g., the *loadbalancing* AT and *caching* AT) reuse concepts of Becker's completion components to delegate requests. However, simple replacements (like in Becker's connector completions and container completions) are often impossible because an AT's refinements are more complex. For example, the loadbalancing AT additionally creates several replicas of the bound component, including their allocation to additional resources. The AT method therefore uses QVT-O transformations to implement completions, which is a more general approach.

6.4.2.4. J. Happe [Hap09]

Like Becker (cf. preceding section), J. Happe provides completions for PCM models. In contrast to Becker, completions are configurable via additional element types. He provides completions for general purpose operating systems schedulers [Hap09, Chap. 3 to Chap. 5] (e.g., for Windows and Linux) and for message-oriented middlewares [Hap09, Chap. 6] (e.g., for implementations of the Java Message Service standard [MHC00]). Similar to Becker's and Verdickt's works, Happe therefore only focuses on lower application layers, i.e., infrastructure layers.

6.4.2.5. L. Happe [Hap11]

L. Happe provides a special kind of completions implemented in QVT-R that allows for variability in completions themselves [Hap11, Sec. 4]. To configure this variability, Happe uses feature models to annotate architectural elements with roles (like Becker; cf. Section 6.4.2.3). Supporting variability is expected to be best suited in situations where multiple completions share common parts that can be reused—only the variable parts then have to be engineered.

Happe's QVT-R-based approach provides an alternative to the AT method's QVT-O-based completions. However, she does not provide empirical evidence that would indicate a preference of QVT-R over QVT-O [Hap11, Sec. 9.3.2]. Indeed, initial empirical evidence that I have previously collected indicates that QVT-O outperforms QVT-R regarding maintainability in uni-directional transformation scenarios [Leh12, Sec. 7.2]—and completions represent uni-directional scenarios. I selected QVT-O for this reason (cf. Section 2.3.2).

Further, L. Happe provides completions that extend J. Happe's message-oriented middleware completions for PCM models [Hap11, Sec. 5.3]. These extensions focus on completions of architectural patterns for concurrency and are, thus, closely related to this thesis. Happe covers patterns for loadbalancing [Hap11, Sec. 5.3.3.1], managing states [Hap11, Sec. 5.3.3.2], communication in pipes and filters architectures [Hap11, Sec. 5.3.4.1], and thread pools [Hap11, Sec. 5.3.5].

Happe's patterns provide formalization opportunities for further ATs. In contrast to her formalization, ATs not only provide completions but also application mechanisms for software architects, including consistency checks of applied architectural knowledge.

6.4.2.6. Rathfelder [Rat13]

Rathfelder provides completions for integrating event-based communication patterns in PCM models [Rat13]. He provides completions for point-to-point and publish/subscribe communication. Similar to J. Happe (Section 6.4.2.4), Rathfelder has integrated elements that conform to these patterns directly in the targeted ADL, i.e., the PCM. His integration enables software architects to directly instantiate event-based connectors in PCM models. The associated completions define the semantics of these new elements by mapping to ordinary PCM constructs (i.e., via translational semantics; cf. Section 2.3.5).

The AT method can be seen as a generalization of Rathfelder's approach. By utilizing profiles and stereotypes, ATs are generically integrated into the targeted ADL. AT completions define the semantics of such integrations, analogously to Rathfelder's approach. AT constraints ensure the consistency of applied architectural knowledge while Rathfelder has enriched the PCM with additional static constraints for this purpose.

6.4.3. Self-Architecting Software Systems (SASSY)

Menascé et al. [MSMG10, GHK+10, MGMS11] introduce Self-Architecting Software Systems (SASSY). In SASSY, an architectural model without applications of architectural patterns is the input to an optimization algorithm. The algorithm optimizes the architectural model by consecutively applying architectural patterns, e.g., the loadbalancing architectural pattern. The optimization finishes when a user-defined utility function is maximized.

SASSY's utility function aggregates values that quantify various quality properties. Supported quality properties are performance, availability, and security. For each of these quality properties, the operations of an architectural models' components have to provide suitable quantification functions. Here, Menascé et al. simply assign each operation a static quantification value per property, e.g., a static execution time to reflect an operation's response time. SASSY's patterns include appropriate functions to propagate such quantifications. For instance, the loadbalancing pattern's execution time function uniformly selects the execution time of the operation in question from one available component replica. This function therefore approximates a simple round-robin strategy (cf. [MSMG10]).

Besides quantification functions, SASSY's patterns include roles to characterize structural and behavioral aspects and an adaptation transformation. The structural descriptions provide a pattern's components and connectors while the behavior is captured via a process algebra (finite state processes [KM98]). SASSY's optimization algorithm applies a pattern's adaptation transformation to weave a pattern's structure and behavior into the targeted architectural model, thus, applying the pattern [GHK+10].

Similar to the feedback for software architects that the AT method provides via architectural analyses, SASSY's utility functions serve as architectural analysis to guide the optimization algorithm. SASSY's utility functions become, however, inaccurate as soon as the assumption that an operation's quantification value can statically be determined is violated. Such violations can indeed occur, e.g., when components are allocated on the same resource and influence each other's QoS properties (cf. [Koz11a, pp. 76-77]). Palladio, as extended by the AT method, does not suffer from this issue because Palladio supports the analysis of such influences [BKR09].

SASSY's adaptation transformations are similar to completions of the AT method. In contrast to completions, however, SASSY's transformations assume that the modeled system is self-adaptive. Transformations can then issue required adaptations to a self-adaptation manager [GHK+10]. Moreover, adaptation transformations are triggered by the optimization algorithm whereas, in the AT method, software architects decide where to apply architectural knowledge. These observations show that SASSY is specialized to the realization of self-adaptive systems; the AT method is a more general engineering method. Nonetheless, SASSY's approach to optimization points to an interesting direction for future extensions of the AT method.

6.4.4. Discussion of Architectural Analyses

Approaches on knowledge-specific transformations to analysis models (Section 6.4.1) are directly depending on their metamodels. This dependence causes problems when additional analysis models and architectural knowledge have to be supported: for each kind of architectural knowledge, transformations to each analysis model have to be engineered.

Instead, completion-based approaches (Section 6.4.2) integrate architectural knowledge on the level of architectural models and subsequently chain transformations to analysis models. This way, completions for architectural knowledge and transformations from architectural model to analysis model can be engineered independently of each other. Unfortunately, completion-based approaches often target infrastructure layer details instead of application layer architectural knowledge and do not exploit such knowledge for designing architectural models, e.g., via conformance checks.

SASSY is a special approach because it automatically applies architectural knowledge to optimize an architectural model. However, it depends on two unsatisfying assumptions: QoS of operations can be statically determined and the modeled system must be self-adaptive.

In the following, these and further differences and commonalities are summarized, discussed, and related to the AT method.

Abstraction level of knowledge integration As mentioned, the approaches discussed in Section 6.4.1 generate knowledge-specific analysis models. In contrast, the approaches discussed in Section 6.4.2 use completions to integrate applied knowledge directly into architectural models, i.e., prior to the architectural model's transformation to an analysis model. Therefore, completions maintain the abstraction level of the architectural modeling language instead of changing it to the level of analysis models.

The benefit of maintaining the abstraction level is that existing tools for this abstraction level can be reused. For example, software architects can use existing model editors to open architectural models that have been extended via completions. Particularly existing transformations to analysis models can completely be reused.

Because of this benefit, the AT method uses completions instead of directly generating analysis models. In consequence, all of Palladio's analysis tools (cf. Section 2.5.3.1) are supported by the AT method.

Abstraction level of captured knowledge The abstraction level of captured knowledge varies over the discussed approaches. Several approaches integrate knowledge about infrastructure layers like middleware and runtime container services into architectural models (Woodside et al. [WPS02], Verdickt et al. [VDGD05], Becker [Bec08], J. Happe [Hap09], L. Happe [Hap11]). Another set of approaches integrates reusable architectural knowledge on a higher level of abstraction, i.e., the application layer. More precisely, these approaches integrate reusable architectural knowledge in terms of architectural styles (Petriu and Wang [PW00], Cortellessa et al. [CG02]) and architectural patterns (Mani et al. [MPW15], Woodside et al. [WPS02], L. Happe [Hap11], Rathfelder [Rat13], SASSY [MGMS11]).

Both abstraction levels are important for achieving a high accuracy when conducting architectural analyses. In that sense, application layer and infrastructure layer approaches complement each other. From the viewpoint of software architects, application layer approaches are especially important in the early actions of architectural model specification (actions (1) to (3) in Section 2.5.1.1) while infrastructure layer approaches become more relevant when specifying deployments (actions (4) in Section 2.5.1.1).

The AT method focuses on reusable architectural knowledge on the application layer. In contrast to the other approaches in this category, ATs additionally exploit constraints of the captured knowledge in their formalization, e.g., to check for a consistent application of ATs.

Explicit vs. implicit element integration Reusable architectural knowledge on the application layer is either explicitly or implicitly integrated into architectural models. In the explicit variant, elements induced by roles of captured knowledge are directly included in the architectural model. In the implicit variant, roles of captured knowledge are played by elements of the architectural model; induced elements are included in subsequent processing steps (e.g., at completion execution time).

Verdickt et al. [VDGD05] and SASSY [MGMS11] follow the explicit variant: on knowledge application, induced elements are directly created. The other approaches all follow the implicit variant.

The implicit variant has the advantage that only core business components have to be explicitly included in the architectural model. The architectural model provides, thus, a compact view on business logic. Applications of reusable architectural knowledge can be separated to a dedicated view, e.g., showing all or only a selection of bound roles. However, a roll-out representation with knowledge-induced elements requires an additional processing step (e.g., by executing a completion).

The explicit variant is useful if a more compact version of the architectural model is unnecessary. For example, in SASSY, the optimization algorithm would not benefit from separating business components with components induced by reusable architectural knowledge—here, it is unnecessary to present software architects a compact version of the architectural model between each optimization step.

The AT method follows the implicit variant because of its focus on software architects and the given benefits. AT tooling particularly supports the creation of a roll-out representation of architectural models by executing all relevant completions (cf. Appendix B.3.5).

Types vs. roles vs. all-or-nothing Architectural knowledge application is either type- or role-based, or follows an "all-or-nothing" paradigm (cf. [Bec08, p. 65]). Four approaches are type-based (Petriu and Wang [PW00], Cortellessa et al. [CG02], J. Happe [Hap09], Rathfelder [Rat13]), five approaches are role-based (Mani et al. [MPW15], Woodside et al. [WPS02], Becker [Bec08], L. Happe [Hap11], SASSY [MGMS11]), and one approach follows the all-or-nothing paradigm (Verdickt et al. [VDGD05]).

Verdickt et al.'s [VDGD05] all-or-nothing approach does not mark architectural elements with knowledge-specific information. Instead, their refinement transformation simply replaces all connectors of the architectural model with knowledge-specific details (in their case with CORBA-specific details). Advantages of this approach are that it requires no adaptations of metamodels (thus, requiring no modifications of modeling editors, for example) and software architects save effort to learn about and use knowledge-specific elements (e.g., additionally requiring a per-element role-binding). The main downside of the all-or-nothing approach is its inflexibility. That is, software architects lose control about where knowledge should be integrated (and where not). Especially for high-level architectural knowledge like architectural styles and architectural patterns, software architects would therefore lose one of their main responsibilities (cf. Section 2.2).

For these reasons, the AT method follows a role-based approach instead of the all-or-nothing approach. In Section 6.2.7, type- and role-based approaches are discussed and related to the AT method.

Variability of knowledge integration: configuration techniques Refinement transformations can be configured for integrating varying knowledge. The following configuration techniques exist; ordered from the least flexible option to the most flexible option:

Configuration via (meta)model elements. (Meta)model elements that are knowledge-specific can provide information to refinement transformations, e.g., allowing to only transform connectors of a "CORBA connector" type. Cortellessa et al. [CG02], J. Happe [Hap09], and Rathfelder [Rat13] employ this option.

Configuration via profiles. Profiles are a lightweight mechanism for extending metamodels (cf. Section 2.3.4). Consequently, dedicated profiles can provide information to refinement transformations (as detailed in Section 2.5.2.2). Woodside et al. [WPS02] indeed suggest UML profiles as a means for parametrizing completions.

Configuration via mark models. Architectural models can be referenced (marked) by dedicated models (mark models) to configure refinement transformations. Software architects have to provide these mark models as an additional input to refinement transformations (action (2) in Section 2.5.1.2). This option is followed by Mani et al. [MPW15], Becker [Bec08], and L. Happe [Hap11].

Configuration via transformation parameters. Transformations for refinements may be parametrized arbitrarily. For example, the number of replicas to be loadbalanced by a loadbalancer may directly be passed to the transformation. Mark models (as discussed in the previous option) are a special case of this option. Woodside et al. [WPS02] describe the possibility of transformation parameters further.

The AT method follows the "configuration via profiles" option. As discussed in Section 6.4.2.3, profiles have the advantage of an easy integration into existing editors without having to change the targeted ADL. Moreover, profiles do not require transformations to request additional inputs.

Variability of knowledge integration: configuration contents The information to configure refinement transformations (via the techniques described above) may be of different kinds. Typical examples include the following:

Element types and attributes. The type and attributes of an element to be refined determine the behavior of a refinement transformation. Verdickt et al. [VDGD05], Cortellessa et al. [CG02], J. Happe [Hap09], and Rathfelder [Rat13] only follow this option. Cortellessa et al. [CG02], J. Happe [Hap09], and Rathfelder [Rat13] particularly extend the targeted ADL with knowledge-specific types for receiving the required information (see previous paragraph). Also the other approaches utilize information about types and attributes but additionally support other options.

Dedicated configuration parameters. Parameters may be introduced with the dedicated purpose of configuring refinement transformations. Woodside et al.'s transformation parameters [WPS02] represent such parameters.

Feature models. Feature models (cf. Appendix A) are a typical means to systematically structure and configure features. For example, a feature model can allow to activate encryption and to select a required encryption algorithm. Feature models are employed by Becker [Bec08] and L. Happe [Hap11]. L. Happe's approach [Hap11] particularly allows to configure whole completion variants via an extended feature model, thus, giving software architects a high flexibility for knowledge integration.

Role models. Reusable architectural knowledge typically uses the concept of roles (cf. Section 2.2.4). Therefore, some approaches use models of roles to parametrize bound elements. Petriu and Wang [PW00] use UML Collaborations (cf. Section 6.2.6.1) and Mani et al. [MPW15] the RBML (cf. Section 6.3.3) as role models.

Besides utilizing information of types and attributes, the AT method uses role models because roles suit the domain of software architecture. In the AT method, roles are bound via stereotypes to architectural elements. These stereotypes provide bound elements with additional attributes (via tagged values) that can be accessed by refinement transformations.

The option to use feature models, e.g., referenced by stereotypes, may be investigated in future work. To maintain the benefit of an easy editor integration, the employed profile framework should then optimally support the configuration of referenced feature models.

Manual vs. automatic knowledge application SASSY (Section 6.4.3) is the only approach that applies reusable architectural knowledge automatically. Automatic applications are useful for SASSY's design space exploration—its optimization algorithm applies reusable architectural knowledge as a heuristic for the most promising design decisions. This heuristic restricts the possible design space, thus, making the optimization more efficient.

The other approaches—like the AT method—require software architects to manually apply architectural knowledge. Here, software architects have more control about which architectural knowledge to apply. An automatic optimization of so-created models is, however, a reasonable and complementary addition to these approaches.

6.5. Feature Model Compiled from Related Works

The previous sections reveal typical features to support reusable knowledge in architectural analysis methods. I have compiled these features into the feature model (cf. Appendix A) illustrated in Figure 6.6.

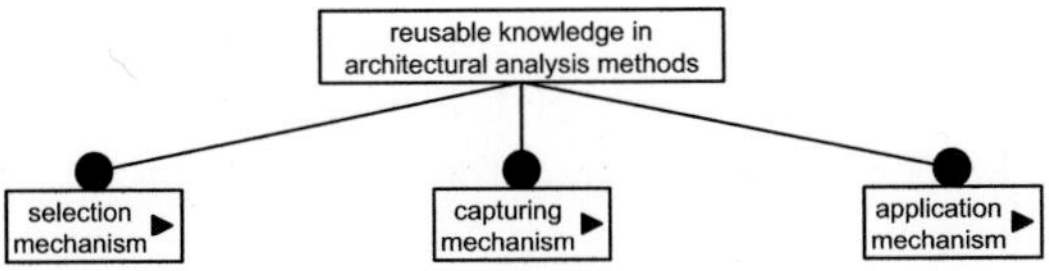

Figure 6.6.: Features to support reusable knowledge in architectural analysis methods.

In Figure 6.6, the features associated to the root feature represent the main mechanisms to select, capture, and apply reusable architectural knowledge. Each of these features references a more detailed feature model (as denoted by the triangle symbol). This section describes and refines these feature models for the selection mechanism (Section 6.5.1), capturing mechanism (Section 6.5.2), and application mechanism (Section 6.5.3). The overall feature model allows to systematically classify and discuss related works and the AT method in subsequent sections (Section 6.6 and Section 6.7).

6.5.1. Features of Selection Mechanisms

Software architects use **selection mechanisms** for selecting knowledge to be applied. Figure 6.7 illustrates the feature model for such mechanisms. Software architects have three complementing selection options: manual, question-based, and (semi-)automatic.

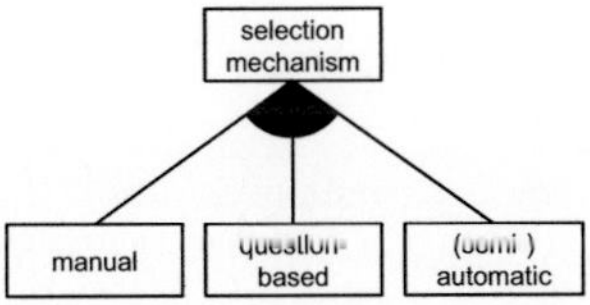

Figure 6.7.: Features of selection mechanisms for reusable architectural knowledge.

In a manual selection, software architects manually select the knowledge from a catalog. Software architects can base their manual selection on their experience, descriptions provided within the catalog, requirements in the form of usage models and SLOs, and previously gathered analysis results (see the development process described in Section 2.5.1). Manual selection is the most simple and common mechanism among the investigated methods.

In a question-based selection, the manual selection of software architects is supported with a question-technique like in ADMD3 (Section 6.1.4). This technique provides an additional means to validate the suitability of the selection.

In a (semi-)automatic selection, an optimization algorithm automatically selects the knowledge to be applied. The algorithm either lets software architects confirm whether the knowledge should indeed be applied (semi-automatic variant) or directly applies the knowledge (fully automatic variant). SASSY (Section 6.4.3) applies the fully automatic variant.

6.5.2. Features of Capturing Mechanisms

Engineers use **capturing mechanisms** to formalize reusable architectural knowledge. Figure 6.8 illustrates the feature model for such mechanisms. The root feature (capturing mechanism) includes four mandatory features (knowledge kind, capturing paradigm, captured decisions, and concrete syntax) and four optional features (process, documentation, reuse mechanism, and quality assurance). In the following, each of these features is described in a dedicated subsection.

6.5.2.1. Capturing Mechanism: Process

An approach may describe a **process** for using the capturing mechanism. Such a description covers each action to be followed by engineers that want to formalize reusable architectural knowledge. For example, the PMF (Section 6.3.5) provides a dedicated process description but the RBML (Section 6.3.3) provides only a description of its specification language for reusable architectural knowledge.

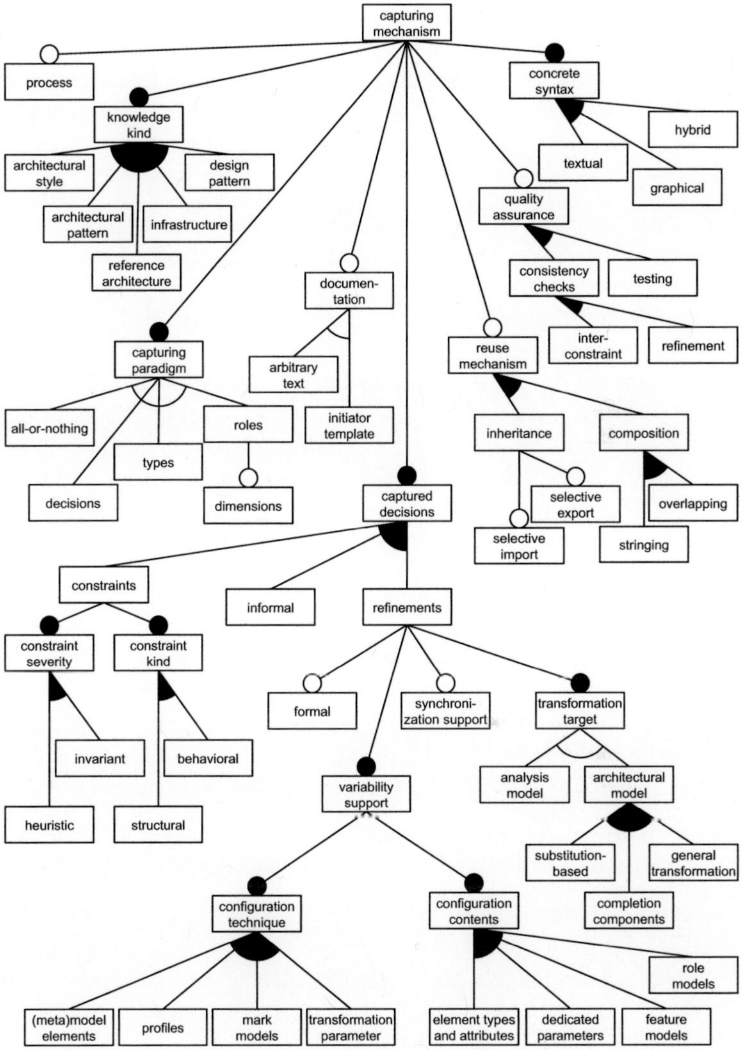

Figure 6.8.: Features of capturing mechanisms for reusable architectural knowledge.

6.5.2.2. Capturing Mechanism: Knowledge Kind

As shown in Figure 6.8 (**knowledge kind** feature), reusable architectural knowledge to be captured can be of different kinds, i.e., targeting different levels of abstraction. An approach may support one or more kinds of knowledge.

Section 2.2.4 describes **architectural styles**, **architectural patterns**, and **reference architectures** as the focus of the AT method. These kinds describe high-level knowledge, especially important for software architects. Knowledge about **infrastructure** is on a lower level of abstraction, which is especially important for system deployers. Most approaches on completions focus on this kind of knowledge (cf. discussion in Section 6.4.4). Similarly, **design patterns** are also on a lower level of abstraction but especially important for component developers. For example, UML Collaborations (Section 6.2.6.1) and several approaches from the pattern community (Section 6.3) focus on design patterns.

6.5.2.3. Capturing Mechanism: Capturing Paradigm

Figure 6.8 (**capturing paradigm** feature) illustrates general paradigms to capture knowledge. The investigated approaches either follow an all-or-nothing approach or use decisions, types, or roles as first-class citizens for capturing knowledge.

All-or-nothing approaches simply refine all elements of the architectural model with knowledge-specific details (where feasible). Therefore, these approaches need no dedicated constructs that can be applied to architectural models.

Decision-based approaches have design decisions as first-class citizens. Architectural knowledge is then captured as a set of such decisions; the application of this set is a design decision on its own. Architectural models can be inferred from the set of made decisions.

Type-based approaches create architectural elements via instances types that are knowledge-specific. Here, first-class citizens of architectural models are defined on a per-knowledge base.

Role-based approaches bind roles to common elements of architectural models, e.g., components and connectors. These roles cover design decisions, e.g., about constraints and refinements. The first-class citizens remain the elements of architectural models. Optionally, role-based approaches support the concept of **dimensions**, which ensures that cardinalities of role assignments are consistent.

Only Verdickt et al. use the all-or-nothing approach (cf. discussion in Section 6.4.4). Some approaches from the domain of knowledge management, e.g., Archium (cf. Section 6.1.2), employ the decision-based approach. The other approaches are either type- or role-based (cf. discussion in Section 6.2.7). DPML is the only approach that additionally makes use of the dimension concept (cf. Section 6.3.2).

6.5.2.4. Capturing Mechanism: Documentation

Knowledge may be informally documented in natural language (optional **documentation** feature in Figure 6.8). Documentation is either based on arbitrary text or on initiator templates.

In the **arbitrary text** variant, knowledge is captured via a generic documentation in natural language. In the **initiator template** variant, knowledge is captured via an initiator template covering typical attributes of reusable knowledge as, e.g., listed in the POSA books (cf. Section 6.3.1). These attributes are informally set via sentences in natural language.

6.5.2.5. Capturing Mechanism: Captured Decisions

At the bottom of Figure 6.8, the **captured decisions** feature illustrates which design decisions are typically captured. The investigated approaches cover decisions captured via formal constraints, informal text, and (semi-)formal refinements.

Design decisions captured via formal constraints Support to capture design decisions about constraints can be classified along supported constraint severities and constraint kinds:

constraint severity. The constraint states whether software architects are only warned about constraint violations (heuristic constraints) or whether software architects receive an error (invariant constraints).

constraint kind. The constraint kind states whether a constraint restricts structural or behavioral properties of an architectural model.

For each of the features, an approach may support one or both of the given options to capture decisions about constraints. Section 6.2.7 discusses both features in detail.

Design decisions captured via informal text Arbitrary decisions may be informally captured via text formulated in natural language. Such decisions are naturally part of an approach's documentation mechanism as described in Section 6.5.2.4.

Design decisions captured via (semi-)formal refinements A cpaturing approach can capture design decisions about the existence of elements via refinements; technically realized as model transformations. Regarding such refinements, the following features vary over the investigated approaches:

formal. A refinement may be defined formally, e.g., via first-order predicate logic. As discussed in Section 6.2.7, formal refinements allow for verifying the conceptual integrity of refinements but are more complex to specify.

variability support. A refinement varies its output depending on its inputs, thus, providing support for variability. Variability support comes with a configuration technique and configuration contents.

The **configuration technique** specifies how a refinement is configured for integrating variations of reusable knowledge. There may be a configuration via metamodel elements, profiles, mark models, and transformation parameters. These options are discussed in Section 6.4.4.

The **configuration contents** specify what information a refinement processes to produce varying output. A refinement may process element types and attributes, dedicated parameters for variation, feature models, and models of roles. These options are discussed in Section 6.4.4 as well.

synchronization support. Information from refinements can be used to synchronize models related to the targeted architectural model, e.g., a previously generated analysis model. The synchronization updates these models with the new elements created by the refinement. Only Mani et al. (Section 6.4.1.3) provide support for such a synchronization mechanism.

transformation target. As discussed in Section 6.4.4, a refinement's transformation can integrate knowledge on two different levels of abstraction: either into **analysis models** or directly into **architectural models**. The latter variant describes a transformation that realizes a completion. If realized as completions, refinements are independent of transformations from architectural model to analysis models. This independence fosters reuse of such transformations (cf. Section 6.4.4).

The investigated approaches use different variants to implement completions; support for multiple variants is also possible. UML templates (Section 6.2.6.2) use a substitution-based variant as Section 2.4.3.3 describes for bound templates in general. Becker's completion components are a similar variant specialized to component-based substitutions of connectors and containers (Section 6.4.2.3). Other approaches that implement refinements via completions use general purpose transformation approaches, e.g., L. Happe uses QVT-R (cf. Section 6.4.2.5).

6.5.2.6. Capturing Mechanism: Reuse Mechanism

The **reuse mechanism** feature shown in Figure 6.8 is an optional means to capture knowledge by reusing previously captured knowledge. The reused abstraction is a *module* [LR10] and is determined by the capturing paradigm. For example, types and roles can represent such modules but also the captured knowledge as a whole (e.g., a set of roles). As discussed in

Section 6.2.7 and Section 6.3.6, the two major reuse techniques for modules are inheritance and composition.[11]

Inheritance as a reuse mechanism Inheritance is a reuse mechanisms in which one or more modules are merged into a reusing module, which can subsequently extend merged elements. Most approaches define a module as the captured knowledge as a whole. Therefore, a reusing module typically inherits all roles (or types) of other modules.

Optionally, modules can be defined more fine-granular, e.g., as a type or role. SADL (Section 6.2.4), for instance, lets a type inherit all constraints and refinement specifications of another type. If defined on such a fine-granular level, modules to be merged can explicitly be selected (**selective import**) and explicitly allowed for being merged (**selective export**).

Composition as a reuse mechanism Composition is a reuse mechanism that puts reused modules into a larger composite module. COMLAN (Section 6.3.4) illustrates two composition variants: stringing and overlapping.

In the **stringing** variant, modules are related to each other via connectors. These connectors define module behavior as the interaction between modules. Another example of the stringing variant is PMF's composition mechanism (cf. Section 6.3.5).

In the **overlapping** variant, reused modules are nested within the reusing module, which allows to create module hierarchies. Reusing modules can delegate to nested modules for defining (parts of) their behavior. Another example (besides COMLAN) of the overlapping variant are POSA's pattern compounds (cf. Section 6.3.1).

[11] Alternatively, "inheritance" may be rephrased as *composition by extension* and "composition" as *composition by connection and containment* [LR10]. The sub features of the latter then correspond to *composition by connection* (stringing) and *composition by containment* (overlapping). I have refrained from this alternative because the investigated approaches follow the here presented terminology.

6.5.2.7. Capturing Mechanism: Quality Assurance

Optionally, a capturing mechanism provides dedicated means for assuring the quality of the captured knowledge (**quality assurance** feature in Figure 6.8). The main quality property targeted is the conceptual integrity of the captured knowledge, i.e., whether the knowledge is consistently captured (cf. Definition 2.14 in Section 2.2.4). Consistency checks and testing are the two concrete quality assurance techniques that have been discussed in Section 6.2.7.

Consistency checks Consistency checks formally proof whether knowledge is captured consistently. These checks can target the consistency between constraints and of refinements.

Checking **inter-constraint** consistency proves that constraints do not contradict each other. Checking **refinement** consistency proves that a refinement from an abstract model to a refined model is correct. That is, the refined model satisfies the abstract model's constraints exactly as the abstract model itself.

The benefit of these consistency checks is that they are able to formally verify consistency properties. Their downside is that they require formally captured decisions (cf. Section 6.5.2.5) and often require conducting proofs manually (cf. Section 6.2.4). Therefore, such consistency checks are often complex and effort-intensive.

Testing In testing, conceptual integrity is not verified but checked against representative examples. Testing is therefore a complementary but more lightweight approach to formal consistency checks.

Section 2.3.3 provides a general description of testing. The AT method integrates testing as described in Section 4.1.3.3.

6.5.2.8. Capturing Mechanism: Concrete Syntax

Section 6.2.7 discusses concrete syntaxes for capturing reusable architectural knowledge. At least one concrete syntax is needed but using several concrete syntaxes is possible as well. Moreover, a concrete syntax can be **textual** (e.g., like in Acme), **graphical** (e.g., like in UML), or a **hybrid** combination of textual and graphical syntax.

6.5.3. Features of Application Mechanisms

Software architects use **application mechanisms** to apply previously captured reusable architectural knowledge to architectural models. Figure 6.9 illustrates the feature model for such mechanisms. The root feature (application mechanism) includes one mandatory feature (application paradigm) and five optional features (element integration, architectural model, analysis support, concrete syntax, and initialization support). In the following, each of these features is described in a dedicated subsection.

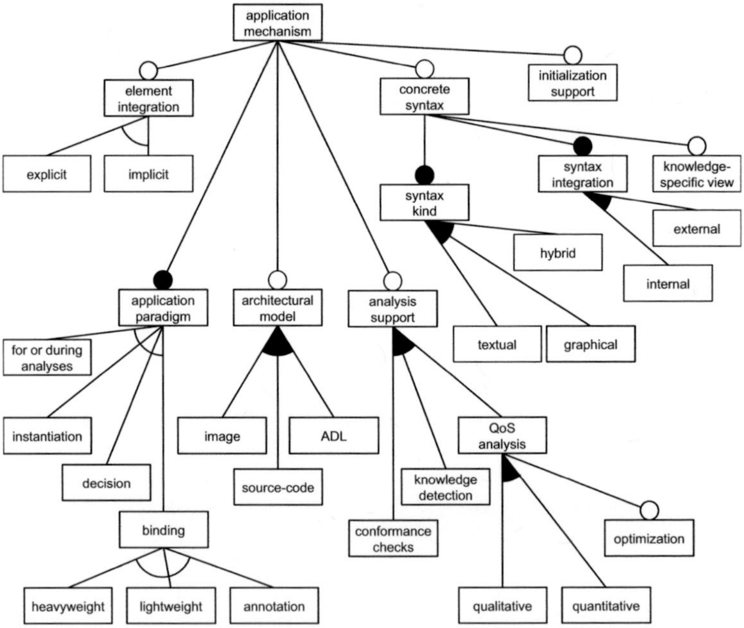

Figure 6.9.: Features of application mechanisms for reusable knowledge.

6.5.3.1. Application Mechanism: Element Integration

When knowledge with formally captured refinements is applied, elements induced by the knowledge's existence decisions need to be integrated into the targeted architectural model (**element integration** feature in Figure 6.9). There are two integration variants: explicit and implicit.

In the case of an **explicit** element integration, induced elements are integrated at the time of knowledge application. In the case of an **implicit** element integration, induced elements are integrated at the time of architectural analysis start. The implicit variant is useful to keep the architectural model compact and suitable if induced elements do not have to be manually altered. Section 6.4.4 discusses the two variants in detail.

6.5.3.2. Application Mechanism: Application Paradigm

The **application paradigm** feature in Figure 6.9 determines the general paradigm with which architectural knowledge is formally applied. The application paradigm is directly influenced by the capturing paradigm (Section 6.5.2.3).

If an all-or-nothing approach is used, knowledge is automatically applied **for or during analyses**. If a type-based approach is used, knowledge is applied by **instantiation**. If a decision-based approach is used, knowledge is applied by a dedicated "knowledge application" **decision** (cf. discussion in Section 6.1.2). If a role-based approach is used, knowledge is applied by the specification of a **binding** between roles and architectural elements. Only Verdickt et al. follow an all-or-nothing approach as discussed in Section 6.4.4. Type- and role-based approaches are discussed in Section 6.2.7 and the only fragment-based approach (Archium) is discussed in Section 6.1.2.

Approaches that follow the binding-based application paradigm have different options to enable bindings between elements of an architectural model and roles. Either the architectural model's metamodel is extended in a **heavyweight** or **lightweight** manner, or an external **annotation** provides the binding information. These options are described and discussed in Section 4.2.4.1.

6.5.3.3. Application Mechanism: Architectural Model

Figure 6.9 shows three representation options of an **architectural model** to which knowledge is applied: as image, in source-code, and via an ADL instance.

In the simplest option, only an informal **image** represents the architectural model. An application mechanisms may document architectural models before and after knowledge applications via such images. Another option is to use **source-code** to represent the architectural model, e.g., by introducing dedicated annotations for architectural elements and design decisions like the application of architectural knowledge. The third option is to specify an architectural model via an **ADL**. Knowledge applications can then be integrated via the various application paradigms (cf. Section 6.5.3.2). Section 6.1.5 discusses each option in detail.

6.5.3.4. Application Mechanism: Analysis Support

The investigated approaches vary in their support for knowledge-based analyses—ranging from conformance checks over knowledge detection to QoS analyses. The OR-feature-group in Figure 6.9 shows that supporting multiple of such analyses is possible.

Some approaches can check previously captured (structural and behavioral) constraints, thus, realizing **conformance checks**. These checks are described and discussed in Section 6.2.7 for approaches on ADLs and in Section 6.3.6 for the pattern community.

A **knowledge detection** of previously captured knowledge within a targeted architectural model is another kind of analysis. For example, PMF (Section 6.3.5) provides a pattern detection mechanism. Knowledge detection is discussed in Section 6.3.6.

Several of the investigated approaches provide means to conduct a **QoS analysis**. Approaches may provide means to conduct **qualitative** QoS analyses like SAAM [KBWA94] and ATAM [KBK+99] only (see introduction of Section 6.4). However, the focus of this work are **quantitative** QoS analyses as investigated throughout Section 6.4. Section 6.4.4 additionally discusses the option to use results from QoS analyses as feedback to an **optimization** as applied by SASSY (Section 6.4.3).

6.5.3.5. Application Mechanism: Concrete Syntax

Analogously to the capturing mechanism, the application mechanism can have one or more **concrete syntaxes** as shown in Figure 6.9. An approach may lack such a concrete syntax if no application mechanism is supported, e.g., PAKME (Section 6.1.3), or if an approach's refinements only integrate elements explicitly, e.g., Verdickt et al. (Section 6.4.2.2) and SASSY (Section 6.4.3). Approaches with concrete syntax vary in syntax kind, syntax integration, and in support for knowledge-specific views.

The **syntax kind** feature states whether a **textual**, **graphical**, or **hybrid** kind of syntax is supported; support for multiple of these options is also possible. For example, Acme (Section 6.2.1) provides both a textual and a graphical syntax for knowledge application. The **syntax integration** feature states whether integrated syntaxes are **internal**, **external**, or both. For example, most type-based approaches like Acme (Section 6.2.1) provide an internal syntax integration for visualizing knowledge applications directly in architectural model views. Becker (Section 6.4.2.3) instead provides an external integration by referencing architectural models externally from feature models. Section 6.2.7 discusses these features of concrete syntaxes for applying reusable architectural knowledge.

An application mechanism can optionally provide a concrete syntax for a **knowledge-specific view**. Then, a view for the targeted architectural model can be created that only shows elements related to the applied knowledge. COMLAN (Section 6.3.4) exemplifies this optional feature.

6.5.3.6. Application Mechanism: Initialization Support

Optionally, an architectural model can be initialized based on previously captured knowledge (**initialization support** feature in Figure 6.9). Technically, this feature can be realized as an initiator template (cf. Section 2.4.3.1). Default instances of Acme (Section 6.2.1) and ATs (Section 4.2.5.3) provide such initiator templates.

6.6. Classification of Related Works

The feature model introduced in Section 6.5 allows to systematically classify the support for reusable knowledge in architectural analysis methods. Table 6.1 provides this classification for the AT method and the related work investigated from Section 6.1 to Section 6.4. In the following, this classification is described. Subsequently, Section 6.7 discusses this classification to provide a summary of this chapter.

In Table 6.1, the first column gives a representative name of an investigated work. The second column points to the section in which a work is investigated (i.e., described and discussed). The remaining columns denote the leaf features of the feature model.

For each leaf feature, the header of Table 6.1 provides a representative name of the feature (vertical text). The parent features of these leaf features are given above; a horizontal line groups all child features of a parent feature. For example, the capturing mechanism (described in Section 6.5.2) includes eight child features—process, knowledge kind, capturing paradigm, documentation, captured decisions, reuse mechanism, quality assurance, and concrete syntax—and, e.g., the knowledge kind feature (described in Section 6.5.2.2) contains five child features on its own—architectural style, architectural pattern, reference architecture, infrastructure, and design pattern. The header of Table 6.1 follows this hierarchical structure consistently with the feature model of Section 6.5.

The rows below the header point to the investigated works. Horizontal lines separate the investigated domains and the AT method from each other:

- The architectural knowledge management domain (Section 6.1) provides the approaches ADDS, Archium, PAKE, and ADMD3.
- The ADL domain (Section 6.2) provides Acme, Aesop, Rapide, SADL, Wright, and UML.
- The pattern domain (Section 6.3) provides POSA, DPML, RBML, COMLAN, and PMF.
- The architectural analysis domain (Section 6.4) provides the works of Petriu and Wang, Cortellessa et al., Mani et al., Woodside et al.,

Table 6.1.: Classification of related works based on derived feature model

		sel. m.			capturing mechanism																																									application mechanism																				
						knowledge kind					capturing paradigm					doc.		captured decisions																	reuse mechanism					quality assur.			concrete syntax			elem. int.		application paradigm						arch. model			analysis support				concrete syntax						
Name	Sec.	manual	question-b.	automatic	process	arch. style	arch. pattern	ref. arch.	infrastructure	design pattern	all-or-nothing	decisions	types	roles	dimensions	arbitr. text	init. temp.	heuristic	invariant	structural	behavioral	informal	formal	(m)m. elem.	profiles	mark model	trans. param.	types & attr.	dedic. param.	feature mod.	role mod.	sync. sup.	ana. model	arch. model	inheritance	sel. imp.	sel. exp.	stringing	overlapping	inter-constr.	refinement	testing	textual	graphical	hybrid	explicit	implicit	for/dur. ana.	instantiation	decision	heavyweight	lightweight	annotation	image	source-code	ADL	conf. checks	knowl. det.	QoS analysis	optimization	textual	graphical	hybrid	internal	external	knowl.-sp. v.	init. sup.
ADDSS	6.1.1	X	-	-	-	X	X	-	-	-	-	X	-	-	-	X	-	-	-	-	-	X	-	-	-	-	-	-	-	-	-	-	-	-	-	-	-	-	-	-	-	-	-	X	-	-	-	-	X	-	-	-	X	-	-	-	-	-	-	-	-	X	-	X	-	-
Archium	6.1.2	X	-	-	-	X	X	X	X	X	-	X	-	-	-	-	X	-	-	-	-	X	-	-	-	-	-	-	-	-	-	-	-	-	-	-	-	-	-	-	-	-	-	X	-	-	-	-	X	-	-	-	-	X	-	-	-	-	-	X	-	-	X	-	-	-
PAKME	6.1.3	X	-	-	X	-	X	-	-	-	-	X	-	-	-	-	X	-	-	-	-	X	-	-	-	-	-	-	-	-	-	-	-	-	-	-	-	-	-	-	-	-	-	X	-	-	-	-	-	-	-	-	-	-	-	-	-	-	-	-	-	-	-	-	-	-
ADMD3	6.1.4	-	X	-	X	-	X	-	-	-	-	-	-	X	-	-	X	-	-	-	-	X	-	-	-	-	-	-	-	-	-	-	-	-	-	-	-	-	-	-	-	-	-	X	-	-	-	-	-	-	-	X	-	-	X	-	-	-	-	-	X	-	X	-	-	-
Acme	6.2.1	X	-	-	X	X	-	-	-	-	-	-	X	-	-	X	-	X	X	X	-	-	-	-	-	-	-	-	-	-	-	-	-	-	X	-	-	-	-	X	-	-	X	-	-	-	-	-	X	-	-	-	-	-	-	X	X	-	-	-	X	X	-	X	-	-	X
Aesop	6.2.2	X	-	-	-	X	-	-	-	-	-	-	X	-	-	-	-	-	X	X	-	-	-	-	-	-	-	-	-	-	-	-	-	-	X	-	-	-	-	-	-	-	X	-	-	-	-	-	X	-	-	-	-	-	-	X	X	-	-	-	X	X	-	X	-	-	-
Rapide	6.2.3	X	-	-	-	X	-	-	-	-	-	-	X	-	-	-	-	-	X	-	X	-	-	-	-	-	-	-	-	-	-	-	-	-	-	-	-	-	-	-	-	-	X	-	-	-	-	-	X	-	-	-	-	-	-	X	X	-	-	-	X	-	-	X	-	-	-
SADL	6.2.4	X	-	-	-	X	-	-	-	-	-	-	X	-	-	-	-	-	X	X	-	-	X	-	-	-	-	X	-	-	-	-	-	X	X	X	X	-	-	-	X	-	X	-	-	-	X	-	X	-	-	-	-	-	-	X	X	-	-	-	X	-	-	X	-	-	-
Wright	6.2.5	X	-	-	-	X	-	-	-	-	-	-	X	-	-	-	-	-	X	X	X	-	-	-	-	-	-	-	-	-	-	-	-	-	X	-	-	-	-	-	-	-	X	-	-	-	-	-	X	-	-	-	-	-	-	X	X	-	-	-	X	-	-	X	-	-	-
UML	6.2.6	X	-	-	-	-	-	-	-	X	-	-	-	X	-	X	-	-	-	-	-	X	-	-	-	-	-	-	-	-	-	-	-	-	X	-	-	-	-	-	-	-	-	X	-	-	-	-	-	-	X	-	-	-	-	X	-	-	-	-	-	X	-	X	-	-	-
POSA	6.3.1	X	-	-	-	-	X	-	-	-	-	-	-	X	-	-	X	-	-	-	-	X	-	-	-	-	-	-	-	-	-	-	-	-	-	-	-	-	X	-	-	-	-	X	-	-	-	-	-	-	X	-	-	-	-	X	-	-	-	-	-	X	-	X	-	-	-
DPML	6.3.2	X	-	-	-	-	-	-	-	X	-	-	-	X	X	-	-	-	X	X	-	-	-	-	-	-	-	-	-	-	-	-	-	-	-	-	-	-	-	-	-	-	-	X	-	-	-	-	-	-	-	-	X	-	-	X	X	-	-	-	-	X	-	-	X	-	-
RBML	6.3.3	X	-	-	-	-	-	-	-	X	-	-	-	X	-	-	-	-	X	X	-	-	-	-	-	-	-	-	-	-	-	-	-	-	X	-	-	-	-	-	-	-	-	X	-	-	-	-	-	-	-	-	X	-	-	X	X	-	-	-	-	X	-	-	X	-	-
COMLAN	6.3.4	X	-	-	-	-	X	-	-	-	-	-	-	X	-	-	-	-	X	X	-	-	-	-	-	-	-	-	-	-	-	-	-	-	-	-	-	X	X	-	-	-	-	X	-	-	-	-	-	-	-	-	X	-	-	X	X	-	-	-	-	X	-	X	-	X	-
PMF	6.3.5	X	-	-	X	-	X	-	-	X	-	-	-	X	-	-	-	-	X	X	-	-	-	-	-	-	-	-	-	-	-	-	-	-	X	-	-	X	-	-	-	-	-	X	-	-	-	-	-	-	-	-	-	-	-	X	-	X	-	-	-	X	-	X	-	-	-
Petriu & W.	6.4.1.1	X	-	-	-	X	-	-	-	-	-	-	X	-	-	-	-	-	-	-	-	-	-	X	-	-	-	X	-	-	X	-	X	-	-	-	-	-	-	-	-	-	-	X	-	-	X	-	X	-	-	-	-	-	-	X	-	-	X	-	-	X	-	-	X	-	-
Cortellessa	6.4.1.2	X	-	-	-	X	-	-	-	-	-	-	X	-	-	-	-	-	-	-	-	-	-	X	-	-	-	X	-	-	-	-	X	-	-	-	-	-	-	-	-	-	X	-	-	-	X	-	X	-	-	-	-	-	-	X	-	-	X	-	X	-	-	X	-	-	-
Mani	6.4.1.3	X	-	-	X	-	X	-	-	-	-	-	-	X	-	-	-	-	-	-	-	-	-	-	-	X	-	X	-	-	X	X	X	-	-	-	-	-	-	-	-	-	-	X	-	-	X	-	-	-	-	-	X	-	-	X	-	-	X	-	-	X	-	-	X	-	-
Woodside	6.4.2.1	X	-	-	-	-	X	-	X	-	-	-	-	X	-	-	-	-	-	-	-	-	-	-	X	-	X	X	X	-	-	-	-	X	-	-	-	-	-	-	-	-	X	-	-	-	X	-	-	-	-	X	-	-	-	X	-	-	X	-	-	X	-	X	-	-	-
Verdickt	6.4.2.2	X	-	-	-	-	-	-	X	-	X	-	-	-	-	-	-	-	-	-	-	-	-	-	-	-	-	X	-	-	-	-	-	X	-	-	-	-	-	-	-	-	X	-	-	X	-	X	-	-	-	-	-	-	-	X	-	-	X	-	-	-	-	-	-	-	-
Becker	6.4.2.3	X	-	-	-	-	-	-	X	-	-	-	-	X	-	-	-	-	-	-	-	-	-	-	-	X	-	X	-	X	-	-	-	X	-	-	-	-	-	-	-	-	-	X	-	-	X	-	-	-	-	-	X	-	-	X	-	-	X	-	-	X	-	-	X	-	-
J. Happe	6.4.2.4	X	-	-	-	-	-	-	X	-	-	-	X	-	-	-	-	-	-	-	-	-	-	X	-	-	-	X	-	-	-	-	-	X	-	-	-	-	-	-	-	-	X	-	-	-	X	-	X	-	-	-	-	-	-	X	-	-	X	-	-	X	-	X	-	-	-
L. Happe	6.4.2.5	X	-	-	-	-	X	-	X	-	-	-	-	X	-	-	-	-	-	-	-	-	-	-	-	X	-	X	-	X	-	-	-	X	-	-	-	-	-	-	-	-	-	X	-	-	X	-	-	-	-	-	X	-	-	X	-	-	X	-	-	X	-	-	X	-	-
Rathfelder	6.4.2.6	X	-	-	-	-	X	-	-	-	-	-	X	-	-	-	-	-	X	X	-	-	-	X	-	-	-	X	-	-	-	-	-	X	-	-	-	-	-	-	-	-	X	-	-	-	X	-	X	-	-	-	-	-	-	X	-	-	X	-	-	X	-	X	-	-	-
SASSY	6.4.3	-	-	X	-	-	X	-	-	-	-	-	-	X	-	-	-	-	-	-	-	-	-	-	-	-	-	X	-	-	-	-	-	X	-	-	-	-	-	-	-	-	X	-	-	X	-	X	-	-	-	-	-	-	-	X	-	-	X	X	-	-	-	-	-	-	-
AT method	4	X	-	-	X	X	X	X	-	-	-	-	-	X	-	X	-	X	X	X	-	-	-	-	X	-	-	X	-	-	X	-	-	X	X	X	-	-	-	-	-	X	-	X	-	-	X	-	-	-	-	X	-	-	-	X	X	-	X	-	-	X	-	X	-	-	X

Verdickt et al., Becker, J. Happe, L. Happe, Rathfelder, and Menascé et al. (on SASSY).

- The AT method (Chapter 4) is classified in the last row.

An "X" in Table 6.1 marks a feature supported by an approach; a "-" denotes an unsupported feature. For example, the first row below the header of Table 6.1 provides the classification of ADDSS, which Section 6.1.1 describes in detail. As denoted in Table 6.1, ADDSS' selection mechanism is manual. ADDSS' capturing mechanism covers the knowledge kinds architectural style and architectural pattern, follows a capturing paradigm based on informal decisions, supports documentation with arbitrary text, and provides a concrete syntax that is hybrid. ADDSS' application mechanism follows an application paradigm based on decisions, relates to an architectural model represented as image, and provides a concrete syntax that is hybrid and external. ADDSS provides no further features, e.g., does not provide a question-based selection mechanism.

6.7. Discussion of Related Works

The classification of related works in Section 6.6 reflects the discussions for the domains of architectural knowledge management (Section 6.1.5), ADLs (Section 6.2.7), patterns (Section 6.3.6), and architectural analyses (Section 6.4.4). To summarize—and as evident from Table 6.1—the investigated domains each have a different focus:

Informal documentation. In the architectural knowledge management domain, the focus is on the informal but systematic documentation of reusable architectural knowledge.

Conformance checks to architectural styles. The ADL domain has a focus on type-based formalizations of architectural styles. Formalizations allow to check whether architectural models conform to these styles.

Conformance checks to (architectural) patterns. The pattern domain has a focus on role-based formalizations of (architectural) patterns. Formalizations allow to check whether architectural models conform to these patterns.

QoS analysis. In the architectural analysis domain, the focus is on integrating knowledge into architectural models (or directly into analysis models) for quantifying QoS properties via architectural analyses.

The AT method is unique in that it combines these key features. That is, the AT method provides features to capture reusable architectural knowledge both informally and formally. Informally captured knowledge serves for documentation purposes, e.g., allowing software architects to select ATs without having to dive into their technical implementation. Formally captured knowledge serves for conducting conformance checks and QoS analyses, e.g., allowing software architects to consistently apply reusable architectural knowledge while being enabled to quantitatively analyze the impact of the applied knowledge on QoS properties.

In the following, the features of the AT method are briefly summarized and discussed at a more detailed level. The summary and discussion follows the features of Table 6.1 from the left to the right and highlights potential future works.

Selection mechanism Like most other approaches, the AT method follows a manual selection approach for captured knowledge. A potential future work is to complement the AT method's selection mechanism with question-based and (semi-)automatic selection techniques (cf. discussion in Section 6.1.5).

Capturing mechanism: process PAKME (Section 6.1.3), ADMD3 (Section 6.1.4), Acme (Section 6.2.1), PMF (Section 6.3.5), Mani et al. (Section 6.4.1.3), and the AT method provide process descriptions for capturing reusable architectural knowledge. The other approaches lack dedicated process descriptions, which potentially leads to incomplete and inconsistently captured knowledge (cf. [Dur16, p. 100]).

Capturing mechanism: knowledge kind The AT method has a focus on reusable architectural knowledge on the application level, i.e., on architectural styles, architectural patterns, and reference architectures. This focus has allowed to integrate ideas from the ADL and pattern domains into the AT method, e.g., conformance checks. In contrast, several approaches from the domain of architectural analyses focus on the infrastructure level and, thus, do not integrate ideas from the ADL and pattern domains. For example, no approach from the architectural analysis domain also features conformance checks.

Capturing mechanism: capturing paradigm The AT method follows a role-based approach for capturing knowledge because of its flexibility. Section 6.2.7 and Section 6.4.4 discuss advantages and disadvantages of this approach in detail.

Capturing mechanism: documentation In contrast to most approaches, the AT methods acknowledges the need for informal documentation: ATs have a dedicated *documentation* attribute (cf. Section 4.2.5.3). While this attribute can contain arbitrary text, the documentation of ATs created for this thesis refers to a Wiki [Clob] that documents the capture knowledge according to POSA's initiator template. A potential future work is an empirical comparison of the current version of ATs (i.e., with arbitrary text) and a modified version where the documentation of ATs has to strictly follow POSA's initiator template. Section 6.1.5 discusses documentation aspects in more detail.

Capturing mechanism: captured decisions Unlike most other approaches, ATs can capture both constraints and refinements. ATs support heuristic and invariant structural constraints. Support for behavioral constraints like in Rapide and SADL is left as future work.

An AT's refinements can be configured via profiles and utilize information from element types, element attributes, and AT roles. AT refinements are implemented as completions, i.e., as transformations targeting the architectural model level instead of the analysis model level. As discussed in Section 6.4.4, the benefit of this approach is that subsequent transformations from architectural to analysis models can completely be reused. A potential future work is a more formal treatment of refinements like illustrated in SADL (Section 6.2.4). As discussed in Section 6.2.7, the benefit of such a formal treatment is the verification of the conceptual integrity of refinements.

Capturing mechanism: reuse mechanism AT roles can selectively inherit decisions (in the form of constraints and completions) from other AT roles as discussed in Section 6.2.7. This reuse mechanism lowers the effort for AT engineers to specify ATs that share decisions with already specified ATs. The AT method's reuse mechanism is inspired by existing reuse mechanisms from the ADL and pattern domains, e.g., by Acme's (Section 6.2.1) and SADL's (Section 6.2.4) reuse mechanisms. In the domain of architectural analyses, no other approach provides such a reuse mechanism.

Capturing mechanism: quality assurance For the quality assurance of captured knowledge, Acme (Section 6.2.1) provides formal consistency checks between captured constraints and SADL (Section 6.2.4) provides consistency checks for refinements. All other approaches lack dedicated quality assurance features for their capturing mechanism.

The AT method employs testing as a quality assurance technique; a unique feature over all investigated approaches. As discussed in the section about SADL (Section 6.2.4), testing is more practical than more formal approaches. Still, extending ATs with consistency checks between constraints (like in Acme) and refinements (like in SADL) is a reasonable prospect for future works.

Capturing mechanism: concrete syntax For capturing knowledge, the AT language introduces a graphical concrete syntax (Section 4.2.5). This syntax is inspired by graphical syntaxes in related works, e.g., by the UML's graphical syntax (cf. Section 6.2.6).

As Table 6.1 shows, several approaches provide a textual concrete syntax for capturing knowledge. Future works may extend the AT language with such a textual syntax and inspect whether AT engineers can use it effectively and efficiently.

Application mechanism: element integration Naturally, only approaches that capture refinements (e.g., via completions) provide the element integration feature. The AT method integrates elements captured via AT completions implicitly, i.e., at the time an architectural analysis is started. As discussed in Section 6.4.4, an implicit integration is especially useful to keep architectural models focused on business components, without explicitly weaving knowledge-induced elements into the model that potentially obscure the view on business logic.

Most approaches follow the implicit variant; only Verdickt et al. (Section 6.4.2.2) and SASSY (Section 6.4.3) integrate elements explicitly, i.e., at the time of knowledge application. Verdickt et al.'s all-or-nothing approach hinders software architects in marking knowledge applications at architectural elements, which induces the need of an explicit element integration. Moreover, SASSY's optimization algorithm would not benefit from the implicit variant as SASSY's optimization already operates at analysis time.

Application mechanism: application paradigm Only the AT method and Woodside et al. (Section 6.4.2.1) follow a binding-based application paradigm that is lightweight (i.e., based on profiles). As discussed in Section 4.2.4.1, the main benefit of this approach is that it easily allows to extend existing architectural analysis methods like Palladio.

Application mechanism: architectural model The AT method (as most other approaches) represents architectural models in terms of a dedicated ADL. ADDSS and Archium are the only approaches that provide alternatives.

ADDSS (Section 6.1.1) illustrates the use of normal images as a representation of architectural models. Such a feature may complement the documentation of ATs.

Archium (Section 6.1.2) annotates architectural elements and involved design decisions directly to source-code. As discussed in Section 6.1.2, such an approach may complement the AT method in actions following the architectural analysis action.

Application mechanism: analysis support As discussed in the introduction of this section, a unique key feature of the AT method is that it combines conformance checks (of the ADL and pattern domains) with QoS analyses (of the architectural analysis domain). Table 6.1 clearly illustrates this difference at the columns associated to the “analysis support” feature. As the evaluation of the AT method indicates, this combination makes software architects more effective and efficient in conducting architectural analyses.

Table 6.1 particularly points to future work opportunities. First, knowledge detection mechanisms like in PMF (Section 6.3.5) may be combined with ATs as discussed in Section 6.3.6. Second, knowledge-based optimization techniques like in SASSY (Section 6.4.3) may be applied to the AT method as discussed in Section 6.4.4.

Application mechanism: concrete syntax The AT language describes a graphical and internal concrete syntax for applying ATs (Section 4.2.5). Similar to the concrete syntax for capturing architectural knowledge, this syntax is inspired by graphical syntaxes in related works, e.g., by the UML's graphical syntax (cf. Section 6.2.6).

The suitability of this syntax depends on the targeted ADL. For example, the PCM defines a graphical syntax that suits the graphical concrete syntax of AT applications, thus, allowing for an internal integration into PCM model editors.

An extension with a textual syntax for AT applications is left as a future work. Table 6.1 provides several related works that can be used as an inspiration for such a textual syntax, e.g., most approaches from the ADL domain provide a textual syntax. Supporting knowledge-specific views like COMLAN (Section 6.3.4) is also left as future work.

Application mechanism: initialization support Only the AT method and Acme (Section 6.2.1) provide an initialization support for architectural models. This initialization support is realized via initiator templates (cf. Section 2.4.3.1) for architectural models. These initiator templates provide software architects a starting point for creating similar architectural models.

"Knowledge of what is possible is the beginning of happiness."

— George Santayana 1863 – 1952

7. Conclusion

When constructing architectural models suited for architectural analyses, software architects previously had to conduct all or some steps for applying reusable architectural knowledge manually. The high efforts for software architects caused by this manual approach have motivated this PhD thesis.

The thesis introduces the Architectural Template (AT) method as a means to lower manual efforts in scenarios where reusable architectural knowledge can be applied. As the evaluation of the AT method shows, the AT method achieves this goal, thus, making software architects more effective and efficient. Moreover, the evaluation has revealed some limitations and future work opportunities.

This chapter summarizes and discusses these results. Section 7.1 provides a summary, Section 7.2 a discussion of assumptions and identified limitations, and Section 7.3 a list of future work directions.

7.1. Summary

The novel contributions of this thesis are the AT method, its evaluation, and two AT method extensions (a reuse mechanism and an optimization mechanism). Moreover, the thesis provides a novel classification schema for combining reusable architectural knowledge with architectural analyses of QoS properties, evaluated by a classification of related works of the AT method. In the following, each of these novel contributions is summarized.

7.1.1. Summary: The AT Method

The AT method is a software engineering method to make approaches for architectural analyses of QoS properties more effective and efficient. For achieving this goal, AT engineers first have to capture reusable architectural knowledge (e.g., architectural styles, architectural patterns, and reference architectures) in reusable templates—so-called Architectural Templates (ATs). Afterwards, software architects can apply these ATs to initialize and extend architectural models. The two main advantages of this application are that ATs (1) maintain conformance to the captured knowledge by construction and via automated constraint checks and (2) architectural elements captured in the template can automatically be included via completions, i.e., an automatic weaving of such elements into the targeted architectural model. These advantages promise to increase effectivity and efficiency with which software architects model and analyze architectural models, especially if complex architectural knowledge is captured. For example, reference architectures can cover multiple detailed but relevant factors for accurate architectural analyses—ATs can capture and hide such factors from software architects and only expose application-specific variation points that require decision making by software architects.

The AT method is structured into three means: AT processes, AT language, and AT tooling:

(1) AT processes guide software architects and AT engineers in following the AT method.

Software architects select and apply ATs during the creation of architectural models; the integration of AT-induced elements for conducting accurate architectural analyses is automated.

For creating architectural models, software architects commonly select and apply reusable architectural knowledge—this holds already for preexisting methods (cf. Section 2.5.1). However, in contrast to preexisting methods (that require a manual knowledge application), the AT method enables a formal application of knowledge captured within ATs. Software architects only have to select suitable ATs from a pre-specified AT catalog and bind each selected AT to their architectural model, thus, following the concept of bound templates.

This approach has been illustrated for architectural styles and architectural patterns. Additionally, ATs can be used to create a new architectural model from scratch based on a pre-specified model blueprint, thus, following the concept of initiator templates. This approach has been illustrated for reference architectures.

Subsequent modifications of AT-enabled architectural models are checked against formal constraints contained in bound ATs. These checks maintain the conceptual integrity (i.e., the conformance) to the captured reusable architectural knowledge.

For conducting architectural analyses, software architects transform their architectural models to QoS analysis models—just as in preexisting approaches. However, during this transformation, AT-induced elements are integrated. Based on the information available in ATs, this integration can be automated as shown in AT tooling.

In case software architects require new ATs, they request suitable ATs from AT engineers by specifying targeted domains, QoS properties, analysis approaches, and/or concrete architectural knowledge to be captured. Such requests then trigger the process for AT engineers.

AT engineers specify ATs based on requests by software architects and in cooperation with AT testers for quality assurance. The resulting ATs are eventually provided to software architects via AT catalogs.

Before specifying ATs, AT engineers identify the QoS properties and corresponding architectural analysis approaches for which ATs need to be specified. The request by software architects defines the prevailing constraints for this identification. Similarly, AT engineers select and understand the concrete architectural knowledge to be specified based on the request and existing sources for reusable architectural knowledge, e.g., books on software architecture.

While sources for reusable architectural knowledge typically capture knowledge informally, the goal for AT engineers is to interpret and formally capture this knowledge within ATs suited for architectural analyses. Therefore, AT engineers next specify ATs;

consisting of parametrizable roles (for defining variation points), constraints, and completions. The AT language specifies syntax and semantics of these elements, thus, providing AT engineers with the formalisms to specify ATs.

For all kinds of investigated architectural knowledge, the concept of roles has been important to assign responsibilities to elements of architectural models. However, depending on the kind of knowledge to be captured, AT engineers proceed differently in specifying roles of ATs. For architectural styles, roles globally prescribe the types of architectural elements within an architectural model. To specify these types, AT engineers focus on formally capturing design decisions about design constraints (via AT constraints) within roles. For architectural patterns, roles prescribe refinements of individual elements within an architectural model. To specify these refinements, AT engineers focus on formally capturing design decisions about the existence of elements (via AT completions) within roles. For reference architectures, roles expose planned variation points within a blueprint architectural model. The blueprint particularly includes a domain-specific architectural style and architectural patterns. To specify this blueprint, AT engineers focus on creating a reference architectural model that is then captured as an initiator template (via an AT default instance). Such ATs can expose planned variation points via AT roles. Moreover, such ATs can include applied architectural styles and architectural patterns (formalized via dedicated AT roles) coming as part of the reference architecture.

Finally, AT engineers trigger AT testers for assuring the quality for the specified ATs. Quality assurance is important because of two main reasons. First, AT engineers may misinterpret the reusable architectural knowledge to be captured, thus, external parties (e.g., AT testers and software architects) need to assess whether ATs meet the expected behavior. Second, AT engineers may introduce faults in AT roles, e.g., in constraints and completions, which violate the conceptual integrity to the captured reusable architectural knowledge.

The introduced quality assurance process for AT testers is inspired by existing processes for testing model transformations, given the similarity of AT constraints and AT completions to transformation contracts and transformation specifications. Accordingly, AT testers proceed by specifying test goals and adequacy criteria, creating and assessing a test suite, building oracle functions, executing the test suite, and evaluating test results. The outcome of this process is a report of identified faults.

AT engineers resolve identified faults in cooperation with AT testers and software architects. A set of typical root-causes helps AT engineers in finding and resolving the causes for faults efficiently. Once all faults are resolved, AT engineers finally expose quality-assured ATs in AT catalogs to be used by software architects.

(2) The AT language specifies syntax and semantics of ATs and their application to architectural models. For these capabilities, the AT language introduces a type-instance relationship between ATs and AT instances matching the introduced AT processes. While AT engineers specify ATs, software architects specify AT instances to express the application of ATs to architectural models.

ATs are collected in AT catalogs, which allow AT engineers to provide ATs to software architects. The constituents of an AT are its roles, a documentation, and an optional default AT instance. AT roles can include formal parameters (specifying variation points), constraints (expressing restrictions on elements playing the role), and a completion (refining elements playing the role). A completion particularly defines role semantics in a translational way. An AT's documentation provides a natural language description of the captured architectural knowledge. The optional default AT instance defines an initiator template for an AT-based initialization of architectural models.

AT instances describe the application of corresponding ATs to architectural models via bindings. To bind an AT, each of an AT's roles has to be linked to appropriate architectural elements. If an AT role includes formal parameters, actual parameters have to be provided along with the binding.

Technically, the AT language employs profiles and profile applications to realize ATs and AT instances. Each AT contains a profile that extends the metamodel of the targeted architectural model in a lightweight manner. Extensions cover stereotypes for each AT role to be applied; tagged values of stereotypes correspond to formal parameters of the corresponding AT role. Based on such profiles, AT instances can be specified using existing profile application mechanisms.

(3) AT tooling provides tool support for software architects and AT engineers that want to follow the AT method. Moreover, AT tooling defines the semantics of the AT language in a pragmatic way, i.e., via a reference implementation.

Tool support for software architects includes a wizard for AT-based initializations of architectural models and editors for applying ATs to architectural models. Moreover, a job for executing AT completions for the integration of AT-induced elements into architectural models is provided. The editors and the job are specific to Palladio as a concrete architectural analysis approach, despite it is expected that other approaches can be supported similarly. Tool support for AT engineers includes a framework for integrating new metrics into architectural analyses (QuAL), editors for creating AT catalogs, profiles, and completions, and a basic facility for testing completions.

7.1.2. Summary: Evaluation of the AT Method

We have evaluated the AT method with three main case studies (CloudStore, WordCount, and Znn.com), some smaller, special-focused case studies, and a preliminary controlled experiment. Over all of these empirical investigations, we were able to reuse a uniform evaluation design. Our successful reuse indicates that future empirical investigates can reuse (parts of) this design as well.

The main lessons learned from our investigations are:

(1) Software architects require only a few minutes to apply ATs. Efforts slightly increase with AT catalog size, an AT's roles and parameters, and the number of AT roles to be bound.

(2) Software architects typically save more than 90 % of recurring modeling efforts by applying ATs. Effort saving grows with the number of AT-induced elements.

(3) Conformance checks can help software architects maintaining the conformance to the captured architectural knowledge. Moreover, AT tooling often ensures conformance by construction, e.g., by prohibiting role assignments to wrong architectural elements.

(4) Software architects get several further benefits from the AT method. Making the decision to apply knowledge becomes more context-aware and more informed (because of the support for architectural analyses). ATs can hide complexity that is unimportant for designing architectural models but important for producing accurate analysis results. Moreover, ATs are reusable over multiple architectural models. We have observed that particularly novice software architects benefit from an increased effectivity and efficiency and that the AT method can easily be learned based on the provided documentation.

(5) Some issues exist that should be resolved in future works. AT tooling and external tools suffer from some technical issues while lacking an integrated environment for AT application, specification, and debugging; and some of the provided ATs are still immature. Visualization issues exist for elements that will be created by completions but are invisible to software architects; a preview of AT-induced elements is therefore suggested. Finally, we have observed that (even unfounded) distrust in ATs exists in case results from architectural analyses deviated from the expectations of software architects; software architects should therefore get more training and further tool support in understanding analysis results.

By cross-checking these lessons over multiple empirical investigations, we have lowered potential validity threats. We have evaluated the generalizability of our lessons as good given that we have covered the domains of distributed computing, cloud computing, and big data and the QoS properties performance, scalability, elasticity, and cost-efficiency. Further empirical investigations should strengthen and extend these lessons further, e.g., for the automotive domain and for reliability as an additional QoS property.

7.1.3. Summary: Extensions of the AT Method

Two optional mechanisms extend the AT method—a reuse mechanism and an optimization mechanism:

The reuse mechanism allows AT engineers to define AT roles that inherit from multiple other AT roles. The AT specification process is appropriately extended by actions to identify and exploit reuse opportunities. For this exploitation, the AT language is extended by a self-association for AT roles to specify inheritance relationships among roles. AT tooling provides an extended editor support and an implementation of the C3 linearization algorithm to derive the order of inherited properties, e.g., utilized for orchestrating completions.

The reuse mechanism has been evaluated for a set of reuse scenarios. Compared to a realization of these scenarios without reuse mechanism, the reuse mechanism has increased the productivity of AT engineers by 210 % on average. This result points to a significantly increased efficiency for AT engineers in reuse scenarios.

The optimization mechanism allows software architects to automatically determine actual AT parameters based on evolutionary algorithms. For achieving this goal, the optimization framework PerOpteryx has been integrated into the AT method. The integration additionally requires software architects to identify and specify AT parameters as concrete degrees of freedom to be optimized. Moreover, software architects have to configure and execute the optimization itself. AT tooling provides appropriate PerOpteryx plug-ins that enable software architects to execute these actions.

The optimization mechanism has been evaluated via a small proof-of-concept example. The evaluation shows that the optimization mechanism is applicable, however, further evaluations are required for more generalizable results.

7.1.4. Summary: Classification Schema and Related Works

The AT method is related to works that capture reusable architectural knowledge. By inspecting 25 of such related works for common features, I have created a novel classification schema. Subsequently, I have used this schema for classifying all 25 related works and the AT method itself.

At a high level of abstraction, the classification reveals the core features of different domains. The AT method is unique in that it combines all of these core features:

Informal documentation of captured architectural knowledge in natural language and in a systematic manner. The architectural knowledge management domain focuses on this feature.

Conformance checks to architectural styles that are captured as types for elements of architectural models. The ADL domain focuses on such type-based formalizations.

Conformance checks to (architectural) patterns that are captured as roles bound to elements of architectural models. The pattern domain focuses on such role-based formalizations.

Knowledge integration for QoS analyses into architectural models or directly into analysis models. The architectural analysis domain focuses on such integrations of reusable architectural knowledge.

7.2. Assumptions and Limitations

Section 4.5 provides a detailed discussion of assumptions and limitations of the AT method. Briefly summarized, the following assumptions and limitations are discussed: the assumption that AT-induced elements can be specified as completions, the focus on QVT-O for implementing completions, the focus on Palladio for architectural analyses, the observation that ATs can cross-cut different concerns, and technical restrictions of AT tooling. The evaluation of the AT method shows that the AT method can effectively and efficiently be applied within these assumptions and limitations (see Section 4.5 for a detailed discussion on how to cope with them).

7.3. Future Work

Throughout this thesis, future work opportunities are derived: Section 4.5 derives future work from assumption and limitations of the AT method, Section 5.6 from the evaluation of the AT method, and Section 6.7 from related works.

This section highlights and summarizes some of these future works. Section 7.3.1 describes future work on features for software architects and Section 7.3.2 for AT engineers. Afterwards, further empirical evaluations are suggested in Section 7.3.3. Section 7.3.4 briefly highlights future work on architectural analysis approaches in general.

7.3.1. Additional Features for Software Architects

Both the evaluation of the AT method and the investigation of related works have revealed several features that potentially provide additional benefits for software architects:

Question-based and (semi-)automatic selection. The selection of ATs from AT catalogs may be supported by a question-based mechanism like in ADMD3 (cf. Section 6.1.4). Moreover, it would be interesting to investigate (semi-)automatic selection mechanisms like in SASSY (cf. Section 6.4.3). Such (semi-)automatic mechanisms can naturally extend the AT method's optimization mechanism because both mechanisms are based on feedback from architectural analyses.

Integrated documentation. The documentation of ATs currently links to a Wiki. However, the controlled experiment has shown that software architects can easily miss to follow these links, which can result in problems to apply ATs (cf. Section 5.4.2). A tighter integration of an AT's documentation in AT tooling promises to avoid such problems. For example, a context help when binding AT roles may inform software architects directly about valid bindings.

Textual syntax. In addition to the graphical concrete syntax, the AT language can be extended with a textual concrete syntax for AT application like available in most related ADLs inspected in Section 6.6.

Such an extension will especially pave the way to extending architectural analyses with textually specified architectural models with the AT method.

Knowledge-specific views. Because ATs hide AT-induced elements, architectural models can appear incomplete to software architects. A feature for previewing such elements when viewing architectural models can therefore help software architects (cf. Section 5.6). For example, COMLAN provides such knowledge-specific views (cf. Section 6.3.4).

Anti-pattern and hotspot detection. In the Znn.com case study, the software architect has blamed the applied AT to cause unsatisfying QoS analysis results despite the AT has worked correctly (cf. Section 5.3.3.4). This distrust in ATs shows that especially novice software architects have problems in detecting the root-causes of unsatisfying results. For this reason, we have suggested supporting software architects with an automated detection of quality anti-patterns (cf. [BBL17, Chap. 7]) and hotspot detections (cf. [Str13, Sec. 4.3]).

Knowledge detection. A knowledge detection mechanisms like in PMF (cf. Section 6.3.5) is able to support software architects to detect reusable architectural knowledge, captured via ATs, automatically within architectural models. Such a mechanism would particularly allow to detect bad design decisions if an AT captures anti-patterns (see the discussion in Section 6.3.6).

ATs in the full development lifecycle. ATs may be utilized to support software architects in further actions of the analysis-driven development process described in Section 2.5.1.

For example, the generation of QoS prototypes like Palladio's ProtoCom prototypes (cf. Section 2.5.3.1) may utilize information captured in ATs to create knowledge-specific prototypes. In previous works [LLK13, Kla14], we have indeed prepared ProtoCom to be easily extensible, e.g., for generating QoS prototypes for multiple target platforms. We have particularly showcased this extensibility for JavaEE [GL13] and the SAP HANA Cloud platform [Abd14, Kla14, KL14]. Targeted platforms can be seen as reference architectures that can be captured via ATs. Such ATs can then ensure the conceptual integrity to constraints of the captured reference architecture at the level of architectural models while configuring ProtoCom with the necessary information to generate QoS prototypes that accurately reflect the associated QoS properties.

Another example is to support software architects in the provisioning of components (i.e., action (4) of the development process from Section 2.5.1). As shown by Archium (cf. Section 6.1.2), architectural decisions can be annotated to source code. Such annotations have the benefit that vaporization of architectural knowledge is less likely. Accordingly, when provisioning components in green field and forward engineering, architectural decisions captured by ATs may be generated into code skeletons. An appropriate extension of Palladio's code skeleton generator (cf. Section 2.5.3.1) is therefore interesting for future works.

7.3.2. Additional Features for AT Engineers

The evaluation of the AT method and investigated related works have also revealed several future work opportunities for AT engineers:

Behavioral constraints. AT engineers may enrich ATs with behavioral constraints like in Rapide (cf. Section 6.2.3) and SADL (cf. Section 6.2.4). Behavioral constraints would further improve the capability of ATs to maintain the conceptual integrity to the captured reusable architectural knowledge.

Consistency checks between constraints. ATs can be extended with consistency checks between constraints like in Acme (cf. Section 6.2.1). Such checks ensure that constraints do not contradict each other. Especially when combined with the AT method's reuse mechanism for ATs, such checks are expected to become useful [PGH07].

Formal completions. Assuring the quality of refinements captured via completions is currently based on transformation testing. A formal specification of completions like in SADL (cf. Section 6.2.4) would allow to formally ensure the conceptual integrity of the refined architectural model.

Integrated AT specification environment. The evaluation of the AT method indicates that software architects can effectively and efficiently follow the AT method. However, the work of AT engineers is often tedious; caused by technical tooling issues and missing features (cf. Section 5.6). These lacks make it currently impossible to evaluate the potential effectivity and efficiency of AT engineers in a controlled manner. I have therefore suggested to provide an integrated environment for AT specification with additional features (cf. Section 4.5).

The integrated environment should provide the following features:

- graphical editors for AT specification using the graphical syntax defined within the AT language (currently, only tree-based editors exist; cf. Section 4.5); in addition, a textual syntax like available in most related ADLs (cf. Section 6.6) for AT specification can be provided and evaluated,
- profiles that are generated out of AT specifications and kept in sync with these ATs (instead of requiring AT engineers to specify profiles separately; cf. Section 4.5 and Section 5.6),
- editors for specifying completions and tests directly embedded in the environment (instead of depending on external tools; cf. Section 4.5),
- static syntax analysis and highlighting during OCL specification (cf. Section 5.6),
- debugging support for completions (cf. Section 5.6), and
- an automated generation of test models covering typical root causes for AT faults (cf. Section 5.6).

7.3.3. Further Empirical Evaluations

The evaluation of the AT method can be extended in several dimensions (see Section 5.6 for a detailed discussion):

Effort estimation. For estimating the efforts for AT application and AT specification, further experiments on relevant influence factors and accurately weighting their impact need to be conducted.

Quality properties. Further quality properties should be investigated. This holds both for QoS properties, e.g., reliability, and internal quality properties, e.g., maintainability. Particularly the long-term impact of using ATs, e.g., on maintainability, would be interesting to investigate.

Domains. Further domains may be investigated to further assess the generalizability of the AT method, e.g., the automotive domain.

AT reuse. Reusing ATs both within already investigated domains and in different domains needs further investigation.

Additional and improved ATs. Further ATs should be provided and existing ATs should be matured, e.g., the *Hadoop MapReduce* AT.

Reuse mechanism. Additional reuse scenarios for ATs should be investigated for further evaluating the reuse mechanism of the AT method.

Optimization mechanism. The optimization mechanism requires further evaluation, especially for multi-parameter and multi-objective optimizations.

Controlled experiments. The controlled experiment was conducted as a pre-study with a few software architects. Lessons from this pre-study should be taken into account to conduct a full-fledged controlled experiment with more software architects. Moreover, future work may design and conduct a controlled experiment on the effectivity and efficiency of AT engineers as well.

Documentation variants. It should be evaluated whether strictly following POSA's template (cf. Section 6.3.1.1) for documenting ATs helps software architects in applying ATs. The impact of using representative images of the captured knowledge in AT documentation like in ADDSS (cf. Section 6.1.1) should also be evaluated.

7.3.4. Missing Features Within Architectural Analyses

Because the AT method extends existing architectural analyses, analysis effectivity and efficiency is restricted by these analyses. Therefore, a resolution of issues in and with these analyses is required to unfold the full potential of the AT method.

For example, for extending Palladio with the AT method, several issues within Palladio's tooling should be resolved. Examples include SimuLizar's missing support for asynchronous communication, SimuLizar's missing support for debugging reconfiguration rules, and a missing user interface for intuitively configuring the Experiment Automation Framework (cf. Section 5.6).

An interesting future work direction is the composition of analysis results [LB15a]. In a composition approach, software components are assumed to be black boxes that only expose QoS-relevant information, e.g., gained from internally conducted analyses. For systems composed out of such components, compositional analyses can derive overall QoS properties only based on these information. The benefit of this approach is that components do not have to be reanalyzed internally. This saving reduces analysis time and allows component providers to hide component internals, which is important for software-as-a-service providers and in microservice architectures, for example. Therefore, future works should particularly investigate to capture such architectures within ATs, including exposed QoS-relevant information.

A. Feature Models

Feature models are models to describe and analyze domains by means of a hierarchy of variable and common features of the domain [CH06]. Feature models were introduced by Kang et al. [KCH$^+$90] and later extended and described in detail by Czarnecki and Eisenecker [CE00, Chap. 4]. Further, Kim and Czarnecki [CHE04] proposed the "cardinality-based feature modeling notation" which extends feature models by cardinalities for features. Czarnecki et al. [CHE05] formalized these concepts afterwards and applied the cardinality-based feature modeling in several of their papers (e.g., in [KC05] and [CH06]).

This thesis uses the cardinality-based feature modeling notations as applied by Kim and Czarnecki [KC05] and Czarnecki and Helsen [CH06] for two reasons: (1) this thesis refers to the work of Czarnecki and Helsen [CH06] and reuses their feature models that, in particular, include cardinalities, and (2) the feature models introduced within this thesis require cardinalities.

Table A.1 describes the applied elements for visualizing feature models, i.e., their concrete syntax. This thesis makes use of eight distinct feature elements: (1) root, (2) mandatory, (3) optional, (4) mandatory clonable, and (5) grouped features, (6) XOR-feature-groups and (7) OR-feature-groups, as well as (8) feature model references. A diagram that applies these elements for feature models is referred to as *feature diagram*.

The *root feature* is the only feature that has no parent features. The root and the other features can contain children features that can be either solitary or grouped.

Firstly, solitary features include the *mandatory feature* that is always a feature of the parent feature, the *optional feature* that can be a feature of the parent feature, and the *mandatory clonable feature* that occurs at least once as a child feature of the parent.

Table A.1.: Cardinality-based feature modeling notation (derived from [CH06])

Element	Description
	Root feature F
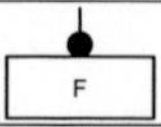	Mandatory feature F (cardinality $[1..1]$)
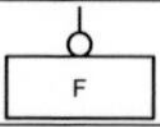	Optional feature F (cardinality $[0..1]$)
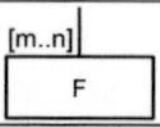	Mandatory clonable feature F (cardinality $[m..n]$; $0 \leq m \leq n$; $n > 1$)
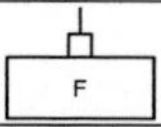	Grouped feature F (cardinality $[0..1]$)
	XOR-feature-group (cardinality $\langle 1 - 1 \rangle$)
	OR-feature-group (cardinality $\langle 1 - k \rangle$ where k is the group size)
	Feature model reference F

Secondly, *grouped features* are optional features of a group of features. Groups of features are either specified via an *XOR-feature-group* that allows exactly one feature to be part of the parent, or via an *OR-feature-group* that allows multiple features to be part of the parent. Table A.1 also shows the cardinalities induced by these descriptions.

A *feature model reference* allows to link to sub-feature models: if it is used as a leaf feature, it links to another feature model representing its sub-features. This feature model is identified via a feature model reference used as the root of the feature model.

B. AT Tooling: Reference Implementation

This appendix provides details on AT tooling as briefly overviewed in Section 4.3. AT tooling covers tool support for software architects to apply ATs (Section B.1), for engineers of analysis tools to integrate support for AT completions (Section B.2), and for AT engineers and AT testers to specify ATs (Section B.3).

B.1. AT Application Support

For applying ATs as described in Section 4.1.1, software architects need a tooling that is integrated with the editors for their architectural models. Palladio's editors have been built with the Graphical Modeling Framework (GMF) [Gro09, Sec. 4.2]. However, GMF's mixture of model-driven code generation and complex manual adjustments make it hard to maintain and extend these editors [SL13], e.g., with an AT support.

In the context of the AT method, we have therefore investigated migration options to more promising editor frameworks. In detail, we have investigated Graphiti [SL13] and Sirius [SJR+16] as alternatives. We have decided for a migration to the Sirius framework because of several advantages such as the layer-based hiding and unhiding of diagram content, improved layouting, an easy customization of graphical nodes, support for extensions, and a lively community [SJR+16].

Our novel Sirius-based editors for Palladio models are publicly available [Pala] and particularly support ATs. The remainder of this section describes the two AT-related features within these editors: initializing architectural models with ATs (Section B.1.1) and applying ATs to architectural models (Section B.1.2).

B.1.1. Initializing Palladio Projects with ATs

As described in Section 4.1.1, software architects can use ATs as initiator templates, i.e., to create initial architectural models. For this creation, ATs are required to provide a default AT instance (cf. Section 4.2.5.3). A template engine—the AT initiator—can then copy the default AT instance to a new project, thus providing an initial architectural model.

In the context of this thesis, the realization of an AT initiator is illustrated with a novel wizard for initializing Palladio projects with ATs.[1] This section describes this wizard.

Figure B.1 shows an excerpt of Eclipse's New Project dialog. The dialog provides various wizards to create new projects. In the Palladio Modeling category, the new and highlighted wizard New Palladio Project - Sirius supports the AT-based initialization of Palladio projects.

After selecting the New Palladio Project - Sirius wizard, the wizard asks for a name of the project to be initialized and the location to store the project. In the example in Figure B.2, the Palladio project is named "MyBookShop" and stored at the default location, i.e., at the current Eclipse workspace.

On the next wizard page, the AT to be used as initiator template can be selected. The wizard only lists ATs that provide a default AT instance. The example in Figure B.3 shows that nine of such ATs (e.g., the Static Resource Container Loadbalancing AT) are currently available. When software architects select an AT from this list, a corresponding description is shown on the right side of the dialog. In the example in Figure B.3, the Book Shop AT (an AT that resembles the book shop example from Chapter 3) is selected.

After software architects have selected an AT, software architects can press the Finish button to start an AT-based initialization. By copying the contents of the default AT instance to the newly defined project location, the AT initiator fills the new project with contents. Figure B.4 shows the resulting

[1] The old Palladio project wizard [Palb] was the basis for the novel wizard; the AT-based initialization is new.

Figure B.1.: In Eclipse's new project dialog, a novel wizard for creating Palladio projects based on ATs is available (highlighted).

project files for the example of the Book Shop AT. Typical Palladio models (cf. Section 2.5.3) are created, e.g., the file BookShop.resourceenvironment provides a model for a Palladio resource environment. Moreover, the AT initiator creates diagrams for each model, e.g., a diagram for the resource environment model as highlighted in Figure B.4.

Figure B.5 illustrates the resource environment diagram for the book shop opened in the Palladio editor with support for ATs. The illustrated initial architectural model includes three resource containers (Web & Application Server, Database Server, and Image Server) with CPUs that are interconnected via the LAN network. The Static Resource Container Loadbalancing AT (a realization of the loadbalancing AT exemplified in Section 3.2.4) has been applied

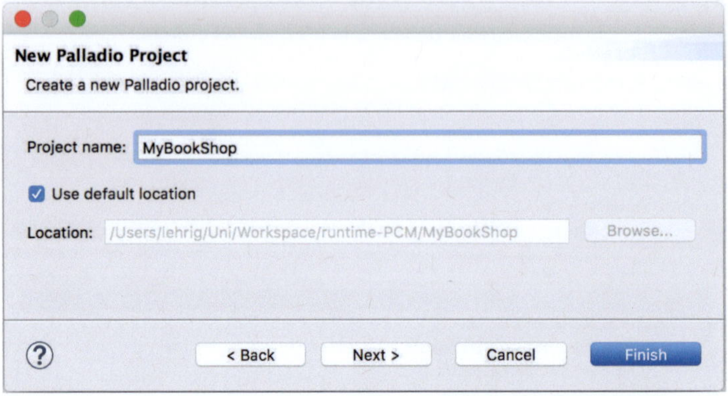

Figure B.2.: The wizard allows to set a custom name for the Palladio project.

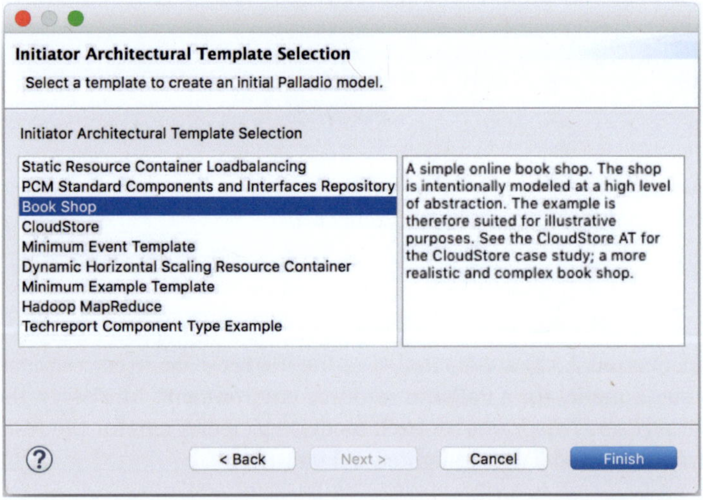

Figure B.3.: The wizard lists each AT that provides a default AT instance, e.g., the Book Shop AT (highlighted).

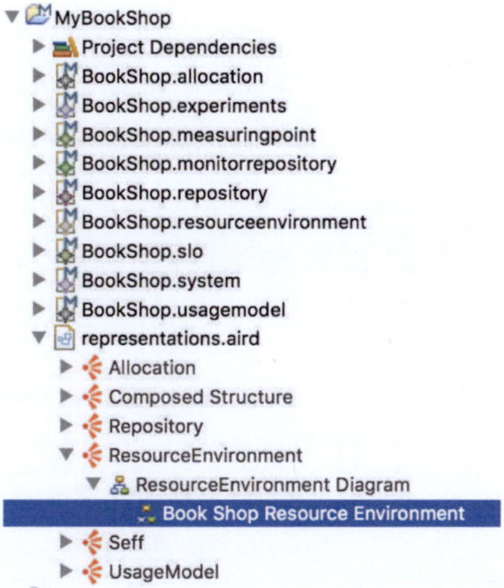

Figure B.4.: The wizard creates an initial Palladio project from the selected AT. Diagrams are also created, e.g., for resource environments (highlighted).

to the resource environment as shown at the top of Figure B.5. Moreover, the Static Loadbalanced Resource Container role of this AT (corresponding to the Loadbalanced Container role of the loadbalancing AT) has been applied to the Web & Application Server. The role parameter numberOfReplicas has been set to 2, which models that the Web & Application Server (including components allocated on this server) is replicated two times while a loadbalancer distributes workload over these replicas. Overall, the automatically initialized resource environment, thus, reflects the book shop example from Section 3.2.4.

Given this starting point, software architects may adapt specifications of resource containers, exchange components, apply further ATs, etc. to create custom book shops. The advantage of specifying a book shop model based on a default AT instance is that parts of the AT instance can be reused, e.g., the bound AT role for introducing the loadbalancing architectural pattern.

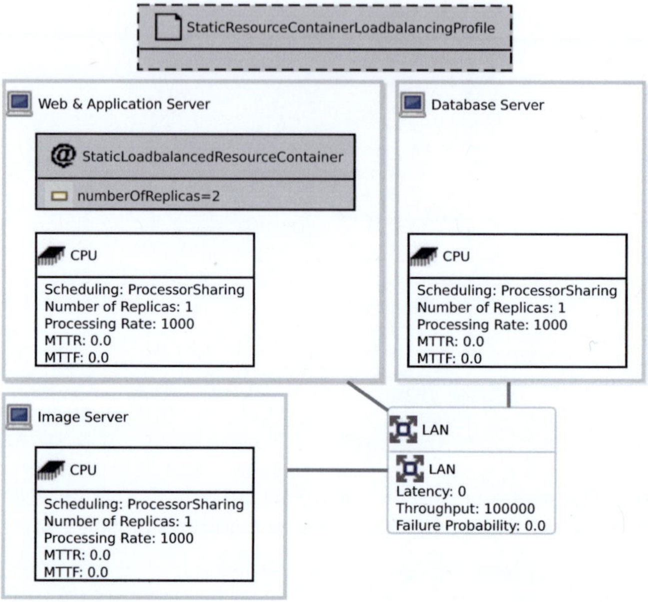

Figure B.5.: A Palladio resource environment diagram automatically initialized from a default instance of the Book Shop AT.

B.1.2. Applying ATs to Palladio Models

Besides initializing architectural models from ATs, software architects can also manually apply ATs to architectural models (cf. Section 4.1.1). In the context of this thesis, AT tooling provides novel Sirius-based Palladio editors with support for such AT applications. This section describes these editors.

Palladio projects can include various diagrams to view and edit models. These diagrams are stored in a project's representations.aird file. For example, Figure B.4 shows an expanded view on the book shop's representations.aird file where a diagram for the book shop's resource environment is selected.

Figure B.6 shows the view of the Sirius-based Palladio editor for resource environments when software architects open this diagram. The top of the view provides a tool bar for configuring and rearranging the view. The left side of the view shows the resource environment diagram from Figure B.5. The right side of the view provides a palette with elements that software architects can use to edit the resource environment model.

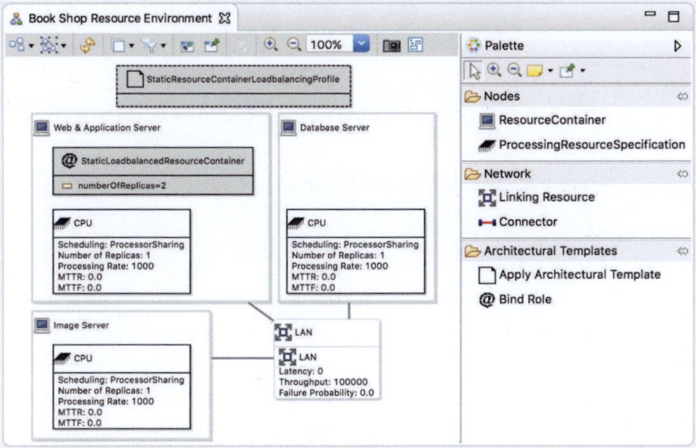

Figure B.6.: A view on the resource environment of the book shop example within the corresponding Sirius-based Palladio editor.

In addition to common Palladio elements, the palette particularly includes the novel Architectural Templates category. This category allows software architects to apply ATs and to bind roles of ATs.

Figure B.7 shows the dialog that opens when software architects select the Apply Architectural Template action from the palette and then click on the resource environment diagram. The dialog lists the available ATs that software architects can apply to their architectural model. For example, the highlighted Static Resource Container Loadbalancing AT has already been applied to the model illustrated in Figure B.6.

Figure B.8 shows the dialog that opens when software architects select the Bind Role action from the palette and then click on an architectural element.

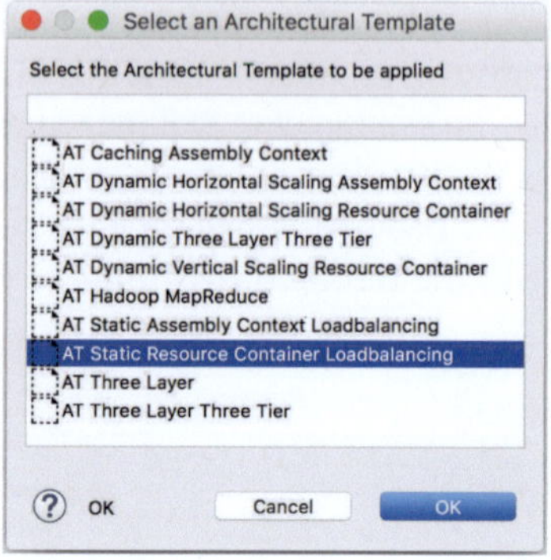

Figure B.7.: The dialog for selecting and applying an AT.

The dialog lists only those roles that belong to already applied ATs and that can be bound to the selected architectural element. For example, the highlighted StaticLoadbalanceResourceContainer role in Figure B.6 belongs to the already applied Static Resource Container Loadbalancing AT and the selected element is a resource container, i.e., an element for which this role can legally be bound.

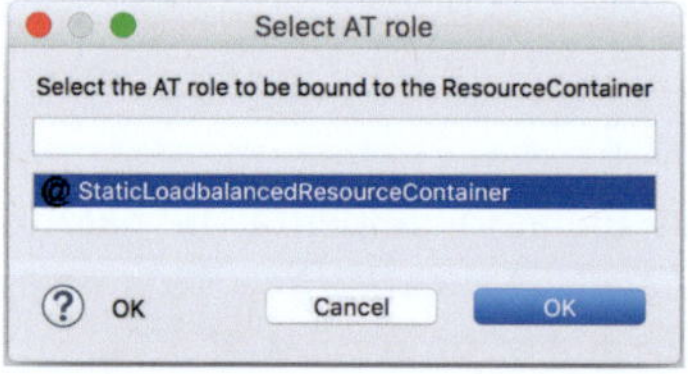

Figure B.8.: The dialog for selecting and binding roles of ATs.

Once software architects have applied ATs and bound AT roles to a resource environment model, the corresponding elements of AT instances are shown within the resource environment diagram of the editor. For example, the diagram in Figure B.6 shows the applied Static Resource Container Loadbalancing AT and the bound Static Loadbalancing Resource Container role.

Figure B.9 shows the view of the Sirius-based Palladio editor for systems. In the example in Figure B.9, a software architect opened the diagram of the book shop's system model. As shown, the editor is structured like the editor for resource environments (with a tool bar at the top, the diagram on the left, and a palette on the right). The editor's palette particularly includes the novel Architectural Templates category. Using the actions of this category, software architects can apply ATs and bind AT roles as analogously described for the resource environment editor. The excerpt of the system diagram of Figure B.9 shows that the Three Layer AT has been applied to the book shop system and that AT roles have been assigned to the system's assembly contexts, e.g., the Presentation Layer AT role to the assembly context of the Book Shop Web Pages component.

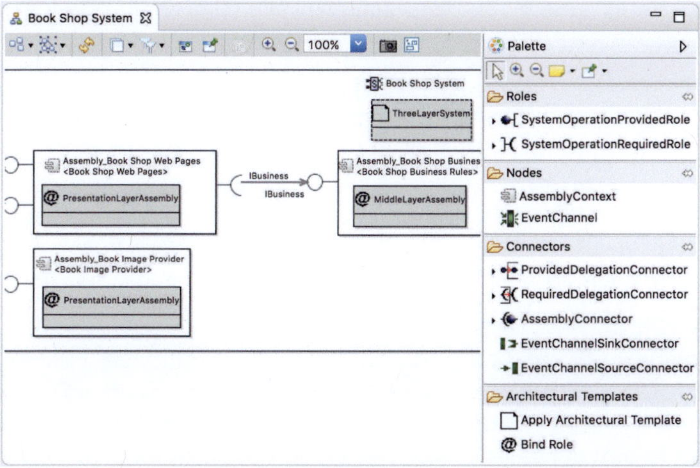

Figure B.9.: A view on the system of the book shop example within the corresponding Sirius-based Palladio editor.

As described in Section 4.1.1, software architects apply ATs to system models. Moreover, software architects integrate information from resource environment and allocation models to create complete architectural models. As part of this integration, software architects have to assign appropriate AT roles to non-system elements, e.g., to resource containers of resource environments like shown in Figure B.6. The described Sirius-based editors for system and resource environment models enable software architects to realize these tasks. The Sirius-based editors for the other models have currently no support for applying ATs because these models are not specified by software architects, thus, out of this thesis' focus. Section 4.5 discusses this limitation.

B.2. AT Integration Support

As described in Section 4.1.2, AT-induced elements have to be integrated into architectural models prior to the transformation to analysis models. Here, tool support can ensure that completions of ATs are executed, which integrates AT-induced elements automatically. This section describes this tool support for Palladio.

In Palladio, a workflow engine [Palc] takes care of transforming PCM models into analysis models and of evaluating QoS properties. The workflow engine structures this workflow in consecutive jobs. Because each of Palladio's analysis tools (cf. Section 2.5.3.1) requires a different analysis model and is started differently, each tool provides different jobs for these tasks. Given the requirement that all of these tools shall support ATs, one option is thus to integrate an additional job for executing completions in each of these tools.

Alternatively, Palladio's Experiment Automation Framework (described in [Leh16, Chap. 9]) can be extended. The Experiment Automation Framework provides a generic workflow for transforming to analysis models, configuring and running analysis tools, and for storing measurements. Concrete analysis tools can provide adapters between the framework and their tool-specific jobs [Leh16, Sec. 9.2]. For example, the analysis tools SimuCom and SimuLizar provide such adapters [Leh16, Sec. 9.2]. Subsequently, software architects can use the Experiment Automation Framework to configure and run workflows for adapter-providing analysis tools.

In the context of the AT method, an additional job for executing completions can directly be integrated into the generic workflow of the Experiment Automation Framework. The Experiment Automation Framework provides a dedicated extension point for hooking-in such additional jobs [Leh16,

Sec. 9.3]. This integration option requires only a single extension of the Experiment Automation Framework while the requirement that all analysis tools shall support ATs is fulfilled (as long as these tools provide a suitable adapter).

For this reason, AT tooling follows the integration option to extend the Experiment Automation Framework. AT tooling provides a further job that additionally takes care of executing completions. For robustness, the job also validates all constraints of ATs prior to completion execution. AT tooling registers this job before the job that transforms PCM models to analysis models.

Listing B.1 and Listing B.2 exemplify the workflow's console output of the integrated AT job using the book shop example. Listing B.1 reports results on validated constraints. For example, line 24 shows that the number of replicas constraint (as described in the context of Figure B.12) validated successfully. Listing B.2 reports the successful execution of the StaticResourceContainerLoadbalancing completion. Only after these tasks have been executed successfully, the workflow continues to transform the architectural model, into which AT-induced elements have been integrated, to analysis models.

B.3. AT Specification Support

For specifying ATs as described in Section 4.1.3, AT engineers need tool support that is compliant with the tooling for AT application. AT tooling provides such a tool support as described in this section. With the provided tool support, AT engineers can integrate new metrics into QoS analyses (Section B.3.1) and create AT catalogs (Section B.3.2), profiles (Section B.3.3), and completions (Section B.3.4). Moreover, AT testers are provided with tools for testing completions (Section B.3.5).

B.3.1. Integrating New Metrics

In action (1) of the AT specification process (Section 4.1.3.2), AT engineers may be required to extend or implement an analysis approach with a novel

Listing B.1: Console output of the integrated AT job: validated constraints.

```
...
INFO : Validating AT Constraints.
INFO : Constraint: Middle Layer Assemblies do not require ↩
    functionality from Presentation Layer Assemblies succeeded.
INFO : Constraint: Three Layer System has at least one Data ↩
    Layer Assembly succeeded.
INFO : Constraint: Data Layer Assemblies do not require ↩
    functionality from Presentation Layer Assemblies succeeded.
INFO : Constraint: No Provided Infrastructure Delegation ↩
    Connectors to Middle Layer Assemblies succeeded.
INFO : Constraint: Three Layer System has at least one ↩
    Presentation Layer Assembly succeeded.
INFO : Constraint: All Assemblies are stereotyped as ↩
    Presentation Layer Assembly, Middle Layer Assembly, or Data↩
     Layer Assembly succeeded.
INFO : Constraint: Presentation Layer Assemblies do not require ↩
    functionality from Data Layer Assemblies succeeded.
INFO : Constraint: Three Layer System has at least one Middle ↩
    Layer Assembly succeeded.
INFO : Constraint: No Provided Delegation Connectors to Middle ↩
    Layer Assemblies succeeded.
INFO : Constraint: No Provided Infrastructure Delegation ↩
    Connectors to Data Layer Assemblies succeeded.
INFO : Constraint: No Provided Delegation Connectors to Data ↩
    Layer Assemblies succeeded.
INFO : Constraint: Three Layer System has at least 3 Assemblies ↩
    succeeded.
INFO : Constraint: Data Layer Assemblies do not require ↩
    functionality from Middle Layer Assemblies succeeded.
INFO : Constraint: System is Three Layer System succeeded.
INFO : Constraint: Resource Environment has exactly one Static ↩
    Loadbalanced Resource Container succeeded.
INFO : Constraint: Static Loadbalanced Resource Container has ↩
    Assembly Contexts succeeded.
INFO : Constraint: System is Static Resource Container ↩
    Loadbalancing System succeeded.
INFO : Constraint: Presentation Layer Assembly is not another ↩
    Layer Assembly succeeded.
INFO : Constraint: Presentation Layer Assembly is not another ↩
    Layer Assembly succeeded.
INFO : Constraint: Middle Layer Assembly is not another Layer ↩
    Assembly succeeded.
INFO : Constraint: Data Layer Assembly is not another Layer ↩
    Assembly succeeded.
INFO : Constraint: Number of Replicas greater 0 succeeded.
...
```

Listing B.2: Console output of the integrated AT job: completion execution.

```
...
INFO : Executing QVTO Transformation...
INFO : AT Completion "StaticResourceContainerLoadbalancing" started
INFO : AT Completion "StaticResourceContainerLoadbalancing" finished
INFO : Transformation executed successfully
INFO : Task Sequential Job Execution completed in 1.124E-6 seconds
...
```

QoS metric. In this case, AT engineers profit from analysis frameworks that allow for an easy integration of new metrics.

Unfortunately, Palladio did not provide an extensible analysis framework; supported metrics were hard-coded. The AT method's requirement to extend analysis approaches with additional metrics therefore motivated the development of such a framework. The developed framework—the Quality Analysis Lab (QuAL) [Leh16]—is now integrated into Palladio. AT engineers can use this framework for extending Palladio with new metrics or as a framework for new analysis tools. QuAL's developer guide [Leh16] describes the necessary steps for integrating new metrics.

B.3.2. Creating AT Catalogs

AT engineers specify ATs as described in action (3) of the AT specification process in Section 4.1.3.2. For practically realizing such specifications, AT tooling provides a simple tree-based editor [ATt]; generated via EMF from the AT metamodel (cf. [SBPM09, Sec. 3.2]). Figure B.10 exemplifies an AT catalog opened within this editor.

The upper part of Figure B.10 shows the editor's tree view while the lower part shows a properties view. In the tree view, AT engineers can select, add new, and remove existing elements. In the properties view, AT engineers can edit attributes of selected elements.

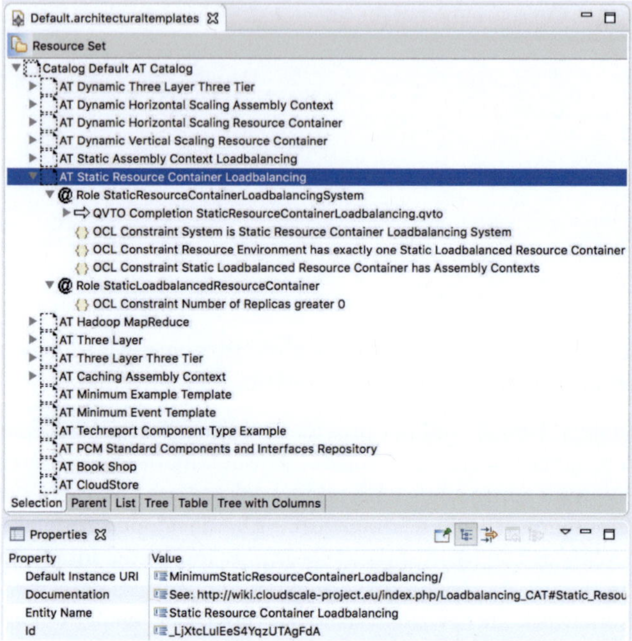

Figure B.10.: The tree-based editor for AT catalogs.

The tree view in Figure B.10 shows an expanded AT catalog (Default AT Catalog) that includes several ATs (Dynamic Three Layer Three Tier, Dynamic Horizontal Scaling Assembly Context, etc.). Because the Static Resource Container Loadbalancing AT is selected, the properties view in Figure B.10 shows the attributes of this AT. For example, the AT has a default instance pointing to the (project-relative) URI MinimumStaticResourceContainerLoadbalancing/.

Moreover, the AT Static Resource Container Loadbalancing is expanded, which instructs the tree view to show its contained roles. The AT includes the roles Static Resource Container Loadbalancing System and Static Loadbalanced Resource Container. When, for instance, selecting the second role in the tree viewer, the properties view adapts as shown in Figure B.11. Besides attributes for a unique identification (ID), an entity name, and a list of included roles, the view shows the stereotype referenced by the selected role. In the example in Figure B.11, the stereotype StaticLoadbalancedResourceContainer is referenced.

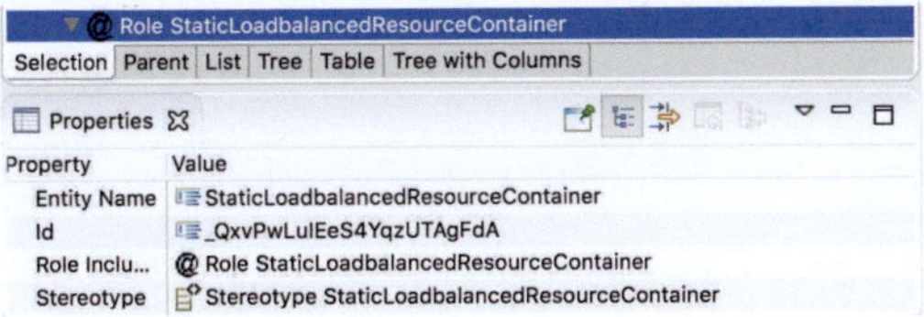

Figure B.11.: The properties view when selecting an AT role.

For both roles, contained elements are shown, i.e., completions and constraints. The first role contains a completion specified as a QVT-O model transformation (linking to the project-relative URI StaticResourceContainer-Loadbalancing.qvto) and three constraints formulated via OCL. The second role contains only one OCL constraint.

When, for instance, selecting this OCL constraint in the tree viewer, the properties view adapts as shown in Figure B.12. The Entity Name provides a description of the constraint in natural language while the Expression specifies the constraint in correct OCL syntax. In the example in Figure B.12, the constraint demands that the actual value for the number of replicas parameter of the constraint's role is strictly greater than zero. The evaluation context for this constraint is the stereotype referenced by the role of the constraint. Because this stereotype defines the formal parameter numberOfReplicas, the OCL expression self.numberOfReplicas>0 accordingly formalizes the constraint in OCL.

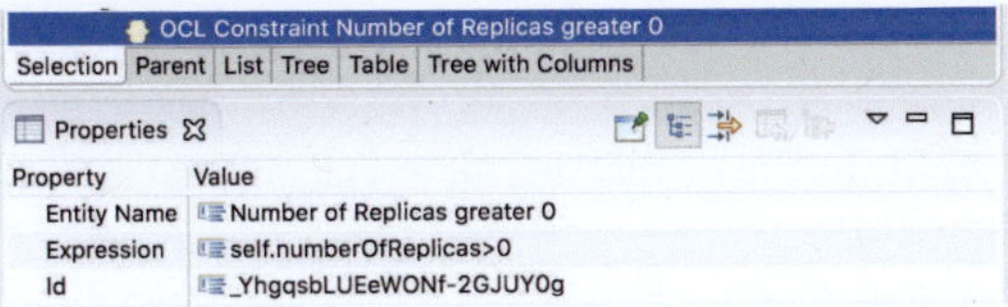

Figure B.12.: The properties view when selecting an OCL constraint.

The tree editor allows AT engineers to specify elements of AT catalogs by opening an element's context menu and then adding appropriate child nodes. Figure B.13 exemplifies this context menu for the AT catalog element (i.e., the root element). As shown, the New Child entry allows to add a new AT to the catalog.

Figure B.13.: Context menu for adding an AT to an AT catalog.

Besides the tree-based specification of AT catalogs, AT engineers need to create suitable profiles and completions that can be referenced from such catalogs. The following sections detail the creation of these artifacts.

B.3.3. Creating Profiles

As described in Section 4.2.4, ATs extend architectural models via profiles. Accordingly, AT engineers have to create a dedicated profile for an AT where each of the AT's roles references its corresponding stereotype within the profile (e.g., shown in Figure B.11). Because AT tooling is based on EMF profiles [KDH+12], AT engineers can also reuse EMF profiles' editor for creating suitable profiles. Figure B.14 exemplifies a profile opened within this editor; this section briefly describes the editor along this figure. Further details on the specification of EMF profiles are provided by the original authors [KDH+12].

The upper part of Figure B.14 shows the editor's graphical specification view while the lower part shows a properties view. In the graphical specification view, AT engineers can select, add new, and remove existing elements. For additions, AT engineers have to select the appropriate element from the palette on the right. In the properties view, AT engineers can edit attributes of selected elements.

The graphical specification view illustrates the profile used for applying the loadbalancing AT in Section B.1.2. As shown in the properties view, the profile is named Static Resource Container Loadbalancing Profile. Moreover, the graphical specification view shows that the profile includes two stereotypes: Static

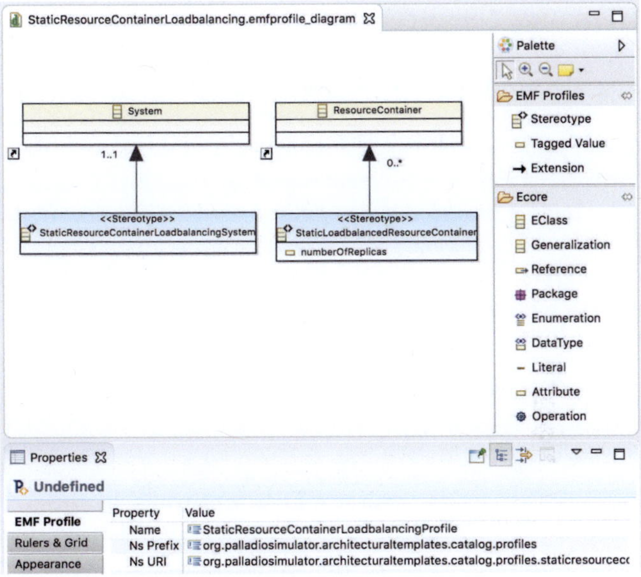

Figure B.14.: The graphical editor for creating profiles.

Resource Container Loadbalancing System and Static Loadbalanced Resource Container. These stereotypes extend Palladio's System and Resource Container metaclasses, i.e., the stereotypes can be bound to instances of these metaclasses. The cardinality denoted along with the extension arrow states that a correct profile application requires that the Static Resource Container Loadbalancing System stereotype needs to be bound to exactly one Palladio System instance and that the Static Loadbalanced Resource Container stereotype can be bound to an arbitrary number of Palladio Resource Container instances.

Figure B.6 exemplifies a correct profile application for the book shop example. The roles of the applied AT—the loadbalancing variant called Static Resource Container Loadbalancing—particularly reference the stereotypes of the applied profile. For instance, Figure B.11 shows that the Static Loadbalanced Resource Container role references its corresponding and equally named Static Loadbalanced Resource Container stereotype.

B.3.4. Creating Completions

AT tooling supports completions specified in QVT-O (cf. Section 2.3.2): if specified in QVT-O, AT tooling ensures that the completions of AT roles are executed prior to architectural analyses of architectural models with bound roles. AT engineers can create completions in QVT-O using the QVT Operational tooling provided by the Eclipse Modeling Project [Ecl16]. This section briefly describes AT-specific specification aspects when creating such completions. Further details on the editor of QVT Operational are provided by the Eclipse Modeling Project [Ecl16].

Listing B.3 shows an excerpt of the QVT-O transformation that defines the completion for the Static Resource Container Loadbalancing AT from Section B.3.2. Lines 1 to 6 in Listing B.3 provide imports and declarations; lines 7 to 27 define the transformation itself.

The import in line 1 loads a reusable library provided by the AT tooling. The library provides operations for working with profiles and stereotypes within QVT-O transformations. These operations allow to check for profile and stereotype applications, to apply and unapply profiles and stereotypes, and to read and write tagged values. For example, the hasAppliedStereotype operation (line 21 in Listing B.3) stems from this library and allows to check whether a given model element has a specific stereotype applied.

The declarations of model types (lines 3 and 4 in Listing B.3) specify which metamodels can be accessed by the transformation. Besides others, the transformation in Listing B.3 can access Palladio's metaclasses for allocation models (line 3) and resource environments (line 4). The name of the model type, e.g., PCM_ALLOC (line 3), can then be used as type of models within transformation parameters.

The transformation signature (line 7 in Listing B.3) indeed uses the allocation's model type (PCM_ALLOC) as parameter of the StaticResourceContainerLoadbalancing transformation. The parameter is marked as inout because the completion is defined as an in-place transformation, i.e., the transformation can read and write pcmAllocation's actual parameter.

Figure B.15 shows the declarative specification of the completion within the corresponding AT catalog. For the Static Resource Container Loadbalancing System role, the QVT-O completion is linked via a project-relative URI (see the

Listing B.3: Example completion specified as QVT-O transformation (excerpt).

```
1  import org.palladiosimulator.architecturaltemplates.catalog.↩
       black.ProfilesLibrary;
2
3  modeltype PCM_ALLOC uses "http://palladiosimulator.org/↩
       PalladioComponentModel/Allocation/5.1";
4  modeltype PCM_RES_ENV uses "http://palladiosimulator.org/↩
       PalladioComponentModel/ResourceEnvironment/5.1";
5  ...
6
7  transformation StaticResourceContainerLoadbalancing(inout ↩
       pcmAllocation : PCM_ALLOC) {
8
9    property allocation:Allocation = pcmAllocation.rootObjects()![↩
         Allocation];
10   property resourceEnvironment:ResourceEnvironment = allocation.↩
         targetResourceEnvironment_Allocation;
11   ...
12
13   main() {
14     log("AT Completion started");
15     ...
16     // Get resource containers that shall be loadbalanced
17     var originalResourceContainers : Set(ResourceContainer) :=
18       resourceEnvironment
19       .resourceContainer_ResourceEnvironment
20       ->select(container : ResourceContainer |
21         hasAppliedStereotype(container,"↩
               StaticLoadbalancedResourceContainer")
22       );
23     ...
24     log("AT Completion finished");
25   }
26   ...
27 }
```

properties view in Figure B.15). Moreover, the expanded QVT-O completion element in Figure B.15 shows that the completion's parameters conform to the declaration from line 7 in Listing B.3. That is, the only parameter is a PCM blackbox parameter of type allocation. As defined in Section 4.2.5.6, PCM blackbox parameter particularly allow completions to read and write, thus, complying to the transformation parameter's inout characterization.

The properties of the transformation (lines 9 and 10 in Listing B.3) store model elements within global variables. In line 9, the variable allocation holds a model element of the Allocation metaclass. The model element is received from the allocation model (pcmAllocation) by requesting exactly one (denoted by the exclamation point in line 9) root object of type Allocation. In line 10, the variable resourceEnvironment analogously holds a model element of the ResourceEnvironment metaclass. Because the allocation references a target resource environment, this environment can directly be requested via metamodel navigation (allocation.targetResourceEnvironment_Allocation).

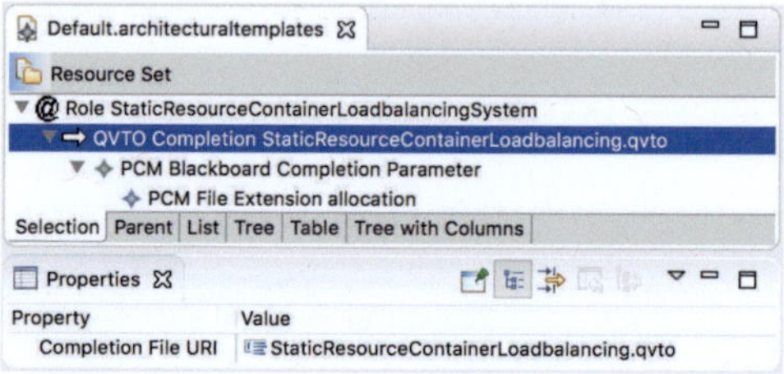

Figure B.15.: Configuration of a completion with an allocation PCM blackbox parameter.

Lines 13 to 25 in Listing B.3 specify the main operation, i.e., the transformation's entry point. The log operations in lines 14 and 24 generate messages informing about the start respectively the end of the completion. The QVT Operational transformation engine prints these messages to a console.

Between those logging operations, the completion logic is specified. An example for such a logic is given in lines 17 to 22 where the resource containers that shall be loadbalanced are queried. As specified in line 17, these containers are stored inside the originalResourceContainer variable that can hold a set of resource containers (Set(ResourceContainer)). The query starts from the globally stored resource environment model element (line 18). From the resource environment, each contained resource container is received (line 19). From these containers, only those are selected (line 20) that have the Static Loadbalanced Resource Container stereotype applied (line 21). This stereotype corresponds to the AT's Static Loadbalanced Resource Container role, thus, marking resource containers that shall be loadbalanced.

While Listing B.3 outlines the completion for the Static Loadbalanced Resource Loadbalancing AT, AT engineers can similarly specify other completions. For example, the import in line 1, the model type declarations in lines 3 and

4, and the declaration of global variables in lines 9 and 10 can be reused for each Palladio-related completion. Particularly the library imported in line 1 helps AT engineers to access AT-related information via profiles and stereotypes.

B.3.5. Testing Completions

The specification of ATs involves AT testers that ensure that ATs are of high quality. As described in Section 4.1.3.3, AT testers specify oracle functions via QVT-O transformations and run these transformations against the in- and output models of completions. Transformation outputs subsequently report test results. AT tooling supports AT testers in this task by an option to store relevant models in a temporary project. These models can then be tested against oracle functions. This section exemplifies these tooling aspects.

Palladio provides a dialog for starting architectural analyses. As shown in Figure B.16, AT tooling enriches this dialog with a dedicated tab for ATs. This tab allows AT testers to enable the Store completed models option, which ensures that in- and output models of completions are stored at the specified location when running an analysis.

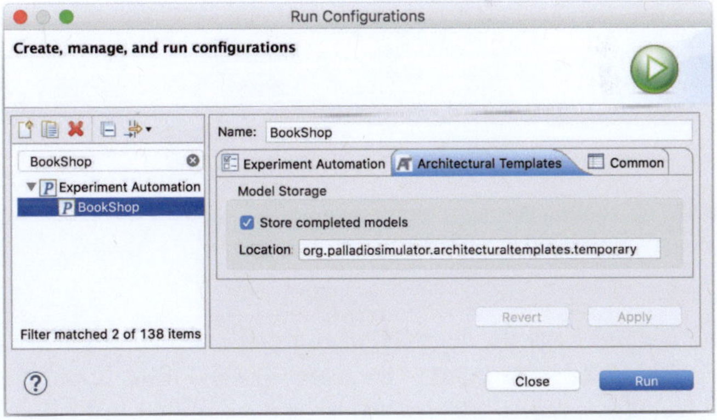

Figure B.16.: Palladio's run dialog for conducting architectural analyses includes an AT tab to configure the storage of a completion's in- and output models.

For example, when running an architectural analysis for the book shop example, AT tooling creates the temporary project illustrated in Figure B.17. Inside the project's model-gen folder, the highlighted folders beforeCompletion and afterCompletion store in- respectively output models of the executed completion.

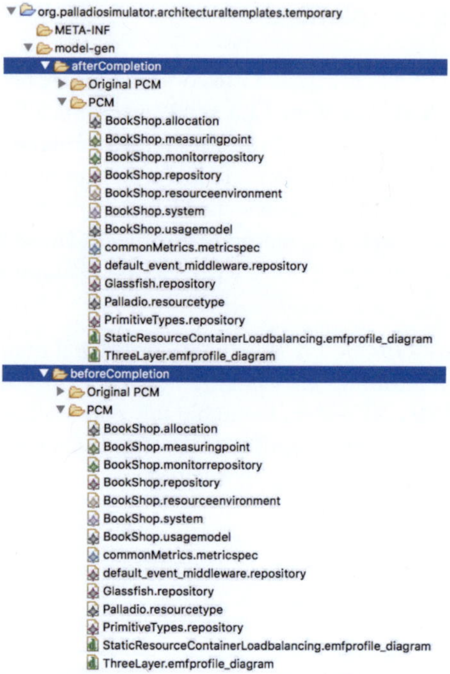

Figure B.17.: AT tooling creates a temporary project where a completion's in- and output models are stored.

Next, AT testers check the completion contract's source-target-conditions by using these models as input to dedicated QVT-O transformations. Such QVT-O transformations are structured as exemplified in Listing B.4 (cf. [Gia16, Sec. 5.3.3]).

AT testers can specify imports and model types (lines 1 to 4 in Listing B.4) as well as global properties (lines 9 to 12) analogously to completions

Listing B.4: Example for using QVT-O transformations as oracle functions (excerpt).

```
1  import org.palladiosimulator.architecturaltemplates.catalog.↩
       black.ProfilesLibrary;
2
3  modeltype PCM_ALLOC uses "http://palladiosimulator.org/↩
       PalladioComponentModel/Allocation/5.1";
4  modeltype PCM_RES_ENV uses "http://palladiosimulator.org/↩
       PalladioComponentModel/ResourceEnvironment/5.1";
5  ...
6
7  transformation StaticResourceContainerLoadbalancingTest(in ↩
       allocationBeforeCompletion : PCM_ALLOC, in ↩
       allocationAfterCompletion : PCM_ALLOC);
8
9    property oldAllocation:Allocation = allocationBeforeCompletion↩
         .rootObjects()![Allocation];
10   property newAllocation:Allocation = allocationAfterCompletion.↩
         rootObjects()![Allocation];
11   property oldResourceEnvironment := oldAllocation.↩
         targetResourceEnvironment_Allocation;
12   property newResourceEnvironment := newAllocation.↩
         targetResourceEnvironment_Allocation;
13   ...
14
15   main() {
16     log("Test started");
17     ...
18     testCorrectNumberOfLoadbalancerResourceContainers();
19     ...
20     log("Test finished");
21   }
22   ...
23 }
```

(cf. Section B.3.4). The transformation signature (line 7), however, has to request both models before (allocationBeforeCompletion) and models after the completion (allocationAfterCompletion). The global properties (lines 9 to 12) store model elements belonging to models before the completion (oldAllocation and oldResourceEnvironment) respectively after the completion (newAllocation and newResourceEnvironment).

The main operation (lines 15 to 21 in Listing B.4) defines the test by calling various test queries, e.g., testCorrectNumberOfLoadbalancerResourceContainers in line 18. Test queries are defined separately from the main operation in a dedicated QVT-O query as illustrated in Listing B.5.

Listing B.5: Example test query in QVT-O.

```
1 // Test whether the number of resource containers with bound loadbalancer roles equals the number of created loadbalancer resource containers
2 query testCorrectNumberOfLoadbalancerResourceContainers() {
3   var loadbalancedResourceContainers : Set(ResourceContainer) :=
4     oldResEnvironment
5     .resourceContainer_ResourceEnvironment
6     ->select(container |
7       hasAppliedStereotype(container, "StaticLoadbalancedResourceContainer")
8     );
9
10  var loadbalancerResourceContainers : Set(ResourceContainer) :=
11    newResEnvironment
12    .resourceContainer_ResourceEnvironment
13    ->select(container |
14      hasAppliedStereotype(container, "LoadbalancerResourceContainer")
15    );
16
17  assert error(loadbalancedResourceContainers->size() = loadbalancerResourceContainers->size())
18    with log("The number of resource containers with bound loadbalancer roles ("+loadbalancedResourceContainers->size().toString()+") does not equal the number of created loadbalancer resource containers ("+loadbalancerResourceContainers->size().toString()+")!");
19 }
```

The testCorrectNumberOfLoadbalancerResourceContainers query is exemplified in lines 2 to 19 in Listing B.5. First, the resource containers to be load-balanced are collected in the loadbalancedResourceContainers variable (line 3). These containers are queried from the original resource environment (line 4) that provides all resource containers (line 5) that have the StaticLoadbalancedResourceContainer stereotype applied (lines 6 to 8). Second, the resource containers that act as loadbalancer server are collected in the loadbalancerResourceContainers variable (line 10). These containers are queried from the newly created resource environment (line 11) that provides all resource containers (line 12) that have the LoadbalancerResourceContainer stereotype applied (lines 13 to 15). The latter stereotype application is created by the completion under test in order to explicitly mark created loadbalancer servers. Third and finally, the number of resource containers hold by the two variables are asserted for equality (line 17). In case this assertion fails, an appropriate error message is logged (line 18).

Once the QVT-O transformation is specified, AT testers only have to specify a normal QVT Operational run for this transformation (cf. [Ecl16]). As input models, AT testers select appropriate models from the temporary project that was created by AT tooling. For the transformation in Listing B.4, AT testers can, for instance, select the BookShop.allocation models from the beforeCompletions/PCM and afterCompletion/PCM folders shown in Figure B.17. If the test is successful, the transformation only outputs "Test started" and "Test ended" according to lines 16 and 20 in Listing B.4. If a test query failed, the transformation outputs the corresponding error message, e.g., the one specified in line 18 in Listing B.5.

C. Case Study Reports

This appendix provides detailed reports of the case studies conducted on the AT method. Section C.1 reports the CloudStore case study, Section C.2 the WordCount case study, and Section C.3 the Znn.com case study.

C.1. Case Study Report: CloudStore

CloudStore [LSB+17] represents a distributed, CPU-bound online book shop where customers can search and order books, similar to (but more complex than) the book shop example from Chapter 3. CloudStore's implementation is based on a legacy implementation of the TPC-W benchmark [Tra02]. In our previous efforts [LB16, LSB+17], we have conducted a case study to migrate this legacy version to a version that operates in a cloud computing environment. We have applied the AT method for planning this migration, e.g., to analyze whether CloudStore would benefit from the loadbalancing architectural pattern inside the cloud computing environment. Accordingly, CloudStore has two main advantages: (1) it refers to the well-specified TPC-W benchmark [Tra02] that is popular both in academia and industry and (2) it represents a typical distributed legacy system for which a migration needs to be planned, thus, fitting to one purpose of architectural analyses.

This section reports this case study on CloudStore. The CloudStore case study refines the overall evaluation goal by focusing on planning a migration within the distributed and cloud computing domains. Therefore, the AT method's effectivity and efficiency is evaluated in these domains and their typical QoS properties (performance, scalability, elasticity, and cost-efficiency). By including this refinement into the GQM template for the overall evaluation goal, the particular goal of the CloudStore case study is to:

Analyze: the AT method

For the purpose of: conducting architectural analyses *for planning migrations*

With respect to: effectivity and efficiency

From the viewpoint of: software architects and AT engineers

In the context of: realistic *distributed and cloud computing* systems.

To achieve this goal, CloudStore's software architect requests a set of suitable ATs from an AT engineer. In this request scenario, the software architect's request is of the broadest kind (cf. Section 4.1.3.1): the software architect requests ATs for a whole application domain (cloud computing) and is interested in several QoS properties (performance, scalability, elasticity, and cost-efficiency). Therefore, the AT engineer is required to extensively work on each action of the AT specification process (cf. Section 4.1.3).

The remainder of this section is organized according to the reporting guidelines for case studies by Runeson and Höst [RH09]. After Section C.1.1 details the CloudStore application, Section C.1.2 describes the background on cloud computing. Section C.1.3 describes the design of the case study as a refinement of the generic evaluation design from Section 5.2. Afterwards, Section C.1.4 provides the results of the case study, including an interpretation and discussion of threats to validity.

C.1.1. CloudStore

This section details CloudStore based on its architectural model. We have specified this architectural model as PCM instance [LB16] by analyzing the source code of the CloudStore implementation [Jav03]. The model's specification has required us a total effort of approximately 214 hours for its creation (83 hours effort), calibration (121 hours effort), and evaluation (10 hours effort) [LB16].

Figure C.1 illustrates CloudStore's model as a refinement of the previously described model of the online book shop from Chapter 3. Figure C.1 uses the same syntax as the overview of the example book shop in Figure 3.4 by illustrating: (1) the static system structure of the CloudStore system via connected component instances, (2) the allocation of these instantiated components to system resources (Web & Application Server, Image Server, Database Server, and externally hosted External Services), and (3) the system entry point for customers (interfaces for accessing web pages for books, home page, shopping carts, and orders). Moreover, we modeled the dynamic behavior as described next.

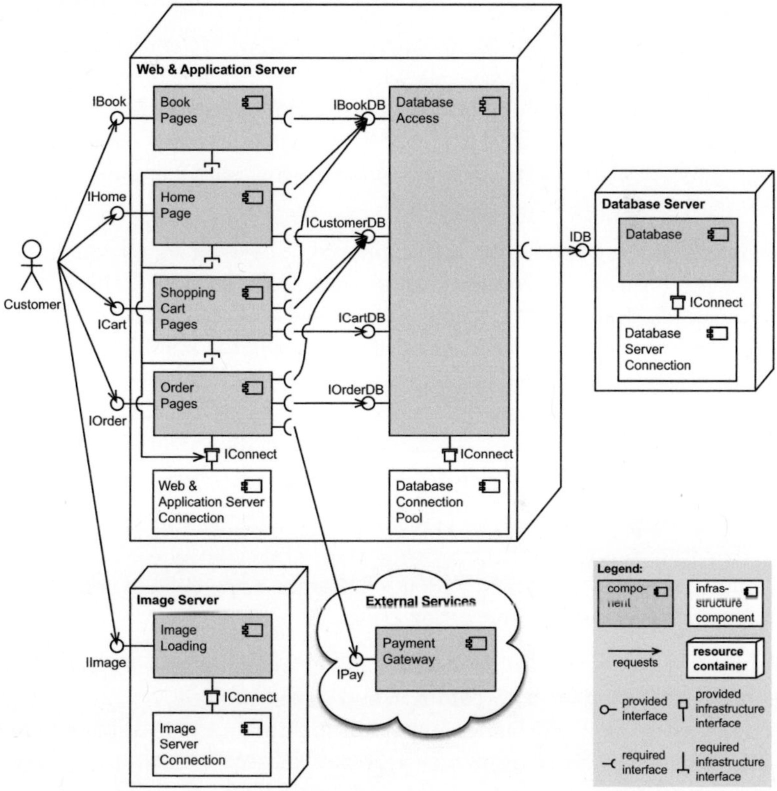

Figure C.1.: PCM model of the CloudStore online book shop.

Customers enter the system via the web pages provided by the Book Pages, Home Page, Shopping Cart Pages, and Order Pages components allocated on the

Web & Application Server. Book Pages provides operations regarding books (e.g., to query book details or search for books). The Home Page component shows CloudStore's home page, which welcomes its customers and displays book categories for browsing. Shopping Cart Pages allows customers to register, add books to a shopping cart, and to check-out the shopping cart. Afterwards, Order Pages allows to follow up on the order. Order pages can particularly request payment services from the externally hosted Payment Gateway.

The aforementioned components require operations of the Database component as allocated on the Database Server. CloudStore's database stores entries for books, customers, shopping carts, and orders. Moreover, if a returned web page references images (e.g., book covers), a customer's browser subsequently fetches these references via the Image Loading component that is allocated on the dedicated Image Server.

Requests to the Database are intercepted by a Database Access component that manages database connections. Database Access receives [returns] such connections from [to] the Database Connection Pool component. Also Web & Application, Image, and Database Server use pools for handling customer requests (Web & Application Server Connection, Image Server Connection, Database Server Connection). These pools (white-colored infrastructure components in Figure C.1) are typical performance factors as their pool-size limits the number of requests that can be processed in parallel.

The PCM supports acquiring and releasing connections from these resource pools within service effect specifications (SEFFs; cf. Section 2.5.3.1). In the CloudStore model, every interaction requires the acquisition of connections and its release once the interaction ends.

Figure C.2 illustrates this schema for SEFFs of web page component operations that interact with database and image components. Actions (1) to (3) model the performance impact of creating an HTML page, while action (4) models the performance impact of subsequently resolving image references. These two phases—receiving an HTML page and subsequently its references—reflect the typical behavior of web browsers [JW04].

CloudStore uses transactions for write operations when creating new customers, books, and orders. Such transactions typically have a major performance impact [JW04]. The CloudStore model again employs the concept of connection pools (with pool-size one) to model these transactions.

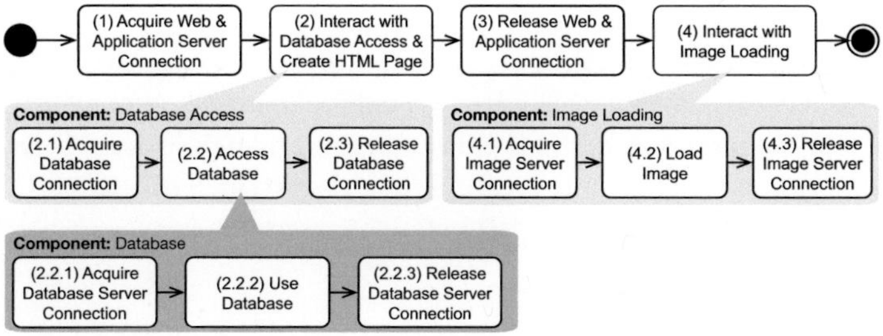

Figure C.2.: Behavior of web page components interacting with database and image components.

Besides modeling the static structure and the behavior of CloudStore, we also modeled the "Browsing Mix" customer workload according to the TPC-W specification [Tra02]. "Browsing Mix" is a workload where customers browse through the book catalog and occasionally order books. We specified the probabilities with which 400 concurrent customers call the 14 CloudStore operations provided by the system interfaces IBook, IHome, ICart, and IOrder. Operations are realized within respective components (each operation is modeled as SEFF according to Figure C.2). For example, the home page is requested in 29.00 % while orders are placed in only 0.69 % of all cases [Tra02].

CloudStore's complete architectural model, documentation, deployment scripts, source code, and raw measurement data are available online at [Clo16a]. Moreover, we have documented the model creation process via online screencasts [Clo16b].

C.1.2. Background: Cloud Computing

Cloud Computing systems extend the distributed computing domain where systems interact over networks [BHS07a, p. 558]. Systems in the cloud computing domain additionally utilize elasticity mechanisms [EPM13], i.e., mechanisms that allow systems to autonomously (de)allocate computing services on demand and in a pay-per-use fashion [MG11].

This section details these concepts and their consequences on software quality in the following. Section C.1.2.1 briefly introduces cloud providers and cloud consumers as main roles in cloud computing. Afterwards, Section C.1.2.2 describes essential cloud computing characteristics. These characteristics induce novel quality properties as described in Section C.1.2.3. To quantify these properties, Section C.1.2.4 describes suitable metrics.

C.1.2.1. Cloud Computing Roles

In the cloud computing domain, **cloud providers** offer computing services to **cloud consumers** [LTM+12]. In the CloudStore case study, the company behind CloudStore acts both as cloud provider (by providing services for browsing and ordering books) and as cloud consumer (by consuming computing services of the targeted cloud computing environment).

C.1.2.2. Cloud Computing Characteristics

For engineering applications of cloud providers, software architects have to consider the essential characteristics of the cloud computing domain. The well-accepted and standardized NIST definition of cloud computing [MG11] states that the following characteristics are essential:

On-demand self-service: A cloud consumer can request additional services on demand, that is, without requiring human interaction on the cloud provider side.

Broad network access: Cloud providers provide access to services through standardized network interfaces, thus supporting both thin and thick clients on the cloud consumer side.

Resource pooling: Cloud providers can group services, e.g., for storage, processing, and memory resources, into pools from which multiple cloud consumers can be served. In such a setup, each cloud consumer is unaware of the activities of other cloud consumers and actual physical resources, so that the number of available services appears to be unlimited.

Rapid elasticity: Services of cloud providers can autonomously scale-in and scale-out, depending on cloud consumer demand, through an elasticity management.

Measured service: Cloud providers measure the usage of services by the cloud consumers. Cloud consumers typically only pay for the services they have used or reserved (pay-per-use).

C.1.2.3. Cloud Computing Properties

Scalability, elasticity, and cost-efficiency are quality properties that cloud providers have to consider to minimize operation costs while fulfilling SLOs as best as possible. These properties are the focus of the CloudStore case study and can be defined based on the concept of capacity. As described in Definition C.1, the capacity of a service defines the amount of workload caused by cloud consumers the service can withstand before violating its SLOs.

Definition C.1 (Capacity) *"Capacity is the maximum workload a service can handle as bound by its SLOs." [LEB15]*

For example, CloudStore may have a capacity of 100 consumers per second with a constant work. The limiting factor that determines this capacity may be a CPU with a too low processing rate or a too strict SLO. Therefore, both increasing the CPU's processing rate and agreeing on less restrictive SLOs can be options to increase capacity.

Based on capacity, the quality properties scalability, elasticity, and cost-efficiency can be defined as follows:

Scalability: As stated in Definition C.2, scalability is a quality property that tells whether a service can increase its capacity by consuming more services provided by cloud providers, i.e., of underlying service layers. Here, only this ability is important—not the degree to which a service can increase capacity.

Definition C.2 (Scalability) *"Scalability is the ability of a service to increase its capacity by expanding its quantity of consumed lower-layer services." [LEB15]*

Examples for underlying services are third-party services (e.g., a payment service for web shops) and directly consumed resources (e.g., servers, CPUs, and hard disk drives). Given a service that consumes all of these lower-level services, it is scalable if an increased consumption of at least one underlying service leads to an increased capacity. That is, consuming either more third-party services (e.g., by issuing more parallel requests to the payment service) or more direct resources (e.g., by using more servers) leads to an increased capacity.

An example of an unscalable service is a service where many consumers share items of the same database and, whenever a change of a single item is made by a consumer, this part of the database is locked. Changes made by other consumers on this item cannot be processed until the first consumer is finished. The capacity of such a service stays at 1 customer per request, independent of the number of additional database servers, CPUs, etc. To make such a service scalable, alternative means to manage database items have to be found, e.g., by using alternative databases with less restrictive constraints on data consistency or by assigning database items to dedicated consumers only.

Elasticity: As stated in Definition C.3, elasticity describes to which extend a service can adapt its capacity to changes in workload. Elasticity needs to be considered over time for changing workloads, e.g., for sudden workload peaks that require an adaptation of capacity. Such an adaptation needs to be timely, i.e., such that potential SLO violations are minimized. Timeliness entails an adaptation process that is autonomous, i.e., is either automated or is guaranteed to be manually realized in time.

Definition C.3 (Elasticity) *"Elasticity is the degree a service autonomously adapts capacity to workload over time." [LEB15]*

Based on this definition, a service needs to be able to adapt its capacity to be elastic. Because exactly this property is captured in scalability, scalability is a prerequisite of elasticity. For example, a service is elastic that dynamically boots a dedicated virtual machine that copes with work-intensive requests (and shuts these machines down once the request has been served).

The benefit of an elastic service is that at each point in time, only the minimal amount of underlying services is used (in the example above: a minimal number of virtual machines). This minimization improves the cost-efficiency of the service.

Cost-Efficiency: As stated in Definition C.4, cost-efficiency measures how many lower-layer services a service consumes to serve the capacity demanded by cloud consumers over time. A cost-efficient service minimizes its service consumption without becoming unable to provide the demanded capacity.

Definition C.4 (Cost-Efficiency) *"Cost-efficiency is a measure relating demanded capacity to consumed services over time." [LEB15]*

For example, CloudStore's application server may provide a capacity of 100 consumers per second. Adding an additional application server for loadbalancing requests is cost-inefficient as long as less than 100 consumers per second arrive.

C.1.2.4. Cloud Computing Metrics

In our previous work [BLB15], we have followed the GQM method to systematically derive metrics for capacity, scalability, elasticity, and efficiency. This section briefly describes these metrics using the book shop example from Chapter 3. In the CloudStore case study, we employ these metrics to specify and analyze SLOs.

Capacity Metrics The following metrics allow to quantify capacity:

Closed Workload Capacity (CWC) quantifies, for a fixed amount of lower-layer services, the maximum closed workload a service can handle as bound by its SLOs. The closed workload is quantified by its number of concurrent users.

For example, a perfectly scalable book shop A can scale up to an infinite number of customers, i.e., provides $CWC_A = \infty\ customers$. A less scalable book shop B, for example, may scale up to a concurrent number of 100 *customers*, i.e., $CWC_B = 100\ customers$.

Open Workload Capacity (OWC) quantifies, for a fixed amount of lower-layer services, the maximum open workload a service can handle as bound by its SLOs. The open workload is quantified by its request rate.

For example, a perfectly scalable book shop A can scale up to an infinite request rate, i.e., provides $OWC_A = \infty\ requests/minute$. A less scalable book shop B, for example, may scale up to a concurrent number of 100 requests per minute, i.e., $OWC_B = 100\ requests/minute$.

Scalability Metrics The following metrics allow to quantify scalability:

Closed Workload Scalability Range ($CWSR$) quantifies a service's increase in capacity if adding lower-layer services. The metric reuses CWC to quantify capacity.

For example, a book shop A may be able to deal with an additional 100 concurrent customers when distributing workload over an additional application server, i.e., $CWSR_A = 100\ customers$. A non-scalable book shop B will have $CWSR_B = 0\ customers$.

Open Workload Scalability Range ($OWSR$) quantifies a service's increase in capacity if adding lower-layer services. The metric reuses OWC to quantify capacity.

For example, a book shop A may be able to deal with an additional 100 customers per minute when distributing workload over an additional application server, i.e., $OWSR_A = 100\ customers/minute$. In contrast, a non-scalable book shop B will have $OWSR_B = 0\ customers/minute$.

Elasticity Metrics The following metrics allow to quantify elasticity:

Number of SLO violations ($NSLOV$) counts a service's number of SLO violations over a defined time interval. Over time, a service may adapt to workload changes to minimize such violations.

For example, over the whole time an in-elastic book shop A is observed, a total of $NSLOV = 100$ *SLO violations* may be measured. After a modification to an elastic book shop B, the measurement may result in $NSLOV = 10$ *SLO violations*. A more proactive configuration of book shop B may achieve the optimum, i.e., $NSLOV = 0$ *SLO violations*. However, more proactivity may come at the cost of higher operation costs (thus, motivating trade-offs with cost-efficiency metrics).

Mean Time To Quality Repair ($MTTQR$) quantifies the mean time a service needs to re-establish its SLOs when the workload increases/decreases for a defined workload delta (the increase/decrease between two workloads; specified as factor). Because it defines a mean time, $MTTQR$ is specific for a specified time frame in which the mean is calculated.

For example, with a workload increase factor of $1.2\, requests/minute$, a perfectly elastic book shop A will adapt itself to the increasing workload within zero time. That is, $MTTQR_{A,1d}(1.2\, requests/minute) = 0\, minutes$ (calculated over one day). A less elastic book shop B may need a mean time of $10\, minutes$ to adapt itself to increasing workload after it detects the workload increase. In this case, it holds that $MTTQR_{B,1d}(1.2\, requests/minute) = 10\, minutes$.

Cost-Efficiency Metrics The following metrics quantify cost-efficiency:

Resource Provisioning Efficiency (RPE) quantifies the match (in percentage) between a service's resource demand and actual resource utilization while the workload is changing. The baseline for minimal resource utilization for a given demand is derived from dedicated capacity metrics, e.g., the CWC-based number of users that can be served with a given set of resources.

A perfectly cost-efficient book shop A will adapt its resource demand exactly to the resource demand at all times. For example, if the workload increases with factor 1.2, the book shop will provision exactly that amount of additional resources required to cope with this additional workload, i.e., $RPE_A(1.2\, requests/minute) = 1.0$.

Operation costs (OC) quantify a service's operation costs over a defined time interval.

For example, over the whole time a book shop A is observed, a total of $OC = \$100.00$ may be measured.

Marginal costs (MC) quantify a service's operation costs to serve an additional workload unit.

For example, the operation costs to serve 20% additional requests per second (factor 1.2) can be \$1.00 for a book shop A, i.e., $MC_A(1.2) = \$1.00$.

C.1.3. CloudStore: Case Study Design

This section covers the design of the CloudStore case study. Section C.1.3.1 briefly points to relevant research questions and procedures for data collection, analysis, and validation. Afterwards, Section C.1.3.2 describes the CloudStore case as a migration scenario for CloudStore. Suitable human subjects for the case study are selected in Section C.1.3.3.

C.1.3.1. CloudStore: Research Questions and Procedures

In the CloudStore case study, we employ the complete evaluation design introduced in Section 5.2, i.e., we reuse its research questions and the procedures for data collection, analysis, and validity.

C.1.3.2. CloudStore: Case

The CloudStore case—as introduced in this section—describes a scenario where CloudStore is migrated from the distributed computing domain to the cloud computing domain (cf. Section C.1.2).

In the following, we describe this case from the perspective of CloudStore's main software architect. The software architect proceeds in three phases: first, the software architect initiates a collaboration with an AT engineer to identify a suitable architectural analysis approach (Palladio is finally selected); second, the software architect modernizes the legacy version of CloudStore to make it scalable; third, the software architect migrates the modernized CloudStore version to a cloud computing environment to make it more cost-efficient. In phases two and three, the software architect particularly requests and applies suitable ATs from the AT engineer (ATs capturing the three-layer architectural style, the loadbalancing architectural pattern, and knowledge specific to the cloud computing domain).

Figure C.3 provides an overview of these three phases by annotating each phase to the development process with architectural analyses (cf. Section 2.5.1) extended by processes of the AT method (cf. Section 4.1). Each of these phases is detailed in the following.

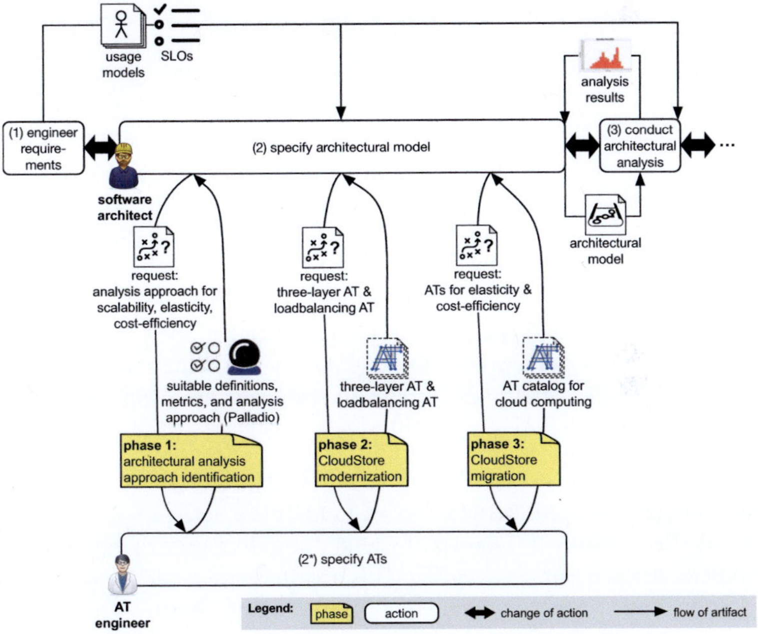

Figure C.3.: Overview of the three phases in the CloudStore case.

Phase 1: Architectural Analysis Approach Identification The goal of CloudStore's software architect is to migrate CloudStore to the cloud computing domain, with a focus on the QoS properties scalability, elasticity, and cost-efficiency. For planning this migration, the software architect wants to apply the AT method and starts a cooperation with an AT engineer.

In the first phase of their cooperation, they want to agree on common definitions of scalability, elasticity, and cost-efficiency and identify a suitable analysis approach for these properties. Table C.1 summarizes this request according to the classification from Section 4.1.3.1.

Table C.1.: Request for a suitable architectural analysis approach

- Requested architectural analysis approach (QoS properties): scalability, elasticity, cost-efficiency

The CloudScale project [BSL⁺13, LB14b] has indeed requested to analyze the QoS properties scalability, elasticity, and cost-efficiency, which triggered the CloudStore case study. The final result were the definitions given in Section C.1.2.3, corresponding metrics described in Section C.1.2.4, and the integration of these metrics into Palladio [LB14a]. Palladio was selected because of its support of QoS properties related to scalability, elasticity, and cost-efficiency (cf. Section 2.5.3). The results section of the CloudStore case study (Section C.1.4) reports further details; the remaining phases assume that Palladio is the finally identified and employed architectural analysis approach.

Phase 2: CloudStore Modernization CloudStore's software architect has created the architectural model of CloudStore illustrated in Figure C.1—a legacy model without applied ATs. This architectural model is the starting point for CloudStore's modernization in the second phase.

As described in Section C.1.1, the software architect knows that customers behave according to the "BrowsingMix" workload; a workload where customers mainly browse and occasionally order books. A maximum of 400 concurrent customers initially use CloudStore; however, a domain analysis has revealed that this number is expected to increase to 500 customers in 1 year.

The software architect therefore wants to analyze whether modifications to CloudStore are needed to cope with the increased workload. To maintain the three-layer structure of the current architectural model during these modifications, the software architect first requests an AT with appropriate constraints from an AT engineer. The software architect particularly requests an AT suitable for Palladio, i.e., the previously identified and employed architectural analysis approach. Table C.2 summarizes this request according to the classification from Section 4.1.3.1.

Table C.2.: Request for AT capturing the three-layer architectural style

- Requested architectural knowledge (direct request): three-layer architectural style
- Requested architectural analysis approach (direct request): Palladio

To improve scalability, the software architect further requests an AT to investigate the option to integrate a loadbalancer and replicated components into CloudStore. As before, the software architect plans to use the AT in conjunction with Palladio. Table C.3 summarizes this request according to the classification from Section 4.1.3.1.

Table C.3.: Request for AT capturing the loadbalancing architectural pattern

- Requested architectural knowledge (direct request): loadbalancer architectural pattern
- Requested architectural analysis approach (direct request): Palladio

After having applied the requested ATs, the software architect finally wants to analyze whether CloudStore has benefited from this application. Therefore, the software architect specifies the SLOs stated in Table C.4. $SLO_{\mathbf{Performance}}$ refers to a classical performance metric (response time) while $SLO_{\mathbf{Capacity}}$ and $SLO_{\mathbf{Scalability}}$ refer to cloud computing metrics from

Section C.1.2.4 (*CWC* and *CWSR*, respectively). Moreover, $SLO_{\textbf{Capacity}}$ and $SLO_{\textbf{Scalability}}$ relate to *number of replicas* as the number of loadbalanced entities; an expected parameter of the requested loadbalancing AT.

Table C.4.: CloudStore's SLOs for phase 2 (modernization)

$SLO_{\textbf{Performance}}$: 90 % of CloudStore's responses for browsing and ordering books shall have a maximum response time of 1 second.

$SLO_{\textbf{Capacity}}$: CloudStore shall handle up to 400 concurrent customers without violating $SLO_{\textbf{Performance}}$ for number of replicas = 1.

$SLO_{\textbf{Scalability}}$: CloudStore's capacity shall increase to 500 concurrent customers for number of replicas = 2.

Phase 3: CloudStore Migration In the third and final phase, the software architect wants to analyze whether CloudStore can benefit from a migration to a cloud computing environment. The software architect expects that the environment's elasticity mechanisms help to increase CloudStore's capacity in peak workloads while lowering operation costs during periods of lower workloads.

Therefore, the software architect requests ATs that capture reusable architectural knowledge to foster typical cloud computing properties (cf. Section C.1.2.3). The software architect again wants to use resulting ATs in conjunction with Palladio. Table C.5 summarizes this request according to the classification from Section 4.1.3.1.

Table C.5.: Request for ATs capturing reusable architectural knowledge that fosters cloud computing properties

- Requested architectural knowledge (application domain): cloud computing
- Requested architectural analysis approach (direct request): Palladio

To analyze whether CloudStore has benefited from the application of the resulting ATs, the software architect specifies the additional SLOs stated in Table C.6. $SLO_{\textbf{Elasticity}}$ and $SLO_{\textbf{Cost-Efficiency}}$ refer to cloud computing metrics from Section C.1.2.4 (*NSLOV* and *OC*, respectively).

Table C.6.: CloudStore's additional SLOs for phase 3 (migration)

$SLO_{\textbf{Elasticity}}$**:** At most 1 violation of $SLO_{\textbf{Performance}}$ occurs per 100 requests.

$SLO_{\textbf{Cost-Efficiency}}$**:** Over a period of one year, the migrated CloudStore version has lower operation costs than the modernized CloudStore version from phase 2.

C.1.3.3. CloudStore: Subjects

In the CloudStore case study, subjects acting as software architects, AT engineers, and AT testers are required. Several subjects have participated.

I acted both as software architect and as lead AT engineer. Because I introduced the AT method, I am expected to have deep knowledge about the AT method and minimal learning efforts.

A student worker, Daria Giacinto, cooperated with me in creating ATs as additional AT engineer during an overall timeframe of one year. Moreover, she acted as AT tester for all ATs in the CloudStore case study. She has introduced testing as quality assurance approach to the AT method in her Master's thesis [Gia16] and is therefore expected to have deep knowledge especially in this area.

Another student worker, Hendrik Eikerling, has cooperated with me in identifying QoS properties as part of the first action of the AT specification process (cf. Section 4.1.3.2), He conducted a systematic literature review to identify definitions and metrics for the QoS properties scalability, elasticity, and cost-efficiency in his Bachelor's thesis [Eik14]. We particularly published the systematic literature review at a conference on software architecture [LEB15] and received a distinguished paper award. The publication and the award are indicators for a successful conduction of the first action of the AT specification process.

A colleague and PhD student, Matthias Becker, has cooperated with me in deriving further metrics for scalability, elasticity, and cost-efficiency. We used a GQM plan for this derivation and published our results at a conference on software architecture [BLB15]. This publication is an additional indicator for a successful conduction of the first action of the AT specification process.

A colleague and senior researcher, Steffen Becker, has participated in extending tools and in discussions, coauthored papers on our findings [LEB15, BLB15], and reviewed several results. He therefore conducted quality assurance steps throughout the CloudStore case study; related to actions of both software architects and AT engineers.

C.1.4. CloudStore: Results

This section reports the results of the CloudStore case study. The report starts in Section C.1.4.1 to Section C.1.4.3 with the execution of each of the three phases of the CloudStore case. The empirical data created during this execution is analyzed in Section C.1.4.4 and interpreted in Section C.1.4.5. Both analysis and interpretation follow the GQM plan from Section 5.2, which eventually allows to answer the GQM plan's research questions and to assess the case study's goal attainment. Potential threats to validity of the CloudStore case study are finally discussed in Section C.1.4.6.

C.1.4.1. CloudStore: Execution of Phase 1

In phase 1 of the CloudStore case (cf. Section C.1.3.2), the software architect's request for an architectural analysis approach for scalability, elasticity, and cost-efficiency has triggered the first action of the AT specification process from Section 4.1.3: identify QoS properties and suitable analysis approaches. This action ensures that an architectural analysis approach is selected that can analyze the QoS properties of interest.

Acting as AT engineers, we have started by inspecting the support of existing approaches for scalability, elasticity, and cost-efficiency [LEB15]. Because no approach sufficiently provided support for these properties, we decided to integrate such a support into Palladio [LB14a]. We have selected

Palladio as basis for this integration because Palladio is the only architectural analysis approach supporting elastic environments (cf. Section 2.5.3.2) and because we have previous experience with Palladio.

We have integrated support for scalability, elasticity, and cost-efficiency as follows. First, we conducted a systematic literature review to identify suitable definitions [LEB15], which has resulted in the definitions described in Section C.1.2.3. From these definitions, we elaborated a goal-question-metric plan [BLB15], which has resulted in the metrics described in Section C.1.2.4. Next, we integrated these metrics in Palladio [LB14a] via the QuAL framework (cf. Appendix B.3.1). This integration finally enabled analyses of scalability, elasticity, and cost-efficiency in Palladio.

C.1.4.2. CloudStore: Execution of Phase 2

In phase 2 of the CloudStore case (cf. Section C.1.3.2), we modernize CloudStore based on ATs for the three-layer architectural style and the loadbalancing architectural pattern. This section first describes our specification of these ATs, second our application of the resulting ATs to modernize CloudStore, and third our conduction of an architectural analysis to check whether these ATs have helped to satisfy the SLOs of phase 2.

Specifying the three-layer and loadbalancing ATs The software architect's request for ATs has triggered two iterations through the AT specification process from Section 4.1.3: the first iteration for capturing the three-layer architectural style and the second iteration for capturing the loadbalancing architectural pattern. We have executed these two iterations as follows.

Iteration I: Three-Layer AT. Acting as AT engineers, we have executed the actions of the AT specification process from Section 4.1.3 to specify the three-layer AT. After finishing with action (1) in phase 1, we have continued with the subsequent actions of this process:

(2) select reusable architectural knowledge. In cooperation with the software architect, we agreed on a common understanding of the three-layer architectural style. We have agreed on the description previously given in Section 2.2.4.1: the *three-layer* architectural style is a common style to structure a system into three logical layers [BHS07a] (a presentation layer, an application layer, and a data access layer). Each of these layers can only access the respective lower-level layer. Because of this restriction, a three-layer system becomes loosely coupled and therefore more maintainable.

(3) specify ATs (with parametrizable roles, constraints, completions).

In the three-layer AT, we have captured each layer of the three-layer architectural style via dedicated roles. Another dedicated role for a three-layer system captures system-wide constraints (opposed to layer-specific constraints). Because architectural styles involve no decisions about the existence of elements, we only had to formalize such constraints of AT roles—and no completions—to define role semantics. Figure C.4 illustrates the three-layer AT with its roles and constraints using the graphical concrete syntax for ATs (cf. Section 4.2.5.3).

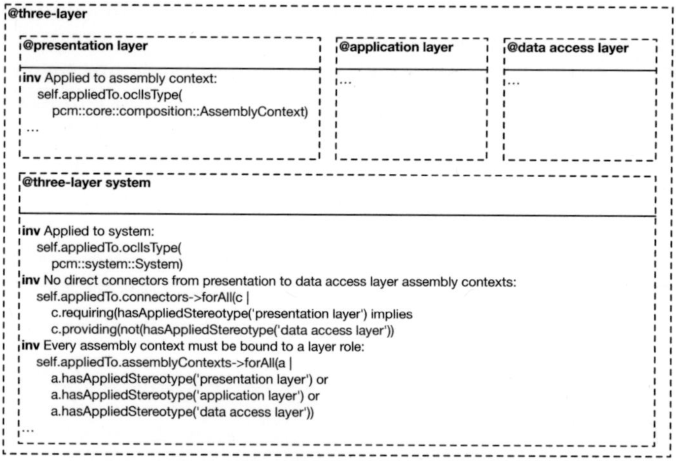

Figure C.4.: The three-layer AT (excerpt).

Figure C.4 depicts several AT constraints formulated via OCL. Each role includes a constraint to ensure that it is bound to the correct architectural element. For example, the presentation layer AT role can only be bound to PCM assembly contexts ("Applied to assembly context" invariant in Figure C.4) and the three-layer system AT role can only be bound to PCM systems ("Applied to system" invariant in Figure C.4). As prescribed by the three-layer architectural style, the three-layer system AT role further includes a constraint to ensure that presentation layer assembly contexts are not directly connected to data access layer assembly contexts ("No direct connectors from presentation to data access layer assembly contexts" invariant in Figure C.4). An additional constraint ensures that each assembly context within a three-layer system is bound to a dedicated layer ("Every assembly context must be bound to a layer role" invariant in Figure C.4).

In sum, we have formulated 17 OCL constraints. Figure C.4 omits the remaining constraints for brevity; the AT catalog coming with AT tooling [ATt] includes all OCL constraints. Moreover, the CloudScale Wiki [Clob] provides a detailed description of the three-layer AT using POSA's initiator template for describing reusable architectural knowledge (cf. Section 6.3.1.1).

(4) assure the quality of the specified ATs, e.g., by testing. We formulated 38 test cases as reported by Giacinto [Gia16, Sec. 6.2], e.g., a test case where presentation layer components directly communicate with data layer components. Thereby, we assured correctness (are constraint violations detected?) and completeness of constraints. We unveiled and added the "Every assembly context must be bound to a layer role" constraint (as illustrated in Figure C.4) only after a corresponding test case has failed.

Iteration II: Loadbalancing AT. Continuing our work as AT engineers, we have reiterated through the actions of the AT specification process from Section 4.1.3 to specify the loadbalancing AT. Analogously to the first iteration, as we have finished with action (1) already in phase 1, we only had to continue with subsequent actions:

(2) select reusable architectural knowledge. In cooperation with the software architect, we agreed on a common understanding of the loadbalancing architectural pattern. We have agreed on the description previously given in Section 2.2.4.2: the *loadbalancing* architectural pattern [BHS07a] requires the existence of a loadbalancer that distributes workload. Variation points include the architectural element to be loadbalanced (e.g., a resource container with all deployed assembly contexts or only a single assembly context), the number of replicas, and the loadbalancing strategy (e.g., round-robin).

(3) specify ATs (with parametrizable roles, constraints, completions). Subsequently, we have formalized two variants of the loadbalancing AT, depending on the architectural element to be loadbalanced. We have formalized a variant for whole resource containers and a variant for single assembly contexts to be loadbalanced.

For resource containers, the loadbalancing AT introduces the role of a "loadbalanced container" with a formal parameter "number of replicas". Figure C.5 illustrates this variant using the graphical concrete syntax for ATs (cf. Section 4.2.5.3). For assembly context, the loadbalancing AT analogously introduces a "loadbalanced assembly context" role.

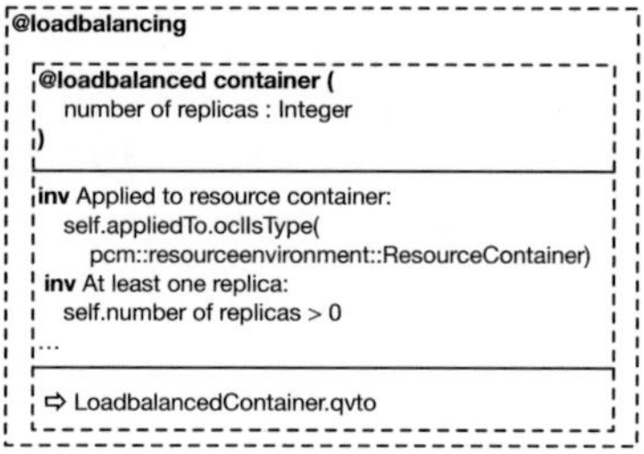

Figure C.5.: The loadbalancing AT for resource containers (excerpt).

Figure C.5 depicts two AT constraints within the "loadbalanced container" role. The first constraint ensures the role can only be bound to resource containers ("Applied to resource container" invariant in Figure C.5). The second constraint ensures that loadbalancers are always configured with a positive "number of replicas" ("At least one replica" invariant in Figure C.5).

Furthermore, we have formalized the semantics to attach a loadbalancer to elements bound to the "loadbalanced container" role. For our formalization, we have specified an appropriate AT completion in QVT-O (one for each variant). For example, Figure C.5 depicts that the resource container variant refers to a completion specified in the "LoadbalancedContainer.qvto" file.

For each variant, the completion identifies the bound element and creates a loadbalancer assembly context on a dedicated loadbalancing server to which all of the element's incoming connectors are reconnected. Next, the completion generates replicas of the bound element according to the actual parameter of "number of replicas". Then, the completion creates connectors from loadbalancer to each of these replicas. Finally, the completion configures the loadbalancer to distribute workload over these connectors in a round-robin manner. Before an analysis is started, the AT engine executes this completion, thus, forcing the existence of the loadbalancer. Using the book shop example, Figure 4.4 exemplifies the result after executing the completion for the resource container variant.

In sum, we have formulated 4 OCL constraints. Figure C.5 omits the remaining constraints for brevity; the AT catalog coming with AT tooling [ATt] includes all OCL constraints and all completions. Moreover, the CloudScale Wiki [Clob] provides a detailed description of both variants of the loadbalancing AT using POSA's initiator template for describing reusable architectural knowledge (cf. Section 6.3.1.1).

(4) assure the quality of the specified ATs, e.g., by testing. With a total of 54 tests (38 tests for the resource container variant and 26 tests for the assembly context variant) [Gia16, Sec. 6.2], we assured that both completions maintain the conceptual integrity to the captured architectural knowledge.

The first iteration has resulted in 39 % (15 of 38) failed tests for resource containers and 27 % (7 of 26) for assembly contexts. The failed tests provided 22 errors, which we pin-pointed to the typical root causes for violations of conceptual integrity described in Section 4.1.3.3. For example, our completion for containers suffered from the "uncovered metamodel elements in completions" root cause when creating replicas. Palladio supports nesting virtual machines (VMs) into resource containers; however, our completion missed to copy VMs from the original container. We successfully unveiled such bugs with the help of tailored test cases, e.g., by testing the border case "if the original resource container includes VMs, are there VMs in its replicas after completion execution?".

We accordingly fixed each detected error, e.g., by integrating the missing functionality into the completion specification. Afterwards, we re-executed all tests in a second iteration, which resulted in 100 % passed tests. This result shows that we removed all identified causes without introducing new errors and, thus, improved conceptual integrity.

Applying the three-layer and loadbalancing ATs Now acting as software architects, we applied the three-layer and the loadbalancing AT for resource containers to the CloudStore model. We have followed the AT application process from Section 4.1.1 as follows.

We bound the roles of the three-layer AT to assembly contexts as illustrated in Figure C.6. Moreover, to distribute workload over the whole Web & Application Server, we bound the loadbalanced container role of the loadbalancing AT for resource containers to this server.

Figure C.6 shows that a validation of AT constraints reveals that we missed to bind a logical layer to the Image Loading assembly context. This is an issue because the three-layer AT requires an assignment for every component (cf. the "Every assembly context must be bound to a layer role" constraint specified in Section C.1.4.2).

As illustrated in Figure C.7, we bound the *presentation layer* role to Image Loading to fix the constraint violation. This binding is appropriate because Image Loading presents images directly to customers. At this point, the *three-layer* AT has helped us to maintain a model conforming to the three-layer architectural style, i.e., it has improved maintainability of the modeled system.

Conducting an architectural analysis for the modernized CloudStore Continuing to act as software architects, we analyzed the fulfillment of the pre-specified SLOs. We have followed the AT-based architectural analysis process from Section 4.1.2 as follows.

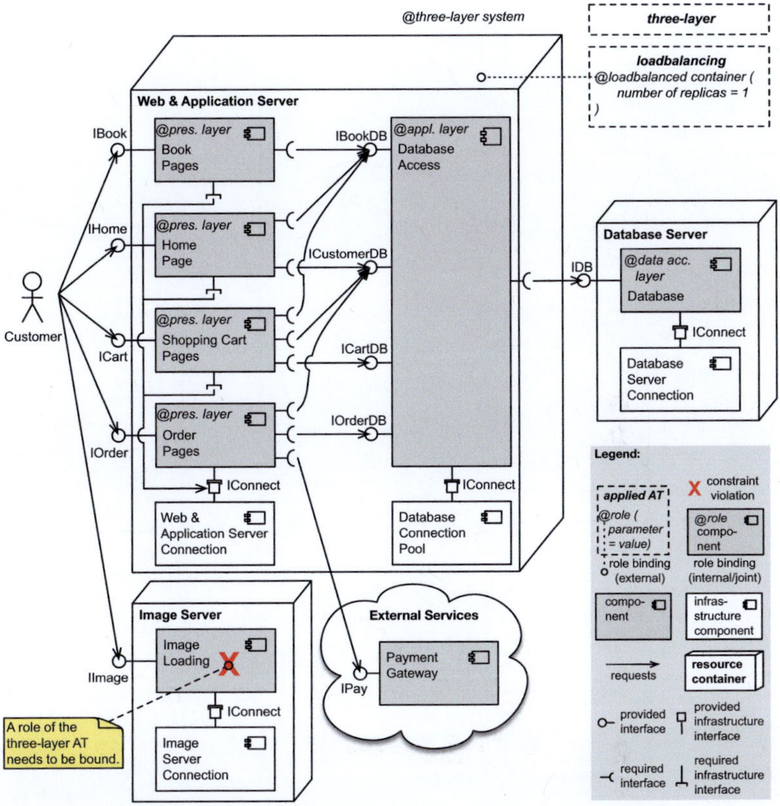

Figure C.6.: The three-layer and loadbalancing ATs applied to the CloudStore model (with constraint violation).

The applied *loadbalancing* AT allows to analyze CloudStore's SLOs by varying the parameter *number of replicas* of the *loadbalanced container* role. First, we configured a capacity analysis with Palladio for *number of replicas = 1* to calculate the maximum number of concurrent customers CloudStore can handle without violating $SLO_{\mathbf{Performance}}$. The result from Palladio was 400 concurrent customers, thus, $SLO_{\mathbf{Performance}}$ and $SLO_{\mathbf{Capacity}}$ were fulfilled.

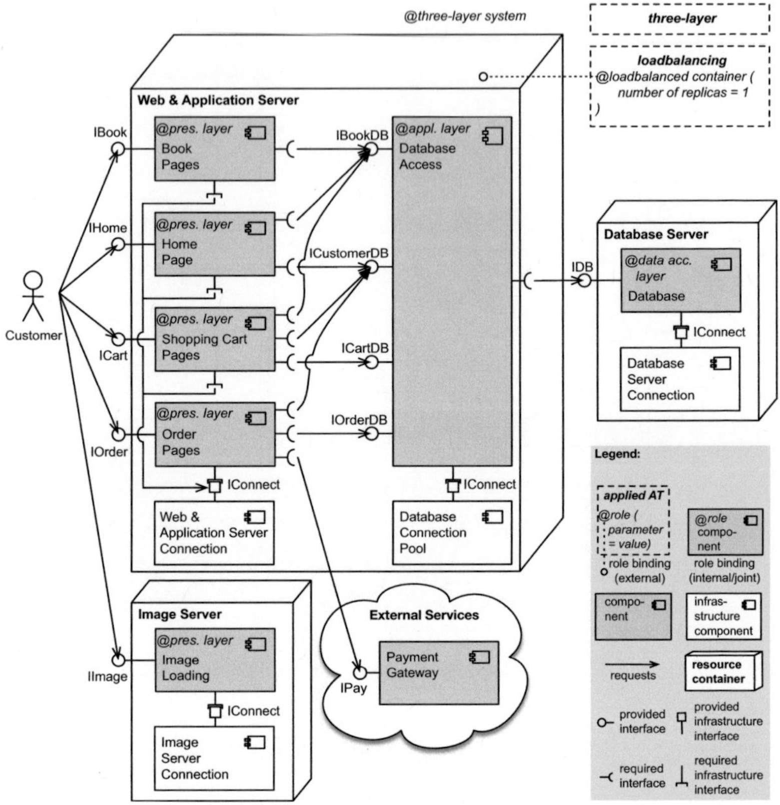

Figure C.7.: The three-layer and loadbalancing ATs applied to the CloudStore model (fixed version).

The capacity analysis particularly reports how response times are distributed. Figure C.8 illustrates these response times as a cumulative distribution function. For 400 customers, Figure C.8 shows that indeed 90 % (y-axis) of the response times are under the 1 second mark (x-axis).

We have repeated this analysis for *number of replicas = 2*. Interestingly, this analysis resulted in a capacity of only 180 concurrent customers, thus, point-

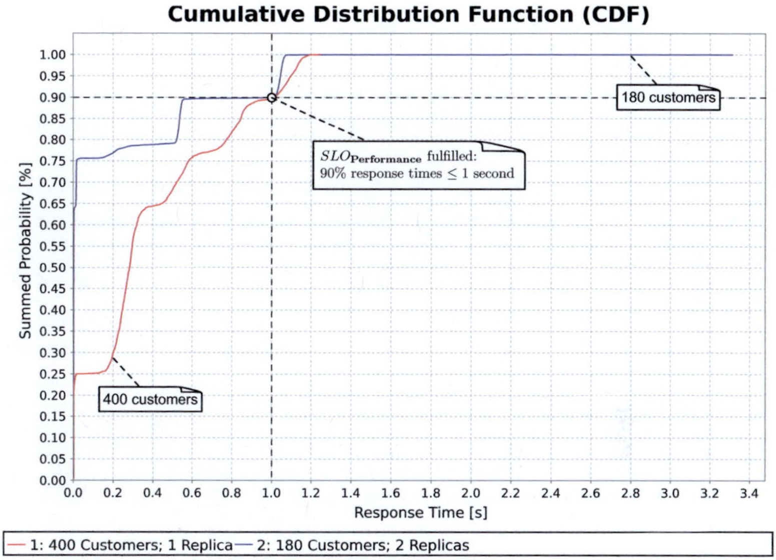

Figure C.8.: Cumulative distribution function of response times for different workloads and configurations of the modernized CloudStore (phase 2).

ing to a violation of $SLO_{\textbf{Scalability}}$. Figure C.8 illustrates the corresponding response time distribution for 180 customers.

To explain this capacity degradation, we additionally investigated the number of jobs waiting at the Database Server: for 400 customers and *number of replicas = 1*, approximately 50 jobs wait at the Database Server; for 180 customers and *number of replicas = 2*, this number increased to 90. This observation points to the Database Server as a reason for the capacity degradation. Because of the replicated Web & Application Server, an increased number of concurrent jobs arrived at the Database Server. The increased workload at the Database Server made this server CloudStore's bottleneck. In the next phase, we therefore investigate the option to use cloud computing knowledge (i.e., the *vertical scaling* architectural pattern on the Database Server) to increase capacity further.

C.1.4.3. CloudStore: Execution of Phase 3

After identifying the capacity degradation in the previous phase, we next analyze whether elasticity mechanisms help to increase capacity while lowering operation costs. Therefore, in phase 3 of the CloudStore case (cf. Section C.1.3.2), we migrate CloudStore to a cloud computing environment. For this migration, we employ ATs that capture reusable architectural knowledge to foster elasticity and cost-efficiency: a stateless variant of the three-layer architectural style and architectural patterns for horizontal and vertical scaling. This section first describes our specification of these ATs, second our application of the resulting ATs to migrate CloudStore, and third our conduction of an architectural analysis to confirm that these ATs have helped to satisfy the SLOs of phase 2 and phase 3.

Specifying the stateless three-layer, horizontal scaling, and vertical scaling ATs The software architect's request for ATs for elasticity and cost-efficiency has resulted in three iterations through the AT specification process from Section 4.1.3: the first iteration for capturing the stateless three-layer architectural style, the second iteration for capturing the horizontal scaling architectural pattern, and the third iteration for capturing the vertical scaling architectural pattern. Each resulting AT is provided by the AT catalog coming with AT tooling [ATt] and documented in the CloudScale Wiki [Clob] using POSA's initiator template for describing reusable architectural knowledge (cf. Section 6.3.1.1).

We have executed the three iterations as follows.

Iteration I: Stateless Three-Layer AT. Acting as AT engineers, we have iterated through the actions of the AT specification process from Section 4.1.3 to specify the *stateless three-layer* AT. Because we finished with action (1) in phase 1, we directly continue with action (2):

(2) select reusable architectural knowledge. In cooperation with the software architect, we agreed on a common understanding of the *stateless three-layer* architectural style. Applications can follow the *stateless three-layer* architectural style [Koz11b] to become elastic. *Stateless three-layer* extends the *three-layer* style by additionally requiring stateless assembly contexts on presentation and application layers.

Because they are stateless, these assembly contexts (and resource containers where they are deployed on) can safely be replicated.

(3) specify ATs (with parametrizable roles, constraints, completions). In the next action, we have formalized the *stateless three-layer* AT analogously to the *three-layer* AT but with an additional OCL constraint to check that components bound to presentation and application layer are stateless: self.appliedTo.hasAppliedStereotype('stateless'). This constraint therefore ensures that software architects directly get warnings when trying to bind stateful assembly context to these layers.

Moreover, as indicated in the constraint specification, we have defined a profile for PCM models that allows to annotate assembly contexts with stereotypes "stateless" or "stateful". Specifying such a profile was necessary because the PCM lacks dedicated constructs for such annotations. ATs that share this constraint (*loadbalancing* AT and *horizontal scaling* AT) can safely be applied in the *stateless three-layer* architectural style.

(4) assure the quality of the specified ATs, e.g., by testing. Giacinto tested the *stateless three-layer* AT analogously to the *three-layer* AT but with additional test cases for triggering violations and fulfillments of the additional constraint [Gia16, Sec. 6.2].

Iteration II: Horizontal Scaling AT. Continuing our work as AT engineers, we have reiterated through the actions of the AT specification process from Section 4.1.3 to specify the *horizontal scaling* AT. As before, because we finished with action (1) in phase 1, we directly proceed with action (2):

(2) select reusable architectural knowledge. In cooperation with the software architect, we agreed on a common understanding of the *horizontal scaling* architectural pattern. The *horizontal scaling* architectural pattern [EPM13, FLR+14] extends the *loadbalancing* pattern such that the loadbalancer dynamically adapts the required number of replicas of containers or components to the current workload. While the *loadbalancing* architectural pattern improves scalability only, the *horizontal scaling* architectural pattern therefore improves elasticity as well.

(3) specify ATs (with parametrizable roles, constraints, completions).

Subsequently, we have formalized two variants of a *horizontal scaling* AT, a variant for resource containers and a variant for assembly contexts. These ATs extend the corresponding *loadbalancing* ATs with parameters that determine their dynamic adaptation behavior with respect to current workload. Instead of a fixed number of replicas, their AT roles therefore include parameters for the *initial number of replicas*, a *scale-in threshold*, a *scale-out threshold*, and a *QoS monitor ID* as illustrated in Figure C.9 for the resource container variant.

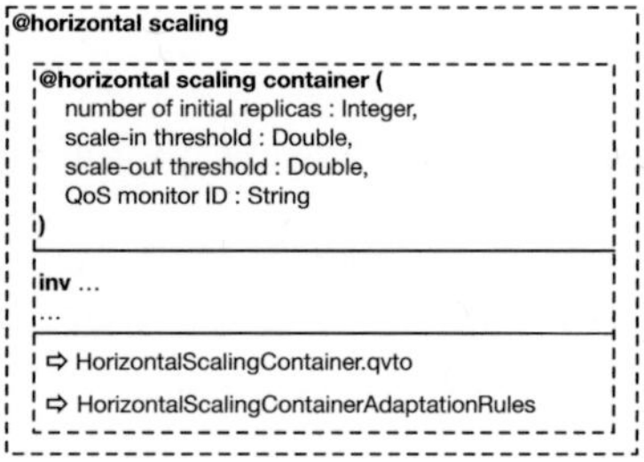

Figure C.9.: The horizontal scaling AT for resource containers (excerpt).

We have formalized completions in QVT-O to define the semantics of these parameters. The completions create loadbalancers that initially distribute workload over the given *number of initial replicas* of the bound element.

Whenever a given threshold with respect to a QoS monitor identified by *QoS monitor ID* is exceeded, the number of these replicas is dynamically adapted. We have formalized this adaptation behavior via QVT-O transformations, e.g., residing in the HorizontalScalingContainerAdaptationRules folder for the resource container variant (as illustrated in Figure C.9). Palladio adapts the architectural model by executing these transformations during analysis (cf. Section 2.5.3.2).

For example, a QoS monitor may measure the utilization of the CPU of CloudStore's Web & Application Server. Thresholds can then be set to a maximum utilization of 80 % and a minimum utilization of 5 %

like shown in Figure C.10. Whenever the Web & Application Server is over-utilized, additional replicas are added and whenever the Web & Application Server is under-utilized, existing replicas are removed.

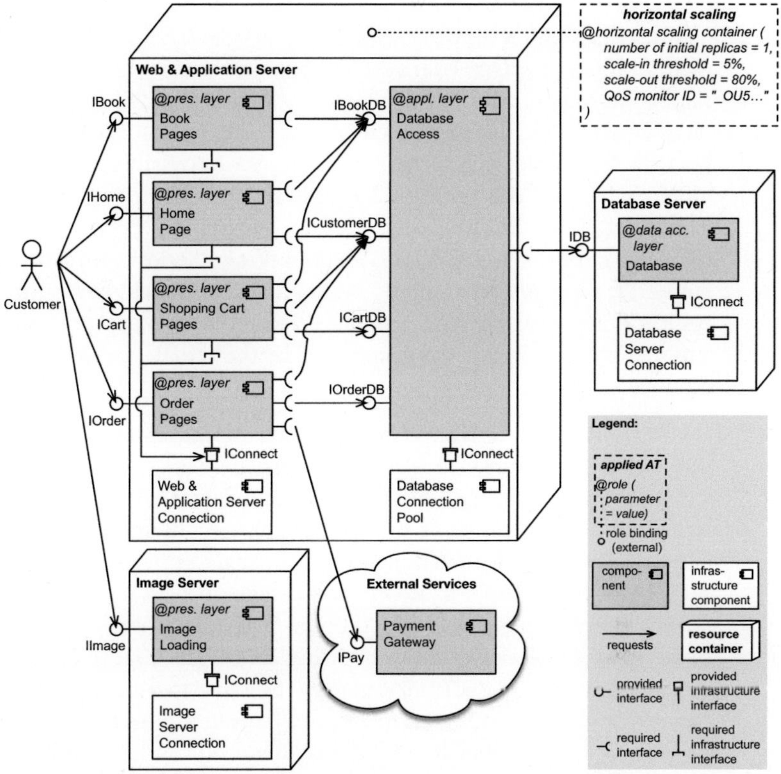

Figure C.10.: The horizontal scaling AT applied to the CloudStore model.

(4) assure the quality of the specified ATs, e.g., by testing. Via 64 tests (38 tests for the resource container variant and 26 tests for the assembly context variant), we have assured the quality of the completions [Gia16, Sec. 6.2]. We proceeded analogously to the tests for the *loadbalancing* ATs (cf. Section C.1.4.2).

Iteration III: Vertical Scaling AT. Continuing our work as AT engineers, we have reiterated through the actions of the AT specification process from Section 4.1.3 to specify the *vertical scaling* AT. As before, because we finished with action (1) in phase 1, we directly proceed with action (2):

(2) select reusable architectural knowledge. In cooperation with the software architect, we agreed on a common understanding of the *vertical scaling* architectural pattern. The *vertical scaling* architectural pattern [EPM13, FLR$^+$14] requires that computing resources of a single resource container can dynamically be (de-)provisioned. For example, when a VM is employed as resource container, higher CPU processing rates can be dynamically provisioned. *Vertical scaling* therefore improves elasticity without requiring stateless components. However, this pattern can only be applied if sufficient computing resources are available. For example, a virtual CPU cannot provision a higher processing rate than supported by the actual (physical) CPU of the VM's host.

(3) specify ATs (with parametrizable roles, constraints, completions). Subsequently, we have formalized the *vertical scaling* AT via a *vertical scaling container* role that can be bound to virtualized resource containers. The parameters of this role enrich containers with self-adaptive behavior for vertical scaling: a *scale-up threshold* and a *scale-down threshold* for a *QoS monitor* (analogously to the *horizontal scaling* AT) to trigger self-adaptations. Self-adaptations vertically scale by in- or decreases the processing rate of the container's processing resources (e.g., CPUs) according to a *rate step size* parameter. Moreover, this self-adaptation respects minimum and maximum processing rates as specified by the *minimal rate* and *maximal rate* parameters. Figure C.11 illustrates the *vertical scaling* AT for resource containers and its parameters.

We have formalized this adaptation behavior via QVT-O transformations, e.g., residing in the VerticalScalingContainerAdaptationRules folder for the resource container variant (as illustrated in Figure C.11). Palladio adapts the architectural model by executing these transformations during analysis (cf. Section 2.5.3.2).

(4) assure the quality of the specified ATs, e.g., by testing. Analogously to previous ATs, we have assured the quality of this AT and its adapta-

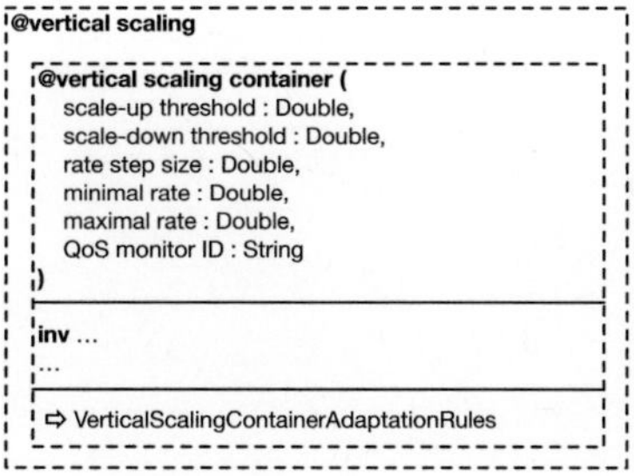

Figure C.11.: The vertical scaling AT for resource containers (excerpt).

tion rules via 22 tests. Giacinto describes these tests in detail [Gia16, Sec. 6.2].

Applying the stateless three-layer, horizontal scaling, and vertical scaling ATs Acting again as software architects, we next applied the *stateless three-layer, horizontal scaling* (for resource containers), and *vertical scaling* ATs to the CloudStore model. We have followed the AT application process from Section 4.1.1 as follows.

We bound the roles of the ATs to the CloudStore like illustrated in Figure C.12. We bound the roles of the *stateless three-layer* AT like we previously bound the *three-layer* AT. To automatically adapt the number of replicas to workload, we bound the *horizontal scaling container* role of the *horizontal scaling* AT for containers to the Web & Application Server (instead of sticking to the previously applied *loadbalancing* AT). To cope with the capacity degradation, we bound the *vertical scaling container* role of the *vertical scaling* AT to the Database Server.

Conducting an architectural analysis for the migrated CloudStore Continuing to act as software architects, we next analyzed the fulfillment of the pre-specified SLOs both for phase 2 and phase 3. We have followed the AT-based architectural analysis process from Section 4.1.2 as follows.

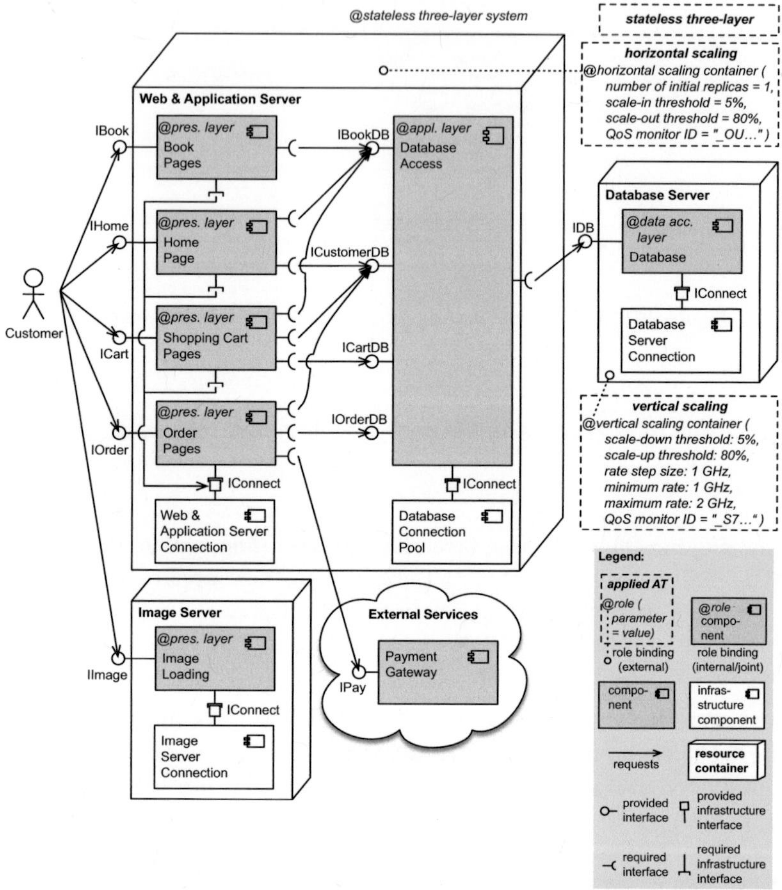

Figure C.12.: ATs for elasticity and cost-efficiency applied to the CloudStore model.

We have repeated the capacity analysis we executed during phase 2. The application of the *horizontal scaling* AT has resulted in the same fulfillment of $SLO_{\mathbf{Performance}}$ and $SLO_{\mathbf{Capacity}}$ as the *loadbalancing* AT for *number of replicas = 1*. The reason is that the AT's self-adaptation rules decrease the number of replicas from initially 2 to 1. Therefore, the application of this AT results in an elastic system that is more cost-efficient than a static configuration of *number of replicas = 2* for the *loadbalancing* AT; it saves 1 unnecessary replica and its operation costs, as confirmed by a run of our cost-efficiency analysis with Palladio [LE15]. $SLO_{\textbf{Cost-Efficiency}}$ is therefore also fulfilled.

The application of the *vertical scaling* AT has additionally increased CloudStore's capacity to over 1,000 concurrent customers (the maximum number we considered for our analysis). Because the CPU of the Database Server scaled-up to 2 GHz, it serviced jobs twice as fast and evidently removed the capacity degradation: even for 1,000 concurrent customers, response times were below the 0.2 seconds mark as we highlight in Figure C.13. In Figure C.13, we particularly see that $SLO_{\textbf{Elasticity}}$ is fulfilled because 100 % of response times were below the 1 second mark.

Being confident that CloudStore will fulfill all specified SLOs, we (as software architect) can continue now to implement, deploy, and operate CloudStore according to its architectural model.

C.1.4.4. CloudStore: Analysis

The empirical data collected during the execution of the CloudStore case study (previous sections) serves as input to the analysis conducted in this section.

Table C.7 provides an overview of this data; depicted measurements directly correspond to the metrics of our GQM plan (cf. Table 5.1 in Section 5.2). The first column specifies the metric of interest while the remaining columns provide the measurements per phase and AT. Rows are grouped via horizontal lines according to the research questions from Section 5.2. For example, the first research question is covered by the first five rows of metric measurements.

Table C.7.: Metric measurements collected in the CloudStore case study

	phase 2 (modernization)	phase 3 (migration)

	three-layer	loadbalancer (resource container)	loadbalancer (assembly context)	stateless three-layer	horizontal scaling (resource container)	horizontal scaling (assembly context)	vertical scaling
$M_{\text{time: AT selection}}$	1 $m.$	2 $m.$	-	1 $m.$	3 $m.$	-	4 $m.$
$M_{\text{time: AT application}}$	4 $m.$	1 $m.$	-	2 $m.$	3 $m.$	-	3 $m.$
$M_{\text{\#ATs}}$	3			7			
$M_{\text{\#AT roles}}$	4	1	1	4	1	1	1
$M_{\text{\#AT parameters}}$	0	1	1	0	4	4	6
$M_{\Delta\text{time}}$	-	-	-	-	-	-	-
$M_{\Delta\text{components}}$	0	1	1	0	1	1	0
$M_{\Delta\text{assembly ctx.}}$ *	0	$1 + 7 \cdot (r\text{-}1)$	r	0	$1 + 7 \cdot (r\text{-}1)$	r	0
$M_{\Delta\text{operations}}$	0	0	0	0	0	0	0
$M_{\Delta\text{self-adapt.}}$	0	0	0	0	803	697	150
$M_{\text{\#detected violations}}$	1	0	0	0	0	0	0
$M_{\text{\#resolved violations}}$	1	0	0	0	0	0	0
M_{benefits}	"detected constraint violations helped to correctly apply the *three-layer* AT", "as an expert, AT application is a matter of a few minutes", "the architectural analysis showed that the application of the *loadbalancing* AT was not beneficial in the given context; without analysis, this issue would have been hard to show"						
$M_{\text{limitations}}$	"creating ATs is cumbersome especially because of the error-prone specification of EMF profiles and complicated debugging mechanisms", "creating only slightly different ATs requires high effort", "specifying OCL constraints is complicated because there is no statical analysis for a correct syntax", "altering the behavior of self-adaptation rules requires an adaptation of the AT; such adaptations should be easier", "conceptually, the *three-layer* AT does not completely fit to CloudStore"						
$M_{\text{time: identification}}$	$\sim 2.5\, person\ months$ (executed in phase 1 for all ATs)						
$M_{\text{time: selection}}$	$\sim 1\,h.$	$\sim 1\,h.$	$\sim 1\,h.$	$\sim 3\,h.$	$\sim 1\,h.$	$\sim 1\,h.$	$\sim 1\,h.$
$M_{\text{time: specification}}$	$\sim 3\,h.$	$\sim 4\,h.$	$\sim 4\,h.$	$\sim 1\,h.$	$\sim 6\,h.$	$\sim 6\,h.$	$\sim 2\,h.$
$M_{\text{time: quality assur.}}$	$\sim 3\,h.$	$\sim 3\,h.$	$\sim 3\,h.$	$\sim 3\,h.$	$\sim 3\,h.$	$\sim 3\,h.$	$\sim 3\,h.$
$M_{\text{\#AT roles}}$	4	1	1	4	1	1	1
$M_{\text{\#AT constraints}}$	17	4	4	19	7	7	10
$M_{\text{\#completion LOC}}$	0	714	693	0	857	752	150
$M_{\text{\#detected errors}}$	1	15	7	10	19	11	12
$M_{\text{\#resolved errors}}$	1	15	7	10	19	11	12

* r denotes the number of (initial) replicas with $r \geq 1$.

Structured along these research questions, the corresponding measurements depicted in Table C.7 are analyzed in the following. The analysis covers a brief description of the measurements and the test of hypotheses associated to each research question. The interpretation of the analysis is left to a dedicated interpretation section (Section C.1.4.5).

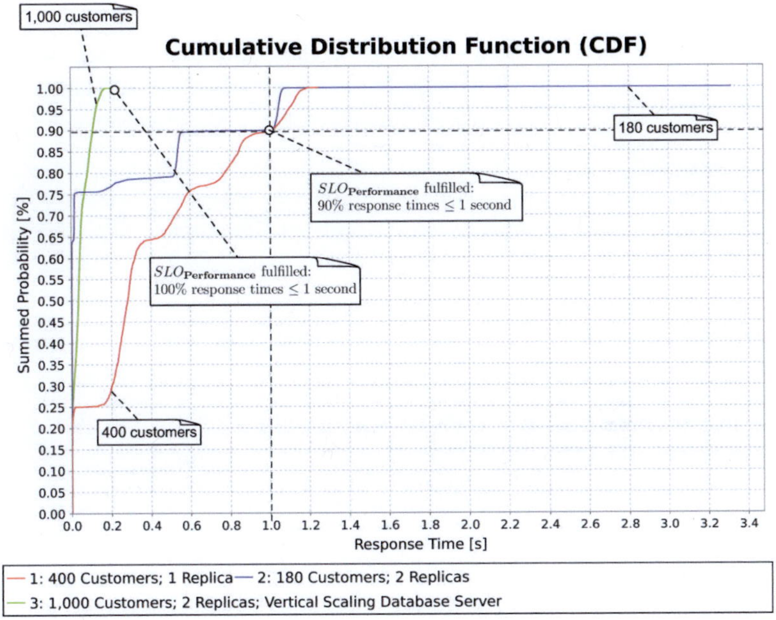

Figure C.13.: Cumulative distribution function of response times for different workloads and configurations of the modernized and migrated CloudStore (phase 2 and phase 3 of the CloudStore case study).

Analysis: How much effort do software architects require to apply ATs?

The measurement on the effort of software architects ($Q_{\textbf{application effort}}$) are depicted in the first measurement group in Table C.7.

Measurement description. We have measured the time for AT selection and application ($M_{\textbf{time for AT selection}}$ and $M_{\textbf{time for AT application}}$) only for the actually applied ATs (i.e., not for the *loadbalancing* and *horizontal scaling* ATs for assembly contexts). The time for selection ranges from 1 to 4 minutes; with an average of approximately 2 minutes per AT. The time for application also ranges from 1 to 4 minutes but with an average of approximately 3 minutes per AT.

We measured the number of ATs within the AT catalog ($M_{\#\textbf{ATs}}$) only once per phase in which we had to select ATs because this selection was always based on the complete AT catalog of the respective phase. As shown in Table C.7, we had 3 ATs available in phase 2 and 7 ATs in phase 3.

For all created ATs, we have measured their number of roles and parameters ($M_{\#\textbf{AT roles}}$ and $M_{\#\textbf{AT parameters}}$). The number of roles ranges from 1 to 4; with an average of approximately 2 roles per AT. The number of parameters ranges from 0 to 6; with an average of approximately 2 parameters per AT.

Hypothesis testing. These measurements allow accepting hypotheses $H_{\textbf{time-size correlation}}$ and $H_{\textbf{effort is low}}$, as described in the following.

Calculating the Pearson correlation coefficient [WRH+00, Sec. 10.1] over the selected and applied ATs yields:

- 0.49 between $M_{\textbf{time for AT selection}}$ and $M_{\#\textbf{ATs}}$,
- 0.32 between $M_{\textbf{time for AT application}}$ and $M_{\#\textbf{AT roles}}$, and
- 0.20 between $M_{\textbf{time for AT application}}$ and $M_{\#\textbf{AT parameters}}$.

Since each calculated correlation coefficient is positive, $H_{\textbf{time-size correlation}}$ is accepted.

The maximum sum of $M_{\textbf{time for AT selection}}$ and $M_{\textbf{time for AT application}}$ aggregates to 7 *minutes* (for the vertical scaling AT). On average, the sum is 4.8 *minutes* (over all selected and applied ATs). In any case, $H_{\textbf{effort is low}}$ is accepted because these values are below the defined threshold of 40 *minutes*.

Analysis: How much creation effort can software architects save when applying ATs? The measurement on effort savings for software architects ($Q_{\textbf{effort saving}}$) are depicted in the second measurement group in Table C.7.

Measurement description. We were unable to measure $M_{\Delta\textbf{time}}$ because we did not let a control group (that would have manually integrated reusable architectural knowledge) redundantly execute the CloudStore case study. However, we were able to take measurements for the remaining difference metrics ($M_{\Delta\textbf{components}}$, $M_{\Delta\textbf{assembly ctx.}}$, $M_{\Delta\textbf{operations}}$, $M_{\Delta\textbf{self-adapt.}}$).

Measurements for $M_{\Delta\textbf{components}}$ yielded either 0 or 1. The only additional component integrated into the CloudStore's repository model (that caused the 1 values) was a component acting as loadbalancer for the *loadbalancing* and *horizontal scaling* ATs.

Measurements for $M_{\Delta\textbf{assembly ctx.}}$ yield 0 for the *three-layer*, *stateless three-layer*, and *vertical scaling* ATs, which do not create new assembly contexts. The *loadbalancing* and *horizontal scaling* ATs for resource containers create a loadbalancer and as many replicas of the 7 assembly contexts from the Web & Application Server as specified by the *number of (initial) replicas* parameter of these ATs. It therefore holds that always $1 + 7(r - 1)$ additional assembly contexts are created where r denotes the actual value of the *number of (initial) replicas* parameter. For example, if $r = 1$, only a loadbalancer is attached in front of the Web & Application Server but no additional assembly contexts have to be created. For $r = 2$, the 7 assembly contexts allocated to the Web & Application Server are replicated once. In contrast, the *loadbalancing* and *horizontal scaling* ATs for assembly contexts create a loadbalancer and replicas for the bound assembly context. It therefore holds that always r additional assembly contexts are created, e.g., only the loadbalancer for $r = 1$ and one additional assembly context for $r = 2$.

Our measurements for $M_{\Delta\textbf{operations}}$ all yielded 0 values. We therefore have not provided an AT that extends an architectural model with additional operations.

The measurements for $M_{\Delta\textbf{self.-adapt.}}$ point to the only self-adaptive ATs (i.e., the ATs for horizontal and vertical scaling) because these are the only ATs with non-zero measurement values. For these ATs, values range from 150 to 803 lines of code; with an average of 550 lines of code.

Hypothesis testing. These measurements allow to accept $H_{\textbf{effort is lowered}}$. In contrast, $H_{\Delta\textbf{time-}\Delta\textbf{size correlation}}$ cannot be tested because of the missing measurements for $M_{\Delta\textbf{time}}$. We leave the testing of this hypothesis therefore to future empirical investigations and describe the test of $H_{\textbf{effort is lowered}}$ in the following.

No measurement for the metrics $M_{\Delta\textbf{components}}$, $M_{\Delta\textbf{assembly ctx.}}$, $M_{\Delta\textbf{operations}}$, and $M_{\Delta\textbf{self-adapt.}}$ is negative. Therefore, $H_{\textbf{effort is lowered}}$ can directly be accepted.

Analysis: Do software architects effectively benefit from checking whether their architectural models violate conformance to applied ATs? The measurement on conformance checking ($Q_{\textbf{conformance}}$) are depicted in the third measurement group in Table C.7.

Measurement description. The measurements for $M_{\textbf{\#detected violations}}$ show that we detected a violation of 1 AT constraint for the *three-layer* AT. For all other ATs, we did not violate AT constraints.

Our measurement of $M_{\textbf{\#resolved violations}}$ shows that we were successful in resolving the detected violation.

Hypothesis testing. We accept both hypothesis $H_{\textbf{violations are detected}}$ and hypothesis $H_{\textbf{violations are resolved}}$ because we detected 1 violation that we were able to resolve.

Analysis: What are effective benefits of the AT method? The measurement on benefits ($Q_{\textbf{benefits}}$) are depicted in the fourth measurement group in Table C.7.

Measurement description. The measurement of $M_{\textbf{benefits}}$ has resulted in the 3 collected benefits given in Table C.7. We, acting as software architects, explicitly observed these benefits during the conduction of the CloudStore case study.

Hypothesis testing. We can directly accept $H_{\textbf{benefits exist}}$ because we identified benefits during the case study.

Analysis: What are effective limitations of the AT method? The measurement on limitations ($Q_{\textbf{limitations}}$) are depicted in the fifth measurement group in Table C.7.

Measurement description. The measurement of $M_{\textbf{limitations}}$ has resulted in the 5 collected limitations given in Table C.7. We observed the first 4 limitations—related to AT tooling—when we acted as AT engineers. We observed the last limitation—a conceptually problematic application of the *three-layer* AT to CloudStore—when we acted as software architects.

Hypothesis testing. We can directly accept $H_{\textbf{limitations exist}}$ because we identified limitations during the case study. These limitations are uncritical because they point to tooling improvements and no conceptual flaws of the AT method.

Analysis: How much effort do AT engineers require for specifying ATs? The measurement on the effort of AT engineers ($Q_{\textbf{specification effort}}$) are depicted in the sixth measurement group in Table C.7.

Measurement description. We structured the measurements for the metric $M_{\textbf{time for AT specification}}$ along the four main AT specification actions from Section 4.1.3: the identification of QoS properties and a suitable analysis approach ($M_{\textbf{time for identification}}$), the selection of reusable architectural knowledge ($M_{\textbf{time for selection}}$), the specification of ATs ($M_{\textbf{time for specification}}$), and the assurance of the quality of the specified ATs ($M_{\textbf{time for quality assur.}}$). Moreover, similar to Koziolek et al.'s effort estimates [KSBH12], our time measurements are post-mortem estimates because we did not use a controlled environment to take these measurements.

In phase 1, we have executed the first action of the AT specification process, which has resulted in the identification of QoS properties (definitions and metrics for scalability, elasticity, and cost-efficiency) and a suitable architectural analysis approach (Palladio extended with support for these QoS properties). Phases 2 and 3 reuse these insights, thus, $M_{\textbf{time for identification}}$ was only measured once in phase 1. We estimate the time we spend on the first action to be approximately 2.5 person months. This estimate is based on the time that Hendrik Eikerling has spent on conducting the systematic literature review in his Bachelor's thesis [Eik14]. At his university, a Bachelor's thesis is account for 15 $ECTS$ (credit points in Europe), which corresponds to 2.5 person months of work on average (1 $ECTS \sim 27.5\, person\ hours$[1], i.e., 15 $ECTS \sim 2.5\, person\ months$).

Our time estimates for $M_{\textbf{time for selection}}$ range from 1 hour to 3 hours; with an average of approximately 1.3 hours. We already had prior experience on most reusable architectural knowledge to be captured, thus, requiring us to spend only 1 hour to agree on a common understanding and its selection. Only for the *stateless three-layer* architectural style, we first had to deeply

[1] See: http://www.kmk.org/fileadmin/veroeffentlichungen_beschluesse/2003/2003_10_10-Laendergemeinsame-Strukturvorgaben.pdf

investigate its description [Koz11b] for achieving an agreement, which has required us approximately 3 hours of time.

Our time estimates for $M_{\textbf{time for specification}}$ range from 1 hour to 6 hours; with an average of approximately 3.7 hours. Moreover, we have estimated the time for $M_{\textbf{time for quality assur.}}$ to be 3 hours per AT. Giacinto provides these estimates in her Master's thesis [Gia16, Sec. 7.1.5].

Being the same metric, the number of AT roles ($M_{\textbf{\#AT roles}}$) yields the same measurements as for the first research question. The number of AT constraints ($M_{\textbf{\#AT constraints}}$) ranges from 4 to 19 constraints; with an average of approximately 10 constraints per AT. The lines of code of an AT's completions ($M_{\textbf{\#completion LOC}}$) range from 0 to 857 lines of code; with an average of 452 lines of code per AT. The *horizontal scaling* ATs and the *vertical scaling* AT include completions with self-adaptations. We included the lines of code of these self-adaptations in our measurement as well.

Hypothesis testing. These measurements require rejecting hypothesis $H_{\textbf{time-size correlation}}$ but to accept hypothesis $H_{\textbf{effort is high}}$ as described in the following.

Calculating the Pearson correlation coefficient [WRH+00, Sec. 10.1] over the specified ATs yields:

- -0.44 between $M_{\textbf{time for AT specification}}$ and $M_{\textbf{\#AT roles}}$,
- -0.51 between $M_{\textbf{time for AT specification}}$ and $M_{\textbf{\#AT constraints}}$, and
- 0.83 between $M_{\textbf{time for AT specification}}$ and $M_{\textbf{\#completion LOC}}$.

Since the first two correlation coefficients are negative, $H_{\textbf{time-size correlation}}$ must be rejected in general. The third correlation coefficient, however, allows to accept $H_{\textbf{time-size correlation}}$ for the special case of the relation between specification time and lines of code of completions.

We have further divided the measurement of $M_{\textbf{time for AT specification}}$ into four more detailed measurements: $M_{\textbf{time for identification}}$, $M_{\textbf{time for selection}}$, $M_{\textbf{time for specification}}$, and $M_{\textbf{time for quality assur.}}$. The sum over these measurements is, for all ATs, greater than the defined threshold of 6.5 *hours*. $H_{\textbf{effort is high}}$ is therefore accepted. Even if not taking $M_{\textbf{time for identification}}$ into account, the sum of the remaining metrics remains above the 6.5 *hours* threshold; only for the *vertical scaling* AT we required less time (6 *hours*).

Analysis: Does quality assurance effectively help AT engineers to improve the conceptual integrity of specified ATs? The measurement on the effectivity of the AT method's quality assurance ($Q_{\textbf{quality assurance}}$) are depicted in the seventh measurement group in Table C.7.

Measurement description. The measurements for $M_{\textbf{\#detected errors}}$ show that we detected 75 errors in total. The number of detected errors ranges from 1 to 19 errors; with an average of approximately 11 errors per AT.

Our measurement of $M_{\textbf{\#resolved errors}}$ shows that we were successful in resolving all detected errors.

Hypothesis testing. We accept both hypothesis $H_{\textbf{errors are detected}}$ and hypothesis $H_{\textbf{errors are resolved}}$ because we detected 75 errors that we were able to resolve.

C.1.4.5. CloudStore: Interpretation

Based on the data analysis in the previous section, this section proceeds with answering the questions of our GQM plan (cf. Table 5.1 in Section 5.2).

Answering $Q_{\textbf{application effort}}$: How much effort do software architects require to apply ATs? The acceptance of $H_{\textbf{effort is low}}$ indicates that software architects have only low effort for applying ATs (compared to the overall efforts for specifying architectural models). Indeed, on average, we have required only about 5 *minutes* to apply ATs. This result is in line with the AT method's goal to make software architects more efficient because only low effort is introduced for benefiting from the exploitation of reusable architectural knowledge (cf. Section 1.2).

The acceptance of $H_{\textbf{time-size correlation}}$ indicates that effort for software architects varies depending on the number of ATs in the employed AT catalog and the number of roles and parameters of the applied AT. When we applied the *three-layer* AT, we additionally noted that effort is caused by the number of *applied* roles: the *three-layer* AT includes only 4 roles but we have bound these roles to total of 8 architectural elements. Therefore, a metric for the number of applied roles may be applied for future empirical investigations.

According to Evans' classification [Eva96], the correlation of AT selection time to the number of ATs in AT catalogs is "moderate"; the correlations from AT application time to the number of roles and parameters are "weak". Therefore, predicting the time for selecting and applying ATs solely based on the identified correlation will result in inaccurate estimates. Future work may investigate whether metrics with stronger correlations can be defined, e.g., similar to the complexity metrics by Martens et al. [MKPR11].

Answering $Q_{\text{effort saving}}$: How much creation effort can software architects save when applying ATs? The acceptance of $H_{\text{effort is lowered}}$ indicates that effort can effectively be lowered by applying ATs. In terms of saved creation efforts of architectural elements, the *loadbalancing* and *horizontal scaling* ATs save creation efforts for assembly contexts. Moreover, ATs can save efforts for specifying self-adaptive behavior by providing generic self-adaptation rules like the *horizontal* and *vertical scaling* ATs.

As we were unable to measure $M_{\Delta\text{time}}$ and to test $H_{\Delta\text{time-}\Delta\text{size correlation}}$, we cannot, based on our empirical data, provide estimates of the saved time when applying ATs. Future empirical investigations may systematically quantify this time with the help of control groups *not* following the AT method. The controlled experiment outlined in Section 5.4 exemplifies such an investigation.

Answering $Q_{\text{conform.}}$: Do software architects effectively benefit from checking whether their architectural models violate conformance to applied ATs? The acceptance of $H_{\text{violations are detected}}$ and $H_{\text{violations are resolved}}$ indicates that software architects can effectively benefit from the AT method's conformance checks. Our results for M_{benefits} particularly indicate that conformance checks help to apply ATs correctly.

However, during the CloudStore case study, we only detected one conformance violation. Therefore, no conclusive insights have been gained—especially regarding the long-term benefits of conformance checks (e.g., regarding maintainability) and regarding software architects that have not participated in creating the applied ATs. Future investigations may focus on these aspects.

Answering Q_{benefits}: What are effective benefits of the AT method? The 3 benefits collected during the case study ($M_{\textbf{benefits}}$) have confirmed expected and revealed unexpected benefits of the AT method.

The first benefit ("detected constraint violations helped to correctly apply the *three-layer* AT") shows that conformance checks not only maintain and ensure conformance but also help software architects to apply ATs. We expect that such a help will be most beneficial for software architects not involved in AT specification and, especially, novice software architects.

The second benefit ("as an expert, AT application is a matter of a few minutes") confirms that AT application can come with low efforts (cf. the answer to $Q_{\textbf{application effort}}$). It would, however, be interesting to inspect whether such benefits are observed by non-experts on the AT method as well.

The third benefit ("the architectural analysis showed that the application of the loadbalancing AT was not beneficial in the given context; without analysis, this issue would have been hard to show") empirically confirms that architectural analyses help in making context-aware informed decisions. During the case study, we were actually surprised that an increased number of loadbalanced replicas can degrade capacity. This degradation is in contrast to what the loadbalancing architectural pattern promises. However, the architectural analysis has revealed that CloudStore's Database Server—a context factor for the loadbalancer—actually becomes overloaded when too many replica exist. Here, the combination of reusable architectural knowledge with architectural analyses was beneficial.

Answering $Q_{\text{limitations}}$: What are effective limitations of the AT method? The 5 limitations collected during the case study ($M_{\textbf{limitations}}$) point to technical issues in AT tooling (first 4 limitations) and an issue in selecting suitable ATs (last limitation).

AT tooling issues relate to EMF profiles and debugging mechanisms (first limitation), missing reuse mechanisms for ATs (second limitation), lack of in-editor syntax checks when specifying OCL constraints (third limitation), and customizability of self-adaptations (fourth limitation). Fortunately, all of these issues are of technical nature and do not render the AT method infeasible. However, for making the AT method more practically relevant, these issues should be resolved. Openkowski has—meanwhile—already resolved the second limitation by introducing reuse mechanisms for the specification of ATs (see the extension described in Section 4.4.1). Resolving the remaining limitations remains as a future work.

The fifth and last limitation ("conceptually, the *three-layer* AT does not completely fit to CloudStore") is not of technical nature but relates to a conceptual mismatch between the selected AT and the targeted system. In CloudStore, assembly contexts for web pages, e.g., Home Page, communicate over a dedicated Database Access assembly context to CloudStore's Database. Because this structure defines three logical layer, we have applied the *three-layer* AT to CloudStore as illustrated in Figure C.7. While all constraints of the captured knowledge are fulfilled, the role names of the *three-layer* AT do not perfectly fit to CloudStore: the *application layer* role is applied to CloudStore's Database Access assembly context and the *data access layer* role is applied to CloudStore's Database assembly context. We may argue that Database Access also includes application layer logic and that Database models the access to CloudStore's database. However, the alternative (and common) role names "presentation layer", "middle layer", and "data layer" of the *three-layer* architectural style may be more intuitive in the context of CloudStore. A next step in the CloudStore case would therefore be to let software architects and AT engineers re-agree on this terminology. We conclude that, in general, software architects and AT engineers must steadily cooperate to avoid confusion due to unsuitable role names.

Answering $Q_{\textbf{specification effort}}$: How much effort do AT engineers require for specifying ATs? The acceptance of $H_{\textbf{effort is high}}$ indicates that AT engineers have high efforts for specifying ATs (compared to the overall efforts for specifying architectural models). The identification of suitable QoS properties and their integration into Palladio has caused the most effort, i.e., approximately $2.5\,person\,months$. We had high efforts in this step because neither established metrics for scalability, elasticity, and cost-efficiency nor a suitable architectural analysis have existed when we started with the case study. However, we expect that only little effort is required in domains with well-established metrics and analysis approaches; for the cloud computing domain, our work has contributed such metrics and analysis approaches.

Once we had finished with our integration into Palladio, on average, we have required about 8 *hours* to select, specify, and quality-assure a single AT. Given the potential effort that software architects save when applying the AT method, we believe that 8 *hours* are affordable. Moreover, as indicated by the answer to $Q_{\textbf{limitations}}$, resolving some limitations in AT tooling promises to lower AT specification efforts.

The rejection of $H_{\textbf{time-size correlation}}$ indicates that not all suspected effort-causing factors indeed cause effort. The negative correlation between specification time and the number of AT roles and constraints even suggests that "the more roles and constraints an AT needs to capture, the less time is required for its specification". Because such a statement makes no causal sense, we suggest a more controlled inspection of these factors. Furthermore, the positive correlation between specification time and completion lines of code indicates that the size of completions indeed influences the effort for specifying ATs. According to Evans' classification [Eva96], this correlation (of 0.83) is even "very strong"; thus, making completions a primary factor for specification efforts.

Answering $Q_{\textbf{quality assurance}}$: Does quality assurance effectively help AT engineers to improve the conceptual integrity of specified ATs? The acceptance of both $H_{\textbf{errors are detected}}$ and $H_{\textbf{errors are resolved}}$ indicates that the AT method's quality assurance helps in effectively improving conceptual integrity of specified ATs: testing has revealed faults in the specification of several ATs. This testing is a lightweight quality assurance technique because it requires little effort compared to a full-blown formal verification. The typical root causes for AT faults (cf. Section 4.1.3.3) particularly have helped to efficiently detect the actual faults. Once detected, we have shown that faults can be removed, thus, leading to an improved conceptual integrity. We therefore suggest to always include the proposed quality assurance steps in any AT specification efforts.

Given its importance, future work should target a more extensive support for quality assurance. For example, an automated generation of test cases that cover the typical root causes for AT faults is a promising future work direction.

C.1.4.6. CloudStore: Evaluation of Validity

This section evaluates the most important threats to validity of the CloudStore case study. The section focuses on the four types of validity described by Wohlin et al. [WRH+00, Sec. 8.7]: (1) conclusion validity, (2) internal validity, (3) construct validity, and (4) external validity.

Wohlin et al. [WRH+00, Sec. 8.7] apply the terminology illustrated in Figure C.14 to describe the four types of validity. Firstly, they generally distinguish between the theory (i.e., the posed hypotheses) and the observation (i.e., the collected empirical data) of an empirical study. For the evaluation of the AT method, the *theory* (upper half in Figure C.14) are the hypotheses stated in Section 5.2.3. Each *hypothesis* is related to the experiment objective (defined via a GQM goal) and describes a relationship between a *cause* and an *effect* construct. For instance, the hypothesis $H_{\textbf{effort is low}}$ states that the application of ATs (cause) causes only low effort for software architects (effect).

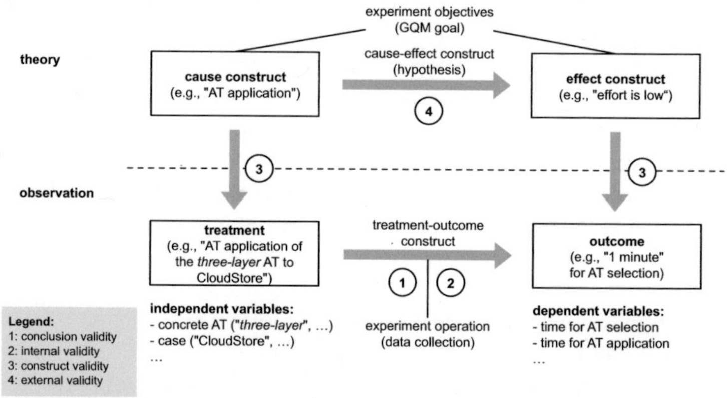

Figure C.14.: Experiment principles and threats to validity (based on [WRH+00, p. 103]).

The *observation* (lower half in Figure C.14) describes the experiment to test these hypotheses. The experiment consists of treatments and outcomes. A *treatment* selects the concrete independent variables of the study. Examples for independent variables are the concrete AT (e.g., the *three-layer* AT) and the concrete case (e.g., CloudStore) investigated during the experiment. Executing an "AT application of the *three-layer* AT to CloudStore" is a possible treatment. The *outcomes* are the values that the *dependent variables* can take. For the evaluation of the AT method, dependent variables are specified by the metrics from Section 5.2.2 and their measurements correspond to above outcomes. For instance, the metric "time for AT selection" ($M_{\textbf{time for AT selection}}$) is an example for a dependent variable and the concrete measurement result "1 minute" is the corresponding outcome for the execution of the "AT application of the *three-layer* AT to CloudStore".

The arrows in Figure C.14 depict relationships between causes, effects, treatments, and outcomes. These relationships have an influence on the validity of the experiment. Therefore, Figure C.14 additionally illustrates which types of validity need to be considered for the respective relationship: each number within a circle corresponds to exactly one type of validity ("1" for conclusion validity, "2" for internal validity, "3" for construct validity, and "4" for external validity). Each validity type is applied to CloudStore in the following.

(1) Conclusion Validity Conclusion validity is the degree to which conclusions relating treatments to outcomes are correct. For example, when measuring the time it takes subjects (e.g., software architects) to execute a task (e.g., applying ATs), variations because of the individual performance form such a threat. Circle "1" in Figure C.14 annotates the corresponding relationship that is affected by conclusion validity.

Wohlin et al. [WRH+00, Sec. 8.8.1] provide a list of threats to conclusion validity. In the following, the most important items of this list with respect to CloudStore are discussed:

Low statistical power: Being typical for case studies, our main threat to conclusion validity is "low statistical power" [WRH+00, Sec. 8.8.1]—we were only a few subjects that executed the CloudStore case study. This threat is especially relevant for time-based effort metrics like $M_{\textbf{time for specification}}$—other subjects may need significantly more or less time for the tasks we conducted. As we are software architects with an average of ten year's experience, we expect that our effort measurements can serve as first base line for software architects with similar experience. Additional studies and controlled experiments are needed to confirm this hypothesis.

Similarly, we have so far only investigated the CloudStore case—whether our results can be generalized to other cases remains to be shown. Still, we expect that web applications and applications deployed in cloud computing environments are comparable to CloudStore.

Reliability of measures: Measurements should optimally be reproducible; otherwise, derived conclusions can be unreliable random observations. Naturally, this threat especially concerns experiments that involve human subjects.

Given that we have measured the time of human subjects executing actions of the AT method (e.g., $M_{\textbf{time for specification}}$), our results potentially suffer from reproducibility issues. We have however tried to conquer these issues by closely following the described AT processes.

Measurements of artifacts, on the other hand, provide a better reproducibility and, thus, suffer less from this threat. For example, the measurement of an AT's number of roles ($M_{\textbf{\#AT roles}}$) can easily be reproduced.

Random irrelevancies in experimental setting: For our case study, we have not used a controlled environment. Therefore, during the execution of our measurements, random factors can have occurred that have disturbed the measurements. For example, AT engineers may have been interrupted by phone calls or lunch and coffee breaks. Our results on human-based measurements provide therefore only a first base line for further empirical investigations, e.g., employing a more controlled environment.

Random heterogeneity of subjects: We had different knowledge about the AT method, architectural analyses, research methods like systematic literature reviews, and software engineering in general. This heterogeneity is particular evident from our context—our team includes student workers at the Bachelor's and Master's levels, PhD students, and a senior researcher. On the other hand, the fact that I have closely cooperated with all members of our team over longer periods of time lowers their heterogeneity.

While factors that indicate a high heterogeneity potentially have a negative effect on conclusion validity, they generally have a positive effect on external validity (see below). It is therefore important to characterize the subjects involved in the study; Section C.1.3.3 provides such a characterization for CloudStore. Further experiments can then set a different focus, e.g., by conducting a study with a more heterogeneous team.

(2) Internal Validity Internal validity is the degree to which conclusions relating treatments to outcomes are causal (given a correctly observed relationship; cf. conclusion validity). For example, experiments without control group (like in our case) are threatened by the possibility that external factors (e.g., not the AT method) have caused the observed outcome. Circle "2" in Figure C.14 annotates the corresponding relationship that is affected by internal validity.

Wohlin et al. [WRH+00, Sec. 8.8.2] provide a list of threats to internal validity. In the following, the most important items of this list with respect to CloudStore are discussed:

History: We conducted the CloudStore case study over a period of one year. During this time, ("historic") events like public holidays and longer business trips have intervened with our efforts. These interrupts can have influenced our performance and, thus, the outcomes of our case study. Again, future work can alleviate such threats by replicating our case study and by conducting studies in more controlled settings.

Maturation: As time has passed during the case study, our behavior matured. Our maturation can have both positively and negatively influenced our effort and our time-based measurements in particular.

For example, we performed repetitive tasks for sighting 418 sources during our systematic literature review (cf. [LEB15]). We countered tiring effects for such repetitive tasks by limiting the amount of continuous work on these tasks to 3 *hours*; however, we acknowledge that such tasks are indeed tiring.

On the other hand, we have also observed a learning effect when specifying ATs. For example, compared to the ATs we specified in phase 2, we have required less time in phase 3 for the initial configuration steps of ATs (e.g., creating role stubs and attaching profiles).

Selection: As described in Section C.1.3.3, we have selected all involved subjects from an academic context. Moreover, our team had a general research interest in common and was motivated to apply and mature the AT method. Because the high motivation will generally not represent the whole population of software architects and AT engineers, outcomes can have been impacted by our selection.

(3) Construct Validity Construct validity is the degree to which conclusions relating theory to observations are correct. Correctness includes that (1) the treatment sufficiently reflects the cause construct, and (2) the outcome sufficiently reflects the effect construct. For example, the number of AT roles ($M_{\mathbf{\#AT\ roles}}$) may be a poor measure for AT specification effort while the time for AT specification ($M_{\mathbf{time\ for\ AT\ specification}}$) may be a better measure. The two circles "3" in Figure C.14 annotate the corresponding relationships that are affected by construct validity.

Wohlin et al. [WRH+00, Sec. 8.8.3] provide a list of threats to construct validity. In the following, the most important items of this list with respect to CloudStore are discussed:

Inadequate preoperational explication of constructs: Some metrics (for example, the size-based metrics in Section 5.2.2) have not been applied before. Therefore, these metrics can suffer from unclear definitions or are inadequate to measure the effect construct of interest. For example, our rejection of $H_{\mathbf{time\text{-}size\ correlation}}$ even indicates that both $M_{\mathbf{\#AT\ roles}}$ and $M_{\mathbf{\#AT\ constraints}}$ are inadequate metrics to measure AT specification effort (cf. Section C.1.4.5).

Fortunately, we have identified strong correlations as well, for example, between the measurements for $M_{\mathbf{time\ for\ AT\ specification}}$ and $M_{\mathbf{\#completion\ LOC}}$. These strong correlations provide evidence for the adequacy of introduced metrics. Future empirical investigations can extend and externally validate these initial insights.

Mono-operation bias: Like most case studies, we face the risk that sticking only to a single case may under-represent the derived theory. In our case study, we only investigated the CloudStore case as a migration scenario. Based on our results, we derived that, in such scenarios, architectural models can effectively and efficiently be created by following the AT method. Whether the CloudStore case was under-representative to draw such conclusions needs to be clarified in further empirical studies.

Interaction of testing and treatment: Because I have participated in the case study on my own, I knew the particular testing goals of applying the AT method—testing the AT method's effectivity and efficiency. This knowledge has potentially led me to avoid AT application errors, e.g., by applying ATs more carefully than other software architects would have applied ATs. Further studies should therefore be conducted with external subjects that are unaware of the tested goals.

(4) External Validity External validity is the degree to which internally valid results can be generalized to industrial practice. For instance, if the results of the CloudStore case study have a high external validity, they will also hold for other cases like different kinds of online shops and non-migration scenarios. Circle "4" in Figure C.14 annotates the corresponding relationship that is affected by external validity.

Wohlin et al. [WRH+00, Sec. 8.8.4] provide a list of threats to external validity. In the following, the most important items of this list with respect to CloudStore are discussed:

Interaction of selection and treatment: Our selection of subjects is based on their availability at our university and on the fact that they had previous experience on model-driven technologies and architectural analyses. For software architects with different contexts that want to learn the AT method, our results can therefore be biased (e.g., regarding effort).

Interaction of setting and treatment: The total number of ATs within the CloudStore case can be seen as small. Therefore, it is unclear whether gained outcomes also hold for more AT applications, especially within an industrial context. Moreover, as mentioned above, the generalizability to different kinds of online shops and non-migration scenarios has not been investigated.

Discussion of Threats to Validity The preceding descriptions show that most validity threats result from the explorative nature of case studies. In summary, our main threats are caused by the focus on a single case, involved human subjects (especially regarding time-based measurements), and the novelty of the introduced metrics.

We have conquered threats related to the novelty of our metrics by taking care of avoiding the "mono-method bias" threat [WRH⁺00, Section 8.8.3]. The mono-method bias describes the threat of using only a single type of metric, which involves the risk of misleading experimentation results. By generally employing several metrics, we were able to cross-check results against each other and to detect inconsistencies. For example, for quantifying AT specification effort ($Q_{\textbf{specification effort}}$), we employed both time-based metrics (e.g., $M_{\textbf{time for selection}}$) and size-based metrics (e.g., $M_{\textbf{\#AT roles}}$ and $M_{\textbf{\#completion LOC}}$). On the one hand, the lack of positive correlation between our measurements for $Q_{\textbf{specification effort}}$ and $M_{\textbf{\#AT roles}}$ enabled us to reject $M_{\textbf{\#AT roles}}$ as a good indicator for AT specification effort. On the other hand, the positive correlation between our measurements for $Q_{\textbf{specification effort}}$ and $M_{\textbf{\#completion LOC}}$ enabled us to identify $M_{\textbf{\#completion LOC}}$ as a good indicator for AT specification effort.

To conquer the remaining threats, we have suggested to focus on these threats in further empirical investigations. Concretely, we have suggested further case studies and the conduction of controlled experiments. Motivated by this suggestion, the subsequent sections describe our initial work on such studies and experiments.

C.2. Case Study Report: WordCount

This section describes a case study that we have conducted in the big data domain; a domain concerned with processing large data sets [Whi09]. In our case study, we have created and analyzed an architectural model for WordCount [Whi09]; a commonly used example application that is able to count the number of word occurrences over a huge set of input texts. We have created this model based on an AT that captures a typical reference architecture for big data applications. The reference architecture is based on Apache's Hadoop framework [Whi09] that implements the MapReduce architectural style [DG08]. Compared to the ATs specified during the CloudStore case study, the unique feature of the *Hadoop MapReduce* AT is that it provides a default AT instance (cf. Section 4.2.5.3), i.e., can be used as initiator template.

Accordingly, the goal of the WordCount case study was to:

Analyze: the AT method

For the purpose of: conducting architectural analyses *based on initiator templates*

With respect to: effectivity and efficiency

From the viewpoint of: software architects and AT engineers

In the context of: realistic *big data* systems.

We have achieved this goal in three consecutive steps. First, in the context of his Master's thesis [Sax15], Manoveg Saxena has acted as software architect to create a reference model for Hadoop applications—with full support for Palladio-based analyses. Second, I have acted as AT engineer to extract the *Hadoop MapReduce* AT from this reference model. Third, I have acted as software architect to showcase the application of this AT to the WordCount case. The third and last step has required only minor effort (less than 1 *hour*) compared to setting up, running, and analyzing the WordCount application on an actual computing cluster. Therefore, our results point to an improved efficiency when using ATs as initiator templates.

The remainder of this section describes the WordCount case study in detail. Analogously to the CloudStore case study, the section follows the reporting guidelines for case studies by Runeson and Höst [RH09]. After Section C.2.1 details the WordCount application and Hadoop, Section C.2.2 describes the design of the case study as a refinement of the generic evaluation design from Section 5.2. Section C.2.3 provides the results of the case study, including an interpretation and discussion of threats to validity.

C.2.1. WordCount and Hadoop MapReduce

As previously described, WordCount [Whi09] is a commonly used example application in the big data domain. The WordCount application counts the number occurrences of each word over a set of input texts. For example, the texts "software architects apply an AT" and "AT engineers create an AT" may be processed. WordCount then outputs a count of 3 for the word "AT", a count of 2 for the word "an", and a count of 1 for the remaining words.

In big data, a huge amount of such texts is processed. The MapReduce architectural style is commonly applied to make such a processing performant and scalable [Whi09]. MapReduce requires that data sets can be processed independently from each other within so-called mapper and reducer functions. Mapper functions filter and sort such data and reducer functions summarize collected data. Based on data independence, multiple of these functions can run in parallel, thus, improving performance and scalability.

A common open-source framework that implements this architectural style is Hadoop MapReduce [Whi09]; developed by the Apache Software Foundation. Hadoop MapReduce can particularly be seen as a reference architecture for similar implementations. As a reference architecture, it essentially describes a processing pipeline for the control and data flow of the MapReduce style.

Figure C.15 illustrates the control and data flow of Hadoop's MapReduce processing pipeline using the WordCount example. The seven actions (depicted as rounded rectangles) of the pipeline are consecutively executed from left to right according to the thick, filled arrows in Figure C.15. The first four actions are associated to the mapper function while the remaining three actions are associated to the reducer function of the MapReduce architectural style. Underneath these actions, associated artifacts (denoted as rectangles) are exemplified based on WordCount. Artifact flow is denoted via straight lines and can involve access to hard disk drives (denoted as cylinder).

In Figure C.15, the focus is on the actions that impact performance as identified by Zhang et al. [ZCL14]:

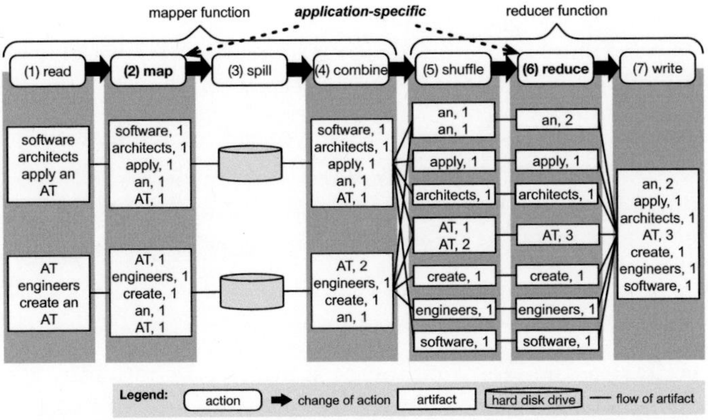

Figure C.15.: Performance-impacting actions of Hadoop's MapReduce processing pipeline exemplified for the WordCount application (based on [ZCL14]).

(1) read: Receives an input stream from which input data is read. For example, the previously described texts ("software architects apply an AT" and "AT engineers create an AT") may be read.

(2) map: Extracts keys and values from the input data. In WordCount, the map action creates a new key for each word of the input data and associates a 1 as value; denoting that the word was found once. For example, the key-value pair ("software", 1) is the first pair found for the first input text in Figure C.15.

(3) spill: Stores intermediate data on a hard disk drive in case an internal buffer gets too full.

(4) combine: Executes the reduce action (see below) for key-value pairs within one artifact. In consequence, the number of key-value pairs to be passed to the next action is lowered. In the example in Figure C.15, the two occurrences of the ("AT", 1) key-value pair are combined into a single pair ("AT", 2); denoting that—in the lower artifact—the word "AT" has occurred twice.

(5) shuffle: Merge-sorts the input key-value pairs by key and transfers all output belonging to the same key to the subsequent reducer action. For example, the key “an” occurs twice over the whole input data in Figure C.15, thus, the corresponding two key-value pairs are transferred together to the next action.

(6) reduce: Calls for each unique key a reduce function that can produce zero or more key-value pairs. In the WordCount example, the reduce function sums up all values belonging to a key, e.g., resulting in the key-value pairs (“AT”, 3) and (“an”, 2).

(7) write: Stores the output from the reduce action, e.g., on a hard disk drive.

In the context of the WordCount case study, it is important to note that only the map and the reduce actions are application-specific (the combine action generically reuses information from the reduce action). Therefore, the remaining actions are generically recurring in architectural models of Hadoop MapReduce applications. The *Hadoop MapReduce* AT captures exactly these recurring actions (in dedicated components) and only requires software architects to supply custom map and reduce components.

C.2.2. WordCount: Case Study Design

In this section, I describe the design of the WordCount case study. Section C.2.2.1 briefly points to relevant research questions and procedures for data collection, analysis, and validation. Afterwards, Section C.2.2.2 describes the WordCount case as a scenario for initiator templates. Involved human subjects (i.e., Saxena and I) are characterized in Section C.2.2.3.

C.2.2.1. WordCount: Research Questions and Procedures

In the WordCount case study, we employ the complete evaluation design introduced in Section 5.2, i.e., we reuse its research questions and the procedures for data collection, analysis, and validity.

C.2.2.2. WordCount: Case

For statistical analyses, a company that is hosting an online book shop needs to count the number of occurrences of each word in its database of digitalized books ("WordCount"; cf. Section C.2.1). The texts of these books sum up to 2 GB in total. Because the company often wants to run WordCount, the company limits the total execution time of WordCount to 10 minutes. The SLO in Table C.8 covers these requirements.

Table C.8.: WordCount's SLO

$SLO_{\textbf{Performance}}$: The total execution time of WordCount for 2 GB of text is at most 10 minutes.

The responsible software architect for WordCount plans its realization from scratch. Being popular in the big data domain, the software architect wants to assess the option to use Apache's Hadoop framework [Whi09]. For this assessment, the software architect requests an AT from an AT engineer that reflects the performance impact of Hadoop—the architect only wants to customize the AT with the special characteristics of WordCount.

C.2.2.3. WordCount: Subjects

In the WordCount case study, both Saxena and I have acted as software architects. Furthermore, I have acted as AT engineer.

In the role of a software architect, Saxena has created a reference model for Hadoop applications—with full support for Palladio-based analyses. He has created this model as the main contribution of his Master's thesis [Sax15]. Saxena's knowledge on architectural modeling and conducting architectural analyses was based on previous experience in our software engineering group (a half-year seminar) and based on papers on Palladio [BKR09] and SimuLizar [BBM13]. In the mentioned seminar, he particularly investigated Hadoop and WordCount in detail, thus, is expected to have good knowledge about the targeted domain.

In my role as AT engineer, I have extracted the *Hadoop MapReduce* AT from Saxena's reference model. In my role as software architect, I have applied the *Hadoop MapReduce* AT to the WordCount case. As for the CloudStore case study, I am expected to have deep knowledge about the AT method and minimal learning efforts.

C.2.3. WordCount: Results

This section reports the results of the WordCount case study. The report starts in Section C.2.3.1 with the execution the WordCount case. The empirical data created during this execution is analyzed in Section C.2.3.2 and interpreted in Section C.2.3.3. Potential threats to validity of the WordCount case study are finally discussed in Section C.2.3.4.

C.2.3.1. WordCount: Execution

In the WordCount case study, we have specified an AT capturing Hadoop MapReduce as a reference architecture and subsequently used this AT as initiator template to model and analyze the WordCount application. This section first describes our specification of the *Hadoop MapReduce* AT, second our application of this AT to model WordCount, and third our conduction of an architectural analysis to check WordCount's SLO (cf. Table C.8).

Specifying the Hadoop MapReduce ATs The software architect's request for an AT capturing Hadoop MapReduce has triggered an iteration through the AT specification process from Section 4.1.3. We have executed this iteration as follows:

(1) identify QoS properties and suitable analysis approaches. We have selected Palladio for this case study because Palladio fully supports performance analyses like required for analyzing $SLO_{\textbf{Performance}}$. Further QoS properties were not required to be identified.

(2) select reusable architectural knowledge. The software architect, as described in the WordCount case, has directly requested an AT for capturing Hadoop MapReduce. Therefore, we only had to understand Hadoop's processing pipeline (see Section C.2.1).

(3) specify ATs (with parametrizable roles, constraints, completions).
Next, we have specified the *Hadoop MapReduce* AT (available at [ATt]) to capture Hadoop's processing pipeline as a reference architecture. The AT introduces a default AT instance (cf. Section 4.2.5.3) along with the roles *map assembly context*, *reduce assembly context*, and *Hadoop MapReduce system*. Figure C.16 illustrates the AT.

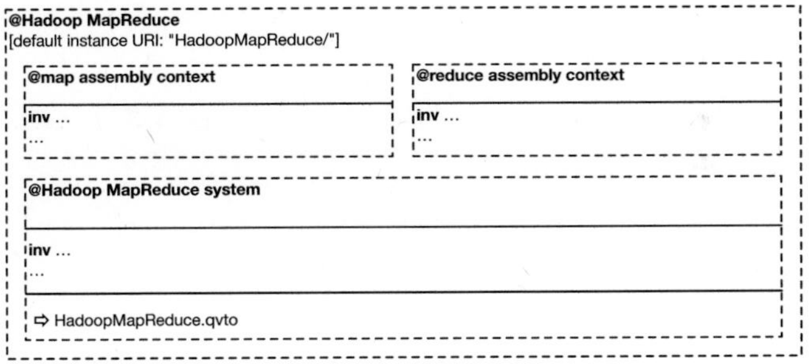

Figure C.16.: The Hadoop MapReduce AT (excerpt).

The default AT instance provides an architectural model that includes a system with map and reduce assembly contexts bound to the respective roles; Figure C.17 shows the corresponding PCM system diagram. After an AT-based initialization, this default AT instance serves as a starting point for software architects. Architects only have to adapt the instance to their concrete scenario. For example, they can easily modify the behavior specification of map and reduce components and the characterization of their resource containers, e.g., the processing rates of CPUs.

Moreover, as shown in Figure C.16 (bottom), the *Hadoop MapReduce system* role includes a completion HadoopMapReduce.qvto that we have formalized in QVT-O. The completion weaves the bound map and reduce assembly contexts into a pre-specified architectural model of Hadoop's processing pipeline (cf. Section C.2.1). To give an impression of the resulting model, Figure C.18 outlines the resulting system with a PCM system diagram. Light-grey assembly contexts are two replicas of the bound map assembly context and the dark-grey assembly context is a replica of the bound reduce assembly context. In the current version of the AT, these numbers are fixed; future work may introduce appropriate AT parameters similar to the *loadbalancing* AT. The remaining assembly context are generic parts of Hadoop's processing pipeline. Saxena has created this reference model—with full support for Palladio analyses—in his Master's thesis [Sax15]; details are described there.

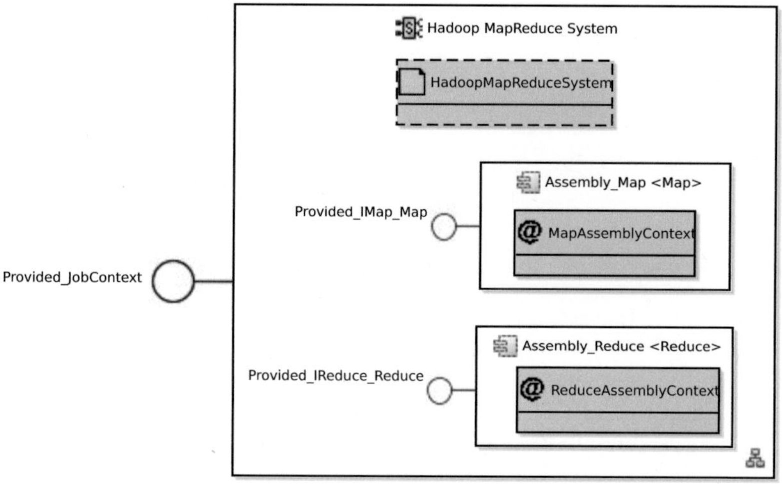

Figure C.17.: PCM system created by the default AT instance of the Hadoop MapReduce AT.

(4) assure the quality of the specified ATs, e.g., by testing. Based on 2 tests [ATt], we assured that custom map and reduce components are correctly integrated; similar to our quality assurance in the CloudStore case study. For each test, we manually inspected the architectural model after executing the mapping. We discovered faults in the implementation of the AT's completion: we failed to correctly connect the map and reduce assembly contexts in the targeted reference archi-

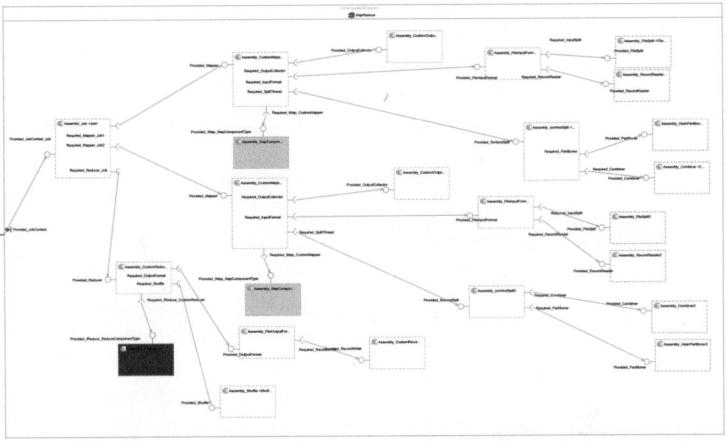

Figure C.18.: System after execution of the Hadoop MapReduce AT's completion.

tectural model. However, after discovery, we successfully removed these faults.

Applying the Hadoop MapReduce AT Acting as architects, we have used the *Hadoop MapReduce* AT as an initiator template to start modeling the WordCount system (action (1*) of AT application described in Section 4.1.1). After instantiation, we have customized the architectural model with a map and reduce component that accurately reflect the behavior of WordCount (cf. [Sax15]). As described in the previous paragraph, the AT's completion takes care of weaving these components into an architectural model of Hadoop's MapReduce processing pipeline. Subsequently, we were therefore able to analyze this architectural model with Palladio.

Conducting an architectural analysis for WordCount Finally, we have analyzed the fulfillment of the pre-specified SLO ($SLO_{\textbf{Performance}}$). We have followed the AT-based architectural analysis process from Section 4.1.2 as follows.

For analyzing the SLO, we have configured a performance analysis with Palladio. Palladio has reported a total execution time of approximately 9.2 minutes for WordCount. Therefore, we concluded that $SLO_{\textbf{Performance}}$ (defining an upper bound of 10 minutes) is fulfilled, thus, successfully finished with the analysis conduction.

C.2.3.2. WordCount: Analysis

In this section, I analyze the empirical data that we have collected during the WordCount case study. Table C.9 provides an overview of this data; depicted measurements directly correspond to the metrics of the GQM plan (cf. Table 5.1 in Section 5.2). The first column specifies the metric of interest while the second column provides the measurements for the application of the *Hadoop MapReduce* AT to WordCount. Rows are grouped via horizontal lines according to the research questions from Section 5.2, e.g., the first research question is covered by the first five rows of metric measurements. Structured along these research questions, the corresponding measurements depicted in Table C.9 are analyzed in the following. The analysis covers a brief description of the measurements and the test of hypotheses associated to each research question. The interpretation of the analysis is left to a dedicated interpretation section (Section C.2.3.3).

Table C.9.: Metric measurements collected in the WordCount case study

	Hadoop MapReduce
$M_{\textbf{time for AT selection}}$	1 $min.$
$M_{\textbf{time for AT application}}$	1 $min.$
$M_{\textbf{\#ATs}}$	8
$M_{\textbf{\#AT roles}}$	2
$M_{\textbf{\#AT parameters}}$	0
$M_{\Delta\textbf{time}}$	-
$M_{\Delta\textbf{components}}$	13
$M_{\Delta\textbf{assembly ctx.}}$	22
$M_{\Delta\textbf{operations}}$	29
$M_{\Delta\textbf{self-adapt.}}$	0
$M_{\textbf{\#detected violations}}$	0
$M_{\textbf{\#resolved violations}}$	0
$M_{\textbf{benefits}}$	"we had very little effort with the AT-based instantiation of the architectural model", "the bound AT heavily reduces the complexity of the underlying Hadoop infrastructure"

$M_{\textbf{limitations}}$	"the AT is currently inflexible and misses parameters, e.g., for configuring the number of map and reduce replicas", "the AT-annotated architectural model appears incomplete because map and reduce assembly context are unconnected", "the applied analysis tool (SimuLizar) lacks support for asynchronous map and reduce tasks, which can generally lead to inaccurate analysis results"
$M_{\textbf{time for identification}}$	$\sim 1\,h.$
$M_{\textbf{time for selection}}$	$\sim 2\,h.$
$M_{\textbf{time for specification}}$	$\sim 2.5\,person\ months$
$M_{\textbf{time for quality assur.}}$	$\sim 4\,h.$
$M_{\textbf{\#AT roles}}$	2
$M_{\textbf{\#AT constraints}}$	2
$M_{\textbf{\#completion LOC}}$	244
$M_{\textbf{\#detected errors}}$	2
$M_{\textbf{\#resolved errors}}$	2

Analysis: How much effort do software architects require to apply ATs?
The measurement on the effort of software architects ($Q_{\textbf{application effort}}$) are depicted in the first measurement group in Table C.9.

Measurement description. Given that the software architect in the WordCount case directly requests an AT for Hadoop MapReduce (Section C.2.2.2), we directly knew which AT to select from the available options. Therefore, we have spent at most 1 *minute* for this selection ($M_{\textbf{time for AT selection}}$).

According to the measurement for $M_{\textbf{time for AT application}}$, also the AT-based initialization has only required at most 1 *minute*. The initialization required us to use the wizard for initializing Palladio projects with ATs (cf. Appendix B.1.1). We simply had to select the *Hadoop MapReduce* AT and start the initialization process.

As shown in Table C.7, we have selected the *Hadoop MapReduce* AT from the catalog of 8 ATs ($M_{\textbf{\#ATs}}$) that we have created during the CloudStore case study plus the novel *Hadoop MapReduce* AT. The *Hadoop MapReduce* AT contains 2 roles and 0 parameters ($M_{\textbf{\#AT roles}}$ and $M_{\textbf{\#AT parameters}}$).

Hypothesis testing. These measurements alone make it impossible to test hypothesis $H_{\textbf{time-size correlation}}$. To test $H_{\textbf{time-size correlation}}$, more time and size samples are needed to calculate the Pearson correlation coefficient.

The sum of $M_{\textbf{time for AT selection}}$ and $M_{\textbf{time for AT application}}$ is 2 *minutes*. This value is below the defined threshold of 40 *minutes*, thus, $H_{\textbf{effort is low}}$ is accepted.

Analysis: How much creation effort can software architects save when applying ATs? The measurement on effort savings for software architects ($Q_{\textbf{effort saving}}$) are depicted in the second measurement group in Table C.9.

Measurement description. As in the CloudStore case study, $M_{\Delta\textbf{time}}$ was not measured because of a missing control group. However, we have taken measurements for the remaining difference metrics ($M_{\Delta\textbf{components}}$, $M_{\Delta\textbf{assembly ctx.}}$, $M_{\Delta\textbf{operations}}$, $M_{\Delta\textbf{self-adapt.}}$).

The measurement of $M_{\Delta\textbf{components}}$ has yielded 13 components to acknowledge for the additional components of Hadoop's processing pipeline. Similarly, the measurement of $M_{\Delta\textbf{assembly ctx.}}$ has yielded 22 assembly contexts (21 assembly contexts for Hadoop's processing pipeline and 1 assembly context for an additional replica of the map assembly context). Moreover, the measurement of $M_{\Delta\textbf{operations}}$ has yielded 29 operations because of additional operations used by the processing pipeline. Because we modeled a static pipeline, i.e., a non-self-adaptive system, the measurement of $M_{\Delta\textbf{self.-adapt.}}$ has yielded 0 lines of code.

Hypothesis testing. These measurements allow to accept $H_{\textbf{effort is lowered}}$. In contrast, $H_{\Delta\textbf{time-}\Delta\textbf{size correlation}}$ cannot be tested because of the missing measurements for $M_{\Delta\textbf{time}}$—analogously to the CloudStore case study.

No measurement for the metrics $M_{\Delta\textbf{components}}$, $M_{\Delta\textbf{assembly ctx.}}$, $M_{\Delta\textbf{operations}}$, and $M_{\Delta\textbf{self-adapt.}}$ is negative. Therefore, $H_{\textbf{effort is lowered}}$ can directly be accepted.

Analysis: Do software architects effectively benefit from checking whether their architectural models violate conformance to applied ATs? The measurement on conformance checking ($Q_{\textbf{conformance}}$) are depicted in the third measurement group in Table C.9.

Measurement description. We did not detect conformance violations, thus, the measurement of $M_{\textbf{\#detected violations}}$ is 0. Consequently, the measurement for $M_{\textbf{\#resolved violations}}$ must be 0 as well.

Hypothesis testing. Because no violations were detected, hypothesis $H_{\textbf{violations are detected}}$ is rejected. Testing $H_{\textbf{violations are resolved}}$ is useless for the case of 0 detected violations.

Analysis: What are effective benefits of the AT method? The measurement on benefits ($Q_{\mathbf{benefits}}$) are depicted in the fourth measurement group in Table C.9.

Measurement description. The measurement of $M_{\mathbf{benefits}}$ has resulted in the 2 collected benefits given in Table C.7.

Hypothesis testing. Because benefits were identified, $H_{\mathbf{benefits\ exist}}$ is accepted.

Analysis: What are effective limitations of the AT method? The measurement on limitations ($Q_{\mathbf{limitations}}$) are depicted in the fifth measurement group in Table C.9.

Measurement description. The measurement of $M_{\mathbf{limitations}}$ has resulted in the 3 collected limitations given in Table C.7.

Hypothesis testing. Because limitations were identified, $H_{\mathbf{limitations\ exist}}$ is accepted.

Analysis: How much effort do AT engineers require for specifying ATs? The measurement on the effort of AT engineers ($Q_{\mathbf{specification\ effort}}$) are depicted in the sixth measurement group in Table C.9.

Measurement description. Like in the CloudStore case study, we have structured the measurements for $M_{\mathbf{time\ for\ AT\ specification}}$ along the four main AT specification actions from Section 4.1.3: (1) the identification of QoS properties and a suitable analysis approach ($M_{\mathbf{time\ for\ identification}}$), (2) the selection of reusable knowledge ($M_{\mathbf{time\ for\ selection}}$), (3) the specification of ATs ($M_{\mathbf{time\ for\ specification}}$), and (4) the assurance of the quality of the specified ATs ($M_{\mathbf{time\ for\ quality\ assur.}}$). Again, our time measurements are post-mortem estimates because we did not use a controlled environment to take these measurements.

The QoS property of interest (performance) was given in the WordCount case, which allowed us to quickly agree on using Palladio as a suitable architectural analysis approach. The time we spend on the first action was therefore only approximately 1 *hour*.

We already had prior experience with Apache's Hadoop MapReduce, which required us to spend only 2 *hours* to agree on a common understanding and its selection ($M_{\textbf{time for selection}}$). We have mainly spent the time to understand the generic and custom parts of Hadoop's processing pipeline as described in Section C.2.1.

Moreover, we have estimated the time for $M_{\textbf{time for specification}}$ to be approximately 2.5 *person months*. This estimate is based on the time that Saxena was expected to have spent in this Master's thesis [Sax15] on creating a reference architectural model. My work of creating an AT that utilizes this reference architectural model as initiator template sums up to approximately 4 *hours*, which are included in the given estimate.

Moreover, I have spent approximately 4 *hours* on quality assurance (metric $M_{\textbf{time for quality assur.}}$). After the initial specification of the AT, I had to fix 2 detected faults in the completion of the AT; other elements were correct.

Being the same metric, the number of AT roles ($M_{\textbf{\#AT roles}}$) yields the same as for the first research question (i.e., 2 roles). Moreover, the AT includes 2 constraints that ensure that the map and reduce roles can only be applied to assembly contexts ($M_{\textbf{\#AT constraints}}$). The lines of code of the AT's completions ($M_{\textbf{\#completion LOC}}$) are 244 lines of code.

Hypothesis testing. These measurements allow to accept $H_{\textbf{effort is high}}$. $H_{\textbf{time-size correlation}}$ cannot be tested because more time and size samples are needed to calculate the Pearson correlation coefficient.

We have further divided the measurement of $M_{\textbf{time for AT specification}}$ into four more detailed measurements: $M_{\textbf{time for identification}}$, $M_{\textbf{time for selection}}$, $M_{\textbf{time for specification}}$, and $M_{\textbf{time for quality assur.}}$. With over 2.5 *person months*, the sum over these measurements is greater than the defined threshold of 6.5 *hours*. $H_{\textbf{effort is high}}$ is therefore accepted.

Analysis: Does quality assurance effectively help AT engineers to improve the conceptual integrity of specified ATs? The measurement on the effectivity of the AT method's quality assurance ($Q_{\textbf{quality assurance}}$) are depicted in the seventh measurement group in Table C.9.

Measurement description. The measurements for $M_{\#\textbf{detected errors}}$ show that we detected 2 errors in total. Our measurement of $M_{\#\textbf{resolved errors}}$ shows that we were successful in resolving these errors.

Hypothesis testing. We accept both hypothesis $H_{\textbf{errors are detected}}$ and hypothesis $H_{\textbf{errors are resolved}}$ because we detected 2 errors that we were able to resolve.

C.2.3.3. WordCount: Interpretation

Based on the data analysis in the previous section, this section proceeds with answering the associated questions of the GQM plan (cf. Table 5.1 in Section 5.2).

Answering $Q_{\textbf{application effort}}$: How much effort do software architects require to apply ATs? The acceptance of $H_{\textbf{effort is low}}$ shows that the application of the *Hadoop MapReduce* AT involves minor effort for software architects—the AT-based initialization of WordCount's architectural model took us less than 2 *minutes*. We expect that this result can be generalized to other AT-based initializations because the initialization wizard requires no complicated configuration and automates most creation tasks; selecting a default AT instance is enough.

Answering $Q_{\textbf{effort saving}}$: How much creation effort can software architects save when applying ATs? The acceptance of $H_{\textbf{effort is lowered}}$ indicates that effort can effectively be lowered by applying ATs. An interesting observation is that, compared to the size-based metric measurements in the CloudStore case study, the measurements of size-based metrics are significantly higher for the *Hadoop MapReduce* AT. Furthermore, the *Hadoop MapReduce* AT is the first inspected AT for which $M_{\Delta\textbf{operations}}$ is positive.

We account both of these observations to the fact that we captured a reference architecture within the AT; opposed to the architectural styles and architectural patterns captured during the CloudStore case study. As described in Section 2.2.4.3, reference architectures can provide additional component interfaces with additional operations, define an architectural style, and group sets of architectural patterns. Based on this definition, the higher values for the taken metric measurements can be explained.

We conclude that ATs of reference architectures can save software architects more effort than ATs that capture different kinds of architectural knowledge. However, we note that reference architectures have the downside of being domain-specific (cf. Section 2.2.4.3), thus, being not as universally applicable as architectural styles and architectural patterns.

Answering $Q_{\textbf{conform.}}$: Do software architects effectively benefit from checking whether their architectural models violate conformance to applied ATs? The rejection of $H_{\textbf{violations are detected}}$ indicates that—at least for WordCount and the *Hadoop MapReduce* AT—no benefits were gained from automated conformance checks. However, that such benefits generally exist has been shown during the CloudStore case study.

Two factors about the *Hadoop MapReduce* AT make it hard to cause conformance violations at all. First, the AT contains only two constraints; each checking that roles are bound to the correct architectural element (i.e., to assembly contexts). However, AT tooling allows only to bind roles to the correct elements; the tool does not allow binding roles to wrong target elements. Second, the AT-based initialization also prevents software architects from violating conformance compared to a completely manually created architectural model.

In such situations, software architects do not necessarily require conformance checks. Fortunately, software architects then face situations where conformance violations are unlikely—grounded in the capabilities of applied ATs and AT tooling.

Answering $Q_{\textbf{benefits}}$: What are effective benefits of the AT method? The 2 benefits collected during the case study ($M_{\textbf{benefits}}$) confirm the answers that we have given for $Q_{\textbf{application effort}}$ and $Q_{\textbf{effort saving}}$: we were clearly impressed by the little effort we have spent to model a complex Hadoop-based system.

The first benefit ("we had very little effort with the AT-based instantiation of the architectural model") covers the effort aspect. As our measurements show, we only required 2 *minutes* for the instantiation of the model, which confirms our impression.

The second benefit ("the bound AT heavily reduces the complexity of the underlying Hadoop infrastructure") covers the complexity aspect. Indeed, we had minor analyzing effort using our architectural model; compared to setting up, running, and analyzing the Apache Hadoop application on actual hardware.

We conclude that we were able to confirm the main promise of the AT method, i.e., to make software architects more efficient.

Answering $Q_{\text{limitations}}$: What are effective limitations of the AT method?
The 3 limitations collected during the case study ($M_{\textbf{limitations}}$) point to current drawbacks of the *Hadoop MapReduce* AT and in SimuLizar.

The first limitation ("the AT is currently inflexible and misses parameters, e.g., for configuring the number of map and reduce replicas") shows that the AT is only a first proof-of-concept for an AT-based initialization. Future work is needed to make the AT more flexible, however, the proof-of-concept of an AT-based initialization was successful.

The second limitation ("the AT-annotated architectural model appears incomplete because map and reduce assembly context are unconnected") points to a potential visualization issue of AT-based architectural models. Due to the fact that missing elements are created by AT completions, AT-based architectural models potentially appear incomplete as, e.g., shown in Figure C.17. A possible solution to this issue is to provide software architects with a view on the architectural model that previews the elements to be generated, e.g., by depicting missing elements in a greyed-out form along with the remaining elements. Future work may inspect this issue further.

The third limitation ("the applied analysis tool (SimuLizar) lacks support for asynchronous map and reduce tasks, which can generally lead to inaccurate analysis results") relates to a tooling issue in SimuLizar; i.e., a tool on which AT tooling depends. Saxena [Sax15, Sec. 7] has identified this issue in his Master's thesis and reports on it in detail. Because the issue influences prediction accuracy, Saxena suggests improving SimuLizar with support for asynchronous communication. Rathfelder [Rat13] provides a good starting point for such an improvement because he describes such an improvement for other Palladio analysis tools, e.g., for SimuCom.

Answering $Q_{\textbf{specification effort}}$: How much effort do AT engineers require for specifying ATs? The acceptance of $H_{\textbf{effort is high}}$ again confirms that AT engineers have high efforts for specifying ATs (compared to the overall efforts for specifying architectural models). In contrast to the CloudStore case study, the specification of the AT itself has caused the most effort, i.e., approximately 2.5 *person months*.

We had high efforts in this step because Saxena's reference model has required extensive investigations of and experimentation with Hadoop's processing pipeline. We suspect that such an amount of effort can even be generalized to most reference architectures, given their typically high amount of (domain-specific) design decisions. However, we expect that such efforts pay-off when captured in ATs that are reused often.

Our inability to test $H_{\textbf{time-size correlation}}$ suggests more experiments that can provide the required data. In the CloudStore case study, we have established first results in this direction, however, not with focus on an AT-based initialization of architectural models. Future work may continue with investigations in this direction.

Answering $Q_{\textbf{quality assurance}}$: Does quality assurance effectively help AT engineers to improve the conceptual integrity of specified ATs? The acceptance of hypothesis $H_{\textbf{errors are detected}}$ and hypothesis $H_{\textbf{errors are resolved}}$ indicates that the AT method's quality assurance helps in effectively improving conceptual integrity of specified ATs. The discussion of this result is analogous to the CloudStore case study in Section C.1.4.5.

C.2.3.4. WordCount: Evaluation of Validity

Compared to the CloudStore case study, we conducted the WordCount case study with an AT that can be used as initiator template. The WordCount case study therefore provides an additional view on the AT method, thus, reducing threats of uncovered properties of the AT method.

Threats in this case study mainly relate to the fact that only a single AT is investigated. For example, the "low statistical power" threat as described in Section C.1.4.6 is even more crucial in the WordCount case study and motivates the conduction of further experiments on ATs with default AT instances. Also other threats are similar to the threats described for the CloudStore case study; these threats are therefore not discussed again in this section.

C.3. Case Study Report: Znn.com

In this section, we outline a case study where a student, Igor Rogic [Rog16], has applied ATs to analyzing the elastic news service Znn.com [CGS09]. The Znn.com case study serves as an external validation of AT application; I only interacted with the student via mail in case of concrete questions.

In summary, the goal of the Znn.com case study was to:

Analyze: the AT method

For the purpose of: conducting architectural analyses *for determining suitable parameters for elasticity mechanisms*

With respect to: effectivity and efficiency

From the viewpoint of: *external software architects*

In the context of: realistic *distributed and cloud computing* systems.

The context of the goal particularly shows that the goal's context has not changed compared to the CloudStore case study (Section C.1). Therefore, the expectation is that ATs that we have specified during the CloudStore case study can be reused for Znn.com. Rogic has indeed applied the *horizontal scaling* AT for resource containers to model and analyze Znn.com's elasticity mechanism [Rog16, Sec. 4.2], thus, meeting this expectation. However, he was only partially successful in interpreting architectural analysis results, which points to learnability problems of architectural analysis approaches.

To summarize and detail these results, the remainder of this section describes the Znn.com case study. Analogously to the preceding case studies, the section follows the reporting guidelines for case studies by Runeson and Höst [RH09]. After Section C.3.1 details the Znn.com service, Section C.3.2 describes the design of the case study as a refinement of the generic evaluation design from Section 5.2. Section C.3.3 provides the results of the case study, including an interpretation and discussion of threats to validity.

C.3.1. Znn.com

Znn.com [CGS09] represents a typical news service with the goal of providing news content to customers within reasonable response time. Figure C.19 illustrates Znn.com via an architectural model. The model contains two assembly contexts: News Service and News Database Access. Each assembly context is allocated to a dedicated resource container, i.e., to Application Server and Database Server, respectively. News customers can request news via the INews interface. To answer such requests, News Service requests appropriate news items via the IDB interface from News Database Access.

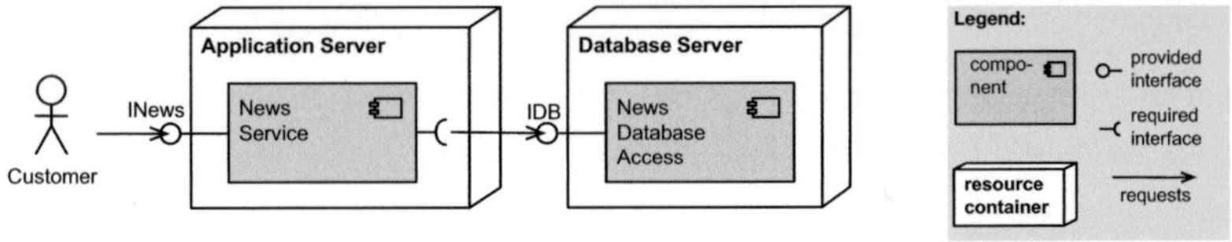

Figure C.19.: PCM model of the Znn.com news service (based on [Rog16, Sec. 4.2.7]).

C.3.2. Znn.com: Case Study Design

This section describes the design of the Znn.com case study. Section C.3.2.1 briefly points to relevant research questions and procedures for data collection, analysis, and validation. Afterwards, Section C.3.2.2 describes the Znn.com case as a parametrization problem of Znn.com's elasticity mechanism. Involved human subjects (i.e., Rogic and I) are characterized in Section C.3.2.3.

C.3.2.1. Znn.com: Research Questions and Procedures

The Znn.com case study provides data to answer the research questions of Section 5.2 related to AT application: $Q_{\textbf{application effort}}$ (How much effort do software architects require to apply ATs?), $Q_{\textbf{effort saving}}$ (How much creation effort can software architects save when applying ATs?), $Q_{\textbf{conformance}}$ (Do software architects effectively benefit from checking whether their architectural models violate conformance to applied ATs?), $Q_{\textbf{benefits}}$ (What are effective benefits of the AT method?), and $Q_{\textbf{limitations}}$ (What are effective limitations of the AT method?). The procedures for data collection, analysis, and validity from Section 5.2 are used to gather, analyze, and validate this data.

C.3.2.2. Znn.com: Case

Due to the nature of news, Znn.com is expected to face varying workloads (cf. [CGS09]), e.g., peak workloads in the event of breaking news. To cope with these varying workloads cost-efficiently, the provider of Znn.com requires that the Znn.com service shall employ elasticity mechanisms. The elasticity mechanisms shall be able to dynamically adapt the number of Znn.com's load-balanced server replicas and Znn.com's content mode (multimedia vs. textual).

Therefore, in the Znn.com case, a software architect has to determine suitable parameters for Znn.com's elasticity mechanisms. Parameters to be determined can relate to the dynamic load-balancing strategy (e.g., the determination of a threshold when a scale-out should be triggered) and the selection strategy of the content mode (e.g., determining a peak workload when content mode should optimally be switched to textual).

Parameters are suitable if Znn.com's SLO—as stated in Table C.10—is fulfilled. The SLO $SLO_{\textbf{Performance}}$ refers to a classical performance metric (response time). In the SLO, Rogic has defined a hard threshold of 0.3 seconds for this metric [Rog16, Sec. 4.2.8]. Moreover, Rogic investigates the fulfillment of this SLO for a workload of 300 concurrent customers [Rog16, Sec. 4.2.6].

Table C.10.: Znn.com's SLO (from [Rog16, Sec. 4.2.8])

$SLO_{\text{Performance}}$: Znn.com responds with a maximum response time of 0.3 seconds.

C.3.2.3. Znn.com: Subjects

The case study on Znn.com was externally conducted by Rogic in the context of his Master's thesis [Rog16]. In the case study, Rogic has acted as software architect following the AT method to determine a suitable configuration of Znn.com's elasticity mechanism. For making the validation external, Rogic and I just agreed on evaluation goals and, subsequently, restricted our interaction to emails (in case of issues with applying the AT method).

Rogic has started the case study with prior experience on Palladio because he worked over half a year on Palladio-related source code as a student worker. His knowledge on conducting architectural analyses was based on papers on Palladio [BKR09], SimuLizar [BBM13], and the AT method [Leh14a]. However, Rogic has not conducted architectural analyses before, thus, can be seen as a novice software architect in this thesis' context.

C.3.3. Znn.com: Results

This section reports the results of the Znn.com case study. The report starts in Section C.3.3.1 with the execution the Znn.com case. The empirical data created during this execution is analyzed in Section C.3.3.2 and interpreted in Section C.3.3.3. Potential threats to validity of the Znn.com case study are finally discussed in Section C.3.3.4.

C.3.3.1. Znn.com: Execution

Acting as software architect, Rogic has applied the *horizontal scaling* AT to the Znn.com model. For this application, he has bound the AT's *horizontal scaling container* role to the Application Server as shown in Figure C.20.

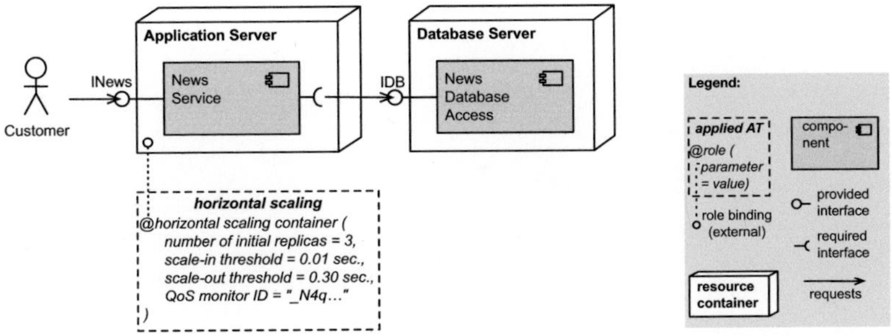

Figure C.20.: The horizontal scaling AT applied to the Znn.com model (based on [Rog16, Sec. 4.2.7]).

In Figure C.20, the actual AT parameter number of initial replicas specifies that Znn.com starts with 3 replicas of the Application Server. This number is dynamically aligned to the response times of the News Service as specified by the *QoS monitor ID* parameter. Replicas are scaled-in if average response times drop below 0.01 *seconds* and scaled-out if they increase beyond the 0.30 *seconds* mark. Therefore, Rogic has defined the 0.30 *seconds* mark according to Znn.com's performance SLO.

Figure C.21 and Figure C.22 show Rogic's results from an architectural analysis of the Znn.com model for a closed workload of 300 *customers*. Over simulation time (X-axis), the Y-axis of Figure C.21 depicts Znn.com's response times while the Y-axis of Figure C.22 depicts the number of Znn.com's resource containers.

Figure C.21 shows that Znn.com's performance SLO is repeatedly violated: most response times are above the 0.30 *seconds* mark. Nonetheless, Figure C.22 shows that, over simulation time, more and more resource containers are added to Znn.com, thus, indicating that the replication mechanism of the applied AT works correctly. At this point, Rogic has however concluded that the applied AT does not behave as expected [Rog16, Sec. 5.1.3] and has stopped his investigation.

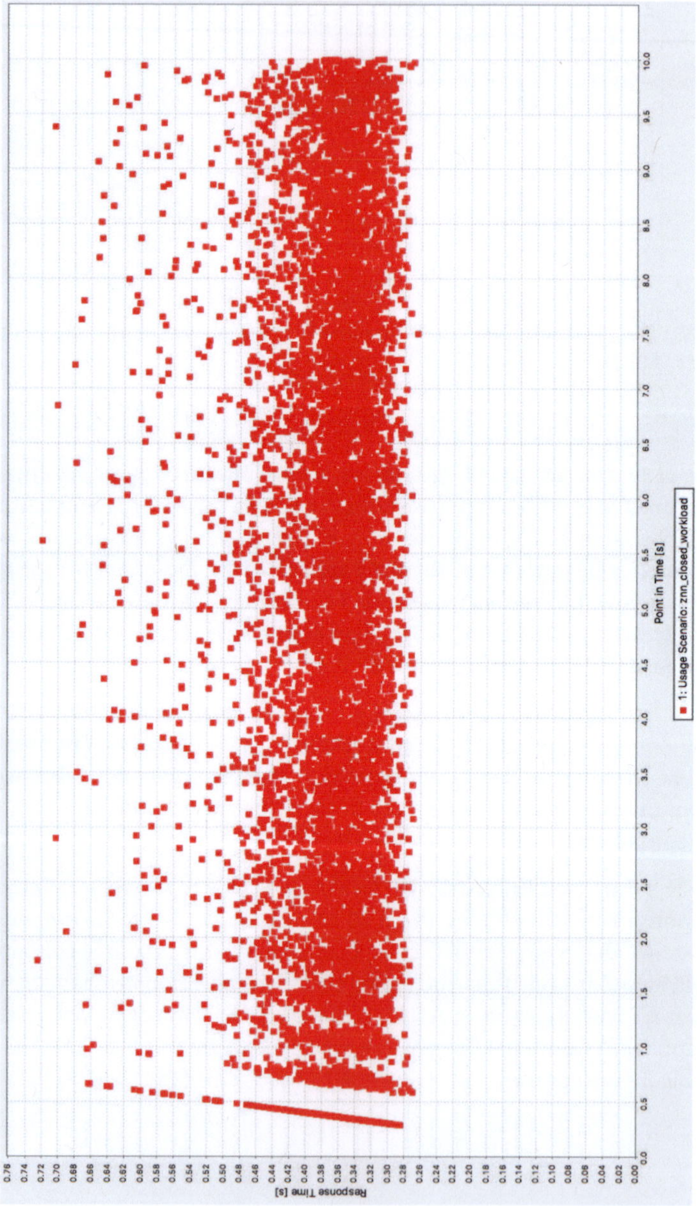

Figure C.21.: Znn.com's response times over simulation time for 300 concurrent customers (from [Rog16, Sec. 5.1.3]).

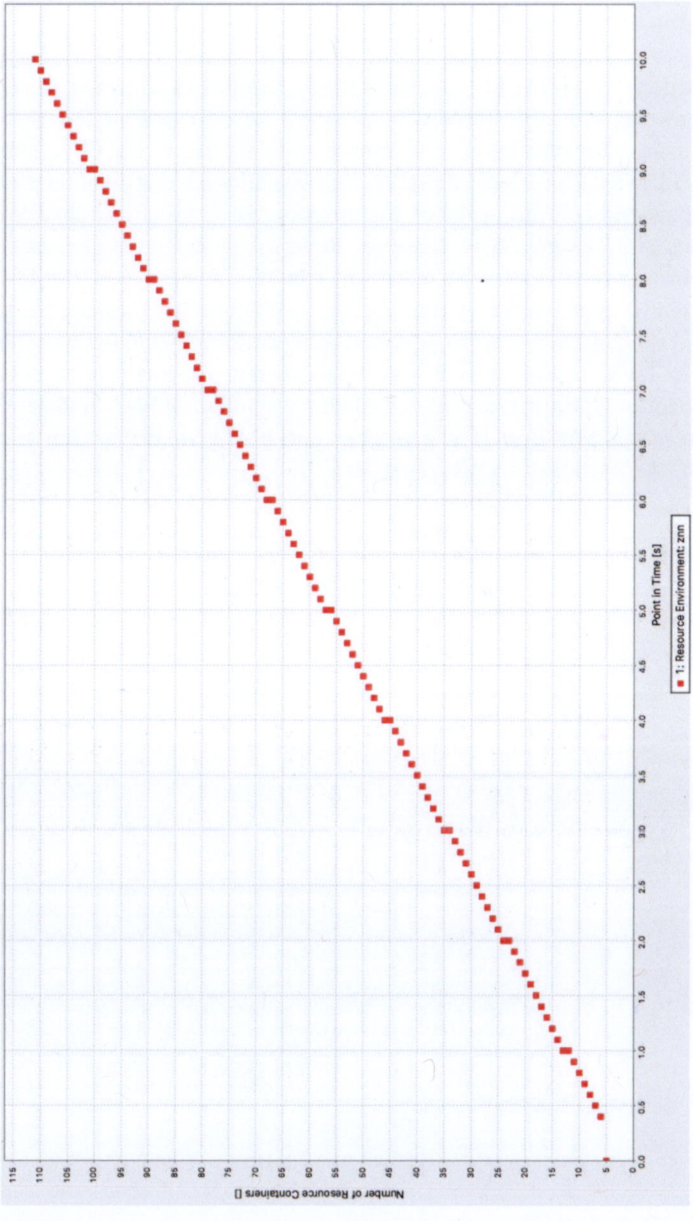

Figure C.22.: Znn.com's number of resource containers over simulation time (from [Rog16, Sec. 5.1.3]).

C.3.3.2. Znn.com: Analysis

In this section, I analyze the empirical data that Rogic has collected during the Znn.com case study. Table C.11 provides an overview of this data; depicted measurements directly correspond to the metrics of the GQM plan (cf. Table 5.1 in Section 5.2). The first column specifies the metric of interest while the second column provides the measurements for the application of the *horizontal scaling* AT to Znn.com. Rows are grouped via horizontal lines according to the research questions from Section 5.2, e.g., the first research question is covered by the first four rows of metric measurements. Structured along these research questions, the corresponding measurements depicted in Table C.11 are analyzed in the following. The analysis covers a brief description of the measurements and the test of hypotheses associated to each research question. The interpretation of the analysis is left to a dedicated interpretation section (Section C.3.3.3).

Table C.11.: Metric measurements collected in the Znn.com case study

	horizontal scaling (resource container)
$M_{\textbf{time for modeling and analysis}}$	46 *hours*
$M_{\textbf{\#ATs}}$	7
$M_{\textbf{\#AT roles}}$	1
$M_{\textbf{\#AT parameters}}$	4
$M_{\Delta\textbf{time}}$	-
$M_{\Delta\textbf{components}}$	1
$M_{\Delta\textbf{assembly ctx.}}$ *	r
$M_{\Delta\textbf{operations}}$	0
$M_{\Delta\textbf{self-adapt.}}$	803
$M_{\textbf{\#detected violations}}$	0
$M_{\textbf{\#resolved violations}}$	0
$M_{\textbf{benefits}}$	"the *horizontal scaling* AT—specified in the context of the CloudStore case study—has been reused during the Znn.com case study", "a novice software architect was able to correctly apply an AT and to conduct an AT-based architectural analysis"
$M_{\textbf{limitations}}$	"the software architect has suspected the AT to be faulty based on unsatisfying analysis results; however, the unsatisfying results were caused by a performance bottleneck unrelated to the applied AT", "mail support was required pointing to the Experimentation Automation Framework for conducting AT-based analyses"

* r denotes the number of initial replicas with $r \geq 1$.

Analysis: How much effort do software architects require to apply ATs?
The measurement on the effort of software architects ($Q_{\textbf{application effort}}$) are depicted in the first measurement group in Table C.11.

Measurement description. For specifying the complete architectural model, Rogic reports an effort of approximately 46 *hours* [Rog16, Sec. 5.2]. However, he provides no per-action information about the consumed time for AT selection and application. Therefore, Table C.11 only reports the total of 46 *hours* that Rogic required for modeling and analyzing Znn.com ($M_{\textbf{time for modeling and analysis}}$).

As shown in Table C.7, Rogic selected the *horizontal scaling* AT from the catalog of 7 ATs ($M_{\textbf{\#ATs}}$) that we have created during the CloudStore case study. As before, the *horizontal scaling* AT contains 1 role and 4 parameters ($M_{\textbf{\#AT roles}}$ and $M_{\textbf{\#AT parameters}}$).

Hypothesis testing. These measurements alone make it impossible to test hypotheses $H_{\textbf{time-size correlation}}$ and $H_{\textbf{effort is low}}$. To test $H_{\textbf{time-size correlation}}$, more time and size samples are needed to calculate the Pearson correlation coefficient. To test $H_{\textbf{effort is low}}$, per-action information about the consumed time for AT selection and application are needed.

Analysis: How much creation effort can architects save when applying ATs?
The measurement on effort savings for software architects ($Q_{\textbf{effort saving}}$) are depicted in the second measurement group in Table C.11.

Measurement description. As in the CloudStore case study, $M_{\Delta\textbf{time}}$ was not measured because of a missing control group. However, Rogic [Rog16, Sec. 5.2] has taken measurements for the remaining difference metrics ($M_{\Delta\textbf{components}}$, $M_{\Delta\textbf{assembly ctx.}}$, $M_{\Delta\textbf{operations}}$, $M_{\Delta\textbf{self-adapt.}}$).

The measurement of $M_{\Delta\textbf{components}}$ has yielded 1 component to acknowledge for the additional component acting as loadbalancer. The *horizontal scaling* ATs for resource containers create a loadbalancer and as many replicas of the News Service assembly contexts as specified by the *number of (initial) replicas* parameter of these ATs. Therefore, the measurement of $M_{\Delta\textbf{assembly ctx.}}$ has yielded r assembly contexts. For example, if $r = 1$, only a loadbalancer is attached in front of the Application Server but no additional assembly contexts have to be created. For $r = 2$, an additional instance of the News Service assembly context is allocated to the Application Server. The measurement of $M_{\Delta\textbf{operations}}$ has yielded 0 operations because no additional operations were introduced in the AT. The measurement of $M_{\Delta\textbf{self.-adapt.}}$ has yielded 803 lines of code; the same value as was measured during the CloudStore case study.

Hypothesis testing. These measurements allow to accept $H_{\textbf{effort is lowered}}$. In contrast, $H_{\Delta\textbf{time-}\Delta\textbf{size correlation}}$ cannot be tested because of the missing measurements for $M_{\Delta\textbf{time}}$—analogously to the CloudStore case study.

No measurement for the metrics $M_{\Delta\textbf{components}}$, $M_{\Delta\textbf{assembly ctx.}}$, $M_{\Delta\textbf{operations}}$, and $M_{\Delta\textbf{self-adapt.}}$ is negative. Therefore, $H_{\textbf{effort is lowered}}$ can directly be accepted.

Analysis: Do software architects effectively benefit from checking whether their architectural models violate conformance to applied ATs? The measurement on conformance checking ($Q_{\textbf{conformance}}$) are depicted in the third measurement group in Table C.11.

Measurement description. Rogic does not report on detected conformance violations, thus, the measurement of $M_{\textbf{\#detected violations}}$ is 0. Consequently, $M_{\textbf{\#resolved violations}}$ must be 0 as well.

Hypothesis testing. Because no violations were detected, hypothesis $H_{\textbf{violations are detected}}$ is rejected. Testing hypothesis $H_{\textbf{violations are resolved}}$ is useless for the case of 0 detected violations.

Analysis: What are effective benefits of the AT method? The measurement on benefits ($Q_{\textbf{benefits}}$) are depicted in the fourth measurement group in Table C.11.

Measurement description. The measurement of $M_{\textbf{benefits}}$ has resulted in the 2 collected benefits given in Table C.7. Because Rogic has not explicitly collected benefits on his own, I derived these benefits from Rogic's conduction of the case study.

Hypothesis testing. Because benefits were identified, $H_{\textbf{benefits exist}}$ is accepted.

Analysis: What are effective limitations of the AT method? The measurement on limitations ($Q_{\mathbf{limitations}}$) are depicted in the fifth measurement group in Table C.11.

Measurement description. The measurement of $M_{\mathbf{limitations}}$ has resulted in the 2 collected limitations given in Table C.7. Similar to benefits, I derived these limitations from Rogic's conduction of the case study.

Hypothesis testing. Because limitations were identified, $H_{\mathbf{limitations\ exist}}$ is accepted.

C.3.3.3. Znn.com: Interpretation

Based on the data analysis in the previous section, this section proceeds with answering the associated questions of the GQM plan (cf. Table 5.1 in Section 5.2).

Answering $Q_{\mathbf{application\ effort}}$: How much effort do software architects require to apply ATs? The data provided by Rogic unfortunately does not allow an interpretation based on the posed hypotheses, especially since Rogic has only measured the total time for creating and analyzing Znn.com's architectural model and not the exclusive time for AT-related actions.

However, Rogic's total time of 46 *hours* can be compared to the total time of 214 *hours* for the creation of the CloudStore model (cf. Section C.1.1). Because we required approximately 4.5 times more time to create the CloudStore model, CloudStore can be considered significantly more complex than Znn.com.

A lowered complexity of Znn.com (compared to CloudStore) implies different expectations for its evaluation. For example, it is less likely that conformance to applied reusable architectural knowledge is violated and less benefits and limitations may be observed during the conduction of the case study. When answering the subsequent questions, the lowered complexity of Znn.com is therefore taken into account.

Answering $Q_{\text{effort saving}}$: How much creation effort can software architects save when applying ATs? The acceptance of $H_{\text{effort is lowered}}$ indicates that effort can effectively be lowered by applying ATs. The interpretation of this result is analogous to the CloudStore case study because the *horizontal scaling* AT was applied there as well.

Answering $Q_{\text{conform.}}$: Do software architects effectively benefit from checking whether their architectural models violate conformance to applied ATs? The rejection of $H_{\text{violations are detected}}$ indicates that—at least for Znn.com and the *horizontal scaling* AT—no benefits were gained from automated conformance checks. That such benefits generally exist has been shown during the CloudStore case study, however, even in the CloudStore case study, only other ATs than the *horizontal scaling* AT have triggered conformance violations.

A possible explanation for these observations is that software architects apply the *horizontal scaling* AT correctly because it involves no complex constraints. Indeed, the constraints of this AT mainly check that actual parameters are set correctly, e.g., that the *number of initial replicas* is positive. Software architects potentially do not violate such constraints as parameter names often suggest valid values intuitively. Future investigations may provide more conclusive answers for this question.

Answering Q_{benefits}: What are effective benefits of the AT method? The 2 benefits collected during the case study (M_{benefits}) indicate that even novice software architects can reuse pre-specified ATs and correctly apply these ATs to architectural models.

The first benefit ("the *horizontal scaling* AT—specified in the context of the CloudStore case study—has been reused during the Znn.com case study") covers the reuse aspect. Because Rogic was able to reuse the previously specified *horizontal scaling* AT within another case study, reuse of ATs is possible. This result holds at least for intra-domain reuse: both CloudStore and Znn.com are located in the context of distributed and cloud computing systems. The *horizontal scaling* AT particularly captures a typical cloud computing architectural pattern [EPM13, FLR+14]. More general ATs like the *three-layer* AT potentially allow for an inter-domain reuse; however, this expectation requires confirmation in future empirical studies.

The second benefit ("a novice software architect was able to correctly apply an AT and to conduct an AT-based architectural analysis") points to a main benefit of the AT method—an increased efficiency of software architects. As the benefit shows, an increased efficiency (due to the time-efficient application of reusable architectural knowledge) is not only achieved for expert software architects. An increase efficiency is particularly achieved for novice software architects without deep architectural knowledge—because the required architectural knowledge is correctly captured within ATs.

Answering $Q_{\text{limitations}}$: What are effective limitations of the AT method?
The 2 limitations collected during the case study ($M_{\textbf{limitations}}$) show that software architects may distrust ATs and that the tooling extended by the AT method requires improvement.

The first limitation ("the software architect has suspected the AT to be faulty based on unsatisfying analysis results; however, the unsatisfying results were caused by a performance bottleneck unrelated to the applied AT") covers the distrust aspect. An inspection of Znn.com's Database Server after re-analyzing the Znn.com model shows that this server is over-utilized and cannot cope with the number of requests. Therefore, Znn.com is unable to scale by adding additional Application Servers—a similar results as we have observed during the CloudStore case study (Section C.1). To resolve this issue Rogic could have, for example, increased the processing rate of the Database Server's CPU. The interesting observation, however, is that Rogic did not resolve the issue at all but suspected a faulty AT.

A solution to lower such distrust in ATs is to train software architects more in interpreting analysis results and inspecting the causes of quality issues such as performance bottlenecks. Software architects can also be supported by an automated detection of quality anti-patterns (cf. [BBL17, Chap. 7]) and hotspot detections (cf. [Str13, Sec. 4.3]). Again, further empirical investigations are needed to analyze the impact of these solutions on the trust in ATs of (novice) software architects.

The second limitation ("mail support was required pointing to the Experimentation Automation Framework for conducting AT-based analyses") relates to a tooling issue in the Experimentation Automation Framework as extended by AT tooling (cf. Appendix B.2). In its current form, the Experimentation Automation Framework provides the required functionality to extend architectural analyses with AT support. However, the Experiment Automation Framework lacks an intuitive user interface for configuring architectural analyses. Due to this lack, Rogic has particularly ran into problems to create a correct configuration and, consequently, has requested my support via mail. Upon having received this request, I have pointed Rogic to an example configuration. Based on this example, Rogic finally managed to create a correct configuration to run architectural analyses with the Experimentation Automation Framework.

Given the observed issue, future work should target improving the usability of the Experiment Automation Framework. A promising direction for such an improvement is provided by the CloudScale Environment [Cloa]: the CloudScale Environment also extends the Experiment Automation Framework but enriches it with a dedicated and intuitive user interface. An integration of this user interface into the Experiment Automation Framework itself is, however, missing at the moment.

C.3.3.4. Znn.com: Evaluation of Validity

Compared to the CloudStore case study, the Znn.com case was conducted by an external subject. Therefore, threats related to biases caused by my involvement are less crucial in the Znn.com case study. For example, the "interaction of testing and treatment" threat as described in Section C.1.4.6 is less relevant for the Znn.com case study.

However, most other threats are similar to the threats described for the CloudStore case study. Most prominently, threats related to the fact that only a single subject has executed the case study are relevant. For example, it remains unknown whether other subjects would face the same, different, or no issues when executing the Znn.com case. Given that this threat remains a main threat to the evaluations conducted so far, Section 5.4 pays special attention on this threat by outlining a controlled experiment for evaluating the AT method.

D. Controlled Experiment: Material

This appendix provides the experiment material for a controlled experiment for the AT method as introduced by Nützel [NÏ5, Sec. 3.3]: installation guides for AT tooling and SimuLizar, workshop document, CloudStore description, and task descriptions for the treatment and the control group. In the following, each of these materials is provided in a dedicated section; the materials are described in Section 5.4.1.2

D.1. Installation Guide for AT Tooling

CloudStore Experiment: Installation Guide

1. Download and install the current »Eclipse Modeling Tools« edition available at http://www.eclipse.org/downloads/ (last tested with Eclipse 4.5.1/Mars.1 Release).
2. Start your newly installed Eclipse and go to your update sites (Help -> Install New Software...).
3. Click »Add...« and Enter »Palladio« as »Name« and »https://sdqweb.ipd.kit.edu/eclipse/palladiosimulator/releases/latest/« as »Location«.
4. Click »Select All«, hit »Next >« (2 times), accept the licencse agreement, and click »Finish«.
5. After restart, add another update site (Help -> Install New Software...) with »Architectural Templates« as »Name« and »https://github.com/PalladioSimulator/Architectural-Templates« as »Location«.
6. Click »Select All«, hit »Next >« (2 times), accept the licencse agreement, and click »Finish«.
7. After a successful installation, switch to the »Palladio« perspective for executing the next steps (Window -> Open Perspective -> Other... -> Palladio).
8. Import the CloudStore model from the zip-file we provided to you (File -> Import... -> Existing Projects into Workspace -> Next > -> Select archive file: CloudStoreWithATs.zip -> Finish)

CloudScale 1

D.2. Installation Guide for SimuLizar

CloudStore Experiment: Installation Guide

1. Download and install the current »Eclipse Modeling Tools« edition available at http://www.eclipse.org/downloads/ (last tested with Eclipse 4.5.1/Mars.1 Release).
2. Start your newly installed Eclipse and go to your update sites (Help -> Install New Software...).
3. Click »Add...« and Enter »Palladio« as »Name« and »https://sdqweb.ipd.kit.edu/eclipse/palladiosimulator/releases/latest/« as »Location«.
4. Click »Select All«, hit »Next >« (2 times), accept the licencse agreement, and click »Finish«.
5. After restart, add another update site (Help -> Install New Software...) with »Architectural Templates« as »Name« and »https://github.com/PalladioSimulator/Architectural-Templates« as »Location«.
6. Click »Select All«, hit »Next >« (2 times), accept the licencse agreement, and click »Finish«.
7. After a successful installation, switch to the »Palladio« perspective for executing the next steps (Window -> Open Perspective -> Other... -> Palladio).
8. Import the CloudStore model from the zip-file we provided to you (File -> Import... -> Existing Projects into Workspace -> Next > -> Select archive file: CloudStoreWithSimuLizar.zip -> Finish)

Screencapture

Finally, we'd like you to capture your screen for all tasks you conduct within the controlled experiment. The experiment description explicitely states the point in time when you need to activate the capture tool. (If you are unwilling to capture, please provide a brief rationale.)

Use the capture tool of your preferenece. On Windows, we suggest the free capture tool »CamStudio« (http://sourceforge.net/projects/camstudio/). On Mac, we suggest the commercial capture tool »Camtasia« (ask Sebastian for a license).

CloudScale 1

D.3. Workshop Document

Engineering a Web Application with Palladio (Version 2.0)

The goal of this workshop is to engineer a web application with Palladio. For this workshop, a web application consists of a web interface allowing users to submit their fore- and surname into a database.

The workshop presents the tasks of modeling the web application and performing performance analyses step-by-step. It is based on the Palladio screencast series available at http://www.palladio-simulator.com/tools/screencasts/ .

1. Installation [Estimated Time: 20 – 40 min.]

1. Download and install the current »Eclipse Modeling Tools« edition available at http://www.eclipse.org/downloads/ (last tested with Eclipse 4.5.1/Mars.1 Release).
2. Start your newly installed Eclipse and go to your update sites (Help -> Install New Software...).
3. Click »Add...« and Enter »Palladio« as »Name« and »https://sdqweb.ipd.kit.edu/eclipse/palladiosimulator/releases/latest/« as »Location«.
4. Click »Select All«, hit »Next >« (2 times), accept the licencse agreement, and click »Finish«.
5. After restart, add another update site (Help -> Install New Software...) with »Architectural Teamplates« as »Name« and »http://cloudscale.xlab.si/cse/updatesites/architecturaltemplates/nightly/« as »Location«.
6. Click »Select All«, hit »Next >« (2 times), accept the licencse agreement, and click »Finish«.
7. After a successful installation, switch to the »Palladio« perspective for executing the next steps (Window -> Open Perspective -> Other... -> Palladio).

General Information can also be found here: http://sdqweb.ipd.kit.edu/wiki/PCM_Installation

2. Buttons [Estimated Time: 1 min.]

This workshop will refer to these buttons available in a Palladio installation:

From left to right, these buttons are named as follows:

1. New Repository Model Diagram ( )
2. New System Model Diagram ( )
3. New Resource Model Diagram ( )
4. New Allocation Model Diagram ( )
5. New Usage Model Diagram ( )

3. Repository Model [Estimated Time: 15 min.]

A component developer uses the repository model to specify a set of components that can later be deployed within a system. Let us model a database component for storing fore- and surnames as well as a web component allowing to access the database via a web interface.

1. Create a new general project »PalladioProject« (Right-click at the Project Explorer view -> New -> Project... -> General -> Project -> Project Name: »PalladioProject« -> Finish).
2. Select the newly created project and click the »New Repository Model Diagram« ( ) button.
3. Select the newly created project folder and click »Next« (this determines the place to store the repository diagram). You may leave the name (»default.repository_diagram«) as it is.
4. Select the newly created project folder and click »Finish« (this determines the place to store the repository model). You may leave the name (»default.repository«) as it is. The diagram should open; on its right is a palette allowing to add elements to the diagram.
5. Add an »Interface« to the diagram and name it »IWeb«. Add a »Signature« from the palette to this interface. Go to the Properties view and set the signature to »void submit(string name, string forename)«. This models the interface to the web component.
6. Repeat step 5 for the »IWeb« interface providing a service with the signature »void store(string name, string forename)«. This models the database interface providing a service to store a fore- and a surname within a database.
7. Next, we will add the components providing and requiring these interfaces. Add a »BasicComponent« to the diagram. Name it »Web«.
8. Add another »BasicComponent« to the diagram. Name it »Database«.
9. Connect the Database component to the IDatabase interface via a »ProvidedRole« from the palette. Connect Web and IWeb similarly.
10. As the Web component needs to write into a database, connect the Web component with IDatabase via a »RequiredRole« from the palette. Your diagram should look like shown below.

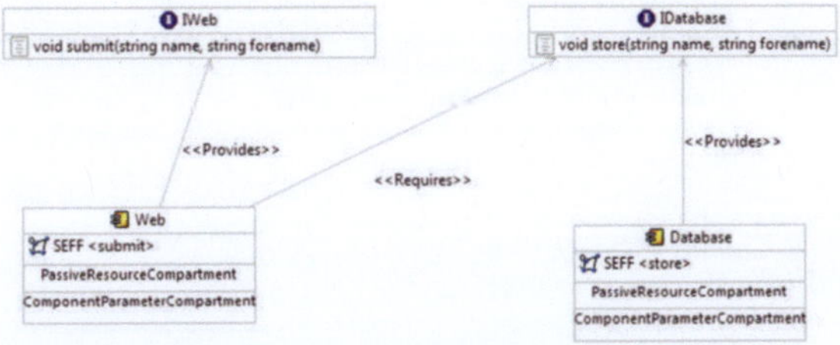

11. Next, we need to specify the behavior of the services our components provide. Therefore, we specify »Service Effect Specifications« (SEFFs) that model the performance-relevant behavior of our services. They are similar to activity diagrams.

- Double click the »SEFF <store>« entry of the Database component. A SEFF diagram editor with a predefined start and stop action opens. Remove the link between these two actions. Next, add an »InternalAction« from the palette to the diagram and name it »storeInternally«.
- Add a »ResourceDemand« from the palette to this action. Select »CPU« and press »OK«. As a stochastic expression, enter »`DoublePMF[ (10;0.3) (20;0.4) (30;0.3) ]`«. This models that our database needs 10 CPU workunits in 30% of the cases to store a name. In 40% of the cases, it needs 20 CPU workunits and in 30% of the cases, it needs 30 CPU workunits. You may use the »Help« button as an online help within the stochastic expression editor to look up the meaning of these stochastic expressions.
- Add another »Resource Demand« to the action. This time, select »HDD« and enter »`100`« as a stochastic expression. This models that the database also needs 100 HDD workunits (constantly, in all of the cases).
- Connect the start action with the »storeInternally« action via a »Control Flow« link from the palette. Analogously, connect »storeInternally« with the end action. Your diagram should look like shown below. You can save and close the diagram now to get back to the repository diagram.

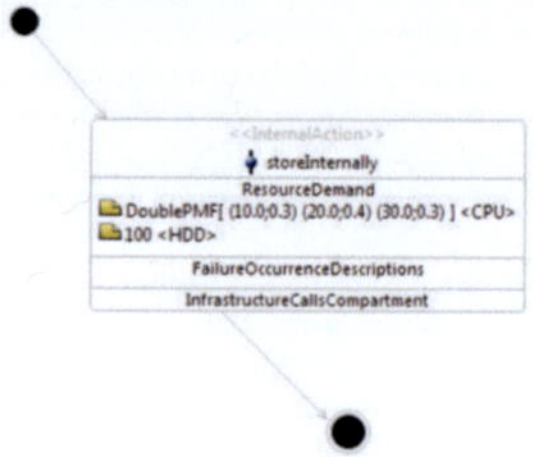

12. Let us also specify the SEFF of the Web component's »submit« service.
    - Double click the »SEFF <submit>« entry of the Web component.
    - Add an »ExternalCallAction« from the palette to the diagram and select the »store« OperationSignature from the dialog that opens. Confirm with »OK«. By this, we model the call to the database from our Web component.
    - Connect the Actions appropriately via »Control Flow« such that you get a diagram like shown below. Save and close the diagram.

13. Save and close the repository diagram.

4. System Model [Estimated Time: 5 min.]

A system architect uses the available components in component repositories (cf. Step 3 – Repository Model) to compose a concrete component-based software system. Let us build such a system for the the components we just created.

1. Click the »New System Model Diagram« () button.
2. Create a new system diagram and model within the »PalladioProject« project folder. The diagram opens with a »defaultSystem« allowing to specify our web application system.
3. Add an »AssemblyContext« from the palette to the »defaultSystem«. Load the repository we created before (Load Repository -> Browse Workspace... -> PalladioProject / default.repository -> OK -> OK). Select the »Database« component and confirm with »OK«.
4. Analogously repeat 3. to add the »Web« component.
5. Connect the two assemblies by using an »AssemblyConnector« from the palette: connect the required interface of »Assembly_Web« with the provided interface of »Assembly_Database«. We now assembled our components within the system.
6. Finally, we need to provide an interface to our system such that it gets accessible by users. Add a »SystemOperationProvidedRole« from the palette to the »defaultSystem« and select the »IWeb« interface. Use an »OperationProvidedDelegationConnector« from the palette to connect the system's provided role to the providing role of the Web assembly.
   You should get a system like shown below. You can save and close the system diagram now.

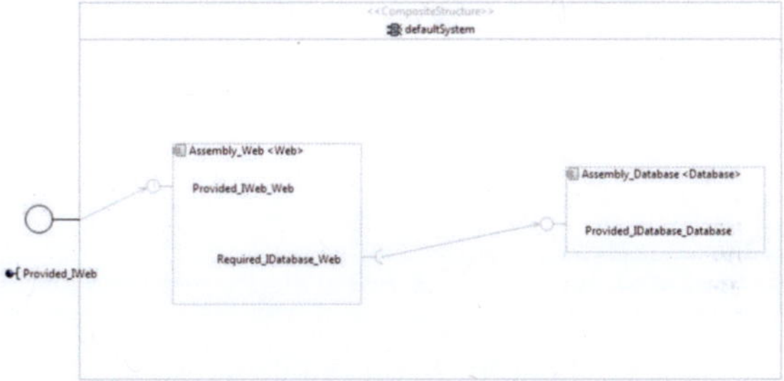

5. Resource Environment [Estimated Time: 5 min.]

A system deployer uses the resource environment to model CPUs, hard disk drives, networks, etc. Let us first consider a single server for our simple web application where we will deploy both, the web and the database components.

1. Click the »New Resource Model Diagram« () button.
2. Create a new resource environment diagram and model within the »PalladioProject« project folder. The diagram opens automatically.

3. Add a »ResourceContainer« from the palette to the diagram and name it »WebServer«.
4. Next we add a CPU specification to the latter container.
   - Add a »ProcessingResourceSpecification« to the newly created resource container. Select »CPU« as processing resource type and confirm with »OK«.
   - A stochastic expression editor pops up in which you specify a processing rate of »10«. This models that our CPU can handle 10 CPU workload units per second. Confirm with »OK«.
   - A new dialog pops up enabling us to select a scheduling policy for our CPU. Select »Processor Sharing« which is a round-robin strategy. This models the scheduler behavior of operating systems in a simplified form. Confirm with »OK«.
5. Analogously repeat 4. for adding a hard disk drive to the WebServer: Select »HDD«, specify a processing rate of »10« modeling that our hard disk drive can handle 10 HDD workload units per second, and select »First-Come-First-Serve« as scheduling policy which models a typical behavior of hard disk drives.

   You should get a resource environment like shown below. You can save and close the resource environment diagram now.

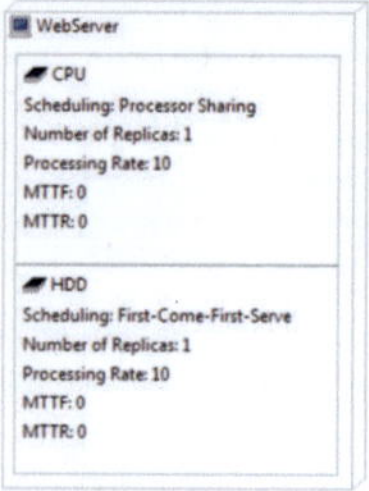

6. Allocation Model [Estimated Time: 5 min.]

Another task for the system deployer is to allocate the components assembled within the system to the resource environment. Let us allocate the system's components to our WebServer.

1. Click the »New Allocation Model Diagram« ( ) button.
2. Create a new allocation diagram and model within the »PalladioProject« project folder. You also have to select the resource environment (»default.resourceenvironment«) and system (»default.system«) from our workspace. The diagram opens automatically after pressing »Finish«. It already includes the WebServer we specified before.
3. Add an »AllocationContext« from the palette to the WebServer. Select the »Assembly_Database« component and confirm with »OK« to allocate it to the WebServer.
4. Proceed analogously with adding the »Assembly_Web« component.

   You should get an allocation like shown below. You can save and close the allocation diagram now.

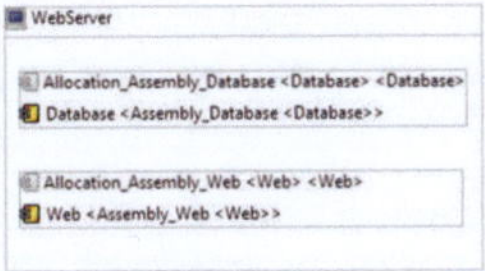

7. Usage Model [Estimated Time: 5 min.]

A domain expert specifies the behavior of users that will use our system. Let us specify that one user repeats submitting fore- and surenames to our web application. After each submit, the user pauses for 10 seconds.

1. Click the »New Usage Model Diagram« ( ) button.
2. Create a new usage diagram and model within the »PalladioProject« project folder. The diagram opens automatically. The diagram already includes a default usage scenario that we will extend.
3. Resize the diagram to your needs. Then add an »EntryLevelSystemCall« from the palette to the diagram. Select the system we specified from your workspace (»default.system«). Then, select the »Provided_IWeb« provided interface of our system and click »OK«. In the next dialog, choose the »submit« operation and confirm with »OK«. This models the call to our system via its provided submit service.
4. Connect the actions appropriately by using the »Usage Flow« links from the palette.
5. Add a »ClosedWorkload« from the palette to our »defaultUsageScenario«. Specify a population of »1« user and a think time of »10« seconds. This models that one user is within our system, calls the submit service of our system, waits for 10 seconds, and finally repeats this process.

   You should get a usage model like shown below. You can save and close the usage diagram now.

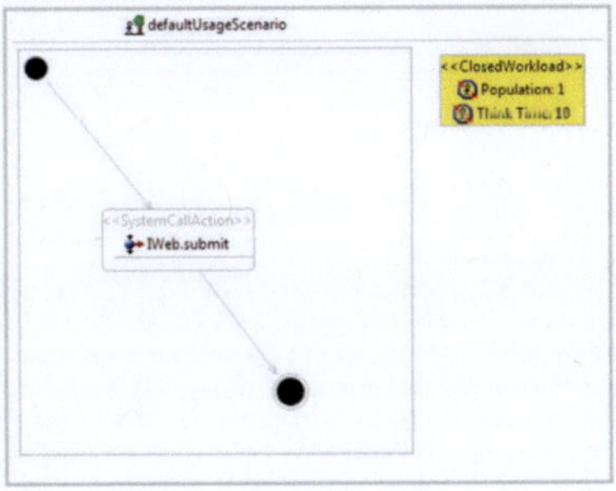

8. Performance Predictions [Estimated Time: 30 min.]

We are now prepared to execute performance predictions of the web application we modeled. This task is usually performed by system architects such that they can evaluate different design alternatives.

1. Open the »Run Configurations« dialog (Run -> Run Configurations...).
2. Doubleclick the »SimuBench« configuration category to create a new run configuration for the SimuCom solver, an often applied solver in Palladio.
3. Name the configuration »SimuCom-WebApplication«.
4. In the »Architecture Model(s)« tab, select the allocation (»default.allocation«) and usage (»default.usagemodel«) models we created from the workspace.
5. In the »Simulation« tab, set the »Experiment Name« to »SimuCom-WebApplication« and set the »Maximum measurement count« to »1000« for shorter simulation times. Finally, browse available »Data sources« for the »Experiment Data Persistency & Presentation (EDP2)« by pressing the »Browse...« button. Press »Add...«, select »In-Memory data source«, and press »Finish«. Select the new »LocalMemoryRepository« for storing our measurement results in main memory.
6. Apply your changes and press the »Run« button. The simulation may take a short while. You can follow the simulation status in the »Console« and the »Simulation Dock Status« views.
7. After the simulation, go to the »Experiments« view. Expand your datasource completely if not already expanded. You should be able to see different entries with measurements taken by different monitors.
8. Let's investigate some of these measurements.
    a. Doubleclick the »Usage Scenario: defaultUsageScenario« entry. Doubleclick the »XY Plot« entry in the dialog that pops up. You will get a diagram similar to the one shown below.

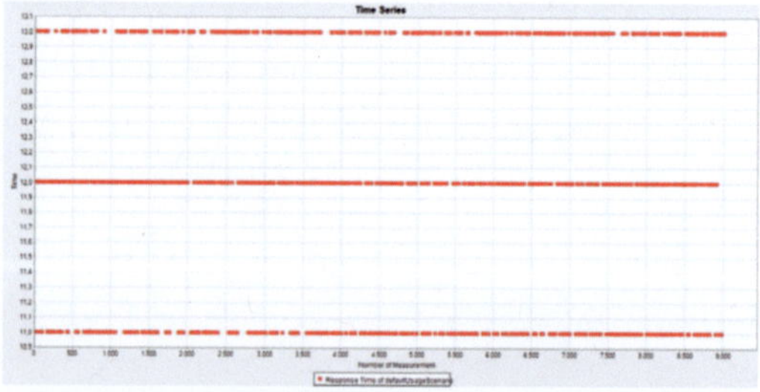

On the x-axis you see the time when the measurement was taken and on the y-axis the response time as measured for the usage scenario. In our scenario, the response time of one measurement is the time that is needed for getting the result of »IWeb.submit« when calling it. The three horizontal lines result from our specification of the demanded CPU workunits as a PMF (10 in 30%, 20 in 40%, and 30 in 30% of the cases). With a CPU processing rate of 10 workunits per second, the CPU can cause 1, 2, or 3 seconds response time. The remaining 10 seconds are caused by the hard disk drive demand (we demanded 100 workunits and have a hard disc processing rate of 10 workunits per second).

b. Let's open a different diagram to see an alternative to an XY Plot. Doubleclick the »Usage Scenario: defaultUsageScenario« entry, again. This time, doubleclick the »Histogram« entry next. You will get a diagram similar to the one shown below.

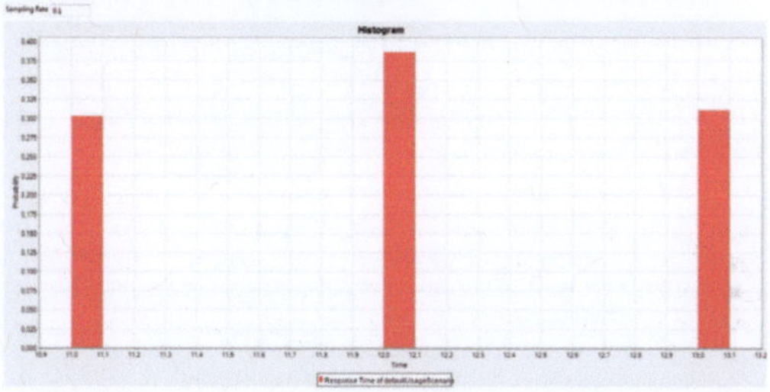

On the x-axis you see response times and on the y-axis the measured probability of a given response time. Here, we clearly see the correspondence of the probabilities we set in the CPU's PMF and the actual measurements (they closely lie around the 30%, 40%, and 30% marks).

c. Let us now have a closer look on the utilization of the CPU. Doubleclick the »CPU [0] in WebServer (State of Active Resource Tuple)« entry for this. Doubleclick the »Pie Chart« entry next. You should get a diagram similar to the one shown below.

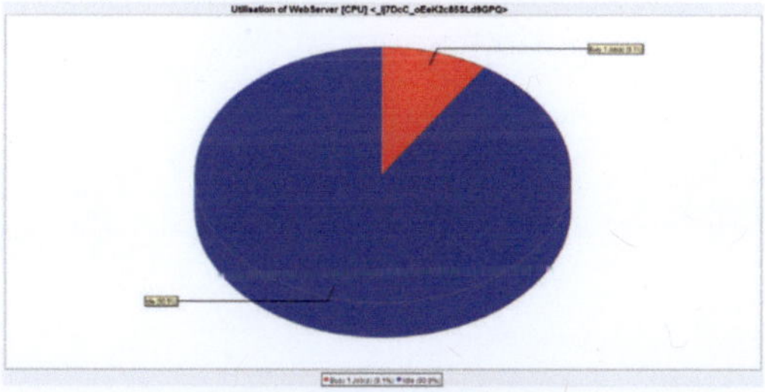

In approximately 9% of the time, the CPU handles 1 job and in 90% of the time, the CPU is idle. Therefore, we do not observe an overload situation here.

d. Now we will similarly investigate the hard disc's utilization. Doubleclick the »HDD [0] in WebServer (State of Active Resource Tuple)« entry for this. Again, doubleclick the »Pie Chart« entry next. You should get a diagram similar to the one shown below.

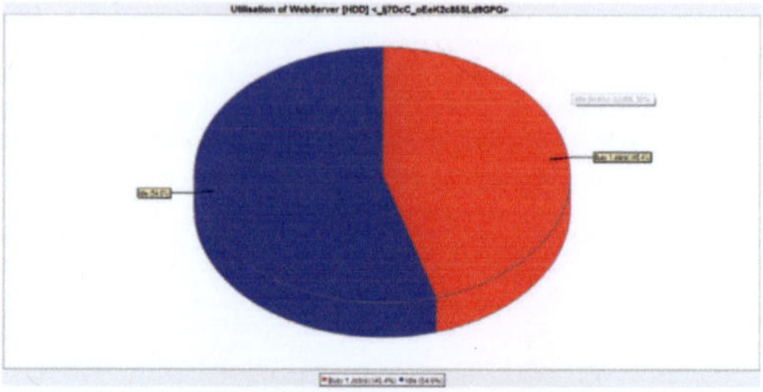

In approximately 45% of the time, the hard disk drive handles 1 job and in 55% of the time, the hard disk drive is idle. Therefore, we also do not observe an overload situation here.

9. At least for one user within our system, the system is predicted to be stable. We may think about using a cheaper CPU as it is in 90% of the time idle.
   However, let's consider another scenario instead: What happens, if the system is used by three users instead of only one? To investigate this issue, change the »Population« of the ClosedWorkload in the usage model from »1« to »3« and rerun the simulation. In the »Experiments« view, navigate to the newly created experiment run. Doubleclick the »HDD [0] in WebServer (State of Active Resource Tuple)« entry and doubleclick the »Pie Chart« entry afterwards. You should get a diagram similar to the one shown below.

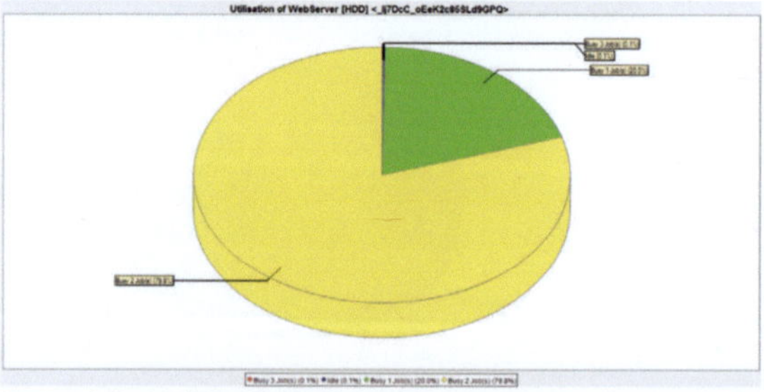

   This time, the hard disk drive is hardly idle but needs to handle 1 job in approximately 20% of the time and 2 jobs in 80% of the time. This means that we have an overload situation here because the hard disk drive is inable to handle the amount of jobs fast enough. An investigation of the response times of the defaultUsageScenario confirms this as the response times increased to approximately 20 seconds per measurement.
10. A straight-forward idea to cope with the overload situation is to use a faster hard disk drive within our WebServer, i.e., to scale the hard disk drive up. Therefore, change the processing rate of the hard disk drive from »10« workunits to »100« workunits within the resource

environment and rerun the simulation. The resulting utilization pie chart for the hard disk drive should look like the one below.

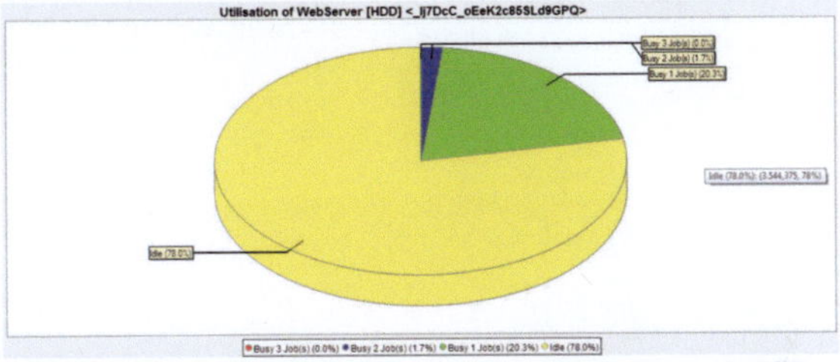

We see that our faster hard disk drive can handle a situation with three users as it is idle for 78% of the time.

11. As a side-remark: we could optimize the processing rate of the hard disk drive to perfectly fit a situation with three users. We could, for instance, aim at having the hard disk drive idle for only 10% of the time such that no over-provisioning occurs.
    To automate this, Palladio provides a sensitivity analysis within a SimuCom run configuration. Within a SimuCom run configuration, go to the »Analysis Configuration« tab and enter appropriate values to the »Sensitivity Analysis Parameters« edit fields. For instance, select the »ProcessingRate« PCM Random Variable of the hard disc as »Variable« and enter »10« into the »Minimum« field, »100« into the »Maximum« field, and »10« into the »Step Width« field. By this, the simulation run performs ten measurements with hard disc processing rates of 10, 20, ..., 90, and 100 workunits.
    The results can nicely be compared via a histogram-based cumulative distribution function (CDF) as follows. Doubleclick the »Response Time of defaultUsageScenario« entry of the first experiment run (with a hard disc processing rate of »10« workunits). Afterwards, doubleclick the »JFreeChart Response Time Histogram-based CDF«. Next, drag and drop each the »Response Time of defaultUsageScenario« of the other nine experiments into the opened CDF diagram. You will get a diagram similar to the one below.

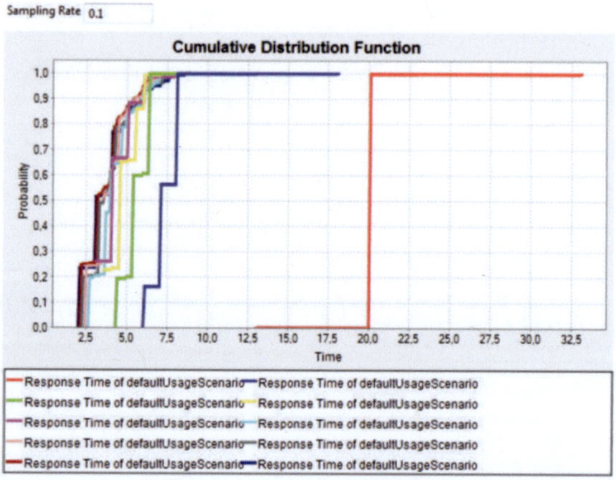

From left to right, the illustrated measurement belong to hard disk drive processing rates of 100, 90, ..., and 10 workunits. Here, we see that a hard disc processing rate of 20 workunits (dark blue values) already improves the response times to a great extend. The corresponding pie chart diagram of the hard disc utilization is shown below.

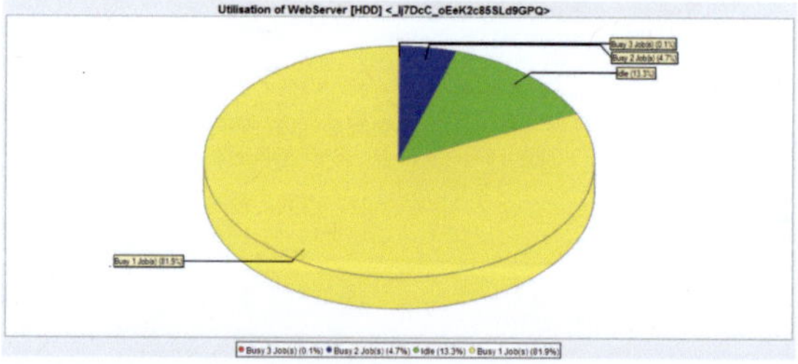

We see that we are close to our goal of having the hard disk drive idle for approximately 10% of the time. Next steps could be to further investigate the relation between the number of users and the hard disc. Alternatively, we may take also the CPU into these considerations as there will also be a point where the CPU becomes the bottleneck of the system. Feel free to experiment on your own regarding these issues.

9. Adding a Loadbalancer [Estimated Time: 20 min.]

Besides scaling available processing resources like CPU and hard disk drives up (vertical scaling), we could also try to scale out via additional servers within our system (horizontal scaling). For achieving this, we will outsource our database component to two dedicated database servers. A load balancer on our webserver then assigns 50% of the requests to the first database server and 50% of the requests the second database server.

1. Modify the repository by adding a »Loadbalancer« BasicComponent to it that provides the IDatabase interface once and requires the interface twice.

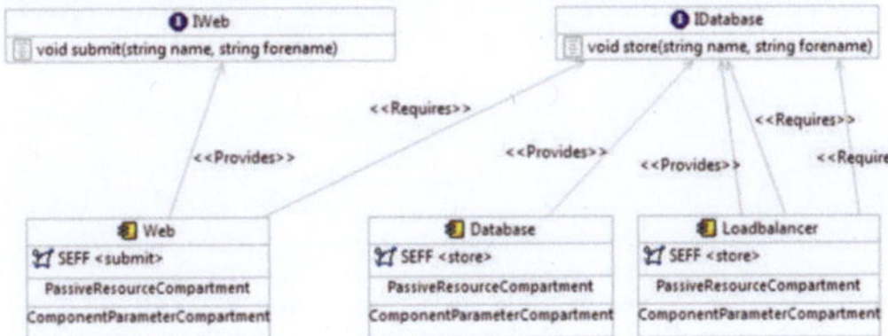

Specify the SEFF for the »store« service of the »Loadbalancer« component as follows. First, add a »BranchAction« from the palette to the SEFF diagram and name it »balance«. Secondly, add two »ProbabilisticBranchTransitions« to the newly created branch action. Name them »dbserver1« and »dbserver2«, respectively. Assign each branch transition a probability of »0.5«. Thirdly, add to each branch transition an »ExternalCallAction«. For the »dbserver1« transition, select the »store« service of the first required role and for the »dbserver2« transition, select the »store« service of the second required role. Finally, connect the added elements appropriately by »Control Flow« links. Your SEFF should look like the one below.

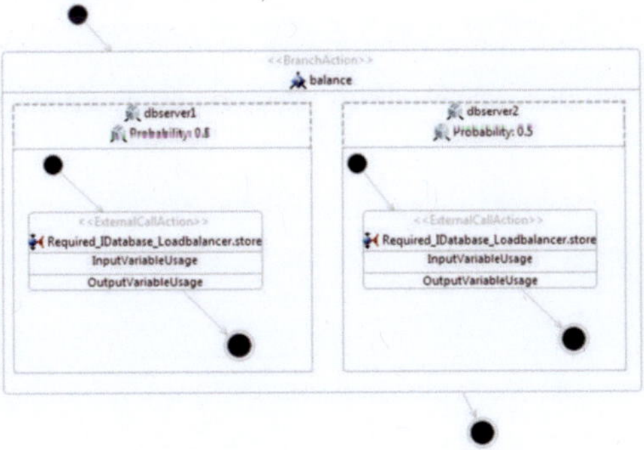

2. Next, we compose a new system by including the load balancer. For this, add the loadbalancer to the system diagram via a new »AssemblyContext«. As we have two databases now, we also add a database component via another new »AssemblyContext« and expand the assemblies name as well as the name of the second provided role of the load balancer by a »2« to ensure a unique naming. We connect the assemblies via »Aseembly Connectors« such that we get a system diagram like shown below.

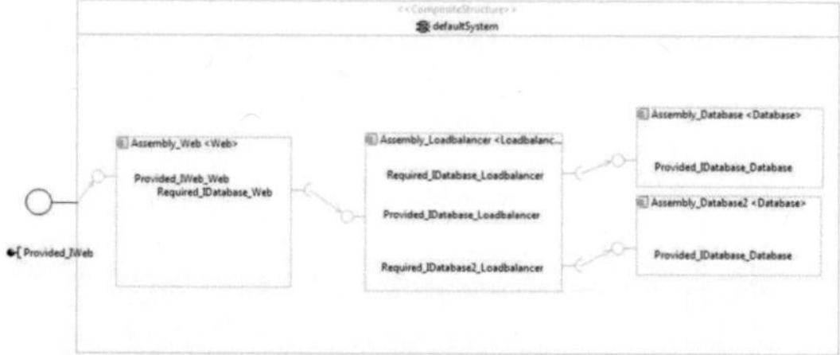

3. In the resource model diagram, we create two new resource containers »DBServer1« and »DBServer2«. Each server gets (1) a CPU with a processing rate of 10 workunits and with a processor sharing strategy as well as (2) a hard disk drive with a processing rate of 10 workunits and with a first-come-first-server strategy.
To connect the three servers, we also add a »LinkingResource« from the palette to the diagram. We set the latency to »0« and the throughput to »1000000«, thus, allowing to neglect network performance influence for the time being. We therefore name it »fastNetwork«. We connect the servers to our network via »Connection« links from the palette. Your diagram should look like the one shown below.

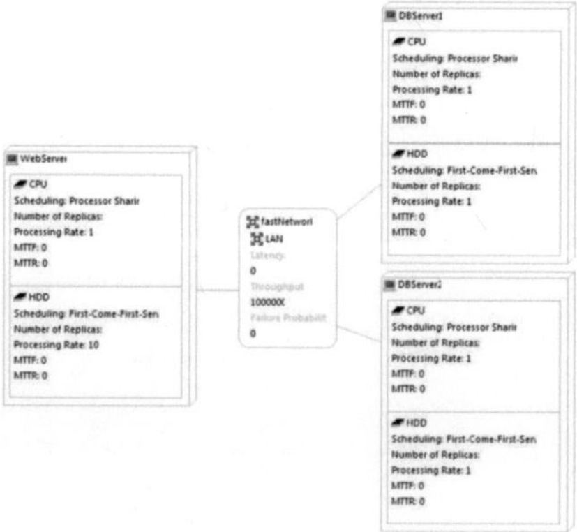

4. In the allocation model diagram, allocate the respective components as planned. You will get an allocation diagram like shown below. Note: you have to delete the »Database« allocation from the »WebServer« and add the »Loadbalancer« component instead.

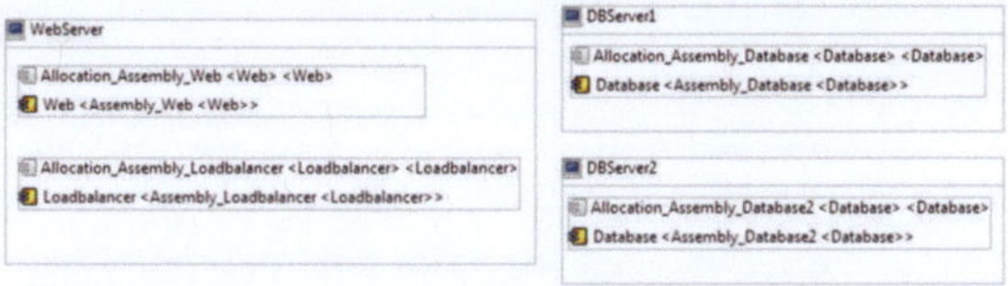

5. We can leave the usage model diagram as it is – our changes were transparent to the users. Therefore, we can run a simulation and investigate the results next.
   After doing so, compare the two pie charts illustrating the hard disk drive utilization of DBServer1 and DBServer2, respectively. Both pie charts should be similarly to the one shown below.

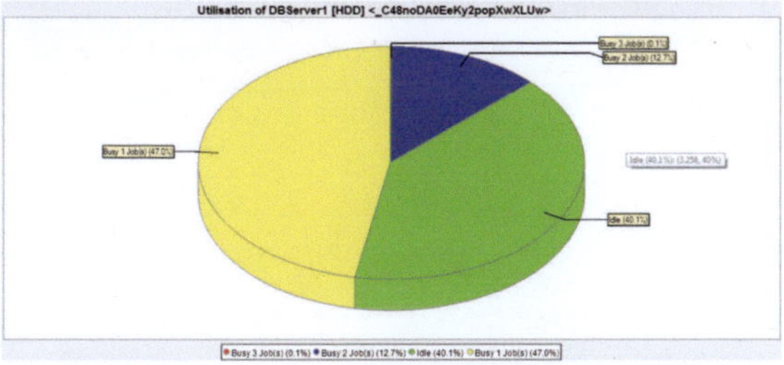

   We see that scaling out to two servers, each having a hard disk drive with a processing rate of 10 workunits, has a similar effect than scaling up a single server's hard disk drive to a processing rate of 20 workunits. Therefore, we found an alternative way of coping with the discovered overload situation.
   Note that there are several other ways to improve our modeling or to test design alternatives. For instance, we could model a "real round-robin" instead of using 50% probabilities within our loadbalancer, which could cause different results. Another possibility would be to extend our model by caches for database accesses. Feel free to experiment on your own with the system.

10. Using New Sirius Editors [Estimated Time: 15 min.]

The so-far discussed graphical Palladio editors were implemented using legacy technologies (the GMF framework). Recently, we reimplemented these editors using a modern technology (the Sirius framework). Owed to this new technology, the usage of editors has changed slightly. In this section, we exemplify this usage based on the new system and resource environment editors. (Note: you already installed these editors from the Architectural Template repository. Also note that we exemplify these steps in the model without loadbalancer.)

To start System model editing, execute the following steps:

1. Switch to the »Modeling« perspective (or open the »Model Explorer« view manually).
2. In the »Model Explorer« view, right-click on your Palladio project and choose »Configure« -> »Convert to Modeling Project« to make your project compatible with the new framework.
3. Next, right-click on your project and choose »Viewpoints Selection«. Check »System Design« in the popup.
4. Expand your System model as shown below, right-click the »System« model element and choose »New Representation« -> »new ComposedProvidingRequiringEntity Diagram«.

5. Enter any name as diagram (i.e., representation) title, e.g., »new ComposedProvidingRequiringEntity Diagram«. The editor will open with your System loaded.

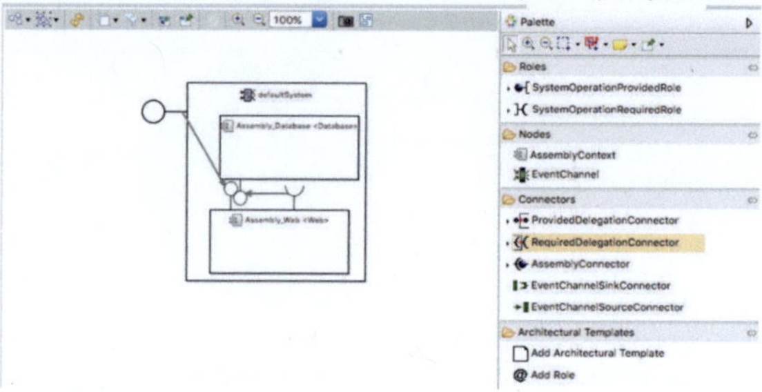

6. Try using the editor as you used the editors before. Generally, the editor should behave the same. Note that some elements of the palette have been reordered and/or grouped together. For example, providing entities roles have now a dedicated group:

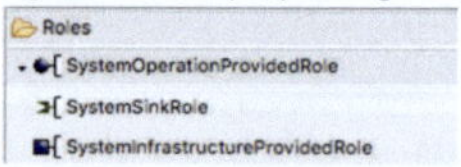

Also note that some elements are new, e.g., the »Architectural Templates« group which is explained in the next section.

Editing resource environments works analogously:

1. Right-click on your project and choose »Viewpoints Selection«. Check »Resource Environment Design« in the popup.
2. Expand your Resource Environment model, right-click the »Resource Environment« model element and choose »New Representation« -> »new Resourceenvironment Diagram«.

3. Enter any name as diagram (i.e., representation) title, e.g., »new Resourceenvironment Diagram«. The editor will open with your Resource Environment loaded.

4. Try using the editor as you used the editors before.

Sirius-based editors for the other Palladio models will appear soon; their usage will be similar.

11. Applying Architectural Templates [Estimated Time: 15 min.]

Architectural Templates allow software architects to apply reusable patterns to their Palladio models. For example, instead of manually modeling the load balancer like we did in Sec. 9, we can also apply the Architectural Template for load balancers. As this application consists only of a few small steps, architects can save a lot of modeling effort.

Execute the following steps on the System model opened with the Sirius-based System model editor:

1. Choose »Add Architectural Template« from the palette and click on the »defaultSystem« to apply a template on your system.
2. In the popup, choose the »AT Static Assembly Context Loadbalancing« Architectural Template to apply the template for a load balancer. Confirm with »OK«.

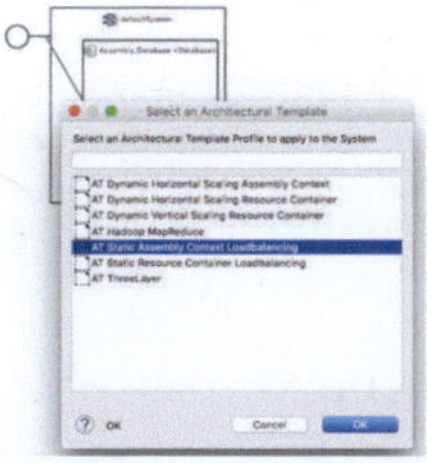

3. The system is now enabled for the load balancer Architectural Template. Whenever we want to work with an Architectural Template, enabling it for the system is the first step. The editor

for the system illustrates the Architectural Template application with a grey box.

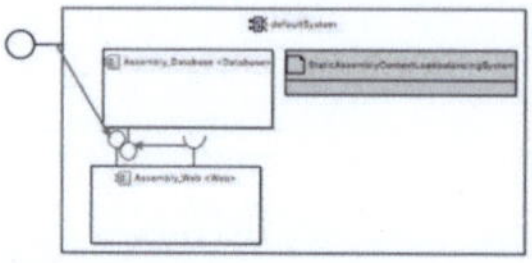

4. Finally, we need to mark the Assembly Context that has to be load-balanced. To do so, choose »Add Role« from the palette and click on the »Assembly_Database <Database>« Assembly Context. In the popup, choose the »StaticLoadbalancedAssemblyContext« role and confirm with »OK«.

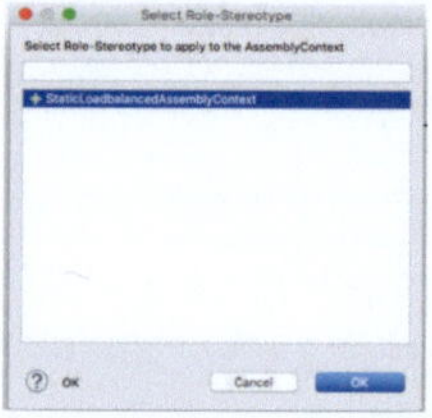

5. The Assembly Context will now be load-balanced during simulation (note: you need to start the simulation using Experiment Automation; see Sec. 13). The editor for the system illustrates this added Role with a grey box within the Assembly Context.

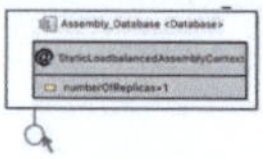

6. The grey box of the added Role allows to set the »Number of Replicas« of the load balancer, i.e., the number of Assembly Context for our database that will be load-balanced. Set it to »2« (by doubleclicking the parameter) to model semantically the same system as we did in Sec. 9 with our manually modeled load balancer.

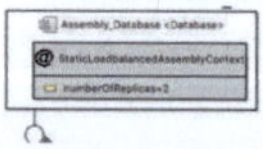

7. Use Experiment Automation (Section 14) to run analyzes based on Architectural Templates.

The complete catalogue of existing Architectural Templates is explained at:
http://wiki.cloudscale-project.eu/index.php/HowTos
As a final task, use this Wiki:

1. Go to http://wiki.cloudscale-project.eu/index.php/HowTos
2. Click on »Loadbalancing« and read the page.
3. Answer this question: What is the difference between »Loadbalanced Resource Container« and »Loadbalanced Assembly Context«?

12. Specifying Usage Evolutions [Estimated Time: 15 min.]

Screencast: https://www.youtube.com/watch?v=k6EKqPyl2Jg

So far, we only modeled *static* usage scenarios. That is, our usage scenarios may used probabilistic characterisations, however, these did not vary over time (thus, the »static«). In contrast, a *dynamic* usage scenario would be characterized as a function of (simulated) time.

We recently filled this gap by introducing so-called Usage Evolution models, i.e., models that allow to vary usage scenario parameters like arrival rates, number of concurrent users, operation parameters, etc. over time. To create such models, a normal usage scenario model, a Descartes Load Intensity Model (DLIM) model to characterize time-depending variations, and a Usage Evolution model that links the former two are needed:

1. Create a new DLIM model (Right-click at your project -> New -> Other... -> Descartes Load Intensity Model -> Descartes Load Intensity Model -> Next -> File Name: »default.dlim« -> Next -> Only mark »Modify Seasonal Part« -> Next -> Only modify »Number of Peaks« to »1«, »Base Arrival Rate Level« to »1.0«, and »Select Seasonal Shape« to »SinTrend« as shown in the screenshot below -> Finish).

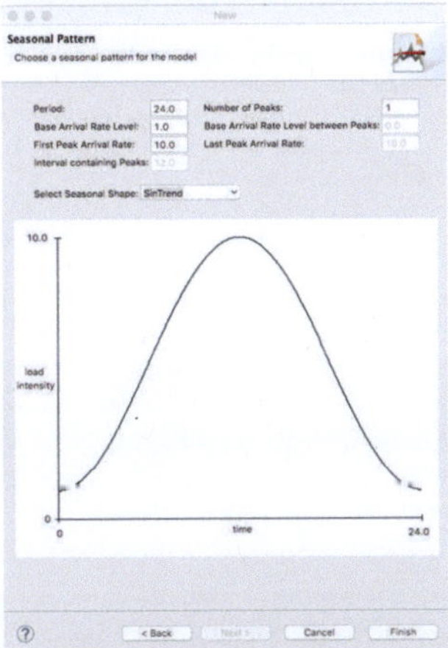

2. You now created a DLIM model where you vary »load intensity« over »time«. You can vizualize the your function by opening the »Load Intensity Plot« (Window -> Show View -> Other... -> Descartes Load Intensity Model -> Load Intensity Plot) and by opening your model in the default editor (double-click on your model if the editor is not already opened).

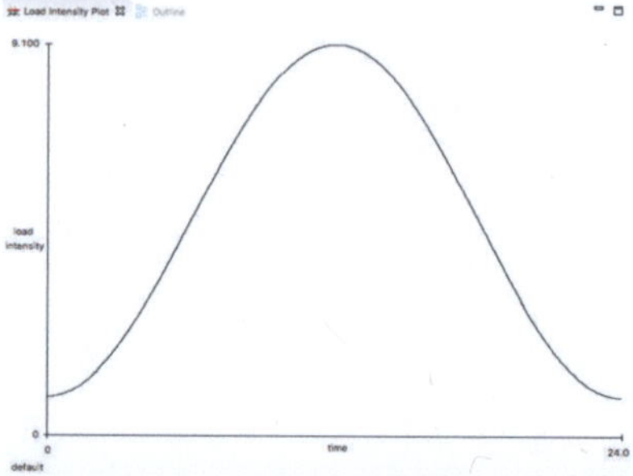

Note that the »9.100« appears to be a bug in the visualization; it should rather be a »10«.

3. Next, let us link this DLIM model to our existing usage model such that we vary the number of users from 1 to 10 until half of the simulation time is over and from 10 to 1 until simulation finishes.
   Create a new Usage Evolution model (Right-click at your project -> New -> Other... -> CloudScale Diagrams -> ScaleDL Usage Evolution -> Next -> File Name: »default.usageevolution« -> Next -> Browse... and select your pre-specified usage model (»/PalladioProject/default.usagemodel«) -> Next -> Browse... and select your pre-specified DLIM model »/PalladioProject/default.dlim«) -> Finish).
4. An editor opens that has everything needed pre-configured (see screenshot below). You may investigate the properties of the »Usage Initial« node to see how we linked DLIM and usage models. Per default, we created a »Load Evolution« for the »defaultUsageScenario« based on the »Sequence default« DLIM model, i.e., we vary the number of users within our open workload (our wizard creates such a configuration by default).

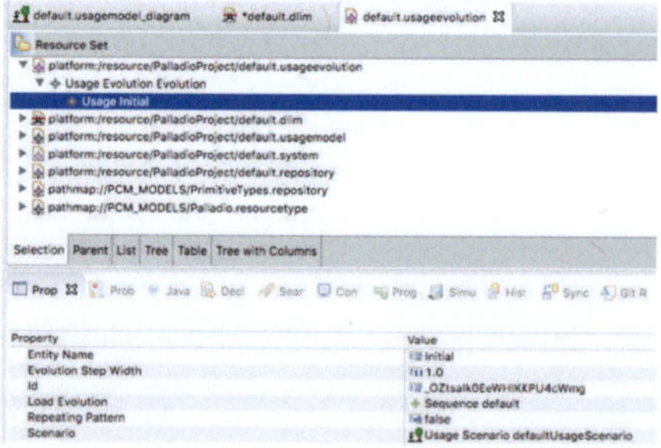

5. Use Experiment Automation (Section 14) to run analyzes based on Usage Evolutions.

13. Specifying Monitor Repositories [Estimated Time: 20 min.]

Ever wondered how we determine what comes out of your simulation? Typically, we use some defaults like usage scenario response times. However, if you need special measurements or do not want to see some default measurements, you can also take full control about that via Monitor Repository models! That is, such models allow you to specify what you are interested in and what should then be measured.

For specifying monitor repositories, you first have to specify a measuring points model, which specifies *where* you want to take measurements (e.g., at the usage scenario). Afterwards, we can specify a monitor repository model that states *what* we want to measure (e.g., response times) at such measuring points:

1. Create a new Measuring Point model (Right-click at your project -> New -> Other... -> Example EMF Model Creation Wizards -> Measuringpoint Model -> Next -> File Name: »My.measuringpoint« -> Next -> Model Object: »Measuring Point Repository« -> Finish).
2. In the now opened tree editor, add a new measuring point for our usage scenario (right click the »Measuring Point Repository« node -> New Child -> Usage Scenario Measuring Point).

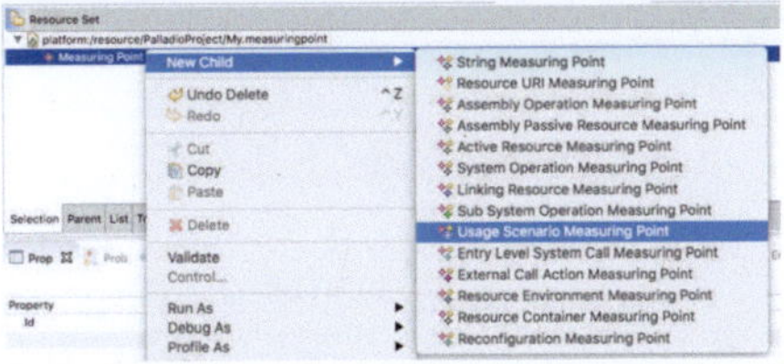

3. Next, configure *our* usage scenario as »Usage Scenario« for this Usage Scenario Measuring Point (drag & drop our usage model into the editor to load the model (»platform://resource/PalladioProject/default.usagemodel« will appear at the bottom of the editor) -> select »Usage Scenario defaultUsageScenario« as »Usage Scenario« within the properties view)

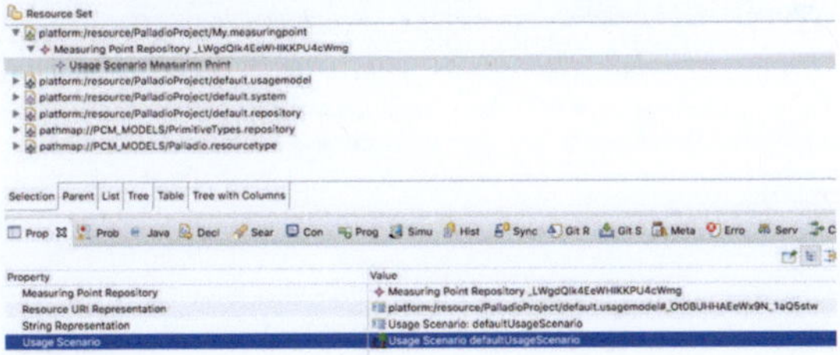

4. Save & close.

5. Create a new Monitor Repository model (Right-click at your project -> New -> Other... -> Example EMF Model Creation Wizards -> MonitorRepository Model -> Next -> File Name: »My.monitorrepository« -> Next -> Model Object: »Monitor Repository« -> Finish).
6. In the now opened tree editor, add a new monitor for our usage scenario (right click the »Monitor Repository« node -> New Child -> Monitor).

7. Next, configure *our* usage scenario measuring point as »Measuring Point« for this Monitor (drag & drop our measuring point model into the editor to load the model (»platform://resource/PalladioProject/My.measuringpoint« will appear at the bottom of the editor) -> select »Usage Scenario Measuring Point Usage Scenario: defaultUsageScenario« as »Measuring Point« and »Usage Scenario Response Times« as »Entity Name« within the properties view)

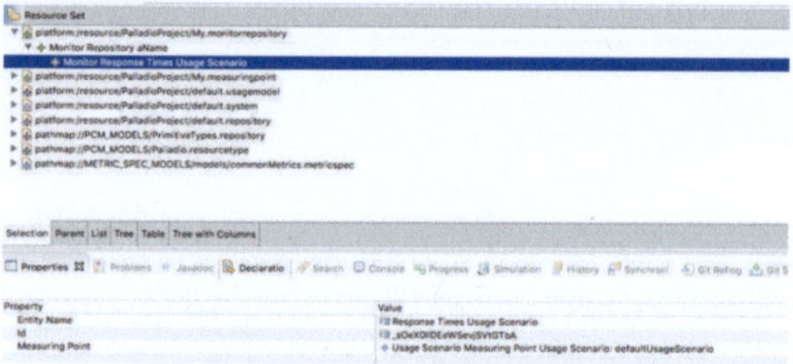

8. Add a new measurement specification for response times to our monitor (right click the »Monitor« node -> New Child -> Measurement Specification).

9. Next, configure Response Times as metrics we are interested in (right-click on the editor -> Load Resource... -> enter »pathmap://METRIC_SPEC_MODELS/models/commonMetrics.metricspec« as »Resource URI« -> OK (»pathmap://METRIC_SPEC_MODELS/models/commonMetrics.metricspec« will appear at the bottom of the editor) -> select »Numerical Base Metric Description Response Time« as »Metric Description« within the properties view)

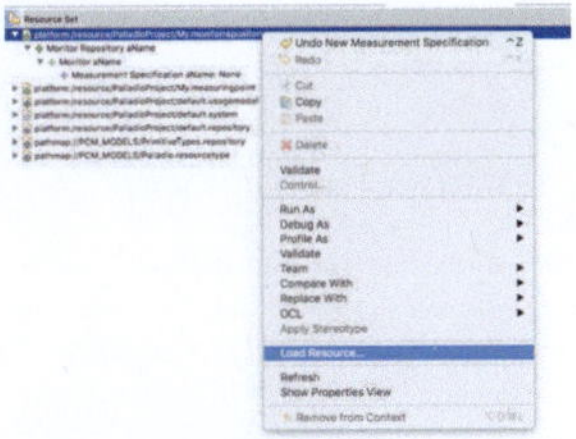

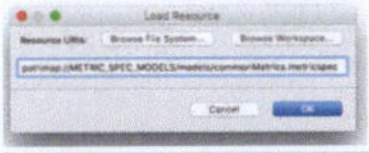

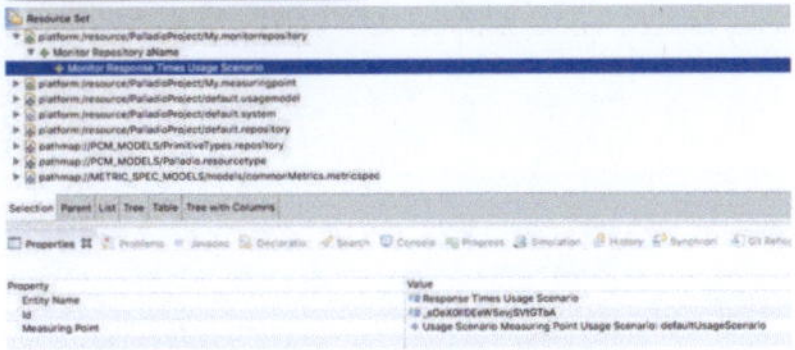

10. Use Experiment Automation (Section 14) to run analyzes based on Monitor Repositories.

14. Using Experiment Automation [Estimated Time: 20 min.]

Screencast: https://www.youtube.com/watch?v=sJSqil9Pwz4

Prerequisite: You specified a monitor repository model (Section 13).

Optional: Experiment Automation optionally supports models with applied Architectural Templates (Section 11) and Usage Evolutions (Section 12).

So far, we always used a »SimuBench« run configuration to start a Palladio-based analysis. Such analyses use Palladio's SimuCom simulator for measuring performance metrics. However, SimuCom run configurations lack support for Architectural Templates, Usage Evolutions, and Monitor Repositories. A dedicated model for runconfigurations – Experiment Automation models – solve this problem.

1. Create a new Experiment Automation model (Right-click at your project -> New -> Other... -> Example EMF Model Creation Wizards -> Experiements Model -> Next -> File Name: »My.experiments« -> Next -> Model Object: »Experiment Repository« -> Finish).

2. In the now opened tree editor, add a Experiment for our Experiment Repository (right click the »Experiment Repository« node -> New Child -> Experiment).

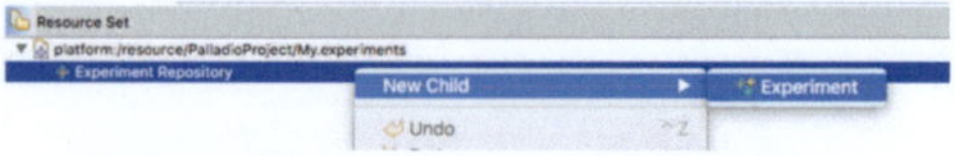

3. Next, configure *our* Experiment (select »My Experiment« as »Description«, »someId« as »Id«, »Usage Scenario Response Times Experiment« as »Name« and »1« as »Repetitions« within the properties view).

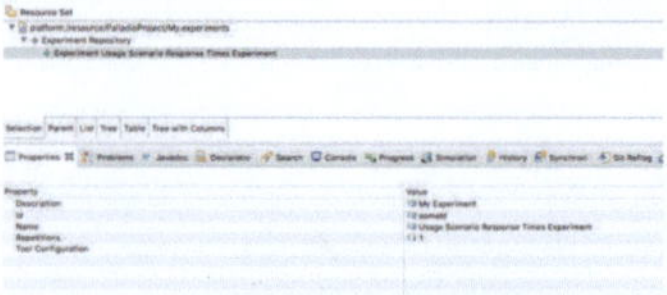

4. In this way, we also have to configure some more child nodes and the »Tool Configuration« to configure an experiment run. As especially the »Tool Configuration« is quite tricky, we stop with our description for manual configuration here.
5. Instead, we now copy an existing Experiment model into our project and only adapt it where we need it. Please do so with a Text Editor (!!) using this experiment model: https://github.com/CloudScale-Project/ArchitecturalTemplates/blob/master/plugins/org.scaledl.architecturaltemplates.examples.dynscalingcontainer/Experiments/Elasticity.experiments
6. Run the experiment (open your run configurations -> double-click »Experiment Automation« -> choose your Experiments model as input -> Run)

15. Adding Variables [Estimated Time: 30 min.]

With Palladio, it is also possible to specify variables to characterize method input parameters as well as their return values. For such specifications, Palladio allows to also model dataflow (besides control flow). See the corresponding screencast at http://www.palladio-simulator.com/tools/screencasts/ for a tutorial on this. This workshop may be extended by a detailed explanation in future versions.

Versions

- V2.1 (2015/11/12; Palladio 4.0; Eclipse 4.5.1/Mars.1): Added new Sirius editors, Architectural Templates, Usage Evolution, Monitor Repository, and Experiment Automation; Sebastian Lehrig (sebastian.lehrig@informatik.tu-chemnitz.de)
- V2.0 (2015/10/08; Palladio 4.0; Eclipse 4.5.1/Mars.1): Revised complete guide to provide up-to-date version; added time estimates; moved from Sensor Framework to EDP2 descriptions; Sebastian Lehrig (sebastian.lehrig@informatik.tu-chemnitz.de)
- V1.3 (2015/09/17; Palladio 4.0; Eclipse 4.5/Mars): Updated to recent Palladio version; Sebastian Lehrig (sebastian.lehrig@informatik.tu-chemnitz.de)

- V1.2 (2013/08/14; Palladio 3.4; Eclipse 4.2/Juno): Corrected typos; Sebastian Lehrig (sebastian.lehrig@uni-paderborn.de)
- V1.1 (2013/01/07; Palladio 3.4; Eclipse 4.2/Juno): Exchanged introduction image to a default Palladio image from website; Sebastian Lehrig (sebastian.lehrig@uni-paderborn.de)
- V1.0 (2012/11/16; Palladio 3.4; Eclipse 4.2/Juno): Initial version; Sebastian Lehrig (sebastian.lehrig@uni-paderborn.de)

D.4. CloudStore Description

CloudStore Description

CloudStore describes a legacy bookshop to be migrated to cloud computing environments. Figure 1 gives a simplified overview of a Palladio model we created for CloudStore. To understand the model, a short description follows.

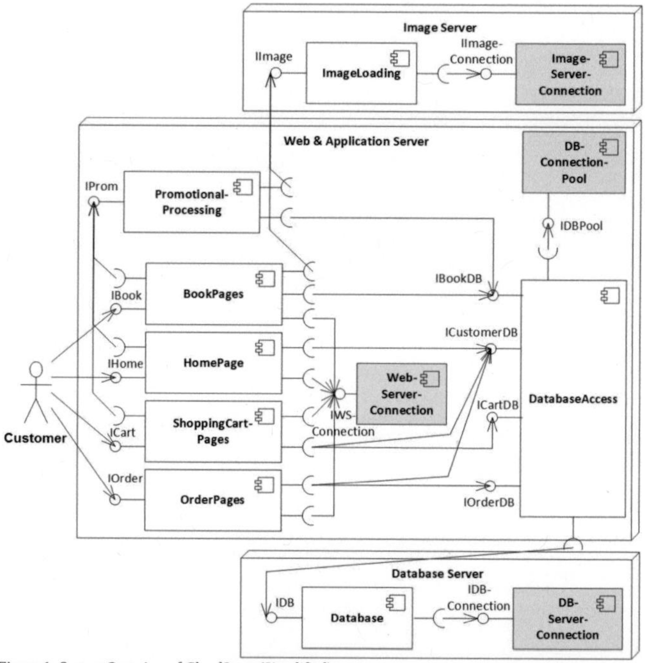

Figure 1: System Overview of CloudStore (Simplified)

Customers enter the CloudStore system via the web pages provided by front-end components. These front-end components are **BookPages**, **HomePage**, **ShoppingCartPages**, and **OrderPages** allocated on the **Web & Application Server**. **BookPages** provides operations regarding books (e.g., to query book details or to search for books). The **HomePage** component shows CloudStore's home page, which welcomes its customers and displays possible book categories for browsing. **ShoppingCartPages** allows customers to register, add books to a shopping cart, and to check-out the shopping cart. Afterwards, **OrderPages** allows to follow-up on the order. **BookPages**, **HomePage**, and **ShoppingCartPages** additionally require the **PromotionalProcessing** component to receive an advertisement area for related books.

These front-end components require operations of the **ImageLoading** and **Database** components as allocated on the **Image** and **Database Server**, respectively. **ImageLoading** provides access to image files, e.g., needed for book covers. CloudStore's **Database** stores entries for books, customers, shopping carts, and orders.

Calls to the **Database** are intercepted by the **DatabaseAccess** component that manages database connections. **DatabaseAccess** receives [returns] such connections from [to] the **DBConnectionPool** component. Also **Web & Application**, **Image**, and **Database Server** use pools for handling customer requests (**WebServerConnection**, **ImageServerConnection**, **DBServer-Connection**). All of these pools (gray-colored components in Fig. 1) are typical factors that influence an application's performance as their pool-size limits the amount of requests that can be processed in parallel.

Palladio supports acquiring and releasing connections from these resource pools in service effect specifications (SEFFs). SEFFs specify the behavior (control and data flow) of component operations. In our model, every interaction requires the acquisition of connections and a subsequent release once the interaction ends. Figure 2 illustrates this pattern for SEFFs of front-end component operations that interact with database and image components. Actions (1) to (3) model the performance impact of creating an HTML page for customers while action (4) models the performance impact of subsequently resolving image references. These two phases—receiving an HTML page and subsequently its references—reflect the typical behavior of web browsers.

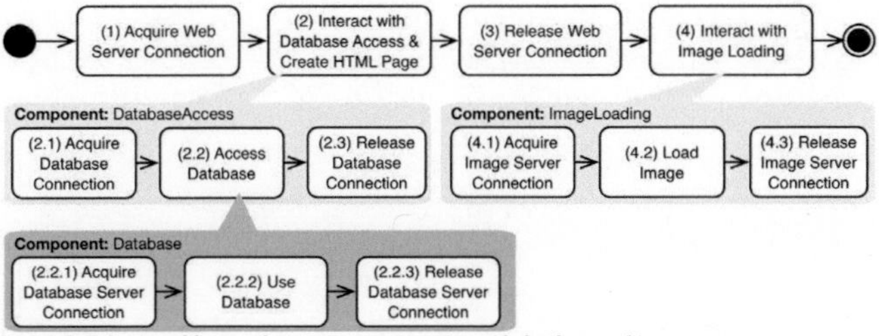

Figure 2: Behavior of front-end components interacting with database and image components

In Figure 3, the load to CloudStore is illustrated. At the x-axis, the simulation time is depicted. At the y-axis, the number of concurrent customers within the system is depicted. Accordingly, at simulation start, there is only one customer within the system. Afterwards, the number of customers linearly increases over time. At the end of the simulation time (200 seconds), there are 1000 customers within the system. The distribution of the customers within CloudStore is defined in the specified usagemodel (UsageScenarios/controlledExperiment.usagemodel).

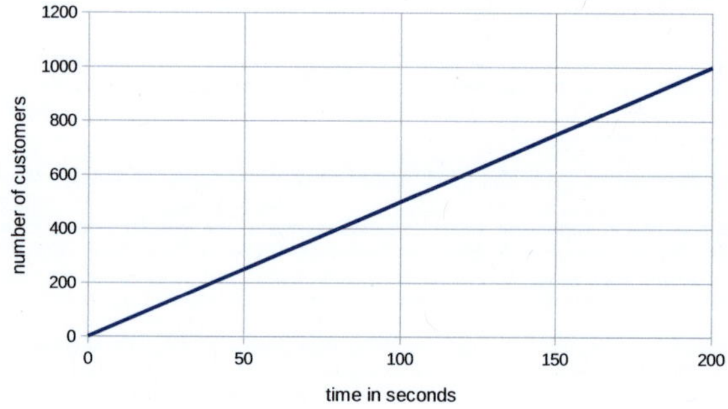

Figure 3: Number of customer over time

D.5. Task description for the Treatment Group (Software Architects Following the AT Method)

Task Description

The goal of this experiment is to detect and resolve a performance problem in a given Palladio model. For detection, we provide a detailed model description and describe the steps to identify the performance problem. For resolving, your task is to apply Architectural Templates and to show based on simulations that you resolved the performance problem.

0 Background Questions

1. For the next steps, use this print for filling it out.
2. Please enter your name

   ____

3. Please enter your e-mail address. We might use this to contact you with regard to your answers to the open questions.

   ____

4. How would you rate your knowledge of Architectural Templates?

none	low	medium	high	expert

5. How many month of experience do you have with Architectural Templates?

   ____

6. How would you rate your knowledge of Eclipse?

none	low	medium	high	expert

7. How many month of experience do you have with Eclipse?

   ____

1 Performance Problem Detection

Please execute the following tasks:

1. Install Palladio (latest release), Architectural Templates (latest release), and configure a new workspace as described in the attached "ATInstallationGuide.pdf". Afterwards, you will have the CloudStore model in your workspace. If you already installed Palladio and Architectural Templates, you have to >>Check for Updates<< and only have to Import the CloudStore model as described into a clean workspace.
   Reminder:
   You can find the Wiki describing available Architectural Templates here:
   http://wiki.cloudscale-project.eu/index.php/Wiki/
2. Please note the starting time.

   ________:hh ________:mm

3. Read the "CloudStoreDescription.pdf" as attached.
4. Please answer the following questions:
   1. How many Assembly Contexts are described in the "CloudStore Description"?
   2. How many Assembly Contexts are specified in the system of the CloudStore model?
   3. How many Resource Containers are described in the "CloudStore Description"?
   4. How many Resource Containers are specified in the resource environment of the CloudStore model?
   5. How many actions are modeled for the "getHome" Operation of the "Homepage" Component of the CloudStore model?
   6. What is the purpose of the "getWorker" and the "returnWorker" Actions in the "getHome" Operation of the CloudStore model?
   7. Why is the "returnWorker" Action not executed as last?

5. Run the "AT-CloudStore.launch" run configuration (right-click → Run As.. → AT-CloudStore) that is part of the imported CloudStore project and investigate the analysis result in the Palladio perspective.
6. Please answer the following questions:
   1. When is the first time that the response time for the usage scenario is above two seconds?

      ____
      ____
      ____

   2. How many CloudStore customers are within the system at that point in time? (note: inspect the DLIM model (see Palladio workshop) for determining an estimate.)

      ____
      ____
      ____

   3. Which system operation call(s) have response times over two seconds?

      ____
      ____
      ____

   4. What is the bottleneck resource causing response time over two seconds?

      ____
      ____
      ____

   5. Given that response times should stay below two seconds, which options do you see to resolve the situation?

      ____
      ____
      ____

7. Please note the current time when you finished all the tasks above.

   ________:hh ________:mm

2 Resolving the Performance Problem

We have the following requirements defined:

- **Performance**: Response times shall stay below two seconds. Violations are allowed in the limits given in the "Elasticity" requirement.

- **Elasticity**: When violations of the performance requirement are detected, CloudStore shall return to a stable state within 20 seconds.
- **Cost-Efficiency**: The operation costs for operating CloudStore shall be minimized.

Next, your task is to resolve the detected performance problem to meet above requirements. You have to investigate two options for resolving: vertically scaling the CPU of the database and horizontally scaling the database.

2.1 Vertical Scaling

In vertical scaling, a fixed server can dynamically speed-up its processing resources over time. Figure 1 illustrates such a scaling for a server.

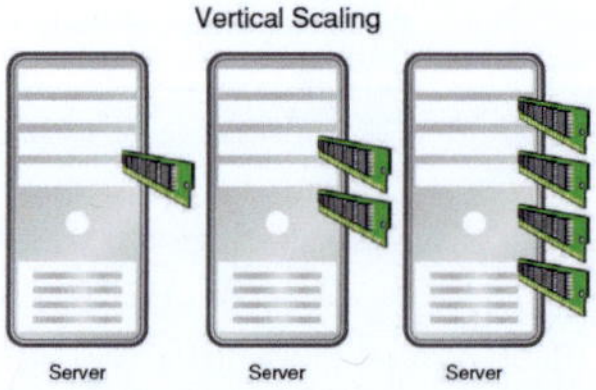

Figure 1: A server scales its processing resources up (from left to right)

In your case, you have to scale-up the CPU of CloudStore's database server. For this task, execute the following steps:

1. Please note the starting time.

   ______:hh ______:mm

2. Apply an appropriate Architectural Template for vertical scaling:
   - Note that the monitor repository (see Palladio workshop) of CloudStore includes a monitor (named: "Response Times – Browsing Mix") that calculates the mean response times for the overall usage scenario in an interval of 5.0 seconds. This calculated value is used by default to determine whether scaling needs to be triggered. Use the values of the following table during your modeling tasks, if feasible:

Scale-Down Threshold	0,1
Scale-Up Threshold	0,8
Step Size	13.350.000.000
Min Rate	13.350.000.000
Max Rate	133.500.000.000

Here, the "Scale-Down Threshold" specifies that the current CPU processing rate should be reduced if the calculated mean response times are lower than 0.1 seconds. Likewise, the "Scale-Up Threshold" specifies that the current CPU processing rate should be increased if the calculated mean response times are higher than 0.8 seconds. The "Step Size" is the rate by which scaling adapts the processing rate. "Min Rate" and "Max Rate" specify lower and upper bounds for this rate, respectively.

- You have a maximum of **1 hour** (starting from the time you noted in step 1) to apply the AT. If you do not manage to provide model with a suitable AT applied in the given time, skip to step 5.

3. Note the current time.

   ______:hh ______:mm

4. Run a CloudStore simulation with your applied AT and inspect the results.
5. Make a screenshot of the "XY Plot" of the "Response Times – Browsing Mix" and store it for later use.
6. Note the current time.

   ______:hh ______:mm

7. Please answer the following questions:
   1. Did you manage to apply a suitable AT? (If yes, name it here; if no, skip to question 5.)

      ____

   2. Is the performance requirement always met?

      ____

   3. In case of a violation of the performance requirement, does the system return to a stable state within 20 seconds?

      ____

   4. Note the current time.

      ______:hh ______:mm

   5. Please list any issues during your task:

      ____

      ____

      ____

2.2 Horizontal Scaling

In horizontal scaling, a given server is dynamically replicated. Each replica is added to an according loadbalancer that distributes workload among them. Figure 2 illustrates such a horizontally-scaled server with three replica.

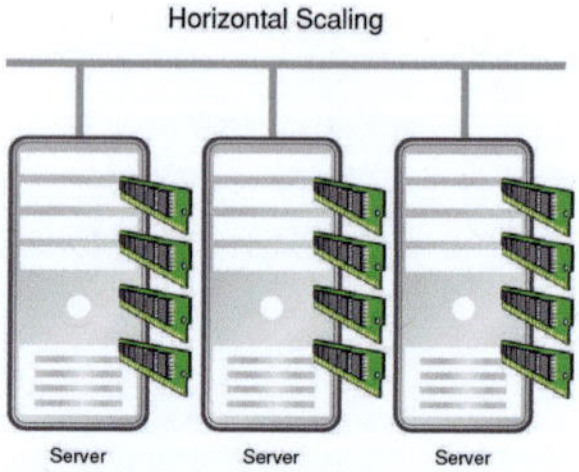

Figure 2: A server is replicated and load-balanced (scale-out)

In your case, you have to scale-out CloudStore's database server. This represents an alternative to vertical scaling and allows you to assess whether it is more cost-efficient. For this task, execute the following steps:

1. Please note the starting time.
   ________:hh ________:mm
2. Apply an appropriate Architectural Template for vertical scaling:
   - Note that the monitor repository (see Palladio workshop) of CloudStore includes a monitor (named: "Response Times – Browsing Mix") that calculates the mean response times for the overall usage scenario in an interval of 5.0 seconds. This calculated value is used by default to determine whether scaling needs to be triggered. Use the values of the following table during your modeling tasks, if feasible:

Scale-In Threshold	`0,1`
Scale-Out Threshold	`0,4`
Number of Initial Replica	`1`

   Here, the "Scale-In Threshold" specifies that the current number of replica should be reduced by 1 if the calculated mean response times are lower than 0.1 seconds. Likewise, the "Scale-Out Threshold" specifies that the number of replica should be increased by 1 if the calculated mean response times are higher than 0.4 seconds. The "Number of Initial Replica" gives the number of database servers at simulation start.
   - The loadbalancer shall work as follows: It forwards workload to a given replica with a probability of 1/(number of current replica).
   - You have a maximum of **2 hours** (starting from the time you noted in step 1) to apply the AT. If you do not manage to provide model with a suitable AT applied in the given time, skip to step 5.
3. Note the current time.

________:hh ________:mm

4. Run a CloudStore simulation with your reconfiguration rule and inspect the results.
5. Make a screenshot of the “XY Plot” of the “Response Times – Browsing Mix” and store it for later use.
6. Note the current time.

   ________:hh ________:mm

7. Please answer the following questions:
   1. Did you manage to apply a suitable AT? (If yes, name it here; if no, skip to question 5.)

      ____

   2. Is the performance requirement always met?

      ____

   3. In case of a violation of the performance requirement, does the system return to a stable state within 20 seconds?

      ____

   4. Note the current time.

      ________:hh ________:mm

   5. Please list any issues during your task:

      ____

      ____

      ____

3 Finalization

In order to finalize this experiment, you have to execute these last tasks:

- Name your above taken screenshots (forename_lastname_vertical.png and forename_lastname_horizontal.png)
- If you have any remarks, feel free to add them here:

  ____

  ____

  ____

  ____

- Hand-in this paper and send the screenshots to Christoph Nützel <**christoph.nuetzel@s2011.tu-chemnitz.de**>. Add Sebastian Lehrig <**sebastian.lehrig@informatik.tu-chemnitz.de**> as CC in your e-mail.

  THANK YOU! :)

D.6. Task description for the Control Group (Software Architects Only Using SimuLizar)

Task Description

The goal of this experiment is to detect and resolve a performance problem in a given Palladio model. For detection, we provide a detailed model description and describe the steps to identify the performance problem. For resolving, your task is to implement suitable self-adaptation rules and to show based on SimuLizar simulations that you resolved the performance problem.

0 Background Questions

1. Print this paper. For the next steps, use your print for filling it out.
2. Please enter your name

   ____

3. Please enter your e-mail address. We might use this to contact you with regard to your answers to the open questions.

   ____

4. How would you rate your knowledge of SimuLizar?

none	low	medium	high	expert

5. How many years of experience do you have with SimuLizar?

   ____

6. How do you prefer to specify reconfiguration rules? (Note: You will have to use your selection for such a specification; if you do not know yet, answer this question after the experiment.)
   1. QVT-O
   2. Storydiagrams
   3. Henshin
7. How would rate your knowledge in the technology you selected in question 6?

none	low	medium	high	expert

8. How many years of experience do you have with the technology you selected in question 6?

____

1 Performance Problem Detection

Please execute the following tasks:

1. Install Palladio (latest release) and configure a new workspace as described in the attached "SimuLizarInstallationGuide.pdf". Afterwards, you will have the CloudStore model in your workspace and a screen capture tool installed.
2. Start recording your actions with the previously installed capture tool.
3. Please note the starting time.

   ______:hh ______:mm

4. Read the "CloudStoreDescription.pdf" as attached.
5. Please answer the following questions:
   1. How many Assembly Contexts are described in the "CloudStore Description"?

      ____

   2. How many Assembly Contexts are specified in the system of the CloudStore model?

      ____

   3. How many Resource Containers are described in the "CloudStore Description"?

      ____

   4. How many Resource Containers are specified in the resource environment of the CloudStore model?

      ____

   5. How many actions are modeled for the "getHome" Operation of the "Homepage" Component of the CloudStore model?

      ____

   6. What is the purpose of the "getWorker" and the "returnWorker" Actions in the "getHome" Operation of the CloudStore model?

      ____

      ____

      ____

   7. Why is the "returnWorker" Action not executed as last?

      ____

      ____

      ____

6. Run the "SimuLizar-CloudStore.launch" run configuration that is part of the imported CloudStore project and investigate the analysis result in the EDP2 perspective.
7. Please answer the following questions:
   1. When is the first time that the response time for the usage scenario is above two seconds?

      ____

      ____

      ____

   2. How many CloudStore customers are within the system at that point in time? (note: inspect the LIMBO model for determining an estimate.)

      ____

      ____

      ____

   3. Which system operation call(s) have response times over two seconds?

      ____

      ____

      ____

   4. What is the bottleneck resource causing response time over two seconds?

      ____

      ____

      ____

   5. Given that response times should stay below two seconds, which options do you see to resolve the situation?

      ____

      ____

      ____

8. Please note the current time when you finished all the tasks above.

   ________:hh ________:mm

2 Resolving the Performance Problem

We have the following requirements defined:

- **Performance**: Response times shall stay below two seconds. Violations are allowed in the limits given in the "Elasticity" requirement.
- **Elasticity**: When violations of the performance requirement are detected, CloudStore shall

return to a stable state within 20 seconds.

- **Cost-Efficiency**: The operation costs for operating CloudStore shall be minimized.

Next, your task is to resolve the detected performance problem to meet above requirements. You have to investigate two options for resolving: vertically scaling the CPU of the database and horizontally scaling the database.

2.1 Vertical Scaling

In vertical scaling, a fixed server can dynamically speed-up its processing resources over time. Figure 1 illustrates such a scaling for a server.

In your case, you have to scale-up the CPU of CloudStore's database server. For this task, execute the following steps:

1. Please note the starting time.

   ________:hh ________:mm

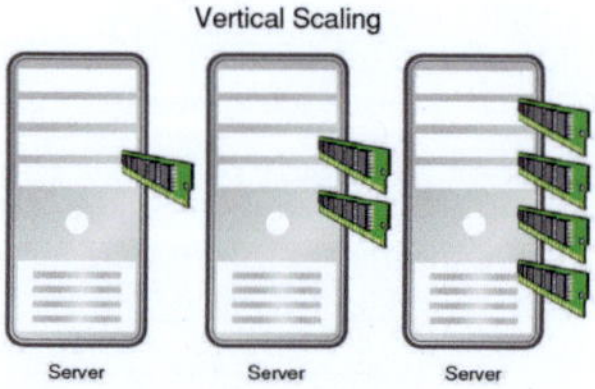

Figure 1: A server scales its processing resources up (from left to right)

2. Implement appropriate reconfiguration rules for SimuLizar for vertical scaling:
   - You may copy transformation code from existing reconfigurations or completely reuse an existing transformation, if you know any.
   - You have to use your preferred transformation language (that is, the one you selected in question 6 in section 0).
   - Note that the monitor repository of CloudStore includes a monitor (named: "Response Times – Browsing Mix") that calculates the mean response times for the overall usage scenario in an interval of 5.0 seconds. Use the calculated value to determine whether a reconfiguration needs to be triggered. Use the values of the following table for your reconfiguration:

Scale-Down Threshold	0.1
Scale-Up Threshold	0.8
Step Size	13,350,000,000
Min Rate	13,350,000,000
Max Rate	133,500,000,000

Here, the "Scale-Down Threshold" specifies that the current CPU processing rate should be reduced if the calculated mean response times are lower than 0.1 seconds. Likewise, the

"Scale-Up Threshold" specifies that the current CPU processing rate should be increased if the calculated mean response times are higher than 0.8 seconds. The "Step Size" is the rate by which scaling adapts the processing rate. "Min Rate" and "Max Rate" specify lower and upper bounds for this rate, respectively.

- You have a maximum of **1 hour** (starting from the time you noted in step 1) to implement the reconfiguration. If you do not manage to provide a working reconfiguration in the given time, skip to step 6.

3. Note the current time.

   ________:hh ________:mm

4. Run a CloudStore simulation with your reconfiguration rule and inspect the results.
5. Make a screenshot of the "XY Plot" of the "Response Times – Browsing Mix" and store it for later use.
6. Note the current time.

   ________:hh ________:mm

7. Please answer the following questions:
   1. Did you manage to implement the reconfiguration? (If not, directly skip to question 5.)

      ____

   2. Is the performance requirement always met?

      ____

   3. In case of a violation of the performance requirement, does the system return to a stable state within 20 seconds?

      ____

   4. Note the current time.

      ________:hh ________:mm

   5. In case you copied or reused an existing reconfiguration, which one?

      ____

      ____

   6. Please list any issues during your task:

      ____

      ____

      ____

2.2 Horizontal Scaling

In horizontal scaling, a given server is dynamically replicated. Each replica is added to an according loadbalancer that distributes workload among them. Figure 2 illustrates such a horizontally-scaled server with three replica.

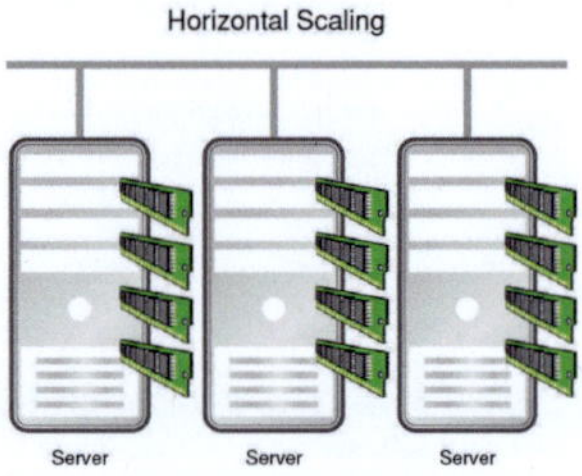

Figure 2: A server is replicated and load-balanced (scale-out)

In your case, you have to scale-out CloudStore's database server. This represents an alternative to vertical scaling and allows you to assess whether it is more cost-efficient. For this task, execute the following steps:

1. Please note the starting time.
   ______:hh ______:mm
2. Implement appropriate reconfiguration rules for SimuLizar for horizontal scaling:
   - You may copy transformation code from existing reconfigurations or completely reuse an existing transformation, if you know any.
   - You have to use your preferred transformation language (that is, the one you selected in question 6 in section 0).
   - Note that the monitor repository of CloudStore includes a monitor (named: "Response Times – Browsing Mix") that calculates the mean response times for the overall usage scenario in an interval of 5.0 seconds. Use the calculated value to determine whether a reconfiguration needs to be triggered. Use the values of the following table for your reconfiguration:

Scale-In Threshold	0.1
Scale-Out Threshold	0.4
Number of Initial Replica	1

Here, the "Scale-In Threshold" specifies that the current number of replica should be reduced by 1 if the calculated mean response times are lower than 0.1 seconds. Likewise, the "Scale-Out Threshold" specifies that the number of replica should be increased by 1 if the calculated mean response times are higher than 0.4 seconds. The "Number of Initial Replica" gives the number of database servers at simulation start.

- The loadbalancer shall work as follows: It forwards workload to a given replica with a probability of 1/(number of current replica).
- You have a maximum of **2 hours** (starting from the time you noted in step 1) to implement the reconfiguration. If you do not manage to provide a working reconfiguration in the given time, skip to step 5.

3. Note the current time.

   _______:hh _______:mm

4. Run a CloudStore simulation with your reconfiguration rule and inspect the results.
5. Make a screenshot of the "XY Plot" of the "Response Times – Browsing Mix" and store it for later use.
6. Note the current time.

   _______:hh _______:mm

7. Please answer the following questions:
   1. Did you manage to implement the reconfiguration? (If not, directly skip to question 5.)

      ____

   2. Is the performance requirement always met?

      ____

   3. In case of a violation of the performance requirement, does the system return to a stable state within 20 seconds?

      ____

   4. Note the current time.

      _______:hh _______:mm

   5. In case you copied or reused an existing reconfiguration, which one?

      ____

      ____

   6. Please list any issues during your task:

      ____

      ____

      ____

3 Finalization

In order to finalize this experiment, you have to execute these last tasks:

- Please ensure that you answered question 6 in section 0.
- Name your above taken screenshots (forename_lastname_vertical.png and forename_lastname_horizontal.png)
- If you have any remarks, feel free to add them here:

- Scan this paper and send it along with the screenshots to Christoph Nützel <**christoph.nuetzel@s2011.tu-chemnitz.de**>. Add Sebastian Lehrig <**sebastian.lehrig@informatik.tu-chemnitz.de**> as CC in your e-mail.

  Send the recorded screen captures to Sebastian via Skype (sebastian.lehrig)

  THANK YOU! :)

E. Controlled Experiment: Report of Preliminary Conduction and Results

This appendix reports the preliminary results of Nützel's controlled experiment [Nï5, Chap. 4–6]. The report starts in Section E.1 with the execution the controlled experiment. The empirical data created during this execution is analyzed in Section E.2 and interpreted in Section E.3. Potential threats to validity of the controlled experiment are finally discussed in Section E.4.

E.1. Controlled Experiment: Execution

The workshop for the treatment group was mainly executed as planned. The only deviation was that the workshop was not executed within one day but split up in two separate workshops, each lasting for 3 hours and 1 week apart from each other. The experiment was conducted another week later.

The controlled experiment was also mainly executed as planned. However, we have required and observed the following deviations (cf. [Nï5, Sec. 4.2]):

- For logistical reasons, we were only physically present in the experiment of the treatment group. To make the experiment of the control group more controlled, we have asked the control group to record their task execution via a screen capturing tool (see the task description Appendix D.6). Unfortunately, 1 subject had technical problems with this tool and did not record the execution.

- Because of other business, 1 subject of the control group was only able to conduct the knowledge application task of the vertical scaling architectural pattern. A result for the horizontal scaling architectural pattern is therefore missing for this subject.
- During the experiment with the treatment group, we have intervened five times:
  - We have informed the subjects that there are some differences between the CloudStore description (Appendix D.4) and the CloudStore model (available at [ATt]); due to the simplifications made for the description. For example, the description does not inform about infrastructure components.

    We informed all subjects about these differences because they have expressed to be confused about these differences. The description in Appendix C.1.1 provides a description of CloudStore that more accurately conforms to the model; future experiments therefore may use this description to avoid confusion.
  - Nützel has observed that some subjects had problems in investigating analysis results [N1̈5, Sec. 4.2]. We have therefore pointed all subjects to the respective section in the workshop document (Section 8 of the document given in Appendix D.3) that explains such investigations.
  - Nützel has observed that some subjects had problems in specifying usage evolution models [N1̈5, Sec. 4.2]. We have therefore pointed all subjects to the respective section in the workshop document (Section 12 of the document given in Appendix D.3) that explains such specifications.
  - All subjects had to pause the experiment because of a technical problem with AT tooling. The problem hindered subjects to apply the *vertical scaling* AT. I provided a quick fix for this problem such that, after 10 *minutes*, each subject was able to continue with the experiment. Moreover, after the controlled experiment, I have released a new version of AT tooling in which the problem is resolved completely.

  - When applying the *vertical scaling* AT, subjects were confused where to apply the *vertical scaling container* AT role; despite of a precise description in the AT's documentation at [Clob] to which the task description points (task 1.1 of the document given in Appendix D.5). After again pointing to this description, each subject was able to apply the AT correctly. In the subsequent application of the *horizontal scaling* AT, the problem did not occur anymore.

- Close to the end of the controlled experiment with the treatment group, 1 subject had to leave earlier than expected. The subject has acknowledged to have selected the wrong AT for applying the horizontal scaling architectural pattern before leaving (i.e., the *horizontal scaling* AT for assembly contexts instead of the AT for resource containers). However, the subject did not manage to fix this issue due to time pressure.

E.2. Controlled Experiment: Analysis

In this section, I analyze the empirical data that Nützel has collected during the pre-study of the controlled experiment. Table E.1 provides an overview of this data; depicted measurements directly correspond to the metrics of the GQM plan (cf. Table 5.1 in Section 5.2). The first column specifies the metric of interest while the second and third column provides the measurements for the application of the *vertical scaling* AT and *horizontal scaling* AT, respectively. Rows are grouped via horizontal lines according to the research questions from Section 5.2, e.g., the first research question is covered by the first four rows of metric measurements. Structured along these research questions, the corresponding measurements depicted in Table E.1 are analyzed in the following. The analysis covers a brief description of the measurements and the test of hypotheses associated to each research question. The interpretation of the analysis is left to a dedicated interpretation section (Section E.3).

Table E.1.: Metric measurements collected in the controlled experiment

	vertical scaling	horizontal scaling (res. container)
$M_{\textbf{time: modeling \& analysis}}$	$20.0\,min.$ (avg.; upper bound)	$9.4\,min.$ (avg.)
$M_{\textbf{\#ATs}}$	7	
$M_{\textbf{\#AT roles}}$	1	1
$M_{\textbf{\#AT parameters}}$	6	4
$M_{\Delta\textbf{time}}$	$36.7\,min.$ (avg.; lower bound)	$110.6\,min.$ (avg.; lower bound)
$M_{\Delta\textbf{components}}$	0	1
$M_{\Delta\textbf{assembly ctx.}}$ *	0	$1 + 7(r\text{-}1)$
$M_{\Delta\textbf{operations}}$	0	0
$M_{\Delta\textbf{self-adapt.}}$	150	803
$M_{\textbf{\#detected violations}}$	0	0
$M_{\textbf{\#resolved violations}}$	0	0
$M_{\textbf{benefits}}$	"the instructions for the experiment were good" [subject of control group], "based on an AT's documentation, AT application is straight-forward" [subject of treatment group]	
$M_{\textbf{limitations}}$	"the main issue is with compilation errors produced when something is wrong with the QVT-O file and with debugging support" [subject of control group], "the reconfiguration engine does not work correctly" [subject of control group], "tooling problems still exist" [our observation]	

* r denotes the number of initial replicas with $r \geq 1$.

Analysis: How much effort do software architects require to apply ATs?
The measurement on the effort of software architects ($Q_{\textbf{application effort}}$) are depicted in the first measurement group in Table E.1.

Measurement description. For modeling and analysis of the architectural model, subjects of the treatment group have required, on average, $20.0\,minutes$ for the *vertical scaling* AT and $9.4\,minutes$ for the *horizontal scaling* AT ($M_{\textbf{time for modeling and analysis}}$).

Unfortunately, Nützel has not measured the time for the *vertical scaling* AT because of the required interventions. I have therefore assigned each participant a pessimistic upper bound of $20.0\,minutes$ in retrospect; based on the subject that finished with the task on the *vertical scaling* AT at last (excluding the time spend for interventions).

For the *horizontal scaling* AT, Nützel has measured $6, 8, 12, 10$, and 11 *minutes* for each respective subject regarding $M_{\textbf{time for modeling and analysis}}$. These values result in the given average of $9.4\,minutes$ with a standard deviation of $2.4\,minutes$

As shown in Table C.7, subjects have selected ATs from the catalog of 7 ATs ($M_{\#\text{ATs}}$) that we have created during the CloudStore case study. As before, the *horizontal scaling* and *horizontal scaling* AT both contain 1 role ($M_{\#\text{AT roles}}$). Moreover, the *vertical scaling* AT contains 6 parameters and the *horizontal scaling* AT contains 4 parameters ($M_{\#\text{AT parameters}}$).

Hypothesis testing. These measurements make it hard to reliably test $H_{\text{time-size correlation}}$ but allow to accept $H_{\text{effort is low}}$, as described in the following.

Calculating the Pearson correlation coefficient [WRH⁺00, Sec. 10.1] over the selected and applied ATs yields:

- no value between $M_{\text{time for modeling and analysis}}$ and $M_{\#\text{AT roles}}$ because each measurement for $M_{\#\text{AT roles}}$ is the same (which does not allow to calculate the Pearson correlation coefficient; however, is an indication for no correlation), and
- 1 between $M_{\text{time for modeling and analysis}}$ and $M_{\#\text{AT parameters}}$ (which is, however, based only on two ATs).

Because of this low amount of data, $H_{\text{time-size correlation}}$ cannot be tested reliably.

In contrast, hypothesis $H_{\text{effort is low}}$ is accepted because each value for $M_{\text{time for modeling and analysis}}$ is below the defined threshold of 40 *minutes*. Here, $M_{\text{time for modeling and analysis}}$ includes all efforts spend on AT actions plus succeeding analysis actions. The hypothesis can therefore be accepted reliably.

Analysis: How much creation effort can software architects save when applying ATs? The measurement on effort savings for software architects ($Q_{\text{effort saving}}$) are depicted in the second measurement group in Table E.1.

Measurement description. In contrast to the previously described case studies, the controlled experiment involves a control group that allows to measure $M_{\Delta\text{time}}$.

For tasks on the *vertical scaling* architectural pattern, the subjects of the control group required 60, 60, and 50 *minutes*. These values result in an average of 56.7 *minutes* with a standard deviation of 5.8 *minutes*. Thus, the resulting value for $M_{\Delta\textbf{time}}$ is 36.7 *minutes*. This value is an upper bound because of the pessimistically estimated upper bound for $M_{\textbf{time for modeling and analysis}}$ and the fact that only one of three subjects of the control group was able to provide correct analysis results (cf. [Nï5, Sec. 5.1]).

For tasks on the *vertical scaling* architectural pattern, both remaining subjects of the control group required the complete allocated time of 120 *minutes* without succeeding. Therefore, the $M_{\Delta\textbf{time}}$ has resulted in an average of 110.6 *minutes* as a lower bound.

The measurements of the remaining difference metrics (i.e., $M_{\Delta\textbf{components}}$, $M_{\Delta\textbf{assembly ctx.}}$, $M_{\Delta\textbf{operations}}$, $M_{\Delta\textbf{self-adapt.}}$) result in the same values as taken during the CloudStore case study (cf. Appendix C.1.4.4). Values must be the same because corresponding measurements are only depending on the applied ATs.

Hypothesis testing. These measurements allow to accept both hypothesis $H_{\Delta\textbf{time-}\Delta\textbf{size correlation}}$ and hypothesis $H_{\textbf{effort is lowered}}$ as described in the following.

As for the previously described research question, testing the hypothesis $H_{\Delta\textbf{time-}\Delta\textbf{size correlation}}$ is hard because of too few data (only on two different ATs). However, the correlation between $M_{\Delta\textbf{time}}$ and $M_{\Delta\textbf{self-adapt.}}$ is likely to be causal, as discussed in the next section.

Regarding $H_{\textbf{effort is lowered}}$, none of the measurements for $M_{\Delta\textbf{components}}$, $M_{\Delta\textbf{assembly ctx.}}$, $M_{\Delta\textbf{operations}}$, and $M_{\Delta\textbf{self-adapt.}}$ is negative. Therefore, hypothesis $H_{\textbf{effort is lowered}}$ can directly be accepted.

Analysis: Do software architects effectively benefit from checking whether their architectural models violate conformance to applied ATs? The measurement on conformance checking ($Q_{\textbf{conformance}}$) are depicted in the third measurement group in Table E.1.

Measurement description. Nützel does not report on detected conformance violations, thus, the measurement of $M_{\#\textbf{detected violations}}$ is 0. Consequently, $M_{\#\textbf{resolved violations}}$ must be 0 as well.

Hypothesis testing. Because no violations were detected, hypothesis $H_{\textbf{violations are detected}}$ is rejected. Testing hypothesis $H_{\textbf{violations are resolved}}$ is useless for the case of 0 detected violations.

Analysis: What are effective benefits of the AT method? The measurement on benefits ($Q_{\textbf{benefits}}$) are depicted in the fourth measurement group in Table E.1.

Measurement description. The measurement of $M_{\textbf{benefits}}$ has resulted in the 2 collected benefits given in Table E.1. The given statements are citations of answers by involved subjects to questions of the task descriptions as given in Appendix D.5 and Appendix D.6.

Hypothesis testing. Because benefits were identified, $H_{\textbf{benefits exist}}$ is accepted.

Analysis: What are effective limitations of the AT method? The measurement on limitations ($Q_{\textbf{limitations}}$) are depicted in the fifth measurement group in Table E.1.

Measurement description. The measurement of $M_{\textbf{limitations}}$ has resulted in the 3 collected limitations given in Table E.1. Analogously to benefits, the first 2 of these limitations were directly collected from subjects involves in the experiment. The third limitation is an observation we made during the experiment.

Hypothesis testing. Because limitations were identified, $H_{\textbf{limitations exist}}$ is accepted.

E.3. Controlled Experiment: Interpretation

Based on the data analysis in the previous section, this section proceeds with answering the associated questions of the GQM plan (cf. Table 5.1 in Section 5.2).

Answering $Q_{\text{application effort}}$: How much effort do software architects require to apply ATs? The acceptance of $H_{\textbf{effort is low}}$ indicates that software architects have low effort in using ATs for architectural analyses (compared to the overall efforts for specifying architectural models). Indeed, with an average of 9.4 *minutes* for the *horizontal scaling* AT, subjects of the controlled experiment were close to our efforts of 6 *minutes* to apply this AT during the CloudStore case study (cf. Appendix C.1.4.4). Given that inexperienced software architects were selected as subjects, our results from Appendix C.3.3.3 are therefore confirmed: the AT method indeed achieves an increase efficiency for novice software architects.

Answering $Q_{\text{effort saving}}$: How much creation effort can software architects save when applying ATs? The acceptance of $H_{\boldsymbol{\Delta}\textbf{time-}\boldsymbol{\Delta}\textbf{size correlation}}$ is based on the positive correlation between $M_{\boldsymbol{\Delta}\textbf{time}}$ and $M_{\boldsymbol{\Delta}\textbf{self-adapt.}}$. Indeed, we can confirm that we had significant efforts for specifying the self-adaptation rules of the investigated ATs (cf. Appendix C.1.4.4) and, thus, reusing these rules saves significant amount of effort. The two investigated ATs indicate that the faced time can range from half an hour to more than two hours. Compared to the typical time for applying ATs (3 *minutes* on average; cf. $M_{\textbf{time for AT application}}$ in the CloudStore case study), the saved time of 36.7 *minutes* (*vertical scaling* AT) and 110.6 *minutes* (*horizontal scaling* AT) is significant because these values range from approximately 92 % to approximately 97 % saved time.

Moreover, the data for these adaptation-intensive ATs shows that rule reuse can render other effort-saving factors less significant. For example, the difference metric for components ($M_{\boldsymbol{\Delta}\textbf{components}}$) is a bad indicator for saved effort of the investigated ATs. The data therefore indicates that combining difference metrics (e.g., via a linear combination) potentially yields a better predictor for effort saving than considering each metric in separation.

The acceptance of $H_{\textbf{effort is lowered}}$ indicates that effort can effectively be lowered by applying ATs. The interpretation of this result is analogous to the CloudStore case study because both the *vertical scaling* AT and the *horizontal scaling* AT were applied there as well.

Answering $Q_{\textbf{conform.}}$: Do software architects effectively benefit from checking whether their architectural models violate conformance to applied ATs? The rejection of $H_{\textbf{violations are detected}}$ indicates that (at least for this setup of the controlled experiment where the *vertical scaling* AT and *horizontal scaling* AT are applied to CloudStore) no benefits were gained from automated conformance checks. Appendix C.3.3.3 discusses this observation in detail.

Answering $Q_{\textbf{benefits}}$: What are effective benefits of the AT method? The 2 benefits collected during the experiment ($M_{\textbf{benefits}}$) indicate that experiment tasks were clear and that AT application is manageable in the context of controlled experiments.

The first benefit ("the instructions for the experiment were good") covers the clarity of experiment tasks. A subject of the control group explicitly wrote this statement in a free text field of the task description. The fact that the subject did so without being asked explicitly about the quality of the instructions is an indication that the task description is indeed comprehensible. Another indication for comprehensibility is that we received no clarification questions regarding the task description. We conclude that experiments in future work can reuse our task description or create similar ones.

The second benefit ("based on an AT's documentation, AT application is straight-forward") points to the suitability of AT applications within controlled experiments and a good usability of ATs in general. However, for the *vertical scaling* AT, we observed confusion about how to apply the AT. Only after we have again pointed to the Wiki with the AT's documentation [Clob], participants were able to correctly apply the AT. Afterwards, for the *horizontal scaling* AT, participants had no problems to apply the AT. We conclude that AT documentation is essential. While the Wiki [Clob] has the advantage that it is easily accessible, its disadvantage is that it is not tightly integrated into AT tooling—software architects currently have to manually access the Wiki. Future versions of AT tooling should therefore strive for a tight integration of AT documentation in addition to the Wiki, e.g., by offering a context help during AT application.

Answering $Q_{\text{limitations}}$: What are effective limitations of the AT method?
The 3 limitations collected during the experiment ($M_{\text{limitations}}$) mainly point to technical issues in AT tooling and in tools extended by AT tooling.

The first limitation ("the main issue is with compilation errors produced when something is wrong with the QVT-O file and with debugging support") was reported by a subject of the control group and relates to difficulties when specifying reconfiguration rules for SimuLizar. The subject notes that debugging is difficult when using QVT-O in conjunction with SimuLizar. SimuLizar indeed lacks support for a debugging mode in which breakpoints in the QVT-O file are considered; debugging is purely based on logging. Furthermore, we have experienced the same issue when we acted as AT engineers to specify ATs that include reusable self-adaptation rules. While this is only a technical issue and no conceptual one, future work on SimuLizar on improving debugging support can increase SimuLizar's practical relevance.

The second limitation ("the reconfiguration engine does not work correctly") describes an issue observed by a subject of the control group. Instead of using *QVT-O*, the subject tried to use Story Diagrams [vDHP+12] as an alternative M2M transformation language to specify reconfiguration rules (cf. Section 2.5.3.2). Unfortunately, SimuLizar's engine for executing reconfiguration rules for Story Diagrams suffers from bugs causing a wrong reconfiguration behavior. Because of this technical issue, the subject was unable to provide correct analysis result. This issue should be fixed in future works, despite not affecting the utility of ATs as long as QVT-O reconfiguration rules are used.

The third limitation ("tooling problems still exist") is an observation we made during the controlled experiment with the treatment group. As described in Section E.1, we had to intervene because of problems in AT tooling. However, at the time of writing, the reported problem has been already resolved in AT tooling.

This example shows that Nützel's pre-study has helped in improving the AT method. Moreover, despite conceptually unimportant, tooling issues bias subjects in empirical evaluations. These biases can lead to questionable conclusions that, most notably, may not reflect the properties of the concepts under investigation. We therefore conclude that future empirical investigations should optimally first resolve currently known tooling issues or explicitly explain subjects how to handle such issues.

E.4. Controlled Experiment: Evaluation of Validity

Compared to all previously conducted case studies, Nützel's pre-study for a controlled experiment investigates the AT method with multiple software architects executing the same tasks in a between-subjects design, i.e., with a treatment and a control group. Therefore, threats related to internal validity and statistical power are less crucial; due to the fact that insights were not solely based on the performance of a single subject. The more controlled environment has improved internal validity further and has reduced the "random irrelevancies in experimental setting" threat (cf. conclusion validity threats in Appendix C.1.4.6).

However, a main issue still threatens the validity of gained insights: despite more controlled than the cases studies, several random factors occurred during the experiment that have disturbed measurements. These factors are listed in Section E.1, e.g., the intervention due to tooling issues. The occurrence of these factors shows the value of a pre-study—for conducting a controlled experiment in future works, experimenters can plan for suitable countermeasures, e.g., by resolving all known tooling issues before starting the experiment.

Moreover, especially the number of participants in the control group can be considered as low, thus, contributing to the "low statistical power" threat of conclusion validity (cf. Appendix C.1.4.6). Given that only few experts on Palladio and SimuLizar exist, it would even in future experiments be hard to find enough subjects for gaining conclusive results. A potential countermeasure is to let subjects of the control group undergo a preceding training, similar to the treatment group.

Another option is to depart from the between-subjects design in favor of a design with a treatment group only. As the pre-study has shown, insights about the AT method can be gained even when not comparing the treatment group with the control group, e.g., about the time it takes software architects to apply ATs. Such a design has the advantage that less experimentation effort is required for a separate experiment with a control group. The disadvantage is that such a design makes it impossible to directly compare the AT method against conventional approaches. Therefore, the two discussed designs are orthogonal to each other and both point to potential experiments in future works.

Bibliography

The references of this bibliography are structured along my own publication (cited and uncited), theses I have supervised and cited, and externally cited literature.

Own Publications (Cited)

[BBB+16] Steffen Becker, Fabian Brosig, Erik Burger, Axel Busch, Zoya Durdik, Jens Happe, Lucia Happe, Christoph Heger, Robert Heinrich, Jörg Henss, Nikolaus Huber, Oliver Hummel, Benjamin Klatt, Anne Koziolek, Heiko Koziolek, Max Kramer, Klaus Krogmann, Martin Küster, Michael Langhammer, Sebastian Lehrig, Philipp Merkle, Florian Meyerer, Qais Noorshams, Ralf H. Reussner, Kiana Rostami, Simon Spinner, Christian Stier, Misha Strittmatter, and Alexander Wert. *Modeling and Simulating Software Architectures – The Palladio Approach.* MIT Press, Cambridge, MA, October 2016. Contributed to chapters 3, 4, 8, 11, and 15. URL: `http://mitpress.mit.edu/books/modeling-and-simulating-software-architectures`.

[BBL17] Steffen Becker, Gunnar Brataas, and Sebastian Lehrig, editors. *Engineering Scalable, Elastic, and Cost-Efficient Cloud Computing Applications: The CloudScale Method.* Springer, Berlin, Heidelberg, 2017. `doi:10.1007/978-3-319-54286-7`.

[BLB15] Matthias Becker, Sebastian Lehrig, and Steffen Becker. Systematically Deriving Quality Metrics for Cloud Computing Systems. In *Proceedings of the 6th ACM/SPEC International Conference on Performance Engineering*, ICPE '15, pages 169–174, New York, NY, USA, 2015. ACM. `doi:10.1145/2668930.2688043`.

[BSL+13] Gunnar Brataas, Erlend Stav, Sebastian Lehrig, Steffen Becker, Goran Kopčak, and Darko Huljenic. CloudScale: Scalability Management for Cloud Systems. In *Proceedings of the 4th ACM/SPEC International Conference on Performance Engineering*, ICPE '13, pages 335–338, New York, NY, USA, 2013. ACM. doi:10.1145/2479871.2479920.

[BSL16] Gunnar Brataas, Erlend Stav, and Sebastian Lehrig. Analysing Evolution of Work and Load. In *12th International ACM SIGSOFT Conference on Quality of Software Architectures (QoSA)*, pages 90–95, April 2016. doi:10.1109/QoSA.2016.18.

[GL13] Daria Giacinto and Sebastian Lehrig. Towards Integrating Java EE into ProtoCom. In Steffen Becker, Wilhelm Hasselbring, André van Hoorn, and Ralf H. Reussner, editors, *Proceedings of the Symposium on Software Performance: Joint Kieker/Palladio Days 2013, Karlsruhe, Germany, November 27-29, 2013.*, volume 1083 of *CEUR Workshop Proceedings*, pages 69–78. CEUR-WS.org, 2013. URL: http://ceur-ws.org/Vol-1083/paper8.pdf.

[HFL16] Marcus Hilbrich, Markus Frank, and Sebastian Lehrig. Security Modeling with Palladio – Different Approaches. In *Proceedings of the Symposium on Software Performance 2016, 8-9 November 2016, Kiel, Germany*, 2016.

[KHK+17] Jóakim Von Kistowski, Nikolas Herbst, Samuel Kounev, Henning Groenda, Christian Stier, and Sebastian Lehrig. Modeling and Extracting Load Intensity Profiles. *ACM Trans. Auton. Adapt. Syst.*, 11(4):23:1–23:28, January 2017. doi:10.1145/3019596.

[KL14] Christian Klaussner and Sebastian Lehrig. Using Java EE ProtoCom for SAP HANA Cloud. In *Proceedings of the Symposium on Software Performance 2014, 26-28 November 2014, Stuttgart, Germany*, 2014.

[LB14a] Sebastian Lehrig and Matthias Becker. Approaching the Cloud: Using Palladio for Scalability, Elasticity, and Efficiency Analyses. In *Proceedings of the Symposium on Software Performance 2014, 26-28 November 2014, Stuttgart, Germany*, 2014.

[LB14b] Sebastian Lehrig and Steffen Becker. CloudScale – Skalierbarkeit für die Cloud. *ForschungsForum Paderborn*, 17:20–23, February 2014.

[LB15a] Sebastian Lehrig and Steffen Becker. Beyond Simulation: Composing Scalability, Elasticity, and Efficiency Analyses from Preexisting Analysis Results. In *Proceedings of the 2015 Workshop on Challenges in Performance Methods for Software Development*, WOSP '15, pages 29–34, New York, NY, USA, 2015. ACM. doi:10.1145/2693561.2693568.

[LB15b] Sebastian Lehrig and Steffen Becker. The CloudScale Method for Software Scalability, Elasticity, and Efficiency Engineering: A Tutorial. In *Proceedings of the 6th ACM/SPEC International Conference on Performance Engineering*, ICPE '15, pages 329–331, New York, NY, USA, 2015. ACM. doi:10.1145/2668930.2688818.

[LB15c] Sebastian Lehrig and Steffen Becker. Software Architecture Design Assistants Need Controlled Efficiency Experiments: Lessons Learned from a Survey. In *Proceedings of the 1st International Workshop on Future of Software Architecture Design Assistants*, FoSADA '15, pages 19–24, New York, NY, USA, 2015. ACM. doi:10.1145/2751491.2751492.

[LB16] Sebastian Lehrig and Steffen Becker. Using Performance Models for Planning the Redeployment to Infrastructure-as-a-Service Environments: A Case Study. In *2016 12th International ACM SIGSOFT Conference on Quality of Software Architectures (QoSA)*, pages 11–20, April 2016. doi:10.1109/QoSA.2016.17.

[LE15] Sebastian Lehrig and Hendrik Eikerling. Analyzing Cost-Efficiency of Cloud Computing Applications with SimuLizar. In *Proceedings of the Symposium on Software Performance 2015, 4-6 November 2015, Munich, Germany*, 2015. URL: http://pi.informatik.uni-siegen.de/stt/35_3/index.html.

[LEB15] Sebastian Lehrig, Hendrik Eikerling, and Steffen Becker. Scalability, Elasticity, and Efficiency in Cloud Computing: A Systematic Literature Review of Definitions and Metrics. In *Proceedings of the 11th International ACM SIGSOFT Conference on Quality of*

Software Architectures, QoSA '15, pages 83–92, New York, NY, USA, 2015. ACM. **Received distinguished paper award (out of 14 papers in total)**. doi:10.1145/2737182.2737185.

[Leh12] Sebastian Lehrig. Assessing the Quality of Model-to-Model Transformations Based on Scenarios. Master's thesis, Software Engineering Group, Heinz Nixdorf Institute, Paderborn University, October 2012.

[Leh13] Sebastian Lehrig. Architectural Templates: Engineering Scalable SaaS Applications Based on Architectural Styles. In Martin Gogolla, editor, *Proceedings of the MODELS 2013 Doctoral Symposium co-located with the 16th International ACM/IEEE Conference on Model Driven Engineering Languages and Systems (MODELS 2013), Miami, USA, October 1, 2013.*, volume 1071 of *CEUR Workshop Proceedings*, pages 48–55. CEUR-WS.org, 2013. URL: http://ceur-ws.org/Vol-1071/lehrig.pdf.

[Leh14a] Sebastian Lehrig. Applying Architectural Templates for Design-Time Scalability and Elasticity Analyses of SaaS Applications. In *Proceedings of the 2nd International Workshop on Hot Topics in Cloud Service Scalability*, HotTopiCS '14, pages 2:1–2:8, New York, NY, USA, 2014. ACM. doi:10.1145/2649563.2649573.

[Leh14b] Sebastian Lehrig. The Architectural Template Method: Design-Time Engineering of SaaS Applications. In Dimka Karastoyanova, editor, *PhD Session at the Advanced School on Service Oriented Computing 2014 (Summer SOC 2014), At Hersonissos, Crete, Greece, July 1, 2014.*, 2014. doi:10.13140/2.1.1281.1040.

[Leh16] Sebastian Lehrig. Quality Analysis Lab (QuAL): Software Design Description and Developer Guide Version 1.0. Technical report, May 2016. URL: https://sdqweb.ipd.kit.edu/wiki/QuAL.

[LHB17] Sebastian Lehrig, Marcus Hilbrich, and Steffen Becker. The Architectural Template Method: Templating Architectural Knowledge to Efficiently Conduct Quality-of-Service Analyses. *Software: Practice and Experience*, 2017. **Journal paper summarizing this thesis**. doi:10.1002/spe.2517.

[LLK13] Michael Langhammer, Sebastian Lehrig, and Max E. Kramer. Reuse and Configuration for Code Generating Architectural Refinement Transformations. In *Proceedings of the 1st Workshop on View-Based, Aspect-Oriented and Orthographic Software Modelling*, VAO '13, pages 6:1–6:5, New York, NY, USA, 2013. ACM. doi:10.1145/2489861.2489866.

[LSB+17] Sebastian Lehrig, Richard Sanders, Gunnar Brataas, Mariano Cecowski, Simon Ivanšekc, and Jure Polutnik. CloudStore - Towards Scalability, Elasticity, and Efficiency Benchmarking and Analysis in Cloud Computing. *Future Generation Computer Systems*, 2017. doi:10.1016/j.future.2017.04.018.

[LZ11] Sebastian Lehrig and Thomas Zolynski. Performance Prototyping with ProtoCom in a Virtualised Environment: A Case Study. In *Proceedings to Palladio Days 2011, 17-18 November 2011, FZI Forschungszentrum Informatik, Karlsruhe, Germany*, 2011.

[SJR+16] Misha Strittmatter, Michael Junker, Kiana Rostami, Sebastian Lehrig, Amine Kechaou, Bo Liu, and Robert Heinrich. Extensible Graphical Editors for Palladio. In *Proceedings of the Symposium on Software Performance 2016, 8-9 November 2016, Kiel, Germany*, November 2016.

[SL13] Christian Stritzke and Sebastian Lehrig. Why and How We Should Use Graphiti to Implement PCM Editors. In Steffen Becker, Wilhelm Hasselbring, André van Hoorn, and Ralf H. Reussner, editors, *Proceedings of the Symposium on Software Performance: Joint Kieker/Palladio Days 2013, Karlsruhe, Germany, November 27-29, 2013.*, volume 1083 of *CEUR Workshop Proceedings*, pages 1–10. CEUR-WS.org, 2013. URL: http://ceur-ws.org/Vol-1083/paper1.pdf.

[vL13] Markus von Detten and Sebastian Lehrig. Reengineering of Component-Based Systems in the Presence of Design Deficiencies – An Overview. In *Proceedings of the 15th Workshop Software-Reengineering*, page 2. Gesellschaft für Informatik, May 2013.

Own Publications (Uncited)

[FHL15] Markus Frank, Marcus Hilbrich, and Sebastian Lehrig. Improved Scalability for Job-centric Monitoring in Distributed Infrastructures. In Marian Bubak, Michał Turala, and Kazimierz Wiatr, editors, *CGW Workshop '15 Proceedings*, pages 79–80. ACC Cyfronet AGH, October 2015. ISBN 978-83-61433-14-9.

[HLF16] Marcus Hilbrich, Sebastian Lehrig, and Markus Frank. Measured Values Lost in Time—or How I rose from a User to a Developer of Palladio. Technical report, November 2016. Published as technical report. URL: `http://nbn-resolving.de/urn:nbn:de:bsz:ch1-qucosa-213813`.

[Leh15a] Sebastian Lehrig. The Architectural Template Method – Engineering of Software-as-a-Service Cloud Applications, February 2015. Peer-reviewed conference poster presented at the 6th ACM/SPEC International Conference on Performance Engineering (ICPE '15), Austin, Texas, USA. **Received best poster award (out of 15 posters in total)**. `doi:10.13140/2.1.1952.8480`.

[Leh15b] Sebastian Lehrig. CloudScale – Scalability Management for Cloud Computing, May 2015. Peer-reviewed conference poster presented at the 11th International ACM SIGSOFT Conference on Quality of Software Architectures (QoSA '15), Montréal, QC, Canada. `doi:10.13140/RG.2.1.4081.8088`.

Supervised Theses (Cited)

[Abd14] Mohammed Abdulkarim. Performance Engineering for SAP HANA Cloud Applications with Palladio. Master's thesis, Software Engineering Group, Heinz Nixdorf Institute, Paderborn University, February 2014.

[Eik14] Hendrik Eikerling. Scalability, Elasticity, and Efficiency in Cloud Computing – a Systematic Literature Review. Bachelor's thesis, Software Engineering Group, Heinz Nixdorf Institute, Paderborn University, July 2014.

[Gia16] Daria Loana Giacinto. Assuring the Conceptual Integrity of Architectural Pattern and Style Applications for Design-Time Analyses. Master's thesis, s-lab – Software Quality Lab, Paderborn University, February 2016.

[Gop14] Vinay Akkasetty Gopal. Dynamic Environment Model for Performance Analysis of Self-Adaptive Systems. Master's thesis, Software Engineering Group, Heinz Nixdorf Institute, Paderborn University, December 2014. (supervised together with Matthias Becker).

[Kla14] Christian Klaussner. Extensible Performance Prototype Transformations for Multiple Platforms. Bachelor's thesis, Software Engineering Group, Heinz Nixdorf Institute, Paderborn University, July 2014.

[Nï15] Christoph Nützel. An Efficiency Comparison Between Architectural Templates and SimuLizar: A Controlled Experiment. Bachelor's thesis, Software Engineering Chair, Chemnitz University of Technology, December 2015.

[Ope17] Alexander Openkowski. Integrating Reuse Principles in the Engineering of Architectural Templates. Master's thesis, Software Engineering Chair, Chemnitz University of Technology, January 2017.

[Sax15] Manoveg Saxena. Analyzing the Accuracy of Palladio for Dynamic MapReduce Environments. Master's thesis, Software Engineering Group, Heinz Nixdorf Institute, Paderborn University, March 2015.

Cited Literature

[ABGJ05] Muhammad Ali Babar, Ian Gorton, and Ross Jeffery. Capturing and Using Software Architecture Knowledge for Architecture-Based Software Development. In *Proceedings of the Fifth International Conference on Quality Software*, QSIC '05, pages 169–176, Washington, DC, USA, 2005. IEEE Computer Society. doi:10.1109/QSIC.2005.17.

[ABJ+10] Thorsten Arendt, Enrico Biermann, Stefan Jurack, Christian Krause, and Gabriele Taentzer. Henshin: Advanced Concepts and Tools for In-place EMF Model Transformations. In *Proceedings of the 13th International Conference on Model Driven Engineering Languages and Systems: Part I*, MODELS '10, pages 121–135, Berlin, Heidelberg, 2010. Springer-Verlag. URL: http://dl.acm.org/citation.cfm?id=1926458.1926471.

[Abr96] J.-R. Abrial. *The B-book: Assigning Programs to Meanings.* Cambridge University Press, New York, NY, USA, 1996.

[Ale77] Christopher Alexander. *A Pattern Language: Towns, Buildings, Construction.* Oxford University Press, 1977.

[All97] Robert Allen. *A Formal Approach to Software Architecture.* PhD thesis, Carnegie Mellon, School of Computer Science, January 1997. Issued as CMU Technical Report CMU-CS-97-144.

[Ame11] American Heritage Dictionary. *"Template" Definition.* The American Heritage Dictionary of the English Language. Houghton Mifflin Harcourt, 5th edition, November 2011. URL: https://ahdictionary.com/word/search.html?q=template [Visited on 30/07/17].

[APS07] Nuno Amálio, Fiona Polack, and Susan Stepney. Frameworks Based on Templates for Rigorous Model-Driven Development. *Electron. Notes Theor. Comput. Sci.*, 191:3–23, October 2007. doi:10.1016/j.entcs.2007.09.002.

[ASB10] Colin Atkinson, Dietmar Stoll, and Philipp Bostan. *Orthographic Software Modeling: A Practical Approach to View-Based Development*, pages 206–219. Springer Berlin Heidelberg, Berlin, Heidelberg, 2010. doi:10.1007/978-3-642-14819-4_15.

[ATt] AT Tooling. https://github.com/PalladioSimulator/Architectural-Templates [Visited on 30/07/17].

[AWS16] AWS Architecture Center, 2016. https://aws.amazon.com/architecture/ [Visited on 30/07/17].

[Bas07] Victor R. Basili. The Role of Controlled Experiments in Software Engineering Research. In Victor R. Basili, Dieter Rombach, Kurt Schneider, Barbara Kitchenham, Dietmar Pfahl, and Richard W. Selby, editors, *Empirical Software Engineering Issues. Critical Assessment and Future Directions*, volume 4336 of *Lecture Notes in Computer Science*, pages 33–37. Springer Berlin Heidelberg, 2007. doi:10.1007/978-3-540-71301-2_10.

[BBJ+08] Achim Baier, Steffen Becker, Martin Jung, Klaus Krogmann, Carsten Röttgers, Niels Streekmann, Karsten Thoms, and Steffen Zschaler. *Handbuch der Software-Architektur*, chapter Modellgetriebene Software-Entwicklung, pages 93–122. dPunkt.verlag Heidelberg, 2nd edition, December 2008.

[BBM13] Matthias Becker, Steffen Becker, and Joachim Meyer. SimuLizar: Design-Time Modeling and Performance Analysis of Self-Adaptive Systems. In Stefan Kowalewski and Bernhard Rumpe, editors, *Software Engineering 2013: Fachtagung des GI-Fachbereichs Softwaretechnik, 26. Februar - 2. März 2013 in Aachen*, volume 213 of *LNI*, pages 71–84. GI, 2013. URL: http://subs.emis.de/LNI/Proceedings/Proceedings213/article35.html.

[BC87] Kent Beck and Ward Cunningham. Using Pattern Languages for Object-Oriented Programs. Technical Report CR-87-43, Apple Computer, Inc. and Tektronix, Inc., 1987. URL: http://c2.com/doc/oopsla87.html.

[BCH+96] Kim Barrett, Bob Cassels, Paul Haahr, David A. Moon, Keith Playford, and P. Tucker Withington. A Monotonic Superclass Linearization for Dylan. *SIGPLAN Not.*, 31(10):69–82, October 1996. doi:10.1145/236338.236343.

[BCK98] Len Bass, Paul Clements, and Rick Kazman. *Software Architecture in Practice.* Addison-Wesley Longman Publishing Co., Inc., Boston, MA, USA, 1998.

[BCR02] Victor R. Basili, Gianluigi Caldiera, and H. Dieter Rombach. The Goal Question Metric Approach. In John. J. Marciniak, editor, *Encyclopedia of Software Engineering*, pages 578–583. John Wiley & Sons, 2nd edition, 2002.

[Bec08] Steffen Becker. *Coupled Model Transformations for QoS Enabled Component-Based Software Design.* PhD thesis, University of Oldenburg, Germany, January 2008.

[Bel57] Richard Bellman. A Markovian Decision Process. *Indiana Univ. Math. J.*, 6:679–684, 1957.

[BF08] Rainer Böhme and Felix C. Freiling. On Metrics and Measurements. In Irene Eusgeld, Felix C. Freiling, and Ralf Reussner, editors, *Dependability Metrics*, volume 4909 of *Lecture Notes in Computer Science*, pages 7–13. Springer Berlin Heidelberg, 2008. doi:10.1007/978-3-540-68947-8_2.

[BG07a] Muhammad Ali Babar and Ian Gorton. A Tool for Managing Software Architecture Knowledge. In *Proceedings of the Second Workshop on SHAring and Reusing Architectural Knowledge Architecture, Rationale, and Design Intent*, SHARK-ADI '07, pages 11–11, Washington, DC, USA, 2007. IEEE Computer Society. doi:10.1109/SHARK-ADI.2007.1.

[BG07b] Muhammad Ali Babar and Ian Gorton. A Tool for Managing Software Architecture Knowledge. In *Proceedings of the Second Workshop on SHAring and Reusing Architectural Knowledge Architecture, Rationale, and Design Intent*, SHARK-ADI '07, pages 11–18, Washington, DC, USA, 2007. IEEE Computer Society. doi:10.1109/SHARK-ADI.2007.1.

[BGK06] Muhammad Ali Babar, Ian Gorton, and Barbara Kitchenham. *A Framework for Supporting Architecture Knowledge and Rationale Management*, pages 237–254. Springer Berlin Heidelberg, Berlin, Heidelberg, 2006. doi:10.1007/978-3-540-30998-7_11.

[BGMO06] Steffen Becker, Lars Grunske, Raffaela Mirandola, and Sven Overhage. Performance Prediction of Component-Based Systems: A Survey from an Engineering Perspective. In Ralf Reussner, Judith Stafford, and Clemens Szyperski, editors,

Architecting Systems with Trustworthy Components, volume 3938, pages 169–192, 2006.

[BHS07a] Frank Buschmann, Kevlin Henney, and Douglas Schmidt. *Pattern-Oriented Software Architecture: A Pattern Language for Distributed Computing*. John Wiley & Sons, Inc., 2007.

[BHS07b] Frank Buschmann, Kevlin Henney, and Douglas Schmidt. *Pattern-Oriented Software Architecture: On Patterns and Pattern Languages*. John Wiley & Sons, Inc., 2007.

[BJPW99] Antoine Beugnard, Jean-Marc Jézéquel, Noël Plouzeau, and Damien Watkins. Making Components Contract Aware. *Computer*, 32(7):38–45, July 1999. doi:10.1109/2.774917.

[BK98] Falko Bause and Pieter S. Kritzinger. Stochastic Petri Nets: An Introduction to the Theory. *SIGMETRICS Perform. Eval. Rev.*, 26(2):2–3, August 1998. doi:10.1145/288197.581194.

[BKBR12] Franz Brosch, Heiko Koziolek, Barbora Buhnova, and Ralf Reussner. Architecture-Based Reliability Prediction with the Palladio Component Model. *IEEE Transactions on Software Engineering*, 38(6):1319–1339, November 2012. doi:10.1109/TSE.2011.94.

[BKR09] Steffen Becker, Heiko Koziolek, and Ralf Reussner. The Palladio Component Model for Model-Driven Performance Prediction. *J. Syst. Softw.*, 82(1):3–22, January 2009. doi:10.1016/j.jss.2008.03.066.

[BM04] Antonia Bertolino and Raffaela Mirandola. *CB-SPE Tool: Putting Component-Based Performance Engineering into Practice*, pages 233–248. Springer Berlin Heidelberg, Berlin, Heidelberg, 2004. doi:10.1007/978-3-540-24774-6_21.

[BMR+96] Frank Buschmann, Regine Meunier, Hans Rohnert, Peter Sommerlad, and Michael Stal. *Pattern-Oriented Software Architecture: A System of Patterns*. John Wiley & Sons, Inc., New York, NY, USA, 1996.

[Boe78] Barry W. Boehm. *Characteristics of Software Quality*. TRW series of software technology. North-Holland Pub. Co., 1978.

[Bri96] Sjaak Brinkkemper. Method Engineering: Engineering of Information Systems Development Methods and Tools. *Information & Software Technology*, 38(4):275–280, 1996. doi:10.1016/0950-5849(95)01059-9.

[BT03] Barry Boehm and Richard Turner. *Balancing Agility and Discipline: A Guide for the Perplexed.* Addison-Wesley Longman Publishing Co., Inc., Boston, MA, USA, 2003.

[BTN+14] Alexander Bergmayr, Javier Troya, Patrick Neubauer, Manuel Wimmer, and Gerti Kappel. UML-Based Cloud Application Modeling with Libraries, Profiles, and Templates. In Richard F. Paige, Jordi Cabot, Marco Brambilla, Louis M. Rose, and James H. Hill, editors, *Proceedings of the 2nd International Workshop on Model-Driven Engineering on and for the Cloud co-located with the 17th International Conference on Model Driven Engineering Languages and Systems, CloudMDE@MoDELS 2014, Valencia, Spain, September 30, 2014*, volume 1242 of *CEUR Workshop Proceedings*, pages 56–65. CEUR-WS.org, 2014. URL: http://ceur-ws.org/Vol-1242/paper7.pdf.

[Bur14] Erik Burger. *Flexible Views for View-Based Model-Driven Development.* PhD thesis, Karlsruhe Institute of Technology, Karlsruhe, Germany, July 2014. doi:10.5445/KSP/1000043437.

[BW84] Victor R. Basili and David M. Weiss. A Methodology for Collecting Valid Software Engineering Data. *Software Engineering, IEEE Transactions on*, SE-10(6):728–738, November 1984. doi:10.1109/TSE.1984.5010301.

[BZJ04] Muhammad Ali Babar, Liming Zhu, and Ross Jeffery. A Framework for Classifying and Comparing Software Architecture Evaluation Methods. In *Proceedings of the 2004 Australian Software Engineering Conference*, ASWEC '04, pages 309–318, Washington, DC, USA, 2004. IEEE Computer Society. doi:10.1109/ASWEC.2004.1290484.

[CA05] Krzysztof Czarnecki and Michał Antkiewicz. Mapping Features to Models: A Template Approach Based on Superimposed Variants. In *Proceedings of the 4th International Conference on Generative Programming and Component Engineering*, GPCE '05, pages 422–437, Berlin, Heidelberg, 2005. Springer-Verlag. doi:10.1007/11561347_28.

[Car88] Rudolf Carnap. *Meaning and Necessity: A Study in Semantics and Modal Logic.* Midway reprints. University of Chicago Press, 1988.

[CB05] Siobhàn Clarke and Elisa Baniassad. *Aspect-Oriented Analysis and Design: The Theme Approach.* Addison-Wesley Professional, 2005.

[CBBD09] Eric Cariou, Nicolas Belloir, Franck Barbier, and Nidal Djemam. OCL contracts for the verification of model transformations. *ECEASST*, 24, 2009. URL: http://journal.ub.tu-berlin.de/index.php/eceasst/article/view/326.

[CD00] John Cheesman and John Daniels. *UML Components: A Simple Process for Specifying Component-Based Software.* Addison-Wesley Longman Publishing Co., Inc., Boston, MA, USA, 2000.

[CE00] Krzysztof Czarnecki and Ulrich W. Eisenecker. *Generative Programming: Methods, Tools, and Applications.* ACM Press/Addison-Wesley Publishing Co., New York, NY, USA, 2000.

[CG02] Vittorio Cortellessa and Vincenzo Grassi. A Performance-Based Methodology to Early Evaluate the Effectiveness of Mobile Software Architectures. *The Journal of Logic and Algebraic Programming*, 51(1):77–100, 2002. doi:10.1016/S1567-8326(01)00016-9.

[CGS09] Shang-Wen Cheng, David Garlan, and Bradley Schmerl. Evaluating the Effectiveness of the Rainbow Self-Adaptive System. In *Proceedings of the 2009 ICSE Workshop on Software Engineering for Adaptive and Self-Managing Systems*, SEAMS '09, pages 132–141, Washington, DC, USA, 2009. IEEE Computer Society. doi:10.1109/SEAMS.2009.5069082.

[CH06] Krzysztof Czarnecki and Simon Helsen. Feature-Based Survey of Model Transformation Approaches. *IBM Syst. J.*, 45(3):621–645, July 2006. doi:10.1147/sj.453.0621.

[CHE04] Krzysztof Czarnecki, Simon Helsen, and Ulrich W. Eisenecker. *Staged Configuration Using Feature Models*, pages 266–283. Springer Berlin Heidelberg, 2004. doi:10.1007/978-3-540-28630-1_17.

[CHE05] Krzysztof Czarnecki, Simon Helsen, and Ulrich W. Eisenecker. Formalizing Cardinality-Based Feature Models and their Specialization. *Software Process: Improvement and Practice*, 10(1):7–29, 2005.

[CKK02] Paul Clements, Rick Kazman, and Mark Klein. *Evaluating Software Architectures: Methods and Case Studies*. SEI series in software engineering. Addison-Wesley Longman Publishing Co., Inc., Boston, MA, USA, 2002.

[Cloa] CloudScale Environment. http://www.cloudscale-project.eu/results/tools [Visited on 30/07/17].

[Clob] CloudScale Wiki: HowTos. http://wiki.cloudscale-project.eu/wiki/index.php/HowTos [Visited on 30/07/17].

[Clo14] Cloud Select Industry Group on Service Level Agreements Subgroup (C-SIG SLA). Cloud Service Level Agreement Standardisation Guidelines. Technical report, Cloud Select Industry Group (C-SIG), 2014.

[Clo16a] CloudStore Case Study Material: CloudStore Documentation, Source Code, Deployment Scripts, Architectural Model, and Raw Measurement Data, 2016. https://github.com/CloudScale-Project/CloudStore and https://github.com/CloudScale-Project/Examples/tree/master/CloudStore/analyser.

[Clo16b] CloudStore Screencasts, 2016. http://www.cloudscale-project.eu/results/screencasts/.

[CMSD04] Eric Cariou, Raphaël Marvie, Lionel Seinturier, and Laurence Duchien. OCL for the Specification of Model Transformation Contracts. In Octavian Patrascoiu, editor, *OCL and Model Driven Engineering, UML 2004 Conference Workshop, October 12, 2004, Lisbon, Portugal*, pages 69–83. University of Kent, 2004.

[CNPDn06] Rafael Capilla, Francisco Nava, Sandra Pérez, and Juan C. Dueñas. A Web-Based Tool for Managing Architectural Design Decisions. *SIGSOFT Softw. Eng. Notes*, 31(5), September 2006. doi:10.1145/1163514.1178644.

[CS13] Daniel Calegari and Nora Szasz. Verification of Model Transformations. *Electron. Notes Theor. Comput. Sci.*, 292:5–25, March 2013. doi:10.1016/j.entcs.2013.02.002.

[Cza98] Krzysztof Czarnecki. *Generative Programming: Principles and Techniques of Software Engineering Based on Automated Configuration and Fragment-Based Component Models.* PhD thesis, 1998.

[DG08] Jeffrey Dean and Sanjay Ghemawat. MapReduce: Simplified Data Processing on Large Clusters. *Commun. ACM*, 51(1):107–113, January 2008. doi:10.1145/1327452.1327492.

[dGJKK12] Thijmen de Gooijer, Anton Jansen, Heiko Koziolek, and Anne Koziolek. An Industrial Case Study of Performance and Cost Design Space Exploration. ICPE '12, pages 205–216, New York, NY, USA, 2012. ACM. doi:10.1145/2188286.2188319.

[Dij82] Edsger W. Dijkstra. *On the Role of Scientific Thought*, pages 60–66. Springer New York, New York, NY, 1982. doi:10.1007/978-1-4612-5695-3_12.

[DK01] Kalyanmoy Deb and Deb Kalyanmoy. *Multi-Objective Optimization Using Evolutionary Algorithms.* John Wiley & Sons, Inc., New York, NY, USA, 2001.

[DLS05] G. Dobson, R. Lock, and I. Sommerville. QoSOnt: A QoS Ontology for Service-Centric Systems. In *31st EUROMICRO Conference on Software Engineering and Advanced Applications*, pages 80–87, August 2005. doi:10.1109/EUROMICRO.2005.49.

[DN02] Liliana Dobrica and Eila Niemelä. A Survey on Software Architecture Analysis Methods. *IEEE Trans. Softw. Eng.*, 28(7):638–653, July 2002. doi:10.1109/TSE.2002.1019479.

[DR12] Zoya Durdik and Ralf Reussner. Position Paper: Approach for Architectural Design and Modelling with Documented Design Decisions (ADMD3). In *Proceedings of the 8th International ACM SIGSOFT Conference on Quality of Software Architectures*, QoSA '12, pages 49–54, New York, NY, USA, 2012. ACM. doi:10.1145/2304696.2304706.

[Dry07] David Drysdale. *High-Quality Software Engineering*. Lulu.com, 2007.

[Dur16] Zoya Durdik. *Architectural Design Decision Documentation through Reuse of Design Patterns*. PhD thesis, KIT Scientific Publishing, Karlsruhe, 2016. doi:10.5445/KSP/1000043807.

[EBL06] Maged Elaasar, Lionel C. Briand, and Yvan Labiche. A Metamodeling Approach to Pattern Specification. In *Proceedings of the 9th International Conference on Model Driven Engineering Languages and Systems*, MoDELS '06, pages 484–498, Berlin, Heidelberg, 2006. Springer-Verlag. doi:10.1007/11880240_34.

[Ecl16] Eclipse Modeling Project. Operational QVT (Version 3.6.0). http://www.eclipse.org/mmt/qvto [Visited on 30/07/17], 2016.

[EPM13] Thomas Erl, Ricardo Puttini, and Zaigham Mahmood. *Cloud Computing: Concepts, Technology & Architecture*. Prentice Hall Press, Upper Saddle River, NJ, USA, 1st edition, 2013.

[Eva96] James D. Evans. *Straightforward Statistics for the Behavioral Sciences*. Brooks/Cole, 1996.

[FH86] Gillian D. Frewin and Barbara J. Hatton. Quality management - procedures and practices. *Software Engineering Journal*, 1(1):29–38, January 1986. doi:10.1049/sej:19860006.

[FLR+14] Christoph Fehling, Frank Leymann, Ralph Retter, Walter Schupeck, and Peter Arbitter. *Cloud Computing Patterns: Fundamentals to Design, Build, and Manage Cloud Applications.* Springer Publishing Company, Incorporated, 2014.

[GAO94] David Garlan, Robert Allen, and John Ockerbloom. Exploiting Style in Architectural Design Environments. *SIGSOFT Softw. Eng. Notes*, 19(5):175–188, December 1994. doi:10.1145/195274.195404.

[Gar03] Gartner, Inc. and/or its Affiliates. The Gartner Glossary of Information Technology Acronyms and Terms. Technical report, Gartner Inc., 2003.

[Gar14] David Garlan. Software Architecture: A Travelogue. In *Proceedings of the on Future of Software Engineering*, FOSE 2014, pages 29–39, New York, NY, USA, 2014. ACM. doi:10.1145/2593882.2593886.

[GHJV95] Erich Gamma, Richard Helm, Ralph Johnson, and John Vlissides. *Design Patterns: Elements of Reusable Object-Oriented Software.* Addison-Wesley Longman Publishing Co., Inc., Boston, MA, USA, 1995.

[GHK+10] Hassan Gomaa, Koji Hashimoto, Minseong Kim, Sam Malek, and Daniel A. Menascé. Software Adaptation Patterns for Service-Oriented Architectures. In *Proceedings of the 2010 ACM Symposium on Applied Computing*, SAC '10, pages 462–469, New York, NY, USA, 2010. ACM. doi:10.1145/1774088.1774185.

[Gie08] Simon Giesecke. *Architectural Styles for Early Goal-Driven Middleware Platform Selection.* PhD thesis, Carl von Ossietzky University of Oldenburg, 2008. URL: http://oops.uni-oldenburg.de/volltexte/2008/796/pdf/dissertation_final.pdf.

[GMW00] David Garlan, Robert Thomas Monroe, and David Wile. Foundations of Component-Based Systems. chapter Acme: Architectural Description of Component-Based Systems, pages 47–67. Cambridge University Press, New York, NY, USA, 2000. URL: http://dl.acm.org/citation.cfm?id=336431.336437.

[Gro09] Richard C. Gronback. *Eclipse Modeling Project: A Domain-Specific Language (DSL) Toolkit.* The Eclipse Series. Addison-Wesley Professional, 1st edition, 2009.

[GTWJ03] Jerry Zayu Gao, Jacob Tsao, Ye Wu, and Taso H.-S. Jacob. *Testing and Quality Assurance for Component-Based Software.* Artech House, Inc., Norwood, MA, USA, 2003.

[Hap09] Jens Happe. *Predicting Software Performance in Symmetric Multi-Core and Multiprocessor Environments.* PhD thesis, Carl von Ossietzky University of Oldenburg, 2009. URL: http://oops.uni-oldenburg.de/volltexte/2009/882/.

[Hap11] Lucia Happe. *Configurable Software Performance Completions through Higher-Order Model Transformations.* PhD thesis, Karlsruhe Institute of Technology, Karlsruhe, Germany, 2011. URL: http://digbib.ubka.uni-karlsruhe.de/volltexte/1000031034.

[Har97] Frank A. Harmsen. *Situational Method Engineering.* PhD thesis, University of Twente, Utrecht, January 1997.

[HAZ07] Neil B. Harrison, Paris Avgeriou, and Uwe Zdun. Using Patterns to Capture Architectural Decisions. *IEEE Softw.*, 24(4):38–45, July 2007. doi:10.1109/MS.2007.124.

[HBR+10a] Jens Happe, Steffen Becker, Christoph Rathfelder, Holger Friedrich, and Ralf H. Reussner. Parametric Performance Completions for Model-Driven Performance Prediction. *Performance Evaluation*, 67(8):694 – 716, 2010. Special Issue on Software and Performance. doi:http://dx.doi.org/10.1016/j.peva.2009.07.006.

[HBR+10b] Nikolaus Huber, Steffen Becker, Christoph Rathfelder, Jochen Schweflinghaus, and Ralf H. Reussner. Performance Modeling in Industry: A Case Study on Storage Virtualization. In *SE '10*, volume 2, pages 1–10, May 2010. doi:10.1145/1810295.1810297.

[HFBR08] Jens Happe, Holger Friedrich, Steffen Becker, and Ralf H. Reussner. A Pattern-Based Performance Completion for Message-Oriented Middleware. In *Proceedings of the 7th International Workshop on Software and Performance*, WOSP '08, pages 165–176, New York, NY, USA, 2008. ACM. doi:10.1145/1383559.1383581.

[HHK02] Holger Hermanns, Ulrich Herzog, and Joost-Pieter Katoen. Process Algebra for Performance Evaluation. *Theor. Comput. Sci.*, 274(1-2):43–87, March 2002. doi:10.1016/S0304-3975(00)00305-4.

[HJS+09] Florian Heidenreich, Jendrik Johannes, Mirko Seifert, Christian Wende, and Marcel Böhme. Generating Safe Template Languages. In *Proceedings of the Eighth International Conference on Generative Programming and Component Engineering*, GPCE '09, pages 99–108, New York, NY, USA, 2009. ACM. doi:10.1145/1621607.1621624.

[HK05] Alan Hartman and David Kreische, editors. *Model Driven Architecture - Foundations and Applications, First European Conference, ECMDA-FA 2005, Nuremberg, Germany, November 7-10, 2005, Proceedings*, volume 3748 of *Lecture Notes in Computer Science*. Springer, 2005.

[HNS99] Christine Hofmeister, Robert L. Nord, and Dilip Soni. Describing Software Architecture with UML. In *Proceedings of the TC2 First Working IFIP Conference on Software Architecture (WICSA1)*, WICSA1, pages 145–160, Deventer, The Netherlands, The Netherlands, 1999. Kluwer, B.V. URL: http://dl.acm.org/citation.cfm?id=646545.696368.

[Hoa78] Charles A. R. Hoare. Communicating Sequential Processes. *Commun. ACM*, 21(8):666–677, August 1978. doi:10.1145/359576.359585.

[IEE10] Systems and Software Engineering – Vocabulary. *ISO/IEC/IEEE 24765:2010(E)*, pages 1–418, December 2010. doi:10.1109/IEEESTD.2010.5733835.

[ISO01] ISO/IEC Standard. Software Engineering – Product Quality – Part 1: Quality Model. ISO/IEC Standard 9126-1, ISO/IEC, 2001.

[ISO03b] ISO/IEC Standard. Software Engineering – Product Quality – Part 3: Internal Metrics. ISO/IEC Standard 9126-3, ISO/IEC, 2003.

[ISO07] ISO/IEC Standard for Systems and Software Engineering - Recommended Practice for Architectural Description of Software-Intensive Systems. *ISO/IEC 42010 IEEE Std 1471-2000 First edition 2007-07-15*, pages c1–24, July 2007. doi:10.1109/IEEESTD.2007.386501.

[ISO11] ISO/IEC Standard. Systems and Software Engineering – Systems and Software Quality Requirements and Evaluation (SQuaRE) – System and Software Quality Models. ISO/IEC Standard 25010:2011, ISO/IEC, 2011.

[ISO14] ISO/IEC Standard. Systems and Software Engineering – Systems and Software Quality Requirements and Evaluation (SQuaRE) – Guide to SQuaRE. ISO/IEC Standard 25000:2014, ISO/IEC, 2014.

[ISO16b] ISO/IEC Standard. Systems and Software Engineering – Systems and Software Quality Requirements and Evaluation (SQuaRE) – Measurement of System and Software Product Quality. ISO/IEC Standard 25023:2016, ISO/IEC, 2016.

[JABK08] Frédéric Jouault, Freddy Allilaire, Jean Bézivin, and Ivan Kurtev. ATL: A Model Transformation Tool. *Science of Computer Programming*, 72(1-2):31–39, 2008. Special Issue on Second issue of experimental software and toolkits (EST). doi:10.1016/j.scico.2007.08.002.

[Jac12] Daniel Jackson. *Software Abstractions: Logic, Language, and Analysis.* The MIT Press, 2012.

[Jav03] Java Middleware Open Benchmarking (JMOB). TPC-W Benchmark: Java Servlets/MySQL Implementation, August 2003. http://jmob.ow2.org/tpcw.html.

[JB05] Anton Jansen and Jan Bosch. Software Architecture As a Set of Architectural Design Decisions. In *Proceedings of the 5th Working IEEE/IFIP Conference on Software Architecture*, WICSA '05, pages 109–120, Washington, DC, USA, 2005. IEEE Computer Society. doi:10.1109/WICSA.2005.61.

[JCP08] Andreas Jedlitschka, Marcus Ciolkowski, and Dietmar Pfahl. Reporting Experiments in Software Engineering. In Forrest Shull, Janice Singer, and DagI.K. Sjøberg, editors, *Guide to Advanced Empirical Software Engineering*, pages 201–228. Springer London, 2008. doi:10.1007/978-1-84800-044-5_8.

[Jon90] Cliff B. Jones. *Systematic Software Development Using VDM (2nd Ed.)*. Prentice-Hall, Inc., Upper Saddle River, NJ, USA, 1990.

[JP05] Andreas Jedlitschka and Dietmar Pfahl. Reporting Guidelines for Controlled Experiments in Software Engineering. In *International Symposium on Empirical Software Engineering, 2005*, pages 10–pp, November 2005. doi:10.1109/ISESE.2005.1541818.

[JvdVAH07] Anton Jansen, Jan van der Ven, Paris Avgeriou, and Dieter K. Hammer. Tool Support for Architectural Decisions. In *Proceedings of the Sixth Working IEEE/IFIP Conference on Software Architecture*, WICSA '07, pages 4–4, Washington, DC, USA, 2007. IEEE Computer Society. doi:10.1109/WICSA.2007.47.

[JW04] Ian Jacobs and Norman Walsh, editors. *Architecture of the World Wide Web, Volume One*. The World Wide Web Consortium (W3C), December 2004. URL: http://www.w3.org/TR/webarch/.

[KBK+99] Rick Kazman, Mario Barbacci, Mark Klein, S. Jeromy Carrière, and Steven G. Woods. Experience with Performing Architecture Tradeoff Analysis. In *Proceedings of the*

21st International Conference on Software Engineering, ICSE '99, pages 54–63, New York, NY, USA, 1999. ACM. doi:10.1145/302405.302452.

[KBK+05] Rick Kazman, Len Bass, Mark Klein, Tony Lattanze, and Linda Northrop. A Basis for Analyzing Software Architecture Analysis Methods. *Software Quality Journal*, 13(4):329–355, December 2005. doi:10.1007/s11219-005-4250-1.

[KBWA94] Rick Kazman, Len Bass, Mike Webb, and Gregory Abowd. SAAM: A Method for Analyzing the Properties of Software Architectures. In *Proceedings of the 16th International Conference on Software Engineering*, ICSE '94, pages 81–90, Los Alamitos, CA, USA, 1994. IEEE Computer Society Press.

[KC05] Chang Hwan Peter Kim and Krzysztof Czarnecki. Synchronizing Cardinality-Based Feature Models and Their Specializations. In Hartman and Kreische [HK05], pages 331–348.

[KC07] Barbara Kitchenham and Stuart Charters. Guidelines for performing Systematic Literature Reviews in Software Engineering. Technical Report EBSE 2007-001, Keele University and Durham University Joint Report, 2007.

[KCH+90] Kyo C. Kang, Sholom G. Cohen, James A. Hess, William E. Nowak, and A. Spencer Peterson. Feature-Oriented Domain Analysis (FODA) Feasibility Study. Technical report, Carnegie-Mellon University Software Engineering Institute, November 1990.

[KCSS02] Mohamed M. Kandé, Valentin Crettaz, Alfred Strohmeier, and Shane Sendall. Bridging the Gap Between IEEE 1471, an Architecture Description Language, and UML. *Software and Systems Modeling*, 1(2):113–129, 2002. doi:10.1007/s10270-002-0010-x.

[KDH+12] Max E. Kramer, Zoya Durdik, Michael Hauck, Jörg Henss, Martin Küster, Philipp Merkle, and Andreas Rentschler. Extending the Palladio Component Model using Profiles and Stereotypes. In Steffen Becker, Jens Happe, Anne Koziolek, and Ralf Reussner, editors, *Palladio Days 2012 Proceedings (appeared as technical report)*, Karlsruhe Reports in Informatics; 2012,21, pages 7–15, Karlsruhe, 2012. KIT, Faculty of Informatics. URL: `http://nbn-resolving.org/urn:nbn:de:swb:90-308043`.

[KFGS03] Dae-Kyoo Kim, Robert France, Sudipto Ghosh, and Eunjee Song. A Role-Based Metamodeling Approach to Specifying Design Patterns. In *Proceedings 27th Annual International Computer Software and Applications Conference. COMPAC 2003*, pages 452–457, November 2003. `doi:10.1109/CMPSAC.2003.1245379`.

[KG10] Jung Soo Kim and David Garlan. Analyzing Architectural Styles. *J. Syst. Softw.*, 83(7):1216–1235, July 2010. `doi:10.1016/j.jss.2010.01.049`.

[KH06] Heiko Koziolek and Jens Happe. A QoS Driven Development Process Model for Component-Based Software Systems. In *Proceedings of the 9th International Conference on Component-Based Software Engineering*, CBSE '06, pages 336–343, Berlin, Heidelberg, 2006. Springer-Verlag. `doi:10.1007/11783565_25`.

[KJ04] Michael Kircher and Prashant Jain. *Pattern-Oriented Software Architecture: Patterns for Resource Management.* John Wiley & Sons, Inc., 2004.

[KKR11] Anne Koziolek, Heiko Koziolek, and Ralf Reussner. PerOpteryx: Automated Application of Tactics in Multi-Objective Software Architecture Optimization. In *Proceedings of the Joint ACM SIGSOFT Conference – QoSA and ACM SIGSOFT Symposium – ISARCS on Quality of Software Architectures – QoSA and Architecting Critical Systems – ISARCS*, QoSA-ISARCS '11, pages 33–42, New York, NY, USA, 2011. ACM. `doi:10.1145/2000259.2000267`.

[Kle08] Anneke Kleppe. *Software Language Engineering: Creating Domain-Specific Languages Using Metamodels.* Addison-Wesley Professional, 1st edition, 2008.

[KLvV06] Philippe Kruchten, Patricia Lago, and Hans van Vliet. Building Up and Reasoning About Architectural Knowledge. In *Proceedings of the Second International Conference on Quality of Software Architectures*, QoSA '06, pages 43–58, Berlin, Heidelberg, 2006. Springer-Verlag. doi:10.1007/11921998_8.

[KM98] Jeff Kramer and Jeff Magee. Analysing Dynamic Change in Software Architectures: A Case study. In *Proceedings of the Fourth International Conference on Configurable Distributed Systems, 1998*, pages 91–100, May 1998. doi:10.1109/CDS.1998.675762.

[Kom98] Andrew Kompanek. Modeling a System with Acme. School of Computer Science, Carnegie Mellon University, http://acme.able.cs.cmu.edu/html/WORKING-%20Modeling%20a%20System%20with%20Acme.html [Visited on 30/07/17], 1998.

[Koz08] Heiko Koziolek. *Parameter Dependencies for Reusable Performance Specifications of Software Components.* PhD thesis, University of Oldenburg, Germany, March 2008.

[Koz10] Heiko Koziolek. Performance Evaluation of Component-Based Software Systems: A Survey. *Performance Evaluation*, 67(8):634–658, 2010. Special Issue on Software and Performance. doi:10.1016/j.peva.2009.07.007.

[Koz11a] Anne Koziolek. *Automated Improvement of Software Architecture Models for Performance and Other Quality Attributes.* PhD thesis, Institut für Programmstrukturen und Datenorganisation (IPD), Karlsruher Institut für Technologie, Karlsruhe, Germany, 2011. URL: http://digbib.ubka.uni-karlsruhe.de/volltexte/1000024955.

[Koz11b] Heiko Koziolek. The SPOSAD Architectural Style for Multi-Tenant Software Applications. In *Proceedings of the 2011 Ninth Working IEEE/IFIP Conference on Software Architecture*, WICSA '11, pages 320–327, Washington, DC, USA, 2011. IEEE Computer Society. doi:10.1109/WICSA.2011.50.

[KPP06] Dimitrios S. Kolovos, Richard F. Paige, and Fiona A.C. Polack. Model Comparison: A Foundation for Model Composition and Model Transformation Testing. In *Proceedings of the 2006 International Workshop on Global Integrated Model Management*, GaMMa '06, pages 13–20, New York, NY, USA, 2006. ACM. doi:10.1145/1138304.1138308.

[Kri98] Anders Kristensen. Template Resolution in XML/HTML. *Comput. Netw. ISDN Syst.*, 30(1-7):239–249, April 1998. doi:10.1016/S0169-7552(98)00023-3.

[Kru95] Philippe Kruchten. Mommy, Where do Software Architectures Come From? In *Proceedings of the 1st International Workshop on Architectures for Software Systems*, IWASS1, 1995.

[KSBH12] Heiko Koziolek, Bastian Schlich, Steffen Becker, and Michael Hauck. Performance and Reliability Prediction for Evolving Service-Oriented Software Systems. *Empirical Software Engineering*, pages 1–45, 2012. doi:10.1007/s10664-012-9213-0.

[Küh06] Thomas Kühne. Matters of (Meta-)Modeling. *Software and System Modeling*, 5(4):369–385, 2006. doi:10.1007/s10270-006-0017-9.

[LCM06] Christian Lange, Michel Chaudron, and Johan Muskens. In Practice: UML Software Architecture and Design Description. *IEEE Softw.*, 23(2):40–46, March 2006. doi:10.1109/MS.2006.50.

[LK15] Michael Langhammer and Klaus Krogmann. A Co-evolution Approach for Source Code and Component-Based Architecture Models. In *Proceedings of the 17th Workshop of Software-Reengineering and -Evolution*, volume 4. Gesellschaft für Informatik, May 2015. URL: http://fg-sre.gi.de/fileadmin/gliederungen/fg-sre/wsre2015/WSRE2015-Proceeedings-preliminary.pdf#page=40.

[LKA+95] David C. Luckham, John J. Kenney, Larry M. Augustin, James Vera, Doug Bryan, and Walter Mann. Specification and Analysis of System Architecture Using Rapide. *IEEE Trans. Softw. Eng.*, 21(4):336–355, April 1995. doi:10.1109/32.385971.

[Loa] Minimal Example for the Loadbalancing AT. https://github.com/PalladioSimulator/Architectural-Templates/tree/master/org.palladiosimulator.architecturaltemplates.examples.staticresourcecontainer [Visited on 30/07/17].

[LR10] Kung-Kiu Lau and Tauseef Rana. A Taxonomy of Software Composition Mechanisms. In *Proceedings of the 2010 36th EUROMICRO Conference on Software Engineering and Advanced Applications*, SEAA '10, pages 102–110, Washington, DC, USA, 2010. IEEE Computer Society. doi:10.1109/SEAA.2010.36.

[LTM+12] Fang Liu, Jin Tong, Jian Mao, Robert Bohn, John Messina, Lee Badger, and Dawn Leaf. *NIST Cloud Computing Reference Architecture: Recommendations of the National Institute of Standards and Technology (Special Publication 500-292)*. CreateSpace Independent Publishing Platform, USA, 2012.

[LWWC12] Philip Langer, Konrad Wieland, Manuel Wimmer, and Jordi Cabot. EMF Profiles: A Lightweight Extension Approach for EMF Models. *Journal of Object Technology*, 11(1):8:1–29, April 2012. doi:10.5381/jot.2012.11.1.a8.

[LZGS84] Edward D. Lazowska, John Zahorjan, G. Scott Graham, and Kenneth C. Sevcik. *Quantitative System Performance: Computer System Analysis Using Queueing Network Models*. Prentice-Hall, Inc., Upper Saddle River, NJ, USA, 1984.

[Mar04] Moreno Marzolla. *Simulation-Based Performance Modeling of UML Software Architectures*. PhD thesis, Università Ca' Foscari di Venezia, February 2004.

[Mar07] Anne Martens. Empirical Validation of the Model-Driven Performance Prediction Approach Palladio. Master's thesis, Carl-von-Ossietzky Universität Oldenburg,

2007. URL: http://sdqweb.ipd.kit.edu/publications/pdfs/martens2007a-complete.pdf.

[MCF+95] Richard J. Mayer, John W. Crump, Ronald Fernandes, Arthur Keen, and Michael K. Painter. Information Integration for Concurrent Engineering (IICE) Compendium of Methods Report. Technical report, DTIC Document, 1995.

[MDA04] Daniel Menascé, Lawrence W. Dowdy, and Virgilio Almeida. *Performance by Design: Computer Capacity Planning By Example.* Prentice Hall PTR, Upper Saddle River, NJ, USA, 2004.

[Mey97] Bertrand Meyer. *Object-Oriented Software Construction (2nd Ed.).* Prentice-Hall, Inc., Upper Saddle River, NJ, USA, 1997.

[MG11] Peter Mell and Timothy Grance. The NIST Definition of Cloud Computing. *NIST Special Publication*, 145(6):7–7, 2011.

[MGMS11] Daniel Menascé, Hassan Gomaa, Sam Malek, and João Sousa. SASSY: A Framework for Self-Architecting Service-Oriented Systems. *IEEE Software*, 28(6):78–85, November 2011. doi:10.1109/MS.2011.22.

[MHC00] Richard Monson-Haefel and David Chappell. *Java Message Service.* O'Reilly & Associates, Inc., Sebastopol, CA, USA, 2000.

[MHG01] David Maplesden, John Hosking, and John Grundy. A Visual Language for Design Pattern Modelling and Instantiation. In *Proceedings IEEE Symposia on Human-Centric Computing Languages and Environments (Cat. No.01TH8587)*, pages 338–339, 2001. doi:10.1109/HCC.2001.995285.

[MHG02] David Maplesden, John Hosking, and John Grundy. Design Pattern Modelling and Instantiation Using DPML. In *Proceedings of the Fortieth International Conference on Tools Pacific: Objects for Internet, Mobile and Embedded Applications*, CRPIT '02, pages 3–11, Darlinghurst, Australia, Australia, 2002. Australian Computer Society, Inc.

[MKBJ08] Brice Morin, Jacques Klein, Olivier Barais, and Jean-Marc Jézéquel. A Generic Weaver for Supporting Product Lines. In *Proceedings of the 13th International Workshop on Early Aspects*, EA '08, pages 11–18, New York, NY, USA, 2008. ACM. doi:10.1145/1370828.1370832.

[MKPR11] Anne Martens, Heiko Koziolek, Lutz Prechelt, and Ralf Reussner. From Monolithic to Component-Based Performance Evaluation of Software Architectures. *Empirical Softw. Eng.*, 16(5):587–622, October 2011. doi:10.1007/s10664-010-9142-8.

[Moh12] Farmeena Khan Mohd Ehmer Khan. A Comparative Study of White Box, Black Box and Grey Box Testing Techniques. *International Journal of Advanced Computer Science and Applications (IJACSA)*, 3(6), 2012. URL: http://ijacsa.thesai.org/.

[Mon99] Robert Thomas Monroe. *Rapid Development of Custom Software Architecture Design Environments.* PhD thesis, Pittsburgh, PA, USA, 1999.

[MPW15] Nariman Mani, Dorina C. Petriu, and C. Murray Woodside. Exploring SOA Pattern Performance using Coupled Transformations and Performance Models. In Haiping Xu, editor, *The 27th International Conference on Software Engineering and Knowledge Engineering, SEKE 2015, Wyndham Pittsburgh University Center, Pittsburgh, PA, USA, July 6-8, 2015*, pages 552–557. KSI Research Inc. and Knowledge Systems Institute Graduate School, 2015. URL: http://dx.doi.org/10.18293/SEKE2015-140, doi:10.18293/SEKE2015-140.

[MR97] Mark Moriconi and Robert A. Riemenschneider. Introduction to SADL 1.0: A Language for Specifying Software Architecture Hierarchies. Technical Report SRI-CSL-97-01, Computer Science Laboratory, SRI International, March 1997.

[MRW77] Jim A. Mccall, Paul K. Richards, and Gene F. Walters. *Factors in Software Quality*, volume I, II, III. Rome Air Development Center Reports, 1977.

[MSMG10] Daniel A. Menascé, João P. Sousa, Sam Malek, and Hassan Gomaa. QoS Architectural Patterns for Self-architecting Software Systems. In *Proceedings of the 7th International Conference on Autonomic Computing*, ICAC '10, pages 195–204, New York, NY, USA, 2010. ACM. `doi:10.1145/1809049.1809084`.

[MT00] Nenad Medvidovic and Richard N. Taylor. A Classification and Comparison Framework for Software Architecture Description Languages. *IEEE Trans. Softw. Eng.*, 26(1):70–93, January 2000. `doi:10.1109/32.825767`.

[MWR14] Connie Morrison, Dolores Wells, and Lisa Ruffolo. *Computer Literacy BASICS: A Comprehensive Guide to IC3*. Cengage Learning, 5th edition, 2014.

[New15] Sam Newman. *Building Microservices*. O'Reilly Media, Inc., 1st edition, 2015.

[Obj11] Object Management Group (OMG). OMG Unified Modeling Language (OMG UML), Superstructure Specification (Version 2.4.1). Technical Report OMG Document Number: formal/2011-08-06, Object Management Group, August 2011.

[Obj12] Object Management Group (OMG). Common Object Request Broker Architecture (Version 3.3). Technical report, Object Management Group, http://www.omg.org/spec/CORBA/3.3/, November 2012.

[Obj14] Object Management Group (OMG). Object Constraint Language (OCL) Specification (Version 2.4). Technical Report OMG Document Number: formal/2014-02-03, Object Management Group, February 2014. URL: `http://www.omg.org/spec/OCL/2.4`.

[Obj15] Object Management Group (OMG). OMG Meta Object Facility (MOF) Core Specification (Version 2.5). Technical Report OMG Document Number: formal/2015-06-05, Object Management Group, http://www.omg.org/spec/MOF/2.5/, June 2015.

[Obj16] Object Management Group (OMG). *Meta Object Facility (MOF) 2.0 Query/View/Transformation Specification – Version 1.3*. June 2016. URL: http://www.omg.org/spec/QVT/1.3.

[OGW+14] Per-Olov Östberg, Henning Groenda, Stefan Wesner, James Byrne, Dimitrios S. Nikolopoulos, Craig Sheridan, Jakub Krzywda, Ahmed Ali-Eldin, Johan Tordsson, Erik Elmroth, Christian Stier, Klaus Krogmann, Jorg Domaschka, Christopher B. Hauser, Peter J. Byrne, Sergej Svorobej, Barry Mccollum, Zafeirios Papazachos, Darren Whigham, Stephan Rüth, and Dragana Paurevic. The CACTOS Vision of Context-Aware Cloud Topology Optimization and Simulation. In *6th IEEE International Conference on Cloud Computing Technology and Science (CloudCom), 2014*, pages 26–31, December 2014. doi:10.1109/CloudCom.2014.62.

[OVDPB01a] James Odell, H. Van Dyke Parunak, and Bernhard Bauer. Representing Agent Interaction Protocols in UML. In *First International Workshop, AOSE 2000 on Agent-Oriented Software Engineering*, pages 121–140, Secaucus, NJ, USA, 2001. Springer-Verlag New York, Inc. URL: http://dl.acm.org/citation.cfm?id=370834.370852.

[OVDPB01b] James Odell, H. Van Dyke Parunak, and Bernhard Bauer. Representing Agent Interaction Protocols in UML. In *First International Workshop, AOSE 2000 on Agent-Oriented Software Engineering*, pages 121–140, Secaucus, NJ, USA, 2001. Springer-Verlag New York, Inc. URL: http://dl.acm.org/citation.cfm?id=370834.370852.

[Oxf16a] Oxford Dictionaries. "Blueprint" Definition. Oxford University Press, 2016. URL: http://www.oxforddictionaries.com/definition/blueprint [Visited on 30/07/17].

[Oxf16b] Oxford Dictionaries. "Template" Definition. Oxford University Press, 2016. URL: http://www.oxforddictionaries.com/definition/template [Visited on 30/07/17].

[Pala] Sirius-Based Editors for Models of the Palladio Component Model (PCM). https://github.com/PalladioSimulator/Palladio-Editors-Sirius [Visited on 30/07/17].

[Palb] Palladio—The Software Quality People. Palladio Project Wizard. https://sdqweb.ipd.kit.edu/wiki/Palladio_Project_Wizard [Visited on 30/07/17].

[Palc] Palladio—The Software Quality People. Palladio Workflow Engine. http://sdqweb.ipd.kit.edu/wiki/Palladio_Workflow_Engine [Visited on 30/07/17].

[Pan10] Rajesh K. Pandey. Architectural Description Languages (ADLs) vs UML: A Review. *SIGSOFT Softw. Eng. Notes*, 35(3):1–5, May 2010. doi:10.1145/1764810.1764828.

[Par04] Terence John Parr. Enforcing Strict Model-View Separation in Template Engines. In *Proceedings of the 13th International Conference on World Wide Web*, WWW '04, pages 224–233, New York, NY, USA, 2004. ACM. doi:10.1145/988672.988703.

[Pera] PerOpteryx Integration: Actual AT Parameters. https://svnserver.informatik.kit.edu/i43/svn/code/Palladio/Addons/PerOpteryx/trunk/de.uka.ipd.sdq.pcm.designdecision/; user: anonymous; password: anonymous [Visited on 30/07/17].

[Perb] PerOpteryx Integration: Experiment Automation. https://svnserver.informatik.kit.edu/i43/svn/code/Palladio/Addons/PerOpteryx/branches/simulizarAnalysisDSE/de.uka.ipd.sdq.dsexplore.analysis.experimentautomation/; user: anonymous; password: anonymous [Visited on 30/07/17].

[PGH07] Claus Pahl, Simon Giesecke, and Wilhelm Hasselbring. An Ontology-Based Approach for Modelling Architectural Styles. In Flávio Oquendo, editor, *First European Conference on Software Architecture, ECSA 2007, Aranjuez, Spain, September 24-26, 2007, Proceedings*, volume 4758 of *Lecture Notes in Computer Science*, pages 60–75. Springer, 2007. doi:10.1007/978-3-540-75132-8_6.

[Pre01] Lutz Prechelt. *Kontrollierte Experimente in Der Softwaretechnik: Potenzial Und Methodik.* Springer, 2001.

[PW00] Dorina C. Petriu and Xin Wang. *Deriving Software Performance Models from Architectural Patterns by Graph Transformations*, pages 475–488. Springer Berlin Heidelberg, Berlin, Heidelberg, 2000. doi:10.1007/978-3-540-46464-8_33.

[Rat13] Christoph Rathfelder. *Modelling Event-Based Interactions in Component-Based Architectures for Quantitative System Evaluation*. PhD thesis, Karlsruhe Institute of Technology, Karlsruhe, Germany, 2013. URL: http://www.ksp.kit.edu/shop/isbn2shopid.php?isbn=978-3-86644-969-5.

[RBKR12] Christoph Rathfelder, Stefan Becker, Klaus Krogmann, and Ralf Reussner. Workload-Aware System Monitoring Using Performance Predictions Applied to a Large-Scale E-Mail System. In *WICSA/ECSA '12*, pages 31–40, August 2012. doi:10.1109/WICSA-ECSA.212.11.

[RH09] Per Runeson and Martin Höst. Guidelines for Conducting and Reporting Case Study Research in Software Engineering. *Empirical Softw. Eng.*, 14(2):131–164, April 2009. doi:10.1007/s10664-008-9102-8.

[RH11] John Rhoton and Risto Haukioja. *Cloud Computing Architected: Solution Design Handbook*. Recursive Press, 2011.

[Rie03] Dirk Riehle. The Perfection of Informality: Tools, Templates, and Patterns. *Cutter IT Journal*, 16(9):22–26, 2003.

[Rog16] Igor Rogic. Scalability and Elasticity Prediction of Self-Adaptive Systems Using SimuLizar and Architectural Templates: Industrial Case Study. Master's thesis, Software Engineering Group, Heinz Nixdorf Institute, Paderborn University, August 2016.

[SBPM09] David Steinberg, Frank Budinsky, Marcelo Paternostro, and Ed Merks. *EMF: Eclipse Modeling Framework 2.0*. Addison-Wesley Professional, 2nd edition, 2009.

[SCD12] Gehan M. K. Selim, James R. Cordy, and Juergen Dingel. Model Transformation Testing: The State of the Art. In *Proceedings of the First Workshop on the Analysis of Model*

Transformations, AMT '12, pages 21–26, New York, NY, USA, 2012. ACM. doi:10.1145/2432497.2432502.

[SDAH08] Dag I. K. Sjøberg, Tore Dybå, Bente C. D. Anda, and Jo E. Hannay. Building Theories in Software Engineering. In *Guide to Advanced Empirical Software Engineering*, pages 312–336. Springer London, 2008. doi:10.1007/978-1-84800-044-5_12.

[Sea99] Carolyn B. Seaman. Qualitative Methods in Empirical Studies of Software Engineering. *IEEE Trans. Softw. Eng.*, 25(4):557–572, July 1999. doi:10.1109/32.799955.

[Som10] Ian Sommerville. *Software Engineering*. Addison-Wesley Publishing Company, USA, 9th edition, 2010.

[Spi92] John Michael Spivey. *The Z Notation: A Reference Manual*. Prentice Hall International (UK) Ltd., Hertfordshire, UK, UK, 1992.

[SS12] Priya Shanmuga and Rajesh M. Suresh. Software Architecture Evaluation Methods - A Survey. *International Journal of Computer Applications*, 49(16):19–26, July 2012. doi:10.5120/7711-1107.

[SSRB00] Douglas C. Schmidt, Michael Stal, Hans Rohnert, and Frank Buschmann. *Pattern-Oriented Software Architecture: Patterns for Concurrent and Networked Objects*. John Wiley & Sons, Inc., New York, NY, USA, 2nd edition, 2000.

[Sta73] Herbert Stachowiak. *Allgemeine Modelltheorie*. Springer Verlag, Wien, 1973.

[Str13] Misha Strittmatter. Feedback-Driven Concurrency Improvement and Refinement of Performance Models. Diploma thesis, Karlsruhe Institute of Technology (KIT), Germany, March 2013.

[SW02] Connie U. Smith and Lloyd G. Williams. *Performance Solutions: A Practical Guide to Creating Responsive, Scalable Software*. Addison Wesley Longman Publishing Co., Inc., Redwood City, CA, USA, 2002.

[Szy02] Clemens Szyperski. *Component Software: Beyond Object-Oriented Programming*. Addison-Wesley Longman Publishing Co., Inc., Boston, MA, USA, 2nd edition, 2002.

[TA05b] Jeff Tyree and Art Akerman. Architecture Decisions: Demystifying Architecture. *IEEE Softw.*, 22(2):19–27, March 2005. doi:10.1109/MS.2005.27.

[Tai07] Toufik Taibi. *Design Pattern Formalization Techniques*. IGI Global, Hershey, PA, USA, 2007.

[TAJ+10] Antony Tang, Paris Avgeriou, Anton Jansen, Rafael Capilla, and Muhammad Ali Babar. A Comparative Study of Architecture Knowledge Management Tools. *J. Syst. Softw.*, 83(3):352–370, March 2010. doi:10.1016/j.jss.2009.08.032.

[TFS10a] Chouki Tibermacine, Régis Fleurquin, and Salah Sadou. A Family of Languages for Architecture Constraint Specification. *J. Syst. Softw.*, 83(5):815–831, May 2010. doi:10.1016/j.jss.2009.11.736.

[TMD09] Richard N. Taylor, Nenad Medvidovic, and Eric M. Dashofy. *Software Architecture: Foundations, Theory, and Practice*. Wiley Publishing, 2009.

[Tra02] Transaction Processing Performance Council (TPC). TPC-W Benchmark (Web Commerce) Specification Version 1.8, February 2002.

[Tri82] Kishar Shridharbhai Trivedi. *Probability and Statistics with Reliability, Queuing and Computer Science Applications*. Prentice Hall PTR, Upper Saddle River, NJ, USA, 1982.

[TSO12] Minh Tu Ton That, Salah Sadou, and Flavio Oquendo. Using Architectural Patterns to Define Architectural Decisions. In *Proceedings of the 2012 Joint Working IEEE/IFIP Conference on Software Architecture and European Conference on Software Architecture*, WICSA-ECSA '12, pages 196–200, Washington, DC, USA, 2012. IEEE Computer Society. doi:10.1109/WICSA-ECSA.212.28.

[TSOB15] M.T.T. That, S. Sadou, F. Oquendo, and I. Borne. Preserving Architectural Pattern Composition Information Through Explicit Merging Operators. *Future Gener. Comput. Syst.*, 47(C):97–112, June 2015. doi:10.1016/j.future.2014.09.002.

[TTSOF16] Minh Tu Ton That, Salah Sadou, Flavio Oquendo, and Régis Fleurquin. Preserving Architectural Decisions Through Architectural Patterns. *Automated Software Engineering*, 23(3):427–467, September 2016. doi:10.1007/s10515-014-0172-0.

[VCC15] Gilles Vanwormhoudt, Olivier Caron, and Bernard Carré. Aspectual templates in UML. *Software & Systems Modeling*, pages 1–29, 2015. doi:10.1007/s10270-015-0463-3.

[VDGD05] Tom Verdickt, Bart Dhoedt, Frank Gielen, and Piet Demeester. Automatic Inclusion of Middleware Performance Attributes into Architectural UML Software Models. *IEEE Trans. Softw. Eng.*, 31(8):695–711, August 2005. doi:10.1109/TSE.2005.88.

[vDHP+12] Markus von Detten, Christian Heinzemann, Marie C. Platenius, Jan Rieke, Dietrich Travkin, and Stephan Hildebrandt. Story Diagrams - Syntax and Semantics. Technical report, Software Engineering Group, Heinz Nixdorf Institute, University of Paderborn, 2012.

[VJ02] David Vandevoorde and Nicolai M. Josuttis. *C++ Templates*. Addison-Wesley Longman Publishing Co., Inc., Boston, MA, USA, 2002.

[Vli98] John Vlissides. *Pattern Hatching: Design Patterns Applied*. Addison-Wesley Longman Ltd., Essex, UK, UK, 1998.

[vSB99] Rini van Solingen and Egon Berghout. *The Goal/Question/-Metric Method: A Practical Guide for Quality Improvement of Software Development*. McGraw-Hill, 1999.

[VSC06] Markus Völter, Thomas Stahl, and Krzysztof Czarnecki. *Model-Driven Software Development: Technology, Engineering, Management*. John Wiley & Sons, 2006.

[Whi09] Tom White. *Hadoop: The Definitive Guide.* O'Reilly Media, Inc., 1st edition, 2009.

[Wie13] Springer Automotive Media Wiesbaden. AUTOSAR – The Worldwide Automotive Standard for E/E Systems. *ATZextra worldwide*, 18(9):5–12, 2013. doi:10.1007/s40111-013-0003-5.

[Wil12] Bill Wilder. *Cloud Architecture Patterns: Using Microsoft Azure.* O'Reilly Media, 2012.

[WPS02] Murray Woodside, Dorina Petriu, and Khalid Siddiqui. Performance-related Completions for Software Specifications. In *Proceedings of the 24th International Conference on Software Engineering*, ICSE '02, pages 22–32, New York, NY, USA, 2002. ACM. doi:10.1145/581339.581346.

[WRH+00] Claes Wohlin, Per Runeson, Martin Höst, Magnus C. Ohlsson, Bjöorn Regnell, and Anders Wesslén. *Experimentation in Software Engineering: An Introduction.* Kluwer Academic Publishers, Norwell, MA, USA, 2000.

[WS03] Lloyd G. Williams and Connie U. Smith. Making the Business Case for Software Performance Engineering. In *CMG '03, December 7-12, 2003, Dallas, Texas, USA*, pages 349–358, 2003.

[WSK+11] Manuel Wimmer, Andrea Schauerhuber, Gerti Kappel, Werner Retschitzegger, Wieland Schwinger, and Elizabeth Kapsammer. A Survey on UML-Based Aspect-Oriented Design Modeling. *ACM Comput. Surv.*, 43(4):28:1–28:33, October 2011. doi:10.1145/1978802.1978807.

[ZCL14] Zhuoyao Zhang, Ludmila Cherkasova, and Boon Thau Loo. Parameterizable Benchmarking Framework for Designing a MapReduce Performance Model. *Concurr. Comput. : Pract. Exper.*, 26(12):2005–2026, August 2014. doi:10.1002/cpe.3229.

The Karlsruhe Series on Software Design and Quality

Edited by Prof. Dr. Ralf Reussner // ISSN 1867-0067

Band 1 **Steffen Becker**
Coupled Model Transformations for QoS Enabled Component-Based Software Design.
ISBN 978-3-86644-271-9

Band 2 **Heiko Koziolek**
Parameter Dependencies for Reusable Performance Specifications of Software Components.
ISBN 978-3-86644-272-6

Band 3 **Jens Happe**
Predicting Software Performance in Symmetric Multi-core and Multiprocessor Environments.
ISBN 978-3-86644-381-5

Band 4 **Klaus Krogmann**
Reconstruction of Software Component Architectures and Behaviour Models using Static and Dynamic Analysis.
ISBN 978-3-86644-804-9

Band 5 **Michael Kuperberg**
Quantifying and Predicting the Influence of Execution Platform on Software Component Performance.
ISBN 978-3-86644-741-7

Band 6 **Thomas Goldschmidt**
View-Based Textual Modelling.
ISBN 978-3-86644-642-7

Band 7 **Anne Koziolek**
Automated Improvement of Software Architecture Models for Performance and Other Quality Attributes.
ISBN 978-3-86644-973-2

Die Bände sind unter www.ksp.kit.edu als PDF frei verfügbar oder als Druckausgabe bestellbar.

Band 8 **Lucia Happe**
Configurable Software Performance Completions through Higher-Order Model Transformations.
ISBN 978-3-86644-990-9

Band 9 **Franz Brosch**
Integrated Software Architecture-Based Reliability Prediction for IT Systems.
ISBN 978-3-86644-859-9

Band 10 **Christoph Rathfelder**
Modelling Event-Based Interactions in Component-Based Architectures for Quantitative System Evaluation.
ISBN 978-3-86644-969-5

Band 11 **Henning Groenda**
Certifying Software Component Performance Specifications.
ISBN 978-3-7315-0080-3

Band 12 **Dennis Westermann**
Deriving Goal-oriented Performance Models by Systematic Experimentation.
ISBN 978-3-7315-0165-7

Band 13 **Michael Hauck**
Automated Experiments for Deriving Performance-relevant Properties of Software Execution Environments.
ISBN 978-3-7315-0138-1

Band 14 **Zoya Durdik**
Architectural Design Decision Documentation through Reuse of Design Patterns.
ISBN 978-3-7315-0292-0

Band 15 **Erik Burger**
Flexible Views for View-based Model-driven Development.
ISBN 978-3-7315-0276-0

Band 16 **Benjamin Klatt**
Consolidation of Customized Product Copies into Software Product Lines.
ISBN 978-3-7315-0368-2

Band 17 **Andreas Rentschler**
Model Transformation Languages with Modular Information Hiding.
ISBN 978-3-7315-0346-0

Band 18 **Omar-Qais Noorshams**
Modeling and Prediction of I/O Performance in Virtualized Environments.
ISBN 978-3-7315-0359-0

Band 19 **Johannes Josef Stammel**
Architekturbasierte Bewertung und Planung von Änderungsanfragen.
ISBN 978-3-7315-0524-2

Band 20 **Alexander Wert**
Performance Problem Diagnostics by Systematic Experimentation.
ISBN 978-3-7315-0677-5

Band 21 **Christoph Heger**
An Approach for Guiding Developers to Performance and Scalability Solutions.
ISBN 978-3-7315-0698-0

Band 22 **Fouad ben Nasr Omri**
Weighted Statistical Testing based on Active Learning and Formal Verification Techniques for Software Reliability Assessment.
ISBN 978-3-7315-0472-6

Band 23 **Michael Langhammer**
Automated Coevolution of Source Code and Software Architecture Models.
ISBN 978-3-7315-0783-3

Die Bände sind unter www.ksp.kit.edu als PDF frei verfügbar oder als Druckausgabe bestellbar.

Band 24 **Max Emanuel Kramer**
Specification Languages for Preserving Consistency between Models of Different Languages.
ISBN 978-3-7315-0784-0

Band 25 **Sebastian Michael Lehrig**
Efficiently Conducting Quality-of-Service Analyses by Templating Architectural Knowledge.
ISBN 978-3-7315-0756-7